D0446351

# THE PAST BEFORE US

# THE PAST BEFORE US

## Contemporary Historical Writing
## in the United States

EDITED FOR THE
AMERICAN HISTORICAL ASSOCIATION
BY MICHAEL KAMMEN

*Cornell University Press*

ITHACA AND LONDON

First published 1980 by Cornell University Press.
Published in the United Kingdom by Cornell University Press Ltd.,
Ely House, 37 Dover Street, London W1X 4HQ.

*First printing, Cornell Paperbacks, 1982.*
*Second printing, 1982.*
*Third printing, 1982.*

International Standard Book Number (paper) 0-8014-9231-9
International Standard Book Number (cloth) 0-8014-1224-2
Library of Congress Catalog Card Number 79-25785
Printed in the United States of America
*Librarians: Library of Congress cataloging information appears
on the last page of the book.*

*The paper in this book is acid-free, and meets the guidelines for permanence and durability
of the Committee on Production Guidelines for Book Longevity of the Council on Library
Resources.*

*This volume of essays was prepared for presentation on the occasion
of the Fifteenth International Congress of Historical Sciences,
held in Bucharest, Romania, August 1980.*

Perhaps the mass of students are more skeptical now than they were thirty years ago of the possibility that such a science [of history] can be created. Yet almost every successful historian has been busy with it, adding here a new analysis, a new generalization there; a clear and definite connection where before the rupture of idea was absolute; and, above all, extending the field of study until it shall include all races, all countries, and all times. Like other branches of science, history is now encumbered and hampered by its own mass, but its tendency is always the same, and cannot be other than what it is. That the effort to make history a science may fail is possible, and perhaps probable; but that it should cease, unless for reasons that would cause all science to cease, is not within the range of experience. Historians will not, and even if they would they can not, abandon the attempt.

> —Henry Adams, "The Tendency of History," an open letter to the American Historical Association, dated December 12, 1894, while Adams was president of the Association

In the history of history a myth is a once valid but now discarded version of the human story, as our now valid versions will in due course be relegated to the category of discarded myths. With our predecessors, the bards and story-tellers and priests, we have therefore this in common: that it is our function, as it was theirs, not to create, but to preserve and perpetuate the social tradition; to harmonize, as well as ignorance and prejudice permit, the actual and the remembered series of events; to enlarge and enrich the specious present common to us all to the end that "society" (the tribe, the nation, or all mankind) may judge of what it is doing in the light of what it has done and what it hopes to do.

> —Carl Becker, "Everyman His Own Historian" (1932)

# CONTENTS

Acknowledgments                                                              9
Foreword, by John Hope Franklin                                             11
Introduction: The Historian's Vocation and the State of the
    Discipline in the United States, by Michael Kammen   19

### PART ONE: UNITS OF TIME AND AREAS OF STUDY

1. Fragmentation and Unity in "American Medievalism," by
    Karl F. Morrison                                     49
2. Early Modern Europe, by William J. Bouwsma                               78
3. Modern European History, by William H. McNeill                          95
4. African History, by Philip D. Curtin                                    113
5. The History of the Muslim Middle East, by Nikki R. Keddie               131
6. East, Southeast, and South Asia, by John Whitney Hall                   157
7. Latin America and the Americas, by Charles Gibson                       187

### PART TWO: EXPANDING FIELDS OF INQUIRY

8. Toward a Wider Vision: Trends in Social History, by
    Peter N. Stearns                                    205
9. The New Political History in the 1970s, by Allan G. Bogue               231
10. Labor History in the 1970s: Toward a History of the
    American Worker, by David Brody                     252
11. Community Studies, Urban History, and American Local
    History, by Kathleen Neils Conzen                   270
12. The Negro in American History: As Scholar, as Subject,
    by Jay Saunders Redding                              292
13. Women and the Family, by Carl N. Degler                                308
14. Intellectual and Cultural History, by Robert Darnton                   327
15. Marking Time: The Historiography of International
    Relations, by Charles S. Maier                       355

*Contents*

PART THREE: MODES OF GATHERING AND
ASSESSING HISTORICAL MATERIALS

16. Oral History in the United States, *by Herbert T. Hoover*     391
17. Psychohistory, *by Peter Loewenberg*     408
18. Quantitative Social-Scientific History, *by J. Morgan Kousser*     433
19. Comparative History, *by George M. Fredrickson*     457
20. The Teaching of History, *by Hazel Whitman Hertzberg*     474

The Contributors     505
Index     511

# ACKNOWLEDGMENTS

PHILIP FRENEAU, author of *The Rising Glory of America* (1771) and poet of the American Revolution, had a low opinion of scholars. He regarded them as "the most insipid companions in the universe," and found them almost always in a "childish fret." He said so in an essay that he called "The Antiquarian." My experience in preparing this volume suggests otherwise. The twenty contributors have been good-natured, stimulating, and cooperative. At least, most of them were, most of the time. (Unfortunately, the scholar who promised to contribute an essay on the new economic history failed to prepare it, despite repeated assurances that he would.) Needless to say, we do not share a common program or point of view about recent historical writing and the state of the discipline. Such a consensus would be impossible even if it were desirable. We are in agreement on many points, however, and the contributors supplied valuable suggestions and responses to several drafts of my introductory essay. It is much improved as a consequence; and I wish to acknowledge what a pleasure it has been to collaborate with them. I am indebted to four additional colleagues for their helpful responses to my essay: Steven L. Kaplan, Walter F. LaFeber, and Joel H. Silbey of Cornell, and David H. Pinkney of the University of Washington.

Five individuals must be singled out for particular expressions of appreciation: John Whitney Hall, who first suggested, in 1977, that such a volume be prepared; Mack Thompson, executive director of the American Historical Association, who acted on Hall's suggestion and is a most congenial administrator to work with; Edmund H. Worthy, Jr., assistant executive director of the AHA in 1977–78, who helped to prepare the grant application for this project to the National Endowment for the Humanities; and William J. Bouwsma and

John Hope Franklin, presidents of the AHA in 1978 and 1979—wise men who gave me good counsel.

*The Past before Us* has also been the beneficiary of guidance from the AHA's Committee on International Historical Activities, chaired by Robert Forster of The Johns Hopkins University; from the AHA's Research Division, chaired by Nancy L. Roelker until 1978 and by Eugene F. Rice thereafter; and from an ad hoc advisory board that included Bernard Bailyn of Harvard, Philip D. Curtin of Johns Hopkins, Natalie Z. Davis of Princeton, Carl N. Degler of Stanford, Felix Gilbert of the Institute for Advanced Study, Edmund S. Morgan of Yale, and C. Vann Woodward of Yale.

*The Past before Us* would not have been possible without generous support from the National Endowment for the Humanities (grant no. RO-32374-78-887). Bernhard Kendler, Barbara Salazar, Marilyn Sale, and Kay Scheuer of Cornell University Press have been splendidly thoughtful and meticulous throughout the editorial and production phases of the project. Their efforts extended far beyond the call of duty, and I regard them as joint editors of the volume. My assistant, Anne-Marie Garcia, who is a paragon of efficiency, has patiently done much of the inevitable photocopying, collating, typing, proofreading, telephoning... in sum, all the details that must be attended to in bringing a project such as this one to fruition in record time. She has, as always, my deep appreciation.

MICHAEL KAMMEN

*Ithaca, New York*

1 0

# FOREWORD

## John Hope Franklin

THE officers and Council of the American Historical Association originally conceived this volume to be a report on the part of historians in the United States to their colleagues in other parts of the world. We intended the birth of the book to coincide with the fifteenth meeting of the International Congress of Historical Sciences. That organization convenes at five-year intervals; and its impending sessions at Bucharest, Romania, in August 1980, seemed an ideal target for the first succinct assessment of American historical scholarship during the 1970s.

As the project has developed since 1977, however, it has grown broader and deeper than anyone envisioned at the outset. Consequently, in addition to serving as a report to historians all over the world, it should also serve as an invaluable guide and reference work for teachers of history, and their students, throughout the United States.

*The Past before Us* describes a panoramic range of the interests, activities, problems, and achievements of historians in the United States, with particular attention to the 1970s, a period that has witnessed the transformation of historical scholarship. The book makes no claim to be all-inclusive, however. Many thousands of historians in the United States are unaffiliated with educational institutions, public agencies, or historical societies, so although their work may be highly significant, it is nearly impossible to characterize their interests as a group. Moreover, even historians who have contact with one another and exchange views regularly do not always agree about major developments, or the importance of new approaches, or the validity of various interpretations. In recent years historians in a broad field have tended to pursue their own specialty and then to argue that the specialty itself has become a field. The historians reporting here have taken cognizance of these specialties to the extent that it was possible for them to do so.

Professional historians apart, the people of the United States have always had a consuming interest in their own past. That interest has greatly intensified in recent years. As emigrants from Europe, Africa, and Asia became more assimilated, they grew less absorbed in the history of the lands of their ancestors and devoted more attention to their New World home and its history. Later they were to return to a study of their more remote past—to discover their "roots," as it were.

The impressive fact about the study of history in the United States in the twentieth century, and especially in the 1960s and 1970s, has been the seriousness with which so many people have approached it. This has been the case not only in the universities, which have awarded large numbers of doctorates in history, but also at lower educational levels and even among people unconnected with educational institutions.

For many years there were only a few major historical societies and museums in various parts of the country. In addition to the American Historical Association, founded in 1884, there were important regional organizations, notably the Organization of American Historians—founded in 1907 as the Mississippi Valley Historical Association—and the Southern Historical Association, organized in 1934. Among the well-established state societies were those in Massachusetts, New York, Pennsylvania, Virginia, South Carolina, Kentucky, and Wisconsin. Later, such organizations came into being in every state of the Union. Some were privately endowed while others were supported by state governments. In addition, city and town historical societies emerged, often supported by private funds. The many activities of these organizations raised the historical consciousness of people other than professional historians regarding their history. This was especially true after the founding of the American Association for State and Local History in 1940. By 1976 there were approximately 4,500 historical societies in the United States. Some of them published attractive and well-edited periodicals, such as *American Heritage*, that enjoyed wide readership among lay persons as well as among professionals.

The establishment of archives and museums and the preservation of historic sites provide further evidence of Americans' interest in history. Some archives and museums are affiliated with historical societies; for example, the Essex Institute in Salem, Massachusetts, and the New-York Historical Society. Others are unaffiliated with any society; two leading examples are the Henry Francis du Pont Winterthur Museum in Delaware and the Henry E. Huntington Library and Art Gallery in California. The beginning of the restoration of Colonial Williamsburg in 1926, with the support of John D. Rockefeller, Jr., was a great stimulus for the preservation of historic sites in other parts of the country.

Few developments did more to stimulate interest in history than did the transformation of various state archives. No longer a political sinecure, they are now the domain of the professional archivist and historian. While some archives had been administered by trained historians, not until the years following World War II did most of them become important educational and cultural institutions with trained personnel and diversified programs aimed at making historical information available to the rank and file of the citizenry.

By establishing the National Archives in 1935, the federal government set an excellent example for states and cities that wished to institute programs to further the preservation and dissemination of historical knowledge. Presidential libraries, under the supervision of the National Archives, date from the administration of Franklin D. Roosevelt. As the depositories of the papers of modern presidents and their associates, they are scattered across the country, from Hyde Park, New York, to Austin, Texas. Meanwhile, the federal government has encouraged a national interest in the papers of earlier presidents (as well as of a large number of other citizens) through assistance provided by the National Historical Publications and Records Commission. Various agencies in the federal establishment, ranging from the Department of State to the National Park Service, have worked to promote the preservation of historical materials and have demonstrated the responsibility that the federal government can effectively assume in writing institutional history. It now seems that the involvement of the United States government in the promotion of historical studies need be limited only by the resourcefulness and the ingenuity of the civil servants and other participants involved.

During the last two decades, the activities of government at every level, and of many parts of the private sector, did much to set the stage for an acceleration of historical activities in the United States. In 1961 the nation began to observe the centennial of its Civil War. Most states established Civil War centennial commissions, composed of historians and interested lay people whose duties involved the promotion of the observance throughout the land. Historians, novelists, and others wrote numerous books. Civil War round tables and clubs composed of devotees of the military aspects of the war took on new life. Editors launched fresh periodicals. Educational institutions, radio, and television set up countless programs. In dozens of ways, the American people were made painfully aware of the turbulent events of the middle of the last century that had torn the nation apart.

It did not take much prompting from organized groups for the launching of a full-scale observance of the bicentennial of the nation's independence in 1976. Seemingly, all of the historical organizations that had emerged in previous years—national, regional, and local associations, historical museums, and groups to preserve historic sites—were poised to celebrate the event. From the federal government's American Revolution Bicentennial Authority on down to the most modest elementary school history club, people were looking back to the earlier struggle not only to celebrate independence but also to search for relevant meaning for their own time. Perhaps nothing more clearly epitomized this interest in the American Revolution than the television series *The Adams Chronicles,* the saga of one of the prominent families of the Revolution whose influence has extended to our own day. Sponsored by the National Endowment for the Humanities, the series was seen on national educational television stations by an audience estimated at eight million people.

Public interest in history, especially when presented on television, continued into the postbicentennial years. *Holocaust,* an account of the travail and death of six million Jews in Europe, held the attention of some 120 million viewers when it was shown in the United States in 1978. A year earlier more than 130 million people watched *Roots,* the television version of a book by Alex Haley that traced a black family's history from capture in Africa through slavery and emancipation in the United States. Defying both tradition and predictions, it held its audience for eight consecutive nights. On its final evening 51 percent of all television sets in the United States were tuned to it. Two years later 110 million people viewed the week-long sequel, *Roots: The Next Generations.* In anticipation of an increased interest in family history, the National Archives and Records Service prepared free family history research packets to assist anyone who wanted to become a family historian. The development of American concern for family history, genealogical research, and even family reunions has increased to the point at which some refer to this development as "the *Roots* phenomenon."

While professional historians may continue to regard themselves as custodians of the nation's past, the average person's awareness of his own history and the history of the United States has come from a number of influences and has intensified in the last two decades. Some history is learned in the schools and universities, to be sure, but some through motion pictures and television as well. One cannot always vouch for the authenticity of such history or, indeed, measure how it is perceived and how much the viewer absorbs. But it cannot be denied that such influences have been considerable. True to their reputation for inventiveness, however, Americans have sought new ways of popularizing history in much the way way that they have sought to promote some new product for home use. Thus History Day in Ohio has been greeted with enthusiasm, particularly in the secondary schools, and is "celebrated" throughout the state. The Metro History Fair in Chicago seeks to create interest in, even excitement over, national as well as local history.

As readers of this volume become acquainted with the areas of interest of today's professional historians, they would do well to reflect upon the relationship between these historians and the general public. Surely, the influence of the professionals is direct and important. In due course what they discover, write about, and teach will affect the average person's understanding of history in the United States and elsewhere. Meanwhile, other influences—government, historical societies, museums, historic sites, television, motion pictures, and even historical fiction—will also affect the manner in which the average person perceives and appreciates the role of the professional historian. If distortions and misperceptions occur as a result of the wealth and variety of sources of historical information, the professional historian can be expected once again to correct and clarify the picture.

# THE PAST BEFORE US

# INTRODUCTION

## The Historian's Vocation and the State of the Discipline in the United States

### Michael Kammen

I

HISTORY has been written in what is now the United States ever since the early seventeenth century, when Captain John Smith and Governor William Bradford first began to record the circumstances of exploration and colonization in North America. The emergence of history as an avowedly professional discipline, however, took place about a hundred years ago—partly as a result of the desire for a more "scientific" form of historical scholarship, and signaled by the development of graduate programs in history at the major universities. The founding of the American Historical Association in 1884–85 is symptomatic of History's coming of age as a vocation.

Ever since then, the guild has had a penchant for introspection. One consequence of that tendency has been the appearance of periodic reports on the state of the discipline. One thinks of *The Writing of History* (1926), which resulted from the work of an AHA committee created in 1920, and which contained a long essay by John Spencer Bassett entitled "The Present State of History-Writing"; or *Historical Scholarship in America*, a report by the committee of the AHA on the planning of research, which appeared in 1932; or *The Social Sciences in Historical Study*, a report of the committee on historiography of the Social Science Research Council (1954); or *History* (1965), by John Higham, Leonard Krieger, and Felix Gilbert; or *Historical Studies Today* (1971), sponsored by the American Academy of Arts and Sciences. Montaigne's tart remark comes inevitably to mind: "There is more to-do about interpreting interpretations," he wrote, "than interpreting the facts themselves. There are more books about books than about anything else. We do nothing but make commentaries on one another."

Be that as it may, the current need for a fresh and systematic evaluation is perhaps greater than ever. Why? Because the profession has grown rapidly in recent years; because its geographical scope and methodological sophistication have increased dramatically; and, most of all, because a creative proliferation of new historical literature is altering our perceptions of the past. During the 1970s a marked transition occurred within the guild of historians in the United States. Although we cannot speak with precision about a particular "generation" or "cohort" of historians, neither can we escape the sense that a changing of the guard took place in that period. A younger group of practitioners emerged—among them many of the contributors to this volume—who have profoundly influenced the discipline. *Pari passu*, an older group of distinguished scholars disappeared from the scene. To recite just a few of their names is to recall an honor roll of the generation that achieved maturity and professional prominence during the second quarter of the twentieth century: Samuel Eliot Morison (1887–1976); Allan Nevins (1890–1971); Samuel Flagg Bemis (1891–1973); Herbert Feis (1893–1972); James Phinney Baxter III (1893–1975); Edward C. Kirkland (1894–1975); Roy F. Nichols (1896–1973); William L. Langer (1896–1977); Constance McLaughlin Green (1897–1975); Louis Gottschalk (1899–1975); David M. Potter (1910–71); Richard Hofstadter (1916–70); and Mary C. Wright (1918–70).

Although it would scarcely surprise these doyens to learn that major changes occurred in the profession during the 1970s—it is, after all, an aspect of the historian's vocation to anticipate changes, in prospect as well as in retrospect—they would perhaps raise their eyebrows at the reasons for those changes. Some of the shifts might have been predictable, but many were not. Let us look first at the predictable portion, and then at the surprises. "If there is a single way of characterizing what happened in our historical writing since the 1950's," Richard Hofstadter wrote in 1968, "it must be, I believe, the rediscovery of complexity in American history: an engaging and moving simplicity, accessible to the casual reader of history, has given way to a new awareness of the multiplicity of forces."[1] If those words seemed true more than a decade ago, how much more compelling they are today!

On the other hand, it is also fair to say that even the most perceptive

1. Hofstadter, *The Progressive Historians: Turner, Beard, Parrington* (New York, 1968), 442.

observers of historiographical change could not have predicted the particular configuration of reasons why Clio's wardrobe is now as new and extensive as it has become. In 1960, for example, C. Vann Woodward published a penetrating and widely noted essay called "The Age of Reinterpretation."[2] After reviewing the sequence of momentous developments that had occurred since the end of World War II, he concluded with a wistful plea that historians usher in a major era of historical reassessment.

What strikes us with particular force, looking back after two decades, is that his plea *cum* prophecy is rapidly being fulfilled, but not for the reasons he anticipated. Woodward called attention to the close of a long era of "free security"—a transformation he likened in importance to Frederick Jackson Turner's emphasis on the closing of the American frontier—and, in general, Woodward's focus highlighted the crucial role of changes in international relations. Most American historians would now contend, as the essays in this volume suggest, that alterations in the position of the United States as a world power and changes in man's capacity for destruction bear a relatively modest responsibility for the historiographical whirlwind that transformed our profession during the 1970s.

There is no reason why Woodward, in 1960, should have anticipated the vocational shifts that would be brought about by quantitative methods and computer technology; by the "discovery" of women, blacks, ethnic groups, the laboring and so-called dangerous classes; by the application of social theory and psychoanalysis; by the striking growth of area studies programs; by the development of urban and rural history as sophisticated genres that have been enhanced by the application of historical geography; and by the emergence of local history and historical archaeology as innovative subdisciplines with far-reaching implications.

One might apply to the historical profession, ever since the mid-1960s, E. B. White's pithy observation about Americans during the early years of their romance with the Model T Ford: "They rode in a state of cheerful catalepsy."[3] That is to say, we have moved so swiftly through so many exciting developments that there have been, perhaps inevitably, some loss of contact with the cultural environment and a suspension of sensation. The time has come, therefore, to look around, reevaluate the ground we have covered, and reestablish con-

2. Woodward, "The Age of Reinterpretation," *American Historical Review*, LXVI (1960), 1–19.
3. White, "Farewell, My Lovely!" (1936) in *Essays of E. B. White* (New York, 1977), 164.

Michael Kammen

tact between the historian's vocation and its social context. What are the salient characteristics of a guild that is undergoing the most creative ferment in its entire lifetime?

One of the more interesting anomalies in the evolution of American historical writing from its professionalization in the 1880s until the 1960s lies in the coexistence of two prominently cherished values: nationalism and detachment. J. Franklin Jameson, for instance, upheld the highest critical standards as a scholar, yet he was also a staunch patriot and believed that a knowledge of American history should undergird national pride.[4] Most members of his successor generation, practicing their craft during the middle third of the twentieth century, also felt a powerful attachment to the national past. "Attachment," as R. Jackson Wilson has written, "took the form of attributing certain values, such as 'democracy' or 'Anglo-Saxon constitutional principles,' to the nation at large and viewing American history as the emergent triumph of the principles."[5]

Simultaneously, however, practitioners also expressed admiration for detachment because they associated it with objectivity. Thus Carl Becker was widely admired for his ironic style of historical detachment; and Bernard De Voto, the cultural historian and prolific specialist on the westward movement, proclaimed the virtue of what he called "literary skepticism."[6]

In our time, however, there has been a stunning inversion with respect to these two traditional values. National chauvinism has given way to national self-criticism in historical writing. Liberalism and the liberal tradition in the United States have been challenged. The motives of national leaders are discussed cynically; and the makers of American foreign policy have been fiercely chastised on the basis of revisionist historical research. Unqualified affirmations of the national past now seem simplistic and embarrassing. Members of the guild have become more critical in order to achieve greater insight, but also more understanding in order to judge others as they would wish to be judged themselves.

4. See Allan Nevins, *James Truslow Adams: Historian of the American Dream* (Urbana, Ill., 1968), 59–60; Maurice Isserman, "'God Bless Our American Institutions': The Labor History of John R. Commons," *Labor History*, XVII (1976), 309–328.
5. Wilson, "United States: The Reassessment of Liberalism," in Walter Laqueur and George L. Mosse, eds., *The New History: Trends in Historical Research and Writing since World War II* (New York, 1967), 92. See Wilcomb E. Washburn, "Samuel Eliot Morison, Historian," *William and Mary Quarterly*, XXXVI (1979), 331.
6. See John Spencer Bassett, "The Present State of History-Writing," in J. J. Jusserand et al., *The Writing of History* (New York, 1926), 101; Phil L. Snyder, ed., *Detachment and the Writing of History: Essays and Letters of Carl L. Becker* (Ithaca, N.Y., 1958), esp. 3–28; De Voto, *Mark Twain's America* (Boston, 1932), xv.

The traditional goal of detachment, meanwhile, has also gone a-glimmering, in at least two very notable respects: the linked issues of whether or not the historian ought to make moral judgments, and whether or not the historian ought to admit (and even profess) an emotional or ideological engagement with his or her subject. Contemporary historians of the city, or of agriculture, or of the environment and rural values, or of technology, or of architecture often have a subjective relationship to their chosen topic. They may feel a sense of regret about its condition or decline. They often feel that they have a stake in its survival. This tendency is by no means new. Samuel Eliot Morison's love for the sea and fine horses is reflected in his historical writing, just as Marc Bloch's love of the field and vine is reflected in his. But practitioners today tend to be ever more explicit, even autobiographical, in explaining where they stand in relation to their subject. As Henry F. May put it in 1976: "One thing that has been forced on university teachers by their students in recent years is that they abandon the comforting pose of academic impartiality and declare their allegiances, even—contrary to all their training—admit their emotions."[7]

Similarly, there has been a shift in our climate of opinion concerning the propriety or desirability of the historian's making moral judgments. As recently as the mid-1960s, when this shift began to occur, persuasive voices could be heard on behalf of both points of view. John Higham argued the affirmative, and was answered in 1966 by Henry Steele Commager. "The historian is not God," declared Commager. "He is not called upon to judge the quick or the dead. If he sets himself up as a judge he changes the whole pattern of his intellectual and professional role from one dedicated to objective inquiry to one devoted to prosecution or defense."[8] Within a decade, however, the balance in that debate had been decisively tipped; and advocates of "history as a moral science" could be found among prac-

7. May, *The Enlightenment in America* (New York, 1976), xvii; see also Jerrold Seigel, *Marx's Fate: The Shape of a Life* (Princeton, 1978), 9; Martin Duberman, "On Becoming an Historian," in Duberman, *The Uncompleted Past* (New York, 1971), 336–356; and Duberman, *Black Mountain: An Exploration in Community* (New York, 1972).

8. Higham, "Beyond Consensus: The Historian as Moral Critic," *American Historical Review*, LXVII (1962), 609–625; Commager, "Should the Historian Make Moral Judgments?" *American Heritage*, XVII (February 1966), 92–93. For a transitional dialogue, between David M. Potter and John A. Garraty, see Garraty, ed., *Interpreting American History: Conversations with Historians* (New York, 1970), II, 330. Garraty: "History is indeed amoral, isn't it? As historians, we seek to discover and record what happened." Potter: "I suppose I agree, though I think that there is a moral value in recognizing how circumstances enhance or limit human potentialities. The historian should be mindful of the moral implications of that fact."

titioners in every subdiscipline, and among historians of all age groups. As Gordon Wright put it in his presidential address to the American Historical Association: "Our search for truth ought to be quite consciously suffused by a commitment to some deeply held humane values."[9]

The movement of American scholars in this direction has been stimulated by the work of foreign authors. For example, in the controversy that developed during the 1960s over the impact of industrialization on the standard of living in England, 1790–1850, such distinguished historians as E. J. Hobsbawm and E. P. Thompson invoked moral criteria in arguing their views.[10] Their call for the use of humanistic values in judging the socioeconomic impact of industrialization has been heeded by historians in the United States and has been applied in turn to a broad range of comparable issues.

It is a commonplace observation that many American historians during the later 1960s and 1970s, inspired by egalitarian zeal, rediscovered history "from the bottom up," by which they meant the story of "ordinary" or working-class people (sometimes misleadingly designated as "the inarticulate").[11] The word "rediscovered" is significant here because social historians of the 1930s and 1940s, especially historians of immigration and of various ethnic groups, had actually devoted a great deal of attention to what they called "grass-roots history." It is noteworthy, also, that at that time Henry Ford established Greenfield Village (in Dearborn, Michigan), because he "wanted to preserve what he appreciated as the contribution of plain men who never got into history."[12]

Interest in the history of ordinary people was sustained throughout the 1970s; yet it was accompanied by the growing recognition that elites must also continue to be studied because of their determinative role in shaping the lives of so many members of their societies. Radical

9. Wright, "History as a Moral Science," *American Historical Review*, LXXXI (1976), 1–11; see also Richard M. Morse, "The Care and Grooming of Latin American Historians, or: Stop the Computers, I Want to Get Off," in Stanley R. Ross, ed., *Latin America in Transition: Problems in Training and Research* (Albany, 1970), 36; and Francis Jennings, *The Invasion of America: Indians, Colonialism, and the Cant of Conquest* (Chapel Hill, 1975), x.

10. See Georg G. Iggers, *New Directions in European Historiography* (Middletown, Conn., 1975), 166–167.

11. See, e.g., Tamara K. Hareven, ed., *Anonymous Americans: Explorations in Nineteenth-Century Social History* (Englewood Cliffs, N.J., 1971).

12. See Theodore C. Blegen, *Grass Roots History* (Minneapolis, 1947); Oscar Handlin, *Boston's Immigrants: A Study in Acculturation* (Cambridge, Mass., 1941); William Greenleaf, *From These Beginnings: The Early Philanthropies of Henry and Edsel Ford, 1911–1936* (Detroit, 1964), 85.

historians, in particular, owing to their desire to uncover patterns of hegemony in human history, have sought to examine the powerful as well as the powerless, and, most important of all, the vectors of interaction between them.[13]

Many of the radical historians, but by no means all, style themselves as Marxist scholars. Although they do not appear to agree upon any single definition of "Marxist historiography," and although they address diverse problems from varied angles of vision, they have joined together to establish several new journals in which their research can more easily find expression.[14] As their work has become less deterministic and more subtle, it has grown more influential in the profession. During the later 1970s, many non-Marxists began to share with them an intense interest in Karl Marx and his theories of historical development.[15]

Despite the gains made by Marxist scholars in the United States, however, they still comprise a relatively small (though highly vocal) segment of the profession. There are important fields, such as urban history and the "new political history," where Marxist influence has been relatively slight. The reasons are not entirely clear; but it would appear that the ethnocultural emphasis of historians interested in voting behavior has tended to minimize an economic or class interpretation of American political history.

The extent to which a Marxist approach *has* spread among universities in the United States is symptomatic of a breakdown in distinctively national styles of historical scholarship. Clio is a citizen of the world, and History is increasingly an international guild. Just as Marx-

13. See Lee Benson, "Political Power and Political Elites," in Benson et al., *American Political Behavior: Historical Essays and Readings* (New York, 1974), 280–310; William N. Parker and Eric L. Jones, eds., *European Peasants and Their Markets: Essays in Agrarian Economic History* (Princeton, 1975); and J. H. Broomfield, *Elite Conflict in a Plural Society: Twentieth-Century Bengal* (Berkeley, 1968).

14. See *The Radical History Review*, which began in 1973/74; *Marxist Perspectives*, the first issue of which appeared early in 1978; and Ronald Radosh, "The Rise of a Marxist Historian: An Interview with Eugene Genovese," *Change*, x (November 1978), 31–35. The Marxist view of American history may appeal to some scholars because of the collapse of the quondam liberal syntheses: either the progressive (Beardian) or the consensus school. The current lack of an integrated vision of how all the pieces fit together creates problems for many who teach a survey course or try to plan a coherent syllabus. The Marxist approach, however imperfect, at least offers a holistic explanation of United States history in its entirety.

15. See William H. Shaw, *Marx's Theory of History* (Stanford, 1977); Martin Seliger, *The Marxist Conception of Ideology: A Critical Essay* (New York, 1977); Martin Berger, *Engels, Armies, and Revolution: The Revolutionary Tactics of Classical Marxism* (Hamden, Conn., 1977); Seigel, *Marx's Fate*; Melvin Rader, *Marx's Interpretation of History* (New York, 1979).

ist historians are now to be found in many countries that do not have socialist governments, so the *Annales* school in France, stressing total history, has had a pervasive impact, particularly in the United States and in Eastern Europe.[16]

Heavy borrowing from the methods and theories of social science has resulted in pluralism and greater cosmopolitanism in contemporary American historical activity. This surge of cosmopolitanism is salutary because it serves, in some measure, as an antidote to the rapid growth of specialization, which threatens at times to effect the fragmentation of History as a cohesive discipline.[17] That former danger of national chauvinism has been replaced by the high risk of subdisciplinary parochialism. The proliferation of specialties, each with its own journal, is evidence of the enormous creativity of the profession, but also is a harbinger of the malaise that results when scholars cannot communicate because they fail to follow fields beyond their own.

The intellectual curiosity and eager borrowing—from historians of other cultures as well as from other disciplines—characteristic of American historians in recent years have resulted in an eclecticism that contributes to the decentralization of the discipline here. There is no single, dominant, national "school" of historical thought in the United States. The result may be somewhat less "teamwork" than elsewhere; or possibly a duplication of effort on occasion; or even direct competition. On the other hand, the result may also be greater diversity and autonomy in the selection of topics for research and methods to be used. Nor can a small group of senior professors determine research or control the appointment of younger scholars to junior positions—certainly not to the extent that such groups do in other cultures.

The profession is no longer dominated by the history departments at a few prestigious universities. First-rate scholars are to be found throughout the country. Whereas the "new political history" may have had its genesis and received special support at Iowa, Pittsburgh,

16. See Iggers, *New Directions in European Historiography*, 31–32, 110, 115, 118, 172–173; Traian Stoianovich, *French Historical Method: The Annales Paradigm* (Ithaca, N.Y., 1976); Robert Forster, "Achievements of the Annales School," *Journal of Economic History*, XXXVIII (1978), 58–76.

17. See Charles F. Delzell, ed., *The Future of History: Essays in the Vanderbilt University Centennial Symposium* (Nashville, 1977). Although it is difficult to demonstrate with precision, the claim has been made that a higher percentage of historians who are Americans research or teach the history of other nations than is true of historians in any other culture. If this claim is valid, it is impressive evidence of the enhanced cosmopolitanism of the profession in the United States. Compare the contents of this volume, for example, with Jacques Le Goff and Pierre Nora, eds., *Faire de l'histoire*, 3 vols. (Paris, 1974).

Pennsylvania, Wisconsin, and Michigan, the "new economic history" developed at Purdue, the University of Washington, Chicago, Rochester, MIT, and Stanford; and the "new social history" at Harvard, Berkeley, Princeton, Johns Hopkins, and Carnegie-Mellon, among others. UCLA and Northwestern have unusual strength in African history; Cornell in Southeast Asian history; Texas and Wisconsin in Latin American history; Princeton and UCLA in the history of the Middle East; Harvard, Yale, and Washington in East Asian history, and so on.

The relationship between historical scholarship, on the one hand, and the teaching of history (at the graduate, undergraduate, and secondary school levels), on the other, is so complex that to discuss it properly would require a separate essay—indeed, a book-length monograph.[18] Some critical generalizations can be made, however.

First, contact and communication are still insufficient between research-oriented scholars and those who are primarily teachers of history, especially teachers in the secondary schools, community colleges, and junior colleges. Historians in the United States have yet to achieve the successful integration that occurs, for instance, through the Historical Association in Great Britain. There remains a considerable time lag between the development of important new emphases or interpretations and their assimilation into textbooks.[19] The American Historical Association has attempted to remedy these problems by cosponsoring conferences, at universities throughout the country, on the teaching of history; by cosponsoring regional institutes on women's history; and by undertaking a reevaluation of introductory and survey courses in history as they are now taught. The National Endowment for the Humanities made an important contribution during the 1970s by supporting an extensive program of summer institutes for college teachers.

Second, most of our Ph.D.s in history still receive little or no formal training designed to prepare them to be effective teachers. Although students who wish to become secondary school teachers of history or

18. For points of contrast with the situation a century and a half-century ago, see Felix Gilbert, "Reflections on the History of the Professor of History," in Gilbert, *History: Choice and Commitment* (Cambridge, Mass., 1977), 449; Bassett, "Present State of History-Writing," 120–121, 122–25; Dexter Perkins et al., *The Education of Historians in the United States* (New York, 1962); and Walter Rundell, Jr., *In Pursuit of American History: Research and Training in the United States* (Norman, Okla., 1970).

19. One hopeful sign is the appearance of a journal called *Trends in History: A Review of Current Periodical Literature in History*, published by the Institute for Research in History. Its editorial board consists of university scholars as well as secondary school teachers. The first issue appeared in May 1979.

social studies do received formal training and participate in internship programs, the quality of their instruction is often woefully inadequate, particularly with respect to new developments in subject areas they will be assigned to teach.

Third, although there has been a severe shortage of jobs for history Ph.D.s, and although demographic projections about the undergraduate population in decades to come do not portend an alleviation of the employment crisis in colleges and universities, many institutions with Ph.D. programs continue to train too many Ph.D. candidates.[20] Despite a great deal of lamentation about the desperate circumstances of younger scholars, little has been done to adjust the relationship between supply and demand. Nor has there been sufficient effort to reorient university professors to a predominant emphasis on undergraduate teaching.

Nevertheless, despite these shortcomings, some positive steps have been taken, with results that suggest that with sufficient patience the patient may be healed. A National Coordinating Committee for the Promotion of History was formed in 1976 to gather information and augment job opportunities for historians in fields other than teaching: for example, historical administration, preservation and archival work, and jobs in the commercial sector. Although it is too early to assess what effect the NCC will have, it enjoys the support of a broad array of scholarly organizations and serves a valuable role as a clearinghouse for information about jobs and related historical activities and programs.

Yet another auspicious sign is the fact that the Ph.D. dissertation, regarded for so long as a dry and routine exercise—merely an application for a "union card"—is alive and well. Not only are a number of first rate dissertations being written, but it is fair to say that a remarkable proportion of the seminal books of the 1970s originated as Ph.D. dissertations.[21]

II

Useful as it may be to survey the sociology of a discipline in flux, the changes in modes of historical inquiry and discourse are even more

20. For a somewhat different point of view see John Hope Franklin, "On the 'Oversupply' of Graduate Students," *Daedalus*, CIII (Fall 1974), 265–268.

21. Here are simply a few examples selected from an impressive field: Philip J. Greven, Jr., *Four Generations: Population, Land, and Family in Colonial Andover, Massachusetts* (Ithaca, N.Y., 1970); Richard Jensen, *The Winning of the Midwest: Social and Political Conflict, 1888–1896* (Chicago, 1971); Peter Wood, *Black Majority: Negroes in*

important. The twenty essays that comprise *The Past before Us* examine a significant number of those shifts. The next two sections of this introduction attempt to identify some broad patterns that pertain to many of the subfields and therefore seem characteristic of the discipline as a whole. This section, in particular, takes a closer look at three developments that are more complex than they seem at first glance: (1) the apparent shift from descriptive to analytical history; (2) the proliferation of methodological innovations; and (3) the changing relationship of the "new social history" to other subdisciplines—their similarities, their differences, and a common theme that pervades them all.

The key group of creative historians who came of age after World War II eschewed traditional narrative history (as well as biography, its individualized companionate form) in favor of analytical history. They valued explanatory power above expressive power. To write in the mode of a Parkman, a De Voto, or a Morison seemed as futile as trying to compose music in the fashion of Mozart, Beethoven, or Brahms. Admiration for "sophisticated" history—taking the past apart and reassembling it to show *how* and *why* things happened—caused in many quarters a mistrust or even denigration of "mere storytelling."

A closer look at developments during the 1970s, however, reveals just how muted this transformation has actually been. Why? First, because some of our most respected colleagues continue to sing the praises of traditional history (albeit modified and modernized appropriately), and of the need for expressive power.[22] Second, because so many of the major prize-winning books of the 1970s have been, in one

*Colonial South Carolina from 1670 through the Stono Rebellion* (New York, 1974); Joan W. Scott, *The Glassworkers of Carmaux: French Craftsmen and Political Action in a Nineteenth-Century City* (Cambridge, Mass., 1974); J. Morgan Kousser, *The Shaping of Southern Politics: Suffrage Restriction and the Establishment of the One-Party South, 1880–1910* (New Haven, 1974); Edward M. Cook, Jr., *The Fathers of the Towns: Leadership and Community Structure in Eighteenth-Century New England* (Baltimore, 1976); Douglas S. Greenberg, *Crime and Law Enforcement in the Colony of New York, 1691–1776* (Ithaca, N.Y., 1976); Robert A. Gross, *The Minutemen and Their World* (New York, 1976); Melvyn Hammarberg, *The Indiana Voter: The Historical Dynamics of Party Allegiance during the 1870's* (Chicago, 1977); Merritt Roe Smith, *Harpers Ferry Armory and the New Technology: The Challenge of Change* (Ithaca, N.Y., 1977); and James H. Kettner, *The Development of American Citizenship, 1608–1870* (Chapel Hill, 1978).

22. See the letters from J. H. Hexter in William O. Aydelotte, *Quantification in History* (Reading, Mass., 1971), 155–179; J. H. Hexter, *The History Primer* (New York, 1971), especially chap. 6; Peter Gay, *Style in History* (New York, 1974); and John Clive, "Why Read the Great Nineteenth-Century Historians?," *American Scholar*, XLVIII (Winter 1978/79), 37–48. Jonathan D. Spence of Yale University is the leading figure in a movement to restore the rich tradition of descriptive history in the East Asian field. See, especially, *Emperor of China: Self-Portrait of K'ang-hsi* (New York, 1974) and *The Death of Woman Wang* (New York, 1978).

form or another, exemplars of descriptive history.[23] Third, because of the powerful influence of the *Annales* school; for, as Charles Tilly has pointed out, the French use quantitative techniques, by and large, for descriptive purposes. Most *Annalistes* are more humanistic than scientific; and, in the words of one sympathetic scholar, "There are times when one wonders whether *Annales* historians care about 'explanations' at all, in the sense of weighing factors or variables."[24] Keep in mind, also, Fernand Braudel's special notion of time, the *longue durée*, and his concern for evolutionary patterns of change over time—patterns that can be perceived only through the scrupulous accumulation and juxtaposition of descriptive materials.

What happened during the 1970s, then, and what is surely one of the profession's most impressive efforts, is that historians in the United States have sought to be both more analytical *as well as* richly descriptive. Many have tried harder than ever before to theorize and generalize, but also to respect the particularities of place and time—in sum, not to violate the pastness of the past. They have sought to reintegrate society and polity, economy and geography, institutions and ideas. They have learned much about what it really means to pose historical problems, and to respond to them, if not always to resolve them, by means of an expanded historical consciousness.[25] The standards applied in historical exposition, explanation, and argument have grown steadily more rigorous. Historians have achieved greater precision in defining the social units under investigation, and in making inferences from various kinds of historical evidence. Historians are more inclined to ask, for example, "How representative is this or that piece of evidence?"[26] Waggish types have been known to say, on occasion, that history is too important to be left to the historians. We contend that there is too much at stake in achieving an accurate ren-

23. See Don E. Fehrenbacher, *The Dred Scott Case: Its Significance in American Law and Politics* (New York, 1978); David G. McCullough, *The Path between the Seas: The Creation of the Panama Canal, 1870–1914* (New York, 1977); David M. Potter, *The Impending Crisis, 1848–1861* (New York, 1976); Paul Horgan, *Lamy of Santa Fe: His Life and Times* (New York, 1975); Bernard Bailyn, *The Ordeal of Thomas Hutchinson* (Cambridge, Mass., 1974); John Clive, *Macaulay: The Shaping of the Historian* (New York, 1973); and Daniel J. Boorstin, *The Americans: The Democratic Experience* (New York, 1973).

24. See Forster, "Achievements of the Annales School," 61, 63, 69–70, 74.

25. For several excellent examples of what is meant by posing historical problems, see Charles Gibson, "Conquest, Capitulation, and Indian Treaties," *American Historical Review*, LXXXIII (1978), 1–15; Peter Wood, *Black Majority*, 36–37, 56, 62; and Robert Heilbroner's review of Alfred D. Chandler, Jr., *The Visible Hand: The Managerial Revolution in American Business* (Cambridge, Mass., 1977), in *The New York Review of Books*, February 9, 1978, 36.

26. See, however, the critical comments by Michael Katz in a review, *Journal of Interdisciplinary History*, IX (1979), 754.

dering of the past for that responsibility to be left in the hands of ahistorical, present-minded persons.[27]

Although it might be exaggerating the case to speak of a methodological revolution in the 1970s, a revolution in methodological *awareness* surely has occurred. We can see it in the burst of books on how History ought to be done;[28] in the proliferation of new journals that emphasize methodology;[29] in books and essays that plead for greater self-consciousness on the part of historians about their assumptions and procedures;[30] and in the appeal being made by some that historical methodology itself be recognized as a discrete subdiscipline.[31]

Whereas most historians active during the middle third of the twentieth century did not feel obliged to explain their frames of reference, their methodological orientations, or their theoretical constructs, the pendulum of opinion has now swung heavily in the opposite direction. How to achieve the proper balance between theory and an adequate "data base" has become a frequent issue requiring protracted discussion. Should the historian posit questions and hypotheses, and *then* accumulate and correlate the data? Or should he first collect the data pertinent to his topic, and only then ask questions of them?[32]

27. For recent examples of misuse of the past by policy makers, politicians, military leaders, jurists, and journalists, see Ernest R. May, *"Lessons" of the Past: The Use and Misuse of History in American Foreign Policy* (New York, 1973); Charles A. Miller, *The Supreme Court and the Uses of History* (Cambridge, Mass., 1969); John Shy, "The American Experience in War: History and Learning," *Journal of Interdisciplinary History,* I (1971), 205–228; and Bruce Kuklick, "History as a Way of Learning," *American Quarterly,* XXII (1970), 609–628.

28. In addition to works cited earlier, see Robert F. Berkhofer, Jr., *A Behavioral Approach to Historical Analysis* (New York, 1969); J. H. Hexter, *Doing History* (Bloomington, Ind., 1971); Lee Benson, *Toward the Scientific Study of History: Selected Essays* (Philadelphia, 1972); and Carl G. Gustavson, *The Mansion of History* (New York, 1976).

29. Notably *Historical Methods Newsletter* (1967), *Journal of Social History* (1967), *Journal of Interdisciplinary History* (1970), *Reviews in American History* (1973), *Social Science History* (1976), and *Review: A Journal of the Fernand Braudel Center for the Study of Economies, Historical Systems, and Civilizations* (1977). *History and Theory* was established in 1960–61.

30. See David Hackett Fischer, *Historians' Fallacies: Toward a Logic of Historical Thought* (New York, 1970); Murray G. Murphey, *Our Knowledge of the Historical Past* (Indianapolis, 1973); and Peter D. McClelland, *Causal Explanation and Model Building in History, Economics, and the New Economic History* (Ithaca, N.Y., 1975).

31. See Gene Wise, *American Historical Explanations: A Strategy for Grounded Inquiry* (Homewood, Ill., 1973); J. Morgan Kousser, "The Agenda for 'Social Science History,'" *Social Science History,* I (1977), 383–391. See also Cecil F. Tate, *The Search for a Method in American Studies* (Minneapolis, 1973).

32. See R. Richard Wohl, "Intellectual History: An Historian's View," *The Historian,* XVI (1953), 67; the remarks by David M. Potter in Garraty, *Interpreting American History,* II, 330–331; Robert P. Swierenga, "Towards the 'New Rural History': A Review Essay,"

Michael Kammen

We have learned that historical models must be more than internally consistent, and must offer more than explanatory power for a particular case in point—even though it may be an especially significant case. Models must be tested against *various* historical episodes and situations—various in their geographical locations and in their stages of socioeconomic development, for example—before they become truly persuasive and enable us to extrapolate conclusions with long-range validity.[33]

The consequences of such knowledge are in some respects surprising. Few historians have been impelled, contrary to what one might have expected, to take a greater interest in the philosophy of history. Moreover, the long-standing question whether History is or can be a scientific discipline seems farther than ever from resolution. Some tough-minded practitioners—such as Lee Benson, Allan Bogue, Richard Jensen, and Morgan Kousser—say yes; others—such as Jacques Barzun, Robert W. Fogel, Arthur M. Schlesinger, Jr., and Hayden White—have said no. Although it is still fair to claim, as Robert P. Swierenga did in 1974, that "American historians lead their European counterparts in the application of computer technology,"[34] the result among most prominent practitioners has been more humility rather than more arrogance.

There is a growing recognition that some of the quantitative work that has been done is very imprecise or methodologically flawed, and that most sciences require qualitative as well as quantitative forms of analysis. Those most experienced in the use of quantitative methods now readily concede that their data often reveal ambiguous conclusions—and sometimes none at all. As David S. Landes declared in his 1978 presidential address to the Economic History Association: "Many, if not most, of the important questions that we have to deal with do not lend themselves—at least not as yet—to quantitative treatment. Sometimes the numerical data are lacking. There are

*Historical Methods Newsletter*, VI (June 1973), 118; Swierenga, "Computers and American History: The Impact of the 'New' Generation," *Journal of American History*, LX (1974), 1063; and J. Morgan Kousser, "The 'New Political History': A Methodological Critique," *Reviews in American History*, IV (1976), 1-14.

33. See Michael P. Weber and Anthony E. Boardman, "Economic Growth and Occupational Mobility in Nineteenth-century Urban America: A Reappraisal," *Journal of Social History*, XI (1977), 52-74, a case study of Warren, Pennsylvania, which indicates that mobility was greater in developing industrial communities than in those that were stabilizing.

34. "Computers and American History," 1051. See also Robert W. Fogel, "The Limits of Quantitative Methods in History," *American Historical Review*, LXXX (1975), 329-350.

whole areas of history where we probably will never have the numbers we need. Sometimes we have the numbers, but they do not tell us enough."[35]

Extraordinary consequences have resulted from this added measure of realism within the profession. The first has been to make all sorts of historians, and not just the quantifiers, self-conscious and careful about matters of methodology. A second is that, in many instances, analysis of literary evidence has become much more precise: we have been shown ways to be rigorous in the use of qualitative materials.[36] A third is that many of the leading scholars in various fields have been inclined to weed their own gardens; that is, historians of slavery apply very high standards in criticizing one another; so do the "new political historians," social and urban historians, and historians of white–Indian relations. It is a sign of good health that the subdisciplines are capable of diagnosing themselves. No one should complain today, as Hayden V. White did in 1966, about "a resistance throughout the entire profession to almost any kind of critical self-analysis."[37]

In sum, although collectively we may know more about the past than our predecessors did, and more about how to do History well,

35. "On Avoiding Babel," *Journal of Economic History*, xxxviii (1978), 6–7. Gilbert Shapiro has recently conceded that the central problems that concern most historians—social change, the dynamics of institutional growth, the nature and configuration of cultural values—"escape the relatively simplistic theoretical models implicit in most quantitative work"; and he goes on to say that "our most important theoretical ideas are, as yet, in no way linked with measurable quantities" ("Prospects for a Scientific Social History: 1976," *Journal of Social History*, x [1976], 197, 203).

36. See Richard Reinitz, "A Note on the Impact of Quantification on the Methodology of Non-quantitative History," *Pennsylvania History*, xxxix (1972), 362–366; David Lundberg and Henry F. May, "The Enlightened Reader in America," *American Quarterly*, xxviii (1976), 262–293; Norman S. Fiering, "The Transatlantic Republic of Letters: A Note on the Circulation of Learned Periodicals to Early Eighteenth-Century America," *William and Mary Quarterly*, xxxiii (1976), 642–660; David Grimsted, *Melodrama Unveiled: American Theater and Culture, 1800–1850* (Chicago, 1968), chap. 5 and Appendixes I and II; and Peter Karsten, *Patriot-Heroes in England and America: Political Symbolism and Changing Values over Three Centuries* (Madison, Wis., 1978), esp. chap. 5.

37. See, e.g., Maris A. Vinovskis, "Recent Trends in American Historical Demography: Some Methodological and Conceptual Considerations," *Annual Review of Sociology*, iv (1978), 603–627; Herbert G. Gutman, *Slavery and the Numbers Game: A Critique of "Time on the Cross"* (Urbana, 1975); Kousser, "'New Political History,'" 1–14; James Henretta, "The Study of Social Mobility: Ideological Assumptions and Conceptual Bias," *Labor History*, xviii (1977), 165–178; William O. Aydelotte, "Lee Benson's Scientific History: For and Against," *Journal of Interdisciplinary History*, iv (1973), 263–272; David C. Stineback, "The Status of Puritan-Indian Scholarship," *New England Quarterly*, li (1978), 80–90; White, "The Burden of History," *History and Theory*, v (1966), reprinted in White, *Tropics of Discourse: Essays in Cultural Criticism* (Baltimore, 1978), 28.

our claims have become less strident. We find ourselves listening to notes of caution and of skeptical criticism, to calls for judicious reassessment and the remapping of terrain recently traveled. As vast amounts of primary and secondary source material accumulate, as new monographs crowd the acquisition shelves, we realize that familiar explanatory frames of reference have broken down and cease to explain the past adequately. In reviewing *The Future of History* in 1978 (see footnote 17), John Higham referred to the disintegration of "the familiar enclosures—national, chronological, and provincial—within which most historians still design their work."[38]

What is called the "new social history" may very well qualify as the cynosure of historical scholarship in the United States during the 1970s. The history of social structure, mobility, the family, sexuality, and such social institutions as factories, prisons, towns, hospitals, and churches has attracted immense attention and application. In the process our retrospective gaze has been diverted from the public sector to what Carroll Smith-Rosenberg has called "private places," that is, the household, the bedroom, the nursery, kinship systems, and voluntary associations. Here, too, we find the humility and methodological concern to which I referred a moment ago. Social historians have become increasingly self-aware in their handling of the historical evolution of social functions: for example, the search for the origins of declining functions (such as the family as a unit of production), or the stubborn persistence of certain other functions (such as the family's role in the socialization of children), or the growing differentiation of functions (as between the family and the church in providing children with religious instruction). What is at issue here? As Elizabeth H. Pleck has demonstrated, historians too readily employ a model of decay or of progress, search for proof accordingly, and then wrench the evidence out of its historical context. An evolutionary approach to social history, however inevitable, involves a high risk of anachronistic interpretation.[39]

One of the most striking developments of the 1970s was the steady expansion of the reach of social history. If it has not actually encircled its sibling disciplines, it has, at the very least, affected them profoundly. Some practitioners of urban and rural (or agricultural) history have recently changed their identification tags and now prefer to

38. *Journal of Southern History*, XLIV (1978), 95–96.
39. See Smith-Rosenberg, "The New Woman and the New History," *Feminist Studies*, III (1975), 185–198; Pleck, "Two Worlds in One: Work and Family," *Journal of Social History*, X (1976), 180.

be called social historians.[40] The central questions they are asking make that designation more appropriate. They want to expand our understanding of the impact of urbanization upon the growth of social and political consciousness. They want to know how people who migrated from rural to urban areas reconstructed their lives in the "urban villages" that they created within the cities.

It comes as no surprise that the histories of women and of various minority groups are part of the "new social history," even though there are, undeniably, important political aspects to the evolution of those segments in our society. It may be more surprising to learn that the "new military history" has become, in some respects, a suitor of social history.[41] Even the "new political history," with its relentless search for what Samuel P. Hays has called "the social basis of politics," has become a half brother (or stepsister) of social history: the most important variables, for historians of voting behavior in the United States, have been cultural identity and religious affiliation.

It seems fair to say that political history is no longer the focal point for historical scholarship. In part that is because *Annales* historians have argued that political history is "surface" history. Most people under the spell of the *Annales* school, therefore, have lacked a model for the reinterpretation of politics. The *Journal of World History*, published by UNESCO since 1962, largely excludes political history. And as public figures were discredited and political institutions became unpopular in the United States during the decade following 1965, the history of politics became a distasteful subject to many.[42]

In another sense, however, the decline of political history has surely been exaggerated; many of the other subdisciplines have, in fact, been "politicized." Class and other intergroup relationships are described in terms of "hegemony by elites." Economic relationships (involving mercantilism, for example) are described in terms of "power" and "control." Historians have suddenly begun to discover crises of authority throughout the American past. The point, therefore, is that political analysis—the study of competition for power, of responses to

40. See Bruce M. Stave, *The Making of Urban History: Historiography through Oral History* (Beverly Hills, 1977), 21; and Laurence Veysey, "The 'New' Social History in the Context of American Historical Writing," *Reviews in American History*, VII (1979), 1–12.

41. See Russell F. Weigley, ed., *New Dimensions in Military History* (San Rafael, Calif., 1975), 38; Allan R. Millett, "The Study of American Military History in the United States," *Military Affairs*, XLI (1977), 58–61; and Reginald C. Stuart, "War, Society, and the 'New' Military History of the United States," *Canadian Review of American Studies*, VIII (1977), 1–10.

42. See Jacques Le Goff, "Is Politics Still the Backbone of History?" *Daedalus*, C (Winter 1971), 1–19.

power, and of power relationships—has scarcely disappeared from historical inquiry. It has simply added manifold dimensions to the public sector, where it is more obvious; and augmented our understanding of private sectors, where power relationships are pervasive though often covert.[43]

Even the disciplines of intellectual history and psychohistory, which became popular in the profession during the 1950s and 1960s, respectively, discovered by the mid-1970s that they were being vigorously challenged and consequently were very much in need of reassessment.[44] For some practitioners the best solution seemed to be more interdisciplinary borrowing—especially from literary theory and post-Freudian psychiatry as well as social psychology. Other practitioners, however, found useful alternatives in a rapprochement with social history: deepening our understanding of the social context of ideas in order to move from the analysis of ideas and values held by individuals to those of social groups—or even, ideally, masses of people.[45] Disciples of the *Annales* school are especially important here because of the attention they give to *mentalités* in times past.

Some historians have argued that if the *Annales* school is characteristically French, and if Marxist historiography has its roots in Central and Eastern Europe, then "the cliometric school is characteristically American." Although scholars may differ on that point, there *is* a consensus that cliometrics involves more than mere numerology. The critical ingredient is economic theory, that is, the application of theory in analyzing statistics relating to prices, foreign trade, the money supply, and economic productivity. Disputes may occur over the causes of depressions, for example, or the reasons for retardation in rates of economic growth; but such disputes simply send historical-minded economists in search of better theories. There is, however, an important distinction to be made between economic historians and historical economists in the United States, a clarification

43. See, e.g., David C. Hammack, "Problems in the Historical Study of Power in the Cities and Towns of the United States, 1800–1960," *American Historical Review*, LXXXIII (1978), 323–349.

44. See, e.g., Morton White, "Why Annalists of Ideas Should be Analysts of Ideas," *Georgia Review*, XXIX (1975), 930–947, which became a new Introduction to White's *Social Thought in America*; Fred Weinstein and Gerald M. Platt, "The Coming Crisis in Psychohistory," *Journal of Modern History*, XLVII (1975), 202–228.

45. See Dominick La Capra, *A Preface to Sartre* (Ithaca, N.Y., 1978); Hayden White, "The Tasks of Intellectual History," *Monist*, LIII (1969), 606–630; J. G. A. Pocock, *Politics, Language, and Time: Essays on Political Thought and History* (New York, 1971), esp. chap. 1; Robert Darnton, "The High Enlightenment and the Low-life of Literature in Prerevolutionary France," *Past and Present*, no. 51 (1971), 81–115; and Benjamin B. Wolman, ed., *The Psychoanalytic Interpretation of History* (New York, 1971).

succinctly put by David Landes in 1978: "The difference is not only one of method. Quantitative methods are only a tool; they are not the heart of the matter. . . . The economist seeks abstraction, the better to order and systematize and build models. He wants sufficient explanation. . . . The historian, on the other hand, revels in complexity, is happy to incorporate new unknowns in his problem . . . and generally follows the law of conservation of evidence. The explanation should try to account for as many pieces of evidence as possible and are known."[46]

As I suggested earlier, one thematic emphasis has pervaded and affected nearly all the subdisciplines of historical writing in the United States during the past decade. I have in mind the widespread concern for intergenerational relations—often involving conflict—and social change. This theme is to be found in literature written by Americans about every period of their own country's history, but in American scholarship dealing with other cultures as well. To say that an emphasis on intergenerational conflict was a natural outgrowth of domestic turmoil during the 1960s in no way depreciates the insights, importance, and enduring value of so many of these studies. Nor should we neglect the seminal importance of family history and the history of childhood—specialties that only began to mature during the 1970s. We now have, all in all, a substantial body of literature with which to test Gloria Main's assertion that "application of the concept of age cohorts sharing similar life experiences throws a flood of light on historical events which have hitherto stood outside the traditional explanatory apparatus of scholars."[47]

III

The essays that follow reveal significant changes in historians' assumptions about their craft: that is, from which other disciplines they

46. Donald N. McCloskey, "The Achievements of the Cliometric School," *Journal of Economic History*, XXXVIII (1978), 15, 23; Landes, "Avoiding Babel," 8–9.

47. See Alan B. Spitzer, "The Historical Problem of Generations," *American Historical Review*, LXXVIII (1973), 1364; and "Generations," a special issue of *Daedalus*, CVII (Fall 1978), esp. the section "Generations in Historical Perspective." For Main, see *Reviews in American History*, IV (1976), 379. For selected examples of the burgeoning literature on intergenerational relations, see Erich Gruen, *The Last Generation of the Roman Republic* (Berkeley, 1974); Catherine Albanese, *Sons of the Fathers: The Civil Religion of the American Revolution* (Philadelphia, 1976); Steven J. Novak, *The Rights of Youth: American Colleges and Student Revolt, 1798–1815* (Cambridge, Mass., 1977); Joseph F. Kett, *Rites of Passage: Adolescence in America, 1790 to the Present* (New York, 1977); David Hackett Fischer, *Growing Old in America* (New York, 1977); and George B. Forgie, *Patricide in the House Divided: A Psychological Interpretation of Lincoln and His Age* (New York, 1979).

can borrow most profitably; just how complex the process of historical explanation needs to be; and the ways in which those first two necessarily affect the working definitions of History as an instrument for understanding patterns of human behavior over long periods of time.

There are almost as many definitions of History as there are practicing historians. According to June Goodfield, writing in 1977,

> History is the study of the human past as a form of collective self-understanding of human beings and their world. It is the story of human activities, what men did, what they thought, what they suffered, what they aimed at, what they accepted, what they rejected or conceived or imagined. It tells us about their motives, their purpose, their ambitions, their ways of acting and their ways of creating.[48]

Even as Goodfield uttered those unexceptionable phrases, however, practitioners attempting to come to terms with the explosion of new information about the past were deepening and redefining in more subtle ways the meaning of the phrase "historical events." Here is a pertinent excerpt from an essay about a long-term project under the direction of Bernard Bailyn.

> The amount of quantitative information available has become so great that *latent* events—events of which contemporaries were largely unaware and which become discernible only in quantitative terms (shifts in birth rate, changes in family size or structure)—have become centers of attention; and they have become important independent of any framework of interpretation that can bring them together with the course of *manifest* events,—that is, events that were matters of conscious concern. The basic problem, in other words, created by the outpouring of numbers which are badly if at all integrated into general lines of interpretation, is the difficulty of relating latent to manifest events. In the absence of effective linkages, facile formulations grow into received assumptions before their validity can be assessed. . . . The problem of relating latent events, especially those detected and expressed in quantities, to events that register in the awareness of contemporaries . . . is, I believe, becoming the central methodological problem of modern historiography. . . . For the essence and drama of history lie precisely in the relationship between latent conditions, which set the boundaries of human existence, and the manifest problems with which people consciously struggle.[49]

48. Goodfield, "Humanity in Science: A Perspective and a Plea," [Phi Beta Kappa] *Key Reporter*, XLII (Summer 1977), 4, 8.
49. Bailyn, "The Peopling of British North America: Thoughts on a Central Theme in Early American History—A Working Paper," (Harvard University, 1978), 5-6.

The successful integration of these two types of historical "events" is surely a major challenge to historical scholarship during the decades ahead. There is a sense in which the great Enlightenment historians—Voltaire, Hume, and Gibbon, for example—tried to do so but without success. A number of the most prominent scientific historians in the nineteenth century became wedded to the study of manifest events, and tended to neglect deep structures. During the later 1960s and especially the 1970s, momentum swung the other way with driving force. Our task in the 1980s, therefore, is to strike a balance: to bring events and structures into a sensible and mutually explanatory relationship; to make our knowledge of events less superficial and our understanding of structures more purposeful and personalized; to clarify major questions involving continuity and discontinuity in human history. An emphasis on events tends to put people into the foreground, whereas an emphasis on structures and series calls our attention to large socioeconomic forces. Both, therefore, are essential in achieving a fully rounded perception of the past.

Historians are also becoming more sensitive to the variability in rates of change over time, and want to know much more about the reasons why change fails to occur during the so-called quiescent periods and comes so rapidly at others. As Laurence Veysey has asserted,

> The fundamental fact of history is the unevenness of rates of change. History, like the landscape of Mars, is composed of broad plateaus which give way to sudden jagged ruptures. Patterns emerge, but they seldom enable prediction. . . . The historian can try in a more careful way to use past time as a yardstick, but he is nearly as helpless in discovering the edge of a future precipice. In the main, the historian understandably retreats to the task of seeking patterns in past outcomes, hoping at best to reveal a measure of coherence *ex post facto*.[50]

Implicit in Veysey's statement is recognition of one of the most fascinating trends in contemporary historical thought: namely, the growing appreciation of nonrational elements in man's history and behavior—what James Boswell called, even as the Enlightenment reached its peak, "the unaccountable nature of the human mind."[51] Throughout its history, Western civilization has placed a high value

50. Veysey, *The Communal Experience: Anarchist and Mystical Counter-Cultures in America* (New York, 1973), 72–73.
51. February 27, 1763, in Frederick A. Pottle, ed., *Boswell's London Journal, 1762–1763* (New York, 1950), 206.

on rationality. That tendency began to crest—Boswell to the contrary notwithstanding—with the eighteenth-century concept of "an appeal to reason"; and reached its culmination, perhaps, in the belief shared by Progressive historians during the first half of the twentieth century that men and women act purposefully. Conyers Read expressed such a view in his presidential address to the American Historical Association in 1950: "If historians, in their examination of the past, represent the evolution of civilization as haphazard, without direction and without progress, offering no assurance that mankind's present position is on the highway and not on some dead end, then mankind will seek for assurance in a more positive alternative whether it be offered from Rome or from Moscow."[52]

Oh, how swiftly the climate of opinion changed in less than a generation! As Ernest R. May remarked in 1973, so many professional historians are now inclined to argue that "if history teaches anything, it is how uncertain and unpredictable are the consequences of what men do." Historians of science are increasingly aware that the story of discovery and invention in their field has been, all too often, an attempt to clarify and rationalize a set of events that was frequently muddled, filled with mistakes and dead ends. "Much of economic history," David Landes concedes, "with its abstraction from complex reality, its suiting of behavior to theory rather than theory to behavior . . . is an exercise in tidying up rather than an effort to see people whole."[53]

The acknowledgment of unexplainable elements in human history, and the recognition that people often took actions or held views for reasons they did not fully understand, have had salutary consequences. One such consequence has been to make historians more cautious about uncritically borrowing their explanations of human behavior from the social sciences and thereby perpetuating the simplifications and misunderstandings that originated in those disciplines. A second has been to make them more mindful of the inadequate explanatory power of certain concepts and metaphors. "Political culture," "modernization," "watershed," and "image" do

52. See Miller, *Supreme Court and the Uses of History*, 81; Read, "The Social Responsibilities of the Historian," *American Historical Review*, LV (1950), 284.
53. May, *"Lessons" of the Past*, 179, 191; Landes, "Avoiding Babel," 10. See also Arthur M. Schlesinger, Jr., "On the Inscrutability of History," *Encounter*, XXVII (November 1966), 10–17; Forster, "Achievements of the Annales School," 74–75; Weigley, *New Dimensions in Military History*, 9, 26–34, 39; Laurence R. Veysey, *The Emergence of the American University* (Chicago, 1965), 267–268; and C. Vann Woodward, *American Counterpoint: Slavery and Racism in the North-South Dialogue* (Boston, 1971), 36.

not, in fact, explain very much because so often they are invoked too vaguely.[54]

A third consequence is very likely to be the most significant of the three because it adds much more than just a cautionary note: it contributes a way of dealing with the complexity of human history. I have in mind the use of typologies in order to take fully into account the diversity and particularity of elements that constitute any given historical phenomenon. We are less interested now in the archetype and more interested in the elements themselves. One finds this utilization of typologies, for example, in Reformation history, in the study of Puritanism, in the latest analyses of early American communities, in the study of race relations in the Americas, and in discussions of industrial development in historical perspective.[55]

An important point to be made about the significance of the 1970s in historical scholarship is that historians have actually begun to do things—to implement suggestions systematically—which they had been exhorted to do for a very long time. The call for a "new urban history," not to mention extravagant claims for its promise, goes back as far as 1940 at least. Nevertheless, for more than a generation urban historians continued to disregard a great deal of their own best advice. Similarly, the call for historians to study and borrow from anthropology was first heard in the 1930s. Yet that call, too, went largely unheeded until the 1970s. In the past decade, however, many historians have been reading in ethnography, enthnohistory, and cultural and symbolic anthropology. Clio has been introduced to Clifford Geertz, Victor Turner, Mary Douglas, A. F. C. Wallace, and Sidney Mintz. Such phrases as "deep change" and "thick description" have begun to appear in the vocabulary of historians. It is now acceptable for them to plot kinship and child-rearing patterns, analyze festivals and describe the idiosyncrasies of village celebrations. Having discovered cultural ecology, we are in a better position to understand the inter-

54. Christopher Lasch, *Haven in a Heartless World: The Family Besieged* (New York, 1977), xvii; Ronald P. Formisano, "Deferential-Participant Politics: The Early Republic's Political Culture, 1789-1840," *American Political Science Review*, LXVIII (1974), 475n10, 487n76; Alexander Gerschenkron, *Continuity in History and Other Essays* (Cambridge, Mass., 1968), 1,7.

55. See Lewis W. Spitz, "History: Sacred and Secular," *Church History*, XLVII (1978), 13; Richard R. Beeman, "The New Social History and the Search for 'Community' in Colonial America," *American Quarterly*, XXIX (1977), 426; Woodward, *American Counterpoint*, 242-245; and Gerschenkron, "The Typology of Industrial Development as a Tool of Analysis," in Gerschenkron, *Continuity in History*, 77-79. For the use of typologies in studying the history of the family, see Tamara Hereven, "Cycles, Courses, and Cohorts: Reflections on Theoretical and Methodological Approaches to the Historical Study of Family Development," *Journal of Social History*, XII (1978), 97-109.

play between values and customs on the one hand and their social environment on the other.[56]

Two closely related breakthroughs have also taken place. The first one can be found in the strangely belated emergence of historical geography: belated because our forebears more than three centuries ago fully appreciated its importance. That canny Captain John Smith, for example, wrote: "As Geography without History seemeth a carkasse without motion; so History without Geography wandreth as a Vagrant without a certaine habitation." Historical geography, which was neglected for so long in the United States, though widely used in Great Britain and France, is at last coming into its own. Innovative historical atlases are starting to appear alongside superb microhistorical studies. The consequence has been to make even those historians who lack training in geography far more sensitive to the role of environment, material resources, and land use in human history.[57]

The other big breakthrough has come in a related variant of microhistory: community and town studies. In the process, an interesting reversal has occurred in the dominant rationale for writing local history. For a long time, the primary purpose was to demonstrate that a given locality was really the nation writ small. Authors sought to encapsulate national themes, and so the cheeriest claim seemed to be that one's chosen place was "typical." For more than a decade, however, the purpose of serious scholars engaged in community studies has been to *test* prevailing generalizations about some region or the nation as a whole, rather than to reaffirm mindlessly the conventional wisdom.

The writing of local history and the writing of ethnic history have undergone roughly similar and parallel transformations—from their traditional antiquarianism to the most sophisticated professionalism. Ethnic history, as John Higham has pointed out, for many years could not transcend the limitations of parochialism and chauvinism. "Every group naturally wants to know its own special story and little more.

56. See Natalie Zemon Davis, "The Historian and Popular Culture," in Jacques Beauroy et al., eds., *The Wolf and the Lamb: Popular Culture in France from the Old Regime to the Twentieth Century* (Saratoga, Calif., 1977), 9–16; Richard P. Horwitz, *Anthropology toward History: Culture and Work in a Nineteenth-Century Maine Town* (Middletown, Conn., 1977); Neil Harris, ed., *The American Culture* (New York, 1970–73), 8 vols.

57. See Lester J. Cappon et al., eds., *Atlas of Early American History: The Revolutionary Era, 1760–1790* (Princeton, 1976); Carville Earle, *The Evolution of a Tidewater Settlement System: All Hallow's Parish, Maryland, 1650–1783* (Chicago, 1975); Edward W. Fox, *History in Geographic Perspective: The Other France* (New York, 1971); and David Ward, ed., *Geographic Perspectives on America's Past: Readings on the Historical Geography of the United States* (New York, 1979).

Relatively few historians... have inquired seriously into common themes that connect one group with another." That situation has begun to change; and the consequences are comparable in importance to the revolution in local historiography. The proliferation of colonial town studies, and of monographs on various immigrant groups or on nineteenth-centuries cities, enables us to make illuminating comparisons and contrasts, and even to construct typologies. "Careful comparison," as Laurence Veysey has so aptly declared, "lies close to the heart of historical explanation."[58]

## IV

What, then, can be said in summary about the historian's vocation, historical knowledge, and contemporary American culture? During the 1970s a great wave of nostalgia washed over the American people, whose mood became one of apprehension about the present mingled with affection for the receding past. Although a dramatic growth of tradition-orientation could be seen in museum-going, antique collecting, television programming, and book buying in certain categories (for example, Gore Vidal's *Burr*, Alex Haley's *Roots*, and Barbara Tuchman's *A Distant Mirror*), this reawakening of popular interest in the past, from all indications, failed to dissipate the woeful ignorance on the part of most Americans about the basic narrative structure of their national history.[59]

A glance at the history of History should provide us with a soupçon of comfort, however, for it will readily reveal that both History as a professional discipline and public historical consciousness have several times before languished and then flourished in rhythmic cycles. In 1869, John Lothrop Motley, one of our greatest and most influential narrative historians, lamented that "there is no such thing as human history. We have a leaf or two, which we decipher as best we can, with purblind eyes, and endeavor to learn their mystery as we float along to the abyss; but it is all confused babble—hieroglyphics of which the key is lost." A historiographical renaissance occurred in the age of Turner, Beard, and Becker; yet in 1953 Howard K. Beale

58. Higham, *Send These to Me: Jews and Other Immigrants in Urban America* (New York, 1975), vii; Timothy L. Smith, "Religion and Ethnicity in America," *American Historical Review*, LXXXIII (1978), 1155–1185; Veysey, *Communal Experience*, 7; David H. Miller and J. O. Steffen, eds., *The Frontier: Comparative Studies* (Norman, Okla., 1977). Comparative history served as the focal theme for the annual meeting of the American Historical Association in December 1978.

59. See *New York Times*, November 30, 1975, and May 2, 3, and 4, 1976.

could complain that "history is fast losing the place of importance it once held," and then observe that if we professionals "do not interpret and seek lessons from history out of our knowledge, [then] journalists, commentators, and popularizers are going to do it for us out of their ignorance of history."[60]

History in our time confronts grave challenges as well as great opportunities. The challenges are to be found in the job crisis for history Ph.D.s; in the decline of undergraduate enrollment in history courses at many colleges; in the way that history has been subsumed under social studies in so many of our secondary schools; in the way that church history has been pushed away from the core of theological studies in our divinity schools; in the misuses of history by politicians, policy makers, and jurists; and finally, in the dangers of vocational diversion and distraction. Noel Annan has described this last problem very well. He had the United Kingdom in view, but his words are equally applicable to the United States.

> Another major change has been the seduction of the artist and the intellectual by the life of consumption. In days gone by you pleased yourself [with] what you created, and as what was paid was usually derisory you wrote to express yourself. But now the market is arbiter. So are the norms of work. Intellectuals are busier than they were—or rather more involved in busy-ness. Dons advise foreign governments and departments in Whitehall, they are engaged in the administration of big science, they are consultants to industry, manage investment trusts, conduct polls, work for cultural agencies, write for and appear on the mass media, organize experiments in education, fill seats on countless national and local committees—all this in addition to their academic work whose rituals and committees multiply rather than diminish.[61]

There is a silver lining, of course, to Lord Annan's dark cloud. Insofar as historians do make themselves useful to society and find employment outside of academe, they not only help to counteract the job crisis for new Ph.D.s but help to demonstrate the imperative of a historical perspective as well. Thus the Federal Power Commission has a historian-in-residence who is concerned with environmental matters and historical and archaeological sites. Similarly, full-time his-

60. Motley, *Democracy: The Climax of Political Progress and the Destiny of Advanced Races* (London, 1869), 4; Beale, "The Professional Historian: His Theory and His Practice," *Pacific Historical Review*, XXII (1953), 227, 230; Woodward, "Age of Reinterpretation," 18–19.

61. Annan, *The Disintegration of an Old Culture*, Romanes Lecture (Oxford, 1966), 23–24.

44

torians are now employed by the U.S. Forest Service, the U.S. Energy Research and Development Administration, the Nuclear Regulatory Commission, the U.S. Senate, and the U.S. Food and Drug Administration.[62]

There are still other signs that Clio's current health is robust. We find them in the extraordinary proliferation of societies now affiliated with the American Historical Association—sixty-eight by 1980—and in the burgeoning subdisciplines that might very well have received autonomous essays in this volume but could not because of limitations of space: for example, educational history, legal history, ethnohistory, metahistory, military history, environmental history, and the histories of science and technology. Many historians now find that they have cross-cutting interests and multiple allegiances in the profession. If it was true, as Crane Brinton declared in 1964, that History has many mansions, it now would seem that History has suburbs and shantytowns, trailer parks and condominiums as well.[63]

Two other signs of vocational vigor deserve mention. One is the growing desire for cooperation and the attendant awareness of our interdependence. Team research and collaborative analysis are inevitable as we seek to delineate what Bernard Bailyn has called latent events and their relationship to manifest events. As long ago as 1904, Theodore Roosevelt expressed the fear that "the ideal history of the future will consist not even of the work of one huge pedant but of a multitude of small pedants." There is an element of truth to that anticipation, perhaps, but cooperation has also brought benefits to the profession and to our culture which Roosevelt could not anticipate.[64]

The final achievement to be noted is attributable to a fundamental shift in the angle of vision of so many historians practicing their craft in the United States today. During previous generations, most historians—whether or not they avowed E. A. Freeman's dictum that "History is Past Politics"—tended to describe and define structures of power (administrative, economic, ecclesiastical, social, or intellectual) in times past. The newer modes of historical inquiry, by contrast, are just as likely to describe human *responses* to those structures of power.

---

62. See the new journal entitled *The Public Historian*, produced by the Graduate Program in Public Historical Studies of the University of California at Santa Barbara.

63. Brinton, "Many Mansions," *American Historical Review*, LXIX (1964), 309–326.

64. See Jacob M. Price, "Recent Quantitative Work in History: A Survey of the Main Trends," *History and Theory*, supplement 9 (1969), 8–9; Aydelotte, "Lee Benson's Scientific History," 269–270; Roosevelt to George Otto Trevelyan, January 25, 1904, in *The Letters of Theodore Roosevelt*, ed. Elting E. Morison et al., III (Cambridge, Mass., 1951), 708.

The new modes build upon the old because the two are, quite obviously, complementary. One result is a discipline that is more responsive to the pluralistic and increasingly egalitarian society in which it functions. A second result, we hope, will be a more cosmopolitan discipline in a shrinking world—a world that is rapidly discovering just how interdependent its past, present, and future prospects are.

# PART ONE

# UNITS OF TIME AND
# AREAS OF STUDY

# 1

# Fragmentation and Unity in *"American Medievalism"*

## Karl F. Morrison

Y task is to describe an intellectual landscape. In what ways have historians in the United States explored the history of Europe between the fourth and the fifteenth centuries?[1] Our discussion of this subject is roughly limited to one decade, the 1970s. Even so, the terrain presents anomalous, and complex, fea-

For assistance during the writing of this essay I am grateful to the staffs of the libraries of the Garrett-Evangelical Theological Seminary, the Seabury-Western Theological Seminary, Northwestern University, and the University of Chicago, and of the Newberry Library. A number of colleagues were kind enough to give me the benefit of advice; I hope that the others will forgive me for naming only two, Paul Meyvaert and Robert S. Nelson.

1. A comprehensive survey entitled *Medieval Studies in North America: Past, Present, and Future* is now in the making. It is to be edited by Francis Gentry and Christopher Kleinhenz, and it will consist of about eleven chapters, by various scholars, on different aspects of the subject. Quite properly, it will take account of the close collaboration that has grown up between medievalists in the United States and Canada. Stocktaking has been a regular practice of medievalists in the United States, and I may mention here articles in that genre in which readers can find information on the field in general and on its subfields. The list follows chronological order: C. W. David, "American Historiography of the Middle Ages, 1884-1934," *Speculum*, x (1935), 125-137; James L. Cate, "A Decade of American Publication on Medieval Economic History," *Progress of Medieval and Renaissance Studies in the United States and Canada* [hereafter *PMRS*], xvi (1941), 8-26; J. R. Cresswell, "Recent American Scholasticism," *PMRS*, xvii (1942), 6-26; Guido Kisch, "A Decade of American Research in Medieval Legal History," *PMRS*, xvii (1942), 27-34; Ruth J. Dean, "Latin Palaeography: 1929-1943," *PMRS*, xviii (1944), 6-18; Francis J. Carmody, "Ten Years of American Scholarship in Medieval Science." *PMRS*, xviii (1944), 19-27. Gray C. Boyce, "American Studies in Medieval Education," *PMRS*, xix (1947), 6-30; Loren MacKinney, "Medieval History and Historians during World War II," *Medievalia et Humanistica*, v (1948), 24-35; S. Harrison Thomson, "The Growth of a Discipline: Medieval Studies in America," in Katherine Fisher Drew and Floyd Seyward Lear, eds., *Perspectives in Medieval History* (Chicago, 1963); David M. Nicholas, "Medieval Urban Origins in Northern Continental Europe: State of Research and Some Tentative Conclusions," *Studies in Medieval and Renaissance History*, vi (1969), 55-114 (not limited to research in the United States); Michael

tures. One of the strangest is the contrast between the ideal of inter-disciplinary coherence and the reality of fragmentation.[2]

If the impulse toward wholeness were recent, one might interpret it as a sign of an emerging science. If extreme segmentation were recent, one might foresee the disintegration of community. In fact, the effort to minimize fragmentation—geographical as well as intellectual—appeared together with the historical profession itself, at the end of the nineteenth century; and the creation of the Medieval Academy (1925) was among its first major achievements. Ancient poets knew the kind of paradox with which we have to deal. They recognized it as *concordia discors*, a conflict or dissonance of individual elements in the world that both generated and concealed a fundamental harmony.[3]

My contention is that the study of medieval history displays characteristics shared by many areas of historical inquiry represented in this volume. Beneath all the formal discontinuities that divide styles and generations of historical inquiry, there are common habits of thinking that change very slowly and that, in fact, make general discourse possible. Historical writing, too, has its virtual immobilities, its *longue durée*. Our business is to describe this general feature in one particular field.

But the landscape that we are to survey—our scenic *concordia discors*—presents a special anomaly. How is it possible to distinguish an area of "American medievalism"? Certainly, on the level of formal analysis and expression, such a distinction from scholarship in other countries is unreasonable in almost every way, except with regard to indigenous conditions under which medievalists in the United States work, and, of course, with regard to ways in which those conditions have colored ways of thinking.

In an earlier generation, the eminent American medievalist Charles Homer Haskins thought that there were distinctively American ways

---

Altschul, "Kingship, Government, and Politics in the Middle Ages: Some Recent Studies," *Medievalia et Humanistica*, n.s. II (1971), 133–152; Braxton Ross, "Latin Palaeography in the Later Middle Ages," *Medievalia et Humanistica*, n.s. II (1971), 153–163; David Herlihy, "The Economy of Traditional Europe," *Journal of Economic History*, XXXI (1971), 153–164 (not limited to research in the United States). The same volume of the *JEH* contains two other essays relevant to our subject that are not, strictly speaking, bibliographical reviews: Robert S. Lopez, "Agenda for Medieval Studies," 165–171, and Harry Miskimin, "Agenda for Early Modern Economic History," 172–183.

2. See Boyce, "American Studies," 29; Cate, "Decade of American Publication," 9; MacKinney, "Medieval History, and Historians," 34. The gulf between branches of inquiry has often been commented on; e.g., Theodore K. Rabb, "The Historian and the Art Historian," *Journal of Interdisciplinary History*, IV (1973), 107–117.

3. Horace, *ep.* 1.12.19; Lactantius, *Institutiones Divinae*, 2.9.17.

of writing history. Haskins believed in national mentalities.[4] "The American mind," he said, had certain features that appeared in historiography—openness to new ideas and modes of scholarship, independence from the inherited customs (or prejudices) of Europe, and freedom of inquiry. Detachment had enabled Americans to evaluate some past events more equitably than their European colleagues. And yet it also had its costs. Detachment meant separation from "the seething life of an older civilization," loss of the immediate familiarity "without which history is bloodless and untrue."[5] More recently, European scholars have also detected broad national traits in American perspectives, traits that have even pervaded the works of colleagues translated from Europe to the United States.[6] Clearly, the concept of American medievalism should be taken seriously, and it bears on the mental topography that we have to trace. Just as clearly, since we are dealing with a mentality built up over time, we cannot isolate the decade of the 1970s from the cumulative experience that preceded it and of which it was an extension.

What were the predicates of discord? The insight that, as a whole, "American historiography is a reflex of fragmentation"[7] is particu-

4. "European History and American Scholarship," *American Historical Review*, XXVIII (1923), 225. Cf. Haskins's statement: "For the most part the characteristics of our work are individual and personal rather than distinctively American," which the very next sentences appear to contradict.

5. Ibid., 215-16, 224-27.

6. The German philologist Ernst Robert Curtius invented the term "American medievalism" to describe what he considered to be distinctive configurations of medieval studies in the United States. See "Appendix: The Medieval Bases of Western Thought," in *European Literature and the Latin Middle Ages* (New York, 1963), 585. Among other perspectives offered from outside the United States, see T. F. Tout, "History and Historians in America," *Transactions of the Royal Historical Society*, 4th ser., XII (1929), 1-17; Eberhard Demm, "Neue Wege in der amerikanischen Geschichtswissenschaft," *Saeculum*, XXII (1971), 343-376; Herwig Wolfram, "'Medieval Studies in America' und 'American Medievalism,'" *Frühmittelalterliche Studien*, XI (1977), 396-408; and Geoffrey Barraclough, "History," in Jacques Havet, ed., *Main Trends of Research in the Social and Human Sciences*, pt. 2, vol. 1 (New York, 1978), esp. 258, 270. On indigenous ways of thinking observed by émigré scholars, see the comments by Erwin Panofsky and Paul Tillich in Franz L. Neumann et al., *The Cultural Migration: The European Scholar in America* (Philadelphia, 1953), 90, 101, 104, 150; Arnaldo Momigliano, *Studies in Historiography* (London, 1966), 230-231, 233. On the assimilation of imported norms and of individual scholars, see Jürgen Herbst, *The German Historical School in American Scholarship* (Ithaca, N.Y., 1965), 233; Momigliano, *Studies in Historiography*, 226-227; Charles Diehl, *Americans and German Scholarship, 1770-1870* (New Haven, 1978), passim. For a general account of cultural assimilation at work, consult Hans Rudolf Guggisberg, *Das europäische Mittelalter im amerikanischen Geschichtsdenken des 19. und des frühen 20. Jahrhunderts* (Basel, 1964).

7. I borrow the phrase from Louis Hartz, "American Historiography and Com-

larly true of American medievalism in its formative period. Haskins and his contemporaries lived in the shadow of two divisive events: the American Revolution and the Civil War. It was natural that their historical inquiries dealt so regularly with formal mechanisms by which society deliberately maintains or reconstructs itself, and with those two supreme moments of transformation, the end of the Roman world and the Renaissance. In a narrower sense, however, their work was a reflex of professional affiliation, dispersal, and fragmentation.

We cannot here enter into the extraordinary careers of men and women in the decades before the 1960s, careers that in the earliest days led Americans as far afield as Constantinople and Tiflis, and that drew Europeans to the New World. Nor can we describe the peripatetic career patterns that led individual scholars across the United States, thus spreading enthusiasm for a subject that many at first denounced as detached from popular culture, impractical, and elitist.

We should register an essential point, however. Through all the divisions among them and through their "long struggle for professional validation,"[8] medievalists did cherish broad, mutual aspirations for their field. They formed the Medieval Academy as a focus and instrument of those aspirations. At a deeper level, they also drew elements of their heritage together into a common methodological repertoire.

Working independently, many minds converged, carving out three modes of integrating data. According to the first, historians of social order inclined to study the facts before them as functions: that is, as variables reacting on one another and making up a vast social context. According to the second mode, philologists tended to examine their data as texts, taking their stand inside the evidence, so to speak, and operating within its terms. Finally, scholars developed a symbolic mode of integrating data. Explored largely by art historians, this mode gave access to changes in cultural mentality expressed in styles of architecture and the plastic arts. Regardless of dominant methodology, it was not uncommon for a writer to employ more than one of these modes in a given study.

All three modes of integrating data could be called "structuralist in conception, positivist in development, and yet orthodox humanist in final purpose and allegiance."[9] The essential point was that medie-

---

parative Analysis: Further Reflections," *Comparative Studies in Society and History*, v (1963), 373.

8. See the forewords to *Progress of Medieval Studies in the United States* (hereafter cited as *PMS*), III (1925), and *PMRS*, XXII (1953).

9. Jeremy Y. du Q. Adams, *The Populus of Augustine and Jerome* (New Haven, 1971), vii, speaking of his own book.

valists read their data on at least two levels: the message that they found on the surfaces of their individual fragments of evidence, and a second message running beneath the surface that they could recover by analyzing whole classes of data. The similarities among the three modes of integration are important clues to the method within the methods that counteracted the atomization of learning and drew so many disparate enterprises together into a common area of discourse.

Haskins's generation led the field of medieval history into the 1940s. Indeed, its longest lived members survived into the decade with which we are primarily concerned.[10] Understandably, therefore, the professional ethos that they created early in the twentieth century persisted among them and the students who succeeded them; after a fashion, it became institutionalized. Still, in what Haskins had called its openness to fresh ideas, American medievalism was also in the process of transforming itself. Amid this intensive self-examination, new branches of inquiry appeared. Like the debate over historicism, however, the promotion of additional fields and subjects of research tended to multiply the idioms of medieval studies without enhancing the flexibility of common discourse.

There was one exception: the social history taught in France by Lucien Febvre and Marc Bloch, and transplanted to the United States, largely in the 1940s. Mainly from their German intellectual forebears, American scholars had inherited the vision of a total history, cutting across the boundaries of academic disciplines. They cherished that vision, but their experience and their existing methods ran counter to it. Febvre and Bloch, too, inherited the dream of wholeness, from German predecessors among others,[11] but they had a method that promised to fulfill their vision. In the United States, there were some intrepid demographers, the advance guard of social history, in the 1940s; they gained followers and companions in the 1950s;[12] and, in the 1960s, they achieved, by means of computers, a technique required for the full development of their method.

And yet this reflex of fragmentation was not universally accepted. Febvre and Bloch quite deliberately rejected the old humanism—largely confined as it was to classical traditions in literature and to

10. Charles Howard McIlwain (1871–1968); George La Piana (1878–1971); E. A. Lowe (1879–1969).

11. Bryce D. Lyon, *Henri Pirenne: A Biographical and Intellectual Study* (Ghent, 1974), 128–136, on Lamprecht's influence.

12. Barraclough, "History," 264–270. Cf. Sylvia L. Thrupp and Dietrich Gerhard, "Comparative Study at Stockholm," in *Comparative Studies in Society and History*, III (1960), 483: "Comparative study may well prove to be the best counter-force we can oppose to the danger of the fragmentation of historical knowledge through over-specialization."

53

institutions of literate classes—in favor of a wider humanism that would include the entire range of human endeavor, society's inarticulate as well as its educated components. Some scholars welcomed their emphasis on collective phenomena and their approbation of social-scientific methods. But others deplored these innovations as dehumanizing. Bloch attacked the "idol of origins" that, he thought, classical humanism had erected; but critics alleged that social historians were blinded by their own devotions, including one to "that Bitch-goddess, Quantification."[13]

As the 1970s began, therefore, divisions were more obvious than common discourse. Further, the endemic disruption of academic life and the unusual experience of conducting classes under the protective rifles of the National Guard heightened the sense of discord. When one of the most distinguished American medievalists took stock in 1969, he therefore struck a menacing tone. In general, Joseph R. Strayer said, history had fallen into disrepute with the wider public. Justifying techniques as ends in themselves (indeed, bound to outmoded techniques) and parading its antiquarianism, the special enterprise of medieval history faced the prospect of "being shoved into the back corner along with Sanskrit, Assyriology, and other subjects that are kept alive only through the efforts of a handful of specialists." The statistically unreliable state of much evidence used by medievalists precluded rejuvenation through "new sociological and statistical techniques." Even when they were most successful, medievalists applying such techniques might appear to other scholars and the public to be playing "esoteric games." Was there any way out of this cul-de-sac? The answer proposed lay in the accumulation of fresh data through precise techniques and exacting studies, and in analogies that medievalists could thereby discover between early Europe and the diverse cultures of their own day, analogies that would yield "some insights into the problems of a troubled world."[14]

13. Marc Bloch, *Apologie pour l'histoire, ou Métier d'historien* (Paris, 1949), 5; Carl Bridenbaugh, "The Great Mutation," *American Historical Review*, LXVIII (1963), 326.
14. Joseph R. Strayer, "The Future of Medieval History," *Medievalia et Humanistica*, n.s. II (1971), 179, 181–182, 185, 188. Alarmed by academic overspecialization—which he held responsible for "the retarded progress and the lessening appeal of medieval studies"—Walter Ullmann, at Cambridge University, addressed the same subject in *The Future of Medieval History* (Cambridge, Eng., 1973) not long after Strayer. The differences between American and continental perspectives on the Middle Ages are suggested when one compares Strayer's call for an increasing number of detailed studies with Ullmann's call for the creation of an "integrative history" centered on the study of law and institutions. The detachment implicit in Strayer's search for analogies—a trait in "American medievalism" noted earlier—contrasts with Ullmann's

Strayer's lecture illustrates, in miniature, how some traits of thought that characterized earlier decades in American medievalism persisted also in the one just past: an openness to experimentation, a search in the past for analogies to the present, and a sense of potentially harmful detachment from the social environment. There is, of course, other evidence of continuity. Great endeavors often mature slowly, and the 1970s saw the fulfillment of several enterprises begun between twenty and fifty years earlier. Kenneth John Conant undertook exploratory excavations at Cluny in the 1920s and completed his great study with the publication of *Cluny: Les églises et la maison du chef d'ordre* in 1968. The last volumes of E. A. Lowe's *Codices Latini Antiquiores* have antecedents almost as old; and a massive revision of Louis Paetow's *Guide to the Study of Medieval History*, one of the first books published under the auspices of the Medieval Academy, has just been compiled. In the 1930s Millard Meiss began research for what became, by 1974, the five volumes of his *French Painting in the Time of Jean de Berry*. It would be easy to enlarge the list of works of long maturation that were accomplished between 1968 and 1978.[15] (By its nature, the Index of Christian Art, instituted by Charles Rufus Morey in 1917, has remained in a state of continual maturation.) The massive contributions of senior scholars to historical knowledge is emphasized by another list: of the ten historians who have received the Haskins Medal of the Medieval Academy in the period under review, four were born between 1894 and 1904, and two others in 1914 and 1916. (The remaining four were born between 1921 and 1929.)[16] The topography of American medievalism therefore retained personal and disciplinary elements of its past.

view that by studying medieval evidence "we can find out what we were before we have become what we are today" (29).

15. One could add, for example, Blanche Boyer and Richard McKeon, eds., *Peter Abailard, Sic et Non: A Critical Edition* (Chicago, 1976, 1977), dedicated to Charles H. Beeson, who died in 1949; a new edition of the multivolume *History of the Crusades*, under the general editorship of Kenneth Setton (Madison, Wis., 1969-); George Forsyth and Kurt Weitzmann, *The Monastery of St. Catherine at Sinai: The Church and Fortress of Justinian* (Ann Arbor, n.d.); and Kurt Weitzmann, *The Monastery of Saint Catherine at Mount Sinai: The Icons, I: From the Sixth to the Tenth Century* (Princeton, 1976); and Robert Ignatius Burns's volumes on the Christian conquest of Valencia (see note 28 below). It is only right to point out that new works have been initiated on the monumental scale so characteristic of earlier generations. One thinks, for example, of Jaroslav Pelikan's *Christian Tradition: A History of the Development of Doctrine*, of which the first four volumes are (or will be) within the chronological limits of the Middle Ages; and of the *Dictionary of the Middle Ages*, which is being compiled under the auspices of the American Council of Learned Societies.

16. In the order in which they received the Haskins Medal, the historians mentioned are: 1968, Marshall Clagett (b. 1916); 1969, Giles Constable (b. 1929); 1970, Robert Brentano (b. 1926); 1971, S. Harrison Thomson (1895-1975); 1972, Kenneth John

The few examples that I have cited also indicate that it retained characteristics of geographical and intellectual dispersal that were already apparent in 1926. I have alluded to authors who completed or launched slowly maturing works on the eastern seabord (Dumbarton Oaks, Harvard, The Institute of Advanced Study and Princeton University, Yale), in the Middle West and the Rocky Mountain region (Chicago, Michigan, University of Colorado), and on the west coast (University of San Francisco). My second list—that of Haskins medalists—adds the South (Emory).[17] The two lists also suggest the range of intellectual dispersion. The authors have studied particular areas—England, France, Italy, Iberia, and Asia Minor under Byzantium and the Turks—as well as the Mediterranean society of medieval Judaism. Their learning has included Arabic (or Islamic), Greek, and Jewish culture, as well as Latin. Their subjects have formed a brilliant, kaleidoscopic array—military and political mechanisms, church history, literature, the history of science, philosophy, art and archaeology, ethnography, and palaeography. This inventory of subjects might well suggest a much fuller range than was apparent in 1926.

But a sampling of exceptional—and therefore rare and unrepresentative—materials will not give us the details that our topography requires, and that, in fact, demonstrates marked continuity in patterns both of geographical and of intellectual endeavor. Let us turn, therefore, to a well-populated class of data, and one that is most sensitive to institutional changes: doctoral dissertations. Tables 1–4 have been constructed on the premises that doctoral dissertations in history are completed, on the average, about nine years after a student enters a graduate program,[18] and that his place in the numerical sorting of cohorts within the profession is conditioned by his place in a series beginning when he matriculates. With an eye on doctorates received in and after 1967/68, the tables therefore begin with 1960/61. The most obvious feature of Tables 3 and 4 is the double peak of doctorates awarded in 1972/73 and 1975/76, followed by a sharp de-

Conant (b. 1894); 1973, S. D. Goitein (b. 1900); 1974, Kurt Weitzmann (b. 1904); 1975, Speros Vryonis, Jr. (b. 1928); 1976, Robert Ignatius Burns (b. 1921); and 1979, George Cuttino (b. 1914).

17. Burns, Conant, and Thomson appear on both lists. The 1926 survey appeared in *PMS*, IV (1929), 15–45. This was the first list that James F. Willard, the editor of *PMS* (later *PMRS*), considered representative, though he acknowledged that it was incomplete.

18. American Council on Education, *A Fact Book on Higher Education*, 4th issue (1976), 76.259. Fluctuations in the average between 1920 and 1970 are indicated in U.S. Department of Commerce, Bureau of the Census, *Historical Statistics of the United States: Colonial Times to 1970*, ser. H 751–765, Bicentennial Edition, pt. 1 (Washington, D.C., 1975), 385.

cline in the number of dissertations under way and completed. We shall return to this feature when we examine evidence for prognostication. At the moment, we need to observe the statistical breaks in Table 2. It is clear that a great number of institutions have awarded between one and six doctorates in medieval history during the period under review, while another grouping has awarded between nine and eleven; a third, between fourteen and eighteen; and a fourth, between twenty-one and twenty-seven. Wisconsin is in a class by itself with forty. During our period, a number of history departments sharply reduced the size of their graduate programs. Consequently, it would be wrong to read qualitative judgments into these figures (which cannot, in any case, be regarded as final),[19] but the figures at least indicate where programs of advanced instruction have been sustained, and with what rhythm.

Regarding the more populous programs, it is obvious that the densities of geographical dispersion represented here repeat those that had emerged by 1926. As earlier, there are primary concentrations in the New England and Middle Atlantic regions, in the tier of midwestern states bordering the Great Lakes, and in California, though the extraordinary branching out of the University of California in the last thirty years extends contours that appeared in 1926 down the length of the state from Berkeley to Los Angeles. Closer inspection reveals some topical concentrations, reflecting the special interests of eminent scholars, such as the series of dissertations in ecclesiology and canon law written at Cornell University under Brian Tierney's direction, or that on Carolingian luminaries written under the supervision of Richard Sullivan at Michigan State University, or the dissertations written under David Herlihy's direction during his tenure at Wisconsin (1964–72), in a class almost by themselves by virtue of their attention to largely illiterate social classes.

From the bird's-eye view, the recent intellectual dispersion, like the geographical one, continues an earlier pattern, but with modifications. Among the dissertations accounted for in the period 1967/68–1977/78, the largest individual segment (73) comprised works on England, predominantly in the late Middle Ages. (Ten of the 73 dealt with Anglo-Saxon topics.) Nearly half (31) were studies of law and institutions. The next largest segment was devoted to France (62), again in

19. This is partly the result of unpredictable classifications in *American Doctoral Dissertations*. For example, Joseph H. Lynch's "Simoniacal Reception in Religious Houses, 1050–1215" (Harvard, 1970–71) appeared under the heading "Education, Religion"; and Emily Z. Tabuteau's "Transfers of Property in Eleventh-Century Norman Law" (Harvard, 1975) under "Literature, Medieval."

*Table 1.* Doctorates awarded in medieval history, United States, 1960/61–1977/78

| Institution | 1960/61 | 1961/62 | 1962/63 | 1963/64 | 1964/65 | 1965/66 | 1966/67 | 1967/68 | 1968/69 | 1969/70 | 1970/71 | 1971/72 | 1972/73 | 1973/74 | 1974/75 | 1975/76 | 1976/77 | 1977/78 | Total |
|---|---|---|---|---|---|---|---|---|---|---|---|---|---|---|---|---|---|---|---|
| Boston University | | | | | | | | | 1 | | 1 | 2 | 1 | 1 | 2 | | 2 | 1 | 11 |
| Brandeis | | | | | | | | | | 1 | 1 | | | | | | | | 2 |
| Brown | | | | | | | 2 | | | | 1 | | | | | 1 | | | 4 |
| Bryn Mawr | | | | | 2 | 2 | | | | | | | | | | | | | 4 |
| California–Berkeley | | 3 | 1 | 2 | 2 | 2 | | | | 2 | 3 | 1 | 1 | 2 | 2 | 2 | | 2 | 25 |
| California–Davis | | | | | | | | | 1 | 2 | 1 | | | | | | | | 4 |
| California–Irvine | | | | | | | | | | | | | | | | | | 1 | 1 |
| California–Los Angeles | 2 | | | | | | | | 2 | 2 | 2 | 4 | 1 | 1 | 1 | 5 | 3 | 2 | 25 |
| California–Riverside | | | | | | | | | | | | | | | | 1 | | | 1 |
| California–San Diego | | | | | | | | | | | | | 1 | 1 | | | | | 2 |
| California–Santa Barbara | | | | | | | | | | | | | 1 | | 1 | | | | 2 |
| Carnegie-Mellon | | | | | | | | | | | | | | 1 | | | | | 1 |
| Case–Western Reserve | | | | | | | | 1 | | | | | | | | | | | 1 |
| Catholic University | | 1 | 2 | | 1 | | 2 | | | | | | | 2 | 1 | 1 | | | 10 |
| Chicago | | 3 | 3 | | 1 | | | 1 | | 1 | | | 1 | 2 | 1 | 6 | 3 | 2 | 24 |
| Cincinnati | | | | | | | | 1 | | | | | 1 | | 1 | | | | 3 |
| City University of New York | 2 | | | 3 | | | | | | | | | | | 1 | | | | 6 |
| Colorado–Boulder | | | | | | | | 2 | | 1 | | | | 5 | | | | 1 | 9 |
| Columbia | | 1 | 1 | 2 | | | 2 | 1 | 3 | 3 | 1 | 3 | 4 | 1 | 1 | 3 | 1 | 1 | 28 |
| Connecticut | | | | | | | | | | | | | | | | 1 | | | 1 |
| Cornell | 2 | | | | | | | | 1 | 1 | 1 | 7 | 1 | 1 | 1 | | | 3 | 18 |
| Denver | | | | | | | | | | | | | | | | | 2 | | 2 |
| Duke | | | | | | | | | 1 | | | 1 | 2 | 1 | | 2 | | 2 | 9 |
| Emory | 1 | | 1 | | 1 | | 1 | 1 | 1 | 1 | | 1 | 1 | 1 | | 1 | | | 11 |
| Fordham | 1 | | | | | | 2 | 1 | | | | | | | | | | | 4 |
| Georgetown | | | | | | | | | | | | | | | 1 | | | | 1 |
| Georgia | | | 1 | | | | 1 | | 2 | | | | | | | | | | 4 |
| Harvard | 1 | | 1 | | | | | 2 | 2 | 3 | | | 2 | 1 | 1 | 1 | | | 14 |
| Hawaii | | | | | | | | | | | | | | | | | 1 | | 1 |

Table 1. (Continued)

| Institution | 1960/61 | 1961/62 | 1962/63 | 1963/64 | 1964/65 | 1965/66 | 1966/67 | 1967/68 | 1968/69 | 1969/70 | 1970/71 | 1971/72 | 1972/73 | 1973/74 | 1974/75 | 1975/76 | 1976/77 | 1977/78 | Total |
|---|---|---|---|---|---|---|---|---|---|---|---|---|---|---|---|---|---|---|---|
| Illinois–Urbana | | 1 | | | 1 | | 1 | | 1 | 1 | | 1 | 4 | | | | | | 10 |
| Indiana | | | | | | | | | 1 | 1 | | 1 | 1 | | 1 | 1 | 1 | 2 | 9 |
| Iowa | | | 1 | | | | | | | | | 1 | 1 | 1 | 1 | | 2 | | 6 |
| Jewish Theological Seminary | | 1 | | | | | | | | | | | | | | | | | 1 |
| Johns Hopkins | | | 3 | | | | | 3 | | 1 | 1 | 1 | | 1 | 1 | 1 | 3 | 1 | 16 |
| Kansas | | | | | | | | | | 1 | | | | 2 | 1 | 2 | | | 6 |
| Kent State | | | | | | | | | | | | | | 2 | | | | | 2 |
| Kentucky | | | | | | | | | | | | | | | | | 1 | | 1 |
| Loyola of Chicago | | | | | | | | | | | | | | 1 | | | 1 | | 2 |
| Maryland | | | | | | | | | | 1 | 1 | | | 2 | | | | | 3 |
| Massachusetts | | | | | | | | | | | | | | | | | | 2 | 2 |
| Miami of Ohio | | | | | | | | | | | 1 | | | | | | | | 1 |
| Michigan | | | 1 | | 1 | 1 | 1 | 1 | | 1 | 1 | 1 | 1 | | | | | | 10 |
| Michigan State | | | 1 | | | 1 | | 1 | 2 | 3 | 2 | 2 | | 2 | | 2 | 1 | 1 | 17 |
| Minnesota | | | 1 | | | | | | 2 | 2 | 2 | | | 2 | | | | | 9 |
| Mississippi State | | | 1 | | | | | 2 | | 1 | 2 | | 2 | | | 1 | | 2 | 9 |
| Missouri–Columbia | | | | | | | | | | | | | | | | | | 2 | 2 |
| Nebraska–Lincoln | | | | | | | | | | | 1 | | | | | | | | 1 |
| New York University | | | | | 1 | | 2 | | 2 | 2 | 2 | 2 | 4 | 2 | | 2 | 1 | 1 | 21 |
| North Carolina | | 2 | 2 | | 1 | | | | | | | | | | | | | | 5 |
| Northwestern | | | | | | 2 | | | | | | | | | | | | | 2 |
| Notre Dame | | | | | | | 1 | | | 1 | 1 | | | | | | | | 4 |
| Ohio State | | | | | | | | | | | | | | | | | | | 4 |
| Oklahoma | | | | | | | 1 | | | | 1 | | | | | 1 | 2 | | 3 |
| Pennsylvania | | | | | | | | | 2 | 1 | | | | | | | | | 4 |
| Pennsylvania State | | | | | | | 1 | | | | | | | | | | 1 | | 1 |
| Pittsburgh | | | | | | | | 1 | | | | | | 1 | | | | | 2 |
| Princeton | | 1 | | 2 | 1 | | 3 | | | 3 | 2 | 4 | 2 | 1 | | 3 | 1 | 1 | 23 |
| Rice | | | | | | | | | | | | | | 1 | | 1 | | | 2 |

Table 1. (Continued)

| Institution | 1960/61 | 1961/62 | 1962/63 | 1963/64 | 1964/65 | 1965/66 | 1966/67 | 1967/68 | 1968/69 | 1969/70 | 1970/71 | 1971/72 | 1972/73 | 1973/74 | 1974/75 | 1975/76 | 1976/77 | 1977/78 | Total |
|---|---|---|---|---|---|---|---|---|---|---|---|---|---|---|---|---|---|---|---|
| Rochester | | | 1 | | | | | | 2 | 1 | 1 | 2 | 1 | | | 2 | | | 4 |
| Rutgers | | 2 | 2 | | | | | | 1 | 1 | 1 | 2 | 1 | | 2 | | 1 | | 11 |
| St. Louis | | | 2 | | 1 | 1 | 1 | 2 | | 1 | 2 | | 1 | | 1 | | | 1 | 10 |
| Southern California | | | | | | | | | | | | | | 3 | | 2 | 1 | | 6 |
| Stanford | | | | | | | | | | | | | 3 | 3 | | | 1 | | 9 |
| SUNY–Binghamton | | | | | | | | | | | | | | | | | 1 | | 1 |
| Syracuse | | | | | | | 2 | | | | | 1 | | | 1 | 1 | 1 | 1 | 3 |
| Texas–Austin | | | | 1 | | | | | | | | | 1 | | 1 | 1 | | | 5 |
| Tufts | | | | | | | | | | | 1 | | | | | | | | 1 |
| Tulane | | | 1 | | | | | | | | | | 1 | | 1 | | | | 3 |
| Union Theological Seminary | | | | | | | | | | | | | | | | | | 1 | 1 |
| Utah | | | | | | | | | | | | 2 | | | | | 1 | | 3 |
| Virginia | | | | | | 2 | | | | | 1 | | | | 2 | | | 1 | 4 |
| Washington (Seattle) | | 1 | 1 | | 1 | 1 | 2 | | | | 1 | | 2 | | | | | | 9 |
| Washington University (St. Louis) | | | | | | | | | | | | | 2 | 1 | 1 | | | | 4 |
| Wayne State | | | | | | | | | | | | | | | | | 1 | | 1 |
| Wisconsin–Madison | 1 | 2 | 1 | 3 | 4 | 4 | 2 | 2 | 3 | 6 | 1 | 4 | 6 | | 2 | | 1 | | 40 |
| Yale | | | | | 1 | | | 2 | 2 | 2 | 2 | 2 | 2 | 4 | 1 | | 1 | | 23 |
| Yeshiva | | | | 1 | 1 | | 2 | | | | | | | | 2 | 3 | 1 | | 5 |

Total institutions: 77
Total dissertations: 549

Sources: *American Doctoral Dissertations; Dissertation Abstracts; List of Doctoral Dissertations in History in Progress in the United States* for the years noted. The information displayed in this table may be compared with that provided by S. Harrison Thomson in "A Note on American Doctoral Dissertations," *Progress of Medieval and Renaissance Studies in the United States and Canada*, xx (1949), 53–54.

*Table 2*.    U.S. institutions awarding doctorates in medieval history, 1960/61–1977/78, in order of frequency

| Doctorates awarded | Institution |
| --- | --- |
| 40 | Wisconsin |
| 28 | Columbia |
| 25 | California–Berkeley; California–Los Angeles |
| 24 | Chicago |
| 23 | Princeton; Yale |
| 21 | New York University |
| 18 | Cornell |
| 17 | Michigan State |
| 16 | Johns Hopkins |
| 14 | Harvard |
| 11 | Boston University; Emory; Rutgers |
| 10 | Catholic University; Illinois–Urbana; Michigan; St. Louis |
| 9 | Colorado–Boulder; Duke; Indiana; Minnesota; Mississippi State; Stanford; Washington (Seattle) |
| 6 | City University of New York; Iowa; Kansas; Southern California |
| 5 | North Carolina; Texas–Austin; Yeshiva |
| 4 | Brown; Bryn Mawr; California–Davis; Fordham; Georgia; Notre Dame; Ohio State; Pennsylvania; Rochester; Virginia; Washington (St. Louis) |
| 3 | Cincinnati; Maryland; Oklahoma; Syracuse; Tulane; Utah |
| 2 | Brandeis; California–San Diego; California–Santa Barbara; Denver; Kent State; Loyola of Chicago; Massachusetts; Missouri–Columbia; Pittsburgh; Rice |
| 1 | California–Irvine; California–Riverside; Carnegie–Mellon; Case–Western Reserve; Connecticut; Georgetown; Hawaii; Jewish Theological Seminary; Kentucky; Miami of Ohio; Nebraska–Lincoln; Northwestern; Pennsylvania State; suny–Binghamton; Tufts; Union Theological Seminary; Wayne State |

the later period (3 concerned Merovingian history and 15 Carolingian). In order of size, these two categories were followed by Italy (42), ecclesiology and church order including canon law (40), Byzantium (21), textual studies (20, including editions), "Germany" (19), Iberia (18), and various smaller categories, among which were the histories of science, philosophy, and hagiography. If we turn to dissertations announced as being in progress since 1975 but not yet reported as having been completed, much the same relative strengths occur, though the numbers are of course far smaller, and the proportions correspondingly less distinct.[20]

By and large, the titles of dissertations indicate the well-trodden

20. The numbers are: England, 15 (including 1 Anglo-Saxon); France, 11 (including no Merovingian topics and 1 Carolingian); Italy, 5; Byzantium, 6; textual analyses, 2; "Germany," 2; Iberia, 6; church order, canon law, and spirituality, 11.

*Table 3.* Number of U.S. doctorates in medieval history and number of awarding institutions, 1960/61–1977/78

| Year | Doctorates | Institutions |
|---|---|---|
| 1960/61 | 8 | 6 |
| 1961/62 | 14 | 9 |
| 1962/63 | 24 | 16 |
| 1963/64 | 13 | 6 |
| 1964/65 | 17 | 13 |
| 1965/66 | 18 | 10 |
| 1966/67 | 30 | 19 |
| 1967/68 | 24 | 16 |
| 1968/69 | 28 | 17 |
| 1969/70 | 42 | 24 |
| 1970/71 | 30 | 22 |
| 1971/72 | 50 | 25 |
| 1972/73 | 54 | 30 |
| 1973/74 | 52 | 32 |
| 1974/75 | 28 | 22 |
| 1975/76 | 49 | 27 |
| 1976/77 | 34 | 25 |
| 1977/78 | 34 | 24 |
| Total | 549 | |

*Table 4.* Dissertations reported as being in progress, 1975–78

| Period | Dissertations |
|---|---|
| May 1967–May 1970 | 97 |
| May 1970–May 1973 | 102 |
| May 1973–June 1975 | 64 |
| July 1975–June 1978 | 53 |

Note: In a small way, the decline indicated here contributed to the general decline in the number of doctoral degrees conferred in all branches of history, from a peak of 1,358 in 1973 to 1,082 in 1977 (Association of Research Libraries, *American Doctoral Dissertations,* 1976–77, Table II, xxv).

Source: *List of Doctoral Dissertations in History in Progress in the United States.*

ways of politics and institutions, biography and textual analysis. Through all the broad, familiar categories, however, are scattered titles that reflect social concerns and commitments unknown, at least in recent intensity, to earlier generations. I have just referred to some studies written at Wisconsin in which agricultural and artisan classes figure. Other investigations concerned the history of women, of families, and of elites, the births of various professions, the repressive and demonic sides of spirituality, and the social impact of disease. To say that such subjects, developed in the social sciences, have been investigated is also to say that the techniques of quantitative analysis used by social scientists have played a great role, as dissertations that have now been published amply demonstrate.

It is also worth noting, among new characteristics, the proportionately large number of dissertations devoted to Byzantine culture. When Haskins addressed the American Historical Association in 1922, that field was by no means active. "The Byzantine Empire," Haskins said, "appears to have left America cold."[21] Circumstances began to change through the work of A. A. Vasiliev, Peter Charanis, and other distinguished, if isolated, scholars. As the change accelerated through the establishment (1940) and later the splendid achievements at Dumbarton Oaks, instruction was begun and research libraries established in centers of learning that had unconsciously ignored half of medieval Europe. Our figures indicate some results of this long collective effort. The number of dissertations (31) is perhaps less telling than the number of institutions at which they were submitted (17). It is right to add that by 1975, instead of a handful, more than 200 scholars formed the Byzantine Studies Conference.

The multiplication of specialisms and the facilities that they require for graduate programs was paralleled in other fields that Haskins saw lying fallow. The history of science is another such instance. "Whereas in 1950 the scholars engaged in serious research into the history of medieval science could be counted on the fingers of two hands, by 1975 they numbered in the scores. This has meant an enormous increase in the quantity of research and has brought us to the point where virtually every scientific discipline pursued during the Middle Ages has attracted a coterie of historians."[22] Still, the number of dissertations completed in such fields as Byzantine history and the history of science leaves the dominant areas in the intellectual topography of American medievalism the same as they were fifty years ago: England (particularly law and institutions), France, and Italy.

Thus far, we have recognized two persistent traits in our landscape: geographical dispersal, and a complex intellectual dispersal among academic specialisms and—it can be added—among coteries of

21. "European History and American Scholarship," 220.
22. David C. Lindberg, *Science in the Middle Ages* (Chicago, 1978), ix. The history of technology has not advanced as much as might have been expected. See Lynn White, Jr., *Medieval Technology and Social Change* (Oxford, 1962), and "Cultural Climates and Technological Advances in the Middle Ages," *Viator*, II (1971), 172-201. For a valuable review of changing attitudes toward medieval science, see Richard C. Dales, *The Scientific Achievement of the Middle Ages* (Philadelphia, 1973), esp. 170-176 and the bibliographical essay, 177-182.

scholars within specialisms. We may now turn to the further subject that figured in our earlier discussion. All historians, we then said, were engaged in a common enterprise: the integration of historical data. Three modes of integration appeared to constitute a common methodological repertoire at the beginning of the century. All three modes addressed the characteristic enigma of historical inquiry: development, a mingling of continuity and change. To unravel the enigma, they postulated that data could be read on two levels—the surface (what they say) and below the surface (the meaning, or meanings, embedded in what they say). Whether approached as functions, texts, or symbols, data lent themselves to breaking apart and reconstructing, so that the interior level of tacit assumptions and unspoken coherence could be disclosed and made to illuminate the outer level of material evidence. Of course, any representational art operates on two tiers, in just this way. The habit of segmenting the past into problems, however, which became firmly implanted during the 1930s, colored the ways in which the three modes have been subsequently applied.

A few remarks on the three modes as recently employed may illustrate points at which works about very different subjects converge. From the beginning, the approach to data as functions was designed for analysis of developments on the grand scale. It has continued to serve that purpose. In the period with which we are concerned, it has been applied to one salient but perplexing aspect of medieval culture: the conquest and domination of peoples by minorities, not infrequently by aliens. Our sample consists of four books on extremely varied subjects. Two concern the Christianization of the Roman Empire;[23] a third describes the conversion of Anglo-Saxon England to Christianity;[24] and the fourth, the Turkish conquest and "de-Hellenization" of Asia Minor.[25] Because of the diversity of their themes, the books draw on the most varied kinds of evidence. The transition from pagan to Christian Latin poetry is treated entirely with reference to literary remains. The creation, diffusion, and transformation of Christian motifs in art has been described with reference to a selective range of evidence drawn from many media, but leaving aside nonvisual evidence. Poetry and art can be thought of as symp-

23. Ernst Kitzinger, *Byzantine Art in the Making: Main Lines of Stylistic Development in Mediterranean Art, 3rd–7th Century* (Cambridge, Mass., 1977); Charles Witke, *Numen Litterarum: The Old and the New in Latin Poetry from Constantine to Gregory the Great* (Leiden, 1971).

24. William A. Chaney, *The Cult of Kingship in Anglo-Saxon England: The Transition from Paganism to Christianity* (Berkeley, 1970).

25. Speros Vryonis, Jr., *The Decline of Medieval Hellenism in Asia Minor and the Process of Islamization from the Eleventh through the Fifteenth Century* (Berkeley, 1971).

toms; but study of a systemic change requires a far wider base of evidence. Thus, the conversion of the Anglo-Saxons to Christianity is approached through a daunting array of data—literature, archaeology, folklore, numismatics, place names, and others. And the de-Hellenization of Asia Minor is described by means of the massive apparatus of ethnology.

And yet, at the interpretive level, these four books exemplify common traits. As we have indicated, they are reductive in their selection of data for the purpose of defining, resolving, and appraising a problem isolated by the historian. For an antiquarian, the integrity of the individual piece of evidence counts. For a historian working in any of our three modes, the individuality of a fact or event or life matters less than its formal, objective relation to other evidence and to other categories of evidence bearing on the problem. Through this emphasis on formal context, it is possible to exclude whole bodies of evidence from the discussion of poetry and art, and, in the wider studies, to dissect the data and rearrange the *disjecta membra* in the way that is most germane to the logical exposition of a theme. The data are seen first as functions of interpretive or thematic unity. Only after the reductive stage does the exposition become inductive. At this moment, selected, dissected, and reconstituted, the data are portrayed as functions once again, this time in the general course of development.

Breaking the past down into problems naturally has its costs. Narrative linkages, such as chronology, are among the casualties. Chronology plays a very subordinate role in these four books. In one (Chaney's) there is no chronological sequence at all. In another (Witke's), development is retrograde, the fullest form of Christian Latin poetry (in Prudentius) coming among its earliest practitioners. In the other books, a progressive direction gradually takes shape. Functions vary, however, and some classes of data remain almost static, while others sustain fundamental changes. Some artistic styles, for example, become immobilized for generations; some are revived after long intervals. Ethnography displays many similar examples in the conservatism of custom, language, and religion. When the clock stands still or is turned back, and when the course of development is seen as a series of problematic ebbs and flows extending over centuries, chronology ceases to be a major analytical tool, though it may remain an expository one.[26]

26. See Witke, *Numen Litterarum*, 145. A distinguished example of how chronology can be used to achieve narrative unity is John Bell Henneman's two-volume study of French fiscal history, *Royal Taxation in Fourteenth-Century France: The Development of War Finances, 1322–1356* (Princeton, 1971) and *Royal Taxation in Fourteenth-Century France:*

Chronology sustains simplistic themes of "decline and fall" or "conquest and consolidation," but it fails to capture the problematic nonlinear sequences described in our four books. The studies do cover development over long reaches of time—roughly between 200 and 500 years—and development emerges in their pages as the sum of analogies, parallels, and exchanges in many aspects of life. It is portrayed as occurring through a process of mediation—or, more precisely, of translation[27]—which may or may not be dialectical, but which alters both parties, victor and vanquished alike.

One object of employing data as functions is to elucidate the intellectual or social context within which development occurs. If a scholar surveys not the whole course of reculturalization but only the moment of conquest itself, he has a different perspective, and, correspondingly, different heuristic needs. What then meets the eye, especially if the conqueror is an alien minority, is not so much the elaborate reciprocal process of mediation as the one-sided assertion of control. Such treatment is exemplified in Robert Ignatius Burns's massive study of the Christian conquest of Valencia, a work that has struck so many readers "par la vivacité de l'exposé et la facilité brillante du style, ainsi que par l'abondance et l'information de l'annotation."[28]

Dealing with the first forty years after the conquest, this work characterizes development as an organic unity, "a plurality of separate thrusts, combining with apparent fortuity to the same end."[29] The thrusts occurred within the Christian camp. It is not evident how they reacted upon and modified one another. Nor is there any clear linkage between the Christians and the Muslims. Indeed, the Muslim majority vanishes from sight in the documents that Burns had at his disposal, and only the most painstaking reconstruction of evidence has recov-

*The Captivity and Ransom of John II, 1356–1370* (Philadelphia, 1976). The results were partly disintegrative, however, as Frederic Cheyette pointed out (*Speculum*, LIII [1978], 379): "Methodologically, this means that research in the history of the late medieval monarchy cannot be limited to the archives of the central institutions but must be pursued—as Henneman has done—in local monographs, and in town and departmental archives."

27. The simile of translation is used, e.g., by Kitzinger, *Byzantine Art*, 18, and Witke, *Numen Litterarum*, 200.

28. Robert Ignatius Burns, *The Crusader Kingdom of Valencia: Reconstruction on a Thirteenth-Century Frontier*, 2 vols. (Cambridge, Mass., 1967); *Islam under the Crusaders: Colonial Survival in the Thirteenth-Century Kingdom of Valencia* (Princeton, 1973); *Medieval Colonialism: Post-crusade Exploitation of Islamic Valencia* (Princeton, 1975). A final volume, *The Crusader-Muslim Predicament: Colonial Confrontation in the Conquered Kingdom of Valencia*, is in progress. The comment is quoted from a review by Charles Verlinden in *Revue belge de philologie et d'histoire*, LV (1977), 560.

29. Burns, *Crusader Kingdom of Valencia*, 1, 301.

ered something of its institutions, its life, and the impact that, en route
to oblivion, it had on the small élite of Christian rulers. Although his
subject is dynamic, Burns's data describe static episodes rather than
the process of development. Accordingly, he sets forth his data in an
interlocking series of case studies, integrating them syntactically, as
though they comprised a text of immobilized parts of speech, through
which the moving discourse could become apparent. He therefore
leads us from the first mode—data as functions—to the second—data
as texts.

As I implied, seekers after functional contexts practice forms of
external criticism, while those who regard their data as texts can be
called internalists. They operate within "the interconnected structure
of thought, the internal self-propelling factors" in a fragment, or a
body, of evidence.[30] In other words, they regard their data as documents, or even as one great composite document, and, so far as possible, they criticize a text in its own terms. This way of thinking lends
itself quite easily to the study of a given problem in a monographic
case study, and it is the most widely and diversely applied among our
three modes of integrating data. During the 1970s it has been applied,
for example, in semantics, in the history of ideas, and in art history,
and it has also figured in the dispute over the merits of quantification.

Jeremy Adams's study of the words *populus* and *gens* in the vo-
cabularies of SS Augustine and Jerome provides an example of how
the textual mode has been applied in semantics. The object of this
study was to penetrate beneath the level of the individual text to the
wider syntax of thought. For "some of the most powerful and persistent of human convictions operate just beneath the level of formula
construction, and in patterns interestingly different from statements
held up for public exhibit." To achieve his purpose, Adams assembled
a comprehensive file of instances in which the two fathers employed
the critical terms, and he sorted them by connotation. Since he did not
sort them chronologically, he in effect regarded the entire *oeuvres* of
Augustine and Jerome as two vast texts informed by consistent habits
of thought. But, despite important similarities, each father had his
own "central concept or set of notions,"[31] and one result of disclosing
this content hidden beneath written words was to sift common from
idiosyncractic connotations. But development is not part of Adams's
theme; for the syntax of the "central concept" does not move.

30. Cf. Felix Gilbert, "Intellectual History: Its Aims and Methods," in Felix Gilbert
and Stephen R. Graubard, eds., *Historical Studies Today* (New York, 1972), 145.
31. Adams, *Populus of Augustine and Jerome*, 3, 174.

67

In the history of ideas, the task has often been not so much to establish a text as to unpack it. When the philosopher Paul Ricoeur speaks of "unpacking" a metaphor, he means that a verbal statement encases a complex array of meanings that analysis can disclose. The historical version of this exercise rests on the proposition that an idea is what its experience in the world has made it. Quite often, one begins with a crystalline statement of this idea—a text—and describes, by extended exegesis, the experience encapsulated in that statement, the experience that *is* the meaning of the statement.

An outstanding example of this address to data occurs in a book by Brian Tierney on the doctrine of papal infallibility.[32] In effect, the work is a historical exegesis on the text "Whether the Roman pontiff is . . . unerring in faith and morals." It aroused both approval and controversy because Tierney concluded that the doctrine of papal infallibility did not belong to the original and enduring faith of the Roman church, but rather emerged out of polemical opportunism in the thirteenth century, and that the papacy, having also embraced it for pragmatic reasons in the nineteenth century, might be well advised to discard it in the twentieth.

For our purposes, the essential point is that, desiring "to understand the past in its own terms,"[33] Tierney reconstituted the syntax of those terms by studying documents as the products of variable circumstances.[34] To be sure, the documents did form a series, but their direction took shape by accident rather than by design or by the unfolding of some primordial truth. They remained disjointed until congealed in the aspic of theology. An empiricism such as David Hume's, without Hume's dogmatic skepticism, operates in this historical exegesis, and with its familiar isolating effects. Development is crucial to the argument, but development is perceived in retrospect. Hindsight sifts what is permanent from what is ephemeral. The actual movement of events, while it is going on, is a series of discontinuous, idiosyncratic episodes; and, for an idea as for a person, the experience is intrinsic, unique, and incommunicable.

32. Brian Tierney, *Origins of Papal Infallibility, 1150–1350: A Study on the Concepts of Infallibility, Sovereignty, and Tradition in the Middle Ages* (Leiden, 1972).
33. The comment forms part of Tierney's response to a critique by Father Alfons M. Stickler, published in *Catholic Historical Review*, LX (1974), 427–441, and further developed in *CHR*, LXI (1975), 265–279. Tierney's comment occurs in the latter volume, at 271. The exchange was translated and published again in the *Rivista di storia della chiesa in Italia*, XXVIII (1974), 585–594, and XXIX (1975), 221–234.
34. As was suggested in a review by John J. Ryan, *Journal of Ecumenical Studies*, XIII (1976), 38: "He makes the shift [from infallibility to irreformability] as early as pages three and four of his book by treating infallibility as an attribute of *documents* rather than of the *persons* of the pontiffs involved."

A third approach to data as texts is represented by Millard Meiss's study of the brothers Limbourg, superb artists employed by Jean duc de Berry, at the beginning of the fifteenth century. The object of this work was to identify and appraise the Limbourgs' miniatures as documentary evidence, to parse "the rhetoric of painting,"[35] and to make it speak not only in terms of color and composition but also in those of the spiritual, intellectual, and social cosmos that orbited around the flamboyant duke. If paintings were to be studied as documents, it was necessary to edit them, thereby making them conveniently accessible to other scholars, and Meiss's work indeed carries, in a separate volume, about 900 illustrations. Through the use of color films, Meiss was able for the first time to collate the miniatures, as one would written texts. By thus analyzing the miniatures as individual texts comprising an *oeuvre*, Meiss was able to distinguish the styles of the three brothers, and changes in their individual styles. He was able to portray the originality that they allowed themselves in the use of earlier models, including works by a contemporary, the sculptor Claus Sluter, and by great Tuscan painters of the fourteenth century, and perhaps also remains of classical antiquity in Jean de Berry's magnificent treasury.

The achievement of this work is to locate in northern France the earliest appearance of some characteristics formerly ascribed to the art—and to the mentalities—of Renaissance Italy. Strangely, this general and important conclusion has corollaries that restrict generalization. Meiss has surveyed the works of three men, an oeuvre in a single medium produced over the course of about sixteen years. The culmination of the oeuvre (the *Très riches heures*) was left fragmentary. Thus, the state of the evidence presents certain inherent cautions against generalization. Furthermore, Meiss has disputed the coherence and pervasiveness of an "international style" in the early fifteenth century, judging that "the local or regional qualities of French painting . . . [are] far more interesting and historically of much greater importance." The final and highest point in the oeuvre, he argued, had nothing to do with an international style, but was "absolutely unique in European painting."[36]

35. Millard Meiss, *French Painting in the Time of Jean de Berry: The Limbourgs and Their Contemporaries*, 2 vols. (New York, 1974), I, 249.

36. Ibid., I, 5–6, 241. An excellent study that replaces uniformity with regionalism in another branch of study—church history—is Robert Brentano, *Two Churches: England and Italy in the Thirteenth Century* (Princeton, 1968). Borrowing the term from architecture (and art), Brentano describes the English and the Italian churches as expressing two "styles," working with the same basic elements, but differing in episcopal and

As in our other examples, therefore, the integration of data as texts served to emphasize what was problematic and therefore singular, and especially to portray development as something intrinsic to the data and occurring in their own terms, according to the rules of their own rhetoric.

A very powerful revulsion from this point of view has taken shape among social historians, notably demographers; it focuses on the use of quantifying techniques. As our example of semantic analysis indicates, the point at issue is not whether statistical methods have merit.[37] The issue is not even whether data—of whatever genre—should be integrated as texts. The issue is whether the historian is limited to such exegetical or even allegorical[38] analyses as we have considered. Can he, or should he, free himself from the terms and rhetoric of the past, which dictate questions that may be asked and infer the answers that may be given? Should he dare to ask questions undreamed of earlier, and to generate new data with which to answer them?

At least superficially, the generation and manipulation of data resemble the exercise that we have been considering: specifically, the reconstitution of an implicit text lying hidden within the explicit text of written documents. Another point of resemblance is the difficulty in generalizing beyond the problematics of the individual case study. The basis for quantitative analysis, however, exacerbates this difficulty. Statistical evidence is rare, fragmentary, and highly localized, and the conclusions of studies based on it are necessarily limited to specific places and periods. Furthermore, individual studies rest on categorically distinct bodies of evidence—one on tax rolls, another on wills, a third on official surveys, and so forth. The data are both "highly fragmentary"[39] and incommensurable. Moreover, in the absence of any common frame of reference, no broad configuration of constants and variables could emerge from the aggregate of monographic case studies.[40] Finally, given the partial and abstract nature of the evidence, it is natural that statistical studies portray Europe in

---

monastic order, modes of writing and preserving documents, paradigms of sanctity, and other important aspects of individual and collective life.

37. See also Gerhart B. Ladner, "Gregory the Great and Gregory VII: A Comparison of Their Concepts of Renewal, with a note on the computer methods used by David W. Packard," *Viator*, IV (1973), 1–31.

38. Michel Foucault, *The Archaeology of Knowledge*, trans. A. M. Sheridan Smith (London, 1972), 139.

39. John B. Freed, *The Friars and German Society in the Thirteenth Century* (Cambridge, Mass., 1977), 119. See Lopez, "Agenda for Medieval Studies," 167.

40. Barraclough, "History," 310–320, 440, provides a sober analysis of the promise and achievement of quantification, not limiting his comments to medieval history.

ways that appear "incomplete, cold, and wholly dehumanized,"[41] all the more since they portray it in limited, immobile cross sections that, like snapshots of disparate subjects, betray neither continuity nor change.[42]

And yet the powers, objectives, and achievements of statistical analysis are beyond dispute. As an example of this mode of reconstituting data as texts, we may refer to a comprehensive study of the Florentine census, or *catasto*, of 1427–30. In its own time, the catasto was a spectacular bureaucratic miscarriage. Eventually it accounted for about 60,000 households and more than 260,000 persons, with their property. But the bulk of information was too enormous to be used in the fifteenth century; the catasto appears never to have been mentioned in another public document; the reforms toward which it was intended to lead were never initiated. Armed with computers, collaborating American, French, and Italian scholars were able to generate their data and to constitute a major sociological text.[43]

Defects found in less vast demographic sources also characterize the catasto, and, with meticulous care, the collaborating scholars attended to them. The catasto provides very incomplete data on mortality; these were supplemented from the records of burial societies and other sources. The catasto offers little about the rites of passage in Florentine life, and family memoirs, chronicles, and literary texts were drawn on to supply this section of the picture. A vast panorama results, displaying patterns of the distribution of wealth, structures of professions for men and women, conventions regarding marriage, old age, and death.

The value of this study is all the greater because its authors considered and stated its limitations. There are defects in the data that could not be rectified. The migrant population is all but ignored, and not only the marginal members of society but even the clergy are most inadequately represented.[44] These gaps and the singular nature of the catasto make it difficult and hazardous to generalize from the data contained in and generated from it, or even to collate it with such evidence as exists from other places. Above all, there is the effect of immobility. The authors return again and again to the problem of

41. Charles T. Wood's review in *Speculum*, LII (1977), 964.
42. The phenomenon of immobility was certainly known in other lines of inquiry, including canon law. See Richard Helmholz, *Marriage Litigation in Medieval England* (Cambridge, Eng., 1974), 165, 186.
43. David Herlihy and Christiane Klapisch-Zuber, *Les Toscans et leurs familles: Une étude du catasto florentin de 1427* (Paris, 1978), 11–12, 101, 106, 614–615.
44. Ibid., 137, 151–161, 164, 308.

7 1

giving chronological depth to their data, of animating the snapshots—the fixed and immobile images—provided by their evidence.[45] It may be true that, despite all efforts, their account does not capture the deep realities that ceaselessly formed and reformed Tuscan society, dynamic impulses of which statistics were merely a reflection. But, with its residual immobilities, the study is by no means "dehumanized" in its reconstructed text about "les réactions des différentes classes sociales à la menace du déclin ou de l'anéantissement."[46]

Thus far, we have considered two modes of integrating data. Each of them has been applied in widely diverse lines of inquiry and can therefore be regarded as belonging to a general level of discourse, cutting across formal specialisms. The same is true of our third mode, in which data are integrated as symbols.

By contrast with the other two modes, the symbolic is inherently appropriate to the quest for multilevel analysis that has been such a persistent aspect of this account. To regard data as symbols is, from the start, to anticipate two levels of discourse, the one literal and the other figural, an implicit meaning within the explicit meaning of the evidence. It is hard to escape this two-tiered way of reasoning if one expects material evidence to yield meaning. This is so even in the history of science when, stripping away the trappings of scriptural allegory in a medieval text, a scholar finds, on another level, a set of operating assumptions and procedures—"basic conceptualizations"—that anticipated modern scientific theories.[47]

Indeed, the symbolic mode occurs in many of the works that we have already consulted. In studies representing the functional mode, it was used to indicate major changes in collective thought and belief (Kitzinger, Witke) or analogues that facilitated communication and exchanges between two alien cultures (Chaney, Vryonis). In studies that exemplified the textual mode, it appeared in the use of metaphors to elucidate informing concepts (Adams) or to justify, through scriptural exegesis, claims of administrative or doctrinal authenticity in the church (Tierney). It also figured in the attribution of paintings to specific artists on grounds of iconography (Meiss). Thus, the symbolic mode appears incidentally in many areas of inquiry, but few authors have employed it as a primary tool.

Fascinating as it is in its own right, symbolic analysis chiefly remains

45. Ibid., 4, 12, 165.
46. Ibid., 521, 617.
47. Nicholas H. Steneck, *Science and Creation in the Middle Ages: Henry of Langenstein (d. 1397) on Genesis* (South Bend, Ind., 1976), 6, 31, 148–151.

(as it was early in the twentieth century for two founders of art history, Norton and Morey) a key to collective mentalities. Symbols have life cycles, and sensitive readings of an emblem or a ritual at various points in its career can disclose fundamental changes in the guiding assumptions—the unspoken language—of a society. Seismic changes are evident without symbols, but attention to the transformations of symbols does illuminate the character, direction, and inner repercussions of those discontinuities. In a distinctive way, they clarify the paradoxical equivalence of continuity and change in development.

During the 1970s a scattering of studies was written in the symbolic mode on special problems in language,[48] art,[49] political thought,[50] and literature. The interests of this decade are reflected in the fact that research has been devoted to the varying representations of woman as a symbol in literature,[51] and to the symbolic world of religious imagery. Indeed, the latter has characterized a new, widespread, and compelling attraction to the logical but nonrational area of spirituality, both among orthodox religious orders and among groups that in their own times were condemned for heresy.[52]

The symbolic mode therefore belongs to the medievalist's repertoire of general discourse, and studies applying it mark out an area where diverse branches of historical inquiry coincide and where they also intersect with other disciplines, such as semiology, theology, and anthropology. And still, no more than studies cast in the functional or textual mode do individual studies in the symbolic mode have a common frame of reference. In the symbolic mode, too, the problematic approach has left aside the narrative unity of chronology. Chronology

48. Marcia L. Colish, *The Mirror of Language: A Study in the Medieval Theory of Knowledge* (New Haven, 1968).

49. Anthony Cutler, *Transfigurations: Studies in the Dynamics of Byzantine Iconography* (University Park, Pa., 1975); Meyer Schapiro, *Words and Pictures: On the Literal and the Symbolic in the Illustration of a Text* (The Hague, 1973).

50. Edward Peters, *The Shadow King, 751–1327* (New Haven, 1970), esp. 18–19, 244, "the formation of political typology between the eighth and the fourteenth centuries."

51. Joan Ferrante, *Woman as Image in Medieval Literature: From the Twelfth Century to Dante* (New York, 1975).

52. E.g., Bernard McGinn, *Three Treatises on Man: A Cistercian Anthropology* (Kalamazoo, 1977); Robert E. Lerner, *The Heresy of the Free Spirit in the Later Middle Ages* (Berkeley, 1972); Richard Kieckhefer, *European Witch Trials: Their Foundations in Popular and Learned Culture, 1300–1500* (Berkeley, 1976) and *Repression of Heresy in Medieval Germany* (Philadelphia, 1979). An important aspect of the renewed interest in spirituality, and particularly in monasticism, has been the attention paid to practical matters. See, for example, the distinguished studies by Giles Constable, *Monastic Tithes from Their Origins to the Twelfth Century* (Cambridge, Eng., 1964), and Louis J. Lekai, *The Cistercians: Ideals and Reality* (Kent, O., 1977). Consult also Giles Constable, *Medieval Monasticism: A Select Bibliography* (Toronto, 1976).

has a subordinate, even a negligible, role to play; for the pace of change is plotted in terms of morphology, inherent in the particular symbol, rather than in those of shared, external relations, including time. The studies, therefore, are dispersed on the formal level, however much they may converge on that of preanalytical assumptions.

To conclude: The decade under review has seen the fulfillment of some research begun much earlier, in some instances between thirty and fifty years ago. It has also seen very wide and exciting methods and fields of inquiry open. And still, in some ways, the paradigms of historical inquiry remain unchanged. Toward the beginning of the decade, Sylvia Thrupp observed that "so far, knowing more about medieval society has not produced any radically new way of thinking about it."[53] The same view would apply even now to the *longue durée*, not only of social history but of our entire subject.

Perhaps, in the sphere of paradigms, the sense of a common level of discourse is destined, like so many ideals, never to be realized in practice. Long ago, Frederick William Maitland expressed this dilemma in his celebrated metaphor of history's seamless web. "The web must be rent," he wrote, "but, as we rend it, we may watch the whence and whither of a few of the severed and unravelling threads which have been making a pattern too large for any man's eye."[54] The methods of analysis seem at odds with the goal of wholeness. The impulse to break down the artificial but proprietary limits of disciplines may never be gratified except in conferences or in collaborative volumes in which each scholar speaks from his own pinnacle in the landscape of knowledge.[55] Or perhaps amidst a common reflex of fragmentation there will emerge a fully articulated theory of integrative discontinuities, the joyful harbor that philosophers and theologians saw from afar but never entered.

On the whole, historians lack the gift of prognostication, but they are qualified to identify evidence out of which prognostications can be distilled. Let us briefly mention four.

1. The enormous richness and variety of achievement requires no emphasis. Haskins stressed openness to new ideas and new learning as

53. Sylvia Thrupp, *Society and History*, ed. Raymond Grew and Nicholas H. Steneck (Ann Arbor, 1977), 46. Cf. a similar judgment by Robert P. Swierenga, concerning "the impact of computers on comparative historical studies," in "Computers and Comparative History," *Journal of Interdisciplinary History*, v (1974), 267.

54. Frederick Pollock and Frederic William Maitland, *The History of English Law before the Time of Edward I* (Cambridge, Eng. 1968), I, 2.

55. E.g., Madaleine Cosman and Bruce Chandler, ed., *Machaut's World: Science and Art in the Fourteenth Century* (New York, 1978).

characteristic of American medievalism, and the same fresh inventiveness still runs deep in fascination with interdisciplinary research, and in the constructive anarchy of an egalitarian and free society. Since the late nineteenth century, an environment has existed in which, with luck, works that needed the luxury of time could be matured for decades, and other works that ripened more quickly could be introduced without let or hindrance into the mainstream of discourse. But the momentum thus gained drew on demographic and economic conditions that no longer obtain.

2. The altered social context made itself felt first among scholars at or past the end of their professional training. American medievalism existed, as it still does, within a constellation of colleges and universities, and those institutions largely provided the means by which the profession advanced its intellectual boundaries and filled its ranks. The means included financial support of graduate education, opportunities for long-term employment in history, grants in aid of research and publication, and well-stocked and accessible libraries. There was also an expectation in the "guild" that investment in professional training would, in due course, fetch a return in professional opportunity.

By 1970, these benefits could no longer be taken for granted. By 1974, even the president of Harvard University was constrained to deliver a budget of marked austerity, reducing "the number of Assistant Professors substantially while cutting the size of the graduate student body below the minimum desirable levels."[56] The aggregate result of many such budgets across the country was a sharp reduction in the number of professional openings for medievalists, and an impairment of library acquisitions and other facilities in aid of research. Awareness of this changed climate impelled a large number of advanced students to complete their doctoral dissertations quickly, producing a bulge that is noticeable around 1972–74 in our tables. For many reasons, including the deliberate reduction or suspension of programs in some universities, it also resulted in a decline in the number of graduate students proceeding to the doctorate.

In effect, the historians who became qualified during this period without being able to secure professional employment constitute a generation of scholars that may be in the process of being lost, casualties of abrupt transition. There is no reason to expect that the demographic and economic trends that so sharply reversed their professional expectations will alter before the end of the century, and this

56. Harvard University, *President's Report, 1973–1974*, 4.

projection raises certain quite obvious possibilities regarding the diversity and the renewal of the profession.

3. A further characteristic of American medievalism is understanding the past in terms of problems. In a sense, the practice of history is thought of as an exercise in defining and resolving problems, an exercise that requires technical proficiency joined with a high degree of specialization. This feature appears earliest not at the top but in the middle of professional training—in the university curriculum. The consequences of premature specialization have been clear at least since 1874, when Theodor Mommsen attacked it in his celebrated rectorial address at the University of Berlin. Mommsen deplored a tendency to reform universities into vocational schools, trimming the curriculum to suit the demands of technical proficiency. The results, he said, would be particularly unfortunate for historians, for history was not a self-contained discipline. Rather, it cut across many disciplines, and in his formal studies the prospective historian should not concentrate on history. He should train his integrative powers through the study of law; he should prepare for the research ahead by mastering languages. A nemesis, Mommsen warned, awaited those who regarded history not as the art that it was but as a technical discipline that could be learned and practiced as a craft, the nemesis of narrow-minded, pragmatic work, lacking any vision of distant goals.[57]

One-sided as Mommsen's argument was, his views on premature specialization are germane to undergraduate education at the present day, not because specialization is required, but because it is allowed, and encouraged through the seminar, imported to the United States from Germany in Mommsen's day. It is true, however, that latitudinarianism in undergraduate curricula permits the extremes of specialization and diffusiveness. If—as has so often been observed since the early twentieth century—most medievalists in the United States have no knack for theoretical generalization, part of the explanation is surely to be found in this state of affairs. Either extreme constricts the powers to generalize, and thus to infer meaning. But much will depend on the place that medievalists can find for their enthusiasm and their learning in educational curricula as a whole and in the life of a wider community. Much will depend on whether historians can be more than people who speak *about* cultures, and whether they can function as spokesmen for and to their own culture.

---

57. "Rede bei Antritt des Rektorates, 15 Oktober, 1874," in Theodor Mommsen, *Reden und Aufsätze* (Berlin, 1905), 9-11, 14.

4. Finally, progressing from the top to the bottom, we turn to the disjunction between secondary and higher education. The curriculum and the last stages of professional training present urgent considerations, but like any beginning, the propaedeutic stage is exceptionally important. Yet this stage has been largely ignored by scholars teaching history beyond the high school level. As higher and higher proportions of secondary school graduates enter colleges and universities, the strange dissociation of curricula at the collegiate level from those at earlier levels will present consequences that cannot be deferred, consequences of neglecting the rudiments of the liberal arts as the mind is formed during childhood and adolescence. Whitehead said of the classics in 1923 that "their future will be decided during the next few years in the secondary schools of this country."[58] James Harvey Robinson and others of Whitehead's generation recognized that the same could be said about medieval history, and they made strenuous efforts accordingly. Their example in this regard has fallen into disuse. It might well be revived.

58. Alfred North Whitehead, "The Place of Classics in Education," in *Aims of Education* (New York, 1961), 67.

# 2

## Early Modern Europe

### William J. Bouwsma

Historians of earlier phases in the European past can describe themselves quite naturally as ancient historians or medievalists; but there are no historians—in the same broad sense—of modern or early modern Europe, only specialists of various kinds. This, of course, says something about the subject of the present essay; scholarship in the history of early modern Europe is generally fragmented along national or topical lines, sometimes both. Yet it may be that the historiography of early modern Europe is somewhat less fragmented in the United States than in Europe itself, not only because of the perspective resulting from geographical separation but also because of the special historical relationships between Europe and America. The American perception of European history has inevitably been influenced by the origins of the United States in rebellion against a major European power, as well as by the fact that, although most Americans are the descendants of Europeans, their ancestors inhabited every part of Europe. The result has been both a persistent, if somewhat ambivalent, interest in European history (perhaps especially in the early modern period, which roughly coincides with the colonial period of American history, when "Americans" were still more or less Europeans) and some differences in emphasis.

Among these differences have been a refusal to give privileged treatment to the history of any particular European people and some tendency instead to deal with European developments in general or comparative terms.[1] One consequence has been a special effort by

I have received advice and suggestions for this essay from various colleagues, but I must give particular acknowledgment to the many-sided help of my research assistant, Laurence Dickey.

1. Even English history has now lost most of the special attention it once received in American higher education.

American historians to define the place of Europe, and to describe its activity, within a wider historical world. This effort has been a major element in the interest aroused by Immanuel Wallerstein's *Modern World-System: Capitalist Agriculture and the Origins of the European World-Economy in the Sixteenth Century* (New York, 1974). Other recent works have also dealt with the relations between Europe and the rest of the world. So, in *Venice: The Hinge of Europe, 1081–1797* (Chicago, 1974), William H. McNeill explores the maritime connections between Europe and Asia, as he had earlier explored overland connections in *Europe's Steppe Frontier, 1500–1800* (Chicago, 1964). Similar concerns are evident in Deno John Geanakoplos, *Interaction of the "Sibling" Byzantine and Western Cultures in the Middle Ages and Italian Renaissance (330–1600)* (New Haven, 1976), and Andrew C. Hess, *The Forgotten Frontier: A History of the Sixteenth-Century Ibero-African Frontier* (Chicago, 1978). The latter work is also concerned to sharpen the definition of Europe by emphasizing, against Fernand Braudel's notion of a unified Mediterranean world, the conflict between Christendom and Islam.

Concern with the definition of Europe and the place of Europe in the wider world has been complemented by an interest in generalizing about Europe as a whole. This tendency received a considerable impetus from Robert R. Palmer's *Age of the Democratic Revolution,* 2 vols. (Princeton, 1959–64). Palmer had seen as a limitation of the otherwise abundant scholarship concerned with Europe under the old regime that it "has been carried on in national isolation, compartmentalized by barriers of language or the particular histories of governments and states." He proposed in his own work, therefore, to deal with the "wider reality" that, he argued, all historians acknowledged but few were ready to come to grips with. Most American historians of early modern Europe, I suspect, are sympathetic in principle to the kind of history Palmer advocated, whatever form their own work has taken.

But Palmer's unduly modest description of his method as "simply a putting together of hundreds of excellent studies already in existence"[2] not only suggests a positivism of a kind increasingly unfashionable, but also seems daily less practicable for an individual historian, given the steady proliferation of historical publication; and in practice the kind of history Palmer thought desirable is now being pursued chiefly through symposia in which groups of specialists compare their findings on selected topics. *Preconditions of Revolution in Early Modern Europe*, edited by Robert Forster and Jack P. Greene

2. *Democratic Revolution*, I, 8.

*William J. Bouwsma*

(Baltimore, 1970), and *National Consciousness, History, and Political Culture in Early Modern Europe*, edited by Orest Ranum (Baltimore, 1975), are examples of such comparisons; but, as Ranum's intelligent introduction to the latter volume appears to recognize, such attempts at the comparative study of politics and political institutions have not had much success in moving historiography to a higher level of generalization.

Economic history gives a rather different impression, doubtless in part because it deals, in the early modern period, with an expanding system of international transactions. A sense of the functional unity of Europe is evident in the lucid and general accounts by Harry A. Miskimin, *The Economy of Early Renaissance Europe, 1300–1460* (Englewood Cliffs, N.J., 1969) and *The Economy of Later Renaissance Europe, 1460–1600* (Cambridge, Eng., 1977), and Jan De Vries, *The Economy of Europe in an Age of Crisis, 1600–1750* (Cambridge, Eng., 1976). Robert Brenner's essay "Agrarian Class Structures and Economic Revolution in Pre-Industrial Europe"[3] is an example of the impetus Marxism has given to more general interpretation; as the case of Wallerstein also suggests, much of the attraction of Marxist approaches to early modern European history seems to have less to do with ideology, for American scholars, than with the stimulus they offer by their higher level of generalization.

A further peculiarity of American historiography arises from the size, the decentralization, and hence the relative inertia of the American historical profession. These circumstances tend to insulate American historiography against sudden change; they promote diversity and at the same time keep historiography open to novelties of all kinds without permitting any approach to dominate historical study. One result of this situation is that, to an outsider, much in American historiography may appear remarkably conservative and old-fashioned; Americans continue to produce substantial and respected works of a kind that may have gone quite out of favor elsewhere. Thus political biography has recently been well represented by Nancy Lyman Roelker, *Queen of Navarre: Jeanne d'Albret, 1528–1572* (Cambridge, Mass., 1968); by Donald R. Kelley, *François Hotman: A Revolutionary's Ordeal* (Princeton, 1973); by Peter Pierson, *Philip II of Spain* (London, 1976); and by Herbert H. Rowen, *John de Witt, Grand Pensionary of Holland, 1625–1672* (Princeton, 1978). Even the diplomatic history of early modern Europe, though hardly flourishing, is still alive, facilitated by Charles H. Carter's useful introduction to the

3. *Past and Present*, no. 70 (February 1976), 30–75.

study of diplomatic sources, *The Western European Powers, 1500-1700* (Ithaca, N.Y., 1971). William Roosen, in "A New Way of Looking at Early Modern Diplomacy—Quantification,"[4] suggests that some American historians, far from giving up this venerable branch of historical study, are concerned to breathe new life into it.

A good many American historians thus remain committed to the importance of traditional *histoire événementielle* and the sort of political and institutional analysis that has always accompanied it. This is apparent, to cite a few examples, from such recent studies as Robert E. Ruigh, *The Parliament of 1624: Politics and Foreign Policy* (Cambridge, Mass., 1971); Robert Bireley, *Maximilian von Bayern, Adam Contzen S. J. und die Gegenreformation in Deutschland, 1624-35* (Göttingen, 1975); A. Lloyd Moote, *The Revolt of the Judges: The Parlement of Paris and the Fronde, 1643-1652* (Princeton, 1971); and Sharon Kettering, *Judicial Politics and Urban Revolt in Seventeenth-Century France: The Parlement of Aix, 1629-1659* (Princeton, 1978). Of particular importance because of their relation to large themes in modern political culture—and hence by no means significant only for French history—are William F. Church's revisionist *Richelieu and Reason of State* (Princeton, 1972), which, as it moves back and forth between practical politics and political discussion, develops a far less Machiavellian and more traditionally Christian interpretation of its protagonist; and J. Russell Major, *The Growth and Decline of Representative Government in Early Modern France* (New Haven, 1980), a distillation into general statement of many years' specialized study of an institution obviously pertinent to a modern democratic society.

American historiography's persistent concern with politics is thus also related to other interests that perhaps remain unusually strong in the United States: an interest in the historical backgrounds of our own world and time, a renewed preoccupation with historical identity on the part of a nation of immigrants that had once deliberately severed its connections with the Old World to make a "new beginning," and an impulse therefore to probe and test a traditional kind of historicism that may elsewhere have almost disappeared. These concerns have produced a number of recent works of great scope, often massively erudite, dealing with developments at once (more or less) originating in the early modern world and (supposedly) of central importance for the general history of the West, including the United States. Major examples include Elizabeth L. Eisenstein, *The Printing Press as an*

4. *Proceedings of the Fifth Annual Meeting of the Western Society for French History*, v (1978), 1-13.

*Agent of Change,* 2 vols. (Cambridge, Eng., 1979), an extended argument for the printing press as the essential vehicle for the modernization of European culture between the fifteenth and seventeenth centuries: J. G. A. Pocock, *The Machiavellian Moment: Florentine Political Thought and the Atlantic Republican Tradition* (Princeton, 1975), which traces the civic humanism of the Renaissance from Italy through seventeenth-century England and on to its role in the formation of an independent American republic; and Reinhard Bendix, *Kings or People: Power and the Mandate to Rule* (Berkeley, 1978), a large-scale comparative study, by a historical sociologist in the Weberian tradition, of the transition from a traditional to a modern conception of legitimacy in politics. Clarence J. Glacken, *Traces on the Rhodian Shore: Nature and Culture in Western Thought from Ancient Times to the End of the Eighteenth Century* (Berkeley, 1967), though it stops with the early modern period, responds to the broad contemporary concern about man's understanding of his relations with the natural environment. These are all extraordinarily ambitious books that reflect, perhaps, the same kind of boldness and exuberance as that required to do Palmer's sort of comparative investigation.

The concern in such works to deepen the understanding of peculiarly modern problems through historical study suggests a degree of subjectivity and present-mindedness (terms that American historians might use less pejoratively than other historians) that is also apparent in other interests of American historians in early modern Europe. Notable among these is an interest in the contribution of the early modern age to modern historiography; that is, to the attitudes and methods of the historian himself. This kind of oblique self-exploration has found expression in numerous articles in the journal *History and Theory.*[5] Significant books on this subject include Donald J. Wilcox, *The Development of Florentine Humanist Historiography in the Fifteenth Century* (Cambridge, Mass., 1969), which is particularly concerned with the rhetorical element in Renaissance historical composition; Felix Gilbert, *Machiavelli and Guicciardini: Politics and History in Sixteenth-Century Florence* (Princeton, 1965), which studies the two greatest historians of the Renaissance in their concrete political context; Mark Phillips, *Francesco Guicciardini: The Historian's Craft* (Toronto, 1977), a study of the elements that shaped Guicciardini's art as a historian; Donald R. Kelley, *Foundations of Modern Historical Scholarship: Language, Law, and History in the French Renaissance* (New

5. For a distinguished example, see "Philosophy of History before Historicism," *History and Theory,* III (1964), 291–315, by George H. Nadel, its long-time editor.

York, 1969), which relates historiography to both humanist philology and legal scholarship; George Huppert, *The Idea of Perfect History: Historical Erudition and Historical Philosophy in Renaissance France* (Urbana, Ill., 1970), which emphasizes the Renaissance origins of the notion of scientific history; and Peter H. Reill, *The German Enlightenment and the Rise of Historicism* (Berkeley, 1975), which deals with the positive significance for historical study of at least one dimension of the Enlightenment. The concern of these works with the modern historian's understanding of his craft is suggested by the absence from this list of comparable studies in seventeenth-century historiography, presumably because the seventeenth century is widely regarded as regressive from the standpoint of our own kind of historiography. Even my own book, *Venice and the Defense of Republican Liberty: Renaissance Values in the Age of the Counter Reformation* (Berkeley, 1968), which deals with Paolo Sarpi and other Venetian historians of the earlier seventeenth century at some length, treats their work as an extension of the Renaissance tradition in historiography.

A further indication, perhaps, of the present-mindedness of American historiography in this period is its preoccupation with cities as the basic unit for political and social analysis. Renaissance scholarship has long focused on the city-state, especially Florence; and American historians have devoted a remarkable amount of work to Florence, much of it stimulated by (though not necessarily following) Hans Baron, *The Crisis of the Early Italian Renaissance: Civic Humanism and Republican Liberty in an Age of Classicism and Tyranny* (Princeton, 1955). Important studies of Renaissance Florence have been published by Gene A. Brucker, Marvin B. Becker, Lauro Martines, Anthony Molho, Donald Weinstein, Felix Gilbert, Eric Cochrane, and David Herlihy.[6] But American research has also expanded to include other cities of Renaissance Italy. Herlihy has worked on Pistoia; Werner L. Gundersheimer on Ferrara; William M. Bowsky on Siena; and Frederic C. Lane, Felix Gilbert, Stanley Chojnacki, James C.

6. Brucker, *Florentine Politics and Society, 1343–1378* (Princeton, 1962), *Renaissance Florence* (New York, 1969), and *The Civic World of Early Renaissance Florence* (Princeton, 1977); Becker, *Florence in Transition:* I, *The Decline of the Commune*, and II, *Studies in the Rise of the Territorial State* (Baltimore, 1967–68); Martines, *The Social World of the Florentine Humanists, 1390–1460* (Princeton, 1963) and *Lawyers and Statecraft in Renaissance Florence* (Princeton, 1968); Molho, *Florentine Public Finances in the Early Renaissance, 1400–1433* (Cambridge, Mass., 1971); Weinstein, *Savonarola and Florence: Prophecy and Patriotism in the Renaissance* (Princeton, 1970); Cochrane, "The End of the Renaissance in Florence," *Bibliothèque d'Humanisme et Renaissance*, XXVII (1965), 7–29, and *Florence in the Forgotten Centuries, 1527–1800* (Chicago, 1973). Gilbert's major essays on Renaissance Florence and Venice are included in his *History: Choice and Commitment* (Cambridge, Mass., 1977); for Herlihy, see below.

Davis, and I on Venice.[7] This interest in cities has moved, too, into other periods and regions. Miriam U. Chrisman and Thomas A. Brady, Jr., have studied the impact of the Protestant Reformation on Strasbourg; Robert M. Kingdon and William Monter have studied Geneva during the Reformation; Gerald Strauss has written on Nuremberg and Robert C. Walton on Zurich. Other American studies of early modern cities include books by Ruth Pike on Seville, Richard Tilden Rapp on seventeenth-century Venice, Orest Ranum and Leon Bernard on the Paris of Louis XIV, and Josef W. Konvitz on that ruler's seaports.[8]

Here too, however, though the desirability of such studies is widely recognized, there have been few general or comparative works, so that it has been difficult to assess the significance of the development of any individual city for the process of urbanization itself. A major exception to this observation for the Renaissance is Lauro Martines's *Power and Imagination: City States in Renaissance Italy* (New York, 1979), a comprehensive work that, given the political fragmentation of Italy and the particularlity of the scholarship dealing with its cities, is a major contribution to comparative study; and some of the essays by Marvin Becker offer stimulating generalizations about the urban experience in Renaissance Italy.[9] An important general study of towns during the Reformation is Steven E. Ozment, *Reformation in the Cities: The Appeal of Protestantism to Sixteenth-Century Germany and Switzerland* (New Haven, 1975), which analyzes the attrac-

7. Herlihy, *Medieval and Renaissance Pistoia: The Social History of an Italian Town, 1200–1430* (New Haven, 1967); Gundersheimer, *Ferrara: The Style of a Renaissance Despotism* (Princeton, 1973); Bowsky, in addition to many articles, *The Finance of the Commune of Siena, 1287–1355* (Oxford, 1970); Lane, *Venice: A Maritime Republic* (Baltimore, 1973), in addition to numerous articles collected in *Venice and History* (Baltimore, 1966); Gilbert, see note 6 above; Chojnacki, "In Search of the Venetian Patriciate: Families and Factions in the Fourteenth Century," in J. R. Hale, ed., *Renaissance Venice* (London, 1973), 47–90; Davis, *The Decline of the Venetian Nobility as a Ruling Class* (Baltimore, 1962); Bouwsma, *Venice and Republican Liberty*.

8. Chrisman, *Strasbourg and the Reform: A Study in the Process of Change* (New Haven, 1967); Brady, *Ruling Class, Regime, and Reformation at Strasbourg, 1520–1555* (Leiden, 1978); Kingdon, *Geneva and the Coming of the Wars of Religion in France, 1555–1663* (Geneva, 1956), and *Geneva and the Consolidation of the French Protestant Movement, 1564–1572* (Madison, Wis., 1967); Monter, *Calvin's Geneva* (New York, 1967); Strauss, *Nuremberg in the Sixteenth Century* (New York, 1966); Walton, *Zwingli's Theocracy* (Toronto, 1967); Pike, *Aristocrats and Traders: Sevillian Society in the Sixteenth Century* (Ithaca, N.Y., 1972); Rapp, *Industry and Economic Decline in Seventeenth-Century Venice* (Cambridge, Mass., 1976); Ranum, *Paris in the Age of Absolutism: An Essay* (New York, 1968); Bernard, *The Emerging City: Paris in the Age of Louis XIV* (Durham, N.C., 1971); Konvitz, *Cities and the Sea: Port City Planning in Early Modern Europe* (Baltimore, 1978).

9. For example, "Some Common Features of Italian Urban Experience (c. 1200–1500)," *Medievalia et Humanistica*, n.s. 1 (1970), 175–201, which argues for the importance of war as a general cause of change.

tion of Protestant doctrine to the urban laity. But on early modern cities, as on other subjects where more general accounts are needed, specialization is the rule, although here too specialists may occasionally combine to produce such works as *Violence and Civil Disorder in Italian Cities, 1200–1500* (Berkeley, 1972), in which general chapters by the editor, Lauro Martines, offer some discussion of problems common to the cities treated separately by the other authors.

Much of this attention to cities comes, nevertheless, out of a concern to understand larger historical processes. This may be illustrated by Brucker's *Civic World of Early Renaissance Florence*, a product of extended and meticulous research, which, no less if less explicitly than—for example—Pocock's *Machiavellian Moment*, illuminates developments eventually crucial for modern Western society. By a close analysis of Florence in the late fourteenth and early fifteenth century, Brucker shows how, in one immensely significant case, the transition was made from a communal society and communal modes in politics to patrician oligarchy, from personal and group relations to the bureaucratic state, from a collective ethos to individualism, and from traditional perspectives to a new kind of flexible realism in the conduct of public affairs. And in general the continued clustering of American work in early modern European history around those episodes—the Renaissance, the Protestant Reformation, the English Revolution of the seventeenth century (and for that matter the Enlightenment, which is dealt with elsewhere in this volume)—suggests the persistent influence on American historiography of the famous (or infamous) Whig-liberal vision of the past. I do not mean to suggest that much American work is any longer consciously written within that tradition, which now tends to be dismissed with a degree of scorn, but rather that even the most recent American studies of early modern Europe can again and again be seen obscurely questioning, testing, and otherwise reassessing the old Whig orthodoxies, and thereby demonstrate their continuing importance.

The same desire to test out, and then to reject, to modify, or to renew old orthodoxies, above all those dealing with the relation of past to present, can also be seen in recent American work in Renaissance intellectual and cultural history. This seems to me notably true of the most substantial study published in this area during the 1970s, Charles Trinkaus's *In Our Image and Likeness: Humanity and Divinity in Italian Humanist Thought*, 2 vols. (Chicago, 1970), which demonstrates that Italian humanism was, in one of its dimensions, a broadly significant reaction on the part of devout laymen against a complex of tendencies in later medieval thought. Trinkaus's own reservations

85

about the propriety of the "genetic-modernist" approach to the past[10] seem to me unlikely to deter other scholars from seeing distinctly Weberian overtones in the enthusiastic celebration by the humanists of the creative powers of man. Jerrold E. Seigel, however, in *Rhetoric and Philosophy in Renaissance Humanism: Ciceronian Elements in Early Quattrocento Thought and Their Historical Setting* (Princeton, 1968), by viewing humanism as "mere rhetoric," has tended to deny its larger historical significance; on the other hand, Nancy S. Struever, in *The Language of History in the Renaissance: Rhetoric and Historical Consciousness in Florentine Humanism* (Princeton, 1970), implies that humanism was strikingly modern precisely because of its rhetorical character. Other works on this subject have tended to explore Baron's views on the importance of the civic content of Renaissance humanism for the formation of modern politics; these include Pocock's *Machiavellian Moment* and Ronald G. Witt's studies of Salutati. Witt and James R. Banker are also working toward a clearer understanding of the relation between Renaissance humanism and the medieval rhetorical tradition.[11] But however particular historians regard the long-range significance of the Renaissance, all American study of this subject has been deeply indebted to Paul Oskar Kristeller's well-known views on the rhetorical character of Renaissance humanism.[12]

Another focus of American scholarship in early modern history is the Protestant Reformation. As we have seen, some of this activity is directed to the role of cities in the Reformation; but much of it, in what seems in part an expression of the ecumenical mood following the Second Vatican Council, explores the backgrounds of the Reformation in pre-Reformation Catholicism.[13] A major question here has been the relationship between Renaissance humanism and Protestantism. This has been variously answered in general terms in essays by Charles Trinkaus and by me;[14] it has been dealt with obliquely in

10. "Humanism, Religion, Society: Concepts and Motivations of Some Recent Studies," *Renaissance Quarterly*, xxix (1976), 677, 685–686. This essay goes far more deeply into many of the issues touched on here than I am able to do.

11. Witt, *Coluccio Salutati and His Public Letters* (Geneva, 1976), with references to his other publications; Banker, "Giovanni di Bonandrea and Civic Values in the Context of the Italian Rhetorical Tradition," *Manscripta*, xviii (1974), 3–20.

12. See the implied tribute in the American contributions to two of the recent Kristeller Festschriften: Heiko A. Oberman and Thomas A. Brady, Jr., eds., *Itinerarium Italicum: The Profile of the Italian Renaissance in the Mirror of Its European Transformations* (Leiden, 1975); and Edward P. Mahoney, ed., *Philosophy and Humanism: Renaissance Essays in Honor of Paul Oskar Kristeller* (Leiden, 1976).

13. Cf. the anthology edited by Steven E. Ozment, *The Reformation in Medieval Perspective* (Chicago, 1971).

14. Trinkaus, "The Religious Thought of the Italian Humanists, and the Reformers: Anticipation or Autonomy?" in Charles Trinkaus and Heiko A. Oberman, eds., *The*

Lewis W. Spitz, *The Religious Renaissance of the German Humanists* (Cambridge, Mass., 1963), and Maria Grossman, *Humanism in Wittenberg, 1485–1517* (Nieuwkoop, 1975). There have also been substantial recent American contributions to the vast literature on Erasmus.[15] But the largest body of significant American work on the backgrounds of the Reformation has consisted in a group of recent studies, many by students of Heiko A. Oberman, whose own *Harvest of Late Medieval Theology: Gabriel Biel and Late Medieval Nominalism* (Cambridge, Mass., 1963) became the starting point for this considerable series of investigations of later medieval theology and spirituality.[16]

The mainstream of Reformation scholarship in America among general historians, however, seems to be flowing increasingly toward investigation of the social context of religious movements, as the interest of historians of the Reformation in towns noted above and the titles of two recent collections of Reformation studies would suggest: *The Social History of the Reformation*, edited by Lawrence P. Buck and Jonathan W. Zophy (Columbus, O., 1972),[17] and *Social Groups and Religious Ideas in the Sixteenth Century*, edited by Miriam U. Chrisman and Otto Gründler (Kalamazoo, 1978). Other recent titles also bear witness to this interest: Claus-Peter Clasen, *Anabaptism: A Social History, 1525–1618* (Ithaca, N.Y., 1972); Steven E. Ozment, *Mysticism and Dissent: Religious Ideology and Social Protest in the Sixteenth Century* (New

---

Pursuit of Holiness in Late Medieval and Renaissance Religion (Leiden, 1974), 339–366; Bouwsma, "Renaissance and Reformation: An Essay in Their Affinities and Connections," in H. A. Oberman, ed., *Luther and the Dawn of the Modern Era: Papers for the Fourth International Congress for Luther Research* (Leiden, 1974), 127–49.

15. For example, James D. Tracy, *Erasmus: The Growth of a Mind* (Geneva, 1972), and Alfred Rabil, Jr., *Erasmus and the New Testament: The Mind of a Christian Humanist* (San Antonio, 1972).

16. Among them E. Jane Dempsey Douglass, *Justification in Late Medieval Preaching: A Study of John Geiler of Keisersberg* (Leiden, 1966); David Curtis Steinmetz, *Misericordia Dei: The Theology of Johannes von Staupitz in Its Late Medieval Setting* (Leiden, 1968); John W. O'Malley, *Giles of Viterbo on Church and Reform* (Leiden, 1968); James Samuel Preus, *From Shadow to Promise: Old Testament Interpretation from Augustine to the Young Luther* (Cambridge, Mass., 1969); Michael G. Baylor, *Action and Person: Conscience in Late Scholasticism and the Young Luther* (Leiden, 1977); Thomas N. Tentler, *Sacramental Confession before the Reformation* (Princeton, 1977). *The Pursuit of Holiness* (cited in note 14 above) is also important in this connection, as well as for other aspects of religious history discussed below. Oberman was the Winn Professor of Ecclesiastical History at Harvard University before be became Director of the Institüt für Spätmittelalter und Reformation at the University of Tübingen, and many of these works appeared in "Studies in Medieval and Reformation Thought," published by E. J. Brill in Leiden, of which he is editor.

17. This is an appropriately titled Festschrift for Harold J. Grimm, whose own most recent contribution to the social history of the Reformation is *Lazarus Spengler: A Lay Leader of the Reformation* (Columbus, O., 1978).

Haven, 1973); and Phyllis Mack Crew, *Calvinist Preaching and Iconoclasm in the Netherlands, 1544–1569* (New York, 1978).

The seventeenth century as a whole remains, for American historiography, a relatively underdeveloped borderland between two overdeveloped areas, a century of flux without clear identity, intelligible if at all as a period of desperate but indecisive "struggle."[18] This is apparent in the titles of two broadly interpretive works on the seventeenth century published during the 1970s: Leroy E. Loemker, *Struggle for Synthesis: The Seventeenth-Century Background of Leibniz's Synthesis of Order and Freedom* (Cambridge, Mass., 1972), and Theodore K. Rabb, *The Struggle for Stability in Early Modern Europe* (New York, 1975). This perception of the seventeenth century, which might also be taken as bearing on the migration from the Old World to the New, likewise underlies Carl Bridenbaugh's *Vexed and Troubled Englishmen, 1590–1642* (New York, 1967).[19] Interest in the instability of the century, its pursuit of stability through political absolutism, and the ultimate failure of that solution to the problems of the old regime (again one senses a concern with the larger shape of Western history) are also apparent in Joseph Klaits, *Printed Propaganda under Louis XIV: Absolute Monarchy and Public Opinion* (Princeton, 1976), and Lionel Rothkrug, *Opposition to Louis XIV: The Political and Social Origins of the French Enlightenment* (Princeton, 1965).

The continuing importance for American historiography of the Whig interpretation of history is nowhere more evident, however, than in the cluster of American writings around the English Revolution of the seventeenth century. A particular monument to this interest is the publication by the Yale Center for Parliamentary History, directed by J. H. Hexter, of a magnificent edition of English House of Commons debates.[20] American interest in Puritanism especially points to seventeenth-century England and has found recent expression in such very different works as J. Sears McGee, *The Godly Man in Stuart England: Anglicans, Puritans, and the Two Tables, 1620–1670* (New Haven, 1976), which offers an intelligent and original solution to the delicate problem of distinguishing Puritans from other Englishmen; Michael Walzer, *The Revolution of the Saints: A Study in the*

---

18. Cf. my remarks entitled "The Secularization of Society in the Seventeenth Century," in Thirteenth International Congress of Historical Sciences, Moscow 1970, *Doklady Kongressa*, I, pt. 5 (Moscow, 1973), 90.

19. Bridenbaugh is a distinguished historian of colonial American rather than a historian of Europe. The point is worth making because it calls attention again to the importance of early modern Europe for American history.

20. Robert C. Johnson et al., eds., *Commons Debates, 1628*, 3 vols. (New Haven, 1977).

*Origins of Radical Politics* (Cambridge, Mass., 1965), and David Little, *Religion, Order, and Law: A Study in Pre-Revolutionary England* (New York, 1969), which suggest again the continuing value of Max Weber's insights into the relation of religion and society; Marvin Arthur Breslow, *A Mirror of England: English Puritan Views of Foreign Nations, 1618–1640* (Cambridge, Mass., 1970), which deals with the Puritan contribution to English nationalism; and John F. Wilson, *Pulpit in Parliament: Puritanism during the English Civil Wars, 1640–1648* (Princeton, 1969), and Paul S. Seaver, *The Puritan Lectureships: The Politics of Religious Dissent, 1560–1662* (Stanford, 1970), which analyze Puritan sermons for their political content. The English Revolution of the seventeenth century is approached from other directions in Gerald R. Cragg, *Freedom and Authority: A Study of English Thought in the Early Seventeenth Century* (Philadelphia, 1975), and Joyce Oldham Appleby, *Economic Thought and Ideology in Seventeenth-Century England* (Princeton, 1978). The dynamics of the English Revolution have been freshly analyzed by Perez Zagorin in *The Court and the Country: The Beginning of the English Revolution of the Mid-Seventeenth Century* (New York, 1970), which explains that event as a result of a split in the English ruling class.[21]

Up to this point I have emphasized what seem to me the rather special concerns of American historians of early modern Europe. These concerns may not be altogether unique. English historians too, for example, have particular grounds for continuing to study their own history in the seventeenth century, though rather less reason to stress seventeenth-century Puritanism. But this emphasis on what may be peculiarly American in recent American work in the early modern age would by itself give a somewhat distorted impression of the situation. American historians of Europe (and obviously not only in the early modern age) have also long depended on the example and teaching of European scholars, whom they have tended for obvious reasons to regard as mentors whose questions they too should ask, whose methods they should follow, and whose approval represents the highest form of recognition.

The most recent expression of this dependence of American on European historiography has been the remarkable American response to the approaches to the past associated with the *Annales*. This response has been especially strong among American historians of early modern Europe, the field in which much of the most interesting

21. For fuller discussion of the historiography of this event, see Lawrence Stone, *The Causes of the English Revolution, 1529–1642* (London, 1972).

work of the *Annalistes* themselves has been concentrated. Several volumes of selections from the *Annales* have been published in the United States in English translation,[22] and even strictly undergraduate colleges seek to recruit faculty "trained in the *Annales* approach."

It is my own impression, nevertheless, that—at least so far—the *Annalistes* have, in the United States, been more discussed than emulated; part of the reason is, perhaps, that the relation between mentor and disciple, however close, is likely also to be fraught with an ambivalence analogous to that pervading the relationship between European mother-country and her colonists in the New World. The concern of the *Annalistes* to rewrite history "from below" finds some American counterpart in a number of richly suggestive studies of popular customs and popular religion, including the essays by Natalie Zemon Davis, collected under the title *Society and Culture in Early Modern France* (Stanford, 1975); A. N. Galpern, *The Religions of the People in Sixteenth-Century Champagne* (Cambridge, Mass., 1976); and several essays by Richard C. Trexler.[23] These studies, with their "thick description," seem to be equally stimulated, however, by recent work in social and cultural anthropology. A group of American works on witchcraft, which attempt some statistical study at the local level of a major element in the *mentalité* of the people (though of elites as well), may also roughly parallel the kind of work associated with the *Annales*.[24] But in fact the ahistorical tendencies in the school of the *Annales*, its lack of interest in the explanation of major change, and its indifference to events and elites are too contrary to those tendencies in American historiography that I have tried to identify earlier in this essay to be generally assimilated by historians in the United States; and indeed some reaction against "the new social history" of the *Annalistes* may already be under way in the United States.[25] The major

22. Marc Ferro, ed., *Social Historians in Contemporary France: Essays from Annales* (New York, 1972); and, all edited by Robert Forster and Orest Ranum, *Biology of Man in History: Selections from the Annales* (Baltimore, 1975); *Family and Society: Selections from the Annales* (Baltimore, 1976); *Rural Society in France: Selections from the Annales* (Baltimore, 1977); and *Food and Drink in History: Selections from the Annales* (Baltimore, 1979).

23. For example, "Florentine Religious Experience: The Sacred Image," *Studies in the Renaissance*, XIX (1972), 7–41.

24. H. C. Erik Midelfort, *Witch Hunting in Southwestern Germany, 1562–1684* (Stanford, 1972); E. William Monter, *Witchcraft in France and Switzerland: The Borderlands during the Reformation* (Ithaca, N.Y., 1976); Richard Kieckhefer, *European Witch Trials: Their Foundations in Popular and Learned Culture, 1300–1500* (Berkeley, 1976).

25. Notably from Marxist historians: cf. Eugene Genovese and Elizabeth Fox-Genovese, "The Political Crisis of Social History: A Marxian Perspective," *Journal of Social History*, X (1976), 205–220. But see also the remarkably detached analysis by J. H.

impact of the *Annales* has been, therefore, to deepen what remains for the most part *histoire événementielle* by means of increasingly imaginative and careful strategies of social analysis.

Thus American historians of early modern Europe, even when they may be analyzing the composition of a group or examining its *mentalité* somewhat in the manner of an *Annaliste,* have continued to give particular attention to elites, presumably out of an abiding interest in change. This is suggested by the title of Davis Bitton's *French Nobility in Crisis, 1560–1640* (Stanford, 1969), which examines the predicament of an old elite; while George Huppert, in *Les Bourgeois Gentilshommes: An Essay on the Definition of Elites in Renaissance France* (Chicago, 1977), focuses attention on a new one; and Robert R. Harding, *Anatomy of a Power Elite: The Provincial Governors of Early Modern France* (New Haven, 1978), looks at still another. A similar interest in the more influential elements in early modern society may be seen in Leonard R. Berlanstein, *The Barristers of Toulouse in the Eighteenth Century (1740–1793)* (Baltimore, 1975), and Timothy Tackett, *Priest and Parish in Eighteenth-Century France* (Princeton, 1977). Carolyn C. Lougee, *Le Paradis des Femmes: Women, Salons, and Social Stratification in Seventeenth-Century France* (Princeton, 1976), examines the feminist movement—again a major concern of our own society—in the context of elite culture in the past. The collaborative work edited by Lawrence Stone, *The University in Society* (Princeton, 1975), which gives substantial attention to the universities of early modern Europe, is obviously a further indication of continuing interest in elites.

American studies of various other topics commonly associated with the *Annales*, however much these studies may owe to the *Annalistes*, are also likely to differ considerably from their work. Thus the most ambitious American study of the early modern European countryside, *The Dutch Rural Economy in the Golden Age, 1500–1700* (New Haven, 1974), by Jan De Vries, traces the development of the most thoroughly commercialized agriculture of its time, and is therefore concerned with the dynamic possibilities rather than the static elements in the rural scene. Steven L. Kaplan, again, in *Bread, Politics, and Political Economy in the Reign of Louis XV* (The Hague, 1976), treats the problem of subsistence as an element in the political failure of the old regime. American studies of crime in early modern Europe likewise tend to be concerned less with criminality as a type of mass behavior than with the issues it raises for the maintenance of order in

Hexter, "Fernand Braudel and the *Monde Braudelien*," *Journal of Modern History*, XLIV (1972), 480–539.

early modern society, as in John H. Langbein, *Prosecuting Crime in the Renaissance: England, Germany, France* (Cambridge, Mass., 1974), and Joel B. Samaha, *Law and Order in Historical Perspective: The Case of Elizabethan Essex* (New York, 1974). Again a contemporary American preoccupation seems to be projected back into the past.

Most revealing of all, perhaps, is the attention now being given by American historians to the history of the family, a basic interest (as it points to demography and the relations of mass man to the environment) of the *Annalistes* as well as of English social historians, and at the same time another topic of considerable contemporary interest. Yet only a fraction of American work on families in the past deals with strictly demographic questions, or with the history of the family as such; and even when it is concerned primarily with the changing internal relationships within this fundamental human institution, as in the case of Lawrence Stone, *The Family, Sex, and Marriage in England, 1500–1800* (New York, 1977), it may suggest a kind of Whig interest in the "modernization" of the family.[26] David Herlihy, on the other hand, the co-author (with Christiane Klapisch, in a notable example of European-American collaboration) of *Les Toscanes et leur familles: Une ètude du catasto florentin de 1427* (Paris, 1978), is concerned with the full demographic implications of a uniquely instructive document, but also with a wide range of other matters on which it is informative.

Much of what passes for family history in the United States seems, in fact, to be a more familiar kind of social or political history that happens to be based on family records. Such records have proved useful, for example, in studying the composition and durability of elites. A group of American works has thus been concerned with the wealth of great families, or more precisely with the way in which families have managed to conserve wealth and thereby remain great. Of this kind (though of course they may also touch on other changes in the family) are Richard Goldthwaite, *Private Wealth in Renaissance Florence: A Study of Four Families* (Princeton, 1968); Robert Forster, *The House of Saulx-Tavennes: Versailles and Burgundy, 1700–1830* (Baltimore, 1971); Lawrence Stone, *Family and Fortune: Studies in Aristocrat-*

---

26. See also Randolph Trumbach, *The Rise of the Egalitarian Family: Aristocratic Kinship and Domestic Relations in Eighteenth-Century England* (New York, 1979). There has been special interest in the United States in changing attitudes to children, in part stimulated by Philippe Ariès; see David Hunt, *Parents and Children in History: The Psychology of Family Life in Early Modern France* (New York, 1970); and relevant chapters in the at times eccentric collective work edited by Lloyd de Mause, *The History of Childhood* (New York, 1974).

*ic Finance in the Sixteenth and Seventeenth Centuries* (Oxford, 1973); and James C. Davis, *A Venetian Family and Its Fortune, 1500–1900: The Donà and the Conservation of Their Wealth* (Philadelphia, 1975). More politically oriented are Randolph Starn, "Francesco Guicciardini and His Brothers"; Stanley Chojnacki, "In Search of the Venetian Patriciate: Families and Factions in the Fourteenth Century"; and Melissa Meriam Bullard, "Marriage Politics and the Family in Florence: The Strozzi-Medici Alliance of 1508."[27] The remarkably various uses of family documents are apparent in Helen Nader, *The Mendoza Family in the Spanish Renaissance, 1350–1550* (New Brunswick, N.J., 1979), which brings into focus, through the career of a single powerful family, two centuries of development in the social, political, and cultural history of Spain. In doing so it also raises, with striking results, the same questions about Spanish history that have been fruitfully applied to France and Italy in the same period, so that it is also an illustration of interest in—and the value of—thinking about Europe as a whole.

There is, then, among American historians of the early modern period, little of the sense, sometimes discernable elsewhere, of a need to make a choice between a more conventional history of events and a history that deals with great but slow-moving forces that are at work far below the level at which traditional historiography operates and that can be apprehended only through quantitative investigation. The assumption is rather that these "latent" forces, insofar as they have any significance in human affairs, eventually come to the surface and reveal their presence—in events. From this standpoint there can be no conflict between *histoire structurale* and *histoire événementielle*. Indeed, they need each other; for without the event structural change is in every sense inconsequential, but without a sense of structure the event is inexplicable.

In the Whig vision of history the event *par excellence* was, of course, revolution; but the conception of revolution seems too narrowly political to function effectively in a more comprehensive modern historiography. American historians have recently tended to replace it, therefore, with the more flexible notion of "crisis," a word that occurs with some frequency in the titles of books or articles on every aspect of early modern European history, and even more frequently—if implicitly—as the underlying dramatic principle in the organization

27. In, respectively, Anthony Molho and John A. Tedeschi, eds., *Renaissance Studies in Honor of Hans Baron* (De Kalb, Ill., 1971), 409–444; J. R. Hale, ed., *Renaissance Venice* (London, 1973), 47–90; *American Historical Review*, LXXXIV (1979), 668–687.

of historical narrative.[28] It may be that the resort to the notion of crisis is not only symptomatic of the crises of our own time but also points to some gathering consensus in American historiography about early modern Europe.

28. In addition to the works of De Vries, Baron, and Bitton cited above, examples are Charles G. Nauert, Jr., *Agrippa and the Crisis of Renaissance Thought* (Urbana, Ill., 1965); Benjamin Z. Kedar, *Merchants in Crisis: Genoese and Venetian Men of Affairs and the Fourteenth-Century Depression* (New Haven, 1976); and—a multilayered example—Jerome Friedman, "Sixteenth-Century European Jewry: Theologies of Crisis in Crisis," in *Social Groups and Religious Ideas*, 102–112. For the general point—and it may be relevant that it was made by another historian of early modern Europe—see Randolph Starn, "Historians and 'Crisis,'" *Past and Present*, no. 52 (August 1971), 3–22.

# 3

## Modern European History

### William H. McNeill

THE study and writing of modern European history in the United States grew to massive proportions in the 1970s, and underwent a marked diversification of themes as well. The decade saw an efflorescence of professionalism. In the absence of any unifying vision of the field as a whole, most academic historians addressed themselves to fellow specialists, heedless of murmurs about irrelevancy coming from students and other outsiders. How long an ever more specialized research, frequently deriving its vocabulary from debates originating in Europe, can continue to flourish on American soil is a question for the future. Quantitatively, we may be sure that the first half of the decade of the 1970s constituted at least a temporary crest, measured by the number of books printed. Qualitative judgments are more difficult, and we cannot yet tell how meaningful recent American scholarship will turn out to be for future generations.

It is no simple matter to find out exactly what was produced in the United States during the 1970s. Book publishing is an international business, and the fact that a book gets published in the United States by a university press tells nothing about the national origins of its author, who may live in any of the English-speaking countries of the world, or in Israel, the Netherlands, Scandinavia, or even Germany. The writing of European history in English is, in fact, a transnational enterprise. Many individuals migrate across national boundaries; some, indeed, commute annually across the Atlantic, spending part of the year in the United States and part in Europe. Yet within the English-writing world as a whole, the number of universities in the United States and the scale of Ph.D. training in this country (1,714 Ph.D.s in European history awarded in the five years from 1972 to 1976) clearly give preponderance in most academic fields to historians based in the United States; but one usually cannot tell from bibliographical entries or book reviews whether a given author should be counted as an American or not.

Another no less intractable problem confronts anyone seeking to discover what U.S.-based historians of Europe wrote in the 1970s, for the definition of "history" has become so elastic as to merge into adjacent fields of scholarship by imperceptible degrees. This means that whether one counts a given work as history or as political science, literary criticism, or an example of one of the other systematic sciences becomes a matter of judgment; and deciding on the basis of the title alone is often arbitrary.

To try to meet these difficulties in defining the universe with which this essay is concerned, I decided to consult the book notices and reviews published in a selected group of American-based historical journals during the decade 1968–78, on the theory that what modern European history was could be pragmatically defined by the works deemed worthy of notice in these periodicals.[1] In collecting titles from these sources, however, I excluded authors whom I chanced to recognize as being based outside the United States and also discarded all books published outside the United States, save in a few instances when I happened to know that the author was an American using a Dutch or some other foreign publisher.

The result of this compilation was a card file of 2,044 titles, published between 1968 and 1978, and dealing with some aspect of the history of Europe since 1750. Almost exactly 33 percent (680 books) of this array were by authors whose names appear in the *Directory of American Scholars: History*; but on the basis of considerable card-shuffling, I would estimate that another 20–30 percent are first books—often Ph.D. theses revised for publication—whose authors will, presumably, appear in future editions of the *Directory* but cannot be found there now. If this estimate is correct, our national production of academic books about European history since 1750 in the decade 1968–78 totaled somewhere between 1,100 and 1,300 titles. The balance of my 2,044 card entries divides between books by

1. The periodicals consulted were *American Historical Review, Journal of Modern History, Slavic Review, Central European History, Central Europe Journal, Victorian Studies, French Historical Studies, Eighteenth Century Studies, Journal of Economic History, Economic History Review, Journal of Economic Literature, Journal of the History of Ideas, Isis, American Political Science Review,* and *Past and Present,* a transatlantic enterprise. In addition, the *Bibliography of Russian and East European Studies* was used. In this effort I had the assistance of a class of five students at the University of Chicago: Mark Brusco, James Fuchs, Tod Heath, Deborah Stewart, and Stuart H. Van Dyke, Jr., who worked together with me in trying to attain an overview of the recent historiography of Europe since 1750. This essay owes a great deal to their labors and critical suggestions.

*Table 1*.  Books dealing with European history since 1750 published in the United States, 1968–78, by country

| Country | Number |
|---|---|
| Great Britain | 543 |
| (Scotland 6, Wales 1) | |
| USSR | 311 |
| (Ukraine 9, Balticum 5, Lithuania 4, Latvia 3, Belorussia 1) | |
| France | 304 |
| Germany | 231 |
| Ireland | 50 |
| Italy | 45 |
| (Vatican 2) | |
| Austria | 43 |
| Spain | 35 |
| Poland | 32 |
| Yugoslavia | 28 |
| (Serbia 6, Croatia 5, Slovenia 1, Montenegro 1) | |
| Czechoslovakia | 27 |
| (Slovakia 3) | |
| Hungary | 27 |
| Greece | 17 |
| Romania | 10 |
| Bulgaria | 7 |
| Belgium | 6 |
| Ottoman Empire | 6 |
| Finland | 5 |
| Netherlands | 5 |
| Portugal | 4 |
| Sweden | 4 |
| Armenia | 3 |
| Switzerland | 3 |
| Denmark | 2 |
| Norway | 2 |
| Albania | 1 |
| Comprehensive books | 293 |

nonacademic authors and books written by persons living outside the United States whom I was unable to recognize as foreigners.[2]

Clearly I did not succeed in establishing a register of United States scholarship, pure and undefiled, in collecting these 2,044 titles. Still, they do represent books to which academic historians of the United States paid attention in the decade 1968–78. Most of them were products of the great American Ph.D. machine, either proximate in the form of a dissertation revised for publication or at somewhat greater remove in the form of a book of maturer scholarship, generated within the walls of our universities by professors who, when not writ-

2. British history was the field in which differentiation between American and other authors was most difficult, and it is clear that many of my titles in British history

ing, teach. Breakdown by national focus and by theme may therefore be of some use as a loose indicator of the balance of attention that prevailed within American academic circles.

This table reveals some oddities worth commenting on. Clearly the smaller countries of Western Europe (with the exception of Ireland) get remarkably little attention. Seven West European countries attracted a total of 26 books, fewer than either Hungary or Czechoslovakia. Lands under Communist rule, on the other hand, received very substantial attention, with a total of 482 books (counting 36 that treated Europe and Southeastern Europe on a transnational basis in addition to books dealing with separate countries). But the main focus of scholarly effort remains Britain, France, and Germany (1,078 books), together accounting for more than half the entire output. The preponderance of these three countries would increase if it were possible to assign regional focus to the 293 books that transcended any single country, for most of them related mainly to themes that had their principal expression in these same three lands. Such a concentration makes all the more remarkable the fashion in which their smaller neighbors have been systematically ignored by United States scholarship.

Obviously, these classifications are imperfect.[3] Assigning a book to a particular pigeonhole on the strength of its title alone risks error and distortion. Still, I believe this tabulation is of some value in showing how U.S.-based historians of modern Europe distributed their efforts.

Noteworthy strengths and weaknesses emerge from these figures. Clearly the time-honored focus of history upon past politics retained numerical preponderance despite the claims on professional attention made by newer fields. The fact that histories dealing with the politics of a single country outnumbered those treating international relations almost two to one registers the recent tendency for American historians to confine their researches to a single country. A generation ago, I believe, the prominence of diplomatic and international history would have been greater and the concentration on domestic politics smaller than is here recorded. But in the absence of a parallel search

---

were written by Britishers. Another anomaly was introduced by the inclusiveness of the *Bibliography of Russian and East European Studies*, which lists many nonacademic works that do not usually get noticed by learned journals.

3. In a few instances, a book was counted in more than one category, which accounts for the fact that the grand total of 2,027 falls short of the entire number of titles considered by only 17, whereas works that transcended even the broadest of these thematic categories (mostly textbooks and collections of essays by diverse authors), and were therefore not counted at all, numbered 77.

*Table* 2. Books dealing with European history since 1750 published in the United States, 1968–78, by subject matter

| Subject matter | Number |
|---|---|
| Political history | |
|   National politics | 404 |
|   International politics | 211 |
|   Political biographies | 199 |
|   Military history | 144 |
|   Imperialism | 61 |
|    All political history | 1,019 |
| Cultural history | |
|   Intellectual history | 203 |
|   Political ideologies | 77 |
|   Churches and religion | 73 |
|   History of science | 62 |
|   Media | 35 |
|   Biographies of cultural personalities | 30 |
|   Belles lettres | 22 |
|   Visual arts | 22 |
|   Education | 17 |
|   Musical performance and organization | 6 |
|   Recreation | 4 |
|    All cultural history | 551 |
| Social history | |
|   Women and family | 56 |
|   Ethnic (Jewish 49, other 3) | 52 |
|   Working class | 34 |
|   Urban society | 32 |
|   Elites | 29 |
|   Peasants | 21 |
|   Crime and punishment | 18 |
|   Demography | 17 |
|   Psychohistory (5 on Hitler) | 10 |
|   Slavery and its abolition | 10 |
|   Youth | 9 |
|   Law | 6 |
|   General social history | 29 |
|    All social history | 323 |
| Economic history | |
|   Industry, commerce, and banking | 47 |
|   Technology | 18 |
|   Agriculture | 16 |
|   General economic history | 53 |
|    All economic history | 134 |

of book notices in old journals, this impression lacks statistical backing.

The substantial number of books on military history, as tabulated here, might mislead a casual observer. The fact is that this branch of our discipline flourishes in an intellectual ghetto. The 144 books in question divide into two distinct classes: works aimed at a popular

99

readership, written by journalists and men of letters outside academic circles, and professional works nearly always produced within the military establishment of the United States and published by such official or semiofficial bodies as the Naval Institute. The study of military history in universities remains seriously underdeveloped. Indeed, lack of interest in and disdain for military history probably constitute one of the strongest prejudices of the profession. If war is too important to be left to generals, it seems obvious to me that military history is too important to be left in the sort of isolation from other forms of history that it currently both enjoys and suffers from.

Turning next to cultural history, I was surprised at the prominence of studies of churches and religion (a specialty within British history, by the way, for no fewer than 31 books dealt with churches and religion in Great Britain). This focus of interest is clearly on the increase, whereas studies of nationalism (and liberalism), which once bulked large in U.S. historical consciousness, have almost entirely disappeared. Other political ideologies continue to attract a good deal of attention (anarchism 4, communism 16, socialism 15, Marxism 21, fascism 13), although fascism is clearly fading from the forefront of professional concern.

If the history of churches and religion is specially concentrated in British history, intellectual history belongs, apparently, to France. Fifty-nine books dealing with French intellectual history were published in the decade 1968–78, and no fewer than 49 of them took a biographical approach, treating only a single thinker (Rousseau [9], Sartre [5], Voltaire [5], Montesquieu [4], and Diderot [3] led the pack). Such a concentration on Enlightenment figures and reliance on a biographical approach to intellectual history constitutes the most sharply defined school that I detected within the entire ambit of this survey. Biography was also a popular genre among historians of science. Thirty-three out of a total of 62 volumes on the history of science were biographical (7 dealt with Darwin); but in contrast to the Enlightenment focus of French intellectual history, the main concentration in the history of science was on the nineteenth century, and particularly on nineteenth-century biology.

Branches of cultural history that have been little developed yet seem especially promising are those that focus on the linkages between intellectual/artistic creativity and the popular mind. Histories of education, media, recreation, popular literature, visual arts, and music—each examined in both lowbrow and highbrow manifestations—are but slenderly represented in my tabulations. Yet for recent centuries sources should not be hard to find, and an appropriately imaginative approach to this junction between cultural and social history might offer rich insight into the way the world once was.

The positive accomplishment of those who advocated "history from the bottom up" so vigorously in the 1960s is apparent from the tabulations under the rubric of social history. The substantial number of books dealing with women and the family, the working class, slavery, and peasants attests to their impact. The other notable development in this field was the rise of what may be called ethnic history, though in practice this means Jewish history, which far outstripped the study of other ethnic minorities of Europe, unless the Irish are counted not as a separate nation (as I have counted them here) but as a subject people.

Indeed, the most remarkable growth points in the past decade were Jewish (49 books), Irish (50 books), and women's history (56 books). These three fields drew much of their energy from an inherited grievance, both against historians for neglecting the populations concerned and against constituted authorities for oppressing them. Women's history and Jewish history retained a warm emotional tone for the most part; but Irish history tended to replace moral indignation with political, social, and economic analysis.[4]

Obviously, the cooling of raw emotion and substitution of tepid intellectual discourse for the language of attack and defense tends to immerse any historical subject in ambivalent complexities. The most vital history is likely to be written during the period when emotion remains strong enough to be recollected in tranquillity (Wordsworth's definition of the wellspring of true poetry) and before anger or love have been compeltely obscured by intellectial constructs. So, at least, one may interpret the work of nineteenth-century historians who invented national histories for each of the European nations (and for the United States), or the achieve-kment of seventeenth-century scholars who did the same for the churches into which Christendom divided at the time of the Reformation. I will have more to say about where we stand in this cycle of historiographical development later in this essay, but ought first to comment briefly on the economic history of Europe written on the western side of the Atlantic during the past decade.

First of all, concentration on Great Britain in American study of European economic history remained very marked (67 out of a total

---

4. Emmet Larkin, *The Roman Catholic Church and the Creation of the Modern Irish State, 1878–1886* (Philadelphia, 1975), is a good example.

of 136 titles, or 49 percent). This lopsidedness went along with a noteworthy methodological transition—from what may be called descriptive to a more elaborately analytical and mathematical variety of economic history. David Landes's *Unbound Prometheus: Technological Change and Industrial Development in Western Europe from 1750 to the Present* (Cambridge, Eng., 1969) constituted a summation and synthesis of the older, descriptive form of economic history, distilling generations of work on the industrial revolution. The newer sort of writing, intimately informed by economic theory as developed within U.S. departments of economics, remained monographic,[5] and has not yet achieved much in the way of general overview or large-scale understanding of British, much less of European, economic history.

The gap between the two forms of economic history remained pretty wide. No doubt it arose from a long-standing antipathy between those who count and those who do not, reinforced by the fact that some economic historians are trained in and hired by departments of economics whereas others come up through history departments without being intellectually shaped by intensive exposure to economic theory. This professional bifurcation is an old one, however, and so far as I can tell from my survey of book titles, the decade of the 1970s did nothing to change the situation.

I also tried to distribute the 2,044 titles by genre, but this proved impractical since in too many cases the information at hand was insufficient to allow satisfactory classification. A few impressionistic remarks are all that I am able to offer, therefore, about the distribution of attention among the major forms of historical writing.

First of all, the day of the blockbuster textbook seems to have passed. I noticed only two completely new general European history textbooks in the ten years surveyed, though many others appeared in revised editions. Instead, books of readings, concentrated around some fashionable theme, became the focus of textbook publication. But for all their variety, such books remained relatively few. These changes reflected the fact that textbook firms cut back their investment in new books during the 1970s as the number of students in history courses diminished and as the abandonment of standard introductory courses on most U.S. campuses in the 1960s made its effect felt. As a result, what was formerly a distinctive genre of historical writing in the United States faded into at least temporary insignificance.

5. For example, Donald N. McCloskey, *Economic Maturity and Entrepreneurial Decline: British Iron and Steel, 1870–1913* (Cambridge, Mass., 1973).

At an opposite extreme of generality and scope, the publication of narrowly focused monographs derived from Ph.D. dissertations crested in the early 1970s. Buoyant library budgets, the ambitions of newly founded university presses, and the existence of several subsidized series (most notably in Slavic studies and in the history of science) combined in the late 1960s and early 1970s to make such publication comparatively easy. After about 1974, however, the economics of academic publishing became inhospitable to young scholars, and the tide of monographs began to recede as sharply as it had previously swelled.

It seems clear to me that book publication of the familiar kind cannot serve much longer as the standard means of disseminating the results of specialized historical research. There seem to be three possibilities. Either historians will resort to private circulation of typescripts among friends, acquaintances, and fellow specialists along the lines of *samizdat* in the Soviet Union; or we will learn to exploit the flexibility of photoduplication more systematically through a centralized depository, like that fostered by the Xerox Corporation at Ann Arbor; or universities or some other authority will begin to provide systematic subsidies for publication of specialized historical writing. Otherwise, only books judged likely to sell several thousand copies will see the light of day, and most monographic publication of the kind that has recently become the talisman for tenure among academic historians will come to a halt.[6]

My third impressionistic observation is this: although American historians of modern Europe published many good books of high professional quality between 1968 and 1978, none of them seemed able to command general attention. Fields of specialization have become so diverse that only professional bibliographers can keep track of everything that comes out.[7] In the absence of any common focus of attention, the basis for any secure and generally acceptable estimate of quality also begins to fade away. What seems interesting and pathbreaking to one person may well seem insignificant or even incomprehensible to another reader.

6. This was, of course, only another aspect of the career catastrophe facing young historians in the 1970s, but it is one to which European history was more vulnerable than national United States history, since the assured minimal sale of monographs dealing with European history was smaller than that of monographs treating American themes.

7. One must remember that my figure of 2,044 books for the decade leaves out everything written by Europeans about their own history, and it would be irrational indeed for any student of European history to confine attention to books written by U.S.-based scholars.

*William H. McNeill*

There is, moreover, a very considerable gap between academically written and admired history and historical writing aimed at the general public, or at segments thereof. Thus, for example, the United States continues to produce a considerable World War II literature aimed at war buffs who do not care for footnotes but do like detail. Another well-developed genre comprises books on Eastern Europe designed to further a political cause or attack some existing regime. Such works of historical propaganda presumably appeal to specialized subpublics, and publication may sometimes depend on subsidies.

In addition to these nonacademic varieties of historical literature—which usually commanded no attention at all in academic circles—a good many histories aimed to amuse and instruct a more general readership. Commercial publishers seek out this sort of history when it promises to sell well. A few well-known academic historians[8] competed with journalists and men of letters from outside the teaching profession in this genre, but in the decade 1968–78 no professor succeeded in bridging the gap between town and gown by writing a work that dealt with European history and achieved the status of "best seller." This is another indication of the fact that modern European history currently lacks any sort of common focus able to attract general attention, whether within or outside the groves of academe.

University presses are not indifferent to sales, but their standards of success and the qualities sought after are offset from the criteria that commercial publishers bring to bear. New ideas and data matter more: whether specialized scholars can enthusiastically describe the manuscript as an important contribution to learning becomes a primary consideration. Prospective sales and readership come in only as a secondary, though sometimes decisive, afterthought.

Within this unabashedly academic realm of publication, American historians of Europe interact with local European historiographical traditions in contrasting ways in various parts of the continent. Works dealing with British and German history written in the United States closely resemble books written by the professors of history living in those countries. Similar questions, similar methods, similar conceptions reign on both sides of the Atlantic, so that the national origins of the author or his place of residence usually do not leave much distinctive mark on his work. The extensive interpenetration of American

---

8. Examples include John Clive, *Macaulay: The Shaping of the Historian* (New York, 1973), and Peter Gay, *The Enlightenment: An Interpretation*, 2 vols. (New York, 1966, 1969).

with German scholarship that resulted from the transatlantic migration of refugees from Hitler in the 1930s, together with the fact that
Great Britain has long included academics among its exports to the
United States, goes far to explain the remarkable historiographical
homogeneity that has recently come to prevail across the ocean.

France is different. Though an increasing number of Americans
began to notice and admire the work of *Annalistes* in the course of the
1970s,[9] no one on this side of the water succeeded in matching their
achievement very closely.[10] The finely attuned sense of place that
characterizes their work is almost wholly missing among American
historians, thanks to the nearly total eclipse of geography in our
school and college curricula and to the homogenizing effect of the
mass media. (To be sure, the *Annalistes* themselves have not found
recent centuries very congenial, no doubt because overabundant
sources make total history more and more difficult to write.)

Some themes from their recent past remain too divisive for Frenchmen to handle comfortably. Hence the detachment and insight of
Robert O. Paxton's *Vichy France: Old Guard and New Order* (New York,
1972) won admiration not merely in English-speaking lands but in
France as well. But such recognition remained unusual. For many
topics, a general reliance upon Marxist terminology in France created
an ideological gap between French and American scholarship. Indeed, a good many American books on French history got much of
their bite from the way in which they undertook to challenge Marxist
clichés.[11] A potentially productive dialogue between comparably
sophisticated historiographical traditions seems a possible development from this situation.[12]

Elsewhere in Europe, American historians play what might be un-
kindly described as an "imperialistic" role vis-à-vis local historiog-

9. Publication of an English translation of Fernand Braudel, *The Mediterranean in
the Age of Phillip II*, 2 vols. (New York, 1972), together with a special issue of the *Journal
of Modern History* devoted to an appraisal of Braudel's work (December 1972), did much
to propagate a wider appreciation of this school in the United States.

10. See, for example, such attempts as Edward W. Fox, *History in Geographic Perspective: The Other France* (New York, 1971), or Traian Stoianovich, *A Study in Balkan
Civilization* (New York, 1967).

11. As examples, see David Pinkney, *The French Revolution of 1830* (Princeton, 1972),
and Joan Wallach Scott, *The Glassworkers of Carmaux: French Craftsmen and Political Action
in a Nineteenth-Century City* (Cambridge, Mass., 1974).

12. See the interesting effort to measure French scholarly appraisal of American
writing in David H. Pinkney, "The Dilemma of the American Historian of Modern
France Reconsidered," *French Historical Studies*, XI (1975), 170–81. Pinkney found
American work treated more attentively by French scholars between 1958 and 1973
than in the preceding fifteen years.

raphy. Instead of entering into an ongoing discussion either as equals or as eager apprentices, Americans approach the history of Eastern Europe as outsiders,[13] intent on bringing their own organizing concepts to bear upon any or all of the various national histories, while paying scant attention to the ruling ideas and principal concerns that dominate the work of local historians. The result is to create a loosely defined United States historiographical school that emphasizes characteristics common to the East European and Balkan peoples, and employs terms and concepts derived from the vocabulary of American social science—sometimes anthropological, sometimes economic.[14]

American scholarship directed toward the Communist-ruled lands of Eastern Europe is almost wholly un-Marxist if not anti-Marxist. This is in part a function of official sponsorship. American study of Slavic Europe, which burgeoned markedly after World War II, was inspired in no small degree by the wish to "know the enemy"; and even though individual scholars often sympathized with the Russians and other East Europeans and have usually sought to soften mistrust arising from the Cold War, few indeed have taken official Communist history writing at anything like face value or found fundamental stimulus to their thinking in officially approved party lines about the past.

Official control of access to archives and other sources in the Soviet Union and elsewhere in Eastern Europe means that some sensitive topics are inaccessible to American scholars. Or, more accurately, some topics must be dealt with from without, treating officially published materials, speeches, and the like as a sort of distorting mirror from which, if one is clever enough, one may guess what really happened by correcting for the deliberate distortions and propaganda of the published record. This is what Americans must do for nearly everything since 1917 in Russia, and for politically sensitive subjects in

13. The fact that several leading American historians of Eastern Europe were born there and received part of their formal education in East European lands does not really contradict this observation. Such persons, by leaving the land of their birth (often as refugees), separated themselves from those who remained behind, and consciously accepted American outlooks and values. Acquired identity of this sort is often more emphatic than an inherited one, though, of course, when they visited the land of their birth, reversion to familiar cultural patterns remained possible and sometimes opened doors that would have remained closed to a person of entirely alien background. In this sense, émigrés from Eastern Europe occasionally enjoyed insiders' advantages despite their intellectual commitment to outside approaches.

14. For example, Charles Jelavich and Barbara Jelavich, *The Establishment of the Balkan National States, 1804–1920* (Seattle, 1977); Charles Gati, ed., *The Politics of Modernization in Eastern Europe: Testing the Soviet Model* (New York, 1973).

Eastern Europe at large. In such history writing, evidence is systematically discounted in the light of the historian's own preconceptions, and standards of accuracy attainable in Western countries remain beyond reach.

On the other hand, some topics are "safe" from the point of view of Communist officials, even for Americans. The thoughts and deeds of nineteenth-century revolutionaries usually fall within this category, for example. Scholars who hope to remain sufficiently in the good graces of the authorities to be permitted to return to the archives are constrained to pursue such politically unexceptionable researches. Social and economic themes of a kind that Marxist tradition emphasizes are not easy to investigate, for discrepancies between doctrine and reality which historical research is liable to uncover either embarrass the party or, at best, make changes in its line more difficult to bring about. The result of these restraints on U.S. scholarship is a rather lopsided, sometimes bland, sometimes polemical historiography of the Communist-ruled countries, which has little congruence with historical writing within the USSR or most other East European lands.

Such regional discrepancies are, of course, traditional. Not long ago almost all American scholarly attention was focused on France and Britain, with Germany and more easterly regions of Europe very thinly represented. That pre-World War II distribution of attention was shaped by the view that what really mattered in European and world history was the advance of human liberty, understood constitutionally, legally, politically in the first place, and economically in the second. From this point of view the evolution of the British polity and economy was obviously central (and before 1776, also ancestral to the national history of the United States). The more tumultuous advance of liberty in France pointed the way for other, more backward countries to follow. The Enlightenment and French Revolution were crucial in such a development; and the decades that followed 1789 were, in fact, treated as a theater in which the spread of liberal ideals and institutions clashed in a mighty struggle with the stubborn forces of reaction. The history of modern Europe so conceived had a drama, significance, and relevance to the human condition that no one could deny.

World War I and the Depression, swiftly followed by Hitler and World War II, made such a vision of the meaning and structure of modern European history implausible, to say the least, and a new generation of American historians set busily to work to find out what had gone wrong (here, German history seemed especially critical) or what had really happened (here, Slavic Europe, previously almost terra incognita, took pride of place). This, it seems to me, was the principal agenda of American historians of Europe from 1945 to about 1965. The broadening of vision and accumulation of information that such efforts brought in their train constituted a noteworthy accomplishment indeed, and matched the expansiveness of United States national policy during the post–World War II years.

Yet as World War II faded into the past and European colonial empires were dismantled, the states of Europe ceased to play their former dominating role in world affairs. Reasons for studying European history became correspondingly less obvious. Abysses of ignorance about Asia and Africa often seemed more enticing to venturesome young minds that sought to understand the world beyond the United States' own borders. Consequently, academic study of European history, institutionally entrenched in our universities by the achievements of a past generation, had to feed upon itself.

In this situation, U.S.-based historians often found an invigorating transfusion from historiographical debates that arose in Britain, Germany, and France. The transatlantic airplane, combined with vastly expanded fellowship funds, made this sort of intellectual convergence far easier than it had been before the war. As archival historians, American scholars could begin seriously to compete with Europeans, though obviously persons on the ground year in and year out continued to have a systematic advantage. New ideas, often related to cultural anthroplogy (which had had a distinctive Anglo-American efflorescence in the generation of 1930–60), and new methods[15] could, however, compensate for the handicap of having only sporadic access to local archives, and some fertile and distinguished work resulted. Yet technical virtuosity and statistical ingenuity, applied to smaller and smaller segments of the past, usually had no apparent connection with the American scene. Professionalism, in short, became an end in itself.

Obviously, professionally impeccable historians of this ilk could not do much to answer the simple, naive question people always ask about the past: How did things—meaning the things that matter in *our* lives—get to be the way they are? The result was that the study of European history in this country tended to cut itself off from the mainspring of human curiosity that ultimately, in any society, must

15. I have in mind such things as techniques of family reconstitution from parish records of births, marriages, and deaths as pioneered in France and Great Britain, and computer studies of voting behavior, pioneered in the United States.

undergird whatever historical investigation occurs. Indeed, it seems to me that academic study of European history in the United States is like a powerful fountain whose jet ascended high into the air, only to break up into unstable, inchoate shapes, dispersing in every direction before commencing a glorious descent. The cascade of a descending fountain is entrancing to the beholder—far more spectacular, in fact, than the narrowly focused, ascending jet. But the fountain can persist only if an ascending jet sustains descending multiplicity. It seems to me, for one, that the jet has been turned off. European history has lost the necessary focus on some kind of fundamental meaning such as once was provided by the liberal vision of the human condition—however naive and inadequate it now may seem to have been. Without such an organizing vision of the whole, how long can we expect the variety and technical virtuosity of the decade of the 1970s to be sustained?

This amounts to saying in a slightly different way what I remarked upon in connection with the recent development of Irish, women's, and Jewish history. Emergent organizing ideas and vibrant emotional concerns create a potentially fruitful tension and make writing about any of these subthemes of European history an adventure. But for European history as a whole this is scarcely the case. The mainstream of political, cultural, economic, and social history has been skillfully canalized, subdivided, and locked into place by the work of thousands of scholars across five or six generations. Multitudinous projects for research remain: tasks multiply endlessly as detail gets finer and finer. But the meaning and value of the entire enterprise becomes less and less apparent to ordinary human beings who do not share professionalized interests or care about questions that have been defined by historians' debates rather than by common life experiences or by the course of public events. This surely makes the recent efflorescence of professionalized European scholarship within departments of history in the United States more precarious than most of us wish to believe.

Yet these doubts about the future ought not to detract from appreciation of the spectacle offered by American scholarly achievements in the 1970s. Publication was vast, variegated, and so complex that it becomes invidious to pick out titles for special notice here. Nonetheless, I shall try, risking injustices with each remark I make.

A transatlantic perspective invites U.S.-based historians to cross national and other boundaries. With distance, patterns running across national frontiers may emerge that can scarcely be discerned by observers standing close by. In this way what is a handicap for detailed research may become an advantage for broad-gauged interpretation.

A few books published in the last decade in the United States illustrate this possibility. Jerome Blum's *End of the Old Order in Rural Europe* (Princeton, 1978) offers a good example, for Blum treats the theme of peasant emancipation as a pan-European phenomenon, and what he has to say about events within each sovereignty gains context and meaning because of its place in the larger whole. A geographically even more ambitious work came from the hand of Donald W. Treadgold, the two-volume *The West in Russia and China: Religious and Secular Thought in Modern Times* (Cambridge, Eng., 1973); and John H. Parry's *Trade and Dominion: The European Overseas Empires in the Eighteenth Century* (London, 1971)[16] takes on a literally global theme from a pan-European viewpoint. Charles S. Maier's *Recasting Bourgeois Europe: Stabilization in France, Germany, and Italy in the Decade after World War I* (Princeton, 1975) was more modest geographically but more ambitious analytically in its effort to explain why revolution did not come to Western Europe's principal countries after the shocks of World War I; whereas Charles Tilly, Louise Tilly, and Richard Tilly's *Rebellious Century, 1830–1930* (Cambridge, Mass., 1975) applied sociological methods and concepts on a transnational scale, seeking to discover patterns of and causes for outbreaks of public violence in European society.

A more familiar, indeed old-fashioned, variety of transnational history is represented by such works as Howard Mumford Jones's *Revolution and Romanticism* (Cambridge, Mass., 1974), Maurice Mandelbaum's *History, Man, and Reason: A Study in Nineteenth-Century Thought* (Baltimore, 1971), and Peter Gay's two-volume *Enlightenment: An Interpretation* (New York, 1966, 1969). All three of these authors treat ideas as autonomous, without trying very hard to relate their development to other aspects of human life. As such, these works carry forward an American speciality of long standing, dating back to a time when most U.S.-based historians of Europe had to concentrate on intellectual history because the writings of famous European thinkers were readily accessible in libraries, whereas other sources were scant.

The great bulk of recent American scholarship, however, were concentrated within the boundaries of a single country of Europe. Three works on German history seem especially admirable: Gordon A. Craig's *Germany, 1866–1945* (New York, 1978), James J. Sheehan's

16. Parry's case is a good example of the indeterminacy of national boundaries in recent history writing. Born and educated in England, he has been a professor at Harvard for more than a decade, yet publishes in England and in most respects surely remains British rather than American in outlook, insofar as there is any difference to be discerned between the two national historiographical traditions.

*German Liberalism in the Nineteenth Century* (Chicago, 1978), and Mack Walker's *German Home Towns: Community, State, and General Estate, 1648–1871* (Ithaca, N.Y., 1971). In addition to the previously cited books on French history, Eugen Weber's *Peasants into Frenchmen: The Modernization of Rural France, 1870–1914* (Stanford, 1976) deserves particular notice. In Russian history, Nicholas V. Riasanovsky's *A Parting of Ways: Government and the Educated Public in Russia, 1801–1855* (Oxford, 1976) and Robert C. Tucker's *Stalin as Revolutionary, 1879–1929: A Study in History and Personality* (New York, 1973) impressively exemplify the two strands that have long dominated U.S. study of Russian history, that is, pursuit of the nineteenth-century intelligentsia and practice of the arcane art of Kremlinology. The two-volume work of Michael B. Petrovich, *A History of Modern Serbia, 1804–1918* (New York, 1976), was more intellectually isolated, for it summed up Serbian and European rather than American scholarship, to produce a synthesis that had no real predecessors. More traditional in form and subject matter was Gerhard L. Weinberg's *Foreign Policy of Hitler's Germany: Diplomatic Revolution in Europe, 1933–36* (Chicago, 1970). Weinberg's book offered one of the few impressive examples of the kind of diplomatic history that was, in the 1920s and 1930s, a staple of American scholarship. *Die Grosse Politik* gave a former generation of Americans access to a mass of primary documents; the German archives captured in 1945 by American forces provided Weinberg with a comparable, though vastly larger, basis for his history.

But, as I have insisted in this essay, the cutting edge of new work usually focused on specialized themes that, though they fall within the boundaries of a single nation, cannot properly be described as "national" in scope. I could not, for example, find any American book on a British theme and published since 1968 that deserves to be called "national"; yet such works as Arthur Marder's five-volume *From the Dreadnought to Scapa Flow: The Royal Navy in the Fisher Era, 1904–1918* (London and New York, 1961–70) is assuredly a notable scholarly achievement. Standish Meacham's *A Life Apart: The English Working Class, 1890–1914* (Cambridge, Mass., 1977), and *Oxford and Cambridge from the Fourteenth to the Early Nineteenth Century*, volume I of *The University in Society*, edited by Lawrence Stone (Princeton, 1974), are additional examples of new approaches, new subject matter, and new sensibilities applied to British history.

Other works of similarly restricted scope but wide significance include Keith M. Baker's *Condorcet: From Natural Philosophy to Social Mathematics* (Chicago, 1975); Robert Forster's *House of Saulx-Tavanes*

(Baltimore, 1971); Gregory L. Freeze's *Russian Levites: Parish Clergy in the Eighteenth Century* (Cambridge, Mass., 1977); Gerald Feldman's *Iron and Steel in the German Inflation, 1916–23* (Princeton, 1977); Roger Hahn's *Anatomy of a Scientific Institution* (Berkeley, 1971); Joan Wallach Scott's *Glassworkers of Carmaux: French Craftsmen and Political Action in a Nineteenth-Century City* (Cambridge, Mass. 1974); and Richard Stites's *Women's Liberation Movement in Russia: Feminism, Nihilism, and Bolshevism* (Princeton, 1978).

Needless to say, hundreds of other titles could be set beside these examples of recent American scholarship, adding to the richness and scope of those I have listed here. By any standard, the harvest is abundant. The variety and range of new themes and the vigor of new methods brought within the purview of professional historians were quite extraordinary, and flourished without driving out older ways of writing history.

Clearly, historians of modern Europe in the United States have been riding the crest of a very powerful wave. Their achievements deserve an admiration that is, for me, rendered particularly poignant by the forebodings I feel about the future of highly specialized work of the sort that so successfully engaged the profession in the 1970s.

# 4

## African History

### Philip D. Curtin

AFRICA was the last continent, the last major culture area to emerge into the light of historical knowledge. The darkness of "darkest Africa" for nineteenth-century Europeans was largely that of their own ignorance; by the early twentieth century, however, the colonial powers had to take account of the real estate they had acquired in recent decades. The United States lagged behind and left Africa to the Europeans to govern and exploit as they saw fit. America and Europe alike left African *history* out of account until after World War II. North Africa had, of course, its own version of its past. South Africa had a living historical tradition in the Western mode, though it was largely concerned with the activities of the European settlers from overseas. Europeans who wrote about the recent past wrote "colonial history"—the history of the colonists and administrators from Europe, not the history of the conquered.

The prevalence of colonial history is hardly unexpected for the early twentieth century, when history in the Western world at large was heavily enthnocentric—if not pure national chauvinism in the name of patriotic education for the young. Even though many historians after World War II tried to write within a world-historical perspective, objective enough to be read across national boundaries, the ethnocentric tradition lived on. Only a few years ago, Hugh Trevor-Roper, the Regius Professor of History at Oxford University, described African history as the "unrewarding gyrations of barbarous tribes in picturesque but irrelevant corners of the globe," and that opinion was not simple ignorance. He continued in the same context: "We study . . . history in order to discover how we have come to be where we are."[1] History, in short, was *supposed* to be ethnocentric,

1. Hugh Trevor-Roper in *The Listener*, November 28, 1963.

relevant only to the time and place of the historian. With variations, that view was probably dominant among European historians in the 1960s.

American ethnocentrism took a somewhat different form, because its historians saw their roots in Europe. The "world history" courses that flourished in the secondary schools from the 1930s onward and the "Western civilization" in the universities were directed to a key question of how "we" came to be where we are, and "we" meant twentieth-century Americans. The flight back through time became a flight through space as well—back to Europe, the classical Mediterranean, and the Bronze Age beginnings of city life in Mesopotamia. Room was sometimes made for China or India, but Africa was left out altogether. No offense was intended; it was simply regarded as irrelevant in the line of development that led to the United States. Even so close a neighbor as Canada was also virtually excluded, and for exactly the same reason.

Deplorable as this limited "world history" may have been, it left some room for maneuver. The acceptance of European history was the camel's nose under the tent. Latin America entered hesitantly in the interwar years. After World War II, Americans began to recognize that they should study the history of important places, and Asia, at least, was clearly important. Interdisciplinary area studies programs began to be founded, explicitly to remedy a deficient American knowledge of the world. For all world areas, 14 such university programs had emerged by 1946/47, 25 by 1951, 312 by 1970. Africa was not well represented in the early programs, and African history was even more ignored; but by the late 1950s, as decolonization of the tropical territories took place, Africa was better represented.[2]

A questionnaire circulated by the American Historical Association in 1974 showed 13 percent of its members claiming a special interest in history beyond the United States and Europe. Latin America led with 5 percent, followed by East Asia with 3 percent. Africa came next with 2 percent, leaving the Middle East, South Asia, and Southeast Asia with scores that rounded to 1 percent each.[3]

This growth was to lead on to a body of about 600 Africanist historians in the United States toward the end of the 1970s. The total is astonishing in itself. Even without precise international statistics, it would appear that more than half of the Africanist historians practicing their craft anywhere in the world were then in North America,

2. Richard Lambert, *Language and Area Studies Review* (Philadelphia, 1973).
3. *American Historical Association Newsletter*, XII (1974), 1.

and their increase in numbers had been extremely rapid. In a period when African studies generally were one of the leading growth areas in American universities, historical studies grew even more rapidly, especially in the decade from about 1965 to 1975. The United States had fewer than a dozen Africanist historians in the mid-1950s; the number rose to about 30 by 1960, a little over 100 by 1966, and more than 350 by 1970. In 1968, Norman Bennett founded *African Historical Studies*, the first American journal of African history, with the sponsorship of the African Studies Center at Boston University.

The peak year for doctorates in African history was 1971, when 37 were granted in American universities.[4] And about that time, the number of doctoral candidates in all fields of history began to decline, as American universities stopped growing. The pattern was therefore one of rapid growth followed by rapid contraction in the number of new doctorates—even more in the number of new Ph.D.s entering the profession, since many of those who completed their degrees after 1974 failed to find academic employment.

This pattern is extremely significant for the makeup and achievements of Africanist historians as a group. At least two-thirds of the 600 entered the profession between 1965 and 1975. As of 1980, the same two-thirds of American Africanist historians form a cluster very narrowly concentrated in age from the early thirites to the early forties. One can guess at a median age of about 38 in 1980, with a very narrow standard deviation. This group's age curve appears to be more radically skewed away from a normal distribution than that of any other group in the historical profession.

Such age distribution has had important consequences for its pattern of productivity, its motivation, and its attitudes toward the world at large. The American Africanist historians are of the undergraduate generation who finished their B.A.s between 1960 and 1970. At the beginning of that decade, public attention focused for the first time on African decolonization, with genuine and unguarded optimism about the pace and outcome of African development. The college generation of that time wanted to make a personal commitment to a better world. The Kennedy administration drew successfully on that

4. Most enumerations are on the low side, since they are based on such data as the number of doctorates granted (which leaves out those who changed to African history from some other field) or the membership of the African Studies Association, a voluntary association that did not necessarily include all practicing Africanists. See, nevertheless, African Studies Association, *Roster of Fellows*, 1959 and 1966; Lambert, *Language and Area Studies*, 15; Michael Bratton and Anne Schneller, *American Doctoral Dissertations on Africa, 1886–1972* (Waltham, Mass., 1973), xi. This survey indicated a drop in 1972, but a second peak might possibly have occurred later in the decade.

sentiment in the early years of the Peace Corps, and it was captured by other programs such as Teachers for East Africa (TEA). An inordinate number of those who served in Africa with the Peace Corps or TEA returned to the campuses as graduate students in African studies. The infusion of former Peace Corps members and teachers in East Africa meant a new generation of Africanist historians with unusual personal experience in Africa even before they entered graduate school. Partly as a cause and partly as a result, they were broadly Afrophile; they were left of center in the American political spectrum; they wanted to do something about the world as well as study it.

These attitudes carried on into the second half of the 1960s, even though the American and African scenes both began to change. The American war in Indo-China began to sour relations between the generations in the United States. The continued harshness of racial repression in southern Africa, such internal struggles as the Nigerian civil war, and the prevalence of military regimes in tropical Africa all dampened the earlier optimism. But the depth of American disenchantment with African affairs was not reached until the late 1970s. By then, few young people in America were choosing African history as a career. The generation that staffed African history positions in American universities was a generation that entered in a spirit of optimism and commitment. Their predecessors, the undergraduates of the 1950s, and their successors, the undergraduates of the 1970s, were more conservative, less activist, and far more concerned with their own security and professional advancement.

The group that entered the profession between 1965 and 1970 had to be educated, and the core of American professional Africanist historians of 1960 was far too small to do the job. A cadre of senior staff was recruited mainly from two sources. One group was known in the academic slang of that period as "retreads"; the other was a product of the "brain drain" from Europe and Africa. Retreads were historians who had finished a Ph.D. in some other field and then switched wholly or partly to African history. Some made the transition without apparent difficulty and settled down to a productive career in the new field. Others stayed for a time, taught a course or two, supervised a few Ph.D. dissertations, and then drifted back to their original fields of research. In either case, they began with less depth of training than the younger generation was to receive, but they also sometimes had a breadth of view from their earlier experience that made it possible to see the African past in a broad context of world history—a breadth sometimes missing among those they trained.

The second and larger source of lateral entry was the brain drain from overseas. Salaries in American universities were then attractive to Europeans. Academic jobs were opening in America just as administrative job opportunities for expatriates were closing down in tropical Africa, and just as liberal South Africans of all colors found an increasingly unfavorable political climate at home. In the early 1970s, at least 80 percent of the senior posts in African history at major American universities were held by recruits from overseas. Notable among them were Leonard Thompson, first at the University of California, Los Angeles, and later at Yale (and succeeded at UCLA by Terence Ranger, Boniface Obichere, and Merrick Posnansky); Graham Irwin at Columbia; Jan Vansina at Wisconsin; Ivor Wilks at Northwestern; Kenneth Dike at Harvard—and the list could go on.

By the late 1960s and early 1970s, history departments began to encourage another kind of brain drain by hiring Africans who had originally come to the United States as graduate students intending to complete a doctorate and return home. This group came to be significant, and its rise to importance was closely related to the Afro-American scholarly community and *its* concerns about African history. Even though 12 or 13 percent of all Americans were at least partly of African descent, the Afro-American reaction to Africa had been ambivalent. Other ethnic Americans had some of that ambivalence about their own origins. At one level, assimilation, "Americanization" was the road to success for new immigrants. At another, a search for a special cultural identity or ancestral roots was a source of self-confidence in an alien and often hostile land. Afro-Americans also had to confront the fact that they were not *new* immigrants. The median date of arrival of Africans in the colonies that were to become the United States lay in the distant past, about 1770, while the median date of arrival for European immigrants was about 1900. Given their separate identity but lack of a really significant folk memory of Africa itself—in circumstances where the Euro-American image of Africa stressed its alleged savagery and cultural inferiority—Afro-Americans most commonly chose, before the 1960s, to leave Africa alone.

But a small group of them took another course as early as the 1920s and 1930s and became the only Americans to pay serious attention to African history in those decades. As far back as 1916, Carter G. Woodson had founded the *Journal of Negro History* with a concern for African and Afro-American history alike. Even though Woodson was not able to visit Africa as a field researcher, he wrote widely on African history. The first American historian to do field research in Africa was another Afro-American, George W. Brown, who went to Liberia in 1936 to work on a Ph.D. dissertation for the London School of Economics.[5] Courses in "Negro history" in the segregated black colleges and universities also had African as well as Afro-American content at a time when African history was unheard of in the university world at large.

The civil rights movement of the 1950s and 1960s might have renewed Afro-American interest in African history, and it did to a limited extent; but Afro-American concerns lay elsewhere at that time. The main issues for students and teachers were equal rights in education, the end of segregation in public facilities, and voting rights. The first priority was to get what other Americans already had. As a result, when African history first began to attract interest, it drew comparatively few Afro-Americans, and the proportion of Afro-Americans among historians of Africa actually declined.

By the mid-1960s, and especially after the death of Martin Luther King in 1968, the first goals of the integrationist drive were partly won. Afro-Americans then began to insist more strongly on the culture and values of the black community. This separatist line led straight back to Africa. In the academic year 1968–69, black students began to demand more black faculty members, more courses in Afro-American studies, and separate programs or departments that sometimes took in African history as well. The new separatism spread to the world of scholarly associations. In 1969, many of the Afro-American members of the African Studies Association seceded and formed a separate and segregated African Heritage Studies Association.

Ironically, the demand for black studies came at a time when the proportion of Afro-Americans in the pool of American historians of Africa was near its all-time low. It was to increase in the 1970s, but meanwhile universities had difficulty meeting student demands for black faculty members. The government began to require "affirmative action" from the universities to increase minority representation. Even without a requirement that black history be taught by black people, universities responded in that way. The result was a progressive ghettoization of Afro-American and sometimes of African history. Since comparatively few trained Afro-Americans were available, universities turned to their own African graduate students specializing in African history. Especially from 1968 into the early 1970s, they began to ask these Africans to stay on as staff members, rather than return home after receiving the Ph.D. Some did ultimately go back to Africa,

5. Later published as *The Economic History of Liberia* (Washington, 1941).

but others remained. It was a further irony that the new generation of Afro-Americans trained in African history began to find in the late 1970s that positions were scarce, and many were already filled by African immigrants.

American Africanist scholarship belongs to a worldwide community of scholarship, and one that was still dominated by Europeans at least through the first half of the 1970s. But within this body of scholarship, a few directions or tendencies are clear. Africans, as one might expect, often wrote about their own part of the continent and about the political history of the past century or so.[6] Europeans tended to write about their former colonies—the British about anglophone, the French about francophone, and the Portuguese about lusophone Africa. Anglophone Americans, however, instead of following the British lead, actually spread quite widely into non-English-speaking territories. They concentrated somewhat on countries where the political climate was favorable to foreign researchers, such as Senegal and Kenya, but some were able to work on lusophone Africa even though access to the Portuguese colonies was quite difficult until the early 1970s.[7]

African history in the United States, as elsewhere, began with the history of European activities in Africa. At its worst, "colonial history" concentrated solely on the achievements of the colonizers, but it remained a respectable field of scholarship—so long as writers and readers alike understood that this was a branch of European history, not a balanced African history. Diplomatic historians and historians of the British Empire had dealt with Africa throughout the early part of this century, but in the mid-1950s, Harry R. Rudin at Yale was virtually the only practicing historian at a major university with a background of research on sub-Saharan Africa.[8] Rudin's tradition was partly kept up by his successors and former students, including

6. See, for example, the Ibadan History Series edited by K. Onwuka Dike and later by J. F. Ade Ajayi, now approaching twenty volumes.

7. See, for example, Gerald Bender, *Angola under the Portuguese: The Myth and the Reality* (London, 1978); Allen F. Isaacman, *Mozambique: The Africanization of a European Institution, the Zambesi Prazos, 1750–1902* (Madison, Wis., 1972); Joseph C. Miller, *Kings and Kinsmen: Early Mbundu States in Angola* (Oxford, 1976); Leroy Vail's general history of Mozambique, forthcoming. This list of published works and those that follow are not designed to be exhaustive, nor does it take account of important studies that appeared in the form of articles rather than books.

8. His dissertation, published as *Germans in the Cameroon, 1884–1914: A Case Study of Modern Imperialism* (New Haven, 1938), remains an important study of the way the German empire operated in Africa.

Prosser Gifford, Wm. Roger Louis, and Robert O. Collins.[9] Some of these scholars moved further into African history, while others turned "colonial history" in new directions; one example is Gifford and Louis's recent organization of a large-scale cooperative work on the history of decolonization in Africa.[10]

Another center of colonial history as African history was the Hoover Institution of Stanford University, where Peter Duignan began in the late 1950s to move from European into African history. He was joined by Lewis H. Gann, born in Germany, educated mainly in England, with a research career of more than a dozen years in Northern and Southern Rhodesia before coming to the United States. Their most significant work of the early 1970s was a jointly edited, five-volume coopeative study, *Colonialism in Africa, 1870–1960*,[11] though most of the contributors were, in fact, European. More recently they have concentrated on the nature and practice of colonial administrations.[12] But this is a shadowy zone between fields, and some practitioners, such as William B. Cohen, who writes on French involvement with Africa, consider themselves specialists in European, not African history.[13]

The history of Christian missions in Africa has something in common with administrative history; the emphasis can fall almost entirely on the acts of the missionaries, or it can fall on the responses of the converts (and those who did not convert). African and European historians were quite active on both ends of this continuum; but in America anthropologists were the main group to be concerned with African religious change, and historians tended to neglect missionary history in spite of occasional works such as Marcia Wright's study of German missions in Tanganyika.[14]

By the 1970s, historians of Africa's political, military, and diplomatic affairs had already begun to switch to the African side of things.

9. See, for example, Prosser Gifford and Wm. Roger Louis, eds., *France and Britain in Africa* (New Haven, 1971), a cooperative work drawing on non-American as well as American authors, and Robert O. Collins, *Land beyond the Rivers: The Southern Sudan, 1898–1918* (New Haven, 1971).

10. Wm. Roger Louis and Prosser Gifford, *The Transfer of Power in Africa: Prelude, 1950–1960*, forthcoming.

11. Cambridge, Eng., 1969–76.

12. L. H. Gann and Peter Duignan, *The Rulers of German Africa, 1884–1914* (Stanford, 1977), and *The Rulers of British Africa, 1870–1914* (London, 1978).

13. William B. Cohen, *Rulers of Empire: The French Colonial Service in Africa* (Stanford, 1971), and a study of the French image of Africa, forthcoming.

14. *German Missions in Tanganyika: Lutherans and Moravians in the Southern Highlands* (London, 1971).

The change began in Europe and Africa as well during the decoloniz-
ing 1960s, but with varying rates of speed. One of the problems was
South Africa, with its large population of overseas Europeans and a
history of white South Africa entrenched in the school system. An
important leader in the effort to include the African majority was
Leonard Thompson, who had come to the United States from the
chair in history at the University of Cape Town. With Monica Wilson,
he edited a cooperative work on South African history, explicitly setting out to change the standard view.[15] Most of his collaborators both
in that book and in his other edited volume, *African Societies in Southern Africa*, were either British or South African, but his own work on
the career of Moshoeshoe, the founder of an independent Sotho
state, came during his American years.[16] And some of his American
students have continued research in this tradition, notably Richard
Elphick in his reconsideration of the Khoikhoi confrontation with
their European invaders in the seventeenth century.[17]

A similar though even more marked revisionism appeared in the
historiography of tropical and North Africa. Colonial administration
could be examined from the point of view of particular African
peoples, as in Ralph Austen's work on northwestern Tanzania and
Robert Tignor's on Kenya.[18] Others sought to give an African emphasis by studying an African state in the precolonial or early colonial
period,[19] an individual African leader, or the African dimension of
colonial political life.[20] The revisionist attitude could even extend to
biographical studies of European political figures, if they had a special

15. *The Oxford History of South Africa*, 2 vols. (Oxford, 1969–71).
16. *African Societies in Southern Africa* (London, 1969); *Survival in Two Worlds:
Moshoeshoe of Lesotho, 1786–1870* (Oxford, 1975).
17. *Kraal and Castle: Khoikhoi and the Foundations of White South Africa* (New Haven,
1977).
18. Ralph A. Austen, *Northwest Tanzania under German and British Rule: Colonial Policy
and Tribal Politics, 1889–1937* (New Haven, 1968); Robert L. Tignor, *The Colonial Transformation of Kenya: The Kamba, Kikuyu, and Maasai from 1900 to 1939* (Princeton, 1976).
19. See, for example, Carl L. Brown, *The Tunisia of Ahamd Bey, 1837–1855* (Princeton, 1975); Michael Mason, *Foundations of the Bida Kingdom* (Zaria, forthcoming); Norman R. Bennett, *A History of the State of Zanzibar* (London, 1978); Kenneth C. Wylie, *The
Political Kingdom of the Temne: Temne Government in Sierra Leone, 1825–1910* (New York,
1977); Edward I. Steinhart, *Conflict and Collaboration: The Kingdoms of Western Uganda,
1890–1907* (Princeton, 1977).
20. Norman R. Bennett, *Mirambo of Tanzania, ca. 1840–1884* (London, 1971); James
R. Hooker, *Black Revolutionary: George Padmore's Path from Communism to Pan-Africanism*
(New York, 1967); Leo Spitzer, *The Creoles of Sierra Leone: Responses to Colonialism,
1870–1945* (Madison, Wis., 1974); G. Wesley Johnson, Jr., *The Emergence of Black Politics
in Senegal: The Struggle for Power in the Four Communes, 1900–1920* (Stanford, 1971).

*Philip D. Curtin*

sympathy for the Africans, as in Robert Rotberg's study of Gore-Brown in Northern Rhodesia.[21] Finally, still another group of American historians took up African resistance and rebellion, in the manner of Allen Isaacman's work on resistance in Mozambique.[22] In a rough way, the progression from colonial history of the school of Gann and Duignan to resistance history in the manner of Isaacman reproduced the political spectrum from right to left.

At the same time, American Africanists were less active in the field of social history than might have been expected. Urban history, for example, was underrepresented in the 1970s, in spite of studies by Kenneth L. Brown on Salé and Bruce Fetter on Elizabethville.[23] The history of the family, which became a fashionable subject of study in Europe and America, was hardly represented at all, and women's history had only a bare beginning in a volume edited by Nancy J. Hafkin and Edna C. Bay. Their book included representatives of the other social sciences, but the editors and most of the authors were women historians.[24] Still another kind of social history appeared for the first time in Joseph P. Smaldone's study of northern Nigerian warfare in a broad social setting. Smaldone carried on his social emphasis by editing a volume on quantitative history in Africa.[25]

Much of the change from European to African perspectives in African history was found among historians everywhere, but Africanists in America also pioneered in their own way by broadening the sweep of investigation beyond the conventional limits recognized in Europe or Africa. This tendency came in part from the interdisciplinary area studies idea. Even though the interdisciplinary character of most area studies programs was quite limited, some Africanist historians began to apply the concepts and methods of other disciplines in their own work.

21. Robert I. Rotberg, *Black Heart: Gore-Brown and the Politics of Multi-Racial Zambia* (Berkeley, 1978).
22. Allen F. Isaacman, *The Tradition of Resistance in Mozambique: The Zambesi Valley, 1850–1921* (Berkeley, 1977). See also Edmund Burke III, *Prelude to Protectorate in Morocco: Pre-colonial Protest and Resistance, 1860–1912* (Chicago, 1977); Ross E. Dunn, *Resistance in the Desert: Moroccan Responses to French Imperialism, 1881–1912* (Madison, Wis., 1977); Martin A. Klein, *Islam and Imperialism in Senegal: Sine-Saloum, 1847–1914* (Stanford, 1968); Alf Andrew Heggoy, *Insurgency and Counterinsurgency in Algeria* (Bloomington, 1972); Harry Gailey, *Lugard and the Abeokuta Rising* (London, forthcoming).
23. Kenneth L. Brown, *The People of Salé* (Cambridge, Eng., 1976); Bruce Fetter, *The Creation of Elizabethville, 1910–1940* (Stanford, 1976).
24. *Women in Africa: Studies in Social and Economic Change* (Stanford, 1976).
25. *Warfare in the Sokoto Caliphate: Historical and Sociological Perspectives* (Cambridge, Eng., 1977); J. P. Smaldone, ed., *Explorations in Quantitative African History* (Syracuse, 1977).

Several scholars took the lead in this direction. Daniel McCall, an anthropologist at the African Studies Program of Boston University, published an early and influential guide to method.[26] From within history, the greatest enthusiasm and most striking example came from Jan Vansina, another instance where the brain drain made a crucial impact on African studies in the United States. Vansina was originally Belgian, educated in history at Louvain, with an additional M.A. in anthropology from London University. He then went on to eight years of residence and fieldwork in Rwanda, Burundi, and the then Belgian Congo. One of his first contributions to the development of African historical studies was his theoretical and methodological work on oral traditions and their interpretation.[27] Much of oral history in Africa is different from the oral history discussed in Chapter 17 of this volume. It is not so much a question of witnesses transmitting their own memory of past events as the recitation of formal narratives passed down through generations of specialist intermediaries. The result is often like the corpus of knowledge that Homer recorded for ancient Greece. This kind of evidence had long been used by some historians and anthropologists dealing with the African past, but most historians were still wedded to their documentary sources, and anthropologists had sometimes used oral traditions too uncritically. Among prominent anthropologists, G. P. Murdock claimed that for Africa, "indigenous oral traditions are completely undependable much beyond the personal recollections of living informants," and he tried to set aside all evidence from this source.[28] Vansina's treatise on method helped to show both its weaknesses and its value if used with appropriate care.[29]

It was also important that the search for oral sources brought historians into grass-roots contact with African societies. Few studies could be based entirely on oral traditions, but oral evidence could contribute something to almost any topic in African history. As a result, it be-

26. Daniel McCall, *Africa in Time Perspective* (London, 1964).
27. Jan Vansina, *Oral Tradition: A Study of Historical Methodology* (London, 1965). Translated from the French original of 1961.
28. G. P. Murdock, *Africa: Its Peoples and Their Culture History* (New York, 1959), 43.
29. One of the new problems that emerged with oral data collection in Africa was how to make privately collected material available to a wider world of scholarship. In the mid-1960s, the African Studies Association in the United States, with the cooperation of Indiana University, set up an African Oral Data Center, housed in the Archives of Traditional Music in Bloomington. The center acquires, catalogues, and holds tape recordings and transcriptions for distribution to interested scholars. The aim is to provide a central point for the preservation of oral material collected in Africa by American scholars, and to assure that at least one copy is returned to the country of origin for the use of scholars there.

came customary for American researchers to combine archival and library work with the kind of local investigation that anthropologists alone had done in the past. The consequences for the historiography of Africa went far beyond the mere acquisition of additional evidence. One special problem of cross-cultural research is the need to understand as profoundly as possible the culture of the society under investigation. Historical field research added a dimension of understanding and attitude—a dimension that would otherwise have been hard to come by, though experience in the Peace Corps or TEA sometimes served the same purpose.

The impetus of field research might or might not carry one on to intense training in an additional discipline, but several of the research students who studied with Vansina at one time or another also sought systematic training in anthropology. Steven Feierman earned a Ph.D. in anthropology as well as one in history, at two universities, leading to two separate books on the same African people, from the points of view of the two disciplines.[30] Others stopped short of the double doctorate but nevertheless trained in anthropology to the equivalent of a master's degree or more. David William Cohen used this training as the basis for extensive research on the oral traditions of Busoga, which resulted in two separate publications that are unusual in the degree to which they are based on oral traditions alone.[31] Joseph C. Miller applied similar techniques to the precolonial history of Angola, but with an archival as well as an oral base, and John A. Works, Jr., studied the Hausa community in Chad somewhat in the manner of an anthropologicst doing a community study.[32] But anthropology was not alone as a second discipline. Christopher Ehret moved into linguistics and produced important new findings, published in article form, on the diffusion of cattle and agricultural techniques into East and Central Africa as well as a recent and important hypothetical reconstruction of the early history of East Africa and the Horn, also based largely on linguistic evidence.[33]

Still others among Vansina's former students followed the line of his original contribution to methodology, and particularly the methodology of oral tradition. David P. Henige took up the problems

30. His historical thesis was published as *The Shambaa Kingdom* (Madison, Wis., 1973); the anthropological work is *Symbolism and Change in Shambaa Politics* (Oxford, Eng., forthcoming).

31. *The Historical Tradition of Busoga: Mukama and Kintu* (Oxford, 1972); *Womunafu's Bunafu: A Study of Authority in a Nineteenth-Century African Community* (Princeton, 1977).

32. Miller, *Kings and Kinsmen*; John A. Works, Jr., *Pilgrims in a Strange Land: Hausa Communities in Chad* (New York, 1976).

33. *Ethiopians and East Africans: The Problem of Contacts* (Nairobi, 1974).

of chronology in relation to oral tradition, with Ghana as a principal example,[34] and went on in 1974 to found a new journal, *History in Africa: A Journal of Methodology*, which quickly became a leading journal of methodological criticism not only for Africa but for historical studies in general. The critical discussion of oral traditions is continued in Paul Irwin's forthcoming study of the traditions of Liptako in Upper Volta.

Vansina, meanwhile, went beyond the role of influential teacher to publish an enormous quantity of original research in linguistics and anthropology as well as in history. Two of his most significant books appeared in the 1970s. One was a historical and anthropological study of the Kuba people of central Zaire, the culmination of research going back over several decades. The other was an innovative effort to recapture the nature of society around Stanley Pool in the first years of intense contact with the Europeans.[35]

But all the interdisciplinary ferment was not simply a movement of historians into anthropology or linguistics. The reverse also took place, as people trained in anthropology began to write history. M. G. Smith, a Jamaican anthropologist who has pursued an international career with appointments in London and Jamaica as well as at UCLA and, more recently, at Yale, began in the 1950s to study the history of northern Nigerian emirates. He recently returned to emirate studies with *The Affairs of Daura*. David Montgomery Hart dealt with part of the Moroccan Rif in an ethnographic study that was also a history of Aith Waryaghar from earliest times to the present.[36] William Y. Adams, an archaeological anthropologist, wrote on an even grander scale in *Nubia: Corridor to Africa*,[37] covering that part of the Nile Valley from the earliest times to the present. Its data base for early periods was the crash program of archaeological rescue work to save the evidence about to be covered by the waters of Lake Nasser behind the Aswan High Dam. Adams himself participated in the American contribution to that work, but his book carried the story down to the present on the basis of archival research. His study repeats a theme of recent African historiography by substituting a Nubia-centered approach for the Egypt-centered view that dominated past writing about the middle Nile.

34. *The Chronology of Oral Tradition: Quest for a Chimera* (Oxford, 1974).

35. *The Children of Woot: A History of the Kuba People* (Madison, Wis., 1978); *The Tio Kingdom of the Middle Congo, 1880–1892* (London, 1973).

36. M. G. Smith, *The Affairs of Daura: History and Change in a Hausa State, 1800–1958* (Berkeley, 1978); D. M. Hart, *The Aith Waryaghar of the Moroccan Rif: An Ethnography and History* (Tucson, 1976).

37. Princeton, 1977.

Quite another approach to African history is embodied in the work of Ivor Wilks and a number of his students and associates. Wilks has devoted a long career to the single-minded study of Asante and its neighbors. He made an early lateral shift from philosophy to history, and a series of shifts of residence, from Britain to Ghana to Northwestern. His most important work, *Asante in the Nineteenth Century: The Structure and Evolution of a Political Order*,[38] belongs in a category by itself. It is intensely Asante-centered, and in that way parallel to Adams' work on Nubia, but it makes little use of the anthropological theory or method found so commonly among American historians of Africa. The conceptual framework is eclectic and idiosyncratic, with some borrowing from the geographers' central place theory and with Weberian overtones. Since 1974, Wilks and his associates have been engaged in the Asante Collective Biography Project, producing a computerized compendium of information on every figure from the Asante past for whom information is recoverable. *Asantesem*, a mimeographed journal of Asante studies, is published in connection with the project, and book-length studies by some of Wilks's former students have also begun to appear.[39]

Wilks's work also belongs on the fringes of another significant body of recent historical literature in its use of African documents in Arabic alongside the European records. Arabic sources have not been well explored, because most of those that might be used are still in the hands of private individuals. Photocopying and collecting this literature for distribution to libraries has only begun, though some documentation in Arabic is available for most of Africa north of the tropical forest, and also for parts of the east coast. So far, comparatively few American scholars specializing in tropical Africa have mastered the language skills needed to deal with these sources, but they have already produced an important body of new historical work.[40] This group is also significant because they are almost the only Ameri-

38. Cambridge, Eng., 1975.
39. See, for example, Thomas J. Lewin, *Asante before the British: The Prempean Years, 1875–1900* (Lawrence, 1978).
40. See, for example, Louis Brenner, *The Shehus of Kukawa: A History of The Al-Kenemi Dynasty of Bornu* (London, 1973); B. G. Martin, *Muslim Brotherhoods in Nineteenth-Century Africa* (Cambridge, Eng., 1976); and E. K. Steward, *Islam and Social Order in Mauritania* (Oxford, 1973); Lansiné Kaba, *The Wahhabiyya: Islamic Reform and Politics in French West Africa* (Evanston, 1974); David Robinson, *Chiefs and Clerics: The History of Adbul Bokar Kan and Futa Toro, 1853–1891* (Oxford, 1975); and the forthcoming works by Arnold Green on the Tunisian 'ulama and by William A. Brown on the caliphate of Hamdullahi.

can historians of Africa who have paid serious attention to African religious change, perhaps because it was Muslim religious leadership that left the records.

Economic history has also been slow in developing, not only in the United States but among Africanists everywhere. One kind of research, however, has been popular for some time. This is the "trade and politics" school modeled on the pioneering study of K. Onwuka Dike in the 1950s.[41] Available European sources made it possible to learn a great deal about the nature of political and commercial relations between Africans and Europeans at the points of contact on the African coast in the era of the slave trade, and these studies have been extremely valuable; but they are not really studies of the African economy. They tell more about the politics of trade than about trade itself; they asked little help from economic theory and contributed little to economic anthropology.[42]

To say this is not to detract from their intended contribution, which was considerable, but to set them in contrast to some of the newer trends, which are moving toward an interdisciplinary approach often involving the manipulation of new kinds of source material in order to make possible the study of societies beyond the reach of direct European evidence. My own work on Senegambia from the middle of the seventeenth to the middle of the nineteenth century was done from the point of view of historical economic anthropology.[43] Moving inland from the Niger Delta and the Cross River, which Dike had explored, David Northrup took up the trade of the Igbo and Ibibio peoples.[44] Other scholars also dealt with commercial penetration inland. Robert Harms worked with the Bobangi of the Congo River above Kinshasa, while Edward A. Alpers studied the trade routes of the Yao and others that fed the coastal trading cities of Mozambique and southern Tanzania.[45] Even farther into the East African interior, Gerald Hartwig examined the patterns of long-distance trade in the

41. *Trade and Politics in the Niger Delta* (London, 1956).

42. See, for example, Phyllis M. Martin, *The External Trade of the Loango Coast, 1576-1870: The Effects of Changing Commercial Relations on the Vili Kingdom of Loango* (Oxford, 1972); Edward Reynolds, *Trade and Economic Change on the Gold Coast, 1807-1874* (London, 1974); K. David Patterson, *The Northern Gabon Coast to 1875* (Oxford, 1975).

43. Philip D. Curtin, *Economic Change in Pre-Colonial Africa: Senegambia in the Era of the Slave Trade*, 2 vols. (Madison, Wis., 1975).

44. David Northrup, *Trade without Rulers: Pre-Colonial Economic Development in South-Eastern Nigeria* (Oxford, 1978).

45. Edward A. Alpers, *Ivory and Slaves in East Central Africa* (London, 1975); Harms on the Bobangi is forthcoming.

region of Lake Victoria.[46] And Frederick Cooper broke new ground with a study of precolonial slave plantations on the Kenya coast and the islands of Zanzibar and Pemba, fitting these plantations into the broader comparative context of slave studies in the New World.[47] This new wave of interest in economic history led in 1976 to the establishment of a new specialized journal, *African Economic History*, under the sponsorship of the African Studies Program at the University of Wisconsin.

The new interest in economic history was related, in turn, to a remarkable resurgence of slave-trade studies with an Atlantic rather than an African focus. In 1969 my *Atlantic Slave Trade: A Census*[48] tried to pull together what was then available in the published literature regarding places of origin, destinations, and the number of people who moved across the Atlantic from the beginning of the trade to its conclusion. In the decade that followed, a great deal of new research was published, revising, contradicting, or commenting on this preliminary survey. American historians were far from alone in this effort, and much of the new work appeared in conference volumes of international scope. Herbert Klein's *Middle Passage*, however, constituted a substantial American contribution, while Henry Gemery and Jan Hogendorn edited a conference volume that had a high proportion of American authors.[49] By the end of the 1970s, the main dimensions of the slave trade were clear, but the quantitative work of that decade suggested still other questions ranging from the comparative slave demography of the New World to the comparative forms of slave recruitment in the Old.

When it came to the economic history of the African colonial period, American research was high in quality but small in quantity. Some was in the style of the precolonial trade studies, such as Paul Lovejoy's work on the kola trade from the Asante forests to Hausaland.[50] But there was also a significant new departure, as economics-trained scholars—who normally served in economics, not in history departments—turned to African economic history for the first time. Sara S. Berry made a trail-breaking study of African entrepreneur-

46. *The Art of Survival in East Africa: The Karebe and Long Distance Trade, 1800–1895* (New York, 1976).

47. Frederick Cooper, *Plantation Slavery on the East Coast of Africa* (New Haven, 1977).

48. Madison, Wis., 1969.

49. Herbert Klein, *The Middle Passage: Comparative Studies in the Atlantic Slave Trade* (Princeton, 1978); Gemery and Hogendorn, eds., *The Uncommon Market: Essays in the Economic History of the Atlantic Slave Trade* (New York, 1979).

50. *Caravans of Kola: The Hausa Kola Trade* (Zaria, forthcoming).

ship in agricultural change.[51] Peter Kilby published an important book on postwar Nigerian industrialization, following up a pilot study of the Nigerian bread industry.[52] Jan Hogendorn examined another kind of entrepreneurship in the development of peanut growing in northern Nigeria.[53] This literature is, of course, overshadowed by an enormous literature on Africa by agricultural and development economists. Some of this work is important for historical knowledge, but even more is ahistorical and disappointing—not merely because it has little value for historians, but also because it could have been immensely stronger if the authors had paid more attention to the patterns of the past. One interesting exception, however, is William I. Jones's *Planning and Economic Policy*,[54] dealing mainly with the planning and execution of Malian economic policies in the 1960s, but taking into account the social and intellectual context of the planners' work.

One other way of broadening the scope of historical inquiry appeared in the late 1970s, perhaps a straw in the wind for future American scholarship about Africa. Gerald W. Hartwig and K. David Patterson put together an impressive set of case studies in historical epidemiology, ranging in location from northern Ghana through Cameroon and Chad to East and Central Africa. It may be indicative that the authors are all comparatively young and came from anthropology and political science as well as history, but none of them had his home base in a medical school, the normal center for epidemiological studies in the United States. Other research on African medical history is also under way. Here, in short, is one more example of American historians broadening the scope of the discipline, not merely by asking help from colleagues but also by learning new skills and using them for historical purposes.

African historical studies in the United States during the 1970s had the vigor and originality one would expect from people closely grouped in the age bracket usually most productive for historians. Partly for this same reason, it is still hard to see precisely where the new leadership will come from—who will be the successors of the retreads and drained brains who founded the field in North America. Nor is it easy to see what directions the mature scholarship of the

51. *Cocoa, Custom, and Socio-Economic Change in Rural Western Nigeria* (Oxford, 1975).

52. *Industrialization in an Open Economy: Nigeria, 1945-66* (Cambridge, Eng., 1969), and *African Enterprise: the Nigerian Bread Industry* (Stanford, 1965).

53. *Nigerian Groundnut Exports: Origins and Early Development* (Zaria, 1978).

54. *Planning and Economic Policy: Socialist Mali and Her Neighbors* (Washington, D.C., 1976).

*Philip D. Curtin*

youthful and numerically dominant group will take. The only cause for concern is, perhaps, the fact that the university community is now growing only slowly or not at all. With very few Africanist historians in line for retirement, the group now clustered around age 38 will cluster around age 58 in 2000, and 68 in 2010, with comparatively few replacements in the meantime.

# 5

## The History of the
## Muslim Middle East

### Nikki R. Keddie

BEFORE 1945 the history of the Muslim Middle East was little written about by American academics; what was written, with very few exceptions, was the work of persons without special training in history. American interest in the history of the Third World has followed political and economic interest; before World War II, the Middle East, Africa, and South Asia were the scholarly preserves of Great Britain, France, Russia, and Germany. Only in the Far East and Latin America, where the United States was deeply involved politically and economically, had U.S. historians begun serious study. After 1945, U.S. interests became global; at the same time travel to and study of Third World areas were facilitated by funds for area studies supplied by foundations and government agencies.

In the Middle East as in other regions, the new U.S. area studies program tended, contrary to expectations that might arise from the name "area studies," to stress specialization in a single academic discipline, such as history or anthropology, rather than continuing the Orientalist approach, in which the language and history of one region were emphasized at the expense of rigorous training in a particular discipline. On the whole the new emphasis, although it did not wholly supersede Orientalist trends and attitudes, is generally regarded as a gain. In its Middle Eastern component, Orientalism had its origins in the Middle Ages, when study of the language and religion of the Muslim "enemy" began, and it has often carried with it a large component of hostility to Islam and its peoples (as Edward W. Said has pointed out in *Orientalism*).[1] In the eighteenth and nineteenth cen-

Thanks to Julia Clancy for her assistance and to Michael Kammen and others for their editorial comments.
1. New York, 1978.

turies Orientalists did important textual and interpretive work, much of it still vital to the field; but most Orientalists were affected by feelings of cultural superiority and often lacked adequate knowledge of non-Islamic cultures. Many traits they considered "Islamic" might better have been called "preindustrial," having existed in similar forms in the medieval West and elsewhere. The recognition that such civilizations as the Chinese and Near Eastern were economically more advanced than the Western until the late Middle Ages, when trends were reversed for some centuries, even today could obviate statements of Western superiority followed by Third World apologetics. The Orientalist attitude just described, however, was a natural ideological concomitant of Western policies, notably imperialism. Scholarly racism remained respectable well into the twentieth century.

Thorough training in language and philology, the strong positive feature of Orientalism, was deemphasized in the area studies approach. Stress on literature and philology outside of historical contexts has led, however, to misreadings of terms that have changed in their economic and social significance, as Claude Cahen, the greatest living historian of the Middle East, has noted. Finally, many Orientalists have, in fact or in spirit, entered the field of Middle Eastern studies instead of, or in addition to, entering religious vocations: as a result, Islam has often been looked at in terms of Christianity or Judaism instead of in its own terms, generally to the detriment of Islam. Here again, the trait continues among some scholars, although a countervailing ecumenical trend has developed in recent decades.

Area studies programs developed steadily in the 1950s and 1960s and continued in the 1970s. The areas most commonly studied are the Far East, South Asia, Eastern Europe, Latin America, Africa, and the Middle East. Few if any universities have programs in all areas, but several have programs in more than one. Princeton's Near East program, building on an existing department and on the work of Philip Hitti, was the first to begin, soon after World War II. It was followed by Michigan, Harvard, Columbia, New York University, Chicago, the University of California at Los Angeles, the University of Pennsylvania, and Texas, to name only some of the more prominent ones (Utah, Washington, and the State University of New York at Binghamton are among others). All major centers have outside support in addition to funds from their own universities; some of the sources are institutions, such as the Ford Foundation; branches of the government; and private corporations and individuals. Though it is rare for funding explicitly to shape policies and programs, some examples of implicit influence have occurred.

As suggested earlier, area studies programs turned away from the stress on language and early Islamic history characteristic of the Orientalist approach and emphasized the social sciences, particularly modern history, sociology, political science, and anthropology. Most students began to specialize and to take Oriental languages only as graduate students, when they also carried a heavy program in a given discipline. This belated exposure, plus the scarcity of good language teachers, meant that languages were generally not learned as well in the United States as in, say, England, where language study is much more intense. The problem still exists, even though there is a simple solution: the setting up of one or two good language centers, within or outside the United States, where students could study language full time for a year or two.

The dominant practice in American area centers, in contrast to centers in most other countries, is to appoint professors of all ranks in such departments as history, Near Eastern languages and literatures, and sociology, while the area center itself does little or no teaching or permanent hiring on its own, but has funds to finance visiting scholars, graduate fellows, and interdepartmental or other programs. A few exceptions to this practice exist, notably at Princeton, where a single department is responsible for the teaching of Near Eastern languages, history, and related subjects. One point in favor of the dominant pattern is that it breaks with the Orientalists' notion that everything Islamic is *sui generis*. It also brings both faculty and students into contact with aspects of a discipline unrelated to the Near East, encouraging them to make comparisons and also to keep abreast of new theories and approaches in other areas. It also encourages scholars in fields other than the Third World to look upon that world as a legitimate part of their own discipline, and to undertake comparative work. The disadvantage of the dominant American departmental pattern has been the refusal of some departments to hire area specialists. History departments, however, have largely been willing to add courses on the Middle East and other parts of the Third World to their formerly Western-centered offerings. The addition of such courses was facilitated by the availability of funds during the expansion of the 1950s and 1960s; even in today's straitened academic circumstances, the Middle East, owing largely to its political and economic importance to the United States, is holding its own and may even be growing relative to most other fields of study.

Most of the great expansion of U.S. study of the Middle East that began after World War II and accelerated after 1950 has been due to a generation of scholars who, after participation in area studies programs, received their doctorates in the middle and late 1950s. The field was fortified by senior scholars trained in the Orientalist tradition who came to the United States from Europe in the years soon before and continuing after World War II, notably G. E. von Grunebaum of the University of Chicago, subsequently head of the UCLA Near East Center from 1957 until his death in 1972; H. A. R. Gibb, head of the Harvard Center; S. D. Goitein of the University of Pennsylvania, later of the Institute for Advanced Study in Princeton; and most recently Halil Inalcik of the University of Chicago and Bernard Lewis of Princeton. Although only works that these men completed in the United States will be considered, their total contribution to Middle Eastern studies is inestimable, however much some members of the new generation may fault some of their work for Orientalist or other biases.

## MEDIEVAL ISLAM

Although (or perhaps because) the area studies emphasis has been modern and contemporary, the ratio of very good works to total works produced by U.S. scholars is higher in the early and medieval Islamic field than in the modern field. The first major work on medieval Islamic history published in the United States was G. E. von Grunebaum's *Medieval Islam*. Like most of his works, it is a collection of interconnected essays in which he tries to catch the essence of a civilization through a multidisciplinary approach, making use of his prodigious knowledge of classical civilization, philosophy, literature, language, and social science.[2] Full of brilliant and important insights and discoveries, the book has nonetheless fallen out of fashion, both with those who prefer a rigorous approach to social and cultural history stressing specific historical contexts rather than "Islamic" universals and with those who find in such books pejorative comparisons of Islam with the classical world or the modern West. Whatever its faults, *Medieval Islam* remains a veritable gold mine of ideas, and it is to be hoped that a new generation will not be so sensitive to the very real weaknesses of Orientalism that they will fail to read works by such giants as von Grunebaum, or will read them with little profit.

More in tune with the postwar emphasis on social history that has affected Middle Eastern history almost as much as Western history is

2. Von Grunebaum, *Medieval Islam: A Study in Cultural Orientation*, 2d ed. (Chicago, 1953).

S. D. Goitein's magisterial multivolume study *A Mediterranean Society,* on the Jewish community in Cairo.[3] A problem in medieval Islamic historical studies has been the relative paucity of documentary material before the fourteenth century. An exception was found in the Cairo Geniza, a storehouse next to a synagogue. In it papers of various sorts that might contain holy words (and hence should not be destroyed) were stored until the nineteenth century, when they were discovered and taken to various libraries. The potential contribution of these documents to social history was long unexploited. Goitein, who had already done other studies of Middle Eastern social history, spent years studying the writings, which included business letters and documents, wills, and a wide variety of other papers. With their aid and the aid of related books and documents, he reconstructed a fascinating picture of a medieval Jewish community in Muslim surroundings—a picture that also reveals much about the surrounding Islamic society. The work is so alive and so accomplished in its depicture of the practicality and rationality, as well as the romance, of both Jewish and Muslim communities that it helps to dispel the notion that these were very different kinds of people, possessing very different motivations, from the people we know today. For this reason alone, everyone interested in history can profit from reading all or part of this remarkable work.

Another major contribution to the history of medieval Islam is Ira M. Lapidus's widely praised *Muslim Cities in the Later Middle Ages,* a study of cities in Syria and Egypt in Mamluk times which refrains from making the global generalizations about "Islamic cities" in all times and places that once were prevalent in Orientalist circles. Lapidus also refrains from the Orientalists' accent on the negative— the crookedness of streets, the absence of squares, the supposed lack of urban autonomy and government, and so forth, and instead tries to find out how cities actually functioned. His emphasis on the role of "informal" networks and quarters, and particularly on the *ulama* (religious class) as a binding force, as well as on urban domination of the countryside, has been found relevant for cities beyond those that he studies. Richard N. Frye, in his fine synthetic volume *The Golden Age of Persia,* speaks of the effects on urban life of the decline in centralized government and in trade and production that accompanied the rise of invasions and of nomadism from the eleventh century on. Like Lapidus, he stresses the increasing importance of the ulama and of religious schools, or *madrasas,* which became the only real schools

3. Goitein, *A Mediterranean Society,* 3 vols. to date (Berkeley, 1967-).

and taught orthodoxy.[4] And, to cite only one other example of similar findings, the urban economic and social dominance of the countryside described in Paul N. English's seminal work, *City and Village in Iran,* makes clear the close parallels that exist to the picture portrayed by Lapidus in this book and elsewhere.[5]

Lapidus has also been one of the scholars who supported the thesis first put forth by Claude Cahen of Paris and the late Samuel Stern of Oxford, that there is no credible evidence that guilds existed in the Middle East during the early Middle Ages, and that the evidence put forth by the late Louis Massignon for early guilds, and for their ties with Sufi orders, does not stand up.[6] (Guilds did exist in the late Middle Ages, although there is no way to date precisely something that developed gradually; their rise may be related to other changes in urban structures.)

Another work by a social historian, Richard Bulliet's *Camel and the Wheel,* might be almost as seminal as that of Lapidus if Islamicists were more interested in the history of material culture.[7] Bulliet makes a number of crucial points about the ways in which the use of the domesticated camel affected Near Eastern history. Even before Islam, wheeled vehicular traffic nearly disappeared from the Near East. Bulliet attributes this development not only to the superiority of camels in the desert but to the fact that they were more economical than animal-drawn carts. Once wheeled carts were unnecessary, so too were broad, angular streets to accommodate them and their turns; in exposed, hot, and windy cities, narrow, crooked streets were more functional. The change in city design began even before Islam (disproving fanciful theories about this characteristic of "Islamic cities"). The camel saddle, perfected in North Arabia slightly before the rise of Islam, increased the efficiency of camels in combat, and contributed to easy victories by Muslim armies.

Bulliet's book is an all-too-rare example of a study of the influence of material culture on Islamic history (neglect of material culture is not confined to U.S.-based historians or to historians of the Middle East, but is characteristic of Western historiography in general). Aside from Bulliet's writings, most of the work in this field by persons based

4. Lapidus, *Muslim Cities in the Later Middle Ages* (Cambridge, Mass., 1967); Frye, *The Golden Age of Persia* (New York, 1975).

5. English, *City and Village in Iran: Settlement and Economy in the Kirman Basin* (Madison, Wis., 1966).

6. See the articles by Stern and Cahen in Albert H. Hourani and Samuel M. Stern, eds., *The Islamic City* (Oxford, 1970).

7. Bulliet, *The Camel and the Wheel* (Cambridge, Mass., 1975).

in the United States has been done by art historians, notably Oleg Grabar and a number of younger scholars—Renata Holod, Lisa Golembek, Ulku Bates, Priscilla Soucek—and by archaeologists, notably Robert McC. Adams.[8] Yet, as both Bulliet's work and a body of work outside the Middle Eastern field demonstrate, although archaeological training is a desideratum for Middle Eastern historians who wish to study some areas of material culture, it is by no means always required. Much past technology can be understood by persons who lack special technical training, and without such understanding our knowledge of the economic and social history of the Middle East is incomplete. Like many other countries, the United States could benefit from programs to train historians in archaeology and in the history of technology.[9]

Another fruitful approach to medieval economic and social history is that represented in an important monograph by Abraham L. Udovitch, *Partnership and Profit in Medieval Islam.*[10] Using legal texts to reconstruct the various forms of partnership and commerical arrangements found and sanctioned in medieval Islam, Udovitch reinforces our respect for the way in which jurists in the early Islamic centuries were able to legitimize, and even to create, arrangements to facilitate commerce. Udovitch also brings forth new evidence to show how certain Islamic trade arrangements, notably the commenda (which apparently has pre-Islamic Arabian origins), were taken over by Western Europe once the need for such relatively sophisticated practices was felt. Udovitch compares legal documents with materials found in the Cairo Geniza and elsewhere and shows how realistically legal documents described actual trade practices.

Among works of social history whose utility goes beyond their immediate field is Speros Vryonis's massive study of the conversion of most of the Greek population of Anatolia after the Turkish invasion.[11]

If the newer fields of social and economic history have produced much of the best work on medieval Islam, new approaches to older fields, such as the history of ideas and of religion, have also had important results. Breakthroughs in the areas of Muslim theology and

8. See especially Grabar, *The Formation of Islamic Art* (New Haven, 1973), and Adams, *Land behind Baghdad: A History of Settlement on the Diyala Plains* (Chicago, 1965).

9. See the survey of achievements and possibilities in Nikki R. Keddie, "Material Culture: A Neglected Aspect of Middle Eastern History", in Keddie, *The Middle East and Beyond* (London, 1980).

10. Princeton, 1970.

11. Vryonis, *The Decline of Medieval Hellenism in Asia Minor and the Process of Islamization from the Eleventh through the Fifteenth Century* (Berkeley, 1971).

education have been made by George Makdisi in his studies of change over time in the dominant Ash'ari theology, and of Muslim institutions of higher learning.[12] The late Marshall Hodgson produced important articles on Shi'ism, as well as a book on one branch of the Ismaili Shi'is, *The Order of the Assassins,* which is a more thorough study of the group than any other, and a more sympathetic one as well. Most people are horrified by the Assassins' killing of a few high-level figures, Hodgson says, but take for granted the launching of wars that kill thousands of people. In the book Hodgson tries to give an internal view of the evolution of Ismaili doctrine and practice.[13]

Political, narrative history of the sort that dominated prewar historical writing has also not been neglected. In 1978 Andrew Ehrenkreutz attacked one of the few positive, and perhaps romanticized, Western images of a Muslim hero, Saladin. A year earlier Stephen Humphreys's book on the Ayyubids had offered a more qualified and perhaps more balanced picture.[14]

A variety of newer fields is represented by ongoing research that has already resulted in important journal publications. Basim Musallam's dissertation, in which he shows that birth control practices were not forbidden and were sometimes even approved by leading classical Muslim jurists, philosophers, and theologians, has aroused interest. Many scholars, however, question Musallam's attempt to tie the use of such practices to population decline, especially in late-medieval Egypt.[15] The decline seems better explained by a falling off in agriculture, documented mainly by non-U.S. scholars, and by such factors as the endemic nature of the plague in warm climates, documented in Michael Dols's important and original book on the Black Death in the Middle East.[16] Dols and Musallam are two of the few American scholars of the Middle East to have seriously raised the demographic questions that have become so prominent in the postwar study of Western history; but it is likely that interest in demography will grow, despite the dearth of reliable records.

12. See especially Makdisi, "Muslim Institutions of Learning in Eleventh-Century Baghdad," *Bulletin of the School of Oriental and African Studies,* XXIV (1961), and "Ash'ari and the Asharites in Islamic Religious History," *Studia Islamica,* XVII (1962) and XVIII (1963).

13. M. G. S. Hodgson, *The Order of the Assassins* (The Hague, 1955).

14. Andrew S. Ehrenkreutz, *Saladin* (Albany, N.Y., 1978); Humphreys, *From Saladin to the Mongols: The Ayyubids of Damascus, 1193–1260* (Albany, N.Y., 1977).

15. Musallam, "Sex and Society in Islam: The Situation and Medieval Techniques of Birth Control," Ph.D. dissertation, Harvard University, 1973.

16. Dols, *The Black Death in the Middle East* (Princeton, 1977).

FOURTEENTH THROUGH EIGHTEENTH CENTURIES

The fourteenth through the eighteenth centuries were the period in which the Ottoman Empire rose and developed. In this period, particularly after most of the Arab world was conquered by the Ottomans in the early sixteenth century, new great capitals first came to prominence in the Ottoman Empire and—particularly after the rise of the Safavid dynasty in 1501—in Iran. An Arab-centered view has often been adopted by Orientalists, who tended to be most interested in the early Islamic centuries, when almost everything was written in Arabic; hence, the period from the eleventh century on, and particularly from the thirteenth (Mongol) century on, has often been regarded as one of almost uninterrupted decline. In fact, although certain kinds of economic decline may be demonstrated for some regions and periods, this later period of Islamic history also witnessed significant new developments, particularly in the administrative and cultural spheres. The Ottoman Empire drew on Islamic, Byzantine, and Turkish elements in creating a new amalgam and set up one of the best-ordered premodern imperial and military systems the world has known, while it gained its exaggerated reputation for oppression during the later phases of what still may be termed "decline." The Safavids were also well administered for a time, and Iranian rulers were particularly noted for their patronage of architecture, painting, and theology. Independent schools of philosophy also flourished under the rule—though not the patronage—of the Safavids. In the new emphasis on the achievements of the later periods of premodern history, even the much-maligned eighteenth century has taken on a new look. Most of the important work, however, has been done by non-U.S. historians, including major Turkish scholars. Americans have tended to favor the earlier and later periods.

American contributions to the study of this "late medieval" period appear greater in the Iranian than in the larger Ottoman sphere. A major contribution to Iranian history in these centuries is John Woods's *The Aqquyunlu: Clan, Confederation, Empire,* a comprehensive study of the rise, apogee, and decline of a Turkic clan in Iran that built a confederation and a state, laying the foundations for the Safavid state that followed.[17] Woods questions the prevalent belief that the Aqquyunlu created an almost purely tribal government, and shows how their administrative and religious practices paved the way

17. Minneapolis, 1976.

for Safavid centralization. In his use of Persian and Turkish sources and his integration of tribal and national history, Woods has made a pioneering contribution. Published before Woods's book but dealing with a later period is Michel Mazzaoui's study of religious movements that preceded and helped to bring about the rise of the Safavids, who came to power as heads of an "extremist" Shi'i Sufi order and established Shi'ism for the first time as Iran's state religion.[18]

While Safavid and eighteenth-century Iranian history have not yet been the subject of major books by American scholars, two special issues of the fine U.S. journal *Iranian Studies* contain important contributions on the Safavid period. One is the two-volume *Studies on Isfahan,* edited by Renata Holod; the other, *State and Society in Iran,* edited by Amin Banani.[19] The Holod collection stresses aspects of cultural history as reflected in the Safavid capital city. The Banani study focuses on power relationships during the whole Islamic period. It contains a paper by Banani on the Safavids and a paper by James Reid on the important and relatively new topic of tribal history, a subject dealt with for later periods by Gene Garthwaite.

As noted, the Ottoman Empire before 1789 has been little studied by Americans. Stanford J. Shaw has been the most productive scholar working on this period, having written a controversial two-volume textbook and a more widely applauded monograph on Ottoman Egypt.[20]

Revisionist views have been expressed about the late medieval period, which looks better if seen from a Turkish, Persian, or Indo-Muslim perspective than from an Arab one. They have even been applied to the eighteenth century, which is usually envisioned as the nadir of decline, from which the Middle East was "revived" only after contact with the West. Recently, however, economic "decline" has been shown to be an ambiguous picture, and the very meaning of "decline" has been called into question. It appears justifiable to speak of economic decline when convincing evidence exists of decreases in agricultural production, trade, and population, but the breakdown of central government should not be taken to mean decline if the smaller units that emerged functioned as well as or better than before. Albert Hourani of Oxford has pioneered in the reconsideration of the eighteenth century (as in other questions), and many once-accepted

18. Mazzaoui, *The Origins of the Safawids: Šī'ism, Sūfism, and the Gulāt* (Wiesbaden, 1972).

19. *Iranian Studies,* VII (1974) and XI (1978).

20. Shaw, *The Financial and Administrative Organization of Ottoman Egypt, 1517–1798* (Princeton, 1962).

ideas about that century and about "decline" are revised and modified in an excellent collection with several U.S. contributors, *Studies in Eighteenth-Century Islamic History,* edited by Thomas Naff and Roger Owen.[21] The volume focuses on Ottoman lands and includes a few papers on Iran. Its overall tone is somewhat revisionist. While it does not deny that decline or problems existed, it shows continuing adaptations to new circumstances and suggests that the transition from the eighteenth century to the more "modern" and Western-influenced nineteenth was far less dramatic than is usually supposed.

This theme is also found in a book by Peter Gran that treats eighteenth- and nineteenth-century Egypt, and tries to show that the rise of trade with the West in the eighteenth century encouraged significant economic changes that were quickly reflected in new intellectual currents.[22] The Napoleonic invasions and Muhammad Ali play less important roles than usual, and continuities between eighteenth- and nineteenth-century economic and intellectual life are shown. While Gran may be overambitious in trying to prove new theses about a vast body of economic and intellectual history, and may not satisfactorily demonstrate ties between the economic and the intellectual, even to those who believe that such ties exist, he performs an important service in breaking with views of modern Middle Eastern history centered on the West and on "great men" which have tended to dominate the field until recently.

NINETEENTH AND TWENTIETH CENTURIES

One of the major contributions of the U.S. area studies approach has been to focus the attention of serious historians on the need for well-documented histories of the modern Middle East. As noted earlier, the average level of U.S. contributions has been higher in medieval than in modern studies, but since far more scholars are engaged in modern studies, the total number of useful books produced in this field is greater than in the others.

The dean of Middle Eastern economic history is Charles Issawi, one of the few modern specialists able to handle all of the major languages needed to study the Middle East. Although most of his primary research has resulted in important books and articles concerning Egypt from 1800 through the Nasser period, he has more recently pub-

21. See Naff and Owen, eds., *Studies in Eighteenth-Century Islamic History* (Carbondale, Ill., 1977), *passim,* and the article by Halil Inalcik in Vernon J. Parry and M. E. Yapp, eds. *War, Technology, and Society* (London, 1975).
22. Gran, *Islamic Roots of Capitalism: Egypt, 1760–1840* (Austin, Tex., 1979).

lished volumes containing selected articles and documents on the
Arab Middle East and on Iran, 1800–1914, and is now preparing a
similar collection on Turkey.[23] Issawi has done pioneering work on
Egypt's lopsided economic development, and his collections have
made available to English-speaking scholars material that they would
otherwise have had great difficulty in finding. Although Issawi's
moderate to conservative and nontechnical approach may be
criticized by some economists and by younger leftist historians, his
contributions to the burgeoning field of economic history have been
immense.

An important work in economic history not limited to American
contributors or to the modern period is the volume on Middle Eastern
economic history edited by A. L. Udovitch, based on a Princeton
conference and containing possibly the most sophisticated group of
papers of any of the several volumes on Middle East economic history
to appear in recent years.[24] The modern section covers Iran, the Arab
countries, and the Ottoman Empire. (Single-country works in economic history will be discussed under the respective countries.)

## Iran

If Western scholarship before World War II centered on the early
periods and on Arab lands, something of a reversal has occurred
since, in terms of both time and space. The emphasis on modern
periods may be largely due to political and social science interests and
to the availability of travel and funding for modern research. The
move by American scholars away from the central Arab lands (except
Egypt), toward Turkey, Iran, and Morocco, is partly explained by the
greater ease of research on the modern period in those areas than in
many of the central Arab countries. By 1979, Turkey and Iran were
no longer so hospitable to American researchers, and we may see
shifts in the focus of scholarship as a result. The emphasis in this essay
on Iran, Turkey, and Egypt, however, is a reflection of the present
state of American research and writing on the modern Middle East,
excluding North Africa.

Modern Iranian studies have undergone a period of extraordinary
growth in the United States since World War II, although much of the
work has been done by social scientists rather than by historians.

23. Issawi, *Egypt at Mid-Century* (London, 1954); *Egypt in Revolution* (London, 1963); *The Economic History of the Middle East, 1800–1914* (Chicago, 1966); *The Economic History of Iran, 1800–1914* (Chicago, 1971).
24. Udovitch, ed., *The Islamic Middle East, 700–1900: Studies in Social and Economic History* (Princeton, 1980).

History has not gone unrepresented, however. For the period since 1890, Richard W. Cottam's *Nationalism in Iran,* far broader in scope than its title suggests, is the best interpretive work.[25] For the Reza Shah period, Amin Banani's *Modernization of Iran,* which treats reforms topically, remains the best analytical work, but much additional study, based on new documentation, remains to be done.[26] The same is true of the post–World War II period. Cottam's work gives the best coverage of the Mosaddeq years, for which new documents are now available. A work referred to earlier, *City and Village in Iran,* by the geographer Paul English, uses historical material to demonstrate the close dependence of the carpet-weaving villages around Kerman on the dominant carpet interests in Kerman city. English sets forth a general theory of urban domination in the Middle East based on this pattern of dependence. Although English has been criticized for assuming that a single recent situation may be used as the basis for long-term and area-wide generalizations, his book has shown Middle East scholars how much the field of geography can contribute to the understanding of history. Carpet weaving is important to the history of modern Iran, where carpets have for decades constituted the largest export apart from oil and have affected the lives of millions of Iranians. English traces the growth of a class of Tabriz merchants who rivaled foreigners as carpet entrepreneurs, and the introduction of carpet workshops into Kerman, which had not been a carpet center but whose chief manufacture, Kerman shawls, had become unfashionable in Europe.

Research on Iranian commerce and exports in the nineteenth century has been carried out mostly outside the United States and in unpublished American dissertations. Combining such studies with material found in books by English, Issawi, and other American scholars, we may conclude that the commercialization of agriculture, with growing exports of cotton, opium, tobacco, and fruits and nuts in particular, was considerable in nineteenth-century Iran, although not so great as in Turkey and Egypt, nations more accessible to Europe. It appears also that a native Muslim entrepreneurial merchant class was probably more important in Iran than in Turkey and Egypt, where merchants tended to be foreign or non-Muslim. And although the sale of handicrafts was undermined by the influx of Western manufactures and enforced low tariffs, the loss in income was compensated

25. Pittsburgh, 1964; 2d ed. with update, 1979.
26. Banani, *The Modernization of Iran, 1921–1941* (Stanford, 1961); see also Donald Wilber, *Riza Shah Pahlavi* (Hicksville, N.Y., 1975).

for, to a degree, by the great expansion of one craft, carpetmaking.[27] The deleterious effects of increased child labor in unhealthy surroundings and the spread of opium consumption were among the negative aspects of these developments.

Two special features of modern Iranian history are the political power of nomadic tribes and the power of the Shi'i ulama, both of which developments were attributable in part to the decentralization characteristic of the Qajar dynasty (1796–1925). I have written several articles on the ulama and their allies, but the fundamental book is Hamid Algar's *Religion and State in Iran, 1785–1906*.[28] While Algar and I, among others, assess the character and motives of the Shi'i ulama differently, we agree that Shi'i doctrine as it evolved in Iran provides a basis for asserting the superiority of pronouncements by the top ulama to those of temporal rulers; that the Shi'i ulama were strengthened through their collection of religious taxes, which in Sunni countries passed through government hands; that the Shi'i ulama and their close allies in the bazaar had grievances that were voiced by the popular and hard-to-punish ulama; and that the relative decentralization of Qajar Iran, the lack of a standing army, and the residence of ulama leaders abroad in Iraq strengthened the hand of the ulama.

The first successful Iranian mass movement, in which the alliance of ulama and bazaar classes initially made itself felt, came in the nationwide protest against a tobacco monopoly awarded to a British subject; the protest is explored in my monograph *Religion and Rebellion in Iran*.[29] The success of the religious-bazaar-intellectual alliance in making the government cancel the concession led to a similar alliance—again successful—in 1905–1911, the period of the constitutional revolution. Among the major nineteenth-century figures whose writing advanced the cause of reform and constitutionalism was Malkum Khan, whose biography has been written by Hamid Algar.[30] Some critics have found Algar too sympathetic to the ulama and too hostile to Malkum, whose practice of Islam was purely nominal, and whose financial and other manipulations are emphasized. Algar is, however, a scholar of prodigious ability who at an early age has produced two books and several articles that cast welcome light on Iran

27. These issues were discussed by G. Gilbar, V. Nowshirvani, and others in a congress at Babolsar, Iran, in June 1978.

28. Berkeley, 1969.

29. Nikki R. Keddie, *Religion and Rebellion in Iran: The Tobacco Protest of 1891–1892* (London, 1966).

30. Algar, *Mirza Malkum Khan: A Study in the History of Iranian Modernism* (Berkeley, 1973).

and the Middle East. His article on the oppositional role of the ulama in twentieth-century Iran, published in 1972, is, its partisanship notwithstanding, considered by many to be the most enlightening work written on the subject.[31]

Firuz Kazemzadeh's book is the outstanding work on Iran's relations in Qajar times with Russia and Great Britain—the powers whose rivalry kept Iran from becoming a colony of either nation, while making it a semicolony of both.[32] While unraveling from primary sources the tangled story of the rivalry, Kazemzadeh minimizes the economic motives for imperialism in Iran. Counterarguments can be made, however. While it is true that Iran presented relatively few opportunities for profit in the nineteenth century, carpets, opium, and cotton and other plants were exported and Western goods, particularly cloth, were imported. Equally important were the Russian desire for access to the Persian Gulf and the British need to protect routes to India, both of which factors had a large economic component.

Although good articles by Mangol Bayat, Ervand Abrahamian, and others deal with aspects of the constitutional revolution (which is also touched on in the Kazemzadeh and Algar books), the only American book devoted entirely to the revolution is that by Robert McDaniel on the Morgan Shuster mission and the last years of the revolution, treating the period not included in E. G. Browne's *Persian Revolution*.[33] Browne wrote as a partisan while the revolution was in progress. McDaniel's more conservative and skeptical view differs from that of most younger scholars. The constitutional revolution—a mass movement that lasted for six years and comprised many diverse ideological currents and events, and that produced a vast amount of newspapers, pamphlets, and documents—seems destined to attract more attention by scholars, particularly in view of its parallels with the events of 1978–1979. Both revolutions contrast with the predominantly military or military-led coups d'état characteristic of most Middle Eastern governmental changes in the twentieth century.

Pierre Oberling wrote the first book on Iranian tribal history, on the Qashqai tribe, a useful pioneering work that is sometimes criticized for concentrating too heavily on tribal leaders and their views.[34] Other useful monographs with a large historical component

31. Algar, "The Oppositional Role of the Ulama in Twentieth-Century Iran," in Nikki R. Keddie, ed., *Scholars, Saints, and Sufis* (Berkeley, 1972).

32. Kazemzadeh, *Russia and Britain in Persia, 1864–1914* (New Haven, 1968).

33. Robert A. McDaniel, *The Shuster Mission and the Persian Constitutional Revolution* (Minneapolis, 1974).

34. Oberling, *The Qashqa'i Nomads of Fars* (The Hague, 1974).

include those by M. D. Entner on Russo-Persian economic relations in Qajar times and by Sepehr Zabih on Iranian communism.[35]

## Turkey

If modern Iran was a nearly unknown quantity to the American public before World War II, Turkey was only slightly less so. The only major American book on the subject was A. H. Lybyer's on the Ottoman Empire in the time of Suleiman the Magnificent, written early in this century.[36] To some degree Americans shared a legacy of anti-Turkish feeling that had largely replaced or become confused with earlier anti-Arab feeling once the Arab threat disappeared and the Ottoman threat to various parts of Europe rose. Although a minority of pre-nineteenth-century Western writings on Ottoman Turkey were sympathetic, most were not. The rise of hostility in the nineteenth century was due to several factors. Among them was the Ottoman oppression of Christian subjects, an oppression that recent research has shown to have been rarely more severe than the government's oppression of the Turkish and Arab masses by a central government weakened and in growing need of money to face the challenge of the West. Revolts by Christian nationalities increased Western hostility to the Ottomans, while expansionist moves into Ottoman territories by Great Britain, Russia, France, and Italy were often justified by tales of Ottoman misrule and by a supposed need for a Western civilizing mission. After the Ottomans sided with the Central Powers in World War I they were stripped of territory and were regarded with distaste by the victors. The interwar Ataturk regime managed to modify somewhat the negative Western image of the Turks, but significant new attitudes appeared in scholarly writing only after World War II. Western scholarship on Turkey was improved by the high level of the Turks' own twentieth-century historical scholarship.

With solid Turkish and European works available to them, and profiting from unusual archival possibilities, U.S. scholars of Turkey began in the 1950s to turn out works that, if not methodologically innovative, were highly revisionist in their view of modern Turkish history. A dominant Western view had held that the seventeenth and eighteenth centuries were periods of nearly total decline in most spheres, punctuated by a brief spell in the early eighteenth century when a number of innovations were introduced, chiefly by Ibrahim

35. Entner, *Russo-Persian Commercial Relations, 1828–1914* (Gainesville, Fla., 1965); Zabih, *The Communist Movement in Iran* (Berkeley, 1966).
36. Albert H. Lybyer, *The Government of the Ottoman Empire in the Time of Suleiman the Magnificent* (Cambridge, Mass., 1913).

Muteferika, a man of European origin. The nineteenth century, according to this view, saw a series of Western-inspired reform efforts, first by two sultans and then by powerful ministers, but apart from their military and bureaucratic aspects, reform decrees were seen as window dressing to halt or delay dismemberment of the empire by the West, and they were not taken seriously in the West. The Ottoman constitution of 1876 and the short-lived parliaments that followed were not given much importance, and the reign of Sultan Abdulhamid (1876–1909) was seen as reversing whatever small good had been accomplished by the reforms and the constitution.

The standard views just summarized have been attacked with impressive documentation by several Turkish, European, and American scholars (only when a point is made primarily in an American work will it be cited). As noted, the seventeenth and eighteenth centuries are no longer seen as periods of absolute decline, inasmuch as some decentralized territories enjoyed considerable prosperity. The decentralization, economic decline, and oppression that did occur are not now blamed solely on the Ottomans but are seen to have roots in relations with Europe: the fall in the price of silver hurt the Ottomans, as did the improvement of European techniques both before the industrial revolution and after. With free trade being enforced for Western goods, crafts were undermined, while European consuls and the non-Muslim Ottomans they protected had advantages over Muslims, undermining artisans and merchants. The empire became increasingly an importer of European manufactures and an exporter of commercial crops, and the government could not control trade. Scholars as diverse as Bernard Lewis and Immanuel Wallerstein have analyzed aspects of this increasingly unbalanced East–West relationship or pattern of "dependency."[37] The trends accelerated after the industrial revolution and after the Turks extended the provisions of the Anglo-Turkish treaty of 1838, which provided for a low 5 percent tariff on imports, to other European nations. American scholars have tended to write political histories concentrating on reform, but they have used the above economic background to help to explain the empire's difficulties, which made many feel keenly the need for reform.

The man generally regarded as the first modern reforming ruler in the empire, Selim III, came to the throne in 1789. His life and career

37. Lewis, *The Emergence of Modern Turkey* (London, 1961); Wallerstein, *The Modern World System: Capitalist Agriculture and the Origins of the European World Economy in the Sixteenth Century* (New York, 1974).

have been minutely studied by Stanford Shaw.[38] In addition to giving details on Selim's Westernizing army reform and the tax reform aimed at supporting it, and on the hostile reaction to these reforms that led to Selim's overthrow, Shaw suggests that Selim was really more of a traditional reforming Ottoman sultan than a modern reformer. Like many sultans, he wished to use new methods to support a system that was essentially traditional. Although this view is not universally accepted, it does provide a corrective to the older approach to the modern Middle East that lays heavy emphasis on the role of the "great modernizers." As noted above, several scholars perceive in the eighteenth century elements of "modern" change, and a number of them refuse to accept Napoleon, the industrial revolution, Muhammad Ali of Egypt, Selim III, and the beginning of the Qajar dynasty as representing crucial breaks with the past. (Other scholars suspect that the trend toward an unperiodized "seamless web" has gone too far and would point at least to the Industrial Revolution and its results as having changed the face of the globe.)

Mahmud II, the next reforming sultan, has not had an American biographer. But the following period of reformist ministers, known as the *Tanzimat*, has been analyzed in articles by several authors and in an important book by Roderic Davison, *Reform in the Ottoman Empire, 1856–1876*.[39] Davison, like most recent scholars, takes Ottoman reforms more seriously than earlier Westerners did, and shows how much was done by reformers to meet their promises of equal treatment for non-Muslims, to appoint reforming governors and elected local administrative councils, to regularize taxes and codify the laws and the like. Davison points out that Europeans were essentially interested in just one aspect of reform, equal treatment of Christians, and in this they were not supported by either Christians or Muslims in the empire. For Christians, equal treatment meant mainly not paying a special tax, but on the other hand, it also meant serving in the army. Because they preferred the tax to the army, they generally paid an equivalent sum to be exempted. More seriously, what the articulate elements of the compact Christian nationalities of Ottoman Europe increasingly wanted was not equality or autonomy but independence, in which ambition they were encouraged by Westerners, so that attempts to grant equality might plausibly be seen by Muslims as en-

---

38. Shaw, *Between Old and New: The Ottoman Empire under Sultan Selim III, 1789–1807* (Cambridge, Mass., 1971).
39. Princeton, 1963.

couraging rebellion. Also, granting non-Muslims tax-exempt status and allowing them equal treatment were against Muslim law and practice, causing resentment, particularly when such concessions were regarded as being forced on the empire by the non-Muslim West.

The Ottoman constitution and parliament, like the major earlier reform decrees, were often viewed as window dressing for the West, but a book by Robert Devereux has shown them to be more serious in their intentions and consequences. The Turkish scholar Serif Mardin had previously established the importance of the so-called Young Ottomans.[40] This group, led by the writer Namik Kemal, originated ideas that later played key roles in the important movements of Islamic modernism, nationalism, and pan-Islamism—such ideas as the existence of Islamic or national roots of modern institutions, including constitutions and parliaments, and the importance of Muslim unity in the face of a threatening, hostile West. The Young Ottomans criticized the idea of reform from above, saying that bureaucrats were copying the West and were creating an elite isolated from the masses. (Such cleavages and criticisms of them are still found in the Middle East today.) The group argued that the Ottoman Empire had in its past the roots of the executive-legislative-judicial division, and what it needed was not autocratic reform but a parliamentary system with Ottoman-Islamic roots. There were also some constitutional figures in the government, notably Midhat Pasha. When, in 1876, a sultan died and his heir proved amenable, a constitution was drawn up. Unfortunately, the new king was insane and had to be deposed. Devereux shows that by insisting on a few crucial changes in the constitution, his successor, Abdulhamid II, acquired the power to rid himself of his enemies and to dismiss parliament without calling new elections. Thus Abdulhamid, more than the framers, undermined the meaning of the constitution. Devereux shows that the first two parliaments displayed maturity, considering the novelty of constitutional institutions, but Turkey's defeats in the Russo-Turkish war of 1877-78 gave Abdulhamid the excuse he needed to prorogue the parliament.

Until recently Abdulhamid has appeared in a very negative light, but works by Niyazi Berkes, Bernard Lewis, and the Shaws have modified this picture, showing that in his actions he exemplified the conservative and antiforeign mood arising after the dismemberment of 1878, and that "modernization" continued to a considerable degree

40. Devereux, *The First Ottoman Constitutional Period* (Baltimore, 1963); Mardin, *The Genesis of Young Ottoman Thought* (Princeton, 1962).

under his rule.[41] Not everyone accepts this more benign portrait, especially in view of the first wave of Armenian massacres.

The Young Turks have been dealt with in two books, the more recent a political study by Feroz Ahmad, while the earlier one by Ernest E. Ramsauer treats their ideas and the antecedents of their revolt. There have been fewer American historical works of stature on the post–World War I period, although it has been dealt with in some of the more general studies. Perhaps the shortage of governmental documents is largely responsible, although works surveying the Ataturk period and Richard D. Robinson's *First Turkish Republic* show how much can be done.[42]

Recent developments in historical scholarship dealing with the Ottoman Empire before World War I include a revision of views attributing bad faith to Ottoman reformers and a realization that reform is a gradual process involving more than the will or decrees of a few men at the top; that the roots of reform and economic change go back into the eighteenth century and before; and that their operation did not stop with Abdulhamid.

Other important contributors to modern Turkish history include Kemal Karpat, who has addressed a number of economic, political and intellectual questions; Carter Findley and Donald Quataert on new views of the nineteenth-century administrative and economic changes; and Dankwart Rustow on Ataturk and political modernization.[43]

## Egypt and Arab Asia

If Egypt has rarely been subject to as much Western hostility as Turkey, it has as frequently been the stage for the exercise of "great man" theories: Egypt is seen as having been transformed by Napoleon's invasion; the invasion provided an opportunity for the great Muhammad Ali to take over Egypt; the country was soon ruined by the spendthrift Khedive Ismail but then partially saved by Cromer. (This sequence represents a slight, not an extreme, caricature.) As in

41. Berkes, *The Development of Secularism in Turkey* (Montreal, 1964); Lewis, *Emergence of Modern Turkey;* S. J. and E. K. Shaw, *History of the Ottoman Empire and Modern Turkey,* vol. II (Cambridge, Mass., 1977).

42. Ahmad, *The Young Turks* (Oxford, 1969); Ramsaur, *The Young Turks* (Princeton, 1957); Robinson, *The First Turkish Republic* (Cambridge, Mass., 1963).

43. Karpat, *Turkey's Politics: The Transition to a Multi-Party System* (Princeton, 1959), and *Social Change and Politics in Turkey* (Leiden, 1973); Rustow, "Ataturk as Founder of a State," in Rustow, ed., *Philosophers and Kings: Studies in Leadership* (New York, 1970); Rustow and Robert E. Ward, *Political Modernization in Japan and Turkey* (Princeton, 1964).

the case of Turkey, simple stereotypes have altered as research has progressed and scholars have come to modify the view that all virtues derive from the West. As compared with Western studies of Turkey, those of Egypt have dealt relatively less with politics and political leaders and relatively more with aspects of social, intellectual, and economic history.

More complex views of the early nineteenth century are found in the Gran book, cited earlier, and in articles by Afaf Marsot on the early-nineteenth-century ulama and on Muhammad Ali, about whose life and times Mansot is undertaking an extensive study.[44] An important and readable work that illustrates the interactions between Western bankers and Egypt's rulers at mid-century is David Landes's *Bankers and Pashas*.[45] Problems in nineteenth-century intellectual history are elucidated by Irene Gendzier's monograph on James Sanua, while Nadav Safran has written a more ambitious work, *Egypt in Search of a Political Community*, which analyzes late-nineteenth- and twentieth-century intellectual and political trends. Charles Wendell covers one major problem of intellectual history over time in his book *The Evolution of the Egyptian National Image*. Robert Tignor's *Modernization and British Colonial Rule in Egypt, 1882–1914* surveys the political and social aspects of British rule in Egypt with attention to both gains and losses.[46]

Twentieth-century liberal Westernizing trends in government are dealt with in Afaf Marsot's *Egypt's Liberal Experiment*, which the author characterizes as an old-fashioned history, but which nonetheless reflects her interest in newer fields such as intellectual and social history.[47] Western-style liberalism in the Muslim world attracted the Westernized upper and new middle classes, and the "return" to a somewhat radicalized version of Islam studied in Richard P. Mitchell's book on the Muslim Brethren appealed to the more numerous and increasingly important traditional urban bourgeoisie, petite bourgeoisie, and subproletariat.[48] Yet the two trends were intertwined. One may trace a descent from the radical reformist vision of Islam of Jamal ad-Din "al-Afghani" (1838–1897) and passing in Egypt via

44. Marsot, "The Ulama of Cairo in the Eighteenth and Nineteenth Centuries," in Keddie, ed., *Scholars, Saints, and Sufis,* and her articles referred to therein.
45. Landes, *Bankers and Pashas: International Finance and Economic Imperialism in Egypt* (Cambridge, Mass., 1958).
46. Gendzier, *The Practical Visions of Ya'qub Sanu'* (Cambridge, Mass., 1966); Safran, *Egypt in Search of a Political Community* (Cambridge, Mass., 1961); Wendell, *The Evolution of the Egyptian National Image, from Its Origins to Ahmad Lutfi al-Sayyid* (Berkeley, 1972); Tignor, *Modernization and British Colonial Rule in Egypt, 1882–1914* (Princeton, 1966).
47. Marsot, *Egypt's Liberal Experiment* (Berkeley, 1977).
48. Mitchell, *The Society of the Muslim Brothers* (London, 1969).

his more moderate, Westernized ex-disciple Muhammad Abduh to the latter's disciple Rashid Rida, who stressed a return to a purified original Islam, then to the Muslim Brethren and other Islamic revival movements that espoused programs combining fundamentalist Islam with radical social and anti-imperialist goals. (Similar trends are found in many Muslim countries, but Egypt was a particular center for them.) The Abduh-Rida part of the story has been covered well in a book by Malcolm Kerr.[49]

Among works in the social sciences that are important for the history of Egypt is the pioneering book on Cairo by Janet Abu-Lughod, which includes a useful and original historical section. Works on Nasser and on recent economic and social change are also important.[50]

The non-Egyptian Arab world has been treated less frequently by Americans. Aspects of nineteenth-century Syria and Lebanon have been covered in monographs by William R. Polk and Malcolm Kerr.[51] Majid Khadduri has written about Iraq, and Michael Hudson about Lebanon and Palestine.[52] Although other works could be mentioned, one cannot point to significant American schools of research dealing with Arab Asia and producing major changes in our image of the area, as one can for Iran, Turkey, and Egypt.

On the other hand, the Arab-Israeli question has produced a vast literature—scholarly, polemical, or both—of uneven merit. There is no space here to survey the literature, only to point out a few well-regarded works, written from various points of view. The oldest among them is Jacob C. Hurewitz's *Struggle for Palestine*; an anthology with Arab, Israeli, and nonpartisan viewpoints has been edited by Irene Gendzier; while Nadav Safran's *From War to War* is an ambitious, well-researched study of this area of controversy, written with a pro-Israeli bias but with some understanding of the Arab case.[53]

Considerations of space also do not allow coverage of the vast literature on the history of Zionism and the state of Israel, which is a very large and important topic in its own right but which has seldom been

49. *Islamic Reform* (Berkeley, 1966).

50. J. Abu-Lughod, *Cairo: 1001 Years of the City Victorious* (Princeton, 1971); R. Dekmejian, *Egypt under Nasir* (Albany, N.Y., 1971).

51. Polk, *The Opening of South Lebanon* (Cambridge, Mass., 1963); Kerr, *Lebanon in the Last Years of Feudalism* (Beirut, 1959).

52. Khadduri, *Independent Iraq* (New York, 1961) and *Republican Iraq* (London, 1969); Hudson, *The Precarious Republic: Political Modernization in Lebanon* (New York, 1968).

53. Hurewitz, *The Struggle for Palestine* (New York, 1950); Gendzier, ed., *A Middle East Reader* (New York, 1969); Safran, *From War to War* (New York, 1969). See also Ibrahim Abu-Lughod, ed., *The Transformation of Palestine: Essays on the Origin and Development of the Arab-Israeli Conflict* (Evanston, Ill., 1971).

closely tied in with the historiography of the Muslim Middle East. The historiography of such minorities as the Armenians and the Kurds has also been omitted because of lack of space.

## Comprehensive Works

Among books that cover more than one modern Middle Eastern area is Wilfred C. Smith's *Islam in Modern History,* a broad survey of religious trends and attitudes in the modern Muslim world. The book is unparalleled for its coverage and insights, although some readers find it difficult to sympathize with the author's religious approach, which contrasts with the social and class approach of Smith's *Modern Islam in India,* written a decade earlier.[54] *Islam in Modern History* notes the apologetic nature of much of modernist Islam, and perceives that modernist Muslims often seem more attached to Islam than to God. Such criticisms are not voiced as "Orientalist" hostility to Islam, and, somewhat ironically, Smith has been criticized by some educated Middle Easterners for giving too much weight to Islam's influence. In view of recent Islamic trends, the book remains very important.

A number of collections of original articles have dealt with the modern Middle East. Among them are *The Beginnings of Modernization in the Middle East,* edited by William Polk and Richard Chambers, which concentrates on nineteenth-century changes; *From Medina to Metropolis,* edited by L. Carl Brown, on urban history and change;[55] and my *Scholars, Saints, and Sufis: Muslim Religious Institutions since 1500. Women in the Muslim World,* which I edited with Lois Beck, offers several chapters of interest to historians, who can thus far find few scholarly works on the history of Muslim women.[56] My *Islamic Response to Imperialism* and *Sayyid Jamal ad-Din "al-Afghani"* also cross national boundaries since Afghani, although born in Iran, spent

---

54. Smith, *Islam in Modern History* (Princeton, 1957) and *Modern Islam in India* (London, 1946).

55. Polk and Chambers, eds., *The Beginnings of Modernization in the Middle East* (Chicago, 1968); Brown, ed., *From Medina to Metropolis* (Princeton, 1973).

56. Beck and Keddie, eds., *Women in the Muslim World* (Cambridge, Mass., 1978). Other scholarly works with historical material on women include Elizabeth W. Fernea and B. Q. Bezirgan, eds., *Middle Eastern Women Speak* (Austin, Tex., 1976); Paul Stirling, *Turkish Village* (New York, 1965); Gregory Massell, *The Surrogate Proletariat: Moslem Women and Revolutionary Strategies in Soviet Central Asia, 1919–1929* (Princeton, 1974); Ruth F. Woodsmall, *Women and the New East* (Washington, D.C., 1960); Nadia Youssef, *Women and Work in Developing Societies* (Berkeley, 1974); R. C. Jennings, "Women in Early Seventeenth-Century Ottoman Judicial Records: The Sharia Court of Anatolian Kayseri," *Journal of the Economic and Social History of the Orient,* XXVIII (1975). Many of the works listed earlier in this essay contain material important to the history of women and the history of the family—notably those by Musallam, and Goitein's *Mediterranean Society,* especially vol. III.

much time in Turkey, Egypt, India, and Europe, and influenced many parts of the Muslim world.[57] *Modern Islam* is a collection of von Grunebaum's articles, which offer frequent brilliant insights mixed with some debatable views.[58] C. E. Dawn's *From Ottomanism to Arabism* centers on the early-twentieth-century origins of Arab nationalism.[59]

One work often used as a text, the late Marshall Hodgson's posthumously edited *Venture of Islam,* is so original as to merit a high place among scholarly works. As pointed out in a review by Edmund Burke, it is part of a larger scheme of world history, adumbrated in earlier articles by Hodgson, that would take Europe out of center stage and treat Western civilization as one among several great civilizations—one that for a span of history became stronger than the others, owing primarily to its technological superiority.[60] The book approaches Islam from both an internal and an all-Islamic viewpoint. Hodgson was one of the first to note the vitality of later Islamic history, which would be more visible if scholars stopped concentrating so exclusively on the early periods, and in his book neither the Arabs nor the Middle East is given special stress. For all its achievements, *The Venture of Islam* has many shortcomings; its neologisms (such as "Islamdom" and "Islamicate," aimed at clarifying the multiple meanings of "Islam") tend to be confusing, while his tendency to assume more knowledge on the part of his readers than most of them are apt to possess makes the book difficult to use as a text. It also has an individualist-idealist bias, with a few great thinkers covered in detail, while postwar findings on economic and social history get short shrift, despite the importance given to the Western use of technology and gunpowder. The book marks a major step away from Europocentric views, however, and toward an appreciation of the vast achievements of Islamic culture.

Finally, Edward Said's *Orientalism,* mentioned at the beginning of this essay, has brought to the United States the kind of critique of Western Islamic scholarship that until recently had been confined almost exclusively to the Muslim world and Europe. Said shows, with telling quotations, the degree to which ignorance, hostility, and often romantic "exoticist" views of the Middle East have permeated Western scholarship from the Middle Ages until the present. His book is

57. Nikki R. Keddie, *An Islamic Response to Imperialism* (Berkeley, 1968) and *Sayyid Jamal ad-Din "al-Afghani"* (Berkeley, 1972).

58. G. E. von Grunebaum, *Modern Islam* (Berkeley, 1962).

59. C. E. Dawn, *From Ottomanism to Arabism* (Urbana, Ill., 1973).

60. M. G. S. Hodgson, *The Venture of Islam,* 3 vols. (Chicago, 1974). The review by Burke is in the *International Journal of Middle East Studies,* x, 2 (1979).

important, and could have a beneficial effect on scholars, but, if read uncritically, it could result in the baby being thrown out with the bathwater. Many young scholars, particularly on the left, are already inclined to reject the works of their predecessors and to identify with critiques of nearly all aspects of the West emanating from the Third World. In addition to the social and class analysis that these young scholars wish to espouse, there has developed a "third-worldism," in which all virtues are sought in the culture, religion, economy, and views of most classes in the Third World, and nearly all vices are found in the West. While Said rejects this position, and while his book's emphasis on the shortcomings of Western scholars (apart from a very few that he approves) may be justified as a useful counterweight to the views of the establishment, his emphasis on the sins and omissions of Western scholars may inadvertently feed an undifferentiated third-worldism. Said's work is an original and substantiated account of many prejudices about the Orient that arose from, and contributed to, Western feelings of superiority to Muslims. One would hope that the book will stimulate works in which the errors of Orientalists are weighed against their contributions. The important achievements of von Grunebaum and Lewis, for example, are not evident from the passages quoted by Said, nor does he claim to give a totally balanced picture of their work. Said shows how reluctant U.S. scholars of the Middle East have been to criticize the writings of their peers. His book should spur Middle Eastern scholars to spend part of their time in rectifying this omission.

Without attempting to define the specifics of such assessments, one may say that if Orientalists had serious limitations, recent historians have not been immune to the temptation to make more subtle assumptions of cultural superiority, in the form of either "modernization" theories that equate Westernization with linear progress or continuing concentration on elites, supported by social science views that implicitly endorse Western middle-class criteria of who is important and progressive. To a degree the third-worldist trend constitutes a reaction to such ideas, but a reaction that can be almost as one-sided and undialectical as the views it attacks. We need more historical studies that take into account developments in all social groups and classes, as well as the contradictory impact—past and present—of the West on the Middle East.

My essay has stressed the progress of recent American historical studies, but far more remains to be done—in showing the impact of imperialism on the Middle East; in understanding the positive features of Middle Eastern culture and society; in elucidating the roles of peasants, nomads, workers, and women; in furthering studies of material culture; in more sophisticated uses of elite and folk art and literature as historical sources; and in many other ways. In such reorientations, critiques and studies by leftists and by scholars from the Third World are already playing vital and stimulating roles.[61]

61. Since the above was written I have read two new works important enough to deserve note. One is Roy P. Mottahedeh, *Loyalty and Leadership in an Early Islamic Society* (Princeton, 1980), a study of social institutions and relations under the Buyid dynasty (945–1055). In its detailed analysis of relationships between individuals and social groups it revises many accepted ideas, particularly regarding the ulama, who are shown in this period to be a fluid group of learned men following a variety of often secular occupations. The other is Thomas Philipp, *Ǧurǧī Zaidān: His Life and Thought* (Wiesbaden, 1979), a two-part book on a major nineteenth-century Arab Christian writer. Zaidan is seen as the first Arab to use a secular approach to historical writing in order to promote a cultural-nationalist Arab identity. Philipp's intellectual analysis is followed by his translation of Zaidan's autobiography.

# 6

## East, Southeast, and South Asia

### John Whitney Hall

THE history of Asia east of Iran and Afghanistan was not widely research or taught in the United States before the end of World War II. The great expansion in this field of historical scholarship occurred after 1945 under the impetus of the so-called area studies movement. Following the war, the horizons of American education and scholarship broadened to encompass the world. But since colleges and universities lacked the personnel needed to teach about so many foreign areas, a conscious effort and the special financial support of philanthropic foundations, and later the federal government, were required to develop this capacity. Under this stimulus a large number of language and area studies programs came into being.[1] These were interdisciplinary programs that combined instruction in language with the study of the history, politics, economy, literature, religion, and arts of a given world area. The result was a remarkable expansion of the ability to produce, among others, historians with the background and training in languages necessary to conduct original research on the cultures and societies of Asia.

The current state of American historical scholarship on the several

I wish to thank Susan B. Hanley, James L. McClain, James H. Cole, James R. Rush, and Alice S. Ilchman for their assistance during the preparation of this essay. They are not responsible, of course, for any of its inadequacies.

1. There is a considerable literature on the subject of area studies in the United States. On the practical thinking behind these programs, see Education and World Affairs, *The University Looks Abroad: Approaches to World Affairs at Six American Universities* (New York, 1965). For the theory behind them, see John W. Hall, "Beyond Area Studies," in Donald E. Thackery, ed., *Research: Definitions and Reflections* (Ann Arbor, 1967), 48–66. For a survey of area studies programs in general, see Richard D. Lambert, *Language and Area Studies Review,* American Academy of Political and Social Science Monograph no. 17 (Philadelphia, 1971), and International Council for Educational Development, *Area Studies on U.S. Campuses: A Directory* (New York, 1971).

regions of Asia should not be judged solely in developmental terms. More specialists teaching more students and writing more books do not necessarily constitute progress. Yet because of the newness of so many of the subfields dealing with Asian history, there is a high degree of correlation between the length of time each subfield has had an active existence in the United States and the degree of authority and sophistication achieved in it by American historians. As new fields seeking to gain acceptance by the established academic disciplines, each has had to go through a developmental process, and they have done so at different rates of speed and with varying degrees of success. First, certain conditions and facilities had to be at hand for the production of language-competent historians. Second, such scholars had to acquire or gain access to the historical materials necessary for original research. Third, having achieved these requirements, the newly trained specialists could begin to prepare the first round of scholarly monographs. Fourth, on the basis of these monographs it was possible to write new synthetic surveys and informed works for the general reader. The stimulus of direct contact between American historians and historians of the country being studied would seem to be essential for the further development of any given subfield. Of course, underlying this whole process has been the imperative of demand as measured by the capacity of these fields to attract talent and of American institutions of higher learning to absorb faculty trained in Asian studies. And this capacity has by no means been equal for all subfields or constant for any given subfield.

The subfields into which Western historians have divided Asia are theoretically based on geographically, nationally, and linguistically defined units. Taken in broadest terms, Asia east of the Indus may be divided into three parts: South Asia (from Pakistan to the border of Burma), Southeast Asia (from Burma to the Philippines), and East Asia (from China through Japan). Each of these large regions is composed of many subareas, so that no one region forms a simple, self-contained national, cultural, or linguistic entity. The annual *Bibliography of Asian Studies,* prepared by the Association for Asian Studies, lists its entries under thirty-three separate political categories, a practice much too unwieldy for use in this essay. The analysis that follows adopts the categories most common to the pedagogical fields found in advanced academic programs: Japan, China, Southeast Asia, and South Asia.[2]

2. These categories correspond to the four divisions recognized by the Regional Councils of the Association for Asian Studies: Northeast Asia, China and Inner Asia,

It is apparent that all four divisions have passed through the phases of language training and materials acquisition. The more slowly developing fields (South and Southeast Asia) are at least at the stage of producing monographs. But they are only now achieving the capacity to generate the kind of synthetic studies exemplified in the fields of Chinese and Japanese history, and they have yet to evolve as close a binational relationship as has developed between American and Japanese historians.

### ORIENTALISM, AREA SPECIALIZATION, AND ASIAN HISTORY

The post–World War II upsurge in Asian studies in the United States could not have taken place without a foundation on which to build. This foundation had been prepared by the end of the nineteenth century, mostly outside of America, by scholars of Asian languages, literatures, religions, mythology, philosophy, and classical history. For India it was the classical tradition of the Vedas and Upanishads that first came under study and translation by scholars in England and Germany. For China, the Confucian classics were the objects of early study and translation into French or English. For Japan, the historical classics, the *Kojiki* and *Nihon shoki,* were among the earliest works translated into English.[3] Such activity by the late-nineteenth- and early-twentieth-century pioneer Western scholars is often referred to as Orientalism. The Orientalists were primarily philological students of the "texts," and as a result of their labors later generations of scholars were given a legacy of basic translations, introductory language studies, dictionaries and glossaries, and the first attempts at systematic historical narrative.

The early generation of scholarly writers on Asia consisted mostly of two types: (1) professional academics who taught philology or comparative religion at the great Western centers of learning in Paris, Berlin, Leiden, Oxford, and Cambridge, and (2) nonprofessional scholars, usually in diplomatic or missionary service. The relatively unhurried life of the diplomat abroad in the years before the tele-

---

Southeast Asia, and South Asia. The present survey omits consideration of Korea and Inner Asia for reasons of space.

3. Examples of early translations that are still standard are Maurice Bloomfield, trans., *Hymns of the Atharva-Veda* (Oxford, 1897); F. Max Muller, trans., *The Upanishads* (Oxford, 1879–82); James Legge, trans., *The Chinese Classics,* 5 vols. (Oxford, 1893–95); Basil H. Chamberlain, trans., "Translation of 'Ko-Ji-ki,'" *Transactions of the Asiatic Society of Japan,* x (Yokohama, 1882); William G. Aston, trans., "Nihongi," *Transactions and Proceedings of the Japan Society, London,* 2 vols. (London, 1896).

159

graph gave opportunity for what in some cases was quite serious study of the country of assignment. George B. Sansom could write books on Japanese historical grammar and legal institutions, as well as his still admired cultural history of Japan, while in the British consular service in Japan.[4]

For the Japanese field, Sansom stands as an example of the type of scholar who provided the transition between the Orientalist tradition and the more recent practice of area-based historical study. Sansom was not a professionally trained historian, although after his retirement from diplomatic service he taught at Columbia University. The secret of his success in breaking out of the tradition of philological and literary studies lay in the early development in Japan of a national school of historiography by Japanese historians trained in Western methodology. Their work not only became the basis for their own synthetic histories but made it possible for an outsider to Japanese culture to write with assurance an authoritative survey of Japan's cultural history. None of the other areas of Asia with which we are here concerned created a modern historiography so rapidly as the Japanese.[5]

Undoubtedly the vastness of China and the sheer length of its history had an intimidating effect on the would-be foreign synthesizer. China's proud classical tradition of official histories provides almost too much material to be easily digested by either modern Chinese or Western historians. C. P. Fitzgerald's *China* does not have the ring of authority and the comprehensiveness that Sansom achieved.[6] For South and Southeast Asia, nearly all of whose societies were colonized by Western powers, the awakening of a sense of a national past came slowly. Until after World War II the synthetic histories of these areas were written by scholars from the colonizing countries, working without benefit of strong native traditions. Native scholars, of course, were educated in varying numbers in British, Dutch, or French universities, and their writings aimed at Western audiences sometimes made up for the lack of an indigenous school of national history.

Thus by the 1940s enough groundwork had been laid so that courses on the several regions of Asia could be taught at a number of colleges, and doctoral programs at a few American universities were beginning to turn out historians trained in the requisite languages so that they could do original work in Chinese and Japanese history, and

4. George B. Sansom, *Japan: A Short Cultural History* (London, 1931).
5. See John W. Hall, "Japanese Historiography," in David L. Sills, ed., *International Encyclopedia of the Social Sciences* (New York, 1960) VI, 413–20.
6. C. P. Fitzgerald, *China: A Short Cultural History* (London, 1935).

to a lesser degree in the other areas. The discipline of history in America had begun to recognize these areas as legitimate subjects of professional study. Asian history in most instances had moved out of departments of linguistics or of language and literature.

While World War II slowed the normal pace of development in American academic institutions, it exerted a tremendous impact on the American mind. Young Americans were trained in languages they had never considered important or were posted in countries that they had hardly known existed. After the war, the wave of returning servicemen with newly stimulated interest in foreign areas combined with educators who during the war had been awakened to the tragic neglect of foreign areas other than the Atlantic community to create a demand for the inclusion of foreign area study in American college and university curricula. Area studies programs emerged to meet the demand by drawing together existing resources and specialized faculty talents by area rather than by discipline, since no single department was capable of mounting a full-scale program on a given foreign area, including language study, on its own. Coming to the assistance of these programs were first a number of private foundations—especially Rockefeller, Carnegie, and Ford—and after 1958 the federal government, through the National Defense Education Act. These stimuli, in addition to the normal growing process of American higher education, were the special circumstances behind the startling increase in numbers and capacity of institutions in which specialized training and research on Asia became available. Not all institutions that offered course work in Asian studies were designated "centers" eligible for government support, but all had created multidepartmental programs of study firmly rooted in language study. And out of these new centers and programs there came from the mid-1950s on a virtual flood of works by American historians on all parts of Asia.

One way to acquire an overview of this postwar boom in the historical study of Asia in America is to follow the course of scholarly associations and the professional journals devoted to Asian subjects published by them. Before World War II, the foremost outlets for scholarly articles on the premodern history of Asia were the *Journal of the American Oriental Society* (published since 1843) and the *American Historical Review* (published since 1895). The first was a distinctly Orientalist journal devoted to classical archaeology, language, and literature. The second, reflecting the main orientation of American historians toward United States history and the histories of England and the West European states, included only an occasional article on Asia. Americans writing about Japan, China, South Asia, or Southeast

Asia more often had to go to journals published in Europe or by Westerners resident in Asia. Noteworthy among journals of the latter type was *Transactions of the Asiatic Society of Japan* (since 1874), a Tokyo-based organization that had several American members. The establishment of the Harvard-Yenching Institute in 1936, under the direction of Serge Elisseeff, occasioned the publishing of the *Harvard Journal of Asiatic Studies*. This journal continues to publish highly academic articles in the European tradition on China, Japan, and Inner Asia.

With the appearance in 1941 of the *Far Eastern Quarterly*, an independent journal edited by the newly formed Far Eastern Association, an entirely new type of scholarly journal came into existence. The journal was mainly concerned with Japan and China but occasionally published articles on Southeast Asia, and its annual "Bibliography of Asian Studies" listed works on South and Southeast Asia. This journal was distinguished by its interdisciplinary and social science orientation. In the statement of intent published in the first issue, its editors stated that they wished to fill the "gap between journals dealing with contemporary opinion and events, and the more specialized professional and academic publications." Still it was aimed at the "increasing numbers of specialists ... who had command of one or more of the languages of the area."[7]

In 1948 the Far Eastern Association transformed itself into a scholarly professional association with the encouragement of the Committee on Far Eastern Studies of the American Council of Learned Societies. The thirteen founding members included seven well known to the fields of Chinese and Japanese history: Knight Biggerstaff (Cornell), Woodbridge Bingham (University of California, Berkeley), Hugh Borton (Columbia), Herrlee G. Creel (Chicago), John K. Fairbank (Harvard), Earl H. Pritchard (Chicago), and Edwin O. Reischauer (Harvard). In 1956 the parent association was renamed the Association for Asian Studies, and its journal became the *Journal of Asian Studies*. By this step the association formally included South Asia in its fold, thereby forestalling the need for the establishment of a separate association for South Asian studies.

In 1948, some 200 scholars had met to join the Far Eastern Association. By 1978 the Association for Asian Studies counted a membership of 5,730. Not all members were faculty engaged in teaching, research, and writing, and there is no way to determine accurately how many could be so described. Data contained in the 1977 mem-

7. *Far Eastern Quarterly*, 1 (1941), 4.

bership roster, however, does provide insight into the types and distribution of specialists within a group of some 4,000 members who responded to a survey in 1977 preceding the compilation of the membership list.[8] Of the respondents, roughly 1,800 were faculty members at colleges or universities with graduate programs in some area of Asian studies; 1,500 identified themselves as historians. Among the 4,000 respondents, those who checked their areas of primary specialization or interest against the areas included in this survey numbered as follows:

| | | | |
|---|---|---|---|
| Japan | 890 | Cambodia | 5 |
| China | 1,400 | Thailand | 89 |
| Philippines | 96 | Burma | 28 |
| Indonesia | 110 | Pakistan | 30 |
| Malaysia | 55 | India | 550 |
| Vietnam | 45 | | |

Articles published in the *Journal of Asian Studies* are extremely diverse, but historians predominate among the authors.[9] Many of the historical works are infused with methods and ideas derived from other disciplines, primarily the social sciences. This is true particularly of the works that consciously or unconsciously adopted the culturally sensitized approach of the social anthropologist and sought to understand the process of historical change in Asia "on Asian terms." The hallmarks of such studies were field research, language competence, and openness to multiple explanations of causation. By extension these were the most common distinguishing features of American scholarship on Asian history during the first three postwar decades.

Beyond this one cannot escape the sense that sheer size, diversity, and vitality were the primary measures of the condition of Asian studies in the 1970s by comparison with the 1940s. At the first annual meeting of the Far Eastern Association, some 70 scholars had participated in the program. Thirty years later the number of program participants was 336, and the total number in attendance was close to 2,000. Furthermore, the 1979 convention was used as a place of meeting for 52 special interest groups and scholarly committees and for 36 book exhibitors. There were clear signs that, although 61 panel sessions were held during the three days of the meeting, the association

---

8. Association for Asian Studies, *Membership Directory* (Ann Arbor, 1977).

9. To get a general sense of the content of the journal, see John A. Harrison, ed., *Enduring Scholarship Selected from the Far Eastern Quarterly—the Journal of Asian Studies, 1941-1971,* I (China), II (Japan and Korea), III (South and Southeast Asia) (Tucson, 1972).

163

and its journal were proving too confining, for either academic or political reasons. Within the association, subgroups had been formed on the basis of problem or area specialization. New journals had been founded, and even new and competing organizations.[10]

But one must ask whether growth and diversity signified more than the simple fact that more areas were being covered—that major areas of American ignorance about the history of Asian societies were being eliminated. Were organizations such as the Association for Asian Studies a sign of area parochialism and separateness on the part of American historians of Asia? What had the new fields of Asian history added to the discipline of history in the United States? These are hard questions to answer. History is not a cumulative field in the scientific sense; it has no widely recognized theoretical base that can be reinforced or modified systematically through the opening up of new fields or newly designed methodologies. Perhaps all we can say is that the discipline of history in postwar America has become "richer by Asia," and that efforts at conceptualizing "world history" or "comparative history" have been undertaken. These efforts may not have been systematic, but their possibility and utility were increasingly recognized.

## JAPAN

Among the areas covered in the survey, Japan has been the most closely associated with the United States. Although English and European scholars were the first to begin the study of Japanese history and literature, Americans soon came to predominate. They found in Japan's past a history not of grand continental proportions as in China, or of influential religious traditions as in India, but rather a story of modest but continuous political and social development, a development in fact that appeared increasingly parallel to that of Western societies the more it was studied. As a consequence, there has been a much less mysterious aura attached to Japanese history than to that of either China or India. Japanese data have been used more directly for the comparative testing of such concepts as feudalism, capitalism, and militarism than one finds in other areas.

As suggested above, one of the prime characteristics of the field of Japanese historical studies in America is that it has grown up in close

10. For example, the *Journal of Japanese Studies* (Seattle) started publication in 1974. The Committee of Concerned Asian Scholars began its *Bulletin* (Cambridge, Mass.) in 1968.

touch with the community of professional Japanese historians. Once historians in the United States became proficient in the Japanese language, there was opened up to them not only a rich source of historical materials but a panoply of research aides and secondary interpretive studies.[11] The prior availability of Japanese scholarship has had two noticeable influences on American studies of Japan. First, it made possible a consistently high level of writing by American scholars, and second, it tended to obscure the academic centers of major influence within the United States. It is true, of course, that American historians of Japan were trained at a relatively few institutions in the first decade or so after the war, the two major programs being at Harvard University, under Serge Elisseeff and Edwin O. Reischauer, and at Columbia University, under George B. Sansom and Ryusaku Tsunoda. It was true also that Harvard Ph.D. dissertations tended to be on political and institutional subjects, while those written at Columbia were on literary and intellectual subjects. But few of the products of these institutions identified themselves with their American mentors to the exclusion of the scholars with whom they read or worked in Japan.

Another example of the close association between American scholars and Japan is the degree to which the Japanese people, both privately and through their government, have supported the efforts of American and other foreign scholars to learn about Japan by offering research and study grants. The most spectacular of these gestures was surely the establishment of the Japan Foundation in 1972.[12]

It is safe to say that the only distinguished general survey of Japanese history in English at the start of the postwar era was G. B. Sansom's *Japan: A Short Cultural History,* first published in 1931, but remarkably durable. In his later years, while associated with Columbia and Stanford Universities, Sansom wrote a much fuller survey in three volumes. The first two were of excellent quality, but the third, which was finished shortly before his death, was weak by comparison with the other two and with his own *Western World and Japan.*[13] Since the late 1940s, however, American historians have published a

11. See John W. Hall, "Japanese History in World Perspective," in Charles F. Delzel, ed., *The Future of History* (Nashville, 1977), 173–188.
12. The Japan Foundation became the channel through which ten university-centered Japan studies programs were given $1 million each for purposes of development. This list of ten provides a good way of identifying the major centers of Japanese studies in the United States. They were: Harvard, Yale, Columbia, Princeton, Michigan, Chicago, Stanford, Berkeley, Washington, Hawaii.
13. George B. Sansom, *A History of Japan to 1334* (Stanford, 1958); *A History of Japan, 1334–1615* (1961); *A History of Japan, 1615–1867* (1963); *The Western World and Japan* (New York, 1950).

number of survey histories covering either all of Japanese history or the modern era. In the main these works have been directed toward the college market. Among them the most authoritative is the two-volume text by John K. Fairbank, Edwin O. Reischauer, and Albert M. Craig, which covers all of East Asia. This work illustrates the best qualities of American scholarship on Japan and China, resting as it does on a large number of monographic works produced since the war by American scholars as well as by Japanese and Chinese historians. Among shorter histories, those by Edwin O. Reischauer and John W. Hall cover the whole of Japanese history, though with different emphases. Those by Peter Duus, Tetsuo Najita, and Kenneth Pyle are especially noteworthy for their new interpretations of the modern era.[14]

It is worth mentioning that one of the few efforts to put the area approach fully to work was made at the University of Michigan's Center for Japanese Studies. Material emanating from the Michigan program provides a useful introduction and guide to the field of Japanese studies as a whole, and to the social science–influenced methodology of American scholars.[15]

In the immediate postwar period the principal focus of interest among American historians of Japan was in the modern era—that is, from the 1850s, when Japan was "opened" to the West, down through the Pacific war and its aftermath. The themes of their concern were the nature and impact of Western influence, the causes and meaning of the Meiji Restoration, and the effort to comprehend the process of modernization in Japan. The most influential interpretations of these themes by non-Japanese scholars at the end of the war were E. H. Norman's *Japan's Emergence as a Modern State* (1940) and Ruth Benedict's *Chrysanthemum and the Sword* (1946).[16] Norman's chief accomplishment was to link the political, economic, and social aspects of the late Tokugawa period (from the 1830s) into a coherent explanation of the causes of the Meiji Restoration and the "settlement" that followed. He claimed that it was the "lower class samurai" backed by the

14. Edwin O. Reischauer and John K. Fairbank, *East Asia: The Great Tradition* (Boston, 1958); John K. Fairbank, Edwin O. Reischauer, and Albert M. Craig, *East Asia: The Modern Transformation* (Boston, 1960); Edwin O. Reischauer, *Japan: The Story of a Nation* (New York, 1970); John W. Hall, *Japan from Prehistory to Modern Times* (New York, 1970); Peter Duus, *The Rise of Modern Japan* (Boston, 1976); Tetsuo Najita, *Japan,* Modern Nation in Historical Perspective Series, ed. Robin W. Winks (Englewood Cliffs, N.J., 1973); Kenneth B. Pyle, *The Making of Modern Japan* (Lexington, Mass., 1975).
15. John W. Hall and Richard K. Beardsley, *Twelve Doors to Japan* (New York, 1965).
16. E. H. Norman, *Japan's Emergence as a Modern State* (New York, 1940); Ruth Benedict, *The Chrysanthemum and the Sword* (New York, 1946).

"moneybags of the merchant princes of Osaka and Kyoto" who provided the motive force behind the Restoration. Once the old regime had been destroyed, Japanese political leadership steered a course toward state centralization and economic and military buildup, which ignored the welfare of the people and led inevitably to war and imperialism. Benedict's work had immense influence as the first coherent effort to understand Japanese national behavior in terms of their social and cultural values. This anthropological approach, which sought to explain the Japanese in their own terms, affected the work of many American historians of Japan.

The first postwar round of monographic studies to be published by the major university centers began to appear by the mid-1950s. The majority touched in some way on the Restoration and the themes of Westernization and modernization. All were influenced by Norman's work. Their authors were also thoroughly grounded in the latest Japanese interpretations of the Restoration: that it marked a counter-revolutionary movement that prevented a full-scale bourgeois revolution from taking place, and imposed on Japan an increasingly militarized and absolutist state structure.

Much of the writing of the late 1950s through the early 1970s took issue with various points of interpretation advanced by Norman and the main line of Japanese scholarship. Albert Craig's study of the Choshu daimyo domain, and Marius Jansen's biography of Sakamoto Ryoma, one of the leading figures of the Restoration movement, found private motivation and a sense of national or local crisis rather than class interest to be the key factors in the attack on the old regime. This conclusion is reinforced in subsequent studies by Harry Harootunian, Richard Chang, and Irwin Scheiner. Joseph Pittau's study of political thought in the 1880s and 1890s and George Akita's inquiry into the political forces leading to the adoption of the Meiji Constitution found that the political leadership was less traditional, conservative, and oligarchic than Norman had implied. The role of the state in Japan's modern economic development was also seen to be less dominant by William W. Lockwood, who placed much of the credit in the hands of small private business entrepreneurs. Thomas C. Smith and James Nakamura, both of whom played down the state's exploitive role in Japan's early economic development, confirmed Lockwood's findings.[17] Another genre of studies that demonstrated

17. Albert M. Craig, *Choshu and the Meiji Restoration* (Cambridge, Mass., 1961); Marius B. Jansen, *Sakamoto Ryoma and the Meiji Restoration* (Princeton, 1961); H. D. Harootunian, *Toward Restoration: The Growth of Political Consciousness in Tokugawa Japan* (Berkeley, 1970); Richard T. Chang, *From Prejudice to Tolerance: A Study of the Japanese*

the danger of judging too hastily the motivations of the Meiji leaders was the biographical. In addition to Jansen's study of Sakamoto Ryoma, Roger Hackett has written about Yamagata Aritomo, Ivan Hall on Mori Arinori, Joyce Lebra on Okuma Shigenobu, and Thomas Havens on Nishi Amane, but many other figures have yet to find their book-length biographers.[18]

Once past the 1890s, American historians have looked less to Norman than to the writings of two political scientists whose works raised, if they did not settle, the most basic questions of interpretation: Robert Scalapino's *Democracy and the Party Movement in Japan: The Failure of the First Attempt* and Maruyama Masao's *Thought and Behavior in Modern Japanese Politics.*[19] Scalapino's thesis was that to create a democratic political order in Japan, a Western-style party system was needed. The Japanese, he claims, made the effort but eventually failed. This thesis called forth a number of studies that have attempted to show that in Japan the political party, though different from the Western model, played an important role. Studies of the major parties before the 1930s by Peter Duus and Tetsuo Najita assessed their functions not as failed institutions but as active brokers in the political competition among the civil bureaucracy, the military, the *zaibatsu,* and labor unions. A collection of essays presented at the 1970 Conference on Taisho (1912–26) Japan and edited by Bernard Silberman and H. D. Harootunian throws further light on this problem. Gordon Berger's study of the New Order era, when Japan was girding for war, has provided the strongest refutation of the weakness of the political party system, which survived through the war despite attack from many directions.[20]

---

*Image of the West, 1826–1864* (Tokyo, 1970); Irwin Scheiner, *Christian Converts and Social Protest in Meiji Japan* (Berkeley, 1970); Joseph Pittau, *Political Thought in Early Meiji, 1868–1889* (Cambridge, Mass., 1967); George Akita, *Foundations of Constitutional Government in Modern Japan, 1868–1900* (Cambridge, Mass., 1967); William W. Lockwood, *The Economic Development of Japan: Growth and Structural Change* (Princeton, 1954); Thomas C. Smith, *Political Change and Industrial Development in Japan: Government Enterprises, 1868–1880* (Stanford, 1955); James Nakamura, *Agricultural Production and the Economic Development of Japan, 1873–1922* (Princeton, 1966).

18. Roger F. Hackett, *Yamagata Aritomo in the Rise of Modern Japan, 1838–1922* (Cambridge, Mass., 1971); Ivan P. Hall, *Mori Arinori* (Cambridge, Mass., 1973); Joyce C. Lebra, *Okuma Shigenobu: Statesman of Meiji Japan* (Cambridge, Mass., 1973); Thomas R. H. Havens, *Nishi Amane and Modern Japanese Thought* (Princeton, 1970).

19. Scalapino's book was published in Berkeley in 1953. Maruyama's essays were translated by Ivan Morris, Andrew Fraser, David Titus, Ronald Dore, Paul Varley, Arthur Tiedeman, Barbara Ruch, and David Sisson—a truly collaborative effort. It was edited by Ivan Morris and published in London in 1963.

20. Peter Duus, *Party Rivalry and Political Change in Taisho Japan* (Cambridge, Mass., 1968); Tetsuo Najita, *Hara Kei and the Politics of Compromise, 1905–1915* (Cambridge,

Maruyama's analysis of totalitarian tendencies in prewar Japan, the emperor system, militarism, and what he called "fascism from above" has stimulated a number of studies that followed or attempted to qualify Maruyama's thesis. Kenneth B. Pyle's study of late Meiji nationalist thinkers and Richard Minear's work on Hozumi Yatsuka, the conservative interpreter of the Meiji Constitution, have shown how naturally the conservative stand could be taken, while Frank Miller's biography of Minobe Tatsukichi, the advocate of constitutionalism, revealed how difficult it was to hold a liberal position in the 1930s. James B. Crowley's study of Japanese military leadership and its perceived assessment of Japan's defensive requirements offered a new way of comprehending Japan's drift toward war during the 1930s, which he viewed as a quest for security and national identity. Covering the more extreme ends of the political spectrum, George Wilson has written on the national socialist Kita Ikki, Hyman Kublin on the socialist leader Katayama Sen, F. B. Notehelfer on the anarchist Kotoku Shusui, and Gail Bernstein on the Marxist Kawakami Hajime.[21]

While most of these works were highly empirical in their methodology, many of their authors have been caught up in the debate over the nature of the changes that so transformed Japan in the century following the Restoration. Initially, historians saw these changes as deriving from Japan's attempt to Westernize, or as the products of an intense class struggle. Troubled by the biases that arose from these sorts of analysis, a number of American writers suggested using the concept of modernization as an analytical tool. In 1960, at a conference held at Hakone, Japan, American and Japanese scholars discussed the theme of modernization, without necessarily agreeing on a definition or on the utility of such a concept. The subsequent debate led to one of the more valuable circumstances in which Japanese and American scholars have directly and publicly shared ideas and aired differences of opinions. The Hakone conference was organized by

Mass., 1967); Bernard S. Silberman and H. D. Harootunian, eds., *Japan in Crisis: Essays on Taisho Democracy* (Princeton, 1974); Gordon M. Berger, *Parties out of Power 1931–1941* (Princeton, 1977).

21. Kenneth B. Pyle, *The New Generation in Meiji Japan* (Stanford, 1969); Richard H. Minear, *Japanese Tradition and Western Law: Emperor, State, and Law in the Thought of Hozumi Yatsuka* (Cambridge, Mass., 1970); Frank O. Miller, *Minobe Tatsukichi* (Berkeley, 1965); James B. Crowley, *Japan's Quest for Autonomy: National Security and Foreign Policy, 1930–1938* (Princeton, 1966); George M. Wilson, *Radical Nationalist in Japan: Kita Ikki, 1883–1937* (Cambridge, Mass., 1969); Hyman Kublin, *Asian Revolutionary: The Life of Katayama Sen* (Princeton, 1964); F. G. Notehelfer, *Kotoku Shusui: Portrait of a Japanese Radical* (Cambridge, Mass., 1971); Gail Bernstein, *Japanese Marxist: A Portrait of Kawakami Hajime* (Cambridge, Mass., 1978).

the Conference on Modern Japan, a group effort of the Association for Asian Studies organized by a committee composed of R. P. Dore, John Hall, Marius Jansen, William Lockwood, James Morley, Donald Shively, and Robert Ward. In subsequent years this group produced six volumes of collected conference papers.[22] Taken together they add up to a comprehensive study of modern Japan by the leading Japan specialists of the 1960s. By the 1970s, however, interest in the use of modernization theory, with its apparently positive appraisal of Japan's post-Meiji development, was on the decline. Historians began to show greater interest in the themes of nationalism, imperialism, and militarism. It was in this context that the works of E. H. Norman were being revived to draw attention back to the negative and tragic aspects of Japan's emergence as a modern state.

Next to the modern period American historians have devoted their greatest attention to the period from the middle of the sixteenth to the middle of the nineteenth century. The traditional view of this period, the immediate "old regime" in the eyes of the people of Meiji Japan, has been colored by two interpretive concepts: feudalism and national seclusion. When Japan closed its doors to free foreign trade and travel in the 1630s, it did so, it was argued, to preserve its feudal institutions and the power of the samurai class at the expense of national stagnation. For Norman the Tokugawa hegemony was the darkest of all times for Japan, especially for the peasantry.

Postwar American scholars have argued differently: that in the face of the amazingly rapid modernization after 1868, the Tokugawa period was surely less feudal and less isolated than had been imagined. Articles brought together on this subject by John W. Hall and Marius B. Jansen are illustrative of this point of view. Thomas C. Smith, in his *Agrarian Origins of Modern Japan,* did much to dispel the view that all peasants were close to starvation, as did the work on demographic change by Susan Hanley and Kozo Yamamura. R. P. Dore's *Education in Tokugawa Japan* showed that the Japanese, including the peasants, were about as well educated in the mid-nineteenth

22. For a report on this Hakone conference, see John W. Hall, "Changing Conceptions of the Modernization of Japan," in Marius B. Jansen, ed., *Changing Japanese Attitudes towards Modernization* (Princeton, 1965). Jansen's was the first of the modern Japan series. The other five were R. P. Dore, ed., *Aspects of Social Change in Modern Japan* (Princeton, 1967); William W. Lockwood, ed., *The State and Economic Enterprise in Japan* (Princeton, 1965); Robert E. Ward, ed., *Political Development in Modern Japan* (Princeton, 1968); Donald H. Shively, ed., *Tradition and Modernization in Japanese Culture* (Princeton, 1971); James W. Morley, ed., *Dilemmas of Growth in Prewar Japan* (Princeton, 1971). The 1975 republication of some of E. H. Norman's works occasioned new interest in his views. See John W. Dower, *Origins of the Modern Japanese State: Selected Writings of E. H. Norman* (New York, 1975).

century as the English, and more so than the French. Works by Charles Sheldon, William Hauser, and Kozo Yamamura have given a clearer picture of Japan's economic and commercial growth despite the country's closure to the outside.[23] Two studies of the Tokugawa political order as it affected the territorial lords (the daimyo) by Conrad Totman and Harold Bolitho help to give a much better picture of the inner workings of Tokugawa government. The two authors differ over the question of why the shogunate was unable to retain, much less improve, its national powers of command, one putting the emphasis on factionalism, the other on the pull of localism.[24]

In addition to the fields of political and economic history, American historians have been active in the study of early modern religion and thought. The period starts with the so-called Christian century (1549–1650). Charles Boxer's book by that name has been greatly elaborated though perhaps not displaced by George Elison's *Deus Destroyed*. In this field, too, Maruyama Masao's works have had an important influence. Tetsuo Najita has written a number of enlightening essays on Confucian-based political thought, while Robert Bellah, in his *Tokugawa Religion*, has attempted to apply the concepts of Max Weber to Japan. Since 1973, a seminar on Tokugawa intellectual history, organized by Tetsuo Najita, Robert Bellah, Irwin Scheiner, and Harry Harootunian, has been at work on the premise that "Tokugawa Japan was one of the great ages of human intellectual endeavor."[25]

Before the late 1960s almost no original work had been done by American scholars on the history of Japan before the Tokugawa era.

23. John W. Hall and Marius B. Jansen, *Studies in the Institutional History of Early Modern Japan* (Princeton, 1970); Thomas C. Smith, *The Agrarian Origins of Modern Japan* (Stanford, 1954); Susan B. Hanley and Kozo Yamamura, *Economic and Demographic Change in Preindustrial Japan, 1600–1868* (Princeton, 1977); R. P. Dore, *Education in Tokugawa Japan* (Berkeley, 1965); Charles D. Sheldon, *The Rise of the Merchant Class in Tokugawa Japan* (Tucson, 1958); William B. Hauser, *Economic Institutional Change in Tokugawa Japan* (Cambridge, Eng., 1974); Kozo Yamamura, *A Study of Samurai Income and Enterprise* (Cambridge, Mass., 1974).

24. Conrad Totman, *Politics in the Tokugawa Bakufu, 1600–1868* (Cambridge, Mass., 1967); Harold Bolitho, *Treasures among Men: The Fudai Daimyo in the Tokugawa Settlement* (New Haven, 1974).

25. Charles Boxer, *The Christian Century in Japan, 1549–1650* (Berkeley, 1951); George Elison, *Deus Destroyed: The Image of Christianity in Early Modern Japan* (Cambridge, Mass., 1973); Robert N. Bellah, *Tokugawa Religion: The Values of Pre-Industrial Japan* (Glencoe, Ill., 1957). Mikiso Hane has translated important studies on Tokugawa thought, especially of Ogyu Sorai, in Maruyama Masao, ed., *Studies in the Intellectual History of Tokugawa Japan* (Princeton, 1974). The seminar on Tokugawa intellectual history published its first set of papers, *Japanese Thought in the Tokugawa Period*, ed. Tetsuo Najita and Irwin Scheiner (Chicago, 1978). In his contribution to this book H. D. Harootunian has sought to apply the ideas of Michel Foucault to Tokugawa thought.

John W. Hall's study of the province of Bizen between 500 and 1700 proved to be the first in a steady flow of new works on the period of Japanese history between the twelfth and seventeenth centuries. The 1972 conference on medieval Japan at Yale University and the establishment of the Institute for Medieval Japanese Studies by Barbara Ruch at the University of Pennsylvania became further stimulants to this field. Among the resulting studies, essays by Barbara Ruch, Cornelius Kiley, G. Cameron Hurst, Jeffrey Mass, Paul Varley, and George Elison illustrate the main themes and capacities of these new entrants into a difficult field of research. Again the use of scholarly conferences as a means of bringing Japanese and American scholars together proved useful. The 1973 conference on Muromachi Japan (1338–1573) and the 1977 conference on Sengoku Japan (roughly equivalent to the sixteenth century) have each resulted in a volume of collaborative studies. Significantly, they have been published in both Japanese and English editions.[26]

CHINA

Of the four regions of Asian history covered by this review, China has received the most attention and has given rise to the longest and most complete tradition of historical study by scholars outside of China. In the United States the field of Chinese studies generally has bulked close to twice as large as Japanese studies, and, as we shall see, many times as large as the other two fields. Furthermore, not only has there been a much longer and more extensive tradition of Sinology in the West, there has been, and continues to be, a vigorous and extensive tradition of Japanese scholarship on China. Thus by the end of World War II, the field of Chinese history was well provided with basic works in English and with the academic resources for further development.

One way to get a sense of the state of the China field by the mid-1940s is through L. Carrington Goodrich's short cultural history, published in 1943.[27] Not only was this an excellent piece of synthesis, it was based, as its footnotes and bibliography demonstrate, on a broad foundation of monographic work, a good deal of which was by

26. John W. Hall, *Government and Local Power in Japan, 500–1700* (Princeton, 1966); G. Cameron Hurst, *Insei* (New York, 1976); John W. Hall and Jeffrey P. Mass, eds., *Medieval Japan: Essays in Institutional History* (New Haven, 1974); Jeffrey P. Mass, *Warrior Government in Early Medieval Japan* (New Haven, 1974); John W. Hall and Takeshi Toyoda, *Japan in the Muromachi Age* (Berkeley, 1976).

27. L. Carrington Goodrich, *A Short History of the Chinese People* (New York, 1943).

Americans, or by European and Chinese scholars working in the United States. Among those cited by Goodrich whose works remain part of the standard bibliography are Woodbridge Bingham, Derk Bodde, Herrlee Creel, Homer Dubs, Fei Hsiao-t'ung, Arthur Hummel, Franz Michael, and C. Martin Wilbur. Among this group one can see already the trend away from Sinology in the literary sense and toward an interest in thought and institutions in the more social scientific sense. The stage was set for a literal explosion of growth under the impetus of the area studies movement of the 1950s and 1960s.

The length of tradition and the vitality of the Chinese studies field also led to other characteristics that distinguished it from the other fields. There have been, it would seem, more recognized "giants" whose particular specialties have given high visibility to the academic institutions to which they were attached: John Fairbank (Harvard, modern institutional history), Arthur Wright (Stanford and then Yale, Sui-T'ang intellectual history), Herrlee Creel (Chicago, ancient China), Franz Michael and George Taylor (Washington, modern political and institutional history), and so forth. American scholars of China have created numerous opportunities for group research. The most conspicuous was the series of conferences leading to the publication of symposia volumes organized by the Committee on Chinese Thought of the Association for Asian Studies.[28] Another has been the Ming Biographical History Project, under American Council of Learned Societies sponsorship. Directed by L. Carrington Goodrich, it has compiled a biographical encyclopedia of Ming China with the cooperation of scholars both in the United States and around the world. Still another group effort is the multivolume *Cambridge History of China,* being edited by, among others, John Fairbank.[29]

There is another feature of Chinese studies in America resulting from historical circumstances affecting relations between the United States and China. To the American, China has epitomized the "mysterious East." The closure of mainland China from direct access by American scholars between 1949 and 1978 made China an even greater object of interest and concern to American intellectuals. Fortunately, access to Chinese materials was available through Taiwan

28. The individual volumes were Arthur F. Wright, ed., *Studies in Chinese Thought* (Chicago, 1953); John K. Fairbank, ed., *Chinese Thought and Institutions* (Chicago, 1957); Arthur F. Wright, ed., *The Confucian Persuasion* (Stanford, 1960); David S. Nivison and Arthur F. Wright, eds., *Confucianism in Action* (Stanford, 1959); and Arthur F. Wright and Denis Twitchett, eds., *Confucian Personalities* (Stanford, 1962).

29. The first volumes to appear in print are John K. Fairbank, ed., vol. X, *Late Ch'ing, 1800-1911, Part I,* and Denis Twitchett, ed., vol. III, *Sui and T'ang China, 589-906, Part I,* both published in 1979.

and the Sinological community in Japan. Publishers on Taiwan were particularly helpful in making primary historical sources available through inexpensive reprints, and this was a key factor in the great expansion of American Sinological libraries during the 1960s.

As previously suggested, the China field has not produced a large or distinguished number of survey histories, perhaps because of the sheer magnitude of the task involved. Carrington Goodrich's work has already been noted. Kenneth S. Latourette's *Chinese: Their History and Culture* provided a detailed reference survey based on existing research as of the mid-1940s. The most characteristically American approaches to Chinese history are to be found in the previously mentioned text *East Asia* by the Harvard group, John K. Fairbank's *United States and China,* and Charles O. Hucker's *China's Imperial Past.*[30] Fairbank's work skillfully relates the main themes of Chinese history to problems of American understanding, while the work by Hucker is an excellent summation of the institutional history of traditional China. American China specialists have written a number of excellent historiographical surveys of scholarship on China. Some of these works have informed this essay.[31]

The most common point of entry into China's premodern history has been through the work of intellectual rather than political historians. Herrlee C. Creel's *Chinese Thought from Confucius to Mao Tse-tung* is an excellent synthetic study of the traditional Chinese systems of thought—Confucianism, Taoism, and Legalism. The important stream of Indian religion which so influenced China, particularly as it became an ingredient of statecraft, is well handled in Arthur F. Wright's *Buddhism in Chinese History.* The previously cited works resulting from the conferences of the Committee on Chinese Thought also focused their attention on interactions between thought and political behavior in imperial China. One manifestation of this ap-

30. Kenneth S. Latourette, *The Chinese: Their History and Culture,* rev. ed. (New York, 1946); John K. Fairbank, *The United States and China* (Cambridge, Mass., 1958); Charles O. Hucker, *China's Imperial Past* (Stanford, 1975).

31. Among the historiographical and interpretive surveys, I have relied on Charles O. Hucker, *Chinese History: A Bibliographic Review,* Service Center for Teachers of History Publication no. 15 (Washington, D.C., 1958); Arthur F. Wright and John W. Hall, "Chinese and Japanese Historiography: Some Recent Trends, 1961–1966," *Annals of the American Academy of Political and Social Science,* CCLXXI (1967), 178–193; John K. Fairbank, "New Views of China's Tradition and Modernization," Service Center for Teachers of History Publication no. 74 (Washington, D.C., 1968); Kwang-ching Liu, "From Feudalism to Imperial Localism: Reflections on Some Recent American Works in Chinese History" (mimeo, 1978). This last work was prepared expressly for the Conference of Japanese and American Historians at the 1978 annual meeting of the American Historical Association in San Francisco.

proach is seen in the number of excellent studies on the state of the Confucian tradition at the end of the imperial period as it came face to face with the forces of Westernization. Joseph R. Levenson's impressive three-volume study *Confucian China and Its Modern Fate,* Benjamin Schwartz's study of Yen Fu, translator of J. S. Mill and Herbert Spencer, and David S. Nivison's biography of the traditionalist scholar Chang Hsüeh-ch'eng reveal aspects of the intellectual crisis faced by the nineteenth-century literati. Mary C. Wright's brilliant *Last Stand of Chinese Conservatism* describes the efforts of Chinese scholar-bureaucrats to hold on to the Confucian tradition in the face of Western pressure.[32]

The influence of social science methodology on postwar American scholarship on China has shown itself particularly well in studies of political and social institutions. Whereas the traditional approach to China's political history proceeded chronologically, telling of the rise and fall of dynasties in more or less cyclical fashion, these later works have, in Kwang-ching Liu's judgment, asked three basic questions: (1) What was the nature of imperial authority? (2) Who were the personnel that made up the government and the bureaucracy? (3) How did this government relate to local society?[33]

On the first question, a logical starting point is the work of Herrlee Creel on the origins of statecraft and the beginnings of bureaucracy. These works ask whether the process can be conceived as a transition from feudal decentralization to imperial centralization. Derk Bodde's prewar work on the founding of the first empire had focused attention on the actions of the main figures in that founding.[34] In the 1960s and 1970s the emphasis has been more on ideological methods used to gain legitimacy. This was the theme of Arthur F. Wright's *Sui Dynasty: The Unification of China, A.D. 581–617,* and his piece "T'ang T'ai-tsung and Buddhism." James T. C. Liu, John W. Haeger, and Conrad Schirokauer have written in this vein on the Sung dynasty, Charles O. Hucker on the Ming dynasty.[35]

32. Herrlee G. Creel, *Chinese Thought from Confucius to Mao Tse-tung* (Chicago, 1953); Arthur F. Wright, *Buddhism in Chinese History* (Stanford, 1959); Joseph R. Levenson, *Confucian China and Its Modern Fate,* 3 vols. (Berkeley, 1958–65); Benjamin Schwartz, *In Search of Wealth and Power* (Cambridge, Mass., 1964); David S. Nivison, *The Life and Thought of Chang Hsüeh-Ch'eng, 1738–1801* (Stanford, 1966); Mary C. Wright, *The Last Stand of Chinese Conservatism: The T'ung-chih Restoration, 1862–1874* (Stanford, 1957).

33. I refer here to the piece cited in note 31 above. The remainder of this section is heavily indebted to Professor Liu's analysis.

34. Herrlee G. Creel, *The Origins of Statecraft in China,* vol. I, *Western Chou Empire* (Chicago, 1970); Derk Bodde, "The Beginnings of Bureaucracy in China: The Origins of the Hsien," in *Statesman, Patriot, and General in Ancient China* (New Haven, 1940).

35. Arthur F. Wright, *The Sui Dynasty: The Unification of China, A.D. 581–617* (New

American historians have shown conspicuous interest in the question of how the imperial bureaucracy was recruited and constituted. On this subject the pace was set by E. A. Kracke, Jr., in his *Civil Service in Early Sung China, 960–1067*. This work was followed by Ho Ping-ti's *Ladder of Success in Imperial China: Aspects of Social Mobility, 1368–1181*.[36] Both scholars have made quantitative calculations from original materials to demonstrate the volume and nature of social mobility in late imperial Chinese society. Other approaches have been through the study of specific administrative organs or the lives of imperial officials as exemplified by the works of Charles Hucker and Jonathan Spence.[37]

Studies of the interaction between central government and local government and society are indicative of the greater penetration of American historians into the process of government in China. Brian E. McKnight's study of village and bureaucracy in the Sung period and Ray Huang's study of taxation in the Ming period are indicative of this capacity. So also is the important set of articles on the transition from Ming to Ch'ing edited by Jonathan Spence and John E. Wells. For the Ch'ing dynasty there is the series of publications by Chinese scholars working at the University of Washington, beginning with Chang Chung-li's description of the "Chinese gentry" of the nineteenth century. This work was followed by Hsiao Kung-chuan's analysis of imperial control in rural China. These studies in turn were to stimulate a new generation of American historians, such as Philip A. Kuhn, John R. Watt, and Frederic Wakeman, Jr., to use local documentation for their analyses of social and political movements of late-imperial China. Another influence that has directed historians toward local or regional studies has been that of the sociologist G. William Skinner and his theories of urbanization and marketing systems.[38]

York, 1978); "T'ang T'ai-tsung and Buddhism," in Arthur F. Wright and Denis Twitchett, eds., *Perspectives on the T'ang* (New Haven, 1973); James T. C. Liu, *Reform in Sung China: Wang An-Shih and His New Policies* (Cambridge, Mass., 1959); John W. Haeger, ed., *Crisis and Prosperity in Sung China* (Tucson, 1975), contains Conrad Shirokauer's work; Charles O. Hucker, *The Traditional Chinese State in Ming Times (1368–1644)* (Tucson, 1961).

36. Cambridge, Mass., 1953; New York, 1962.

37. Charles O. Hucker, *The Censorial System of Ming China* (Stanford, 1966); Jonathan D. Spence, *Ts'ao Yin and the K'ang-hsi Emperor: Bondservant and Master* (New Haven, 1965) and *Emperor of China: Self-Portrait of K'ang-hsi* (New York, 1974).

38. Brian E. McKnight, *Village and Bureaucracy in Southern Sung China* (Cambridge, Mass., 1971); Ray Huang, *Taxation and Government Finance in Sixteenth-Century Ming China* (Cambridge, Mass., 1974); Jonathan D. Spence and John E. Wells Jr., *From Ming to Ch'ing: Conquest, Region, and Continuity in Seventeenth-Century China* (New York, 1979); Chang Chung-li, *The Chinese Gentry: Studies in Their Role in Nineteenth-Century Chinese Society* (Seattle, 1960), and *The Income of the Chinese Gentry* (Seattle, 1962); Hsiao Kung-

Once we enter the field of modern Chinese history, during which traditional intellectual, political, and social institutions were transformed under the impact of Western influence, the historical literature multiplies enormously, so that the works cited below become an even more selective listing. General studies of the early contact between Chinese officials and Western traders and diplomats are portrayed in the works of John K. Fairbank, Teng Ssu-yü, Chang Hsin-pao, and Earl Swisher.[39] Responses to the Western challenge came in a variety of forms. One was outright rebellion. The Taiping Rebellion and its failure has received voluminous coverage in Franz Michael and Chang Chung-li, *The Taiping Rebellion: History and Documents*. Efforts at military and political restrengthening have been treated mainly through the lives of specific reformers, such as Stanley Spector's *Li Hung-chang*. Efforts at economic and military reconstruction have been penetratingly analyzed by Kwang-ching Liu, Albert Feuerwerker, and John Rawlinson. Joseph Levenson's biography of Liang Ch'i-ch'ao is one of several studies of transitional intellectuals. Among others, Jerome Grieder has dealt with the important literary figure Hu Shih, and Thomas Metzger has raised important issues in his new interpretation of Neo-Confucianism as having "transformative leverage." Paul Cohen has described the early impact of the Christian missionary movement on China, while Jonathan Spence has described brilliantly the work of foreign advisers devoted to China's modernization. The title of Guy Alitto's book, *The Last Confucian*, neatly sums up this subject.[40]

chuan, *Rural China: Imperial Control in the Nineteenth Century* (Seattle, 1960); Philip A. Kuhn, *Rebellion and Its Enemies in Late Imperial China: Militarization and Social Structure, 1796–1864* (Cambridge, Mass., 1970); John R. Watt, *The District Magistrate in Late Imperial China* (New York, 1972); Frederic Wakeman, Jr., *Strangers at the Gate: Social Disorder in South China, 1839–1861* (Berkeley, 1966). Skinner has written the seminal article "Marketing and Social Structure in Rural China," *Journal of Asian Studies*, 1964, 1965, and has edited the conference volume *The City in Late Imperial China* (Stanford, 1977).

39. S. Y. Teng and J. K. Fairbank, *China's Responses to the West*, 2 vols. (Cambridge, Mass., 1954); John K. Fairbank, *Trade and Diplomacy on the China Coast: The Opening of the Treaty Ports, 1842–1854* (Cambridge, Mass., 1953); Chang Hsin-pao, *Commissioner Lin and the Opium War* (Cambridge, Mass., 1964); Earl Swisher, *China's Management of the American Barbarians: A Study of Sino-American Relations, 1841–1861, with Documents* (New Haven, 1953).

40. Franz Michael and Chang Chung-li, *The Taiping Rebellion: History and Documents*, 3 vols. (Seattle, vol. I, 1966); Stanley Spector, *Li Hung-chang and the Hwai Army: A Study in Nineteenth-Century Chinese Regionalism* (Seattle, 1964); Kwang-ching Liu, *Anglo-American Steamship Rivalry in China, 1862–1874* (Cambridge, Mass., 1962); Albert Feuerwerker, *China's Early Industrialization: Sheng Hsuan-huai (1844–1916) and Mandarin Enterprise* (Cambridge, Mass., 1958); John L. Rawlinson, *China's Struggle for Naval Development, 1839–1895* (Cambridge, Mass., 1967); Joseph Levenson, *Liang Ch'i-ch'ao and the Mind of Modern China* (Cambridge, Mass., 1953); Jerome B. Grieder, *Hu Shih and*

Study of the Revolution of 1911, once considered primarily the work of Sun Yat-sen, has taken a new turn among American scholars. Lyon Sharman's study of Sun Yat-sen, published in 1934, is still a standard biography, though later works by C. Martin Wilbur and Harold Schiffron offer more details of certain aspects of his life.[41] The more recent emphasis is on the role of the local gentry in providing revolutionary motive power. Papers from the 1965 Conference on the Revolution of 1911, edited by Mary Wright, are an important indication of this new thrust in the work of American scholars. Subsequently there has been a steady flow of monographic studies of local movements during 1911.[42] The failure of central authority and the resulting "warlord period" has attracted a number of scholars to the study of particular warlords: James Sheridan for Feng Yü-hsiang, Donald Gillin for Yen Hsi-shan, Odoric Wou for Wu P'ei-fu, and Garvan McCormack for Chang Tso-lin.[43]

The May Fourth Movement, a turning point in the political and intellectual history of twentieth-century China, is voluminously analyzed by Chow Tse-tsung. The succeeding nationalist phase of the government under the Kuomintang and Chiang K'ai-shek has received only spotty coverage in post-1949 American scholarship. But works by Lloyd Eastman and Suzanne Pepper provide an excellent overview of the 1927–49 period.[44] More numerous have been the

*the Chinese Renaissance: Liberalism in the Chinese Revolution, 1917–1937* (Cambridge, Mass., 1969); Thomas A. Metzger, *Escape from Predicament: Neo-Confucianism and China's Evolving Political Culture* (New York, 1977); Paul A. Cohen, *China and Christianity: The Missionary Movement and the Growth of Chinese Anti-Foreignism, 1860–1870* (Cambridge, Mass., 1963); Jonathan D. Spence, *To Change China* (Boston, 1969); Guy Alitto, *The Last Confucian: Liang Shu-ming and the Chinese Dilemma of Modernity* (Berkeley, 1979). Other works pertinent to this subject are listed in note 32 above.

41. Lyon Sharman, *Sun Yat-sen* (New York, 1934); C. Martin Wilbur, *Sun Yat-sen: Frustrated Patriot* (New York, 1976); Harold Schiffron, *Sun Yat-sen and the Origins of the Chinese Revolution* (Berkeley, 1968).

42. Mary C. Wright, ed., *China in Revolution: The First Phase, 1900–1913* (New Haven, 1968); Edward Rhoads, *China's Republican Revolution: The Case of Kwangtung, 1895–1913* (Cambridge, Mass., 1975); Mary Rankin, *Early Chinese Revolutionaries: Radical Intellectuals in Shanghai and Chekiang* (Cambridge, Mass., 1971); Joseph Esherick, *Reform and Revolution in China: The 1911 Revolution in Hunan and Hubei* (Berkeley, 1976).

43. James E. Sheridan, *Chinese Warlord: The Career of Feng Yü-hsiang* (Stanford, 1966); Donald Gillin, *Warlord Yen Hsi-shan in Shansi Province, 1911–1949* (Princeton, 1967); Odoric Wou, *Militarism in Modern China: The Career of Wu P'ei-fu, 1916–1939* (Dawson, 1978); Gavan McCormack, *Chang Tso-lin in Northeast China, 1911–1928* (Stanford, 1977).

44. Chow Tse-tsung, *The May Fourth Movement* (Cambridge, Mass., 1960); Paul Linebarger, *The China of Chiang K'ai-shek* (Boston, 1941); Lloyd Eastman, *The Abortive Revolution: China under Nationalist Rule, 1927–1937* (Cambridge, Mass., 1974); Suzanne Pepper, *Civil War in China: The Political Struggles, 1945–1948* (Berkeley, 1978).

works on Mao Tse-tung and the Communist movement. *Mao's China* by Maurice Meisner provides the best overview.[45] Monographs by Benjamin Schwartz, Maurice Meisner, Stuart Schram, Chalmers Johnson, Lyman Van Slyke, Robert North, John Lewis, and Franz Schurmann explore the ideological roots of the movement, its leaders, and the reasons for their success.[46] The dramatic normalization of relations between the People's Republic and the United States in 1978 will certainly have an effect on the China field, but it has been slow to assert itself.

## SOUTHEAST ASIA

Of the four fields reviewed in this essay, Southeast Asia has received the least extended attention in the United States, for a variety of reasons. There is first the sheer fact of diversity created by the geographical spread and the multiplicity of languages and cultural traditions to be found in the area. Also, because of the pattern of colonization, it was natural for scholars from Britain, France, and the Netherlands to take the lead in Southeast Asian studies. Nonetheless, under the impetus of the area studies movement, opportunities to research and write about Southeast Asia in the United States improved enormously after World War II. By the 1960s, some fifteen university-based programs had been brought into being, and a growing number of American historians were at work in the field.[47] Among the centers, Cornell University was the obvious leader, with Yale also recognized for the excellence of its teaching staff. The precariousness of the field was evident, however, in the fate of the program at Yale University. There, with the death of Harry Benda in

45. Maurice Meisner, *Mao's China: A History of the People's Republic* (New York, 1977).
46. Benjamin Schwartz, *Chinese Communism and the Rise of Mao* (Cambridge, Mass., 1951); Maurice Meisner, *Li Ta-chao and the Origins of Chinese Marxism* (Cambridge, Mass., 1967); Stuart Shram, *Mao Tse-tung* (New York, 1967) and *The Political Thought of Mao Tse-tung* (New York, 1963); Chalmers Johnson, *Peasant Nationalism and Communist Power: The Emergence of Revolutionary China* (Stanford, 1962); Lyman P. Van Slyke, *Enemies and Friends: The United Front in Chinese Communist History* (Stanford, 1967); Robert C. North, *Moscow and Chinese Communists* (Stanford, 1953); John Wilson Lewis, *Leadership in Communist China* (Ithaca, N.Y., 1963); Franz Schurmann, *Ideology and Organization in Communist China* (Berkeley, 1966).
47. See Gerald S. Maryanov, *The Condition of Southeast Asia Studies in the United States: 1972* (Center for Southeast Asian Studies, Northern Illinois University, Occasional Papers no. 3, 1974). The fifteen institutions with such programs were American University, University of California at Berkeley, Chicago, Columbia, Cornell, Harvard, Johns Hopkins, Kansas, Michigan, Northern Illinois, Ohio, Southern Illinois, Washington, Wisconsin, and Yale.

1971 and the retirement of Karl Pelzer, the program was largely phased out of existence.

Historians of Southeast Asia at the start of the postwar era were still troubled by the difficulty of finding unity in the diversity of the area. Representative efforts in the search for a unifying conception are found in the writings of D. G. E. Hall (British, but writing in the *Journal of Asian Studies*) and Harry Benda.[48] Neither was fully successful, though they worked with such unifying concepts as Hinduization, colonization, and modernization.

A new stage both in the overall development of Southeast Asian studies in the United States and in the conceptualization of the history of the area was evident in the jointly written 1971 survey edited by David J. Steinberg of the University of Michigan.[49] Entitled *In Search of Southeast Asia: A Modern History,* this work took in stride the problem of regional integrity. Its authors found a way, as they put it, to "treat each unit [society] in Southeast Asia as a separate species and the region as a distinct genus."[50] They wrote on the premise that earlier Western writers had obscured the dynamics of Southeast Asian history by too great an emphasis on "external stimuli." They believed that the region should rather be understood in terms of its geographical and ecological foundations and its historic location, "south of China and east of India." The authors found deep and widespread uniformities in the traditional base at the start of the eighteenth century. It was rooted first of all in fishing, rice-growing, and upland societies, in village communities under local headmen, and in religiously venerated rulers. The influence of Western colonization was not at first to enforce Westernization so much as to hasten the process whereby a large number of political centers, small and large, were shaped into incipient national entities. Colonization eventually gave rise to political, social, and technological change: urbanization, education, secularization, political reaction, and nationalist movements. During World War II the area was subjected to Japanese occupation under the slogan "Asia for the Asiatics." The end of the war brought

48. See D. G. E. Hall, "Looking at Southeast Asian History," *Journal of Asian Studies,* XIX (1960), 243–253; Harry J. Benda, "The Structure of Southeast Asian History," *Journal of Southeast Asian History,* III (1962), 106–138.

49. David J. Steinberg, ed., *In Search of Southeast Asia: A Modern History* (Kuala Lumpur, 1971). Though the book was published by Oxford University Press, most of the authors are American and all were at work in the United States at the time of writing. They were David Steinberg (Michigan), David Wyatt (Cornell), John Smail (Wisconsin), Alexander Woodside (Harvard), William Roff (Columbia), and David Chandler (Michigan). This work has an excellent bibliography of Western-language works on Southeast Asian history, which has informed this essay.

50. Ibid., 4.

independence, neocolonialism, and the need to form new governments. The book concludes with an overview of the postwar period. Southeast Asian societies, the authors observe, are still caught between "the cultural predispositions of their long, sophisticated historical pasts" and the realities of modern national life. "The problems of balance are enormous. Most Westerners are ignorant of and behave irresponsibly toward Southeast Asian history and the people who make it. Even uninformed sympathy directed toward 'underdeveloped' nations, which in fact are 'underdeveloped' only in economic and scientific organization, is no longer enough."[51]

This remarkable insight, which exemplifies the "Asiacentric" attitude cultivated by so many scholars touched by the area studies philosophy, came about through the work of a team of specialists on the individual histories of the major cultural entities of the region: Burma, Thailand, Cambodia, Vietnam, Malaya, Indonesia, and the Philippines. For them the unity of the region could be demonstrated by following through common themes and grasped by their own sensitivities to local values learned from residence in one of the countries and mastery of its language. While much of the work of American scholars trained since the start of the 1960s remains unpublished or is to be found in articles only, enough has appeared to give a general sense of the shape of American scholarship on Southeast Asian history.

The starting point is certainly the survey edited by David Steinberg. The earlier survey by John Cady and a collaborative work by John Bastin and Harry J. Benda are also noteworthy.[52] American historians have only begun to make distinctive contributions to the histories of individual Southeast Asian societies. John F. Cady has done distinguished work on Burma, and Joseph Buttinger and Alexander Woodside have written on premodern Vietnam.[53] The best surveys of Indonesian history are still the work of European writers, but the area has engaged the attention of several distinguished American cultural anthropologists and sociologists, among them Clifford Geertz, D. H. Berger, and Lauriston Sharp.[54] Village studies, particularly in Java,

51. Ibid., 342.

52. Steinberg, ed., *In Search of Southeast Asia;* John F. Cady, *Southeast Asia: Its Historical Development* (New York, 1964); John Bastin and Harry J. Benda, *A History of Modern Southeast Asia* (Englewood Cliffs, N.J., 1968).

53. John F. Cady, *A History of Modern Burma* (Ithaca, N.Y., 1960); Joseph Buttinger, *Vietnam: A Dragon Embattled* (New York, 1967); Alexander Woodside, *Vietnam and the Chinese Model* (Cambridge, Mass., 1970).

54. Clifford Geertz, *Agricultural Involution* (Berkeley, 1963); D. H. Burger, *Structural Changes in Javanese Society: The Village Sphere/The Supra-Village Sphere* (Ithaca, N.Y.,

have had considerable influence on historians and their efforts to get a feel of the "little tradition" base of the region.

It is in the modern period, from roughly 1870 to the present, that American historians have made their most notable contributions. Among studies on prewar colonial and political developments, John Cady has written on Burma, David K. Wyatt on Thailand, Milton Osborne on the French in Cambodia, Rupert Emerson and Virginia Thompson on Malaysia.[55]

Nationalism has been a favorite subject and a useful conceptual tool for the study of political movements among colonized peoples. Rupert Emerson's *From Empire to Nation* is a pioneer study; so are Clifford Geertz's *Old Societies and New States* and Daniel Lerner's *Passing of Traditional Society*.[56] (None of these writers, it should be explained, is a historian.) To this period belong also Harry J. Benda and Ruth McVey's volume of documents on Communist uprisings in prewar Indonesia, the volume edited by Frank N. Trager on Marxism in four Southeast Asian countries, and John Whitmore's study of the transformation of a Vietnamese village.[57]

Nationalist movements in individual Southeast Asian societies have been well covered by a number of solid studies. Among them are works by George Kahin, Harry Benda, and Robert Van Niel on Indonesia, John T. McAlister on Vietnam, William R. Roff on Malaya, and Frank Trager on Burma.[58] The period of Japanese occupation and subsequent revolution has been given special attention by David J. Steinberg, Harry Benda, Herbert Feith and Lance Castles, and

1956–57); Lauriston Sharp and Lucien Hanks, Jr., *Bang Chan: A Social History of a Thai Farming Community* (Ithaca, N.Y., 1972).

55. John F. Cady, *A History of Modern Burma* (Ithaca, N.Y., 1960); David K. Wyatt, *The Politics of Reform in Thailand* (New Haven, 1969); Milton Osborne, *The French Presence in Cochinchina and Cambodia* (Ithaca, N.Y., 1969); Rupert Emerson, *Malaysia: A Study of Direct and Indirect Rule* (New York, 1937); Virginia Thompson, *Postmortem on Malaya* (New York, 1943).

56. Rupert Emerson, *From Empire to Nation: The Rise to Self-Assertion of Asian and African Peoples* (Boston, 1960); Clifford Geertz, ed., *Old Societies and New States: The Quest for Modernity in Asia and Africa* (New York, 1963); Daniel Lerner, *The Passing of Traditional Society* (Glencoe, Ill., 1958).

57. Harry J. Benda and Ruth McVey, eds., *The Communist Uprisings of 1926–27 in Indonesia: Key Documents* (Ithaca, N.Y., 1960); Frank N. Trager, ed., *Marxism in Southeast Asia: A Study of Four Countries* (Stanford, 1959); John K. Whitmore, *From Notable to Cadre: The Transformation of a Rural Vietnamese Village* (Ithaca, N.Y., 1965).

58. George McT. Kahin, *Nationalism and Revolution in Indonesia* (Ithaca, N.Y., 1952); Harry J. Benda, *The Crescent and the Rising Sun: Indonesian Islam under the Japanese Occupation, 1942–1945* (The Hague, 1958); Robert Van Niel, *The Emergence of the Modern Indonesian Elite* (The Hague, 1960); John T. McAlister, *Vietnam: The Origins of Revolution* (New York, 1969); William R. Roff, *The Origins of Malay Nationalism* (New Haven, 1967); Frank N. Trager, *Burma: From Kingdom to Republic* (New York, 1966).

John R. W. Smail.[59] An earlier work by George Kahin on the revolution in Indonesia remains a classic.[60]

For the postwar development of independent states in Southeast Asia a number of political and institutional analyses deserve attention. The best overall introduction is probably George Kahin's *Governments and Politics of Southeast Asia*.[61] Robert O. Tilman has written on bureaucracy in Malaya, William J. Siffin on Thai government, and Frank Trager and Lucian Pye on Burma, while Ralph Braibanti has edited a collection of essays on the legacy of British administration in Asia.[62] Again it should be pointed out that many of these books are the works of political scientists whose subject matter has led them to take a historical or developmental view of the process of nation building in Southeast Asia.

## SOUTH ASIA

Like China, the other of the two historical originators of continent-wide civilizations and world religions among the four regions covered in this essay, South Asia has exerted a profound hold on the American imagination. Indian religious writings in translation, for instance, as early as the early nineteenth century played an important role in the Transcendentalist movement in American thought, having influenced the thinking of, among others, Ralph Waldo Emerson. India remained very much on the American mind throughout the 1970s, but the state of academic South Asian studies was still comparatively underdeveloped.

The reasons are obvious. The study of Indian religion and history in the West has from its inception been the preserve of English scholars, and later of Indian scholars trained in England. The fact that nearly all of this scholarship was and continues to be written in English means that the important works of translation and historical interpretation were available to American scholars and teachers in

59. David J. Steinberg, *Philippine Collaboration in World War II* (Ann Arbor, 1967); Benda, *Crescent and Rising Sun;* Herbert Feith and Lance Castles, eds., *Indonesian Political Thinking, 1945–1965* (Ithaca, N.Y., 1970); John R. W. Smail, *Bandung in the Early Revolution, 1945–1946: A Study in the Social History of the Indonesian Revolution* (Ithaca, N.Y., 1964).
60. George McT. Kahin, *Nationalism and Revolution in Indonesia* (Ithaca, N.Y., 1952).
61. Ithaca, N.Y., 1959.
62. Robert O. Tilman, *Bureaucratic Transition in Malaya* (Durham, N.C., 1964); William J. Siffin, *The Thai Bureaucracy* (Honolulu, 1966); Trager, *Burma*; Lucian Pye, *Politics, Personality, and Nation Building: Burma's Search for Identity* (New Haven, 1962); Ralph Braibanti, ed., *Asian Bureaucratic Systems Emergent from the British Imperial Tradition* (Durham, N.C., 1966).

their own language. But conversely any American contribution to this vast field would have to compete with the work of well-established and skilled English and Indian academics. Moreover, as fields of research in South Asia became increasingly more specialized, it became necessary for the student to control a number of local languages in addition to classical Sanskrit.

The fact that so much of the scholarly work on South Asia was available in English had both its advantages and its disadvantages. Teaching about Indian history was made relatively easy, but doing research on it was not. As late as 1958, Robert Crane, in his pamphlet on Indian history prepared for the American Historical Association, included in his bibliography the works of only 27 American writers in a total of 106 citations.[63] Furthermore, of the 27, most were not academic historians but the writers of firsthand accounts of travel or residence in India. Two decades later, one of the few survey histories of India to be written by an American academic, Stanley Wolper's *A New History of India*, was still based more than 90 percent on works by English or Indian authors.[64] The domination of this field by scholars outside the United States is evident in the annual *Bibliography of Asian Studies*. In the 1975 edition of this work, the Far East took up 194 pages, Southeast Asia 171 pages, and South Asia 256 pages. The overwhelming portion of works cited on South Asia were by scholars working outside the United States.[65]

To get a sense of the immediate postwar state of the South Asian field in America it is informative to refer to the career of Professor Wolpert. Having decided to turn his attention from marine engineering to Indian history after a visit to India, Wolpert returned to the United States in 1948 to find that the only recognized program in Indian history was at the University of Pennsylvania under the direction of W. Norman Brown. Under what was a typical regional studies program, Wolpert "approached Indian civilization from many perspectives: linguistic, cultural, geographic, ethnographic, social, political, economic, administrative, and, primarily, historical."[66] This was the kind of "education from scratch" needed to train a specialist in the years when South Asian studies could be started only at the graduate level.

63. Robert I. Crane, *The History of India: Its Study and Interpretation,* Service Center for Teachers of History Publication no. 17 (Washington, D.C., 1958).
64. New York, 1977.
65. Published by the Association for Asian Studies, Ann Arbor, 1978.
66. Wolpert, *New History of India,* xi.

By 1956, when the Far Eastern Association became the Association for Asian Studies and included South Asian scholars in its membership, there was already an obvious need for a professional organization to serve the growing number of South Asian specialists. Since then, the South Asian membership has been one of the most active of any group in the promotion of its field, particularly through study groups. By the end of the 1960s, programs could be found at some seventeen American universities, the most important of which were the University of California at Berkeley, the University of Chicago, Duke University, and the universities of Michigan, Pennsylvania, and Wisconsin. Most of these schools were recognized as NDEA centers and had full-scale area programs that offered undergraduate and graduate degrees based on South Asian language and discipline study.[67]

A survey of the field in 1969 counted some forty full-time historians at American academic institutions. According to a self-evaluation made at that time, however, these scholars were rather narrowly specialized, since half of them were working on the nationalist movement and most of the rest on elite composition or cultural reform. Earlier periods of Indian history were poorly represented.[68] Howard Spodek, in a review of the work of British historians of modern India at Cambridge University, observed that the field was not attracting sufficient students even to hold its own in the future.[69]

Spodek's critique of the Cambridge group points out their use of a number of useful social science models: "(1) pluralist machine politics; (2) patron–client relations; (3) federalism; (4) ideology; (5) diffusion of innovation; (6) conflict in social change."[70] The use of social science models holds true as well for American historians, and perhaps more explicitly so. As in the case of Southeast Asian studies, there has been heavy reliance on interdisciplinary research and on field study. In this context the works of Clifford Geertz and Myron Weiner have been important.[71] The American emphasis on regionalism is well illustrated in the publications resulting from seminars held at Duke University

67. Margaret L. Cormack, *Guidelines to South and Southeast Asia Studies Resources in the U.S.*, Center for South and Southeast Asia Studies, University of California, Occasional Papers no. 3 (1969).

68. Richard D. Lambert, ed., *The Development of South Asian Studies* (Ann Arbor, 1969), 108–109.

69. Howard Spodek, "Pluralist Politics in British India: The Cambridge Cluster of Historians of Modern India," *American Historical Review*, LXXXIV (1974), 688–707.

70. Ibid., 700.

71. Geertz, ed., *Old Societies and New States*; Myron Weiner, *Party Building in a New Nation: The Indian National Congress* (Chicago, 1967).

in 1966 and 1973.[72] As with the Cambridge group, the tendency has been to play down the themes of Westernization, colonialism, nationalism, and imperialism and to "see Indian events primarily through the eyes of the Indians themselves."[73] And this tendency in turn has led to an awareness of the subtle distinction between nationalism and secularization as the prime motive force in modern Indian society.

Aside from the works already cited, mention should be made of a number of noteworthy contributions by American scholars to the field of South Asian historiography. An outstanding analysis of modern South Asian history is W. Norman Brown's *United States and India, Pakistan, Bangladesh*.[74] Another unusual work is Erik Erikson's *Gandhi's Truth*.[75] An early and much publicized attempt at psychohistory, it demonstrates an extreme, and not altogether successful, effort to relate social science theory to historical analysis. Other important works referred to by Stanley Wolpert are listed below.[76] They are indicative of the wide range of interest among Americans, not all of them historians, who have written on South Asia during the 1970s.

72. Robert I. Crane, ed., *Region and Regionalism in South Asian Studies: An Exploratory Study* (Durham, N.C., 1967); Richard G. Fox, ed., *Realm and Region in Traditional India* (Durham, N.C., 1977).

73. Spodek, "Pluralist Politics in British India," 703.

74. 3d rev. ed., Cambridge, Mass., 1972.

75. New York, 1969.

76. J. H. Bloomfield, *Elite Conflict in a Plural Society* (Berkeley, 1968); Bernard S. Cohn, *The Social Anthropology of a Civilization* (Englewood Cliffs, N.J., 1971); Ainslee T. Embree, ed., *The Hindu Tradition* (New York, 1966); Holden Furber, *Indian Governor Generalship* (Cambridge, Mass., 1953); Stephen Hay, *Asian Ideas of East and West: Tagore and His Critics in Japan, China, and India* (Cambridge, Mass., 1970); Robert E. Frykenberg, ed., *Land Control and Social Structure in Indian History* (Madison, Wis., 1969); Lloyd I. Rudolph and Suzanne H. Rudolph, *The Modernity of Tradition: Political Development in India* (Chicago, 1967); Milton Singer, *When a Great Tradition Modernizes: The Anthropological Approach to Indian Civilization* (New York, 1972); Stanley Wolpert, *Morley and India, 1906-1910* (Berkeley, 1967).

# 7

## Latin America and the Americas

### Charles Gibson

THE study of Latin American history has a long tradition in the United States. William H. Prescott inaugurated serious research on the subject in the 1840s and dazzled the English-speaking world with his writings on the conquests of Mexico and Peru. Prescott's principal successor in the late nineteenth century, Hubert H. Bancroft, produced massive, detailed, widely read works on Mexico, Central America, and the western states. In the first half of the twentieth century, when Latin American history had ceased to be a pursuit for gentlemen scholars and had become an academic discipline in colleges and universities, the leading figures, all professors of history, were E. G. Bourne, Herbert E. Bolton, Roger B. Merriman, and Clarence H. Haring.[1] Their foremost accomplishments lay in investigations of colonial institutional and legal history. Most students now, a generation or more later, would identify as their critical weakness a tendency to interpret the postindependence history of Latin America in narrowly national and political terms. It is obvious that the whole tradition from Prescott to Haring left a great deal still to be accomplished. But it is also true that that tradition had a dynamism and character and quality of its own, as any interested reader may determine for himself by consulting the two-volume an-

1. William H. Prescott, *History of the Conquest of Mexico, with a Preliminary View of the Ancient Mexican Civilization, and the Life of the Conqueror, Hernando Cortez,* 3 vols. (Boston, 1843); William H. Prescott, *History of the Conquest of Peru, with a Preliminary View of the Civilization of the Incas,* 2 vols. (New York, 1847); Hubert H. Bancroft, *Works,* 39 vols. (San Francisco, 1875–90); E. G. Bourne, *Spain in America, 1450–1580* (New York, 1904); Herbert E. Bolton's numerous writings may be appreciated via John Francis Bannon, ed., *Bolton and the Spanish Borderlands* (Norman, Okla., 1964); Roger B. Merriman, *The Rise of the Spanish Empire in the Old World and in the New,* 4 vols. (New York, 1918–34); Clarence H. Haring, *The Spanish Empire in America* (New York, 1947).

thology on the study and teaching of Latin American history in the United States edited in 1967 by Howard F. Cline.[2]

After World War II historians of the colonial period increasingly turned their attention away from institutions and laws and toward social history. It was a change that had long been under way in the work of colleagues studying the United States and Europe, and it appeared relatively late in work on Latin America. The delay was the consequence of both the nature of the relevant documentation and the exceptional strength and prestige of the existing tradition. Hispanic archives characteristically emphasized (and still emphasize) the institutional and the legal. They include few private papers, diaries, personal letters, or other types of source material appropriate for social history. The conquests, intuitively singled out by Prescott as subjects for dramatic presentation, had no parallel in the subsequent history, and scholars had come to pride themselves on their concern with the formal arrangements and procedures of viceroyalties, *corregimientos, encomiendas,* and *cabildos.*

The first steps toward a larger "human interest" in Latin American colonial history appeared as intellectual biography, cultural history written from literary evidence, studies of colonial education, and examinations of the "theories" of Spanish colonization. Among the precursors, Irving A. Leonard and John Tate Lanning were important figures.[3] The writings of Lewis Hanke on the Spanish "struggle for justice," the sixteenth-century campaign for the humanitarian treatment of Indians, carried the process further. Bartolomé de Las Casas was not an unknown personage to American students, but Hanke's contributions gave Las Casas's life and writings a fresh significance and assigned to the movement that he represented a more consequential role in Spanish colonial policy. Hanke gave additional impetus within the United States to tendencies already evident outside (one thinks especially of Robert Ricard in France and Silvio Zavala in Mexico).[4] After Hanke's major study of 1949, historians were no

2. Howard F. Cline, ed., *Latin American History: Essays on Its Study and Teaching, 1898–1965,* 2 vols. (Austin, 1967).

3. Irving A. Leonard, *Don Carlos de Sigüenza y Góngora: A Mexican Savant of the Seventeenth Century* (Berkeley, 1929); Irving A. Leonard, *Books of the Brave, Being an Account of Books and of Men in the Spanish Conquest and Settlement of the Sixteenth-Century New World* (Cambridge, Mass., 1949); John Tate Lanning, *Academic Culture in the Spanish Colonies* (London, 1940).

4. Robert Ricard, *La "conquête spirituelle" du Méxique: Essai sur l'apostolat et les méthodes missionaires des ordres mendiants en Nouvelle-Espagne de 1523–24 à 1572* (Paris, 1933); Silvio Zavala, *Las instituciones jurídicas en la conquista de América* (Madrid, 1935).

longer willing to view Spanish imperialism in the earlier terms.[5] The result was a new attention to the theoretical or philosophical aspect of Spanish imperialism, an aspect that proved immediately attractive to students of the postwar generation.

What colonial history still needed was a sense of particularity in time and place and an infusion of method and theory from social science. Social science was already exerting its powerful influence on other branches of historical study. The social science discipline par excellence for the colonial period of Latin American history would be anthropology, for anthropologists had approached and closed in on the subject from all sides, and yet, for various reasons, had refrained from crossing the disciplinary boundaries. Archaeologists had traced Indian prehistory up to the moment of conquest. Ethnologists had examined living Indian communities in the twentieth and in some cases even in the late nineteenth century. Between these periods lay the colonial era, as if ready and waiting for the application of a com- bined anthropological-historical interpretation. In field studies an- thropologists had emphasized characteristic differences between one Indian group and another, and between one community and the next. Some communities, such as Tepoztlán in Mexico, had become celebrated as a consequence of the field studies of anthropologists.[6] It was a situation that made the historian's ignorance of particular and local features of the colonial past even more obvious than before. Such works as *The Indian Background of Colonial Yucatan,* by the an- thropologist Ralph Roys, served as public notice to historians to bring their scholarship up to date.[7]

Responses to these challenges can be traced first through the work of students who were not historians in the narrow professional sense but who profoundly influenced the direction that subsequent histori- cal research would take: Robert Barlow, a devotee of codices and early texts who moved to Mexico, learned Nahuatl, and established the ethnohistorical journal *Tlalocan*; George Kubler, an art historian who in 1949 published his classic work on Mexican sixteenth-century ar- chitecture, rich in names, dates, and details; and Sherburne F. Cook, a geographer who, in conjunction with the historian Lesley B. Simpson,

5. Lewis Hanke, *The Spanish Struggle for Justice in the Conquest of America* (Philadel- phia, 1949).

6. Robert Redfield, *Tepoztlán, A Mexican Village: A Study of Folk Life* (Chicago, 1930); Oscar Lewis, *Life in a Mexican Village: Tepoztlán Revisited* (Urbana, Ill., 1951).

7. Ralph L. Roys, *The Indian Background of Colonial Yucatan* (Washington, D.C., 1943).

initiated the "Berkeley School" of Indian demography.[8] All three were anthropologically oriented, and we can see them now as pioneers in the modern study of the colonial Indian, a subject that has come to loom large and that has given all colonial history, but especially the first hundred years, a distinctive character. Through the 1960s research on the postconquest Indian was one of the principal new developments promoted by Howard Cline, who himself published a number of articles on this subject and who, more than any other person, was responsible for the four ethnohistorical volumes of the *Handbook of Middle American Indians,* edited by the anthropologist Robert Wauchope.[9]

In recent United States work on the history of Indians in Latin America the "Berkeley school," consisting of Cook, Simpson, and Woodrow Borah, has become famous. Using town-by-town population counts, Cook and Borah proposed in 1963 a population figure of approximately 25 million for central Mexico at the time of the Spanish conquest and traced a population decline of over 90 percent during the subsequent century. These dramatic calculations, much criticized at first both within and outside the United States, have since come to be widely accepted. Meanwhile the California researchers have published additional findings on a variety of related topics, including price trends, land grants, soil erosion, labor, and the composition of Mexican Indian society.[10]

Modern techniques of social and economic history, spectacularly illustrated by the work of the Berkeley School, are now being promoted by a number of younger historians of the colonial period. Anthropology continues to be the most prominent of the related disciplines, and historians and anthropologists now cooperate in research projects and in publications. The local archives of Latin America have assumed a new role as studies of communities and regions proliferate. The historians of the 1970s have received training, or have trained themselves, in the advanced techniques of quantification. For the first time they are using in a serious way the notarial documentation and the parochial records of baptism, marriage, and

8. Robert Barlow, *The Extent of the Empire of the Culhua Mexica* (Berkeley, 1949); George Kubler, *Mexican Architecture of the Sixteenth Century,* 2 vols. (New Haven, 1948); Sherburne F. Cook and Lesley B. Simpson, *The Population of Central Mexico in the Sixteenth Century* (Berkeley, 1948).

9. Robert Wauchope, ed., *Handbook of Middle American Indians,* 15 vols. (Austin, 1964–75).

10. Woodrow Borah and Sherburne F. Cook, *The Aboriginal Population of Central Mexico on the Eve of the Spanish Conquest* (Berkeley, 1963). Other works are principally in the Ibero-Americana series published by the University of California Press.

burial that exist in virtually every town in Latin America. The study of Indians and of relations between Indians and whites is expanding now to include blacks, mestizos, mulattoes, and the other mixed classes of the advanced colonial period. Work on family history and the history of women is likewise in progress, though these subjects are still less developed than most. The hacienda, long taken for granted, has become a focus for new research in social and economic history, and with this work have come, or are coming, revisionist interpretations of the economic function of latifundia, peonage, entrepreneurship, elitism, absenteeism, and the relations of employers to laborers. Agricultural production, the supply of cities, marketing, and the export economy are all receiving attention.[11]

Most of these developments began with research in Mexico, but they are currently being carried to Peru and to other parts of South America, and for the first time it is possible to make some precise comparisons between one community and another and among the far-flung regions of the Spanish colonies. Peruvian studies are more popular now than ever before among younger colonial historians. Here the ethnohistorical stimulus comes particularly from the work and students of the anthropologist John Murra, whose researches on precolonial Andean society and on sixteenth-century *visitas* have given rural Peruvian studies something of the specificity previously confined to Mexico. The new Peruvian history is represented in an outstanding fashion by the studies of James Lockhart on the first generation of colonists, and of Frederick Bowser on Peruvian colonial slavery.[12]

11. William B. Taylor, *Landlord and Peasant in Colonial Oaxaca* (Stanford, 1972); Ward J. Barrett, *The Sugar Hacienda of the Marqueses del Valle* (Minneapolis, 1970); Charles Gibson, *Tlaxcala in the Sixteenth Century* (New Haven, 1952); Charles Gibson, *The Aztecs under Spanish Rule: A History of the Indians of the Valley of Mexico, 1519-1810* (Stanford, 1964); Arthur P. Whitaker, "Changing and Unchanging Interpretations of the Enlightenment in Spanish America," *American Philosophical Society Proceedings,* CXIV (1970), 256-271; Richard E. Boyer, *La Gran Inundación: Vida y sociedad en la ciudad de México, 1629-1638* (Mexico City, 1975); Murdo J. MacLeod, *Spanish Central America: A Socioeconomic History, 1520-1720* (Berkeley, 1973); Asunción Lavrin, ed., *Latin American Women: Historical Perspectives* (Westport, Conn., 1978); Meri Kraster, "Women in Latin America: The State of the Research, 1975," *Latin American Research Review,* XI:1 (1976), 3-74; Asunción Lavrin, "Latin American Women's History," *Latin American Research Review,* XIII:2 (1978), 314-318. See also the studies of recent work in social history, "The Social History of Colonial Spanish America," in *Latin American Research Review,* VII:1 (1972), 6-94, with articles by James Lockhart, Karen Spalding, and Frederick P. Bowser.

12. John V. Murra, *Formaciones económicas y políticas del mundo andino* (Lima, 1975); John V. Murra, "Current Research and Prospects in Andean Ethnohistory," *Latin American Research Review,* V:1 (1970), 3-36; Karen Spalding, *De indio a campesino: Cambios en la estructura social del Perú colonial* (Lima, 1974); James Lockhart, *Spanish Peru,*

In both Mexican and South American colonial history, detailed investigations are being extended increasingly into the seventeenth and eighteenth centuries. The seventeenth, long known as the "forgotten" century, is being examined not simply as a continuation of the sixteenth but as a period in its own right and in relation to the parent countries' decline. The connection between the Iberian empires and the European "crisis" has provided a new focal point for seventeenth-century investigations, particularly in economic history. The eighteenth century is undergoing reevaluation in ways that supersede traditional preoccupations with the Enlightenment and the antecedents of independence. Social history, price history, the commercial activities of landholders, and the relations between creoles and Peninsulars are eighteenth-century topics of current interest.[13] English, Mexican, and other scholars elsewhere have so far been prominent in these researches on the middle and late colonial years. But United States historians are being drawn to them in increasing numbers, and an interesting outcome has been a closer cooperation between United States and foreign scholars in academic appointments, in international conferences, in publications, and in programs of joint research.

Innovative work on the nineteenth and twentieth centuries appeared later than that on the colonial period, and the surrounding circumstances were rather different. Anthropology was a less important contributing factor. The principal influences came from economics, political science, and sociology. In the 1960s students in these disciplines conducted many new investigations in Latin America, the result being a burgeoning of information on contemporary politics, attitudes, social classes, and economies. In Latin America the emergence of new authoritarian and military governments, and in the United States the disclosures of official interference and of government-sponsored research on Latin American counterin-

---

*1532–1560: A Colonial Society* (Madison, Wis., 1968); Frederick P. Bowser, *The African Slave in Colonial Peru, 1524–1650* (Stanford, 1974).

13. Woodrow Borah, *New Spain's Century of Depression* (Berkeley, 1951); Peter J. Bakewell, *Silver Mining and Society in Colonial Mexico: Zacatecas, 1546–1700* (Cambridge, Eng., 1971); David A. Brading, *Miners and Merchants in Bourbon Mexico, 1763–1810* (Cambridge, Eng., 1971); Susan M. Socolow, *The Merchants of Buenos Aires, 1778–1810: Family and Commerce* (Cambridge, Eng., 1978); Doris M. Ladd, *The Mexican Nobility at Independence, 1780–1826* (Austin, 1976); Nancy M. Farriss, *Crown and Clergy in Colonial Mexico, 1759–1821: The Crisis of Ecclesiastical Privilege* (London, 1968); Dauril Alden, *Royal Government in Colonial Brazil, with Special Reference to the Administration of the Marquis of Lavradio, Viceroy, 1769–1779* (Berkeley, 1968); Mark A. Burkholder and D. S. Chandler, *From Impotence to Authority: The Spanish Crown and the American Audiencias, 1687–1808* (Columbia, Mo., 1977).

surgency, created an unprecedented public awareness. Political liberalism, a shibboleth of the 1950s, gave way to "development," a process that might (or might not) occur under any of a number of political conditions. These circumstances inevitably affected the attitudes and methods of historians working on Latin America and most especially of those working on the period since independence.

Indian ethnohistory, so important in colonial studies, has had no real counterpart in the work on the modern era, partly because the documentation for it is not comparable, partly because ethnic mixtures progressively reduced the historic Indian role. Slavery, on the other hand, in Brazil, the West Indies, and the other areas where it persisted, has continued to attract attention. In all areas scholars have been drawn to problems relating to race relations and the abolition of slavery.[14] Demographic analysis has been carried into the modern era by the Berkeley scholars and others, and in some instances it has now become possible to establish long-term statistical sequences from the colonial period to the twentieth century.[15] Industrial history and economic modernization are being scrutinized from a number of points of view.[16] And of course the modern period offers opportunities for continuations of the lines of inquiry established for the colonial

14. Franklin W. Knight, *Slave Society in Cuba during the Nineteenth Century* (Madison, Wis., 1970); Arthur F. Corwin, *Spain and the Abolition of Slavery in Cuba, 1817–1886* (Austin, 1967); Gwendolyn Midlo Hall, *Social Control in Slave Plantation Societies: A Comparison of St. Domingue and Cuba* (Baltimore, 1971); John V. Lombardi, *The Decline and Abolition of Negro Slavery in Venezuela, 1820–1854* (Westport, Conn., 1971); Robert Conrad, *The Destruction of Brazilian Slavery, 1850–1888* (Berkeley, 1972); Robert Brent Toplin, *The Abolition of Slavery in Brazil* (New York, 1972); Thomas Skidmore, *Black into White: Race and Nationality in Brazilian Thought* (New York, 1974). On these subjects see the bibliographical article by Magnus Mörner, "Recent Research on Negro Slavery and Abolition in Latin America," *Latin American Research Review*, XIII:2 (1978), 265–289.

15. Sherburne F. Cook and Woodrow Borah, *Essays in Population History: Mexico and the Caribbean*, 2 vols. (Berkeley, 1971–74).

16. Peter Klarén, *Modernization, Dislocation, and Aprismo: Origins of the Peruvian Aprista Party, 1870–1932* (Austin, 1973); Stanley J. Stein, *The Brazilian Cotton Manufacture: Textile Enterprise in an Underdeveloped Area, 1850–1950* (Cambridge, Mass., 1957); Richard Graham, *Britain and the Onset of Modernization in Brazil, 1850–1914* (London, 1968); John D. Wirth, *The Politics of Brazilian Development, 1930–1954* (Stanford, 1970); Warren Dean, *The Industrialization of São Paulo, 1880–1945* (Austin, 1969); Peter Eisenberg, *The Sugar Industry in Pernambuco: Modernization without Change, 1840–1910* (Berkeley, 1974); Robert W. Randall, *Real del Norte: A British Mining Venture in Mexico* (Austin, 1972); John H. Coatsworth, *El impacto económico de los ferrocarriles en el porfiriato: Crecimiento y desarrollo*, 2 vols. (Mexico City, 1976); Rodney D. Anderson, *Outcasts in Their Own Land: Mexican Industrial Workers, 1906–1911* (DeKalb, Ill., 1976); Ramón E. Ruiz, *Labor and the Ambivalent Revolutionaries: Mexico, 1911–1923* (Baltimore, 1976); Peter H. Smith, *Politics and Beef in Argentina: Patterns of Conflict and Change* (New York, 1969); Roberto Cortés Conde and Stanley J. Stein, *Latin America: A Guide to Economic History, 1830–1930* (Berkeley, 1977).

period, in studies of local government, *caudillismo,* intellectual history, the church, and urbanization.[17]

Since the earlier understanding of the nineteenth and twentieth centuries had been primarily political, one might suppose that the revisionist historians of the 1970s would turn from politics to emphasize the nonpolitical features of modern Latin American life and culture. But this is happening only to a limited degree. Politics remains central to much of the contemporary writing on the national period. The political perspective is often fused with other perspectives, and the subjects tend to be examined less for substantive political happenings, in the former fashion, than for what those happenings reveal of a broader political dimension. Historians of the 1970s are no longer content simply to reconstruct the unique political event. Their present aim is to formulate connections among a number of events and to make the whole intelligible in more comprehensive generalizations.

Our historians are now less likely to characterize the political climate of independent Latin America in pejorative terms, as a climate promoting disorder or turbulence or *opéra bouffe* on a national scale. They are less inclined than they were only a few years ago to condemn dictatorship, revolution, unconstitutionality, authoritarianism, militarism, and even graft and corruption on ideological or moral grounds. Increasingly they are questioning the assumption that Latin American governments were unsuccessful imitations of the United States. The classic postindependence query "Why has Latin America been unable to establish firm, peaceful, popular governments?" is seen as a *question mal posée,* for it emphasizes the negative side of political processes whose most obvious features are not negative at all but vibrant and highly charged. The values that the question assumes—peace and order and democracy—have been written into constitutions in Latin America and preached as political propaganda, but they have been less relevant than they once seemed to be in the realities of Latin American political life. The tendency is now to understand Latin American political acts in their own terms, and to

17. Robert L. Gilmore, *Caudillism and Militarism in Venezuela, 1810–1910* (Athens, O., 1964); Charles A. Hale, *Mexican Liberalism in the Age of Mora, 1821–1853* (New Haven, 1968); T. G. Powell, *El liberalismo y el campesinado en el centro de México, 1850–1876* (Mexico City, 1974); Robert J. Knowlton, *Church Property and the Mexican Reform, 1856–1910* (DeKalb, Ill., 1976); Frank Safford, *The Ideal of the Practical: Colombia's Struggle to Form a Technical Elite* (Austin, 1976); Richard M. Morse, *From Community to Metropolis: A Biography of São Paulo, Brazil* (Gainesville, Fla., 1958); James R. Scobie, *Argentina: A City and a Nation* (New York, 1964); James R. Scobie, *Buenos Aires: Plaza to Suburb, 1870–1910* (New York, 1974).

see political legitimacy in functional, relative, or Weberian terms, where the question is one of public attitudes rather than the personal predilection of the writer. Modern structuralism and functionalism and objectivity all combine to induce the view that Latin American revolutions are themselves "legitimate" devices for changing political administrations.[18]

National political history is being reformulated additionally through examinations of subnational regions. Interactions between regions and central governments were already under investigation in the 1940s, as the pioneering work of Miron Burgin on federalism in postindependence Argentina demonstrates. But the regional studies of the 1970s go much further than those of any earlier period in the task of identifying critical topics for study. They include local elites, landholding, and regional industries, especially those with which the national political authority has had to come to terms. Regions provide foci of attention between the community and the nation, and they help to identify those intermediate social and economic levels whose relationships to other levels above and below are matters of concern in the scholarship of the 1970s.[19]

Local peasant rebellion is proving to be a related and much valued topic of the national period, perhaps especially where such rebellion can be attributed to modernization or to an expanding capitalism and where relations between the peasant society and the nation may be subjected to analysis. Studies of the recent history of peasant groups in Latin America characteristically indicate a more active peasant role than would have been possible within the terms of the earlier interpretation. The peasant emerges as an exploited figure, but at the same time a figure of intelligence and volition, to some extent controlling the factors that govern his existence, and in any case capable of making the best of various situations, sometimes at the expense of the

18. See the interesting articles in Richard Graham and Peter H. Smith, eds., *New Approaches to Latin American History* (Austin, 1974). See also Richard M. Morse, "The Heritage of Latin America," in Louis Hartz, ed., *The Founding of New Societies: Studies in the History of the United States, Latin America, South Africa, Canada, and Australia* (New York, 1964), pp. 123-177, and the many insights in Glen C. Dealy, *The Public Man: An Interpretation of Latin American and Other Catholic Countries* (Amherst, Mass., 1977).

19. Miron Burgin, *The Economic Aspects of Argentine Federalism, 1820-1852* (Cambridge, Mass., 1946); Stanley J. Stein, *Vassouras: A Brazilian Coffee County, 1850-1900* (Cambridge, Mass., 1957); Joseph L. Love, *Rio Grande do Sul and Brazilian Regionalism, 1882-1930* (Stanford, 1971); Charles H. Harris III, *A Mexican Family Empire: The Latifundio of the Sánchez Navarros, 1765-1867* (Austin, 1975); Ralph Della Cava, *Miracle at Joaseiro* (New York, 1970); Warren Dean, *Rio Claro: A Brazilian Plantation System, 1820-1920* (Stanford, 1976); John D. Wirth, *Minas Gerais in the Brazilian Federation, 1889-1937* (Stanford, 1977).

larger society. Analogies between the colonial Indian and the modern peasant are relevant here, for both may be viewed as clients and their spokesmen may be viewed as brokers, mediating relations outside, or as patrons in accordance with the models of "patron-client relations." Such social mechanisms likewise help to explain the long-term survival of rural, poverty-stricken, and oppressed classes into the modern period.

The networks of families, regions, urban and rural societies, patrons and clients, and other interest groups relate to the exercise of power, to the allocation of resources, and to social and economic rankings. Without being openly illegal, such networks normally exist outside the law, and they thus provide insight into the daily operation of historical forces in ways that remain inaccessible to students who continue to confine their attention to law and its observance. Historians have seen what can be accomplished on these topics toward an understanding of contemporary societies, and they are striving to project similar inquiries into the past. Modern Latin America is emerging as one of the developing world's most important proving grounds, where theories concerning politics, revolutions, regional economies, elites, "middle sectors," peasants, and the interrelations of all of these, past and present, may be put to the test and compared with equivalent phenomena elsewhere.[20]

In the new studies of both the colonial and national periods, historians are depending heavily on the methods of social science. The process has involved some direct borrowing as well as some adaptation. Two social science procedures that have been especially influential in the new Latin American historiography are quantification and prosopography.

20. David Ronfeldt, *Atencingo: The Politics of Agrarian Struggle in a Mexican Ejido* (Stanford, 1973); Paul Friedrich, *Agrarian Revolt in a Mexican Village* (Englewood Cliffs, N.J., 1970); John Womack, *Zapata and the Mexican Revolution* (New York, 1969); for the Mexican Revolution of 1910, see the important article of David C. Bailey, "Revisionism and the Recent Historiography of the Mexican Revolution," *Hispanic American Historical Review*, LVIII (1978), 62–79; William R. Whyte, "El mito del campesino pasivo: La dinámica de cambio en el Perú rural," *Estudios andinos*, I (1970), 3–28; Arnold J. Bauer, *Chilean Rural Society from the Spanish Conquest to 1930* (Cambridge, Eng., 1975); Stephanie Blank, "Patrons, Clients, and Kin in Seventeenth-Century Caracas: A Methodological Essay in Colonial Spanish American Social History," *Hispanic American Historical Review*, LIV (1974), 260–283; John J. Johnson, *Political Change in Latin America: The Emergence of the Middle Sectors* (Stanford, 1958); Catherine C. LeGrand, "Perspectives for the Historical Study of Rural Politics and the Colombian Case: An Overview," *Latin American Research Review*, XII:1 (1977), 7–36. The emphases indicated are most clearly seen in work in progress and not yet published. The best guide to work in progress is the "Current Research Inventory" published through 1978 (but now no longer to be published) in the *Latin American Research Review*.

Quantified or quantifiable data are to be found in abundance in the published and unpublished sources for the Spanish colonies in America. Spanish imperialism was characteristically meticulous, and its records often include vast amounts of the kinds of data from which quantitative history is now being written. Although this is less true of Portuguese imperialism, Brazilian colonial sources will also permit a substantial measure of quantitative research. The far-reaching demographic—and economic and social—studies of Simpson, Cook, and Borah have been mentioned above. These should occupy first place in any assessment of published statistical research on the colonial period. But many other colonialists are now examining statistical material—on population, labor, landholding, mining, economic productivity, and numerous other subjects. Perhaps the foremost colonial research project now under way anywhere is that of John TePaske and his associates, in which the entire history of royal revenue and expenditure relating to the colonial Spanish American viceroyalties is being studied.[21]

Early national statistics are generally less abundant and less reliable than those of the colonial period. But with industrialization, the development of the complex state, and new positivist philosophies, the data for the later nineteenth century and the twentieth century again lend themselves reliably to quantitative techniques, and the resulting research is becoming at least as extensive and impressive as that on the colonial period. It relates to such subjects as birth and death rates, urbanism, internal migration, voting behavior, slavery, railroads, and export products.[22] A major work is James Wilkie's *Mexican Revolution: Federal Expenditure and Social Change in Mexico since 1910,* which seeks to arrive at the successive emphases that modern Mexican adminis-

21. John V. Lombardi, *People and Places in Colonial Venezuela* (Bloomington, Ind., 1976); David A. Brading and Celia Wu, "Population Growth and Crisis: León, 1720–1860," *Journal of Latin American Studies,* v (1973), 1–36; Edgar F. Love, "Marriage Patterns of Persons of African Descent in a Colonial Mexico City Parish," *Hispanic American Historical Review,* LI (1971), 79–91; David A. Brading and Harry E. Cross, "Colonial Silver Mining: Mexico and Peru," *Hispanic American Historical Review,* LII (1972), 545–579; John J. TePaske et al., *La Real Hacienda de Nueva España: La Real Caja de México (1576–1816)* (Mexico City, 1976); John J. TePaske, "Recent Trends in Quantitative History: Colonial Latin America," *Latin American Research Review,* x:1 (1975), 51–62.
22. Robert McCaa, "Chilean Social and Demographic History: Sources, Issues, and Methods," *Latin American Research Review,* XIII:2 (1978), 104–126; Laura Randall, *An Economic History of Argentina in the Twentieth Century* (New York, 1977); William Paul McGreevey, *An Economic History of Colombia, 1845–1930* (Cambridge, Eng., 1971); Richard N. Sinkin, "The Mexican Constitutional Congress, 1856–1857: A Statistical Analysis," *Hispanic American Historical Review,* LIII (1973), 1–26; William Paul McGreevey, "Recent Materials and Opportunities for Quantitative Research in Latin

trations have placed on the social values deriving from the Revolution of 1910. Wilkie's "poverty index," a series of measurable criteria for determining degrees of deprivation in modern Mexico, has received extensive discussion and has become famous.[23]

Prosopography or collective biography, the technique that permits the identification of salient attributes among groups of persons, is now being widely applied also in Latin American historical study. In its developed state it is a special form of aggregate analysis. Through prosopography one may arrive at the generalized social status of persons who were successful in government or business, or make connections relating to other aspects of career patterns of masses of individuals. Birth data, birthplace, family connections, ethnic status, marriage status, education, occupation, rank, wealth, party affiliation, and votes cast on particular issues are examples of categories that are being compared and correlated in the Latin Americanists' new prosopography. Notable examples include James Lockhart's *Men of Cajamarca*, a full assemblage of data on the origin, age, and occupation of the conquistadores who accompanied Pizarro, with much additional biographical information. Stuart Schwartz's study of the judges of the court of Bahia in the seventeenth and eighteenth centuries and Julia Hirschberg's work on the first settlers of Puebla are further examples of this method. Peter H. Smith has recently published a massive survey of the social background and careers of over six thousand persons who held national political positions in Mexico between 1900 and 1971.[24]

Methodological innovations of such magnitude and such far-reaching implications, appearing on the scene so rapidly, have in-

American History: Nineteenth and Twentieth Centuries," *Latin American Research Review*, IX:2 (1974), 73–82; see also the special section on historical statistics by Laura Randall, Michael Hamerly, and others in *Latin American Research Review*, XIII:2 (1978), 70–221.

23. James W. Wilkie, *The Mexican Revolution: Federal Expenditure and Social Change in Mexico since 1910* (Berkeley, 1967); Thomas E. Skidmore and Peter H. Smith, "Notes on Quantitative History: Federal Expenditure and Social Change in Mexico since 1910," *Latin American Research Review*, V:1 (1970), 71–85; Felix G. Boni and Mitchell A. Seligson, "Applying Quantitative Techniques to Quantitative History: Poverty and Federal Expenditures in Mexico," *Latin American Research Review*, VIII:2 (1973), 105–110; James W. Wilkie, "On Quantitative History: The Poverty Index for Mexico," *Latin American Research Review*, X:1 (1975), 63–75.

24. James Lockhart, *The Men of Cajamarca: A Social and Biographical Study of the First Conquerors of Peru* (Austin, 1972); Stuart B. Schwartz, *Sovereignty and Society in Colonial Brazil: The High Court of Bahia and Its Judges, 1609–1751* (Berkeley, 1973); Julia Hirschberg, "Social Experiment in New Spain: A Prosopographical Study of the Early Settlement at Puebla de los Angeles, 1531–1534," *Hispanic American Historical Review*, LIX (1979), 1–33; Peter H. Smith, *Labyrinths of Power: Political Recruitment in Twentieth-Century Mexico* (Princeton, 1979).

evitably taken a toll by way of psychic dislocation. The leaders of the new movements, with some important exceptions, are the younger scholars. The generation gap, while far from unprecedented in professional life, is more pronounced in this case than it has ever been in the past among Latin American historians. A new organization, the Latin American Studies Association, and its journal, the *Latin American Research Review* (founded 1965), provide a stimulating environment for the cross-fertilization of disciplines. Members of the new generation in their contacts, publications, and conversations naturally and inevitably turn away from the history that was written by their elders, the history that the surviving elders, or many of them, continue to prefer. In some degree we do have in the 1970s the kind of rift between traditionalists and innovators that Howard Cline feared and sought to forestall in his anthology on the study and teaching of this subject.

Traditional historians appear to be less disturbed by the innovative subjects being studied—for everyone knows that our information has been incomplete—than by the attendant changes in perspective and vocabulary. The conventional community of historians of Latin America experienced an initial shock several decades ago when the rural laborer in Latin America began to be called a peasant. The notion of a peasantry in Latin America seemed alien, the result of some fundamental misunderstanding. But the term entered the historical literature because anthropology and sociology and political science and economics, and now history also, were seeking larger categories identifiable in a worldwide nomenclature. To admit "peasant" into the lexicon of the Latin American historian is to gain by way of categorical expansion and to bring history into the sphere of generalized social science research, but it is also to yield some of the distinctiveness and subtlety and local feel of the Latin American specialization. Additionally, in a now familiar turnabout, models ceased being examples to be imitated and became hypothetical conclusions to be tested, and the notion of a scholarly model both lost and gained ground accordingly. Other new or newly employed terms, such as factor and cohort and paradigm, sent students scurrying to their dictionaries. And for still others, such as correlation coefficient, multiple regression, and interpositional transition matrix, the dictionary was of no use. For these one needed a whole new education and a new mentality.

Critics sometimes found it inappropriate and ironic that new categories and new scientific methods should be employed in the study of Latin America. In these critics' view, Latin "character" is just the opposite of scientific, and Latin America remains inaccessible to such avant-garde analyses. Victor Alba, a humanist spokesman for the Hispanic world, has pointed to the obsessive preoccupation with facts and figures that characterizes United States scholarship on Latin America. United States students, in his view, have been afraid of offending their Latin neighbors and have found a false security in their position of *frialdad objetiva*. They have been the more prone to settle for quantitative research because deep down they know that they are incapable of a humanistic understanding of Latin character.[25] In such interpretations the new historiography appears as a behaviorist's refuge, productive of abundant data but incapable of inducing empathy or genuine intellectual understanding.

Among United States scholars there have not been many supporters of these views. The critic who stands out, because of the acuteness of his perceptions and the engaging way in which he expresses his iconoclasm, is Richard Morse. Himself one of our foremost Brazilianists and a profound student of urbanism and urban theory, Morse is equally known for his skepticism concerning the value of quantification. Writing under such titles as "The Strange Career of 'Latin-American Studies'" and "The Care and Grooming of Latin American Historians, or: Stop the Computers, I Want to Get Off," Morse has explored more thoroughly than anyone else in the profession the historical and spiritual bases of the alienation between the United States and Latin America.[26] He advocates a humane and qualitative, as opposed to a scientific and quantitative, appreciation of Latin American history.

Studies involving the whole American hemisphere should be understood against the background of the chauvinism of a hundred years ago. In the late nineteenth century the standard United States interpretation of hemispheric history assumed English America to be superior and Hispanic America to be inferior. Englishmen came as settlers, creating a domestic, agrarian, and democratic society. Spaniards and Portuguese came as soldiers, conquering, searching for gold, and eventually establishing a hodgepodge of backwater states. By the early twentieth century these views were being modified in the direction of a more sympathetic understanding of Latin America.

25. Victor Alba, "The Latin American Mind," *Latin American Research Review*, XIII:2 (1978), 311–313.
26. Richard M. Morse, "The Strange Career of 'Latin-American Studies,'" *Annals of the American Academy of Political and Social Science*, CCCLVI (1964), 106–112; Richard M. Morse, "The Care and Grooming of Latin American Historians, or: Stop the Computers, I Want to Get Off," in Stanley R. Ross, ed., *Latin America in Transition: Problems in Training and Research* (Albany, N.Y., 1970), 27–40.

With respect to hemispheric history the revisionism was expressed in Herbert E. Bolton's thesis of "Greater America," according to which the common Pan-American features of American history received special emphasis and required new study. In a celebrated address in 1932 Bolton summed up his position and enumerated the general themes of Greater America: colonial status, transplantation of European culture, exploitation of natives and resources, national competition, political independence, struggle for political stability and economic well-being, and foreign relations.[27]

Boltonism successfully sloughed off many of the prejudices of the earlier interpretations, but it never stimulated the scholarly response for which its author hoped. In practice the Greater America idea was confined to introductory college courses, courses that attracted students but did little or nothing to develop the new field of scholarship envisaged by Bolton. The best works were comprehensive textbooks, such as John Francis Bannon's *History of the Americas* in 1952. The thesis of a shared hemispheric past was subjected to some scholarly testing in the 1950s, when the Pan American Institute of Geography and History undertook a series of projects to determine the feasibility of a single American history. For more than a decade this inquiry engaged the attention of historians in Latin America, Europe, and the United States. But its results were meager. All of the scholars involved in the project were able to recognize some common features in the history of the Americas. None, however, was willing to argue that the similarities took precedence over the differences. It is probably the case that the political realities of the postwar years gave the coup de grâce to the idea of a unitary history of the American hemisphere. When Lewis Hanke assembled the materials for his anthology *Do the Americas Have a Common History?* (1964), the answer to the title's question for most readers was already clear: "No, they do not."[28] Apart from international relations (see Chapter 15), hemispheric history survives now only with reference to a few selected topics, of which comparative slavery and comparative race relations (see Chapter 19) are the most familiar.[29]

Meanwhile Latin America has come to be widely recognized as part

27. Herbert E. Bolton, "The Epic of Greater America," *American Historical Review*, XXXVIII (1933), 448–474.

28. John Francis Bannon, *History of the Americas*, 2 vols. (New York, 1952); Charles C. Griffin, *Program of the History of the New World: III. The National Period in the History of the New World: An Outline and Commentary* (Mexico City, 1961); Arthur P. Whitaker, *The Western Hemisphere Idea: Its Rise and Decline* (Ithaca, N.Y., 1954); Lewis Hanke, ed., *Do the Americas Have a Common History?: A Critique of the Bolton Theory* (New York, 1964).

29. See also James Lang, *Conquest and Commerce: Spain and England in the Americas* (New York, 1964).

of another of the world's subdivisions, that of the less developed countries ("LDCs"). As formerly with the history of the Americas, efforts are currently being made to identify the common features of the group, and these efforts have so far involved historical generalization at a relatively high level of abstraction. Much attention has been given to what is called dependency theory, which developed in Latin America as an intellectual protest and has been infiltrating United States writing since the mid-1960s. Dependency theory explains the condition of the less developed countries in terms of the expansion of the industrial countries, including Spain and Portugal in the sixteenth century as well as Britain and the United States more recently. It is not just that some nations outdistanced others and left them behind. It is that the developed nations needed to suppress and exploit the undeveloped nations in the process of becoming developed. Just as there can be no upper class without a lower class, so dependency is not simply a by-product of capitalism; it is an inherent feature of the system. In a derivatively Marxist form of dependency theory, the colonial period of Latin American history must be identified as capitalist, not feudal. For the sake of consistency, moreover, those areas of Latin America that first came under the influence of the modernizing outside world and have been dependent for the longest time must be identified as the least developed areas of the twentieth century.

The historical portions of dependency theory include more than their share of misrepresentations, logical fallacies, and errors of fact.[30] But it is as important for Latin Americanists as it is for others to know that large-scale reinterpretations of this type can suddenly flourish and pass as scholarship in our enlightened age. Our historians of Latin America have yet to confront the full implications of dependency theory and allied doctrines. It is not enough simply to criticize the worst of the writings on scholarly grounds. The new writings challenge us to construct alternative interpretations of development, underdevelopment, modernization, and dependency, and beyond that to consider again our own points of view toward the colonial and the national periods and what they imply for us historically and politically.

30. The exception to these statements and the principal historical work on the subject is Stanley J. Stein and Barbara H. Stein, *The Colonial Heritage of Latin America: Essays on Economic Dependence in Perspective* (New York, 1970).

# PART TWO

## EXPANDING FIELDS
## OF INQUIRY

# 8

## Toward a Wider Vision: Trends in Social History

### Peter N. Stearns

ARLY in the 1970s Eric Hobsbawm wrote of the excitement of being a practitioner in the field of social history.[1] This sense of excitement remains, on the whole, among social historians in the United States, despite a growing uncertainty later in the decade regarding the place of history in American culture. Social historians, sharing at the very least a concern for achieving a historical perspective on the everyday activities of ordinary people, have steadily grown in number and expanded the range of their activity.

#### DISSEMINATION OF SOCIAL HISTORY

Courses in social history continue to proliferate at the college and university level. Few are surveys of the field; the big increases in social history courses have come as special-topics offerings, on particular groups of people or segments of the life experience, a trend that is reflected in research in the United States as well. Many courses on women's history and ethnic history were launched as aspects of social history or have come to be so regarded by those who teach them and by historians generally. More recently such subjects as the family and sports have been introduced into the history curriculum, taught with a pronounced sociohistorical emphasis. Some fuzziness remains concerning what subject matter belongs in the field and how it should be taught. New subjects are sometimes touted as social history without serious inquiry into their approach or coverage; the fact that women's history, for example, can be treated sociohistorically leads some to

---

1. Eric Hobsbawm, "From Social History to the History of Society," *Daedalus*, c (1971), 43.

Peter N. Stearns

believe that it necessarily is social history no matter what form it takes. The failure, save in a few graduate programs, to provide rigorous training in the basic methodology and key conceptual issues of social history suggests the absence, thus far, of a systematic approach to the history of society. Students emerge more commonly with a sense of key topics in social history than with a knowledge of the basic social processes that unite those topics.

Social history has penetrated general history courses and texts, and even secondary school curricula, though only to a limited extent. In the schools, some special-topics courses on family, ethnic, and women's history have introduced a sociohistorical component. College admissions tests are now a great deal more concerned with social history.[2] The general emphasis of textbooks, however, has shifted little, and as budgetary restraints have slowed the development of new school texts, the dissemination of social history has been correspondingly delayed. For many secondary schoolteachers, key areas of social history remain terra incognita. At both secondary and college levels, the decline of new hiring in recent years has also disrupted the connection that should exist between an exciting field of research and graduate study on the one hand and what is taught on the other. Many large university departments (though not the most prestigious), their size now frozen, still lack any serious representation of social historians, and so either offer no social history or include it among general courses in somewhat diluted form. The excitement generated by social history has not surmounted the broad difficulties of declining interest in history teaching, though it may in some cases have modified them; and correspondingly the slump of history as a discipline during the 1970s adversely affected the production of sociohistorical researchers and the spread of social history as a teaching subject.

Still, an increasing number of students and teachers, at various levels, are being exposed to social history topics and approaches, even in survey courses. Social history courses have also developed in departments of sociology and anthropology, concerned with such themes as collective protest and family development, on which social historians have provided data, methodologies, and conceptual focus.[3] A number of sociology departments have for some years been hiring specialists in "historical and comparative analysis." Social history in any rigorous sense, however, remains a minor current in American

2. College Entrance Examination Board, *Advanced Placement in History* (New York, 1979).
3. Charles Tilly, *From Mobilization to Revolution* (Boston, 1978).

social sciences and history alike. Its importance relative to the rest of the history curriculum is greatest at such universities as Michigan, Rutgers, and Rochester—universities that are not traditional national pacesetters. Issues first raised almost a decade ago—is social history a subject area, like intellectual history, and therefore to be presented as part of a curricular smorgasbord of topic offerings, or is it an approach to the whole of history that historians must either embrace or reject?[4]—remain unresolved at the teaching level. Some continued ambivalence regarding the curricular role of social history may actually be healthy, permitting the avoidance of confrontations and sterile definitional quarrels. That social history, nonetheless, has a claim to be taught can no longer be disputed, and this situation does reflect its increased general acceptance over the past decade in the United States. Work in social history is indeed now noted in the national media, with some books reaching a popularity normally achieved only by military histories and analyses of recent American politics and diplomacy.[5] Some social historians are personally consulted in media examinations of the status of such entities as the family, youth, and the elderly in the United States.

The strength of social history remains, however, in research. (Indeed, one of the pressing tasks of social historians is to bring their dissemination capacity into closer alignment with their research success; too much social history is deliberately written for fellow researchers and aspires at most to an audience of social scientists.) Larger classes and other signs of growing prestige follow from the continued aura of excitement that surrounds social history as a field of inquiry. The bases for this prestige in the United States remain twofold: the research promises to deepen understanding of subjects vital to contemporary life, from the history of blacks to that of divorce, and it demonstrates that the range of sociohistorical concern is being expanded as additional aspects of the human experience are submitted to the perspective that a knowledge of the past can provide. In very few respects does social history yet offer the comfort of famil-

4. Definitional essays on social history include Samuel P. Hays, "A Systematic Social History," in George Billias and Gerald Grob, eds., *American History: Retrospect and Prospect* (New York, 1971), 315–366; Mario S. DePillis, "Trends in American Social History and the Possibility of Behavioral Approaches," *Journal of Social History* I (1977), 36–66; Neil Smelser, "Sociological History," *Journal of Social History*, I (1967), 17–35; and the papers in *Journal of Social History*, x (1977), no. 2 (issue on social history).

5. Four recent books receiving this kind of attention are Philip J. Greven, Jr., *The Protestant Temperament* (New York, 1978); Christopher Lasch, *Haven in a Heartless World: The Family Besieged* (New York, 1977) and *The Culture of Narcissism: American Life in an Age of Diminishing Expectations* (New York, 1978); and Emmanuel Le Roy Ladurie, *Montaillou: The Promised Land of Error* (New York, 1978).

iar topics available for reformulation and reinterpretation. The field's charm is its enthusiasm for novelty and, some add still, its rawness. That is one reason why their research endeavors are still more significant to social historians than teaching or public recognition, and why their published writings, both in their own journals and in more general outlets, are primarily concerned with issues of research approach.[6] The success of social historians in reaching the "other" social sciences is similarly clearest at the level of research reporting, with historical analyses of industrialization, movements of rebellion, and family structure increasingly appearing in the journals read by sociologists and economists.

## THE RESEARCH FRAMEWORK

Any effort briefly to characterize social history research in the United States must start with some warnings and apologies. The absence of dominant, centralized schools in the field—schools in the institutional sense and also schools of thought and allegiance—makes a survey difficult, though some shortfalls here may be compensated for by the presence in this volume of other essays dealing with what are for the most part subfields of social history, such as family and women's history. It is impossible to define social history adequately by discussing it in terms of period or area. Some of the most exciting American social history still focuses on the colonial period,[7] partly because historians concerned with the nineteenth and particularly the twentieth century have long been drawn to more purely political and diplomatic issues, attracted by their topicality and the masses of data they generate. These disparities are, however, beginning to even out somewhat. Historians initially concerned with such subjects as social mobility and working-class life in the early industrial period are now pursuing their investigations well into the twentieth century,[8] and

6. The *Journal of Social History* and the *Journal of Interdisciplinary History* are the most central outlets for work in social history in the United States; see also *Comparative Studies in Society and History* and *Societas: A Review of Social History*.

7. Philip J. Greven, Jr., *Four Generations: Population, Land, and Family in Colonial Andover, Massachusetts* (Ithaca, N.Y., 1970); John Demos, *A Little Commonwealth: Family Life in Plymouth Colony* (New York, 1970); Kenneth Lockridge, *A New England Town: The First Hundred Years, Dedham, Massachusetts, 1636–1736* (New York, 1970); Michael Zuckerman, *Peaceable Kingdoms: New England Towns in the Eighteenth Century* (New York, 1970); Edmund S. Morgan, *American Slavery, American Freedom: The Ordeal of Colonial Virginia* (New York, 1975).

8. Stephan Thernstrom, *The Other Bostonians: Poverty and Progress in the American Metropolis, 1880–1970* (Cambridge, Mass., 1973); Howard P. Chudacoff, *Mobile Americans: Residential and Social Mobility in Omaha, 1880–1920* (New York, 1972); Michael

some research on still newer topics, such as the history of youth,[9] has focused on relevant developments in advanced industrial societies from its inception. On the whole, sociohistorical inquiry is now fairly well distributed chronologically in the United States, certainly better distributed than it was a decade ago; thus it is less firmly anchored to a concern for premodern societies than French work has been, and less closely concerned with early industrialization than British investigations have tended to be.

Considerable geographical balance also exists. Sociohistorical work, like historical work generally in this country, is predominantly focused on the Western Hemisphere and Western Europe. Problems of data availability and occasionally, as with Latin America, the attractions of studying various political developments have somewhat retarded sociohistorical work on other areas; but social historians are well represented among Russian and East Asian specialists in the United States,[10] and serious work has been done in Indian, Middle Eastern, and other areas as well. On certain topics, notably demography and slavery, Latin American research is quite advanced.[11] But again, to indicate special strengths and weaknesses by area would be to miss the main point. The journals devoted to social history have carefully avoided specialization by area or period. Most social historians are more aware of research on their particular subject in periods and areas other than their own than are toilers in other historical fields; for they are more concerned with topics and methodology than with characterization of a single period or regional culture. The budding field of the history of crime thus happily merges medievalists

---

Weber, *Social Change in an Industrial Town: Patterns of Progress in Warren, Pennsylvania, from the Civil War to World War I* (University Park, Pa., 1976); Tamara K. Hareven and Randolph Langenbach, *Amoskeag: Life and Work in an American Factory City* (New York, 1979).

9. Joseph F. Kett, *Rites of Passage: Adolescence in America, 1790 to the Present* (New York, 1977); John Gillis, *Youth and History: Tradition and Change in European Age Relations, 1770–Present* (New York, 1973).

10. Reginald Zelnik, *Labor and Society in Tsarist Russia: The Factory Workers of St. Petersburg, 1855–1870* (Stanford, 1971); Daniel Chirot, *Social Change in a Peripheral Society: The Creation of a Balkan Colony* (New York, 1976); Jerome Blum, *The End of the Old Order in Rural Europe* (Princeton, 1979). On East Asia, see Thomas C. Smith, *Nakahara: Family Farming and Population in a Japanese Village* (Stanford, 1977); Gary Allinson, *Japanese Urbanism* (Berkeley, 1975); Jonathan Spence, *The Death of Woman Wang* (New York, 1978); Susan Naquin, *Millenarian Rebellion in China: The Eight Trigrams Uprising of 1813* (New Haven, 1976).

11. Carl Degler, *Neither Black nor White: Slavery and Race Relations in Brazil and the United States* (New York, 1971); Herbert S. Klein, *The Middle Passage: Comparative Studies of the Atlantic Slave Trade* (Princeton, 1978); S. F. Cook and Woodrow Borah, *The Population of Mixteca Alta, 1520–1960* (Berkeley, 1968); James Lockhart, *Spanish Peru, 1532–1560* (Madison, Wis., 1968).

and historians of industrial society, Americanists and Europeanists.[12]

One other preliminary point is essential. There is no distinctively American school of social history. Social history has some American antecedents and roots, but its current flowering depended, and depends still, quite heavily on work done in France, Britain, and elsewhere. Colonial family and community studies drew on the work of French and English demographers. Few historians of the working class fail to make their bow to E. P. Thompson, Hobsbawm, and others. References to the *Annales* abound, though the actual practitioners of the *Annales* approach in the United States remain few.[13] It is true that American work, in its methodology and subject matter, has now become internationally influential; its role in Germany as well as in the English-speaking countries is particularly striking. American social history in fact flourishes in an international context. At the same time, the uncentralized state of the field within the United States inhibits the development of a unified national approach. The journals relating to social history now published in the United States focus on topics and methodologies, not on exclusive definitions of the field.[14] None would be comfortable with a single conceptual label or with a completely distinctive national designation. Yet collectively these journals do convey something of an American tone, some particular variants of more widespread motifs in social history. It is possible to delineate certain American impulses and emphases in social history, and doing so is one of the central concerns of this essay.

A second way to approach an examination of the state of sociohistorical research is to consider the label of novelty that continues to be

12. James Cockburn, ed., *Crime in England, 1550–1800* (Princeton, 1977); *Journal of Social History,* VIII:4 (1975) (issue on crime).

13. See, however, Traian Stoianovich, *A Study in Balkan Civilization* (New York, 1967); Immanuel Wallerstein, *The Modern World-System: Capitalist Agriculture and the Origins of the European World Economy in the Sixteenth Century* (New York, 1974); Edward Fox, *History in Geographic Perspective: The Other France* (New York, 1972). Some American work in peasant history also reflects the *Annales* approach: Rudolph Bell, *Fate and Honor, Family and Village: Demographic and Cultural Change in Rural Italy since 1880* (Chicago, 1979); Patrice Higonnet, *Pont-de-Montvert: Social Structure and Politics in a French Village, 1700–1914;* see also Steven Kaplan, *Bread, Politics, and Political Economy in the Reign of Louis XV,* 2 vols. (The Hague, 1976). On a more theoretical basis, Traian Stoianovich, *French Historical Method: The "Annales" Paradigm* (Ithaca, N.Y., 1976). Finally, a new journal, *Review: A Journal of the Fernand Braudel Center for the Study of Economies, Historical Systems, and Civilizations,* obviously bears witness to an interest in the Braudelian approach.

14. Thus the *Journal of Social History, Journal of Interdisciplinary History, Comparative Studies in Society and History;* the new *Review* and *Marxist Perspectives* may modify this conceptual eclecticism a bit, though the latter is not defined by a strict sociohistorical interest and the former insists on a heuristic approach to theory.

applied to social history in the United States, despite fifteen years of steady and substantial development on earlier foundations. Impressions of the "newness" of social history result in part from the lack of a dominant school or a single authoritative journal, which promotes confusion about the field's boundaries even among its own members. Thus one historian, labeled social though trained in cultural history, distinguishes himself from "new" social historians who refuse to use novels as historical evidence.[15] Internecine bickering aside, Americans presumably delight in claims of newness, and practitioners of social history are not exempt. Many historians have been particularly eager to seize upon new topics and approaches in a period when the historical discipline can seem dangerously dated, and in a country where social scientists, often ahistorical in their own thinking, have appeared as prophets of a new future in the understanding of man and his works.

If the field does have a claim to novelty—and the term is often applied misleadingly, sometimes derogatorily—it is because it is continually exploring new facets of the social past, generating many of the topics and responding to many of the new demands that now enliven historical research and teaching. It can be argued, however, that social history is most frequently termed "new" because of a continued uncertainty about its place in the broader historical discipline in the United States, and that the label frequently misses the mark. "Newness" in social history refers most obviously to the use by some social historians of concepts from other social sciences, and, above all, the enthusiasm for quantitative methods. Among some historians, in fact, quantitative history is social history by definition, though the methodology has captured only some facets of social history and is more widely used with political and economic data,[16] save in such areas of social history as demography and social mobility studies. Social historians cannot, in fact, point to a distinctive or uniform methodology.

As well as inquiring into what is American about social history in the United States, then, I shall examine what is new about it. This inquiry will lead us, finally, into a discussion of a characteristic, though still developing, debate over fundamentals among American practitioners, a debate that embraces both methodology and conceptualization.

15. See Lasch, *Haven,* 219, for the comment on the restrictive approach of the "new" social history.
16. Thus the new journal *Social Science History,* heavily quantitative in its orientation, has not manifested a primary or even largely sociohistorical focus; see also Robert Fogel, "The Limits of Quantitative Methods in History," *American Historical Review,* LXXX (1975), 329-350.

Although social history was being written in the United States before 1960, in diverse efforts to describe the behavior and material culture of large numbers of people under the impact of industrialization and urbanization and in discussions of the immigrant experience,[17] a wave of new interest began to swell during the 1960s. The new enthusiasm was not based on a conception of social history as a catch-all category for those subjects that other kinds of history left out. It was fueled, certainly, by the desire to deal historically with topics, such as the family, ordinarily left to sociology; but the primary impulse was twofold, as was evident in the eye-catching work of the students of early American history. First, in a memorable phrase, history was to be seen "from the bottom up," through the experiences and perceptions of ordinary rather than extraordinary actors in the past.[18] The clearest general definition of social history in the United States focuses on its concern with the general membership of a society, and not just individuals among the elite. Second, not only the mass of people but also the framework of their daily lives—their families, artifacts, community life, their births and deaths—was to be studied in order to fill out the historical characterization of a period.

Both of these impulses, which led social historians to new subject matter, also spurred them to connect their findings with more conventional historical topics. Radical historians, for example, were at pains to show that ordinary people had political sentiments of their own that were in turn important factors in the political history of the day. Protest history, seen as a statement of the motives of the participants and not just as a narrative of events, was an early interest here. Those who sought in social history the means of completing a portrait of a period, beyond the findings of strictly political or intellectual history, could try to show the relationship of ordinary property transactions or parent-child contacts to larger religious developments or to political events. Thus Philip Greven used an evaluation of the changing economic relationships between New England fathers and sons as a

17. Marcus Lee Hanson, *The Immigrant in American History* (New York, 1939); Oscar Handlin, *The Uprooted* (Boston, 1951) and *Boston's Immigrants* (New York, 1972). Handlin's influence in forming the interests if not the approach of younger American social historians deserves special note.

18. Jesse Lemisch, "The American Revolution Seen from the Bottom Up," in Barton Bernstein, ed., *Towards a New Past: Dissenting Essays in American History* (New York, 1968), 3–45. See also Pauline Maier, *From Resistance to Revolution: Colonial Radicals and the Development of American Opposition to Britain, 1765–1776* (New York, 1972); Jeffrey Kaplow, *The Names of Kings: Parisian Laboring Poor in the Eighteenth Century* (New York, 1973).

new vantage point from which to evaluate motives for the American revolution.[19]

Embedded in both approaches, and apparent in subsequent work, was a desire not only to extend the relevant range of historical causation—to include popular belief systems, for example—but also to apply more rigorous causal, correlative, or other tests to widely known social processes and mechanisms. A concern for greater precision in social analysis marked the field from its inception; a new set of historical narratives was not the main point.

### SOCIAL HISTORY AND THE COMMON PEOPLE

The "history from the bottom up" approach, shorn sometimes of its initial political implications, has most clearly been directed toward defining an ongoing orientation of social history in the United States. A litmus test for the success of sociohistorical inquiry is whether it adequately conveys the experiences of the people being characterized, independently of (though not necessarily in opposition to) the activities of dominant institutions or the canons of high culture. The approach has led to particular interest in certain lower-class groups, such as slaves, servants, and the industrial working class. It has defined the sociohistorical component of investigations in black history and women's history. Each of these subjects initially commanded a great deal of attention from practitioners of political and intellectual history, whether defined as such or not; biographies of exemplars of the group were followed by discussions of policies directed at the group and ideas that related the group to the larger society. Quite decisively in the case of black history,[20] more tentatively in women's history,[21] social historians changed the orientation, moving toward an

19. Greven, *Four Generations.*
20. The imposing array of work in this area includes Eugene D. Genovese, *Roll, Jordan, Roll: The World the Slaves Made* (New York, 1974); John Blassingame, *The Slave Community: Plantation Life in the Antebellum South* (New York, 1972); Herbert Gutman, *The Black Family in Slavery and Freedom* (New York, 1976).
21. Louise Tilly and Joan Scott, *Women, Work, and Family* (New York, 1978); Patricia Branca, *Silent Sisterhood: Middle-Class Women in the Victorian Home* (Pittsburgh, 1975); Theresa McBride, *The Domestic Revolution: The Modernization of Household Service in England and France, 1820–1920* (New York, 1976); Richard Stites, *The Women's Liberation Movement in Russia: Feminism, Nihilism, and Bolshevism, 1860–1930* (Princeton, 1978); William Chafe, *Women and Equality* (New York, 1977); Nancy Cott, *The Bonds of Womanhood: Woman's Sphere in New England, 1780–1835* (New Haven, 1977); Peter Filene, *Him/Herself: Sex Roles in Modern America* (New York, 1974); Carl Degler, "What Ought to Be and What Was: Women's Sexuality in the Nineteenth Century," *American Historical Review*, LXXIX (1974), 1469–90.

*Peter N. Stearns*

analysis of the life and outlook of the whole group or definable segments of it and testing policies and ideas by their relevance to this analysis. Ideas about race thus became part of the history of slaveholding, which in turn became a part of the history of being a slave. Similarly, in what has been called the "new" labor history, workers are examined directly, rather than through the medium of labor organizations,[22] and a "new urban history" was proclaimed,[23] less decisively, to study the people who actually lived in cities, rather than urban artifacts or administration per se. Labor history, or working-class history, continues its difficult task of examining workers in situations other than protest, apart from and sometimes opposed to labor movements, while also reintegrating labor organizations and classic surges of unrest into this expanded framework.[24] Social historians of the city have focused particularly on measurements and explanations of social mobility, following the pioneering work of Stephan Thernstrom.

The same test is also being applied to a variety of institutional areas. The history of mental illness has thus moved from ideas about mental illness to the dominant assumptions of mental institutions and on, still tentatively, to the actual workings of these institutions and the characteristics of their clientele. Each successive approach has involved new kinds of source material as well as more fully sociohistorical vantage points.[25] A social history of medicine is being sketched that involves

22. Herbert Gutman, *Work, Culture, and Society in Industrializing America* (New York, 1976); Peter N. Stearns, *Lives of Labor: Work in a Maturing Industrial Society* (New York, 1975). See also the essays in Stearns and Daniel Walkowitz, eds., *Workers in the Industrial Revolution: Recent Studies of Labor in the United States and Europe* (New Brunswick, N.J., 1974).

23. Stephan Thernstrom and Richard Sennett, eds., *Nineteenth-Century Cities: Essays in the New Urban History* (New Haven, 1969); Michael D. Katz, *The People of Hamilton, Canada West: Family and Class in a Mid-Nineteenth-Century City* (Cambridge, Mass., 1975); Stuart Blumin, *The Urban Threshold: Growth and Change in a Nineteenth-Century American Community* (Chicago, 1976). An emerging sociohistorical approach to urban history may be seen in the effort to relate architectural developments to social structure and social values; for example, Donald Olsen, *The Growth of Victorian London* (New York, 1976).

24. The list of relevant works here is lengthy: see among others David Montgomery, "Workers' Control of Machine Production in the Nineteenth Century," *Labor History*, XVII (1976), 485–509; Daniel Rodgers, *The Work Ethic in Industrial America, 1850–1920* (Chicago, 1978); John Bodnar, *Immigration and Industrialization: Ethnicity in an American Mill Town* (Pittsburgh, 1977); Alan Dawley, *The Industrial Revolution in Lynn* (Cambridge, Mass., 1976); Daniel Walkowitz, *Worker City, Company Town: Iron and Cotton Worker Protest in Troy and Cohoes, New York, 1855–84* (Urbana, Ill., 1978); Joan Scott, *The Glassworkers of Carmaux* (Cambridge, Mass., 1974); Standish Meacham, *A Life Apart: The English Working Class, 1890–1914* (Cambridge, Mass., 1977).

25. George Rosen, *Madness in Society: Chapters in the Historical Sociology of Mental Illness* (New York, 1968); Gerald Grob, *Mental Institutions in America: Social Policy to 1865* (New York, 1973); David Rothman, *The Discovery of the Asylum: Social Order and Disorder in the New Republic* (Boston, 1971); Jamil S. Zainaldin and Peter Tyor, "Asylum and

consideration of the impact of actual medical practices on the client population and the interaction of popular expectations about medicine with the behavior of medical practitioners.[26] A sociohistorical approach to the history of science involves not only the resonance of scientific ideas among a broader public but also the causal role that popular assumptions and demands play in the development of scientific thinking and scientific institutions.[27] The same sort of thing may be said of more scattered American efforts in the social history of religion,[28] recreation,[29] education,[30] and to a more limited extent military institutions have also been examined sociohistorically, with a view toward establishing a potentially reciprocal interchange between organizational complex and high culture on the one hand and client groups on the other. Increasingly also, mediating elements are being considered as a formal part of this interchange: doctors and teachers have their own histories, partially separate from those of institutional mandates and not circumscribed by an unduly rigid model of professionalization that ignored the initiatives of individuals who served as intermediaries between professional ideologies and the recipients of services.[31]

Society: An Approach to Institutional Change," *Journal of Social History*, XIII (1979); Richard W. Fox, *So Far Disordered in Mind: Insanity in California, 1870–1930* (Berkeley, 1979).

26. Linda Gordon, *Woman's Body, Woman's Right: A Social History of Birth Control in America* (New York, 1976); John S. Haller and Robin M. Haller, *Physician and Sexuality in Victorian America* (Urbana, Ill., 1974); *Journal of Social History*, x:4 (1977) (issue on medicine); Harvey Mitchell, "Rationality and Control in French Eighteenth-Century Medical Views of the Peasantry," *Comparative Studies in Society and History*, XXI (1979), 82–112.

27. Morris Berman, *Social Change and Scientific Organization: The Royal Institution, 1799–1844* (Ithaca, N.Y., 1978); Herbert Leventhal, *In the Shadow of the Enlightenment: Occultism and Renaissance Science in Eighteenth-Century America* (New York, 1976).

28. A. N. Galpern, *The Religions of the People in Sixteenth-Century Champagne* (Cambridge, Mass., 1976); Paul E. Johnson, *A Shopkeeper's Millennium: Society and Revivals in Rochester, New York, 1815–1837* (New York, 1978); Harry S. Stout and Robert Taylor, "Sociology, Religion, and Historians Revisited: Towards an Historical Sociology of Religion," *Historical Methods Newsletter*, VIII (1974), 29–38.

29. Michael Marrus, *The Rise of Leisure in Industrial Society* (St. Louis, 1974); Robert Storch, "The Policeman as Domestic Missionary: Urban Discipline and Popular Culture in Northern England, 1850–1880," *Journal of Social History*, IX (1976), 480–509.

30. Lawrence Stone, ed., *Schooling and Society* (Baltimore, 1976); Fritz Ringer, *Education and Society in Modern Europe* (Bloomington, Ind., 1979); Thomas W. Laqueur, *Religion and Respectability: Schools and Working-Class Culture, 1780–1850* (New Haven, 1976); Janet Wilkie, "Social Status, Acculturation, and School Attendance in 1850 Boston," *Journal of Social History*, XI (1977), 179–192; Selwyn Troen, *The Public and the Schools: Shaping the St. Louis System, 1838–1920* (Columbia, Mo., 1975).

31. Paul Mattingly, *The Classless Profession: American Schoolmen in the Nineteenth Century* (New York, 1975); M. Jeanne Peterson, *The Medical Profession in Mid-Victorian London* (Berkeley, 1978).

An important group of American social historians, working primarily on the nineteenth century, has used a model of social control as a means of cutting through the complexities in this nexus of relationships.[32] A social-control model can allow institutional studies and records of the blandishments of administrators to serve as statements of impact on the affected population. It can also explain situations in which a lower-class group does not respond to an imposed policy with protest. Social-control approaches have been used with particular success in histories of education and of custodial institutions, considerably revising conventional assumptions that the beneficence of reform-minded administrators could be taken for granted—that education, for example, can be seen primarily as a means of social advancement. Rather, the focus is placed on a clash of cultures, of classes or ethnic groups, with the client group not simply clay in the hands of kindly administrative molders. The social-control model is typically used to get behind the facade of upper-class rhetoric and assumptions of social homogeneity or a unified American character.

In its best applications, the concept of social control has advanced the effort toward increased precision in the analysis of historical causation. It has frequently implied a radical critique of American or other capitalist institutions, although, of course, one can grant some of the premises of the approach and still defend both the intentions behind and the results of some kinds of manipulation by institutions in periods of extensive social conflict. Few of the social-control studies, however, have had a larger ideological perspective. Marxist models have appeared in American social history in slightly different contexts, most fully in studies of slavery, where they have been developed with great sophistication to allow simultaneous consideration of slaves and their masters, and to explain through an adaptation of the Gramscian theory of hegemony the relative quiescence of the slave population. The work of Eugene Genovese, most notably, is concerned with a total culture, enmeshing dominator and dominated alike, elaborating the life and outlook of slaves without pretending that they were the prime determinants of their own history.[33]

32. David Tyack, *The One Best System: A History of American Urban Education* (Cambridge, Mass., 1974); Michael B. Katz, *Class, Bureaucracy, and the Schools: The Illusion of Educational Change in America* (New York, 1975) and *The Irony of Early School Reform: Educational Innovation in Mid-Nineteenth-Century Massachusetts* (Boston, 1970); Anthony Platt, *The Child Savers: The Invention of Delinquency* (Chicago, 1969).

33. Eugene D. Genovese, *The Political Economy of Slavery* (New York, 1965) and "Marxist Interpretations of the Slave South," in Bernstein, ed., *Towards A New Past*, 123; Eugene D. Genovese and Elizabeth Fox-Genovese, "The Political Crisis of Social History," *Journal of Social History*, x (1977), 205-220; see also Sanford Elwitt, *The Making of the Third Republic: Chaos and Politics in France, 1868-1884* (Baton Rouge,

Neither the hegemonist nor the less ambitious social-control approach, however, has been typical of sociohistorical analysis of social structure or of key social groups. Generally, American social historians have related their interest in ordinary people to a belief in at least semi-independent, identifiable subcultures that allow popular groups some independent basis for reaction to larger systems and processes. Social-control analysis of education and even of asylums has been criticized for failing to include an examination of the client population or of intermediate professionals as partially autonomous actors, capable of evasion, adaptation, or outright influence in their own perceived interest.[34] Save in some of the slavery studies and some analyses of the European working class, a Marxist stratification model has not predominated. An interesting group of studies of urban elites has appeared, for example, which does not use a rigorous class conceptualization.[35]

Indeed, a great deal of the American contribution to social history has to do with detailing and explaining the adaptations of major elements in society to dominant processes and structures. Protest that dwindled away or that did not occur is almost as common a focus, even in studies of working-class groups, as protest that surged; and a considerable amount of inquiry is devoted to areas in which lower-class groups did exert some control over their own lives. The problem of the stillbirth of socialism in the United States has given way, for example, to examinations of workers' family and community structures as the best means of understanding the social history of American labor.[36]

A concentration on protests that aborted or a consideration of life apart from protest is an almost inevitable outgrowth of the American political experience. Both the social-control and the hegemonist approaches focus on a major adaptive process, seeking among other

---

1975). Walkowitz, *Worker City, Company Town,* applies something of a hegemonic model to working-class history.

34. William Muraskin, "The Social-Control Theory in American History: A Critique," *Journal of Social History,* IX (1976), 559-569.

35. Frederic C. Jaher, ed., *The Rich, the Well-Born, and the Powerful* (Urbana, Ill., 1973); John Ingham, *The Iron Barons: A Social Analysis of an American Elite* (Westport, Conn., 1978). Some interest continues in colonial social structure: Gary Nash, *Class and Society in Early America* (Englewood Cliffs, N.J., 1970). Work on Europe includes Fritz Ringer, *The Decline of the German Mandarins* (Cambridge, Mass., 1969); James Sheehan, "Conflict and Coherence among German Elites in the Nineteenth Century," in R. J. Bezucha, ed., *Modern European Social History* (Lexington, Mass., 1972); Peter N. Stearns, *Paths to Authority: The Middle Class and the Industrial Labor Force in France, 1820-48* (Urbana, Ill., 1978).

36. See, however, John Laslett, *Labor and the Left* (New York, 1970).

things to explain lower-class behavior in terms of domination or cooptation. Both do so also without emphasis on material deprivation as a major explanatory factor. Comparative sociohistorical analysis has reduced a purely materialistic approach to quiescence, particularly in the case of slavery in the southern states. But other studies seek to take adaptation in a more positive sense, to include acceptance of institutional and cultural impositions while also preserving elements of indigenous class or group structures and values. The long-standing fascination with ethnic cohesion has blossomed with the new attention to groups traditionally held to be inarticulate and has become a major factor in explanations of working-class behavior, social mobility rates, and demographic patterns. Ethnicity, summing up a host of shared values and institutions that could coexist with larger structures of power, has become a central focus of American social history and an alternative to the kind of class analysis that seizes on social confrontations or their frustration.[37] Examination of family networks, extending now into the nineteenth century, has served much the same purpose, explaining how groups could sustain themselves materially and even spiritually without regularly confronting the power hierarchy astride them.[38] "History from the bottom up" most definitely describes these inquiries, but now groups at society's lower reaches are deemed to have powers to shape their subcultures and nonpolitical behavior, to serve as determining forces in the realms that they themselves might hold most important.

## MODERNIZATION AS A FRAMEWORK
### FOR SOCIAL HISTORY

For some American social historians, a concern for adaptation, for an explanation of a mutual interaction among social groups, institutions, and ideas, has been written in even larger terms. One or

37. Virginia Yans-McLaughlin, *Family and Community: Italian Immigrants in Buffalo, 1880–1920* (Ithaca, N.Y., 1977); Leonard Dinnerstein et al., *Natives and Strangers: Ethnic Groups and the Building of America* (New York, 1979).
38. Family history, which joins a number of strands of American social history, also well illustrates the quest to merge historical with social-scientific categories in various areas and periods of time, and the steady refinement of conceptual approach. On the nineteenth century specifically, see Tamara Hareven, ed., *Family Transitions and the Life Course in Historical Perspective* (New York, 1979), and Hareven and Maris Vinovskis, eds., *Family and Population in Nineteenth-Century America* (Princeton, 1979). See also Vinovskis, "From Household Size to the Life Course: Some Observations on Recent Trends in Family History," *American Behavioral Scientist*, XXI (1977), 263–288, and David Herlihy and Christiane Klapisch-Zuber, *Les Toscans et leurs familles: Une étude du catasto florentin de 1427* (Paris, 1978).

another of the models of historical modernization developed initially in American sociology has attracted, or at least influenced, a considerable body of social historians in the United States. These models have quintessentially American traits: rather loose and superficially non-ideological, focusing on unifying rather than socially divisive processes, purposeful, often optimistic.

Much of modernization theory, certainly, remains nonhistorical and some applications of the theory, even in history, emphasize political and economic structures[39]—at most a framework for social history—rather than the behavior and culture of definable groups of people. It is important to stress as well that modernization theory (though not primarily in its sociohistorical uses) has been roundly criticized, most cogently in its application to non-Western areas, where its ethnocentrism is faulted, but also as a descriptive or explanatory model in the study of Western history, for which it is held somewhat more vaguely to be too loose or too teleological.[40] By no means can a modernization approach be regarded as dominant in United States social history; for this reason the theory is more often brushed aside than refuted. Even its users do not agree as to whether the concept merely serves as a convenient summary of familiar structural processes—merging, for example, industrialization, urbanization, and expansion of the state bureaucracy into a single package—or whether it goes further to describe social change—in popular outlook, for example.[41] Social history certainly offers no definitive statement of a model.

Yet references to modernization and some serious use of a model appear in a host of efforts by American social historians. A modernization concept has been applied to family history, the history of sexuality, the history of nineteenth-century crime, the history of

39. Cyril Black, *The Dynamics of Modernization* (New York, 1966).

40. Hans-Ulrich Wehler, *Modernisierungstheorie und Geschichte* (Gottingen, 1975); Raymond Grew, "Modernization and Its Discontents," *American Behavioral Scientist*, XXI (1977), 289–312; Joseph Gusfield, "Tradition and Modernity: Misplaced Polarities in the Study of Social Change," *American Journal of Sociology*, LXXII (1967), 351–362; Dean C. Tipps, "Modernization Theory and the Comparative Study of Societies: A Critical Perspective," *Comparative Studies in Society and History*, XV (1973), 199–227.

41. John Gillis, *The Development of European Society, 1770–1870* (New York, 1977); Peter N. Stearns, *European Society in Upheaval* (New York, 1975) and *The Other Side of Western Civilization*, vol. II (New York, 1979); Richard D. Brown, *Modernization: The Transformation of American Life* (New York, 1976). Important specialized uses of modernization are Eugen Weber, *Peasants into Frenchmen: The Modernization of Rural France, 1870–1914* (Stanford, 1976); Mack Walker, *German Home Towns: Community, State, and General Estate, 1648–1871* (Ithaca, N.Y., 1971); Lawrence Schofer, *The Formation of a Modern Labor Force: Upper Silesia, 1865–1914* (Berkeley, 1975).

old age, and women's history—though in none of these areas has it won unqualified approval, and in most, ad hoc models have dominated or no models have been offered at all.[42] The idea of modernization, if only as a summary of broad economic and political processes, continues to be a fairly standard reference point in American work on Eastern European social history, and it has by no means been exorcised from analyses of Asia and Latin America. Most recently, important work on European and American social history in the seventeenth and eighteenth centuries has not only invoked the concept but expanded its definition to include substantial changes in popular mentality and, even more strikingly, a distinctive level of popular emotionality.[43] The effort to date a modernization phenomenon and to explain and define it in sociohistorical terms gives new life to the concept, just as does its application to categories of human experience quite remote from initial social-scientific formulations. Although modernization theory does not define American social history, even for those who do not labor in medieval or non-Western vineyards, it is a recurrent concern, calling for at least casual derision from those who eschew it and organizing at least a conceptual substructure for its diverse users.

## THE EXPLOSION OF SOCIOHISTORICAL TOPICS

The most striking contributions of American social history, while they do not as yet relate to a broad synthesis or center around any particular model, do follow from the determination to see in social history more than a detailing of class stratification and its attendant conflicts. The American contributions relate certainly to the impulse to seek ways to approach history other than from the top down, though they go beyond this precept. They consist of the expansion— extraordinarily rapid during recent years—of sociohistorical inquiry into an unprecedentedly wide range of social groupings and activities, the proliferation of angles of vision on a social experience whose totality is only rarely—by a few Marxists, a few Braudelians, perhaps a

42. Edward Shorter, *The Making of the Modern Family* (New York, 1975); Howard Zehr, *Crime and the Development of Modern Society* (Totowa, N.J., 1976); Patricia Branca, "A New Perspective on Women's Work: A Comparative Typology," *Journal of Social History*, IX (1975), 129–153; W. Andrew Achenbaum and Peter N. Stearns, "Modernization and the History of Old Age," *Gerontologist*, XVIII (1978), 307–313; Roger Lane, "Crime and the Industrial Revolution: British and American Views," *Journal of Social History*, VII (1974), 287–303.
43. Lawrence Stone, *The Family, Sex, and Marriage in England, 1500–1800* (New York, 1977); Randolph Trumbach, *The Rise of the Egalitarian Family* (New York, 1979).

handful of modernization theorists—seen as encompassable. This topical expansion has been accompanied by a diversification of methodology, most notably in the introduction of quantitative methods, although recently some hesitation has been expressed about their range and implications.

There are several reasons for the topical expansion, which has its analogues outside North America. Consideration of group histories, other than those of the social classes, has often been impelled by political pressures. Black history and women's history, though not exclusively sociohistorical domains, have been the focuses of some of the most imaginative research and sophisticated conceptualization in the field. Concern with the young as a social group and with youth as a phase of the life cycle, though less well developed, was obviously fed by the turmoil of the 1960s, which also contributed to a more pervasive interest in generational relations in history. Taking ethnicity, gender, and age as criteria for social grouping has added depth and complexity to the American approach to the study of society, and a key inducement to using them in this way has been the emphasis they have received in contemporary society; the concomitance of the rising consciousness of ethnic and gender groupings and the growing interest in a sociohistorical approach, though in part coincidental, has reinforced both. Once launched, the study of the role of groupings other than by social class can develop its own momentum, as in examinations of ethnicity among white workers or the history of the elderly.[44] Sociohistorical consideration of facets of human life and social behavior ranging from crime to family to death also relates to contemporary American concerns about ways to measure the health of society, a virtual obsession with social temperature-taking that appears in the popular media as well as the social sciences. Christopher Lasch has used study of the American family, leisure practices, and the like to raise a persuasive lament for a society in serious decay; some of the more specifically topical social history may also follow from a growing uneasiness about basic features of American life or life in general.[45] Many social historians have also tried to reproduce in historical inquiry the range of topics developed in sociology, while

44. David Hackett Fischer, *Growing Old in America* (New York, 1977); W. Andrew Achenbaum, *Old Age in the New World: The American Experience since 1780* (Baltimore, 1979). A broader concern for generations in history can be traced in Robert Wohl, *The Generation of 1914: Its Myths and Its History* (Cambridge, Mass., 1979); and the issue devoted to "Generations in Historical Perspective," *Daedalus*, CVII (1978), 53-150, though the articles in this collection deal more with intellectual than with social history.
45. Lasch, *Culture of Narcissism*. The convergence on the family as a central topic for American social historians, whose initial concerns range from demography through

some sociologists have joined the effort in order to give a historical anchor to the overly abstract models of some practitioners in their discipline. Yet the proliferation of studies of aspects of social behavior stems primarily from the dynamics of social history itself. With rare exceptions, American social historians have shied away from the awesome task of dealing with the total history of a society. Rather, they approach the subject through examination of groups of people or of phases of experience. The result lacks an overall conceptualization, but does collectively move toward an ever wider embrace of the segments of totality.

The steady development of topical subfields thus marks social history in the United States and defines much of its taste for novelty. The subfields include, of course, some well-established entries, such as demography, which were of historical concern even before the recent surge of social history.[46] They include some newer specialties, notably the family, which have already come to be central to many American social historians and relevant to almost all. But significant formal or informal groups of historians, steadily developing both methodology and conceptualization, are also at work on histories of crime,[47] sexual-

---

social protest, relates in part, surely, to the particularly troubled state of the contemporary American family.

46. A great deal of American work (mainly by economists and demographers rather than by historians per se) has gone into the question of the nature and extent of fertility decline before 1890 and, to a lesser extent, mortality rates in the nineteenth century. The approach seeks a description of trends and usually a correlation with economic factors, including land availability. See Maris Vinovskis, "Recent Trends in American Historical Demography," *American Review of Sociology*, XLVII (1978), and *Studies in American Demography* (New York, 1978); Richard A. Easterlin, "Population Issues and American Economic History: A Survey and Critique," *Research in Economic History*, supplement 1 (1977), 131–158, and *Population, Labor Force, and Long Swings in Economic Growth* (New York, 1968); Edward Meeker, "The Improving Health of the United States, 1850–1950," *Explorations in Economic History*, IX (1972), 353–374; Robert Higgs, "Mortality in Rural America, 1870: Estimates and Conjectures," *Explorations in Economic History*, X (1973), 177–195; C. Forster and G. S. L. Tucker, *Economic Opportunity and White American Fertility Ratios* (New Haven, 1972); Charles Tilly, ed., *Historical Studies of Changing Fertility* (Princeton, 1979); Louis Kantrow and Etienne Van de Walle, "Historical Demography vs. Demographic History," *Population Index*, XL (1974), 611–623; Richard A. Easterlin and others, "Farms and Farm Families in Old and New Areas: The Northern States in 1860," in Hareven and Vinovskis, eds., *Family and Population*. Early American demography, done more commonly by historians, uses sketchier sources and, often, less elaborate quantitative methods; it is also frequently related to issues of family life as well as factors of economy and land: Daniel Scott Smith and M. S. Hindus, "Premarital Pregnancy in America, 1640–1971," *Journal of Interdisciplinary History*, v (1975), 537–570; Robert V. Wells, "Family Size and Fertility Control in Eighteenth-Century America: A Study of Quaker Families," *Population Studies*, XXV (1971), 78–82, and *The Population of the British Colonies in America before 1776* (Princeton, 1975).

47. Hugh Graham and Ted Gurr, eds., *Violence in America* (New York, 1970) (this book also represents an effort to use social history as part of a policy-relevant analysis);

ity,[48] leisure,[49] education, social mobility,[50] and work. Anthologies are appearing in a number of these areas and journals exist in a few. The topical list promises to grow as additional facets of social behavior are subjected to historical scrutiny; the social history of health[51] and that of death,[52] for example, are clearly burgeoning fields.

Topical varieties of social history are characterized, of course, by a diligent search for appropriate new sources of data. In some cases, the search for facts still seems to overwhelm attention to generalization or theory. Efforts are usually made, however, simultaneously to apply and to test social science models drawn often from anthropology as well as sociology, and to compare results with those of other historical inquiries. The concern is less for the fit of the topic into conventional historical periods (the effects of the Renaissance spirit on crime, for example)—though such conformity may be an intended by-product of research—than for a greatly expanded sense of typologies that will enhance the understanding of the phenomenon itself. Typologies

Eric Monkkonen, *The Dangerous Classes: Crime and Poverty in Columbus, Ohio, 1860–1885* (Cambridge, Mass., 1975); Cockburn, ed., *Crime in England;* Roger Lane, *Violent Death: The Social Significance of Suicide, Accident, and Murder in Nineteenth-Century Philadelphia* (Cambridge, Mass., 1979).

48. Edward Shorter, "Illegitimacy, Sexual Revolution, and Social Change in Modern Europe," *Journal of Interdisciplinary History*, II (1971), 237–272; Cissie Fairchilds, "Female Sexual Attitudes and the Rise of Illegitimacy: A Case Study," *Journal of Interdisciplinary History*, VIII (1978), 627–668; Randolph Trumbach, "London's Sodomites: Homosexual Behavior and Western Culture in the Eighteenth Century," *Journal of Social History*, XI (1977), 1–33; R. P. Neuman, "Birth Control in Wilhelmine Germany," *Comparative Studies in Society and History*, XXI (1978), 408–428, and "Industrialization and Sexual Behavior: Some Aspects of Working-Class Life in Imperial Germany," in Bezucha, ed., *Modern European Social History*, 270–298.

49. John Lucas and Ronald A. Smith, *The Saga of American Sport* (Philadelphia, 1978); Benjamin G. Rader, "Modern Sports: In Search of Interpretations," *Journal of Social History*, XIII (1979).

50. Stephan Thernstrom, *Poverty and Progress: Social Mobility in a Nineteenth-Century City* (Cambridge, Mass., 1964) and *The Other Bostonians;* Chudacoff, *Mobile Americans;* for growing methodological sophistication see Michael P. Weber and Anthony E. Boardman, "Economic Growth and Occupational Mobility in Nineteenth-Century Urban America: A Reappraisal," *Journal of Social History*, XI (1977), 52–74.

51. William McNeill, *Plagues and People* (New York, 1976); Elizabeth Etheridge, *The Butterfly Caste: A Social History of Pellagra in the South* (Westport, Conn., 1972); Andrew B. Appleby, "Nutrition and Disease: The Case of London, 1550–1750," *Journal of Interdisciplinary History*, VI (1975), 1–22; Robert Gottfried, *Epidemic Disease in Fifteenth-Century England* (New Brunswick, N.J., 1978); Kenneth F. Kiple and Virginia H. Kiple, "Slave Child Mortality: Some Nutritional Answers to a Perennial Puzzle," *Journal of Social History*, X (1977), 284–309; Phillips Cutright and Edward Shorter, "The Effects of Health on Completed Fertility of Nonwhite and White U.S. Women Born from 1867 through 1935," *Journal of Social History*, XIII (1979).

52. Charles O. Jackson, ed., *Passing: The Vision of Death in America* (Westport, Conn., 1977); David Stannard, *The Puritan Way of Death* (New York, 1977); David Stannard, ed., *Death in America* (Philadelphia, 1976).

Peter N. Stearns

include factors of region and period, of course, thus preserving an important historical component, but there is little hesitation in using social science models and other historical findings to expand the scope of generalization as well as to isolate peculiarities through comparison. Family history thus regularly tests for structure (nuclear vs. extended), whether in twelfth-century France or the nineteenth-century United States. In this sense not only the questions and analytical issues but also a good bit of the conceptual approach of topical social history is akin to work in the social sciences. The range of topical facets plus the concern for a high level of generalization form the most pervasively novel feature of social history in the United States.

Topical social history has an inherently centrifugal tendency. The topical approach thus not only reflects a lack of broader conceptualization but also positively hinders the development of an appropriate sociohistorical periodization, sometimes even periodization for a single topic. A period is often demarcated according to quite conventional political or intellectual history criteria, without real testing of its applicability to the subject at hand. Here is a pressing analytical task for the future. A concentration on data and generalization within a single topic, plus the development of specific methodologies for handling the data, can produce an isolation combined with a technical complexity that converts a subfield into a discrete field of its own. Some observers regard American social history as a half-dozen separate enterprises (such as the study of the family, of social mobility, and of protest) linked only in the loosest way by concern for the everyday experiences of ordinary people. Historical demography has threatened to become a terra incognita for the general run of social historians, largely because of its high level of quantification but also because of a certain delight taken by some of its practitioners in demographic data for their own sake, in substantial isolation from other aspects of social development.[53]

Even here, however, the splintering is far from complete. Many topical historians have feet in more than one topical camp. Thus many demographers have progressed to a concern with family structure, material conditions, and even values and attitudes, seeing a broader approach as vital to the pursuit of answers to questions about the causation of demographic change, while others use demographic

53. Etienne Van de Walle, *The Female Population of France in the Nineteenth Century* (Princeton, 1974); John E. Knodel, *The Decline of Fertility in Germany, 1871–1939* (Princeton, 1974); Ron J. Lesthaege, *The Decline of Belgian Fertility, 1800–1970* (Princeton, 1977).

data to pose questions about developments in other aspects of life. Furthermore, most topical social historians share a concern for broader social processes, seeing their topic as one facet of an analysis of the social components and impact of large political and economic trends. Use of modernization or hegemony theory can bridge topical gaps. So can concern for testing correlation or causation across subject lines: crime rates and protest rates, for example, or work behavior and the leisure ethic. Topical studies of social mobility, though they have not been entirely exempt from a tendency toward self-containment, obviously demand attention to larger social structure and cultural values. It is true that the pervasive topical approach hinders social historians in the awesome task of constructing total social histories, but the field has by no means been fragmented beyond the prospect of bridging generalizations.

### QUANTITATIVE AND QUALITATIVE APPROACHES

Much of the early research in topical social history relied heavily on quantitative techniques. They were more used in some subfields than others—more in black and working-class history, for example, than in women's or age-group history, which depended more on cultural and institutional materials. Historical demographers were the most obvious users of numerical data. Historical demography has been steadily improving its quantitative methods, not only advancing in accuracy of description but raising the level of interpretation. Thus Thomas McKeown reevaluates the causes of modern Western population growth, rejecting earlier explanations on methodological grounds and emphasizing nutrition.[54] The quantitative emphasis and its sophistication also increased in social mobility studies and, to the extent that data permitted, entered into analysis of crime. Most protest history continued to rely largely on qualitative techniques, but in an exceptionally ambitious undertaking, still in process though it has already given rise to a major work on French strikes, Charles Tilly and various collaborators sought not only to organize descriptive data about protests on the basis of numerical characteristics but also to assess the causes of change in protest behavior and the composition of protest movements through correlation analysis.[55] Tilly and his collaborators have also worked on the general incidence of protest in

54. Thomas McKeown, *The Modern Rise of Population* (New York, 1976).
55. Charles Tilly and Edward Shorter, *Strikes in France, 1830–1968* (Cambridge, Eng., 1974).

Britain, France, and Germany, though here they have used general historical trends rather than quantifiable indices as correlates.[56] A quantitative approach, yielding somewhat different conclusions, has also been applied to British strike trends.[57]

Quantification has also been used by U.S. historians in family studies, particularly those concerned with the structural aspects of households, though on the whole with less enthusiasm than that exhibited by the Cambridge population studies group in England. One can likewise expect to see it widely employed in the social history of health. With time and improved training—several of the leading centers of training in quantification have been involved with social history, a summer program at the Newberry Library in Chicago quite heavily so—not only the range of application but also the sophistication of quantitative methodology has increased. Demographic and mobility studies especially can be held up as models of improvement by social science standards because change has resulted more from the application of new methods than from simple reinterpretation. A massive project in another area was Robert Fogel and Stanley Engerman's attempt to answer by quantitative means some of the most complex questions about the impact of slavery.[58]

On the whole, however, the union of social history with quantification remains incomplete. Many social historians have been disinclined to develop the relevant statistical skills. Some early advocates have turned hostile: Lawrence Stone writes of the need "to be more wary of quantification for the sake of quantification . . . to be passionately determined to combine both quantitative and qualitative data and methods as the only reliable way even to approach truth about so odd and unpredictable and irrational a creature as man."[59] Indeed, much of the expansion of social history's effective range of interests has taken directions that do not seem amenable primarily to quantitative analysis. Most social historians of slavery, for example, were not persuaded by the Fogel-Engerman effort, criticizing it at least on the

56. Charles Tilly, Louise Tilly, and Richard Tilly, *The Rebellious Century, 1830–1930* (Cambridge, Mass., 1975); see also Charles Tilly, *The Vendée* (New York, 1967); David Pinkney, *The French Revolution of 1830* (Princeton, 1972); Robert Bezucha, *The Lyons Revolt of 1834* (Cambridge, Mass., 1975).

57. James Cronin, "Theories of Strikes: Why Can't They Explain the British Experience?" *Journal of Social History,* XII (1978), 194–221; see also Jon Amsden and Stephen Brier, "Coal Miners on Strike: The Transformation of Strike Demands and the Formation of a National Union," *Journal of Interdisciplinary History,* VII (1977), 583–616.

58. Robert Fogel and Stanley Engerman, *Time on the Cross: The Economics of American Negro Slavery,* 2 vols. (Boston, 1974).

59. Lawrence Stone, "History and the Social Sciences in the Twentieth Century," in Charles Delzell, ed., *The Future of History* (Nashville, 1977), 39.

grounds that the data available thus far did not allow strictly quantitative answers to the most difficult interpretive problems and in some cases believing that key issues were not susceptible to thorough quantification even in principle.[60]

In general, historians have found quantification more useful in organizing data to raise vital questions for analysis than actually in providing such analysis. Historians of sexuality, for example, including some initially avid quantifiers, have found illegitimacy statistics most valuable in determining the chronological framework for change in sexual behavior and therefore in identifying the periods that should be investigated for changes in the emotional content of sexual behavior and the causes of such changes.[61] Students of social mobility, although more involved with the quantitative mode, have returned to problems that Stephan Thernstrom's initial study raised concerning the values by which the people affected and the larger society judged the mobility or lack of mobility that occurred (which can, locally at least, be measured).[62] Such historical demographers as Richard Easterlin have used data on birth-rate fluctuations to frame questions about modern motives in deciding whether to have children, and have found answers in the situation-cum-expectations of discrete generational cohorts, in the ways particular mentalities affect demographic behavior. Maris Vinovskis invokes a modernization of outlook as part of the apparatus he sees necessary to explain American demographic behavior during the late nineteenth century.[63] In studies of old age thus far, historians have rather explicitly decided against the primacy of demographic and economic (and thus measur-

60. Herbert Gutman, *Slavery and the Numbers Game: A Critique of "Time on the Cross"* (Urbana, Ill., 1975); Paul A. David and Peter Temin, "Slavery: The Progressive Institution?" *Journal of Economic History,* xxxiv (1974), 739–784.

61. Shorter, *Making of the Modern Family;* Filene, *Him/Herself;* Peter N. Stearns, *Be a Man!: Males in Modern Society* (New York, 1979).

62. Thernstrom, *Poverty and Progress;* recent work reopens the issue of the relationship between mobility and culture. Problems of the meaning of occupational distinctions are treated in Clyde Griffen and Sally Griffen, *Natives and Newcomers: The Ordering of Opportunity in Mid-Nineteenth-Century Poughkeepsie* (Cambridge, Mass., 1978); the community context is stressed in Peter R. Decker, *Fortunes and Failures: White-Collar Mobility in Nineteenth-Century San Francisco* (Cambridge, Mass., 1978).

63. Vinovskis, "Recent Trends," stresses the inadequacy of economic correlates and the need to integrate cultural factors into causal explanation; Richard Easterlin has raised new questions about the motivations behind birth-rate change in "The Conflict between Aspirations and Resources," paper delivered at the 1976 meeting of the Population Association of America; see also H. Leibenstein, "On Easterlin's Intergenerational Hypothesis: The Problem of Characterizing Aspirations," at the same meeting. Another exploration from an economic base is Robert V. Wells, "Family History and Demographic Transition," *Journal of Social History,* ix (1975), 1–20.

able) factors even as determinants of the organization of descriptive phenomena, favoring cultural factors instead,[64] though this preference may reflect the tentative first steps in a very new topical area. Certainly, most social historians are not choosing their topics or their analytical frameworks on the basis of the applicability of quantification. The field tolerates varying degrees of enthusiasm for and expertise in quantification, and in the main its members seem to operate on the principle of counting what is to be counted without being dissuaded from areas where counting does not yet yield much information.[65]

Indeed, if there is movement in the field with regard to quantification, it involves a bit of distancing. There is an increasing tendency to develop, or return to, a close relationship between social and cultural history.[66] The sociohistorical contribution to modernization theory, certainly, consists primarily of emphasis on changes in values and outlook. Genovese's elaboration of a hegemonic model of slave–slave owner relationships stressed cultural expressions. Many, though not all, of the newer additions to the list of sociohistorical topics involve some aspect of mentality: attitudes toward sports, or illness, or death. New efforts to combine the history of work and of family in local studies similarly aim at producing an understanding of working-class outlook. A growing interest in the findings and methods of anthropology, as opposed to quantitative sociology, follows and furthers the same ·trend. Natalie Davis, for example, in her work on early modern France, borrows from the perspective of anthropologists in seeking what Clifford Geertz has called a "thick description" of the multiple layers that form a culture.[67] And some Americans who call themselves social historians are sharing with others who call themselves intellectual historians a renewed interest in tracing the sometimes complex process of the dissemination of ideas in a wide social

64. Fischer, *Growing Old in America;* Achenbaum, *Old Age in the New World;* Peter N. Stearns, *Old Age in European Society* (New York, 1977).

65. Robert Fogel, "Cliometrics and Culture: Some Recent Developments in the Historiography of Slavery," *Journal of Social History,* XI (1977), 34–51, stresses, however, the power of quantification to stretch beyond its current topical limits in social history.

66. Diverse examples are Robert Wiebe, *The Segmented Society: An Introduction to the Meaning of America* (New York, 1975); Greven, *Protestant Temperament;* Weber, *Peasants into Frenchmen;* Robert Forster, "The 'World' between Seigneur and Peasant," *Studies in Eighteenth-Century Culture,* V (1976), 401–221; Natalie Z. Davis, *Society and Culture in Early Modern France* (Stanford, 1975).

67. Davis, *Society and Culture;* Clifford Geertz, *The Interpretation of Cultures* (New York, 1973), 10. Charles Tilly criticizes the turn to what he calls retrospective ethnography in "Sociology, Meet History," University of Michigan Center for Research on Social Organization, Working Paper no. 193 (Ann Arbor, 1979).

context. Social history is separated from intellectual history not only by its explicit concern for the popular resonance of ideas but also by its focus on popular belief systems, by its attention to the variety of sources and artifacts that evidence those belief systems, and by its interest in the interaction of mental attitudes and behavior. Nevertheless, their increasing range of shared interests may relate social historians to more conventional historical approaches in new ways. It can also lead them to a consideration of broad-gauged periodization on the basis of belief and behavior alike.[68]

There is both excitement and danger in this movement that goes beyond a concern for new, more "qualitative" topics in the attempt to grasp human life in the past, to a desire for sweeping interpretations of the basic character of past societies. Interpretive sweep, for example, replaces the earlier sociohistorical concern for methodology in Christopher Lasch's recent work and perhaps in the desire to trace the rise of a new kind of affectionate style in family and sexual life in early modern England. The new quest is exciting and provocative. But it can spin perilously close to a reliance on formal expressions of ideas and culture and the elite sources that offer the most available and dramatic evidence of large swings in social mood, so that the ordinary people who have been the stuff of social history either are forgotten or come to be viewed once again as an inert, uninteresting lump acted upon by their betters.[69] At the same time the new work may usefully challenge the cautious, ingrown quality of some of the narrow, topical social histories.

Certainly, issues remain to be debated, related to but broader than the choice of quantitative or qualitative emphasis. The concern for outlook or mental attitude relates social historians not only to cultural but also to psychological history, in intent if not usually in conceptual arsenal.[70] (One of the challenges of this approach is indeed to deter-

68. William Weber, *Music and the Middle Class* (London, 1975); Jack P. Greene, "Search for Identity: An Interpretation of the Meaning of Selected Patterns of Social Response in Eighteenth-Century America," *Journal of Social History*, III (1970), 189–219.

69. For relevant critiques see Peter N. Stearns, "*Haven in a Heartless World: The Family Besieged,* by Christopher Lasch," *Journal of Social History*, XI (1978), 426–430; Charles Tilly and Louise Tilly, "The Rise and Fall of the Bourgeois Family as Told by Lawrence Stone and Christopher Lasch," University of Michigan Center for Research on Social Organization, Working Paper no. 191 (Ann Arbor, 1979).

70. Greven, *Protestant Temperament;* David Hunt, *Parents and Children in History: The Psychology of Family Life in Early Modern France* (New York, 1970); Leslie Howard Owens, *This Species of Property: Slave Life and Culture in the Old South* (New York, 1976); Stone, *Family, Sex, and Marriage;* and Randolph Trumbach, "Europe and Its Families: A Review Essay," *Journal of Social History*, XIII (1979), illustrate relevant if not always decisive interest in sociohistorical utilization of psychology.

mine what is or can be made useful in psychological as well as sociological theory, a process already tentatively begun.) The turning of attention to the history of affective relationships, in terms of gender and generation as well as of family—perhaps the newest general development in American social history—directly raises questions of emotional as well as cultural causation. Other social historians remain more interested in behavior than in outlook, and seek to relate behavior in turn to objective, rational, and often measurable factors. Historical demographers, broadly construed, thus debate whether sexuality as an emotional characteristic enters into the causation of birth-rate changes.[71] Historians of protest dispute whether their subject is a rational and predictable reaction to objective circumstances in work and organizational opportunity or whether such emotions as anger must be added to the causation equation.[72] Debates of this sort can take place beneath such general theoretical umbrellas as modernization. They can divide students of a single sociohistorical topic, though they also tend to lead toward distinct topical emphases.

What is needed is an increasingly explicit debate over the motors of social behavior, necessarily dealing as well with the questions about periodization and priorities among causal forces that so far have largely been evaded. American social history has shown the possibility of some fundamental alterations in our perception of the mainsprings of social behavior in times past and is working out the empirical and theoretical apparatus to deal with them. Its sometimes inchoate groping for basic approach and its concomitant openness to new subject matter and methodological linkages keep the field fertile and exciting.

71. Tilly, ed., *Historical Studies of Changing Fertility,* Introduction.
72. Tilly and Shorter, *Strikes in France,* go beyond refutation of the frustration/ aggression explanation of strike patterns to attack the attachment of significance to any emotional component in striker behavior.

# 9

## *The New Political History*
## *in the 1970s*

### Allan G. Bogue

I

IN 1976 ten of the contributors to the bibliographical inventory *The Reinterpretation of American History and Culture* answered the question: "What do you consider to be the five books that have most influenced teaching and subsequent publication in American political history since the conclusion of World War II?" A broader group of specialists in American political history responded to the same inquiry during 1977.[1] The replies revealed considerable differences of opinion, as befits a profession in which many members prize nonconformity, but both groups suggested the same four authors and five books most frequently:

| Author and Title | Reinterpretation contributors (percent) | AHA Directory sample (percent) |
|---|---|---|
| Arthur M. Schlesinger, Jr. | | |
| *The Age of Jackson* (Boston, 1945) | 60% | 22% |
| Richard Hofstadter | | |
| *The American Political Tradition and the Men Who Made It* (New York, 1948) | 50 | 40 |
| *The Age of Reform: From Bryan to F.D.R.* (New York, 1955) | 50 | 40 |
| Lee Benson | | |
| *The Concept of Jacksonian Democracy: New York as a Test Case* (Princeton, 1961) | 50 | 34 |
| C. Vann Woodward | | |
| *The Origins of the New South, 1877–1913* (Baton Rouge, 1951) | 50 | 21 |

1. William H. Cartwright and Richard L. Watson, Jr., eds., *The Reinterpretation of American History and Culture* (Washington, D.C., 1973). The cooperation of contributors

*Allan G. Bogue*

The books most often mentioned in the survey do indeed represent major schools of thought in American political history since World War II. The volumes by Schlesinger and Woodward reflected the continuing traditions of progressive scholarship with its emphasis on economic self-interest and on the determinative influence of class and region in politics. Hofstadter and Benson demonstrated a pluralist concern for other aspects of the political process—Hofstadter endeavoring to explain the contribution of ideas and ideology in political life and Benson attempting to approach history as a "policy scientist." Their works exemplified the two most important elements of change in American political history since World War II. Many articles, books, and graduate theses and dissertations reveal the direct influence of these authors. Although the Benson and Hofstadter books illustrated different tendencies, they were not completely alien to each other. Hofstadter borrowed concepts from the social sciences—such as status deprivation—to illuminate *materia historica,* and Benson acknowledged indebtedness to Hofstadter. Both worked in the yeasty intellectual environment of Columbia University during the 1950s.

The phrase "new political history" emerged during the mid-1960s to distinguish political history of the kind typified by *The Concept of Jacksonian Democracy.*[2] It could with equal justice, perhaps, have been used to characterize the work of the scholars who were exploring the significance of political ideas, symbols, and ideologies in American political history.[3] But the phrase was appropriated by historians who saw the growing use of quantification in American political history and the self-conscious borrowing of social science methodology and theory as analogous to the sweeping reorientation in economic history then under way, and to the behavioral revolution that had occurred in most of the social sciences during the 1940s and 1950s. Some of the political historians of this persuasion maintained that they were "be-

---

to this book and that of the members of the sample derived from the listings in the American Historical Association, *Guide to Departments of History, 1976-77* (Washington, D.C., 1976) is much appreciated. Eighty-three historians participated in the latter survey; details of the selection process may be obtained from the author.

2. Allan G. Bogue, "United States: The 'New' Political History," in Walter Laqueur and George L. Mosse, eds., *The New History: Trends in Historical Research and Writing since World War II* (New York, 1967), 185-207.

3. As in the work of Hofstadter and publications of Bernard Bailyn, notably *The Ideological Origins of the American Revolution* (Cambridge, Mass., 1967), or that of such younger scholars as Eric Foner, *Free Soil, Free Labor, Free Men: The Ideology of the Republican Party before the Civil War* (New York, 1970), and James M. Banner, *To The Hartford Convention: The Federalists and the Origins of Party Politics in Massachusetts, 1789-1815* (New York, 1970).

haviqralists" and prided themselves on being more rigorous in their research formulations and analyses than were "traditional" or "conventional" historians.[4] When the History Panel of the Behavioral and Social Sciences Survey published the results of its deliberations in 1971, it described a "social-scientific history," distinguished in its practice by "aggregation, the marriage of theory and empiricism, and systematic comparison."[5] The historians involved in these developments tried aggressively to promote interchange across disciplinary lines at a time when some social scientists were experiencing a revitalization of interest in historical evidence. This essay assumes the work of both groups to be part of the new political history.

When I published the first comprehensive inventory of the new political history in 1967, I categorized the various types of analysis in print at that time as voting or electoral studies, roll-call analyses, and collective biographies of elites; I also noted interest in political ideology and in methodology.[6] Methodology aside, most authors listed in the notes were writing within the context of long-standing problems or debates in American history: Why did some individuals become antislavery reformers? What was the nature of Jacksonian democracy? How and when did sectional forces contribute to the demoralization of American political parties before the Civil War? Who were the Republican radicals in Congress during the Civil War and to what degree did their views dictate party positions? What accounted for the rise of progressivism during the early twentieth century? In their research, however, the new political historians endeavored to marshal and manipulate relatively neglected quantitative evidence— electoral returns, roll calls, biographical data—in order to test, correct, and supplement the findings of predecessors who had built their narratives on the foundation of more conventional research resources— manuscript collections, newspapers, congressional speeches, and the like. Although these historians often used rather simple quantitative procedures, this aspect of their work was sometimes more advanced than their grasp of political and social theory.

The origins of the new political history have been described else-

4. Samuel P. Hays, "History as Human Behavior," *Iowa Journal of History*, LVIII (1960), 193-206.

5. David S. Landes et al., *History as Social Science* (Englewood Cliffs, N.J., 1971), 71-73. The degree to which these components are intermingled still varies greatly, and the proper mix to justify classification as new political history can be the subject of considerable argument. But the use of any new and relevant category of evidence in conjunction with hitherto accepted categories represents a step forward in analytical procedures.

6. Bogue, "'New' Political History," 186-188.

where; the roots go deep and found nourishment in many fertile soils.[7] But in 1948 Thomas C. Cochran sounded the first lonely bugle call, summoning the discontented to rally in the cause of a political history that would be social scientific in orientation and state-level in focus and would repudiate the view of political history as mere presidential synthesis.[8] Those who were to lead initially, both by word and by example, had received their formal training by the early 1950s, often in circumstances or under teachers that led them to question conventional approaches and to look to related disciplines for conceptual guidance. That decade was one of beginnings, of earnest talk and planning at conventions; of enthusiastic expositions and suggestions for new-style doctoral dissertations; of postdoctoral training fellowships from the Social Science Research Council, or leaves spent at the Center for Advanced Study in the Behavioral Sciences; and of publication of a few important articles.

The 1960s were years of solid achievement. Benson's pathbreaking monograph appeared in 1961, and provided an exciting conceptual framework for eager young scholars. Several other important books appeared later in the decade, including those of Joel H. Silbey, Thomas B. Alexander, and Michael F. Holt; and a small flood of articles—substantive, conceptual, and methodological—testified to the willingness of some editors at least to encourage innovation.[9] The first anthology of such materials intended for classroom use had appeared before the end of the decade.[10] An increasing number of able

7. Ibid.; Robert P. Swierenga, ed., *Quantification in American History: Theory and Research* (New York, 1970), xiii–xxi, 1–5, and works cited there. Swierenga's bibliographies in this volume are an excellent inventory of relevant work published up to that time. See also Richard J. Jensen, "History and the Political Scientist," and "American Election Analysis: A Case Study of Methodological Innovation and Diffusion," chaps. 1 and 9 in Seymour M. Lipset, ed., *Politics and the Social Sciences* (New York, 1969), 1–28, 226–243. For a general discussion of recent political history in the United States, see Allan G. Bogue, "Recent Developments in Political History: The Case of the United States," in *The Frontiers of Human Knowledge* (Uppsala, 1978), 79–109. A number of passages in this chapter are derived from that publication.

8. Thomas C. Cochran, "The 'Presidential Synthesis' in American History," *American Historical Review*, LIII (1948), 748–759.

9. Joel H. Silbey, *The Shrine of Party: Congressional Voting Behavior, 1841–1852* (Pittsburgh, 1967); Thomas B. Alexander, *Sectional Stress and Party Strength: A Study of Roll-Call Voting Patterns in the United States House of Representatives, 1836–1860* (Nashville, 1967); Michael F. Holt, *Forging a Majority: The Formation of the Republican Party in Pittsburgh, 1848–1860* (New Haven, 1969). Also of importance were F. Sheldon Hackney, *Populism and Progressivism in Alabama* (Princeton, 1969); Michael Paul Rogin, *The Intellectuals and McCarthy: The Radical Specter* (Cambridge, Mass., 1967); James Sterling Young, *The Washington Community, 1800–1828* (New York, 1966). See Swierenga, *Quantification in American History,* for the relevant periodical literature.

10. Don K. Rowney and James Q. Graham, eds., *Quantitative History: Selected Readings in the Quantitative Analysis of Historical Data* (Homewood, Ill., 1969).

graduate students were attracted to the new style of research. The movement came of age in institutional terms as well. The Inter-University Consortium for Political Research (ICPR) established a Historical Data Archive and, with initial assistance from an Ad Hoc Committee on the Quantitative Data of American Political History of the American Historical Association, under Benson's chairmanship, began the task of processing American electoral data and congressional roll calls into machine-readable form. These two agencies collaborated also in sponsoring an important extended seminar-conference on the analysis of historical quantitative data in 1965 and several conferences on American and foreign quantitative data resources during 1967 and 1968.[11] Following the 1965 summer conference, ICPR placed a course in quantitative methods for historians in its summer program designed to supplement the conventional history graduate curriculum until more history departments decided to introduce their students to the quantitative analysis of data.

Meanwhile, the Mathematical Social Science Board organized a History Advisory Committee which planned and initiated an ambitious program of research conferences designed to generate collections of papers to be published by a distinguished press. During the summer of 1967, the MSSB Advisory Committee administered an eight-week summer program at Cornell University in the methods and models of the social sciences for twenty-five history graduate students selected by a national competition. The National Science Foundation, the National Endowment for the Humanities, the Ford Foundation, and the Social Science Research Council all made contributions to these institutional enterprises. In 1967 the History Department at the University of Pittsburgh began to publish the *Historical Methods Newsletter* to serve as a clearinghouse for information about research projects, methods, and data in the new political, social, and economic histories.

The decade of the 1970s saw continued development in the new political history, which achieved a far greater degree of general professional acceptance than ever before. The institutional structures created in the 1960s flourished. The Historical Data Archive of ICPSR (the word "social" was now added) continued to grow, and facilitated hundreds of historical research projects; the MSSB Quantitative Studies Series, published by Princeton University Press, will apparently terminate with the ninth volume; but two have been devoted to political history, and the introductory volume devoted much

11. For papers presented at two of these conferences, see Val R. Lorwin and Jacob M. Price, eds., *The Dimensions of the Past: Materials, Problems, and Opportunities for Quantitative Work in History* (New Haven, 1972).

space to this subdiscipline as well.[12] The Quantitative Data Committee of the AHA is now a standing committee of the association; the Family and Community History Center at the Newberry Library in Chicago has developed an active summer program in quantitative methods supplementing the ICPSR program and the intradepartmental programs that are emerging, albeit slowly.[13] The *Journal of Interdisciplinary History* and *Social Science History* have emerged to serve the specialized publication needs of the new approaches. The latter is the official organ of the Social Science History Association, which has developed an active program of annual and regional meetings, special-interest networks, and publication activities; political historians were active both in its formation and in its continuing activities. The significance of the achievements of the quantitative political historian, however, must rest upon the degree to which they are reshaping the landscape of political history in the United States; this influence may be assessed by a review of the articles and books that quantitative political historians and historically oriented social scientists published during the 1970s.

II

What are the special concerns of political historians? Obviously they are the political aspects of the human experience—that is, those formal or informal procedures and institutions through which people are governed, or alternatively, the processes by which government, private interests, or organized groups use their power to allocate or redistribute societal resources. But within this broad mandate, the scholar may focus on the actors, ideas and symbols, processes, institutions, and the social and economic contexts of politics as well as combinations of these subjects. Such focusing, however, is seldom performed in a conceptual vacuum.

Despite Thomas C. Cochran's castigation of the presidential synthesis, the thinking of most political historians during the 1940s went beyond this organizational device. Although their commitment might be revealed only implicitly in the completed narrative, they often

12. William O. Aydelotte, Allan G. Bogue, and Robert W. Fogel, eds., *The Dimensions of Quantitative Research in History* (Princeton, 1972); William O. Aydelotte, ed., *The History of Parliamentary Behavior* (Princeton, 1977); Joel H. Silbey, Allan G. Bogue, and William H. Flanigan, eds., *The History of American Electoral Behavior* (Princeton, 1978).

13. Two statistical texts for historians have appeared: Charles M. Dollar and Richard J. Jensen, *Historian's Guide to Statistics: Quantitative Analysis and Historical Research* (New York, 1971), and Roderick Floud, *An Introduction to Quantitative Methods for Historians* (Princeton, 1973).

accepted Frederick Jackson Turner's emphasis on the political importance "of great social and economic areas . . . which have acted as units in political history, and which have changed their political attitudes as they changed their economic organization." Others followed Charles A. Beard in endorsing Madison's formula: "The regulation of . . . various and interfering interests forms the principal task of modern legislation, and involves the spirits of party and faction in the necessary and ordinary operations of government."[14] There were more specific conceptual formulations as well. The distinguished political historian Roy F. Nichols, for example, viewed American politics as an exercise in the acquisition and use of power. American political institutions evolved, he believed, "to meet the needs of a self-governing community becoming increasingly complex." Among the "most elaborate . . . inventions" was the "American political party machine . . . which enabled the community to carry on the periodic contests for power which are one of the chief features of the practice of self-government."[15] Thus Nichols conceived of the American political party as a power-oriented distributive mechanism, hardly anticipated by Madisonian pluralism.

Traces of these seminal formulas are still found in the writing of today's historians, including historians of the social science type. But the dominant conceptual picture that has emerged from the writings of the new political historians, based in both history and social science departments, presents the history of American politics as a succession of different political eras, or party systems, separated by periods of realignment. Within the various eras, the party affiliation and voting of members of the political community reflect social, cultural, and economic reference group values, ideologies, and political concerns or objectives. Although much less clearly formulated, the political system is seen as a policy system, involving inputs (environmental factors), conversion or political processes, and outputs (public policy), which in turn have impact upon, or feed back to, the other segments of the policy system. The new political historians of the 1970s on

14. Frederick Jackson Turner, Editor's Note, in Orrin G. Libby, *The Geographical Distribution of the Vote of the Thirteen States on the Federal Constitution* (Madison, 1894), iii; Charles A. Beard, *An Economic Interpretation of the Constitution of the United States* (New York, 1913; reprinted with new introduction, 1935), 1–18; and for the quote in context, see *The Federalist: A Commentary on the Constitution of the United States . . .* (New York: Modern Library, n.d.), 56.

15. Roy F. Nichols, *The Invention of the American Political Parties* (New York, 1967), xi–xii. Nichols's other major works in this context were *The Democratic Machine, 1850–1854* (New York, 1923); *The Disruption of American Democracy* (New York, 1948); and *Blueprints for Leviathan: American Style* (New York, 1963).

*Allan G. Bogue*

occasion revealed an explicit interest in political power and its ramifications and were also influenced to some degree by the interests of social scientists in "political development" or "modernization."

Historically oriented social scientists performed much of the labor in the development of the electoral realignment formulation. Social scientists have long noted alternations in the control of the national and state governments by competing political parties, but the refinements of the current model are rooted particularly in the work of V. O. Key, Jr., with additional contributions by Angus Campbell and other members of the Center for Political Studies at the University of Michigan. Walter Dean Burnham, Gerald Pomper, and others, including many historians, have further elaborated or tested the model in various periods of United States history.[16]

The "First American Party System" is viewed as something of a special case, as is the transition to the "Second System" in the Jacksonian era; but thereafter realignments occurred, allegedly, in the 1850s, the 1890s, and the 1930s, with some spillover in the first instance into the 1860s and premonitory shifts in the electorate during the 1920s. One social scientist in the 1970s defined a political realignment as a "durable change in patterns of political behavior."[17] More specifically, scholars using this conceptual scheme describe changes of the following kinds: A state of relative stability in the political system is disrupted by a crisis. Elements of the voting population in the United States change allegiance, either permanently or for an extended period, during the realignment that ensues. Such change is effected by patterns—sometimes very complex—of voter shifts that may include the development of third parties. Voters move disproportionately into a party that was out of power at the beginning of the

16. Of a massive bibliography, see particularly James L. Sundquist, *Alignment and Realignment of Political Parties in the United States* (Washington, 1973); Walter Dean Burnham, *Critical Elections and the Mainsprings of American Politics* (New York, 1970); Burnham, Jerome M. Clubb, and William M. Flanigan, "Partisan Realignment: A Systemic Perspective," and Lee Benson, Joel H. Silbey, and Phyllis F. Field, "Toward a Theory of Stability and Change in American Voting Patterns, New York State, 1792–1970," in Silbey et al., eds., *History of American Electoral Behavior*, 31–44, 78–105. A useful collection that includes contributions of both historians and political scientists is Joel M. Silbey and Samuel T. McSeveney, eds., *Voters, Parties, and Elections* (Lexington, Mass., 1972). Although the seminal writings on which the present realignment model rests are V. O. Key, Jr., "A Theory of Critical Elections," *Journal of Politics*, XVII (1955), 3–18, and Angus Campbell, "A Classification of the Presidential Elections," in Campbell, Philip E. Converse, Warren E. Miller, and Donald E. Stokes, *The American Voter* (New York, 1960), 531–538; see W. B. Munro, "The Law of the Pendulum," in *The Invisible Government* (New York, 1928), 58–84, for an earlier illustration of the basic idea of the alternation of parties.

17. Sundquist, *Dynamics of the Party System*, 5.

realignment, and it ultimately captures both the legislative and the executive branches. A reform agenda, developed during the realignment period, although perhaps with more extensive antecedents, becomes the major concern of the lawmakers immediately subsequent to realignment. As the system moves beyond realignment, the initial objectives or ideological commitments of the realignment period are gained, or they lose salience, and political brokerage functions play an increasingly important role in the concerns of party leaders and members. Despite minor interparty movement, both short run and long run, the system is, in general, stable until another major crisis occurs. Within this general context, elections may be described as realigning (V. O. Key's adjective was "critical"), deviating, maintaining, or converting—when a party retains control of the government while the composition of its support changes substantially.

Although the realignment-stability schema has been developed in some detail, scholars have also been aware that fundamental and non-recurrent changes may have occurred in the American electoral system at various points in its development. In an influential article of the mid-1960s, Walter Dean Burnham argued that a basic transformation in mass electoral behavior occurred after the realignment of the 1890s. The electorate of the last sixty years of the nineteenth century had been highly mobilized, but now "an increasingly large proportion of the eligible adult male population either left, failed to enter or . . . was systematically excluded from the American voting universe;" it became a system characterized to a striking degree by "active alienation" or "political apathy."[18] In thus incidentally raising the issue of the role of legal-institutional factors in voter mobilization, Burnham touched a subject that has been of some interest throughout the era of the new political history and various aspects of which were illuminated significantly during the 1970s. In 1970, Jerrold G. Rusk showed that the adoption of the Australian ballot contributed perceptibly to the decline of party voting discipline as reflected in split-ticket voting; four years later he argued the important effects of institutional factors generally in the decline of electoral participation during the twentieth century.[19] The most striking historiographic revision, however, related to such developments in the South. Using somewhat

18. Walter D. Burnham, "The Changing Shape of the American Political Universe," *American Political Science Review,* LIX (1965), 7–28, at 26–27.

19. Jerrold G. Rusk, "The Effect of the Australian Ballot Reform on Split Ticket Voting: 1876–1908," *American Political Science Review,* LXIV (1970), 1220–1238, and "The American Electoral Universe: Speculation and Evidence," *American Political Science Review,* LXVIII (1974), 1028–1049.

different research techniques and foci, J. Morgan Kousser and Rusk and John J. Stucker showed that the imposition of the southern system of voter discrimination not merely was confirmation of a *fait accompli,* as suggested by V. O. Key, Jr., but was highly effective in removing blacks and poor whites from the ranks of the southern electorate.[20] By using regression estimation, Kousser was able to suggest the numbers of the two groups excluded.

Many studies by behavioral historians relating to the various party systems have emphasized the interpretive structure that has been termed—perhaps wrongly—the ethnocultural model of electoral behavior. Here the work of Benson has been of primary importance. Published in 1961, *The Concept of Jacksonian Democracy* climaxed a decade of research, thought, and preliminary publication on the substance and methods of American political history.[21] Enriched by the author's broad reading and by his personal contacts with social scientists interested in the political process, particularly Paul Lazarsfeld, the book was at once an attempt to persuade historians of the value of a behavioral approach and rigorously analytical methods and a reevaluation of Jacksonian Democracy on the basis of additional substantive evidence. Benson incorporated the concept of voting cycles, emphasized the necessity of local analysis, and used quantitative evidence in arguing that ethnocultural (including religious) groupings provided major clues to individual party choice and voting behavior during the Jacksonian era in New York State.

Benson argued that members of the same ethnocultural groups in New York made their political decisions in reference to their fellows and suggested that groups he described as "puritan" tended to make common cause as Whigs against those subscribing to more latitudinarian or "nonpuritan" religious doctrine or practice, marshaled in the Democratic Party. He did not contend that this was universally the

20. J. Morgan Kousser, *The Shaping of Southern Politics: Suffrage Restriction and the Establishment of the One-Party South, 1880–1910* (New Haven, 1974); Jerrold G. Rusk and John J. Stucker, "The Effect of the Southern System of Election Laws on Voting Participation: A Reply to V. O. Key, Jr.," in Silbey et al., eds., *History of American Electoral Behavior,* 198–250. The "Key hypothesis" is found in V. O. Key, Jr., *Southern Politics in State and Nation* (New York, 1949), chaps. 25–28 and pp. 533, 535.
21. Benson's developing ideas appeared in "Research Problems in American Political Historiography," in Mirra Komarovsky, ed., *Common Frontiers of the Social Sciences* (Glencoe, Ill., 1957), 113–183, and two widely circulated papers: "An Operational Approach to Historiography," delivered at the American Historical Association meeting in December 1954, and a preliminary version of the book of 1961, "Public Opinion and the American Civil War: An Essay in the Logic and Practice of Historical Inquiry" (Stanford, 1958). In the latter study Benson used the word "ethnocultural" in describing this category of variables.

case in the United States. Rather, he maintained that the "heterogeneous society," "high personal levels of aspiration," "federal government system," and widespread "agreement on political fundamentals" suggested that "a wide variety of factors" would "significantly determine voting and that political parties" would "function essentially as decentralized aggregates of state and locally based organizations."[22]

Since the publication of *The Concept of Jacksonian Democracy*, many historical analyses of electoral behavior have patently been built on the foundation laid by Benson or on the efforts of Samuel P. Hays to integrate the various analytical trends of the time under the rubric "the social analysis of political life." These studies reveal also the tendency of their authors to browse among the offerings of social scientists interested in the political process.[23]

Research evaluating the importance of ethnocultural elements in American political history was undertaken in a number of graduate seminars during the 1950s and 1960s, but Benson's imprint showed strongly in books of the early 1970s by Paul Kleppner, Richard J. Jensen, and Ronald P. Formisano. Kleppner and Jensen analyzed the political history of several midwestern states during the Third Party System, and Formisano examined political developments in Michigan during the preceding era. Although these works were not monocausal in approach and stressed the importance and uses of political symbolism and ideology and the phenomenon of cross-pressures, their greatest contribution lay in providing an elaborate explication of the religious element in nineteenth-century American politics. As Kleppner wrote, "partisan affiliations were not rooted in economic class distinctions. They were political expressions of shared values derived from the voter's membership in and commitment to ethnic and religious groups." Jensen argued that "religion was the fundamental source of political conflict in the midwest." Formisano maintained that "Evangelical Protestant groups . . . led the movement into the Republican coalition" in Michigan.[24]

---

22. Benson, *Concept of Jacksonian Democracy*, 276.

23. Samuel P. Hays, "New Possibilities for American Political History: The Social Analysis of Political Life" (Ann Arbor, 1964, multilith), delivered at the Annual Meeting of the American Historical Association, December 29, 1964, and "The Social Analysis of American Political History, 1880–1920," *Political Science Quarterly*, LXXX (1965), 373–394. See also note 4 above.

24. Paul Kleppner, *The Cross of Culture: A Social Analysis of Midwestern Politics, 1850–1900* (New York, 1970), 35; Richard J. Jensen, *The Winning of the Midwest: Social and Political Conflict, 1888–1896* (Chicago, 1971), 58; Ronald P. Formisano, *The Birth of Mass Political Parties: Michigan, 1827–1861* (Princeton, 1971), 324; space does not permit a listing of all the relevant articles and books in this and similar notes, but see also Fred C. Luebke, *Immigrants and Politics: The Germans of Nebraska, 1880–1900* (Lincoln, 1969).

These authors used the terms "pietists" and "ritualists," or "evangelical" and "liturgical," rather than "puritan" and "nonpuritan," and suggested that the degree of a religious group's commitment to pietist doctrine predicted the strength of its adherence to the Whig and particularly to the Republican party. Conversely, the political objectives of the Republican party incorporated moral imperatives that reflected the party's constituency base while the Democrats eschewed moral reform and emphasized the rights of the free individual. As in Benson's work, much individual behavior was inferred from aggregate data, but Jensen discovered biographical information about the individual voters of eight Illinois townships and Formisano found a contemporary listing of partisan preference in Lansing, Michigan, that showed members of particular ethnocultural groups or religious affiliations to be committed disproportionately to one major party or the other.

Although alert to cultural variables, a number of other young scholars, such as Samuel McSeveney, Stanley B. Parsons, and James E. Wright, reported that economic or other noncultural determinants played an important role during the realignment processes of the 1890s in Connecticut, in New York and New Jersey, in Nebraska and Colorado.[25] And in a work that offered the most sophisticated statistical analysis then available, Melvyn Hammarberg argued that the biographical information in *People's Guides,* listing the residents of a number of Indiana counties, showed the importance of occupational status as an indicator of political affiliation. Noting the impact of religious affiliations in such matters, he maintained that "religious institutions . . . were important, politically, not for their doctrinal content so much as for their exposure, in terms of communication, of one member to another."[26]

Down to the mid 1970s much electoral research drew conclusions about individual behavior through the analysis of aggregate data; researchers sought to obviate the dangers of such analysis by the use of "banner" or relatively "pure" indicator precincts or counties and other stratagems. To some degree, Jensen, Formisano, and Hammarberg used fragmentary records of identifiable voting or partisan preference. It became clear during the 1960s and 1970s that more exten-

25. Samuel T. McSeveney, *The Politics of Depression: Political Behavior in the Northeast, 1893–1896* (New York, 1972); Stanley B. Parsons, *The Populist Context: Rural versus Urban Power on a Great Plains Frontier* (Westport, Conn., 1973); James E. Wright, *The Politics of Populism in Colorado, 1860–1912* (New Haven, 1974).

26. Melvyn Hammarberg, *The Indiana Voter: The Historical Dynamics of Party Allegiance during the 1870s* (Chicago, 1977), 115.

sive collections of such records existed in the local poll books used in a number of states during the period 1789–1860.[27] During the late 1960s and 1970s also, researchers began to use techniques of regression estimation to measure the numbers within particular social or cultural groups who voted for particular parties or the number of voters in a particular election who voted in particular ways in other elections shortly thereafter. The first book-length work resulting from such research was J. Morgan Kousser's in 1974, and a number of authors have followed suit, particularly in probing the mechanics of realignment.[28] In 1978, Kleppner published an examination of electoral behavior in the greater part of the United States between 1853 and 1892 which used this method of analysis, among others.[29] Although stressing the complexity of electoral behavior, he again emphasized the importance of religious and doctrinal factors; his book may be regarded as an amplification and to some degree a defense of his earlier study.

The quantitative historians who dealt primarily with legislatures, elites, and community political processes were less successful than those concerned with electoral behavior in developing comprehensive conceptual or theoretical frameworks. Although assumptions about the importance, uses, and rewards of power permeate some of their work and they have sometimes made explicit use of the concept, their findings generally have been directed to middle-range reinterpretation. The collective biography was particularly common among the early examples of such research. The authors believed that the social,

27. John M. Rozett, "Racism and Republican Emergence in Illinois, 1848–1860: A Re-Evaluation of Republican Negrophobia," *Civil War History*, XXII (1976), 101–115; Paul F. Bourke and Donald A. Debats, "Identifiable Voting in Nineteenth-Century America: Toward a Comparison of Britain and the United States before the Secret Ballot," *Perspectives in American History*, XI (1977–78), 259–288, and "Individuals and Aggregates: A Note on Historical Data and Assumptions," *Social Science History* (forthcoming); see particularly David H. Bohmer, "The Maryland Electorate and the Concept of a Party System in the Early National Period," in Silbey et al., eds., *History of American Electoral Behavior*, 146–173.

28. Kousser, *The Shaping of Southern Politics* and his seminal "Ecological Regression and the Analysis of Past Politics," *Journal of Interdisciplinary History*, IV (1973), 237–262, and Laura I. Langbein and Allan J. Lichtman, *Ecological Inference* (Beverly Hills, 1978). See also Kevin Sweeney, "Rum, Romanism, Representation, and Reform: Coalition Politics in Massachusetts, 1847–1853," *Civil War History*, XXII (1976), 116–137; Peyton McCrary, Clark Miller, and Dale Baum, "Class and Party in the Secession Crisis: Voting Behavior in the Deep South, 1856–1861," *Journal of Interdisciplinary History*, VIII (1978), 429–458; Dale Baum, "Know Nothingism and the Republican Majority in Massachusetts: The Political Realignment of the 1850s," *Journal of American History*, LXIV (1978), 959–986.

29. Paul Kleppner, *The Third Electoral System, 1853–1892: Parties, Voters, and Political Cultures* (Chapel Hill, 1979).

economic, and political characteristics of the individual members of
particular elite groups, if considered systematically and inclusively,
would help to explain the common behavior and objectives of group
members, the changing locus of power within both society and the
various political arenas, and the linkages among the political, social,
and economic structures of society. Thus various of the political elites
of the Populist and Progressive eras were scrutinized in detail, as were
those of the antebellum South and of various local and community
milieus.[30] Although the assumptions, methods, and conclusions of
some of the early collective biographers were flawed, the collective
portrait of the members of elite groups has been common in the
quantitative political literature of the 1970s. Groups as disparate as
the Founding Fathers, wealthy Jacksonians, southern scalawags, and
the leaders of nineteenth-century Paris, Illinois, and early-twentieth-
century Birmingham, Alabama, have been studied in this way.[31]

The analysis of elite activity in American legislatures was as prevalent in the early days of behavioralism as was interest in electoral
analysis. Roll-call analysis, advocates of the approach suggested,
would allow the definition of voting blocs and voting dimensions, the
scaling of legislators in terms of moderation or extremism on specific
issues or issue areas, and the evaluation of sectional, party, and other
interest group commitments, as well as the influence of leaders and
individual members in effecting particular voting outcomes. And research has continued on these and similar fronts since 1965, often
with interesting and sometimes conflicting results. Historians, for
example, have used the results of roll-call analysis to support the
contention that parties developed at an early date in the United States
Congress, but one scholar has used the technique in denying that
party was important in that era. In studying the Confederate Congress two researchers discovered that "former party, secession stand,
and Exterior or Interior [regional] status" foretold the behavior of the
congressmen. Another investigation found that southern con-

---

30. Swierenga, *Quantification in American History,* 127–130, lists major contributions.
31. Richard D. Brown, "The Founding Fathers of 1776 and 1787: A Collective
View," *William and Mary Quarterly,* 3d ser., XXXIII (1976), 465–480; Edward Pessen,
*Riches, Class, and Power before the Civil War* (Lexington, Mass., 1973), and a critique,
Robert E. Gallman, "Professor Pessen on the 'Egalitarian Myth,'" *Social Science History,*
II (1978), 194–207; Warren A. Ellem, "Who Were the Mississippi Scalawags?" *Journal of
Southern History,* XXXVIII (1972), 217–240; Richard S. Alcorn, "Leadership and Stability
in Mid-Nineteenth-Century America: A Case Study of an Illinois Town," *Journal of
American History,* LXI (1974), 685–702; Carl V. Harris, *Political Power in Birmingham,
1871–1921* (Knoxville, 1977). The latter work is in addition a highly sophisticated
analysis of interest group interaction.

gressmen of the 1870s were more consistently allied to western representatives than had been believed earlier, and so on.[32] The opportunities for research of this kind at the state level are very great. In a pathbreaking article, Herbert Ershkowitz and William G. Shade interpreted the variations in party voting on particular issues to support the contention that state parties had well-developed ideologies during the 1830s, but others maintain that such cohesion is more appropriately considered as being an indication of the desire of party leaders to wield power and bestow patronage.[33]

The social science historian of the 1970s has traversed the full range of American national history, and has also devoted attention to the colonial period.[34] But the relative number of the various types of studies has varied from era to historical era. Popular voting studies, for example, have been less common than legislative studies in the early national period. Studies in general have tended to cover relatively short time periods. Some historians who are critical of this characteristic of the new political history have been attracted by the literature of modernization and political development. Scholars in various social science disciplines have identified a number of political processes at work in the western nations during the last several centuries, and have related them in conceptual schemes of varying complexity. Perhaps because the parent literature is basically concerned with cross-national comparisons, quantitative historians have as yet worked relatively little within the framework.[35] But interest in political development has influenced historians to some degree and will continue to do so.

Indeed, some historians have used concepts of modernization with-

32. Representative publications include Mary P. Ryan, "Party Formation in the United States Congress, 1789 to 1796: A Quantitative Analysis," *William and Mary Quarterly*, 3d ser. XXVIII (1971), 523–542; James S. Young, *The Washington Community* (New York, 1966), and in response to Young, Allan G. Bogue and Mark P. Marlaire, "Of Mess and Men: The Boardinghouse and Congressional Voting, 1821–1842," *American Journal of Political Science*, XIX (1975), 207–230; Thomas B. Alexander and Richard E. Beringer, *The Anatomy of the Confederate Congress* (Nashville, 1972), 337; Carl V. Harris, "Right Fork or Left Fork? The Section-Party Alignment of Southern Democrats in Congress, 1873–1897," *Journal of Southern History*, XLII (1976), 471–508.

33. Herbert Ershkowitz and William G. Shade, "Consensus or Conflict? Political Behavior in the State Legislatures during the Jacksonian Era," *Journal of American History*, LVIII (1971), 591–621; Peter D. Levine, *The Behavior of State Legislative Parties in the Jacksonian Era: New Jersey, 1829–1844* (Rutherford-Teaneck, N.J., 1977). See also Ronald P. Formisano, "Toward a Reorientation of Jacksonian Politics: A Review of the Literature, 1959–1975," *Journal of American History*, LXIII (1976), 42–65.

34. See Robert Zemsky, *Merchants, Farmers, and River Gods* (Boston 1971).

35. For a critique by a historian, see Raymond Grew, "Modernization and Its Discontents," *American Behavioral Scientist*, XXI (1977), 289–312.

out greatly emphasizing the fact. In their studies of state legislative politics during the 1780s, Van Beck Hall and Jackson Turner Main distinguished between political leaders who thought mainly in local or community—that is, traditional—terms and those who reflected a cosmopolitan or "society"—that is, modern—point of view in making political decisions.[36] Alternatives to these attempts to work within the framework of a community–society continuum are to be seen in the efforts of Nelson W. Polsby and others to trace the development of institutionalization and related processes in the United States Congress from the time of its creation to the present and to relate various of the developmental processes to the electoral realignment formulation.[37]

Earlier generations of American historians believed that the concerns of political and constitutional historians were closely related. That is still true in some respects, but during the 1960s and the 1970s the trends in the two subdisciplines have also differed somewhat. Most American historians who are interested in the place of the law and the courts in the United States now describe themselves as legal-constitutional historians or simply legal historians. They are still concerned with important judicial decisions, but they emphasize the necessity of placing law and judicial processes within the context of social and economic development and of exploring the reasons why the law and its interpretation changed, as well as how the alterations occurred. Like the social science historians, legal-constitutional historians have urged that research be set within theoretical frameworks. They have insisted also that historians in the specialty improve their

36. Van Beck Hall, *Politics without Parties: Massachusetts, 1780-1791* (Pittsburgh, 1972); Jackson Turner Main, *Political Parties before the Constitution* (Chapel Hill, 1973). Samuel P. Hays provided an early formulation in "Political Parties and the Community-Society Continuum," in William N. Chambers and Walter Dean Burnham, eds., *The American Party Systems: Stages of Political Development* (New York, 1967).

37. Nelson W. Polsby, "The Institutionalization of the U.S. House of Representatives," *American Political Science Review*, LXII (1968), 144-168; Polsby, Miriam Gallagher, and Barry S. Rundquist, "The Growth of the Seniority System in the U.S. House of Representatives," ibid., LXIII (1969), 787-807; H. Douglas Price, "Congress and the Evolution of Legislative Professionalism," in Norman J. Ornstein, ed., *Congress in Change: Evolution and Reform* (New York, 1975), 2-22, and "Careers and Committees in the American Congress: The Problem of Structural Change," in Aydelotte, *Parliamentary Behavior*, 28-62; Allan G. Bogue, Jerome M. Clubb, Carroll R. McKibbin, and Santa A. Traugott, "Members of the U.S. House of Representatives and the Processes of Modernization, 1789-1969," *Journal of American History*, LXIII (1976), 275-302; Clubb and Traugott, "Partisan Cleavage and Cohesion in the House of Representatives, 1861-1974," *Journal of Interdisciplinary History*, VII (1977), 375-401; Lester G. Seligman and Michael R. King, "Critical Elections, Congressional Recruitment, and Public Policy," in Heinz Eulau and Moshe M. Czudnowski, eds., *Elite Recruitment in Democratic Polities: Comparative Studies Across Nations* (New York, 1976), 263-299.

research tools; this has usually meant more formal training in law. Only a few have used quantitative methods, although there appears to be considerable opportunity for research of this kind. The interest of some scholars in the configurations of ideas or modes of thought underlying lawmaking and judicial decision making, such as formalism or constitutionalism, appear in part to reflect the impact of developments in American intellectual history.[38]

The word "new" implicitly contrasts with "traditional" or "conventional," and the distinction has sometimes been a source of friction, if not outright warfare, in American history departments. On the other hand, a common interest in new quantitative methods and a commitment—in theory, at least—to comparative analysis has encouraged the new political historians to look for guidance to other subareas of the discipline. Thus specialists in United States history have influenced colleagues working in the history of other nations and been influenced in turn. William O. Aydelotte and Charles Tilly, in particular, have been influential in shaping American political history as well as their own areas of research interest, British and French history.[39]

III

In technical terms the quantitative or social science history of the 1970s is much more sophisticated than that of the 1950s and early 1960s. As late as 1955 or even 1960 American political historians

38. Several collections document the broadening process: David H. Flaherty, ed., *Essays in the History of Early American Law* (Chapel Hill, 1969), including particularly the editor's definition of the field, pp. 3-38; Wythe Holt, *Essays in Nineteenth-Century American Legal History* (Westport, Conn., 1976). Donald Fleming and Bernard Bailyn, eds., *Law in American History*, vol. v. of *Perspectives in American History* (Cambridge, Mass., 1971), 3-94, provides a chapter, "Legal Elements in United States History," by James Willard Hurst, whose ideas on the role and substance of legal history have been especially important. The Civil War era is described, particularly, as one in which much stimulating revision has occurred in constitutional history; some conception of these developments is gained by contrasting James G. Randall, *Constitutional Problems under Lincoln* (New York, 1926), with Harold M. Hyman, *A More Perfect Union: The Impact of the Civil War and Reconstruction on the Constitution* (New York, 1973), and Herman Belz, *Emancipation and Equal Rights: Politics and Constitutionalism in the Civil War Era* (New York, 1978). For the use of quantification in this field, see Michael L. Benedict, *A Compromise of Principle: Congressional Republicans and Reconstruction, 1863-1869* (New York, 1974); Gordon M. Bakken, "The Arizona Constitutional Convention of 1910," *Arizona State Law Journal* (1978), 1-30, one of several such articles by this author; and George L. Priest, "Law and Economic Distress: Sangamon County, Illinois, 1837-1844," *Journal of Legal Studies*, II (1973), 469-492.

39. William O. Aydelotte, *Quantification in History* (Reading, Mass., 1971) and *Parliamentary Behavior;* Charles Tilly, Louise Tilly, and Richard Tilly, *The Rebellious Century, 1830-1930* (Cambridge, Mass., 1975).

rarely used correlation coefficients; now such statistics are commonplace in the work of quantitatively oriented scholars, and they understand that other measures, generated in regression analysis, are often more illuminating. We know also that the ecological fallacy—the belief that individual behavior can be inferred from aggregate data—is less to be feared than once thought. Quantitative historians have applied various summary measures to the analysis of legislative behavior—cohesion and likeness coefficients and the Guttman scalogram—and have advanced toward a more sophisticated understanding of those that are most useful in various circumstances. Although some authorities regard factor analysis with suspicion, illustrations of its effective use in historical problems are available, and sampling methods are no longer a mystery to historians. Although they have not yet been used intensively, such techniques as multiple classification analysis, discriminant, probit, and logit analysis, and multidimensional scaling will undoubtedly serve them well in the future. At the moment, additional knowledge of time-series analysis appears to be a major priority. Although the undergraduate and graduate history curricula are still woefully inadequate in their presentation or requirements of offerings in theory, quantitative methods, and data processing, hundreds of history students have had some formal training in quantitative methods, and the publication of articles in methodology by historians is no longer a rarity.[40]

The plaints of latter-day Jeremiahs or Luddites that the new political historians do not write history, that they have abandoned style for "jargon," or that the computer dehumanizes history are obvious exaggerations. But there are responsible critics both within and without the new Jerusalem. The electoral realignment and party systems formulation has attracted some researchers with relatively sophisticated conceptual and empirical skills and the results have been impressive, but the model is based on aggregate data analysis, much of it using state rather than local electoral returns. Research at lower levels of aggregation has tended to modify the picture of abrupt realignments to some degree. Much of the work has been essentially taxonomic in nature and devoted to precise description of the mechanics of the realignment process. Realignment analysis is concerned with political change, but in the hands of most researchers change is initiated by an exogenous shock. Why do some exogenous shocks produce realignment while others do not? Research has shown that elements of realignment may proceed over very long chronologi-

40. See also J. Morgan Kousser, "The Agenda for 'Social Science History,'" *Social Science History*, 1 (1977), 383–391.

cal periods, affect different regions at different times, influence some
electoral groups and leave others untouched. Why has this been the
case? Indeed, David A. Bohmer's poll-book analysis of realignment in
two Maryland counties in the early national period linked the process
to changes in the composition of the electorate rather than to shifts in
the allegiance of individual voters.[41] The reference-group theory incorporated in the electoral survey analysis research at both Columbia
and the University of Michigan may be appropriately applied in this
model, and it may be that a generational succession model will help to
explain cyclical elements in American politics.[42] Finally, realignment
analysis has focused primarily on elections; the precise ways in which
legislative behavior and policy outputs are associated with electoral
realignment remain largely unexplored at this time.[43]

In assessing the research of political historians who have emphasized the influence of cultural determinants in electoral behavior,
one finds much to commend in the efforts of Benson and others to
make explicit use of theory and to incorporate quantitative as well as
literary evidence in their works, thereby improving the processes of
empirical validation. Criticism of their efforts usually takes one or
more of the following lines.[44] First, it is said that the theoretical foundations of this sort of electoral analysis rest explicitly on reference-
group theory, but that these researchers have shown little interest in
developing the full implications of that body of theory. Some scholars,
others suggest, have emphasized ethnocultural variables, particularly
religion, and have largely ignored other types of electoral determinants. The ethnoculturalists have not adequately emphasized the
highly inferential character of the linkages that they posit among
religious group membership, belief systems, and aggregate voting

41. Bohmer, "The Maryland Electorate."
42. Samuel P. Huntington, "Paradigms of American Politics: Beyond the One, the
Two, and the Many," *Political Science Quarterly*, LXXXIX (1974), 1–26; see also Seligman
and King, "Critical Elections."
43. Allan G. Lichtman, "Critical Election Theory and the Reality of American Presidential Politics, 1916–40," *American Historical Review*, LXXXI (1976), 317–348, cites much
of the relevant recent literature.
44. James E. Wright, "The Ethnocultural Model of Voting: A Behavioral and Historical Critique," in Allan G. Bogue, ed., *Emerging Theoretical Models in Social and Political
History* (Beverly Hills, 1973), 35–56; and Richard L. McCormick, "Ethno-Cultural Interpretations of Nineteenth-Century American Voting Behavior," *Political Science Quarterly*, LXXXIX (1974), 351–377. The latter article somewhat misstates the relative contributions of Hays and Benson to the "model." See also Hammarberg, *The Indiana Voter*,
passim. Kleppner responds in *The Third Electoral System*, passim and 357–382: "In
creating an ethnocultural school . . . observers have perpetuated . . . a figment of their
own imagination" (p. 359). But to use a major characteristic of a body of literature as a
means of distinguishing it from other writing is not necessarily to deny that other
matters are discussed in it.

patterns. These scholars have made inadequate use of the foreign-language and religious press and have given scant consideration to the presence of large numbers of voters unaffiliated with any church.

Critics note that the quantitative foundations of ethnocultural research are less firm than they ought to be, owing to the inexperience of historians in the use of empirical methods. Even much of the most recent and statistically sophisticated of this work rests in part on estimates of religious group membership and electorate size that involve troublesome assumptions. The presentations of quantitative evidence are often merely illustrative and are incomplete, and the evidence is sometimes soft when the importance of noncultural factors is acknowledged. Most of the electoral historians view voting behavior within the framework provided by periodic political realignments, but the empirical illustrations of ethnocultural voter shifts at such times have not been completely convincing. There is surely some logical inconsistency in displaying strong correlations between ethnocultural groups and party during periods of political stability and failing to show that realignment was effected by fundamental shifts in the allegiance of such groups. Although the formulation has important implications for the study of legislative behavior and public policy, these research opportunities have been relatively ignored.[45] Electoral historians have achieved an important transformation of the historical landscape, but have no reason to believe that their task is complete.

Historians using the technique of collective biography took some disastrous falls initially, but growing awareness of the need for control groups, better understanding of sampling methods, and a more realistic conception of the technique's potential has enabled them to use it more effectively.[46] The work of the legislative roll-call analysts reached the level of technical sophistication found in related disciplines earlier than did that of the electoral analysts, and if its utility was probably overestimated initially, it has fallen somewhat short of its true potential. Quantitative measures and exhibits sometimes seem to be presented as ends in themselves, or the theoretical implications of findings are ignored. And the same criticism may be applied to much of the new political history.

45. Ballard C. Campbell, "Ethnicity and the 1893 Wisconsin Assembly," *Journal of American History*, LXII (1975), 74-94; "Did Democracy Work? Prohibition in Late-Nineteenth-Century Iowa: A Test Case," *Journal of Interdisciplinary History*, VIII (1977), 87-116, and Owen S. Ireland, "The Ethnic-Religious Dimension of Pennsylvania Politics, 1778-1779," *William and Mary Quarterly*, 3d ser., XXX (1973), 423-448, point the way.

46. Howard Allen and Jerome Clubb, "Collective Biography and the Progressives: A Review Essay," *Social Science History*, I (Summer 1977), 518-534.

In general the new political history has been excessively compartmentalized. If many researchers have viewed the polity as a policy system, that fact has not been much in evidence in their writings. Some electoral analysts seem to assume that once electoral behavior is described, all political phenomena have been explained. The social science historians have made a great contribution in emphasizing the relations between the cultural environment and the electoral process. However, the links between the process of popular voting and legislative activity and the impact of policy upon the social, economic, and political process sectors of the society have been relatively ignored thus far.[47]

Disturbed by what he believed to be unthinking empiricism and even contempt for traditional history at a conference sponsored by the History Advisory Committee of MSSB in 1969, J. H. Hexter acknowledged that eggs must be broken if an omelette is to be made. But, he thundered, "Gentlemen, where is the omelette?"[48] Some ten years later, no thoughtful historian could seriously ask that question. Even if some of the criticisms are valid, much of the work of the social science historians will stand; and our conception of the political past in the United States will remain substantially altered by their efforts. In significant respects nonquantitative work in the field already bears their imprint as well, as its authors proceed, on occasion, from assumptions or consider questions that are rooted in quantitative findings. And manifestly the contention that the quantitative historians destroy but do not rebuild is as erroneous as the suggestion that their measurements have graded down the peaks and valleys of the progressive landscape to provide consensus history. Rather, the new political historians have brought, or promise to bring, a greater sense of perspective to past American politics, a better understanding of the variety of arenas in which American politics are conducted, and an enhanced appreciation of the role of cultural conflict in our political history, as well as popularizing the use of new or improved methods and conceptual formulations.[49]

47. But for a promising start, see J. Morgan Kousser, "Progressivism for Middle-Class Whites Only: The Distribution of Taxation and Expenditures for Education in North Carolina, 1880–1910," *Journal of Southern History* (forthcoming).

48. Aydelotte, *Quantification in History*, 170.

49. For other views, see Lawrence Stone, "History and the Social Sciences in the Twentieth Century," in Charles F. Delzell, ed., *The Future of History* (Nashville, 1977), 3–42. D. N. Sprague's article "A Quantitative Assessment of the Quantification Revolution," *Canadian Journal of History*, XIII (1978), 177–192, rests upon definitions and assumptions that not all can accept. See also Philip R. Vandermeer, "The New Political History: Progress and Prospects," *Computers and the Humanities*, XI (1978), 265–278.

# 1 0

# Labor History in the 1970s: Toward a History of the American Worker

## David Brody

I N the first pages of his pioneering essay "Work, Culture, and Society in Industrializing America," Herbert Gutman set his sights at a history of American workers that would go beyond a study of their trade-union institutions.[1] Gutman thereby expressed what has become a hallmark of labor history in the 1970s: a persistent effort to capture the total historical experience of American working people rather than only that part expressed through the labor movement. This tendency was by no means limited to the study of American workers. That Europeanists were moving in the same direction could be discerned early on by the way Peter Stearns posed the main theme of his *Revolutionary Syndicalism and French Labor* (1971): did the radical ideology of the labor movement actually reflect the thinking of its rank-and-file members? Many of the shaping influences, especially those deriving from social history, have been as strongly felt in recent American scholarship on labor in other industrial societies. The historiography of American labor is, however, the product of certain scholarly dynamics particular to the practitioners and problems of that field. To make plain those dynamics, it seems necessary to slight the work being done on European labor and to focus on the historical study of workers in the United States.[2]

This is a revised version of a paper delivered at the meeting of the Organization of American Historians in April 1978 and published in *Labor History,* xx (1979), 111–126.
1. *American Historical Review,* LXXVIII (1973), 531–587.
2. This is a decision with which I have wrestled in the course of revising this essay. I have been ruled by my sense that the dynamics of American labor historiography—the relation of American scholars to the subject and, to some degree, the nature of the subject itself—have kept it distinct from the American historiography on European labor, notwithstanding strongly shared influences acting on both fields during the past decade. It may well be that those influences will lead to a common labor historiography;

For more than half a century stretching well beyond World War II, labor history in America remained nearly the exclusive province of the institutional economists. The revolt against the formalism of classical economics in the late nineteenth century had included a strong historical component. The pioneering labor economists, greatly influenced by the German historical school, considered historical research to be a major empirical weapon against the abstractions of the prevailing school of laissez-faire economics. John R. Commons, who was in the mainstream of this intellectual development, made history a leading part of his program at the University of Wisconsin, devoting much of his energies to gathering the raw materials for *A Documentary History of American Industrial Society* (1910–11) and then to launching the first comprehensive account in *A History of Labor in the United States* (1918, 1935).

Institutional economics took particularly strong root in the United States. For the Commons generation, there was a prideful sense of mission: by their institutional scholarship the labor economists were contesting not only the classical theorists in the academy but the pernicious message to the public that collective action by workers constituted inadmissible interference with the free play of the market. The practice of labor economics, generally involving fieldwork in the industrial world and often service in government and labor arbitration, sustained the vitality of the institutional approach for many years. And, as an integral part of that approach, labor economists produced a vast historical literature on trade unionism and labor relations. A last great surge after World War II yielded, in addition to many monographs, such major contributions as Lloyd Ulman's *Rise of the National Trade Union* (1955), Walter Galenson's *CIO Challenge to the AFL* (1960), and Philip Taft's *A.F. of L. in the Time of Gompers* (1957) and *A.F. of L. from the Death of Gompers to the Merger* (1959).

The study of trade unionism necessarily rested on assumptions as to the nature of the constituency. Only Selig Perlman, an exceptional practitioner of the Wisconsin tradition in many ways, tried to make those assumptions explicit in his *Theory of the Labor Movement* (1928). A speculative scholar with a wide-ranging knowledge of European history, Perlman was highly sensitive to the American conditions acting on labor, but his characterization of working people was little more

certainly this outcome is suggested by the coverage of some of the journals, especially in social and interdisciplinary history, and by the activities of the Network on Workers and Industrialization, an informal organization of American scholars interested in working-class history. In a treatment of past developments, however, the best I can do is to suggest at appropriate points in the notes the common lines between the two fields.

David Brody

than a reasoning back from his conception of job-conscious unionism.
Perlman's prize student, Philip Taft, in later years took the master to
task for expounding a group psychology of workers that was not
empirically grounded and that "really does not help us to understand
the behavior of workers or employers."[3] Prolific scholar that he was,
however, Taft never ventured into such study himself, and he displayed little patience for those who did try to focus directly on the
worker. A certain amount of such work always was done, of course,
either by people from other disciplines or by labor economists rebel-
ling against the prevailing Wisconsin school, for example, Norman
Ware in his *Industrial Worker, 1840–1860* (1924) and *Labor Movement
in the U.S., 1860–1895* (1929). Until they began to abandon in-
stitutionalism for the headier study of human resources and labor-
market theory, however, the labor economists effectively
monopolized the field of labor history, and engraved on it the institutional stamp of their discipline.

The historical profession was hardly blameless for the arrested state
of American labor history. As with the academic world generally,
history had long been the preserve of a privileged segment of American society, and attention focused mainly on politics, diplomacy, and
war. To the extent that the subject broadened out, it did so mainly in
the direction of the frontier and the South. Only when the profession
became democratized after World War II by an influx of people with
working-class and immigrant backgrounds did the worker become an
active subject of study. The sprinkling of graduate students who chose
labor topics during the 1950s aimed at raising labor history to the
level of excellence being achieved at that time in other fields of
American history. This meant, first of all, opening the subject to the
kind of multicausal analysis to be seen in the scholarship of Oscar
Handlin, C. Vann Woodward, Richard Hofstadter, and others of that
brilliant generation of American historians. It involved, second, applying to labor history the skills of the craft, which on the whole were
sadly lacking in the historical work of the labor economists.

That enterprise succeeded resoundingly. The scholarly superstruc-
ture for labor history is now impressive—major archives in Detroit, in
Atlanta, at Penn State and elsewhere, a first-class journal, and active
regional associations. The volume of scholarship has grown enormously: sixteen pages of *Labor History* were required to list all of the
articles published in the field in 1973, not to speak of additional space
for the fifty-eight doctoral dissertations completed that year. The

3. Philip Taft, "Reflections on Selig Perlman," *Industrial and Labor Relations Review*,
XXIX (1976), 250.

better books of recent years have certainly attained the standard of craftsmanship to be found elsewhere in the profession. Sidney Fine's *Sit-Down: The General Motors Strike of 1935-36* (1969) is a model of historical reconstruction based on exhaustive research. No more vigorous narrative history has appeared in the past decade than Irving Bernstein's *The Turbulent Years: A History of the American Worker, 1933-41* (1970) and Bert Cochran's *Labor and Communism: The Conflict That Shaped American Unions* (1977). Barbara Mayer Wertheimer has written the first comprehensive account (to 1914) of women in the labor movement in *We Were There* (1977). And Melvyn Dubofsky's and Warren Van Tine's *John L. Lewis* (1977) is in the best tradition of American biography and by far the finest life we have of an American labor leader.

Most of the first generation of writing, and much even of the 1970s, deals with the familiar subjects of labor history—leaders, strikes, organizations, politics, the left. From the first, however, the evident intention had been not merely to write better conventional history, but to change the focus of study so that labor history would become a history of workers. That purpose can be readily perceived, for example, in Herbert Gutman's detailed studies of labor conflict in the 1870s,[4] in David Montgomery's *Beyond Equality: Labor and the Radical Republicans* (1967), Melvyn Dubofsky's *We Shall Be All: A History of the IWW* (1969), Irving Bernstein's *The Lean Years: A History of the American Worker, 1920-1933* (1960), and my own *Steelworkers in America* (1960). But the obstacles, both of evidence and of conceptualization, were formidable. The first generation succeeded most fully at the practice of conventional skills, and at setting a standard of craft excellence for future work in the field. The impulse to broaden the focus of study did, however, make that first generation the genuine progenitor of the next, and not only by laying a certain amount of essential groundwork and by encouraging further work. Members of the first generation, Herbert Gutman and David Montgomery in particular, have remained on the frontiers of the labor scholarship of the 1970s. In these years, the long-standing barriers to writing the history of American workers have begun to topple.

Among the forces at work, one clearly was ideological. Labor history, Eric Hobsbawm has remarked, "is by tradition a highly political subject."[5] It had not been so in the United States, at least not in

4. A sample of Gutman's early articles can be found in his *Work, Culture, and Society in Industrializing America: Essays in Working-Class and Social History* (New York, 1976).

5. Eric J. Hobsbawm, "Labor History and Ideology," *Journal of Social History*, VII (1974), 371.

Hobsbawm's sense. Labor history had never been the special province of the American left. From Commons onward, the Wisconsin school had identified itself with the pure-and-simple unionism of Samuel Gompers. It was, indeed, the special skill of a practitioner such as Philip Taft to be able to see the trade-union world from the inside and on its own terms.[6] The first generation of trained historians to enter the field fell, on the whole, within the liberal-pluralist spectrum prevailing during the 1950s. There was, of course, no necessary connection between a radical perspective and a rank-and-file orientation—witness the prolific work of Philip Foner or, of more recent origin, that of the corporate-liberal school associated with James Weinstein.[7] But when a radical impulse did finally infuse the study of American labor history during the 1960s, it did in fact establish this connection. The New Left enthusiasm for participatory democracy translated among historians into rallying cries for "history from the bottom up" and for a "history of the inarticulate."[8] Even though its ideological sources were quickly spent, this impulse has given a younger generation of labor historians an ongoing determination not to be distracted from the task of writing the history of workers. The importance of this commitment has been especially great for the study of the modern period, where other influences encouraging working-class history have been less strongly felt.

The other primary stimulus of the new labor history, rich in powers of insight as well as the capacity to motivate, derives from England. With the exception of Frederick Jackson Turner's frontier thesis, probably no other historical statement has been so eagerly embraced or set off so strong a surge of American scholarly activity as E. P. Thompson's *Making of the English Working Class* (1963), and, along with Thompson, Hobsbawm, George Rudé, Brian Harrison, and others in a brilliant constellation of English social historians. Their work suggested dimensions of working-class experience scarcely dreamed of in American labor historiography. Among the richest Thompso-

6. David Brody, "Philip Taft: Labor Scholar," *Labor History*, xix (1978), 9–22.

7. *The Corporate Ideal and the Liberal State* (Boston, 1968). Although Weinstein's views have enjoyed a continuing vogue, they have not generated much additional labor scholarship during the 1970s. See, however, Bruno Ramirez, *When Workers Fight: The Politics of Industrial Relations in the Progressive Era, 1898–1916* (Westport, Conn., 1978); William Graebner, *Coal-Mining Safety in the Progressive Period: The Political Economy of Reform* (Lexington, Ky., 1976). The fullest exploitation of the corporate-liberal theme, in fact, has been by the West German historian Peter Lösche in his *Industriewerkschaften im organisierten Kapitalismus. Das CIO in der Roosevelt-Ära* (1974).

8. For a fuller statement of the impact of the New Left on labor history, see my review essay on Alice and Staughton Lynd's *Rank and File* (Boston, 1973) in *Labor History*, xvi (1975), 117–126.

nian insights transmitted to the American setting were, first, the idea of an industrial morality rooted in evangelical religion, handled with great sensitivity in Paul Faler's work on the Lynn, Massachusetts, shoemakers;[9] second, the meaning of nineteenth-century labor politics and reform, a central theme, for example, in Alan Dawley's *Class and Community: The Industrial Revolution in Lynn* (1976); and, perhaps most frequently observed, the habits and customs of working people in the transition from a preindustrial to an industrial world.[10] Thompson did more than map out a new terrain of working-class life for exploration. By his own loving attention to the concrete and specific, he helped to legitimize the close local study of workers that characterizes so much of the current research in American labor history. And the example of his historical imagination—his fertile effort to re-create an earlier world of working people—spurred on an entire generation of American scholars. If they were misled, it was only in the easy hope of mastering the concreteness and imagination that were, in fact, properties of Thompson's particular genius.[11]

From initial ventures following English guides, American labor historians began to strike out more independently along lines specific to this country's experience. Ethnic history has exerted a strong influence. The work of Virginia Yans-McLaughlin on the Italians of Buffalo, for example, and John Bodnar's on the Slavs of Steelton, Pennsylvania, have provided a fuller understanding of the ways

9. "Cultural Aspects of the Industrial Revolution: Lynn, Massachusetts, Shoemakers and Industrial Morality, 1826–1860," *Labor History*, xv (1974), 367–394.

10. See, e.g., Susan E. Hirsch, *The Roots of the American Working Class: The Industrialization of Crafts in Newark, 1800–1860* (Philadelphia, 1978).

11. There is no need to emphasize the extent to which American scholarship on English labor history has followed the lead of the English school. See, e.g., Richard N. Price, "The Other Face of Respectability: Violence in the Manchester Brickmaking Trade, 1859–1870," *Past and Present*, no. 66 (February 1975), 110–132; Robert D. Storch, "The Plague of the Blue Locusts: Police Reform and Popular Resistance in Northern England, 1840–57," *International Review of Social History*, xx (1975, pt. 1), 61–90; Standish Meacham, *A Life Apart: The English Working Class, 1890–1914* (Cambridge, Mass., 1977). The English influence seems quite strong on American scholars of French labor history. Thompson, indeed, serves as the rallying cry in William H. Sewell, "Social Change and the Rise of Working-Class Politics in Nineteenth-Century Marseilles," *Past and Present*, no. 65 (November 1974), 75–109. The English influence is present but not predominant in Joan W. Scott, *The Glassworkers of Carmaux* (Cambridge, Mass., 1974), and Robert J. Bezucha, *The Lyon Uprising of 1834* (Cambridge, Mass., 1974). See also Temma Kaplan, *Anarchists of Andalusia, 1868–1903* (Princeton, 1977). As one moves into central and eastern Europe, the English influence becomes more remote, and, in fact, is specifically rejected in Lawrence Schofer, *The Formation of a Modern Labor Force: Upper Silesia, 1865–1914* (Berkeley, Calif., 1975), which, quite uncharacteristic of the labor history being done in this country, relies heavily on labor-market and developmental economics.

ethnic characteristics shaped the entry of immigrant workers into the American industrial world. The studies of Bruce Laurie and Michael Feldberg on Philadelphia workers and the Kensington riots of 1844 reveal the depth of ethnocultural tensions that inhibited class development.[12] In *The Indispensable Enemy: Labor and the Anti-Chinese Movement in California* (1971), Alexander Saxton has identified the animus against the Chinese as a defining experience in California working-class life in the nineteenth century. A growing literature is depicting the ethnic dimension of American working-class life in all its complexity—from the study of conflict between Yankee and French-Canadian textile workers in Webster, Massachusetts, in the 1840s, to the labor boycott as an Irish device in New York City, to the role of ethnic groups in the local labor politics of the Knights of Labor in the 1880s.[13]

Community study has offered a second fruitful strategy for the new labor history. Following Herbert Gutman's pioneering work in this area, labor historians have been drawn into a fuller exploration of the way workers fitted into their communities: because of the strong interest in local history, on the one hand, and on the other, because the cultural aspects of working-class life generally took root in the local community. The logic that leads to community study—as well as the benefits—can be seen, for example, in Daniel Walkowitz's work on the iron molders of Troy, New York, which starts out by treating them as workers, then considers their ethnic and associational activity, and finally reveals the web of relationships with the police and politicians that made the molders a powerful presence in Troy in the years after the Civil War. In his study of Lynn and Fall River, Massachusetts, John T. Cumbler stresses the importance of neighborhoods, residential patterns, and the informal social relations of lunchrooms and cafés for understanding the varying degrees of cohesion among workers.[14]

12. Virginia Yans-McLaughlin, *Family and Community: Italian Immigrants in Buffalo, 1880–1930* (Ithaca, N.Y., 1977); John Bodnar, *Immigration and Industrialization: Ethnicity in an American Mill Town* (Pittsburgh, 1977); Michael Feldberg, *The Philadelphia Riots of 1844: A Study in Ethnic Conflict* (Westport, Conn., 1975); Bruce Laurie, "The Working People of Philadelphia, 1827–1853," Ph.D. dissertation, University of Pittsburgh, 1971.

13. Barbara M. Tucker, "The Force of Tradition in the Southern New England Textile Industry, 1790–1860," unpublished paper, chap. 5; Leon Fink, "Workingmen's Democracy: The Knights of Labor in Local Politics, 1886–1896," Ph.D. dissertation, University of Rochester, 1977; Michael Gordon, "Irish Immigrant Culture and the Labor Boycott in New York City, 1880–1886," in Richard L. Ehrlich, ed., *Immigrants in Industrial America* (Charlottesville, Va., 1977), as well as other essays in this collection.

14. Daniel Walkowitz, *Worker City, Company Town: Iron and Cotton Worker Protest in*

Beyond these planned forays into new terrain, a great deal is being learned from the research of scholars who do not think of themselves as labor historians, that is, whose starting point is not the worker, but political behavior, the city, social mobility, the family, women, blacks. As the focus widens from elites to the "plain people"—to use Peter Knight's phrase—all of these are necessarily generating much fresh information about workers. The compartmentalizing of fields is, in fact, rapidly eroding under what Peter Stearns calls elsewhere in this volume "a concern for a historical perspective on the everyday affairs of ordinary people." Elizabeth Pleck has recently made an explicit plea for an end to the unnatural separation of family and labor history, "as if families existed without workers and workers were devoid of families."[15] It is already possible to record some of the fruits of that intermingling of interests. Tamara Hareven, for example, has studied the influence of the family system of French Canadian cotton workers on recruiting and working patterns in the Amoskeag mill in Manchester, New Hampshire.[16] In Leslie Tentler's *Wage-Earning Women: Industrial Work and Family Life, 1900-1930* (1979), both fields benefit mutually: Tentler's focus on the adolescent stage during which most girls worked throws much light on their adjustment to factory employment, and that experience in turn helps to explain their development as women and wives. Moving in the other direction, Susan Kleinberg has shown the impact of a basic-industry economy on the households of Pittsburgh.[17] The interest in women's and family history, finally, has pushed research into the farther recesses of labor history, as, for example, in David M. Katzman's *Seven Days a Week: Women and Domestic Service in Industrializing America* (1979).[18] This fruitful interchange has occurred, to a greater or lesser degree, in a number of other fields whose focus has shifted to the lives of ordinary

---

*Troy and Cohoes, New York, 1855-1884* (Urbana, Ill., 1978); John T. Cumbler, *Working-Class Community in Industrial America: Work, Leisure, and Struggle in Two Industrial Cities, 1880-1930* (Westport, Conn., 1979). For a similar stress on residential patterns in France, see Mary Lynn McDougall, "Consciousness and Community: The Workers of Lyon, 1830-1850," *Journal of Social History*, XII (1978), 129-45. On the whole, Europeanists have tended to associate community with craft identity rather than ethnicity, neighborhood, or town.

15. "Two Worlds in One: Work and Family," *Journal of Social History*, X (1976), 178-195.

16. "Family Time and Industrial Time," *Journal of Urban History*, I (1975), 365-389.

17. "Technology and Women's Work," *Labor History*, XVII (1976), 58-72.

18. The perspective on women's and family history seems to have an especially strong basis in common with the Europeanists. See, e.g., Joan W. Scott and Louise Tilly, "Women's Work and Family in Nineteenth-century Europe," *Comparative Studies in Society and History*, XVII (1975), 36-64; also Patricia Branca, "A New Perspective on Women's Work: A Comparative Typology," *Journal of Social History*, IX (1975), 129-153.

David Brody

people. To some extent, in fact, even so rarefied a subject as intellectual history has found itself drawn toward labor history, as evidenced by recent studies of the work ethic in industrial America. In a notable melding of ideas and social experience, Daniel T. Rodgers has developed a provocative analysis that turns on the tension between the moral ideal of a work ethic and the dehumanizing reality of factory labor.[19]

For certain fields, a genuine imperative pushes study in the direction of the workers. This is true, for example, of research in social mobility. The original formulations of the subject have come under searching criticism in recent years. Is occupation, without data on income and wealth, an adequate index of socioeconomic standing? Does an occupational scale that is static and limited to a few gross categories measure anything worth measuring? And why trace the social mobility of people who may not live by the American ideology of opportunity in the first place?[20] As social-mobility students respond to these questions, they are sure to advance our understanding of American working-class history. The need for a more exact map of job structures, for example, has drawn attention to the economic context and specific characteristics of particular occupations. Thus a recent article growing out of the Philadelphia Social History Project explores the Philadelphia occupational structure over time and with attention to such factors as wage levels, working conditions, and relative opportunities for advancement. The tentative conclusions are bound to stimulate further work, for they suggest the importance of relative job opportunity—that is, whether a particular industry or region was expanding or not—in the determination of mobility rates. And a key is thus offered to the vexing question of geographic mobility: the high rate of movement may have been a direct, rational response to relative economic opportunity.[21] Concern over the nar-

19. Daniel T. Rodgers, *The Work Ethic in Industrial America, 1850-1920* (Chicago, 1977); James B. Gilbert, *Work without Salvation: America's Intellectuals and Industrial Alienation* (Baltimore, 1977).
20. See, e.g., James A. Henretta, "The Study of Social Mobility: Ideological Assumptions and Conceptual Biases," *Labor History*, XVIII (1977), 165-178; Richard W. Fox, review of Thomas Kessner, *The Golden Door: Italian and Jewish Mobility in New York City, 1880-1915* (New York, 1977), in *Chronicle of Higher Education*, May 23, 1977.
21. Bruce Laurie et al., "Immigrants and Industry: The Philadelphia Experience, 1850-1880," *Journal of Social History*, IX (1975), 219-248. In trying to clarify the puzzle over job classifications, the authors revealed the importance of the Census of Manufactures for a whole range of other questions that concern the labor historian—an example of the cumulative benefits deriving from social history. See also, e.g., Anthony E. Boardman and Michael P. Weber, "Economic Growth and Occupational Mobility in Nineteenth-Century Urban America," *Journal of Social History*, XI (1977), 52-73; Margo Anderson Conk, "Occupational Classification in the United States Census," *Journal of*

row empirical focus of social-mobility studies, as well as over the invisibility of women, has similarly prompted Thomas Dublin to exploit the payroll records of a textile mill in Lowell, Massachusetts, with equally provocative discoveries not only regarding occupational and geographic mobility but also on the impact of industrialization on female workers between 1830 and 1860.[22] To the extent that working people are the subjects of social history, its progress almost by definition will entail an enrichment of the study of labor history.

In one respect, the new social history has already made its mark on the field. As attention has shifted to the workers directly, labor historians have been drawn inevitably into quantification, and their guides have been the social historians. Dawley's study of the Lynn shoemakers, for example, has relied heavily on census manuscripts and city directories. His computer printouts have generated a fund of information hitherto inaccessible—the composition of the labor force, career lines, property ownership, family patterns. It can be instructive to compare two books covering similar ground—for instance, two excellent books on Milwaukee, Gerd Korman's *Industrialization, Immigrants, and Americanizers* (1967) and Kathleen Conzen's more recent *Immigrant Milwaukee* (1976)—to get a sense of what statistics can bring to our grasp of labor history. This applies to quite traditional questions as well. In Dawley's book, the single most striking finding refers to the identity of the Knights of St. Crispin. By the simple expedient of comparing union membership lists with the names on the local census tracts, Dawley discovered that the Crispins represented a cross section of Lynn factory workers and thereby proved wrong the long-standing characterization of the Knights of St. Crispin as a movement of artisans resisting the modernization of the shoe industry. It seems likely, in fact, that quantitative research will score its easiest successes on some of the traditional issues of American labor history. Jonathan Garlock has compiled a data bank on the Knights of Labor that will give a firmer basis to our understanding of American labor reform.

*Interdisciplinary History*, IX (1978), 111–130; Michael B. Katz et al., "Migration and the Social Order in Erie County: 1855," *Journal of Interdisciplinary History*, VIII (1978), 669–701.

22. "Women Workers and the Study of Social Mobility," *Journal of Interdisciplinary History*, IX (1979), 647–666. On social-mobility study, clearly, influence flows from the Americanists to students of European labor history. See, e.g., David Crew, "Definitions of Modernity: Social Mobility in a German Town, 1880–1901," *Journal of Social History*, VII (1973), 51–74; William H. Sewell, "Social Mobility in a Nineteenth-Century City: Some Findings and Implications," *Journal of Interdisciplinary History*, VII (1976), 217–234. Like Crew, Joan Scott credits Stephan Thernstrom's influence on *The Glassworkers of Carmaux*. Hers is an exceptional example of data on social and geographic movement actively put to use in a broader analysis, and not offered as an isolated phenomenon.

Garlock's dissertation has made a good start by dealing with such basic questions as the size and duration, occupational coverage, and geographic representation of the Knights of Labor.[23] Warren Van Tine has similarly used quantitative data to uncover the social origins and career lines of trade-union leaders in his *Making of the Labor Bureaucrat, 1870–1920* (1973). Most of the current statistical work, of course, is devoted not to traditional problems but to measuring the complex dimensions of working-class life. Without minimizing the difficulties in such research, both interpretive and technical, we must recognize that the accumulating data are bound ultimately to provide the means for dealing with that range of questions in labor history that can be answered only by counting.

As one moves into the twentieth century, the scholarly terrain changes. The nineteenth-century resources for local research either become unavailable—as with the census schedules—or much less satisfactory. The main themes of the new labor history—ethnicity, community, working-class culture—grow increasingly submerged or dispersed in the modern urban world. And the guiding hand of the English historians weakens in the twentieth-century context. So modern labor historians have been thrown more completely on their own intellectual resources. As community study becomes unmanageable, they have begun to make the individual plant or local union the unit of intensive study. To replace the rich local and labor press of the nineteenth century, they have sought evidence of what workers thought and experienced in public records, such as hearings before labor boards, in certain kinds of union and industrial-relations records, and, above all, in the oral testimony of surviving participants.[24] In the 1970s, oral history programs have become a major part of labor archival work, and research on recent topics regularly entails interviews in the field.

We have in Peter Friedlander's *Emergence of a UAW Local: A Study of Class and Culture* (1975) an example of the fruitful merging of a nineteenth-century historiographical perspective—the specific influence credited by Friedlander is Paul Kleppner's analysis of midwest-

23. "A Structural Analysis of the Knights of Labor," Ph.D. dissertation, University of Rochester, 1974; Garlock, "The Knights of Labor Data Bank," *Historical Methods Newsletter,* Fall 1973, 149–160. On the application of statistical analysis to strikes, the Europeanists have been decidedly in the lead. See especially Edward Shorter and Charles Tilly, *Strikes in France, 1830–1968* (London, 1974).

24. See, e.g., Robert H. Zieger, "The Limits of Militancy: Organizing Paper Workers, 1933–1935," *Journal of American History,* LXIII (1976), 638–653; Zieger, *Madison's Battery Workers, 1934–1952* (Ithaca, N.Y., 1977).

ern political behavior in the late nineteenth century[25]—with a modern research strategy that focuses on the industrial plant as the unit of intensive study and that makes remarkable use of oral testimony. Friedlander's analysis turns on the ethnocultural identity of workers in his Detroit auto-parts plant, and on the role of second-generation Polish-American workers as union militants. In subsequent work, Friedlander has elaborated on this analysis, and given it a firmer empirical base by the use of plant employment records—a kind of modern counterpart to city directories and census schedules of nineteenth-century study.[26] It remains to be seen how fruitful an ethnocultural approach will be for the history of modern workers, except for groups such as blacks, southern whites, and Mexicans. As the main themes of nineteenth-century research become ever harder to identify and handle for the years after World War I, labor historians are seeking other ways of identifying the experience of workers in the twentieth century—by the advent of consumerism in the 1920s, by unemployment in the 1930s, by rank-and-file militancy within the new industrial unions, by the impact of World War II, by the massive entry of women into the labor force, and so on into contemporary times.

Among the most promising of such approaches is the study of workers within the workplace. Scholars have come to this problem from two directions, starting either from management or from the workers. The managerial approach was greatly stimulated by Harry Braverman's *Labor and Monopoly Capital* (1974). Taking as his text Frederick W. Taylor's *Principles of Scientific Management* (1911), Braverman stressed above all the dominating part that management, by its unceasing compulsion to rationalize the production process, played in shaping the fate of the American worker. Attracted by its implications for corporate capitalism, a group of radical economists has done some historical work on this problem, mainly in the form of articles,[27] but recently also in Richard Edwards' *Contested Terrain: The Transformation of the Workplace in the Twentieth Century* (1979). Among historians, Daniel Nelson has made a good start toward establishing

25. *Cross of Culture: The Social Analysis of Midwestern Politics, 1850–1900* (New York, 1970).

26. "The Social Basis of Politics in a UAW Local: Midland Steel, 1933–1941," paper read at the 1977 meeting of the Organization of American Historians.

27. See especially Katherine Stone, "The Origin of Job Structures in the Steel Industry," *Radical America,* VII (1973), 19–64; Bryan Palmer, "Class, Conception, and Conflict: The Thrust for Efficiency . . . 1903–1922," *Review of Radical Political Economics,* VII (1975), 31–49.

the factory context for the evolution of modern management in his *Workers and Managers: Origins of the New Factory System, 1880–1920* (1976), and Stuart Brandes has surveyed paternalistic policies in his *American Welfare Capitalism, 1880–1940* (1976). Neither book, however, displays quite the sensitivity to the imperatives for managerial control to be found in Braverman's study and in the writing of the radical economists. Two recent books, although only tangentially concerned with the management of labor, lay important groundwork for further work in this area. One is Alfred D. Chandler's magisterial *Visible Hand: The Managerial Revolution in Business* (1977). The other is David F. Noble's *America by Design: Science, Technology, and the Rise of Corporate Capitalism* (1977). Noble's provocative study suggests the need to rethink the impact of technology on labor, with particular attention to the choices made by management among a range of technological possibilities for purposes of maximizing control over the work force.

The response of workers has come under active study during the 1970s. David Montgomery has written seminal essays on the autonomy of the skilled worker in the nineteenth-century factory, on a worker's ethic of manliness underlying that independence, and on the struggle for control that was joined at the opening of the twentieth century.[28] Influenced by the work of E. P. Thompson and Eric Hobsbawm, Montgomery and others have carried the notion of shop-floor history forward in time and made labor's struggles to protect its prerogatives and values a central issue in the age of modern industry. Recent studies have dealt, among other topics, with the transformation of work among telephone employees between 1880 and 1925, with electrical workers during the unionizing era, and with wildcat strikes and battles over production standards in the automobile industry in the 1930s and 1940s.[29]

Of all aspects of American working-class history, the study of shop-floor activity is the least confined to specific time periods. The strug-

28. "Workers' Control of Machine Production in the Nineteenth Century," *Labor History*, xvii (1976), 485–509; Montgomery, "The 'New Unionism' and the Transformation of Workers' Consciousness in America, 1909–1922," *Journal of Social History*, vii (1974), 509–529; and, approaching the problem from the managerial side, "Immigrant Workers and Managerial Reform," in Ehrlich, ed., *Immigrants in Industrial America*, 96–110.

29. Maurine Greenwald, "The Transformation of Work and Workers' Consciousness in the Telephone Industry, 1880–1925," paper delivered at the 1977 meeting of the American Historical Association; Ronald Schatz, "American Electrical Workers: Work, Struggles, Aspirations, 1930–1950," Ph.D. dissertation, University of Pittsburgh, 1977; Nelson Lichtenstein, "Wildcat Strikes in the UAW: Their Ebb and Flow, 1937–1945," paper delivered at the 1978 meeting of the AHA Pacific Coast Branch; Lichten-

gle of workers to retain control over the job and of managers to subordinate them to a rationalized system of production is a continuing story that does not end at any given stage of industrialization. And while a great deal remains to be learned about the formative years, it is for the modern period that shop-floor history holds the greatest significance for labor historians, for it permits them to get at the experience of working people even in the age of mature collective bargaining. From a number of angles, among which the shop-floor approach is probably most important, current work promises to lead to a fuller history of the American worker in the twentieth century than seemed possible a decade or so ago.

Thus far, scholarly energies have been heavily committed to opening up the new areas of working-class research. Little attention has been paid to the larger implications of the accumulating scholarship. The new labor historians find themselves in quite a different intellectual setting from the scholars of the Wisconsin school. The latter knew perfectly well where the bits and pieces of their research fitted. It was in the nature of institutional history to provide for its adherents a clear framwork—and none was clearer than the American trade union, with its well-defined structure and rules. Perlman's *Theory of the Labor Movement* performed the same function on a larger scale. Even when the specific analysis of Perlman's *Theory* fell into disrepute among labor scholars after World War II, for the most part they did not doubt that Perlman had captured the job-conscious character of the American labor movement. As historians have pushed out beyond trade-union history, they have necessarily left the safe haven of Perlman's explicit framework. The thrust of the current scholarship has gone strongly against the construction of a new one. For one thing, research has been narrowly focused, devoted to the intensive, local study of workers. We have, moreover, developed an acute sense of the complexity and variety of American working-class experience, in which all lines of inquiry—family, ethnicity, mobility, technology, tradition, and so on—converge into an intricate network of connections. At its best the monographic literature has been highly imaginative at establishing linkages between various aspects of working-class experience and at assessing the totality of that experience at a given place and time. But such an approach has necessarily been inward-looking, and even when it has not fallen into the error of ignoring the

---

stein, "Auto Worker Militancy and the Structure of Factory Life, 1933–1955," paper delivered at the 1979 meeting of the Organization of American Historians. For a similar tendency among Europeanists, see Peter Stearns, *Lives of Labor: Work in a Maturing Industrial Society* (New York, 1975).

national forces acting on local communities, it has militated against any systematic thinking about a new synthesis for American labor history.

To some degree, too, we have doubtless been lulled by the thought that we already had a future guide in *The Making of the English Working Class*. The enormous enthusiasm for Thompson's great book derived not only from our discovery of the richness of labor history, but equally from the expectation that, once we had acquired a comparable body of information, we would then go on to write our own "Making of the American Working Class." Class, says Thompson, "is a cultural as much as an economic formation. . . . The class experience is largely determined by the productive relations into which men are born—or enter involuntarily." And then: "Class-consciousness is the way these experiences are handled in cultural terms: embodied in traditions, value systems, ideas, and institutional forms." The central event occurs "when some men, as a result of common experiences (inherited or shared), feel and articulate the identity of their interests as between themselves, and as against other men whose interests are different from (and usually opposed to) theirs."[30] In fact, Thompson is much less concerned with the productive relations leading to class identity than with its expression in the form of a working-class culture. Thompson's formulation may serve admirably in the English setting. Certainly his disciples think so. Thus Gareth Stedman Jones, in seeking to push Thompson's analysis into the late nineteenth century, writes confidently of "the basic consistency of outlook reflected in the new working-class culture which spread over England after 1870." And further: "The distinctiveness of a working-class way of life was enormously accentuated. Its separateness and impermeability were now reflected in a dense and inward-looking culture."[31] Like Gareth Stedman Jones, we have been busily gethering the evidence of American working-class culture. But labor historians cannot share Jones's confidence of discovering for American workers a "basic consistency of outlook" and a "distinctive . . . way of life."

The most ambitious American attempt thus far to generalize from a Thompsonian perspective is Herbert Gutman's major essay, "Work, Culture, and Society in Industrializing America" (1973). As with all of Gutman's work, the essay is richly detailed and documented, and offers a superb survey of what was known roughly a decade ago about

30. *The Making of the English Working Class* (New York, 1963), 9–13.
31. "Working-Class Culture and Working-Class Politics in London, 1870–1900," *Journal of Social History*, VII (1974), 498.

the work habits and values of the recruits to American industrialism—rural Americans in the early nineteenth century, artisans in the middle period, peasants immigrants at the end of the industrializing era—and about "preindustrial" forms of collective behavior throughout the industrializing century. Despite its attentiveness to the cultural dimensions of American labor history, the essay actually represents a strategic retreat from Thompson's basic formulation. Class is, in fact, wholly jettisoned from Gutman's analysis. Instead, he relies on a distinction between culture and society derived from anthropology that has the effect of drawing his discussion down to a narrow band of working-class experience—the moment of contact between the industrial society and generation after generation of newcomers bearing with them a preindustrial culture.

Thompson's class analysis turned on the interaction between a settled population of English working people, especially in the clothing and metal trades, and a new industrial order that was demonstrably antagonistic to their customs and values. Early America lacked such a preindustrial laboring population. Colonial workers, especially artisans, have been studied actively in recent years, but from a recognition of the important artisan role in colonial politics and revolutionary activity or as an outgrowth of a strong current interest in the social history of early America, and not on the whole from any conviction that the roots of an American working class are to be found in the laboring population of preindustrial America.[32] In his essay, Gutman hit upon the idea of transferring Thompson's theme onto a different plane—the repetition of an essentially identical experience by recurring generations of recruits to American industrialism. By so doing, Gutman offered a fruitful insight into the particular history of American workers, but not one likely to lead to a working-class history in Thompson's meaning. Even within the narrow terms in which Gutman pitched his argument, in fact, the reliance on the preindust-

32. See, e.g., Jesse Lemisch, "Jack Tar in the Streets: Merchant Seamen in the Politics of Revoluntionary America," *William and Mary Quarterly,* xxv (1968), 343-370; Pauline Maier, "Popular Uprisings and Civil Authority in Eighteenth-Century America," *William and Mary Quarterly,* xxvii (1970), 3-35; James H. Hutson, "An Investigation of the Inarticulate: Philadelphia's White Oaks," *William and Mary Quarterly,* xxviii (1971), 3-25; Charles S. Olton, *Philadelphia Mechanics and the American Revolution* (Syracuse, 1975); G. W. Warden, "Inequality and Instability in Eighteenth-Century Boston: A Reappraisal," *Journal of Interdisciplinary History,* vi (1976), 585-620; Alan Kulikoff, "The Progress of Inequality in Revolutionary Boston," *William and Mary Quarterly,* xxviii (1971), 375-412; Gary B. Nash, "Urban Wealth and Poverty in Pre-Revolutionary America," *Journal of Interdisciplinary History,* vi (1976), 545-584; Nash, "Up from the Bottom in Franklin's Philadelphia," *Past and Present,* no. 77 (November 1977), 58-83.

rial concept raised problems not faced in Thompson's study, especially relating to Gutman's need to assume a commonality among a great variety of groups entering American industry over an entire century. The pertinence of Gutman's essay, in any case, is to the larger point: that, for all we have learned from Thompson and his English colleagues, American labor historians cannot expect to develop a new synthesis along the lines suggested in *The Making of the English Working Class.*

If not through the notion of a unified working-class culture, then where is the alternative approach for American labor history? Only one seems likely wholly to satisfy the requirements for a successful new synthesis: first, defining some common ground applying to all American workers; second, providing an element of continuity running from the opening chapter to the present; and, finally, encompassing the dynamic forces shaping the experience of American workers. Those requirements can probably best be met by an economic approach, taking as its starting point not culture but work and the job, and broadening out from there. This perspective is, in fact, implicit in much of the new labor history, even where its focus is on working-class culture. Work provides the unifying element in Gutman's treatment of culture and society, and so it does in the studies of younger scholars following in Gutman's footsteps. This is true, for example, of Alan Dawley's account of Lynn shoe workers, of Daniel Walkowitz on Troy molders, of Thomas Dublin on Lowell cotton workers. All three have a great deal to say about industrial development and job concerns, and, beyond that, about strike activity and labor organization. David Montgomery's study of workers' control of machine production includes a large dosage of the subject matter of the old labor history: informal work rules turn into the shop agreements of trade unions and, as the struggle with management intensifies, what Montgomery calls "workers' consciousness" manifests itself in sympathy strikes and an impulse toward industrial unionism.

Repeatedly, individual scholars have rediscovered the need to see the workers they are studying in the context of job and industry, and often indeed to define their analyses in terms of collective activity and labor organization. The persistent intrusion of these issues into the new labor history suggests the powerful logic behind an economic approach to the history of American workers. And, to a degree, it suggests also an underlying wisdom in Selig Perlman's *Theory of the Labor Movement.* It was the special character of American unionism (as Perlman saw it) to aim at securing the common economic ground on which workers of the most diverse loyalties and persuasions might unite. A new generation of labor historians may be able to capitalize on Perlman's insight, not so as to return to the older institutional history, but for purposes of constructing a usable framework in which to place their rich findings. With a steady focus on men and women on the job, they may be able to delineate the continuities and dynamic elements in the particular labor history of the United States.

The vitality of the new scholarship is evident on every hand—in the volume of research under way, in the accumulating monographic literature, in the attention labor history receives at scholarly meetings, even, indeed, in the growing list of appointments at leading institutions. Perhaps the strongest testimony to its vigor is the fact that the study of workers should be achieving such prominence at a time of marked conservatism in the country. This momentum can be sustained, however, only if it leads to a synthesis that will provide guidance for future scholarship and, perhaps more important, reshape the existing perception of labor's past in America. The truncated state of the field—rich in its findings, unclear as to larger meaning—places the task of synthesis high on the agenda of American labor history in the 1980s.

# 11

## Community Studies, Urban History, and American Local History

### Kathleen Neils Conzen

AFTER almost a century in the historiographical wilderness, the history of life at the local level emerged in the 1970s as one of the most lively and promising areas of historical inquiry in the United States.[1] What began as a proliferation of case studies in which local data were used to shed light on such traditionally disparate problems in American historiography as New England Puritanism and social mobility in the industrial city has grown into a minor industry that is revising our interpretations of major areas of American history, stimulating methodological and conceptual innovation, and supporting a new openness to cross-cultural comparison. It may also promise to provide, for the first time, the basis for a true local history of the United States—a local history resting on a coherent interpretation of the changing nature of life at the local level and the changing role of the local community in American development.

Not that America has been without a local history tradition. Until very recently, however, it has not been an academic one. In the nineteenth century, booster pride and an awesome recognition of historical change personally experienced led numerous gifted and not-so-gifted amateurs to become compulsive chroniclers of local history and to found a still vital network of historical societies, research collections, and journals. But to the rising historical profession of the 1880s, the important historical questions were national and political ones. Local history as the history of individual communities remained

1. On the local history renaissance, see Michael Kammen, "The American Revolution Bicentennial and the Writing of Local History," *History News*, xxx (August 1975), 179-190.

in the hands of the amateurs, while the history of local life in its broader context was ignored along with social history generally.[2]

Insulated from either the interpretive frameworks or the critical standards of academic historians, most local history writing wavered between sterile antiquarianism and uncritical boosterism "so exclusively localized as to appear to have no meaning for any community but one."[3] It recounted a tale of progress and communal harmony in a conventional formula whose elements included surprisingly elegaic accounts of the Indians whom the community had dispossessed; heroic tales of the sufferings and achievements of the early settlers; chronological narrative of political and governmental milestones; recitation of the community's contributions to such national events as wars and economic crises; brief chronicles of the main economic, social, and cultural institutions of the town; and often a "mug book" celebrating the lives of leading citizens.[4] There was little in such a tradition that could clarify either the distinctive quality of life in a given community or the contribution of trends at the local level to the nation's history. By the 1930s, to be sure, the unmistakable prominence of one particular type of locality led Arthur Meier Schlesinger, Sr., to argue that American history could not be understood if the influence of the city were not taken into account, and prompted the beginnings of serious historical inquiry into various aspects of urban life and the history of individual cities. But the trend was unfocused and slow to gather momentum.[5] "The trained historian is primarily interested in larger areas of research," noted a 1944 Social Science

2. David D. Van Tassel, *Recording America's Past: An Interpretation of the Development of Historical Studies in America, 1607–1884* (Chicago, 1960); John Higham et al., *History* (Englewood Cliffs, N.J., 1965).

3. Constance McLaughlin Green, "The Value of Local History," in Caroline F. Ware, ed., *The Cultural Approach to History* (New York, 1940), 279.

4. The formula was often literally provided to local authors by companies specializing in the production and publication of city and county histories for sale to subscribers, who were rewarded with the inclusion of their biographies in the volume. See Van Tassel, *Recording America's Past,* 168–169; Archibald Hanna, "Everyman His Own Biographer," *Proceedings of the American Antiquarian Society,* LXXX (1970), 291–298. For recent intelligent applications of the same formula (without the mug book section) in Bicentennial publications, see Julia M. Ehresmann, ed., *Geneva, Illinois: A History of Its Times and Places* (Geneva, Ill., 1977), and Nicholas C. Burckel, ed., *Racine: Growth and Change in a Wisconsin County* (Racine, Wis., 1977). Numerous other examples could be cited to testify to the continuing vitality of local history and thus to the popular demand for an appropriate format.

5. Arthur M. Schlesinger, "The City in American History," *Mississippi Valley Historical Review,* XXVII (1940), 43–66; Dwight M. Hoover, "The Diverging Paths of American Urban History," *American Quarterly,* XX (1968), 296–317. See also "Conversation with Bayrd Still" in Bruce M. Stave, ed., *The Making of Urban History: Historiography through Oral History* (Beverly Hills, Calif., 1977), 63–102.

Research Council guide for the study of local history. "If the local history of the United States is to be written at all, it will have to be done by an interested, if amateur, citizen or group of citizens in each community."[6]

By contrast, the guide's 1976 successor could note with excusable hyperbole that "most of the research and writing in American history for some years now has been on topics which are distinctly localized in subject matter and source materials."[7] Dissertations with a local focus listed in *Dissertation Abstracts International*, a useful bellwether of changing fashions in historical research, increased from about 7 percent of American history listings in 1969 to over 20 percent by 1976.[8] Locally oriented published works considered of sufficient interest to the profession to receive reviews in the two major historical journals experienced similar proportional increases.[9] Local studies have received the profession's major awards; seminars and conferences with local themes are increasingly common; courses with a local content have become a respected and popular part of the undergraduate history curriculum; and the subfield received a final accolade of sorts in 1977 with the publication of a survey text in American history structured around the local community.[10]

6. Donald Dean Parker, *Local History: How to Gather It, Write It, and Publish It* (New York, 1944), xi.

7. Thomas E. Felt, *Researching, Writing, and Publishing Local History* (Nashville, 1976), xi.

8. Studies with a locality-related topic leveled off to around 17 percent of the total by 1978; the actual numbers of local studies listed and identified in this very rough tabulation increased from 28 in 1969 to 102 by 1976 before dropping to 70 by 1978. It should be noted that *Dissertations Abstracts International* "is a monthly compilation of abstracts of doctoral dissertations submitted to University Microfilms International by more than 400 cooperating institutions in the United States and Canada. Some institutions do not send all of their doctoral dissertations. Also, the various institutions began to contribute to the doctoral program at different times" (statement, p. iii, monthly volume, *Dissertations Abstracts International, A: The Humanities and Social Sciences*, Ann Arbor). Thus these listings do not include, for all or parts of the period, such universities as Harvard, Berkeley, and Chicago, whose students have produced notable numbers of dissertations in this sphere. Therefore these must be regarded as minimum estimates. "Local focus" is here taken to include topics explored in a local setting, or concerned with issues by definition local—urban government, for example—but excluding biography, histories of individual firms, and the like.

9. Reviews of studies with a local focus in the *Journal of American History* increased from 3.7 percent of all reviews (12) in vol. LVI (1969–70) to 7.5 percent by 1976–77 (31) and 10.4 percent (45) in 1978–79; in the *American Historical Review*, proportions of books reviewed in American history increased from 5.6 percent (17) in vol. LXXIV (1969) to 8.5 percent (37) in 1976 and 10.5 percent (36) in 1978. Again, the classification is necessarily approximate.

10. John G. Clark, David M. Katzman, Richard D. McKinzie, and Theodore A. Wilson, *Three Generations in Twentieth-Century America: Family, Community, and Nation* (Homewood, Ill., 1977).

This trend within the profession has coincided with and fed upon the dramatic upsurge in popular historical awareness within the United States during the 1970s. The American Revolution Bicentennial celebrations encouraged an outpouring of local history at the state, county, city, town, even neighborhood levels; among the 88,892 officially sanctioned Bicentennial projects and events were some 4,387 publications, 115 conferences, 295 seminars and symposiums, 1,071 educational courses, 1,591 exhibits, and 1,201 film and slide shows designed to raise consciousness of local as well as national history.[11] The intertwined popularity of historic preservation and urban "re-gentrification" provide further tangible evidence of the vitality of the popular historical impulse, along with the impetus for some of the most carefully researched and imaginatively interpreted work in local community history presently available.[12] The revitalized and democratized national obsession with genealogy—the so-called *Roots* phenomenon—represents another manifestation of this public mood.[13]

Owing little in its origins to the efforts of academic historians, this mood nevertheless has created an important new market for their services at a time when declining enrollments have eroded the academic employment base of the profession. A new professional identity is emerging among "public historians" as employment opportunities expand in museums, historical agencies, and government, and graduate training programs in "practical history" are being shaped to their needs. Such federal actions as the passage of the National Historic Preservation Act of 1966 and the funding activities of the federal endowments, along with public support from state and local governments, have provided a significant stimulus. The American Association for State and Local History, founded in 1940, at a time when the major professional associations had little interest in the

11. *The Bicentennial of the United States of America: A Final Report to the People* (Washington, D.C., 1977), II, 261–262.

12. Charles B. Hosmer, Jr., "The Broadening View of the Historical Preservation Movement," in Ian M. G. Quimby, ed., *Material Culture and the Study of American Life* (New York, 1978), 121–139; Roger S. Ahlbrandt, Jr., and Paul C. Brophy, *Neighborhood Revitalization* (Lexington, Mass., 1975). Examples of excellent preservation-inspired studies include Arthur J. Krim, *Northwest Cambridge,* Cambridge Historical Commission, Architectual Survey of Cambridge, report no. 5 (Cambridge, Mass., 1977); Mary Louise Christovich et al., *New Orleans Architecture,* vol. II: *The American Sector* (Gretna, La., 1972); Ernest R. Sandeen, *St. Paul's Historic Summit Avenue* (St. Paul, Minn., 1978).

13. Samuel P. Hays, "History and Genealogy: Patterns for Change and Prospects for Cooperation," *Prologue,* VII (Summer 1975), 81–84. David Weitzman, *Underfoot: An Everyday Guide to Exploring the American Past.* (New York, 1976), is just one example of a new genre of "how to do history" guides catering to the new popular interest in local history.

concerns of the nonacademic historians, has an extensive and expanding set of programs to meet the needs of the growing number of institutions recorded in its biennial listings of state and local historical agencies.[14]

All of this means that now, as never before, historians interested in history at the local level can hope to find students for their courses, grant money for local research projects, community enrollment for "how-to-do-it" courses in local history, consulting jobs, and the opportunity to work directly with the public in a growing number of museums, historical societies, and restoration projects.[15] Local history still offers a somewhat precarious, undernourished reed upon which to rest the future of the profession, but for numerous historians it has come to represent not only a way to continue doing the history they have been trained to do, but a serious and exciting commitment to a new kind of people's history.

Despite the apparent promise, however, it would be rash to read in these trends the maturation of a "new local history" subfield within American historiography, let alone the emergence of a historiographical tradition capable of replacing or even recasting the older conventions of local history writing. We have as yet nothing to compare with Britain's Leicester school of local history in either its defined focus or its commitment to uniting the great and little traditions in the writing of local history.[16] American historians in the 1970s found themselves doing history at the local level as an almost incidental by-product of research strategies oriented toward other issues, and formulation of a coherent framework for interpreting social change at the local level has proved slow to emerge among studies splintered by chronology, geography, and topic. The consequence thus far has been not so much a "new local history" as a "new urban history" and (far more tentatively) a "new rural history;" redirection in such traditional fields as colonial, immigrant, and labor history; and the emergence of a strong local orientation within such new subfields as family, demographic, and black history. Nevertheless, such work

14. American Association for State and Local History, *Directory of Historical Societies and Agencies in the United States and Canada* (Nashville). The AASLH monthly, *History News,* is a useful source of information on these trends.

15. See D'Ann Campbell and Richard Jensen, "Community and Family History at the Newberry Library: Some Solutions to a National Need," *History Teacher,* XI (1977), 47–54, for a description of one such program; also Samuel P. Hays, "History and the Changing University Curriculum," *History Teacher,* VIII (1974), 64–72.

16. H. P. R. Finberg, "Local History," in Finberg and V. H. T. Skipp, *Local History: Objective and Pursuit* (Newton Abbot, 1967), 25–44; Alan Everitt, *Ways and Means in Local History* (London, 1971).

shares sufficient commonalities in origin, methods, and the interpretive frameworks that have been developed to suggest the outlines of a structure for an explicitly local history uniting these various approaches, and to support the beginnings of historical generalization concerning the changing character and meaning of life at its most local level in the American past.[17]

The origins of the trend must be sought within the broader context of the rise of the "new social history" and the quantitative revolution. Once the dominant mood of the 1960s led a number of younger historians to approach the past "from the bottom up," their concern for the role of the "nondominant, inarticulate" groups led them also, as Constance M. Green had predicted a generation earlier, to the local community. The inarticulate seemed most accessible through the "scraps of evidence" concerning them that were systematically recorded in such public documents as censuses, directories, and vital records.[18] Since it was the level at which many of these sources were generated, the local community provided a pragmatic limit to necessarily laborious collection and analysis of data. More important, until the present century "society" for all but an elite few was bounded by the local community; only there could the most basic patterns that governed the lives of common folk be traced. The nature of these sources dictated quantitative analysis and encouraged experiments with newly available computer technology. The quantitative revolution, in turn, removed some of the barriers to such research and attracted to the local setting those drawn to the new methods. The search for approaches appropriate to local-level data also led to the borrowing of models from the social and behavioral sciences, and most significant, to stimulating encounters with the innovative work of the *Annales* school in France and its British counterparts in the Cambridge group. The domestication of French and British methods and interpretive frameworks generated much of the excitement with which the first New England community studies were received, and openness to cross-fertilization from European scholars and Americans working within European history has continued to characterize many of the local studies.[19]

17. An initial attempt at such generalization is David J. Russo, *Families and Communities: A New View of American History* (Nashville, 1974).

18. Green, "Value of Local History," 278; the words in quotation marks are hers.

19. Kenneth A. Lockridge, "Historical Demography," in Charles F. Delzell, ed., *The Future of History* (Nashville, 1977), 53-64, describes the excitement of that encounter; see also Pierre Goubert, "Local History," in Felix Gilbert and Stephen R. Graubard, eds., *Historical Studies Today* (New York, 1972), 300-314.

These trends appeared most dramatically in American colonial history with the 1970 publication of three studies examining Puritan life within the context of individual Massachusetts towns: Philip J. Greven's analysis of Andover's founding families over four generations, Kenneth A. Lockridge's anatomy of the closed peasant world of seventeenth-century Dedham, and John Demos' dissection of family life in the Plymouth colony.[20] The larger issues they addressed were derived from the long-standing concern for the nature of the Puritan perfectionist impulse and its decline found in the works of Perry Miller, Edmund Morgan, and others; the specific approach they took was inspired particularly by essays of Morgan and Bernard Bailyn stressing the central role of the family in Puritanism and American history more generally.[21] Previous influential studies of local New England life had used systematic social data to illuminate what appeared to be a gradual decline of community cohesion and increased individualism as the seventeenth century merged with the eighteenth.[22] What proved pathbreaking in the three 1970 studies was the attention paid to the family, and the methods used: family reconstitution, demographic analysis, and explicit comparison derived from studies of traditional communities in France and England, to which Demos added an interest in material culture and theoretical models derived from the behavioral sciences. They found not the individualism of a frontier society posited by Bailyn but a traditional set of familial and communal values nurtured by the conditions of American life and challenged (except in Plymouth, where communal dispersion set in at an early stage) only after the pioneer generations had passed from the scene, when the need for additional land placed new pressures on the communities. Indeed, another 1970 study ar-

20. Greven, *Four Generations: Population, Land, and Family in Colonial Andover, Massachusetts* (Ithaca, N.Y., 1970); Lockridge, *A New England Town: The First Hundred Years* (New York, 1970); Demos, *A Little Commonwealth: Family Life in Plymouth Colony* (New York, 1970). For an extended review, see John Murrin, "Review Essay," *History and Theory*, XI (1972), 226–275.

21. Edmund S. Morgan, *The Puritan Family: Religion and Domestic Relations in Seventeenth-Century New England*, rev. ed. (New York, 1966); Bernard Bailyn, *Education in the Forming of American Society: Needs and Opportunities for Study* (Chapel Hill, N.C., 1960).

22. Charles S. Grant, *Democracy in the Connecticut Frontier Town of Kent* (New York, 1961); Sumner Chilton Powell, *Puritan Village: The Formation of a New England Town* (Middletown, Conn., 1963); Darrett B. Rutman, *Winthrop's Boston: Portrait of a Puritan Town, 1630–1649* (Chapel Hill, N.C., 1965); James A. Henretta, "Economic Development and Social Structure in Colonial Boston," *William and Mary Quarterly*, 3d ser., XXII (1965), 75–92; Richard L. Bushman, *From Puritan to Yankee: Character and the Social Order in Connecticut, 1690–1765* (Cambridge, Mass., 1967).

gued (controversially) that the initial impulse toward consensual communalism survived right up to the time of the Revolution.[23]

The challenge to replicate and improve the method and test the interpretations in other settings proved irresistible; where *Dissertation Abstracts* listed one colonial community study in 1971 and two in 1972, six were completed by 1973 and twelve by 1976.[24] Family reconstitution remained the central technique used to unify data derived from a wide variety of sources; the New England town form of settlement, with its treasure-trove of data accessible to the new methods, along with the appealing ease with which its boundaries defined a social unit, remained the favored setting. The multiplication of studies quickly shattered assumptions that Dedham and Boston comprised the only archetypal patterns, so that by 1976 it was possible to suggest a typology of town types based on stages of economic development, social structure, and the exercise of political power.[25] Some studies focused, like Lockridge's, on the local community per se; others used the local community as Greven and Demos did, as a locus for examining other issues, such as family and social tensions. Localized demographic studies have shown particular sophistication in moving beyond borrowed models and techniques and have helped to establish demographic history as an important new subfield.[26]

23. Michael Zuckerman, *Peaceable Kingdoms: New England Towns in the Eighteenth Century* (New York, 1970), also discussed in the Murrin review.

24. A very rough classification yielded about forty such studies between 1969 and 1978; this number probably includes a few that did not make systematic use of the new approaches, and excludes others completed at universities not included in the listings. The Greven, Demos, and Zuckerman studies were all begun as Harvard dissertations. More than half of the listed dissertations were set in New England (mainly Massachusetts) communities; the remainder were about equally divided between the Middle Colonies and the Chesapeake, with the other southern colonies notable for their absence.

25. Selected examples from the large published literature include Linda Auwers Bissell, "From One Generation to Another: Mobility in Seventeenth-Century Windsor, Connecticut," *William and Mary Quarterly*, 3d ser., XXXI (1974), 79–110; Paul Boyer and Stephen Nissenbaum, *Salem Possessed: The Social Origins of Witchcraft* (Cambridge, Mass., 1974); Richard P. Gildrie, *Salem, Massachusetts, 1623–1683: A Covenant Community* (Charlottesville, Va., 1975); John J. Waters, "The Traditional World of the New England Peasants: A View from Seventeenth-Century Barnstable," *New England Historical and Genealogical Register*, CXXIX (1976), 3–21; Stephen Innes, "Land Tenancy and Social Order in Springfield, Massachusetts, 1652 to 1702," *William and Mary Quarterly*, 3d ser., XXXV (1978), 33–56. For a fuller listing, see Richard R. Beeman, "The New Social History and the Search for 'Community' in Colonial America," *American Quarterly*, XXIX (1977), 422–443. For the typology, see Edward M. Cook, Jr., *The Fathers of the Towns: Leadership and Community Structure in Eighteenth-Century New England* (Baltimore, 1976).

26. E.g., Daniel Scott Smith, "Parental Power and Marriage Patterns: An Analysis of Historical Trends in Hingham, Massachusetts," *Journal of Marriage and the Family*, XXXV

Colonial community studies have also begun to move forward in time to probe links between local history and the coming of the Revolution,[27] and across space to examine local life in colonies outside New England. Community studies of the middle colonies, still few in number, have tended to emphasize the individualistic values, heterogeneity, and weak localism of that area in contrast to New England, although the absence of the town form of settlement and government in that region not only makes research on such questions more difficult but also calls for new means of identifying less obvious foci for local communal life.[28] Such strategies are emerging in the more recent spate of innovative studies examining local life in the colonial Chesapeake. The absence of strong nucleated settlements there through much of the colonial period has forced greater attention to the role of non-neighborhood-based and often intermittent communal phenomena such as the county court, kin networks, and religious congregations in providing the basic structures of local life, and has led to a new emphasis on the rituals of local bonding in the absence of a single pervasive ideology.[29]

Rural communities in the postcolonial period have received far less attention from historians in recent years. Dissertation listings again provide an index of relative popularity: there have been two and a half studies of colonial communities for every one on later nonurban places, with southern local places suffering particular neglect.[30] The published literature is even sparser. Certainly the nineteenth-century

---

(1973), 419–428; see also Smith, "The Estimates of Early American Historical Demographers: Two Steps Forward, One Step Back, What Steps in the Future?" *Historical Methods*, XII (1979), 24–38; Maris A. Vinovskis, "Recent Trends in American Historical Demography: Some Methodological and Conceptual Considerations," *Annual Reviews in Sociology*, IV (1978), 603–627.

27. Robert A. Gross, *The Minutemen and Their World* (New York, 1976).

28. James T. Lemon, *The Best Poor Man's Country: A Geographical Study of Early Southeastern Pennsylvania* (Baltimore, 1972); Stephanie Grauman Wolf, *Urban Village: Population, Community, and Family Structure in Germantown, Pennsylvania, 1683–1800* (Princeton, 1976); Thomas J. Archdeacon, *New York City, 1664–1710* (Ithaca, N.Y., 1976).

29. Richard R. Beeman, "Social Change and Cultural Conflict in Virginia: Lunenburg County, 1746 to 1774," *William and Mary Quarterly*, 3d ser., XXXV (1978), 455–476; Allan Kulikoff, "Population and Economic Growth and Social Change in Early America: A Chesapeake Example," Newberry Papers in Family and Community History, no. 77-41 (Chicago, 1977); Aubrey C. Land et al., *Law, Society, and Politics in Early Maryland* (Baltimore, 1977); and the influential work of an Australian scholar: Rhys Isaac, "Evangelical Revolt: The Nature of the Baptists' Challenge to the Traditional Order in Virginia, 1765 to 1775," *William and Mary Quarterly*, 3d ser., XXXI (1974), 345–368.

30. Sixteen dissertations had explicit local settings; such dissertations were probably less subject to an undercount than were the colonial community studies, since western topics hold less attraction for students at some of the universities not listed.

countryside holds out to the historian neither the novelty of a peasant society nor the drama and present relevance of the industrial revolution. Moreover, the looser political and social organization of the trans-Appalachian countryside bequeathed to the historian very different kinds of sources from those that had yielded so well to the new methodologies of the students of colonial communities. But a major reason for the relative neglect of nineteenth-century rural communities must lie in the inadequacies of the Turnerian framework within which they have traditionally been examined.

What might well be termed the first of the new genre of quantitative histories of the American local community was a study of a rural county in frontier Wisconsin published in 1959 by Merle Curti. Curti saw it as a test of Frederick Jackson Turner's frontier thesis "at the grass roots" and also as a test of the feasibility of quantification in historical research. He used the new technology of the IBM card and the counter-sorter to expand and improve older methods of analyzing frontier social structure and social mobility from the federal manuscript census schedules. His dependent variable was democracy, not community. Despite the high levels of population turnover and the significant social stratification that he found, he concluded that the county evidenced sufficient economic, social, and political opportunity to "support what we believe are the main implications of Turner's thesis about the frontier and democracy."[31] Several subsequent studies, using a similar methodology, have confirmed these findings for other communities, but they are too few and still too loosely conceptualized to do more than vaguely suggest possible variations in levels of opportunity and social stratification dependent on the market structure of the agricultural base.[32]

More promising as local history are studies that have developed the

31. Curti, *The Making of an American Community: A Case Study of Democracy in a Frontier County* (Stanford, Calif., 1959), 448; the origins of this approach can be traced back to James C. Malin, "The Turnover of Farm Population in Kansas," *Kansas Historical Quarterly*, IV (1935), 339–372.

32. William L. Bowers, "Crawford Township, 1850–70: A Population Study of a Pioneer Community," *Iowa Journal of History*, LVIII (1960), 1–30; Peter J. Coleman, "Restless Grant County: Americans on the Move," *Wisconsin Magazine of History*, LXVI (1962), 16–20; William G. Robbins, "Opportunity and Persistence in the Pacific Northwest: A Quantitative Study of Early Roseburg, Oregon," *Pacific Historical Review*, XXXIX (1970), 279–296; Michael P. Conzen, *Frontier Farming in an Urban Shadow* (Madison, Wis., 1971); Ralph Mann, "The Decade after the Gold Rush: Social Structure in Grass Valley and Nevada City, California, 1850–1860," *Pacific Historical Review*, XLI (1972), 484–504. Allen G. Bogue, *From Prairie to Cornbelt: Farming on the Illinois and Iowa Prairies in the Nineteenth Century* (Chicago, 1963), provides a study of the process of social change at the regional level.

communal implications of Turnerian theory. In 1954 Stanley Elkins
and Eric McKitrick sought to find what they called "a meaning for
Turner's frontier" in the democratic consensus that resulted from
cooperative community building, a process that could as readily result
in conflict and stalemate, as Allan G. Bogue later observed.[33] Robert
R. Dykstra used an array of quantitative and literary sources to chart
the development of five Kansas cattle towns after the Civil War from
this perspective, which also informs Don Harrison Doyle's study of
the early years of a small Illinois city.[34] Their work underlines the
need to recast Turner's emphasis on frontier individualism to take
into account the cross-cutting patterns of social order that perforce
developed in new communities of great heterogeneity and high
mobility, in the open settlements of the countryside as well as in the
small towns. But thus far rural history has remained almost entirely
the province of the student of agricultural practices and landholding
patterns, whose work is fundamental to an understanding of the economic basis of local life but which has paid little attention to the local
community as such. There are straws of change in the wind: studies of
colonial communities are beginning to move forward into the
nineteenth century to observe the processes of change under the impact of altered market conditions,[35] and current work on fertility
decline among nineteenth-century rural families is calling attention to
family processes that will require local study for detailed documentation.[36] But at this point the "new rural history" is more hope than
reality, and the most vivid accounts of life outside the large cities
remain untested and impressionistic.[37]

Life in urban settings, by contrast, received considerable attention
from American historians in the 1970s. It was in the previous decade

33. Elkins and McKitrick, "A Meaning for Turner's Frontier," *Political Science Quarterly,* LXIX (1954), 323–348; Bogue, "Social Theory and the Pioneer," *Agricultural History,* XXXIV (1960), 21–34.
34. Dykstra, *The Cattle Towns* (New York, 1968); Doyle, *The Social Order of a Frontier
Community: Jacksonville, Illinois, 1825–70* (Urbana, Ill., 1978). See also Richard S. Alcorn,
"Leadership and Stability in Mid-Nineteenth-Century America: A Case Study of an
Illinois Town," *Journal of American History,* LXI (1974), 685–702; Robert E. Bieder, "Kinship as a Factor in Migration," *Journal of Marriage and the Family,* XXXV (1973), 429–439.
35. James A. Henretta, "Families and Farms: *Mentalité* in Pre-Industrial America,"
*William and Mary Quarterly,* 3d ser., XXXV (1978), 3–32.
36. Richard A. Easterlin, "Population Change and Farm Settlement in the Northern
United States," *Journal of Economic History,* XXXVI (1976), 45–83; John Modell, "Family
and Fertility on the Indiana Frontier, 1820," *American Quarterly,* XXIII (1971), 615–634.
37. Robert P. Swierenga, "Towards the 'New Rural History': A Review Essay," *Historical Methods Newsletter,* VI (1973), 111–121; Page Smith, *As a City Upon a Hill: The Town
in American History* (New York, 1966), and Lewis Atherton, *Main Street on the Middle
Border* (Bloomington, Ind., 1954), provide general histories of the small town.

that urban history finally emerged as the object of intensive historical inquiry and established itself as a significant subfield within history departments in the United States, in large part as a response to growing perceptions of a national "urban crisis." As such origins suggest, much of this urban history was empirical and problem-oriented; studies proliferated of individual city growth and of pathological aspects of urban life—social tensions, inadequate services, minority discrimination, political corruption. Such concerns reflected Schlesinger's earlier emphasis on the urban aspects of broader societal phenomena and his interest in the role of the city in the nation's development. They also appeared to rest upon an implied model of the city as an organism whose essential history lay in its survival and adaptation in the face of continued challenges provoked by its changing relations with its external environment.[38]

But the growing maturity of the subfield also intensified long-standing and self-consciously critical efforts to define a content and a methodology for the study of the history of the city. Too much of what was taken for urban history, critics argued, had little basis in an understanding of the generically urban or of the causes and consequences of the societal processes that created cities. There were calls for more careful attention to the basic demographic, social, and ecological structures of cities and their links with differing economies, technologies, and levels of political organization; for explicitly comparative studies of individual cities as products of broader social processes of urbanization; and for carefully specified studies of the "city-building" decisions that created the individual city as an artifact.[39] Although historians had long been influenced by implicit models of the consequences of urbanization derived from sociological theory,[40] these critiques pointed toward more explicit use of social and behavioral science models, quantification, and consequently the

38. For historiographical reviews, see Hoover, "Diverging Paths," and Raymond A. Mohl, "The History of the American City," in William H. Cartwright and Richard L. Watson, Jr., eds., *The Reinterpretation of American History and Culture* (Washington, D.C., 1973), 165–205.

39. Especially Eric E. Lampard, "American Historians and the Study of Urbanization," *American Historical Review*, LXVII (1961), 49–61; Oscar Handlin, "The Modern City as a Field of Historical Study," in Handlin and John Burchard, eds., *The Historian and the City* (Cambridge, Mass., 1963), 1–26; Roy Lubove, "The Urbanization Process: An Approach to Historical Research," *Journal of the American Institute of Planners*, XXXIII (1967), 33–39; Sam Bass Warner, Jr., "If All the World Were Philadelphia: A Scaffolding for Urban History, 1774–1930," *American Historical Review*, LXXIV (1968), 26–43.

40. Especially as filtered through Louis Wirth, "Urbanism as a Way of Life," *American Journal of Sociology*, XLIV (1938), 1–24; see Hoover, "Diverging Paths."

local case study. A significant core of work in urban history during the 1970s was responsive to these suggestions.

The new departures were heralded by the 1969 publication of *Nineteenth-Century Cities: Essays in the New Urban History.*[41] For its editors, Stephan Thernstrom and Richard Sennett, the "new urban history" involved the explicit use of sociological theory, quantification, and concern for the inarticulate whose voices failed to speak through the more conventional sources of most urban history to date. Thernstrom's 1964 *Poverty and Progress: Social Mobility in a Nineteenth-Century City* provided the point of departure for much of this work in its use of the census-analysis techniques pioneered by Curti to trace the career paths of Newburyport, Massachusetts, workers and their sons in a test of common assumptions about the role of social mobility in mitigating class conflict in nineteenth-century America.[42] A host of studies of social and geographic mobility in other nineteenth-century urban communities followed, particularly for the years between 1850 and 1880, for which census data were readily available, culminating in the 1973 publication of Thernstrom's own large-scale study of mobility in Boston from 1880 to 1970.[43]

Despite considerable controversy over the basic assumptions, data, and methods of the mobility studies, they served to focus dramatically the attention of urban historians upon systematic analysis of social stratification and the social changes accompanying urban growth and industrialization. Some studies, most notably Michael Katz's analysis of mid-nineteenth-century Hamilton, Ontario, went well beyond the simple measurement of mobility to dissect the basic social structures

41. New Haven, 1969; see also Thernstrom, "Reflections on the New Urban History," *Daedalus,* C (1971), 359–375.

42. Cambridge, Mass., 1964; see also "Conversation with Stephan Thernstrom," in Stave, ed., *Making of Urban History,* 221–249. This derived from some of the main concerns of American historians in the 1950s and early 1960s; cf. James A. Henretta, "The Study of Social Mobility: Ideological Assumptions and Conceptual Bias," *Labor History,* XVIII (1977), 165–178.

43. In addition to the essays in *Nineteenth-Century Cities,* a partial listing of this work includes Thernstrom, *The Other Bostonians: Poverty and Progress in the American Metropolis, 1880–1970* (Cambridge, Mass., 1973); Peter R. Knights, *The Plain People of Boston, 1830–1860: A Study in City Growth* (New York, 1971); Clyde Griffen, "Making It in America: Social Mobility in Mid-Nineteenth-Century Poughkeepsie," *New York History,* LI (1970), 479–499; Paul B. Worthman, "Working-Class Mobility in Birmingham, Alabama, 1880–1914," in Tamara K. Hareven, ed., *Anonymous Americans: Explorations in Nineteenth-Century Social History* (Englewood Cliffs, N.J., 1971), 172–213; Howard P. Chudacoff, *Mobile Americans: Residential and Social Mobility in Omaha, 1880–1920* (New York, 1972); Michael P. Weber, *Social Change in an Industrial Town: Patterns of Progress in Warren, Pennsylvania, from Civil War to World War I* (University Park, Pa., 1976).

of a North American city before and during industrialization.[44] The initial effort simply to establish gross levels of mobility has yielded in more recent scholarship to detailed exploration of the variation in opportunity from city to city and within various sectors of the urban economy.[45] Historians are beginning to sort out the shifting contemporary perceptions of the stratification system, and to assess the role played by traditional familial and ethnic values in conditioning responses to the opportunities and constraints of the emerging urban industrial order.[46] Studies of working-class communities, following the leads of Sam Bass Warner, Jr., and Herbert G. Gutman, are also moving well beyond interpretations dependent on mobility rates to assess class consciousness in terms of varying workplace demands, urban industrial and ethnic composition, and local political cultures. The best of this work represents a creative blending of urban history with a labor history tradition heavily indebted to E. P. Thompson and Eric Hobsbawm, and has stimulated among American historians the development of a set of questions and research strategies that have encouraged comparison across national boundaries to a greater extent than in other areas of urban history.[47]

44. Michael B. Katz, *The People of Hamilton, Canada West: Family and Class in a Mid-Nineteenth-Century City* (Cambridge, Mass., 1975); Stuart M. Blumin, *The Urban Threshold: Growth and Change in a Nineteenth-Century American Community* (Chicago, 1972); Doyle, *Social Order of a Frontier Community.*

45. Robert Doherty, *Society and Power: Five New England Towns, 1800–1860* (Amherst, Mass., 1977); Clyde Griffen and Sally Griffen, *Natives and Newcomers: The Ordering of Opportunity in Mid-Nineteenth-Century Poughkeepsie* (Cambridge, Mass., 1978); Peter R. Decker, *Fortunes and Failures: White-Collar Mobility in Nineteenth-Century San Francisco* (Cambridge, Mass., 1978).

46. Richard P. Horwitz, *Anthropology toward History: Culture and Work in a Nineteenth-Century Maine Town* (Middletown, Conn., 1978); John Bodnar, *Immigrants and Industrialization: Ethnicity in an American Mill Town, 1870–1940* (Pittsburgh, 1977); Tamara K. Hareven, "The Laborers of Manchester, New Hampshire, 1912–1920: The Role of Family and Ethnicity in Adjustment to Industrial Life," *Labor History,* xvi (1975), 249–266; Virginia Yans-McLaughlin, "Patterns of Work and Family Organization: Buffalo's Italians," *Journal of Interdisciplinary History,* ii (1971), 299–314; Thomas Kessner, *The Golden Door: Italian and Jewish Immigrant Mobility in New York New York City, 1880–1915* (New York, 1977).

47. David Brody, "Labor History in the 1970s: Toward a History of the American Worker," chap. 11 in this volume; Sam Bass Warner, Jr., *The Private City: Philadelphia in Three Periods of Its Growth* (Philadelphia, 1968); Herbert G. Gutman, "Work, Culture, and Society in Industrializing America, 1815–1919," *American Historical Review,* lxxviii (1973), 531–587, and "Class, Status, and Community Power in Nineteenth-Century American Industrial Cities—Paterson, New Jersey," in Frederic Cople Jaher, ed., *The Age of Industrialism in America* (New York, 1968), 263–287; Daniel J. Walkowitz, *Worker City, Company Town: Iron and Cotton-Worker Protest in Troy and Cohoes, New York, 1855–84* (Urbana, Ill., 1978); Susan E. Hirsch, *Roots in the American Working Class: The Industrialization of Crafts in Newark, 1800–1860* (Philadelphia, 1978); Alan Dawley, *Class and Community: The Indus-*

Historians have also confronted the implications for urban public order of increasing stratification combined with heterogeneity, high geographical mobility, and real if not unlimited economic opportunity. "Social control" has seemingly replaced the previously popular concept of "status revolution" as the prevailing explanation for nineteenth-century reform movements in the considerable body of work dealing with asylums, schools, religious revivals, and the like as middle-class responses to the perceived breakdown of an older social order.[48] Other work has pointed to the role of ethnic and racial subcommunities, and more tentatively networks of family and kin, in providing order within apparent demographic and social chaos.[49] Neighborhoods too have been examined within this context, although Warner's emphasis on the social formlessness of the new suburbs has yet to receive serious challenge, and the significance of the urban ghetto neighborhood itself as a pervasive phenomenon has also been questioned.[50] Attention has also been paid to the entrepreneurial class, whose stability and economic self-interest can be interpreted as

*trial Revolution in Lynn* (Cambridge, Mass., 1976); John T. Cumbler, "The City and Community: The Impact of Urban Forces on Working-Class Behavior," *Journal of Urban History,* III (1977),427–442. Addressing all of these issues is the massive, well-funded Philadelphia Social History Project, directed by Theodore Hershberg, at the University of Pennsylvania, which is compiling a voluminous data bank of information on all aspects of Philadelphia life in the latter half of the nineteenth century; see "A Special Issue: The Philadelphia Social History Project," *Historical Methods Newsletter,* IX (March-June 1976).

48. The literature is voluminous; David J. Rothman, *The Discovery of the Asylum: Social Order and Disorder in the New Republic* (Boston, 1971), is an essential starting point. See also Paul E. Johnson, *A Shopkeeper's Millennium: Society and Revivals in Rochester, New York, 1815–1837* (New York, 1978), and Michael B. Katz, *The Irony of Early School Reform: Educational Innovation in Mid-Nineteenth-Century Massachusetts* (Cambridge, Mass., 1968), for approaches using new urban history data and methods, and for a more traditional treatment, Paul Boyer, *Urban Masses and the Moral Order in America, 1820–1920* (Cambridge, Mass., 1978).

49. Josef Barton, *Peasants and Strangers: Italians, Roumanians, and Slovaks in an American City, 1890–1950* (Cambridge, Mass., 1975); Humbert S. Nelli, *Italians in Chicago, 1880–1930: A Study in Ethnic Mobility* (New York, 1970); Kathleen Neils Conzen, *Immigrant Milwaukee, 1836–1860: Accommodation and Community in a Frontier City* (Cambridge, Mass., 1976); Caroline Golab, *Immigrant Destinations* (Philadelphia, 1977); David Katzman, *Before the Ghetto: Black Detroit in the Nineteenth Century* (Urbana, Ill., 1973); Kenneth L. Kusmer, *A Ghetto Takes Shape: Black Cleveland, 1870–1930* (Urbana, Ill., 1976); Howard N. Rabinowitz, *Race Relations in the Urban South, 1865–1890* (New York, 1978).

50. Sam Bass Warner, Jr., *Streetcar Suburbs:The Process of Growth in Boston, 1870–1900* (Cambridge, Mass., 1962); Warner and Colin B. Burke, "Cultural Change and the Ghetto," *Journal of Contemporary History,* IV (1969), 173–187; Howard P. Chudacoff, "A New Look at Ethnic Neighborhoods," *Journal of American History,* LX (1973), 76–93.

providing a basis for communal continuity and the institutional definition of a new urban culture.[51]

Not all of this work has been quantitative, or even explicitly social science in its orientation, but it seems to have enough in common to permit us to consider it all as a derivative form of the "new urban history." By 1977, Thernstrom acknowledged that much of that history was not new, not really urban in its concern for social processes unbounded by city limits, and perhaps not even history, given its frequent indulgence in quantification for quantification's sake. Another critic, John Sharpless, pointed as well to the disappointing elusiveness of general propositions derived from such work.[52] Certainly the literature abounds in unexamined assumptions about the course of recent social change loosely derived from modernization theories, and even where a conscious effort has been made to sort out the consequences flowing from urbanization per se, there is seldom much effort to specify which defining characteristics of the city—its coordinating functions, its population density and heterogeneity, its physical attributes—give rise to particular hypothesized consequences. For all of the problems, however, it remains significant, as Eric Lampard noted in 1975, that urban historians are attempting to come to grips with the central problem of urbanization, particularly its consequences for the internal organization and social order of the city.[53]

This is evident even in work less readily classified under the rubric of "new urban history." Although American historians continue to pay less attention to the city as a physical artifact than their British counterparts, for example, there is strong interest in the city's social ecology and its relationship to changing social values, transportation technology, and the broader imperatives of the urbanization process, continuing lines of inquiry first laid out in Warner's 1962 *Streetcar*

51. John T. Ingham, "The American Urban Upper Class: Cosmopolitans or Locals," *Journal of Urban History*, II (1975), 67–87; Edward Pessen, "The Lifestyle of the Antebellum Urban Elite," *Mid-America*, LV (1973), 163–83, and "The Social Configuration of the Antebellum City," *Journal of Urban History*, II (1976), 267–306.

52. Thernstrom, "The New Urban History," in Delzell, ed., *Future of History*, 43–52; Sharpless, "In Search of Community: A New Theme for the Old 'New' Urban History," *Reviews in American History*, V (1977), 215–222; see also Sharpless and Sam Bass Warner, Jr., "Urban History," *American Behavioral Scientist*, XXI (1977), 221–244.

53. Lampard, "Two Cheers for Quantitative History: An Agnostic Foreword," in Leo F. Schnore, ed., *The New Urban History: Quantitative Explorations by American Historians* (Princeton, N.J., 1975), 12–48. See also the critical assessment in Theodore Hershberg, "The New Urban History: Toward an Interdisciplinary History of the City," *Journal of Urban History*, V (1978), 3–40.

*Suburbs.*[54] Some fruitful recent work along these lines has involved studies of cities outside the United States; dialogue with historical geographers working on similar problems has also intensified.[55] The long-standing emphasis of Warner and Samuel P. Hays on the essential linkages between the process of urbanization, structural change, societal values, and public action is also beginning to reshape the writing of urban political history.[56] Preoccupation with the prosopography of reform is giving way to studies of the distribution and exercise of power, influenced in their orientation by political science theory.[57] Historians are also beginning to show greater awareness of the necessity of dealing again with the nuts-and-bolts questions of urban governmental structure and functioning in order to determine "who gets what, why, and how."[58] Attention to the decision-making process has encouraged a renewed interest in the old questions of boosterism and attitudes toward the city, informed now by greater

54. Examples include Joel Tarr, *Transportation Innovation and Changing Spatial Patterns: Pittsburgh, 1850-1910* (Pittsburgh, 1972); Roger D. Simon, "Housing and Services in an Immigrant Neighborhood, Milwaukee's Ward 14," *Journal of Urban History,* II (1976), 435-458; Olivier Zunz, "Detroit en 1880: Espace et segregation," *Annales,* XXXII (1977), 106-136; David Owen Wise and Marguerite Dupree, "The Choice of the Automobile for Urban Passenger Transportation: Baltimore in the 1920s," *South Atlantic Urban Studies,* II (1978), 153-179; Harold M. Mayer and Richard C. Wade, *Chicago: The Growth of a Metropolis* (Chicago, 1969); Kenneth T. Jackson, "Urban Deconcentration in the Nineteenth Century: A Statistical Inquiry," in Schnore, ed., *New Urban History,* 110-142.

55. Comparative studies include James R. Scobie, *Buenos Aires: Plaza to Suburb, 1870-1910* (New York, 1974); Gerald Michael Greenfield, "Streetcar Squabbles in Old São Paulo: Urban Transportation Development, 1872-1892," *South Atlantic Urban Studies,* II (1978), 180-202; John P. McKay, *Tramways and Trolleys: The Rise of Urban Mass Transport in Europe* (Princeton, 1976); David Ward, *Cities and Immigrants: A Geography of Change in Nineteenth-Century America* (New York, 1971), has been influential.

56. Sam Bass Warner, Jr., *The Urban Wilderness: A History of the American City* (New York, 1972); Samuel P. Hays, "The Changing Political Structure of the City in Industrial America," *Journal of Urban History,* I (1974), 6-38. The considerable literature on urban political machines and reform in the 1960s was an important step in this direction; for sampling and critical discussion of such work, see Alexander B. Callow, Jr., ed., *The City Boss in America: An Interpretive Reader* (New York, 1976).

57. David Hammack, "Problems in the Historical Study of Power in the Cities and Towns of the United States, 1800-1960," *American Historical Review,* LXXXIII (1978), 323-349; Eugene J. Watts, *The Social Bases of City Politics: Atlanta, 1865-1903* (Westport, Conn., 1978); Carl V. Harris, *Political Power in Birmingham, 1871-1921* (Knoxville, Tenn., 1977); Edward Pessen, "Who Governed the Nation's Cities in the 'Era of the Common Man'?" *Political Science Quarterly,* LXXXVII (1972), 591-614.

58. Michael H. Frisch, *Town into City: Springfield, Massachusetts, and the Meaning of Community, 1840-1880* (Cambridge, Mass., 1972); Estelle F. Feinstein, *Stamford in the Gilded Age: The Political Life of a Connecticut Town, 1868-1893* (Stamford, Conn., 1973); Roger W. Lotchin, *San Francisco, 1846-1856: From Hamlet to City* (New York, 1974); Jon C. Teaford, *The Municipal Revolution in America: Origins of Modern Urban Government, 1650-1825* (Chicago, 1975); Kenneth Fox, *Better City Government: Innovation in American Urban Politics, 1850-1937* (Philadelphia, 1977).

understanding of the structural constraints within which the city builders operated.[59] In this context the promising involvement of economic historians with urban issues should also be noted.[60] One need only contrast the approach taken by the most recent entrant into the American urban history textbook sweepstakes with those of its predecessors to measure the extent to which an explicit urbanization model has gained acceptance in the past decade as a structure for American urban history.[61]

Of course, much of urban history continues to be influenced by currently topical issues approached In more conventional fashion. Something like a quarter of the more than 550 urban-related dissertation listings surveyed consisted of studies of various social phenomena found within urban settings, ranging from welfare to schools to symphony orchestras, with police and urban disorder (at least 26 dissertations) and labor (at least 22) especially well represented, and women and the family (at least 15) a growing trend. Another 11 percent comprised standard urban biographies and studies of the influence of national events on particular cities; and perhaps 15 percent addressed issues of political machines, elites, and reform, with about 4 percent dealing with such broader urban-related topics as the idea of the city. But some 15 percent of the total explored issues of boosterism, urban growth, planning, and urban ecology, and about 8 percent were studies of social structure and mobility clearly in the "new social history" tradition. The largest individual concentrations remained studies of black urban communities and race relations (almost 12 percent of the total) and of immigrant groups in urban settings (11 percent).[62]

To what extent, then, do these trends in the study of local communities begin to add up to a new understanding of American local history? Certainly, a good deal more is known in systematic fashion about life at the local level than was the case a decade ago. The

59. Blaine A. Brownell, *The Urban Ethos in the South, 1920–1930* (Baton Rouge, 1975); David R. Goldfield, *Urban Growth in the Age of Sectionalism: Virginia, 1847-61* (Baton Rouge, 1977); Thomas Bender, *Toward an Urban Vision: Ideas and Institutions in Nineteenth-Century America* (Lexington, Ky., 1975); Sylvia Doughty Fries, *The Urban Idea in Colonial America* (Philadelphia, 1977).

60. Claudia Dale Goldin, *Urban Slavery in the American South, 1820–1860: A Quantitative History* (Chicago, 1976); Diane Lindstrom, *Economic Development in the Philadelphia Region, 1810–1850* (New York, 1978); Alan D. Anderson, *The Origins and Resolution of an Urban Crisis: Baltimore, 1890–1930* (Baltimore, 1977).

61. David R. Goldfield and Blaine A. Brownell, *Urban America: From Downtown to No town* (Boston, 1979).

62. Again, the figures are purposely presented as rough approximations in view of the inevitable difficulties of allocating a large number of studies into a reasonably limited set of categories on the basis of not very detailed abstracts.

magnifying glass of the historian was first focused on the American
local community in order to resolve historiographical problems external to the local setting itself. Consequently certain types of localities
have received relatively short shrift from the historians, either because the data were lacking or because their experiences did not seem
relevant to current historiographical debates. Early-nineteenth-
century communities of all sizes, the towns and villages of the later
nineteenth and early twentieth centuries, the communities of South,
the Southwest, the Mountain West, and the Pacific Coast all remain
virtual terra incognita.[63] To an uncomfortable extent also, available
data have dictated the choice of methods (e.g., family reconstitution
or census-based mobility analysis, mobility analysis within but not between communities) and have thereby determined conclusions.
Nevertheless, the local approach has revised interpretations in several
areas of American history—the basis of social order in the early colonies, the character of the American labor movement, the origins of
Progressivism—and the significance of local life is emerging from
accounts of even such central themes in American history as the origins of the Revolution and the waning of Reconstruction.[64] Local
history in this sense has indeed emerged from the wilderness.

A common thread that runs through many of the case studies has
also provided the basis for a broader thesis concerning the changing
context of life at the local level: the notion of community and its
decline. As several commentators have noted, much of this literature,
implicitly or explicitly, details the transition from *Gemeinschaft* to
*Gesellschaft,* from intensely experienced communal life at the local
level to impersonal involvement in the segmented and secondary relationship of mass society—an idea strongly developed also in the
sociological community studies to which the urban historians, particularly, are heavily indebted.[65] Community becomes an ever declining
phenomenon—in seventeenth-century Boston, eighteenth-century
Philadelphia, nineteenth-century Newburyport, twentieth-century

63. Half of the cities treated in the dissertation listings were eastern cities from
Baltimore north, with New York receiving one-seventh of the attention; about a quarter
of the cities studied were midwestern, one-sixth southern, and only one-twelfth
mountain or Pacific Coast; there were only eleven dissertations listed as dealing with the
rural Midwest and Plains states, and none treating rural communities in the far West.

64. E.g., James A. Henretta, *The Evolution of American Society, 1700–1815: An Interdisciplinary Analysis* (Lexington, Mass., 1973); Morton Keller, *Affairs of State: Public Life in
Late-Nineteenth-Century America* (Cambridge, Mass., 1977). Pioneering in this respect,
and very influential, is Robert H. Wiebe, *The Search for Order, 1877–1920* (New York,
1967).

65. Beeman, "The New Social History"; Thomas Bender, *Community and Social
Change in America* (New Brunswick, N.J., 1978); Darrett B. Rutman, "Community

cities everywhere—and the history of the local community becomes a history of constant adjustment to loss of autonomy as the locus of decision making, and therefore of national history, shifts to ever more centralized levels of decision making, and neighbors become strangers.[66] This is a theme that, paradoxically perhaps, echoes the nostalgic antiurbanism of the articulate middle classes; studies of ethnic and racial subcommunities within the cities have tended rather to emphasize their success in maintaining and perpetuating community despite the destructive forces of modernization.[67] Others have in fact suggested that the very process of urban growth may have created a kind of community where none existed before.[68]

Much of the problem for historians, as both Thomas Bender and Darrett Rutman have recently noted, is a definitional one. "Community" may refer both to a particular place and to relationships of a particularly close and intensive nature. For Bender, the best solution is to reserve the notion of community for such close relationships, regardless of their ties to locality; Rutman would reserve the term for the daily network of relationships, regardless of their emotional content. With that obvious distinction made, the problem of determining change in the involvement of an individual in community-like relationships under either definition becomes an empirical one, and historians can begin to determine whether, indeed, the link between community and locality has varied with time, place, or social group.[69]

But even when "community" is cast loose from local ties, the local place at all of its various levels, from neighborhood to city to metropolitan region and even state, still retains a history and an influence over the lives of its residents. The task of local history thus becomes the analysis of the changing consequences of locality, of place itself,

Study," Newberry Papers in Family and Community History, no. 77-4J (Chicago, 1977); on the sociological tradition, see Jean B. Quandt, *From the Small Town to the Great Community: The Social Thought of Progressive Intellectuals* (New Brunswick, N.J., 1970); Maurice R. Stein, *The Eclipse of Community: An Interpretation of American Studies* (Princeton, N.J., 1960).

66. Rutman, *Winthrop's Boston;* Warner, *Private City;* Thernstrom, *Poverty and Progress.*

67. See the studies cited in note 49 and Rudolph J. Vecoli, "European Americans: From Immigrants to Ethnics," in Cartwright and Watson, *Reinterpretation of American History,* 81–111.

68. Blumin, *Urban Threshold;* Carol Hoffecker, *Wilmington, Delaware: Portrait of an Industrial City, 1830–1910* (Charlottesville, Va., 1974); see also Frisch, *Town into City,* and Doyle, *Social Order of a Frontier Community,* for subtle analyses of the changing base of community within growing cities.

69. Bender, *Community and Social Change;* Rutman, "Community Study"; see also Rutman's earlier "The Social Web: A Prospectus for the Study of the Early American Community," in William L. O'Neill, ed., *Insights and Parallels: Problems and Issues of American Social History* (Minneapolis, 1973), 57–89.

for those living within a place and for society at large.[70] But many of the recent studies are ill suited to that task, however well defined they may be on their own terms. They are not so much local history as what the British historian H. P. R. Finberg has termed "national history localized,"[71] case studies whose local setting is often little more than an unavoidable weakness, to be mitigated as far as possible via comparison, typology, and explicit recourse to theory. Many of them lack any clear conception of what is distinctively local in the phenomena they are examining, and there is seldom, even in the urban biographies and explicit community studies, much interest in what to British local historians makes local history an independent discipline, the organic development of distinctive communal cultures and landscapes.[72] The search for social structures necessarily emphasizes processes of social change common to all localities rather than unsystematic local variation.[73] Yet as Michael Frisch noted a decade ago, studying a universal process of urbanization offers no panacea for the problem of writing the urban history of a particular society, since it leaves as an unexplained residual the very cultural distinctiveness that it is the historian's province to explain.[74] Even generalization from case studies requires an assessment of the way in which the historically defined character of a given locality itself functions as a variable in the lives of its residents.

One path to such a truly local history lies in comparative, system-wide studies to uncover the locally distinctive, a research strategy that is appearing more frequently in some areas of localized research.[75]

70. For a related argument, see Hershberg, "New Urban History." This problem was encountered in the American Association for State and Local History's Bicentennial series of state histories, whose task was to determine for each state "what has mattered about it, to its own people and to the rest of the nation"; see, for example, Richard D. Brown, *Massachusetts: A Bicentennial History* (New York, 1978), ix. On the writing of local history at the state level, see John Alexander Williams, "State History: A New Look at an Old Field," Newberry Papers in Family and Community History, no. 77-3 (Chicago, 1977).

71. Finberg, "Local History," 32.

72. Ibid.

73. For a discussion of the strengths and limits of approaching the history of communities through the analysis of structures, see James A. Henretta, "Social History as Lived and Written: Structure, Problematic, and Action," Newberry Papers in Family and Community History, no. 77-4F (Chicago, 1977).

74. Michael H. Frisch, "L'histoire urbaine américaine: Réflexions sur les tendances récentes," *Annales*, xxv (1970), 880–896.

75. E.g., Sam Bass Warner, Jr., and Sylvia Fleisch, "The Past of Today's Present: A Social History of America's Metropolises, 1960–1860," *Journal of Urban History*, III (1976), 3–118; J. Rogers Hollingsworth and Ellen Jane Hollingsworth, "Expenditures in American Cities," in William O. Aydelotte, Allan G. Bogue, and Robert W. Fogel, eds., *The Dimensions of Quantitative Research in History* (Princeton, 1972), 347–389;

But it will also be necessary to move beyond the analysis of social structures to pay more attention to those nonpatterned facets of local existence that also define a local community and its culture to its residents and to outsiders. This can mean the local landscape, which geographers have found central to contemporary local self-definition;[76] it can mean material culture, patterns of consumption, the "quality of life" more generally;[77] it can mean the quality of relationships with a broader hinterland;[78] it can mean the recurring private rhythms and periodic public rituals to which the residents of the locality respond.[79] The example of Anthony F. C. Wallace's *Rockdale* suggests the rich sense of place that can be communicated when the questions of the anthropologist are harnessed to some of the data of the community study and the new urban history; Norman Clark's *Mill Town* demonstrates the ability of the sensitive historian to achieve the same purpose in more traditional fashion.[80]

Such a truly local history, serving the historian's need to balance broader generalization with particular details, can in defining a community also begin to satisfy its residents' desire to understand how it became what it is. The locally oriented studies of the 1970s, in contributing significantly to the historian's understanding of social change in America, have also provided the common ground on which the professional may be reunited with a local readership.

Richard Bernard and Bradley Rice, "Political Environment and the Adoption of Progressive Municipal Reform," *Journal of Urban History*, 1 (1975), 149-174; Cook, *Fathers of the Towns*.

76. Donald W. Meinig, ed., *The Interpretation of Ordinary Landscapes* (New York, 1979); Frisch, *Town into City*, makes very effective interpretive use of the changing urban landscape.

77. Cary Carson, "Doing History with Material Culture," in Ian M. G. Quimby, ed., *Material Culture*, 41-64; see Hirsch, *Roots of the American Working Class*, 133, for suggestive comments on the role of consumption in defining a satisfactory life-style for workers. Historians have been slow to attempt to analyze status and mobility change in terms of consumption patterns, despite the significance they take on in twentieth-century community studies; cf. Stein, *Eclipse of Community*, esp. 47-69.

78. Johnson, *Shopkeepers' Millennium;* Dykstra, *Cattle Towns*, provide examples of the influence of hinterland values upon townsmen dependent on their trade; the sources of migrants to a town would also seem important.

79. Rhys Isaac, "Dramatizing the Ideology of Revolution: Population Mobilization in Virginia, 1774 to 1776," *William and Mary Quarterly*, 3d ser., xxxiii (1976), 357-385; the case for an anthropological approach advanced in Beeman, "New Social History," and Henretta, "Families and Farms," has equal relevance for the study of urban communities.

80. Wallace, *Rockdale: The Growth of an American Village in the Early Industrial Revolution* (New York, 1978); Norman Clark, *Mill Town: A Social History of Everett, Washington, from Its Earliest Beginnings on the Shores of Puget Sound to the Tragic and Infamous Event Known as the Everett Massacre* (Seattle, 1970).

# 12

# The Negro in American History:
# As Scholar, as Subject

## Jay Saunders Redding

SPECIFICALLY in its relation to the Negro, as both scholar and subject, and despite some interpretive confusion, American history has never been in better state either as an academic discipline or as an exercise in objective chronicle narration. As subject, the Negro is no longer slighted or scorned as a creature of attitudes and actions beyond his comprehension and—frequently—even beyond his concern. He is no longer one to whom things do or do not happen solely at the will of the white man. As inquiring scholar—thanks in great part to the estimable work of John Hope Franklin, Rayford Logan, and Benjamin Quarles—the Negro is no longer dependent on the angle of vision, the perceptions, the insights, and the interpretations—once all too frequently questionable—of white historians and chroniclers.[1] The Negro scholar's involvement in historical studies of America and the methods and materials he employs in his work have resulted in a reevaluation of the American past and of that past's relevance to such qualifying abstractions as "the American way," "the American dream," and "the American national character." As scholar—particularly in the social sciences—the Negro must be given credit for "pioneering the scientific examination of the Afro-American past,"[2] partly in the hope of foreseeing the future, but

1. See John W. Blassingame, "The Afro-Americans: From Mythology to Reality," in William H. Cartwright and Richard L. Watson, Jr., eds., *The Reinterpretation of American History and Culture* (Washington, D.C., 1973), 53–79; and Peter H. Wood, "'I Did the Best I Could for My Day': The Study of Early Black History during the Second Reconstruction, 1960 to 1976," *William and Mary Quarterly*, xxxv (1978), 185–225.

2. Robert L. Harris, Jr., "Segregation and Scholarship: The American Council of Learned Societies' Committee on Negro Studies, 1941–1950," a paper delivered at the Fourth Annual New York State Black Studies Conference, April 20, 1978, Columbia University.

principally in the faith that the solution to the American race problems was "a matter of systematic investigation and intelligent understanding," as W. E. B. DuBois declared in a lecture before the American Academy of Political and Social Sciences in 1897. "The world was
thinking wrong about race, because it did not know. The ultimate evil
was stupidity. The cure for it was knowledge based on scientific investigation."[3]

What DuBois gave voice to has been and remains the rationale
underlying and invigorating the work of the foremost Negro scholars
in many fields, but especially those in history. They were the first to
apply the resources, some of the theories, and the techniques of the
social sciences—sociology itself, social and cultural anthropology, intrapsychic accommodation, sociometry—to the study of American
Negro history and, implicitly, the American past. Primarily because of
their exclusion from organized councils of white scholars, the Negro
scholars and their work(s) did not get the attention they might have
had if for no other reason than their challenge to the prejudiced
perceptions of American history put forth by George Bancroft,
William Dunning, Ulrich B. Phillips, and others. So it was not until the
end of World War I, when a national crisis developed in race relations, that the social sciences were seen as factors in those relations.
The term "race relations" was itself a paradigm, and, indeed, it soon
became practically a synonym for Afro-American history.

This recognition of the social sciences as factors in history (although
in the first instances only in American Negro history), by rendering
history susceptible to "scientific" analysis and interpretation, had un-
anticipated consequences. It led to the application of sociological
hypotheses and reasoning to Afro-American historical, social, and
biographical material and its evaluation by a racial mix of cooperating
scholars, journalists, social workers, and intellectuals as dissimilar in
background, training, and ultimate direction and purpose as can be
imagined.[4] Studies, reports, editorials, news stories on racial matters
streamed from the presses and literally inspired the "New Negro,"
who gave substance to the Harlem Renaissance as well as source material to illustrious creative artists of both races.[5]

3. W. E. B. DuBois, *Dusk of Dawn: An Essay toward an Autobiography of a Race Concept*
(New York, 1940), 58.
4. Among them Franz Boas, Horace Cayton, W. E. B. DuBois, Melville J.
Herskovits, Eugene K. Jones, Howard Odum, Robert E. Park, and Carl Sandburg.
5. Among them Sherwood Anderson, Marc Connelly, Countee Cullen, Rudolph
Fisher, DuBose Heyward, Eugene O'Neill, Frederic Torrence. For extensive treatment
of the period, see Nathan I. Huggins, *Harlem Renaissance* (New York, 1971).

Not intentionally capping this interdisciplinary activity, but nevertheless indisputably establishing the relationship between Afro-American history and the social sciences, a corps of distinguished historians, sociologists, political scientists, economists, and other experts under the direction of Gunnar Myrdal, a Swedish scholar, produced a masterly study of race relations in the United States.[6] The two volumes of *An American Dilemma* (six years in preparation) comprise no more and no less than a social-scientific, deductive examination and interpretation of the *history* of race relations in the United States, which is in effect the history of the Negro in America. After the publication of this work in 1944, the writing of Afro-American history came to be governed by the assumption of that history's importance to the whole history of the United States *and* the need to recycle the American past on the basis of that assumption—to which *An American Dilemma* gave irrevocable authority. And that authority soon began to assert itself with the publication of such works as John Hope Franklin's *From Slavery to Freedom* (New York, 1947), Merl R. Eppse's *The Negro, Too, in American History* (Nashville, 1949), Henry Steele Commager's *American Mind* (New Haven, 1950), Herbert Aptheker's *Documentary History of the Negro People in the United States* (New York, 1951), and C. Vann Woodward's *Burden of Southern History* (Baton Rouge, 1960). A dozen other titles that appeared in the same time frame could be mentioned.

But it was in the 1970s, with the psychic heightening of "soul" and black race-consciousness, that the assertion of the centrality of Afro-American history to the whole of American history found strong expression in historical studies, several of them biographically oriented, some of them so unconventional as to make even the least conventional works published in the two previous decades seem relatively ordinary.

*Time on the Cross* is a case in point. Based on a quantitative method called cliometrics[7] as the touchstone of analysis and interpretation, the first volume of Robert W. Fogel and Stanley L. Engerman's study, subtitled "The Economics of American Negro Slavery," does more than question the economics of slavery formerly accepted as substantially correct: it challenges interpretations of ideology and morality, the attitudes of both masters and slaves, and other matters and con-

6. See author's "Preface," *An American Dilemma: The Negro Problem and Modern Democracy* (New York, 1944), I, x–xi.

7. "Cliometrics" is a term so new that it does not appear in standard dictionaries published in 1972.

cerns that scholars and historians of slavery have generally accepted, rejected, or ignored as inconsequential. According to Fogel and Engerman, the slave system was not "irrational"; it was not inhumane; it was not economically moribund. Quite the contrary. Their interpretation of the facts and especially the figures is that slavery was a humane institution that promoted moral behavior in master and slave and encouraged stability in slave family relationships, and that as an economic arrangement it was profitable for the master without being exploitive of the slave, who typically "over the course of his lifetime . . . received about 90 percent of the income he produced."[8]

These and complementary findings are not set forth tentatively as provisional, but as absolutes. And the second volume, subtitled "Evidence and Methods," with its documentary discussion of technical, methodological, and theoretical bases of the author's findings, is intended to affirm them absolutely.

But neither the authors' methods nor the findings and the bases on which they rest have been widely accepted among highly respected scholars. Kenneth Stampp, whose study entitled *The Peculiar Institution* was published in 1956, referred to one of the authors of *Time on the Cross* as "a bit of an academic huckster," and Kenneth Clark, the reputable social psychologist, dismissed the book as "recommending a return to slavery."[9] C. Vann Woodward, John W. Blassingame, and Nathan I. Huggins, among others, have been adversely critical. Indeed, the consensus among those best qualified to judge seems to be that recycling the history of American Negro slavery in terms of cliometrics destructively interferes with, if it does not altogether prevent, the interpretation of the slavery period in humanistic terms. Slavery was an *effective* experience that produced a range of social, cultural, and psychic consequences not only for masters and slaves and all who lived through the period, but for most of their descendants living today.

A work that deals with these consequences is John W. Blassingame's *Slave Community.* Published in 1972, two years before *Time on the Cross,* Blassingame's carefully researched and cautiously written book can be defined as a historical study of American Negro socialization and identification, and while it testifies to a symbiotic relationship between Afro-American history and the social sciences, it also adds strength to

8. *Time on the Cross* (Boston, 1974), I, 4–6.
9. Both quoted in John W. Blassingame's review "The Mathematics of Slavery," *Atlantic Monthly,* August 1974, 78–82.

the idea—rather obliquely set forth on several occasions in the 1960s by David M. Potter[10]—that a rewriting of the past is necessary to an understanding of the present.

In *The Slave Community,* Blassingame, a Negro who teaches at Yale, explores the sources of black American race-consciousness and explains the sociocultural results of its operation. The author found that some of the sources had their rise in Africa, but that they were adulterated by plantation slavery, which was itself a source (and, quite contrary to *Time on the Cross,* not a rationally organized institution). Other sources he located in the intensification of emotions through physical and mental suffering and in stolen moments of respite; in the sudden, unexpected remembrance of ancestral social forms and practices; in role playing; in the explosion of expletory sounds from an unremembered tribal tongue. Though indisputably on a high level of scholarly investigation, *The Slave Community* is both a response to and an expression of Negro race-consciousness.

*The Black Family in Slavery and Freedom, 1750–1925* is neither, but it is pertinent to both the response and the expression of Negro race-consciousness. Herbert G. Gutman's very convincing book examines aspects of Afro-American history in order to recover a complex of psychological, cultural, and sociological truths that drastically modify—or are certainly intended to modify—the perception and the interpretation of the facts of Afro-American history and culture. Acknowledging that his study "was stimulated by the bitter public and academic controversy"[11] stirred up by Daniel P. Moynihan's *Negro Family in America: The Case for National Action* (New York, 1965), which really amounted to a justification for a political stand on the race issue, Gutman turns to such primary sources as plantation records of births, deaths, "marriages" of slaves, their work assignments and food allotments, and slave letters, and converts the facts they convey (and the meaning of the facts) into readily understable tables, charts, and graphs, which substantiate his primary thesis. Simplified, that thesis is that the American Negroes' adaptive capacities overcame the "tangle of pathology" that, according to Moynihan, accounts for the Negroes' "disorganized" family life and individual behavior.

Gutman's carefully conducted study, described as a major rewriting of history, argues against a "tangle of pathology" and leads to conclu-

10. See "Explicit Data and Implicit Assumptions in Historical Study," "C. Vann Woodward and the Uses of History," "Conflict, Consensus, and Comity," and other essays in *History and American Society: Essays of David M. Potter,* ed. Don E. Fehrenbacher (New York, 1973).

11. *The Black Family in Slavery and Freedom, 1750–1925* (New York, 1976), xvii.

sions that are supported by the findings of such expert and reputable sociologists as Hylan Lewis, Tony Dunbar, and Laura Carper. The few differences that may be found between Negro and white family structures down to the mid-twentieth century have no connection with a "tangle of pathology"; these differences "diminish when controlled for income and ... differences by income are more striking than differences by color."[12]

In the preface to *Roll, Jordan, Roll: The World the Slaves Made*, Eugene D. Genovese declares that "white and black ... have come to form one people in all vital respects," and he quotes C. Vann Woodward in support of that view. Although the author is principally concerned with defining the particulars of the black identity and the working of black racial consciousness, he allows the ethnic concept of American history to prevail, and—perhaps inadvertently (and certainly in metaphysical terms)—the book does for the master class what Blassingame's work did for the slaves. Genovese writes:

> The slaves impaled their masters on the central point of slaveholding hegemonic ideology—the dependency relationship. ... The slaveholders of the Old South ... did everything to instill—or reinforce—a dependency complex in their subjects and then howled with rage when they met ingratitude. But what else should they have expected? ...
>
> Gratitude implies equality. The slaveholder had committed the grotesque blunder of assuming that it could be forthcoming from a people who had had an acceptance of inequality literally whipped into them. ... The slaves had turned the dependency relationship to their own limited advantage. Their version of paternalistic dependency stressed reciprocity. What, then, were they supposed to be grateful for? From their point of view, the genuine acts of kindness and material support ... were in fact their due—payment, as it were, for services rendered. And the crowning irony was that their own services rendered were precisely those offered within the dependency relationship itself.[13]

So although Genovese certainly stresses the working of black consciousness and black identity, he is more than a little concerned—especially in Book One, "God Is not Mocked"—with the masters' efforts to prove their humanity in spite of their dedicated defense of a socioeconomic system that the rest of the Western world was increasingly vociferous in characterizing as grossly inhumane and damnably un-Christian.

Genovese uses standard sources for the study of Afro-American

12. Ibid., p. 462.
13. Genovese, *Roll, Jordan, Roll* (New York, 1974), 146.

slavery: plantation records, notebooks, personal letters, diaries, slave narratives. But he examines and interprets them in the light of comparatively new knowledge provided by social psychology, cultural anthropology, intrapsychic accommodation, and the like, and comes up with some uncommon, myth-destructive conclusions. He makes it clear that the slaveholders' efforts to establish and maintain a reputation for gentility, grace, and benevolence did not represent a defensive reaction. They felt no need to defend themselves against what they considered the outrageous accusations of the abolitionists. Slavery was *not* inhumane. "Slaveholders generally believed that their slaves lived better than the great mass of peasants and industrial workers of the world."[14] Slaveholding was a burden, but it was also a duty. These themes "were reflected even in the prevalent idea of economic interest; they constituted its moral justification. The notion that most slaveholders felt guilt-stricken over owning slaves has no basis in fact."[15] It is ironic that among the things some slaveholders felt had to be done in the best interests of the slaves themselves were whipping, branding, burning, maiming, castrating, and occasionally lynching them.

But there was no agreement between the *classes* of slaves as to what their best interests were. The great majority of field slaves believed their best interests were the "protection," subsistence, and security provided by their masters in return for the work that was exacted of them. But the elite among slaves—the mammies, maids, body servants, craftsmen—were of a different mind. Many indulgent masters and mistresses taught their house slaves to read, carried them to church, and made them feel superior to common slaves. Indeed, many of the elite slaves were blood relatives of masters or mistresses, or somebody white, and only the imbeciles among them did not know this by their complexion and the texture of their hair.

As Genovese points out, there were few if any manor houses that did not have an elite class of slaves, and

life in the Big House, with its affection and hatreds, its interracial attachments and intolerance, its extraordinary kindnesses and uncontrollable violence, represented . . . paternalism in its most heightened form. The house servants' psychological and physical dependence upon their masters and mistresses proceeded hand in hand with their acute awareness of the whites' weaknesses, foibles, and insecurities. The masters' and mistresses' psychological and physical dependence upon their slaves pro-

14. Ibid., 58.
15. Ibid., 84.

ceeded hand in hand with gnawing intimations of the blacks' hostility, resentment, and suppressed anger. . . . Too often, even with good will, the contradictions exploded in sudden violence. A field hand could lower his eyes, shuffle, and keep control of himself in the face of provocation, but a house servant had to live with a master and mistress who knew him or her well enough to read insubordination into a glance. . . .[16]

Although Genovese cites enough instances of recalcitrant and murderous behavior on the part of house slaves to bring into question the *Gone with the Wind* version of loyal household slaves spoiling their "white folks" with tender, loving care and sympathetic understanding, he himself does not raise the question. Rather, he brings forward evidence of the thoughtful concern of some slaveholders for the welfare of their slaves; evidence of a disposition for relief and reform of slavery's worst abuses; and evidence of the slave's and slavery's contributions to a heritage that balances and complements the national heritage. And Genovese does this without for a moment slighting or weakening his primary thesis, that Afro-American slavery is basically "a record of one of history's greatest crimes."[17] *Roll, Jordan, Roll* is a superb accomplishment in historical scholarship.

Very good as scholarship and just as absorbing to read is Leon Litwack's *Been in the Storm So Long* (New York, 1979). Here the ethnic concept of American history also prevails, but what Genovese did more or less inadvertently for the white master class in the slavery period Litwack does with purpose aforethought for the same southern white—as well as for blacks—immediately after slavery. Much of the material is anecdotal and some of it is based on interviews with ex-slaves after emancipation; but Litwack uses the material to define the psychology of southern whites and to demonstrate and document how that psychology operated in their attitudes and behavior vis-à-vis the freed blacks and the northern whites ("the damnyankees") who were responsible for freeing them. What *Been in the Storm So Long* adds up to is the most revealing and equitably balanced account yet written of "race relations"—of the interplay of black and white thought and feeling—in a time of crisis. It is also the most richly detailed.

*Black Odyssey* (New York, 1977), on the other hand, is generally confined to the exploration only of Negro thought and feeling in times of perpetual crisis. Avoiding the use of most of the conventional scholarly apparatus yet firmly committed to high scholarly endeavor,

16. Ibid., 363–364.
17. Ibid., xvi.

Nathan I. Huggins, subtitling his study "The Afro-American Ordeal in Slavery," concerns himself with the experience of that ordeal and with how, out of that experience, a culture developed that is distinctively both Negro *and* American. In the broad sweep of *Black Odyssey*, Huggins specifies enough to document the "Afro-Americanization" of the national culture, and his point of view is that of a professional historian addressing a respected audience of involved laymen. In his earlier book *Harlem Renaissance* Huggins had traced the development of distinctive elements of the Negro-American culture in literature and music, the graphic arts, and the dramatic arts from the point of view of the critic. *Black Odyssey* and *Harlem Renaissance* together lead to a rediscovery of neglected aspects of American social and cultural history.

Published at the same time as *Black Odyssey*, Lawrence W. Levine's *Black Culture and Black Consciousness* (New York, 1977) makes it apparent that rediscovering neglected facets of American social and cultural history depends much less (indeed, scarcely at all) on the unearthing of new historical facts than on a reappraisal of old historical facts, assumptions, and sources in the light of new, mid-twentieth-century social-scientific hypotheses and perceptions. The old facts and sources that Levine reexamines are the folklore, the orally transmitted expression of story, song, and saying, and the folk practices—games, dances, religious and other ceremonials—of the Afro-American people. And the result is an exhaustive history of black American culture and the racial consciousness that informs and inspires it.

Though less directly than Levine, August Meier and Elliott M. Rudwick are also concerned with the "activity" of black consciousness on the Negro experience in America. Their book *Along the Color Line: Explorations in the Black Experience* (Urbana, Ill., 1976) does exactly what its subtitle suggests: it explores Negro-American experiences and how Negroes responded to them mentally and emotionally. Meier and Rudwick's most recent work, *Black Detroit and the Rise of the UAW* (New York, 1979), describes the growth of black participation in the United Auto Workers during the New Deal. It then examines the interaction during World War II among union leaders, black workers, civil rights spokesmen, and federal officials that produced important victories for blacks in their struggle for improved employment opportunities.

*Slaves without Masters,* by Ira Berlin, could be interpreted as an examination of race-consciousness among free blacks in the slaveholding South, but such an interpretation would diminish its primary importance as the first and (at this writing) only book-length work on free Negroes in the antebellum South. There have been state and nonsouthern sectional studies of free Negroes, but the geographical limitations, while perhaps valid for the various authors' purposes, narrowed their relevance as histories of freedom and slavery and reduced Afro-American history to a study of cooperation and conflict between the races. But Berlin's book is more than that. It has two themes. One theme has to do with an analysis of the difference between Negro freedom and Negro slavery—a difference that most whites saw as immaterial, since it did not substantially modify their conception of the Negroes' "place" in society. But for a few whites and for the Negroes themselves, the difference between being slave and being free made for profound (and complicated) alterations in intra-racial and interracial relations. And these complicated alterations comprise the second theme of Berlin's extraordinary work.

Owing in part to a paucity of public records and private letters, Berlin's exposition of the second theme, while certainly painstaking, is less successful than his treatment of the first. For instance, it might have been well known locally that some wealthy slaveholder supported a slave mistress in comfort and sent the children she bore him north or to Europe to be educated and to escape the onus of being "half white," but it is unlikely that this would be a matter of public record or of other than strictly private and confidential letters and conversation. And though a man as prominent in public life as, say, the governor of South Carolina in 1835 might declare that Negroes "have all the qualities which fit them to be slaves, and not one of those that would fit them to be free,"[18] in the light of that declaration, he (and any other man so situated) would not make public the fact that he had emancipated a female slave and sent her to live among freedmen, who were mostly light-skinned men and women who made their livings in the crafts and as industrial workers.

Berlin does examine the development of a color-caste system within the Negro race. Accepting the whites' assumption that they (the whites) were members of a superior race, which slavery and the attitudes and responses it provoked on both sides of the color line seemed to support, Negroes themselves embraced the color-caste system. The more white blood a Negro had, the better, and the more intelligent and personable he or she was considered as a human being. The influence of this thinking did not begin to erode among Negroes until about the second decade of the present century; now, thanks to

18. Berlin, *Slaves without Masters* (New York, 1974), 193.

the scientific evidence that disputes it, and to the development of a positive and constructive racial self-concept, the erosion is complete.

Three recent works by perceptive black scholars exemplify the various approaches currently being used to trace the historic struggle for freedom and equality by Afro-Americans. In *Black over White: Negro Political Leadership in South Carolina during Reconstruction,* Thomas Holt has emphasized the social origins of black leaders and related issues involving class conflict in a single (but critically important) state.[19] By emphasizing differences of class *within* the black community, divergent attitudes between leaders and voters, and divisiveness among the Radicals, he has provided a model for future state studies and a more subtly informed explanation for the failure of Radical Reconstruction.

Nell Irvin Painter has studied the first major migration of former slaves after Reconstruction. During the years 1879–81, thousands of "Exodusters"—so called because of the analogy between their situation and that of the biblical Hebrews in flight from Egypt—left Louisiana, Mississippi, Texas, and Tennessee for Kansas, where homestead land was still available and the state was identified in freedmen's minds with John Brown. The 20,000 ex-slaves who traveled from the deep South to Kansas comprised the greatest American folk movement since the Great Migration of Puritans to Massachusetts Bay in the 1630s. At last their story has been told, filling in a major gap in Afro-American historiography.[20]

*Racial Equality in America,* by John Hope Franklin, originated as the 1976 Jefferson Lectures in the Humanities, a prestigious series sponsored by the National Endowment for the Humanities. Franklin's book is actually concerned with racial *in*equality: the betrayal by the Founding Fathers of the ideal of equality for *all* men; the worsening plight of Negroes in nineteenth-century America; and then the tumultuous struggle for equality during the twentieth century. Franklin's succinct and poignant rendering of a story that is all too familiar by now will be appreciated by students and laymen alike. It stands as one of the best available introductions to the American tragedy of racial prejudice, repression, and human resilience.[21]

If *Slaves without Masters, Roll, Jordan, Roll, Black Culture and Black Consciousness,* and other works published in the 1970s provide evidence that Afro-American history is not simply adjunctive to Ameri-

19. Urbana, Ill., 1977.
20. *Exodusters: Black Migration to Kansas after Reconstruction* (New York, 1977).
21. Chicago, 1976.

can history, biographical and autobiographical works and materials support that evidence, and, moreover, furnish examples of the direct relations between the Negro-American experience and the development of Negro-American race and culture consciousness.

On this point—and at this point—*All God's Dangers: The Life of Nate Shaw* is an appropriate book to cite. It is history as biography and social chronicle; and because it vividly illuminates a social group previously neglected in southern history, it is important. It is oral history edited by Theodore Rosengarten, who was wise enough to know that "real history is simply the record of human adjustments to circumstances," and to realize that Nate Shaw's record of his life is the history of the Negro—and white—people in the South for almost a hundred years, and that Shaw, though unlearned, was intelligent and sensitive enough to understand what that history meant.

Nate Shaw was eighty-four when Rosengarten searched him out in 1969, and all the stories are not stories of what happened to him directly. Some go back to his father and three uncles, but as the editor points out, the stories are built upon one another so that "the sequence expresses the sense of a man 'becoming,'" one who wanted to "set an example to his race"—becoming the Nate Shaw who spent twelve years in prison for joining the Sharecroppers' Union in 1932. Beneath the ribald humor and the whimsy of the stories he heard from his father and uncles, Nate could sense their tragic significance, and when he himself recounted them, he understood their meanings as they related to the experience of both black and white in the South: as they related to "keepin the nigger goin the white man's way," and the white man's fear that "the nigger was gettin to be too smart to just follow the white man's way." They related to discouraging the Negro's ambition by preaching that true righteousness for the Negro meant having so little that it would not hurt to lose it.

There are literally hundreds of stories in *All God's Dangers,* and except for a few that Nate tells as second- or thirdhand anecdotes, the storyteller himself is at the very center of their historical interest and meaning. When he was released from prison in 1945, Nate Shaw was sixty and, though landless, still undefeated. As a matter of fact, life was a bit easier; and if many whites still felt that everything belonged to them and that whatever Negroes got, "includin learnin," they got on the sufferance of whites, "a mite fewer colored did."

I've noticed many things through the past history of my life—uneducated man that I am—that point to a plan. Time passes and the generations die. But the condition of the people that's livin today aint like it was for the people that's gone. And it aint now like it's goin to be for the people that comes after us. . . .

There's a certain element that's workin to please God and overturn this southern way of life. How many people is it today that it needs and it requires to carry out this movement? How many is it knows just what it's goin to take? . . . But it's goin to take a great effort; we ought to realize that. . . . Somebody got to move and remove and it may take—how do I know how many it's goin to take?—I just realize in my mind, it's goin to take thousands and millions of words, thousands and millions of steps, to complete this business.

I'd like to live; and if the Lord sees fit to able me to stay here and see it, I'd love to know that the black race had fully shed the veil from their eyes and the shackles from their feet. And I hope to God that I won't be one of the slackers that would set down and refuse to labor to that end.[22]

Nate Shaw's experiences encompass nearly a century of the history of the Negro in America. His narration of those experiences is vigorous and compelling. Some of the poignancy undoubtedly derives from the language of the telling, but in greater part it derives from the details and the authenticity of the emotions they evoke.

Two other works published in the 1970s, the life of Booker T. Washington and the correspondence of W. E. B. DuBois, are also to the point that biographical and autobiographical works and materials furnish examples of the direct relation between the Negro experience and the development of race- and color-consciousness—as well as to the point that Afro-American history is no longer perceived as adjunctive, but as central to American history.

Louis R. Harlan's sensitive biography, *Booker T. Washington: The Making of a Black Leader, 1856–1901,* is the story of a man born in slavery who affected the course of the nation's history. Booker Washington's life was rooted in his native country's attitudes and institutions, and his career was generated and determined by American national values. Unlike a now decimated school of black-culture extremists of both races, whose enthusiasm is beyond question but whose claims to knowledge and scholarly authority are suspect, Harlan does not digress into explorations of African cultural survivals. There were few African survivals, and most of the few were in the sounds of structural peculiarities of Negro vernacular. But even this vernacular had little currency in the Virginia foothills of the Blue Ridge Mountains, where Booker Washington was born, the son of a

22. Theodore Rosengarten, ed., *All God's Dangers: The Life of Nate Shaw* (New York, 1974, 551.

slave mother and, apparently, a white father, and where there were
relatively few slaves. And the slave vernacular had even less currency
in Malden, West Virginia, where he moved with his mother and step-
father when freedom came.

Growing up as the houseboy of the Lewis Ruffners in "the largest
and best-appointed house in town," Booker "developed a closeness to
upper class whites," whose speech and manners he learned. Later at
Hampton Institute, where he was encouraged to go, Negro dialect
was never heard. Founded by a former general in the Union Army,
Samuel Chapman Armstrong, the Hampton Normal and Agricultural
Institute had only white teachers, and the light-skinned, grey-eyed
Booker Washington soon became their favorite pupil. He saw in S. C.
Armstrong, who was still addressed as "General," the "white father
figure he had been searching for . . . [and] completed his identity with
elite whites" that had begun with the Ruffners in Malden.

It goes without saying that the system of values that operated at
Hampton and in such company was American, and in that system,
matter was favored over mind, action over intellect. General
Armstrong was "an almost fanatical proponent of individualism," who
"comprehended the deep philosophy of *one man power*."[23] In emula-
tion of his white father figure, Booker T. Washington, who was no
intellectual, became "a man of action. . . . Power was his game," and,
his biographer tells us, both his psyche and his personality accommo-
dated the American system of values in which at the time (from the
1870s onward) one of the most important elements was keeping the
Negro in his place. In his historic Atlanta Compromise speech of
1895, twenty years after his graduation from Hampton, his definition
of the Negro's place helped to determine the course of race relations
down to the present time.

*The Correspondence of W. E. B. DuBois,* selected and edited by Herbert Aptheker, adds immeasurably to our knowledge of how turbulent and capricious Afro-American history has been since the period
just after the Civil War.[24] It gradually becomes apparent that the
selection of letters reflects Aptheker's biases, but still the letters' historical relevance and DuBois's involvement as a socially concerned
American citizen emerge undistorted. The collection contains hundreds of letters on subjects ranging from local and national politics to
international affairs to race relations at home and abroad. DuBois's
correspondents were as various as Charles Francis Adams and

23. Harlan, *Booker T. Washington: The Making of a Black Leader, 1856–1901* (New
York, 1972), 61.
24. 3 vols. (Amherst, Mass., 1973–78).

Nnandi Azikiwe, Roger N. Baldwin and Herman Bernstein, William Randolph Hearst and Langston Hughes, Jawaharlal Nehru and Kwame Nkrumah, Henry James and Lyndon Johnson, Lady Kathleen Simon and Albert Schweitzer, Herman Talmadge, Sr., and Dalton Trumbo, Jessie Fauset and Ja-Ja Wachuku. The letters go back to 1874, and the last one—from DuBois to Gertrude Heym, director of a German-based publishing company—is dated July 10, 1963, almost exactly one month before DuBois's death in Accra, Ghana, where, after renouncing his American citizenship, he had gone to live at the special invitation of Kwame Nkrumah. Although there are few personal and "private" letters, one comes to know DuBois close up—his head and his heart, his troubles and triumphs—almost as intimately as one knows a close friend. But make no mistake: *The Correspondence of W. E. B. DuBois* is an indispensable resource for scholars in American history and for those general readers who regard Afro-American history as central.

Two other works should be mentioned as responsive to the themes of ethnic consciousness and the centrality of Afro-American history to American history, which have been at the heart of this essay. The first is *Key Issues in the Afro-American Experience* (New York, 1971). Edited by Nathan I. Huggins of Columbia University and Martin Kilson and Daniel Fox of Harvard, *Key Issues* is a collection of essays on topics that distinguished professionals of both races chose as fundamental to a comprehension of the Negro American experience; and they cover the range from Huggin's "Myths, Heroes, and Reality" in Afro-American history to Stanley Elkins's "Social Consequences of Slavery" and Lawrence Levine's "Concept of the New Negro and the Realities of Black Culture." Linking and elucidating these essays are others—whether treating of sensibility or prima facie historical evidence—that support the readers' understanding that the black American experience and the black American identity are rooted in the history of America. The essays by Huggins, Basil Davidson, Kenneth Stampp, and Joel R. Williamson in Volume 1 are must reading; in Volume 11, the essential essays are those by Robert H. Abzug, Otey M. Scruggs, Francis L. Broderick, and Lawrence W. Levine.

Finally, there can be no question that clinching the fact of the spreading appreciation of the themes has been the general public's reception of a book—later turned into a television motion picture—entitled *Roots*. Fittingly subtitled "The Saga of an American Family," Alex Haley's book is not history in the conventional academic sense.[25]

25. New York, 1976. For a useful essay review, see Richard Price in the *Maryland Historical Magazine*, LXXII (1977), 325–328.

It is the historically documented story of six generations of a Negro family's struggle to live and succeed in an environment that was both physically and spiritually hostile. Though the story alternately plunges into tragedy and rises to high comedy, both tragedy and comedy give insights into the minds of black and white Americans and supply readers with a sense of those elements of vitality and strength, understanding and sympathy, affection and respect that, according to legendary tradition, have fused in the national character and made Americans of all races one people.

# 13

## Women and the Family

### Carl N. Degler

I N an absolute sense the fields of women's history and the history
of the family, including the history of childhood, are not new.
The first comprehensive history of the family in America was
published more than sixty years ago, and the earliest histories of
women in America appeared in the mid-nineteenth century.[1] But
measured by the volume of work and the concentrated attention of
historians, both of these fields in United States historiography can be
said to have been born in the 1960s. The outpouring of new work in
the history of women and of the family has been the most recent
example of the way in which the content of the remembered past is
constantly being reshaped. The subjects of women and the family
have been added to the corpus of historical writing for the same
reasons that other aspects of the American past such as labor organizations, the working class, cities, and blacks have been. As new concerns arise in the present, we ask fresh questions of the past, thereby
bringing novel subjects into the purview of the historian.

The operative question, of course, is how these new historical interests are to be integrated into our conception of the past, into that
which is considered *the* history of a nation or a period. To this large
question of integration we shall return later. For the moment let us
look at the way in which these two fields, with some passing reference
to the history of childhood, have been developing since the 1960s,
when United States historians first began systematically to explore
them. (I shall confine my comments to the literature on the American
past.)

Although these two divisions of United States history are quite

---

1. Arthur W. Calhoun, *A Social History of the American Family,* 3 vols. (Cleveland,
1918); Elizabeth F. Ellet, *Women of the American Revolution,* 3 vols. (New York, 1848–50).

properly linked, they evolved separately and, surprisingly and re-
grettably, have continued to be separated in a number of significant
and ultimately counterproductive ways. An examination of their different origins can serve as a convenient introduction to a consideration of the relative significance of these new interests among historians in the United States. The modern field of family history is
largely a European innovation, the first practitioners being French
and English demographic historians whose earliest work appeared in
the late 1950s. The first articles on family history in the United
States—all of them studies of communities in colonial New
England—did not appear until the mid-1960s, and the first books did
not appear until 1970.[2] Although the output of American scholars in
this area has increased enormously, United States historians are still
only one national group among several in family history circles.

The exact opposite is true of women's history. Its origins are almost
entirely American, with most European historians only beginning at
the end of the 1970s even to consider women as significant figures in
the past. Unlike family history, but very much like black history, the
history of women was brought into being largely by changes within
American society. It is no denigration or even criticism of the subdiscipline, but rather a realistic recognition of a fact of historical life, that
it was the demand for historical recognition, first by blacks and then
by women, that catapulted black and women's history into the consciousness of historians. These presentist or ideological origins
created and continue to create problems for the traditional pursuit of
historical scholarship. For that reason the matter will be returned to
later in this essay.

The quite different origins of these two aspects of United States
history help to explain other differences between them. That most
historians of the family are male and most historians of women are
female reveals in yet another way the ideological or presentist origins
of women's history. Women have an interest in their own past that
men have not displayed even though one might have thought that
professional concerns at least would have opened their eyes. By the
same token, the origins of the history of the family in the techniques
of family reconstitution first worked out by French and English de-

2. John Demos, "Notes on Life in Plymouth Colony," *William and Mary Quarterly*, 3d
ser., XXII (1968), 264–286; Kenneth A. Lockridge, "The Population of Dedham, Massachusetts, 1636–1736," *Economic History Review*, 2d ser., XIX (1966), 318–344; Philip J.
Greven, Jr., *Four Generations: Population, Land, and Family in Colonial Andover, Massachusetts* (Ithaca, N.Y., 1970); John Demos, *A Little Commonwealth: Family Life in
Plymouth Colony* (New York, 1970).

mographic historians helps to explain the continued reliance of the field on quantitative as opposed to literary sources. Demography itself, of course, has long been heavily statistical, and that tradition has been carried over into family history. Moreover, thanks to the computer, which has permitted the exploitation of the rich data contained in the United States manuscript census records, quantification has become a prominent as well as a practical tool for historians of the family. At the same time, the ideological or valuational origins of women's history have predisposed its practitioners to look primarily to literary evidence since that kind of source best reveals the values and ideology of historical figures.

The primary reason for emphasizing the ways in which these two new disciplines differ is because the differences seem to have erected impediments to the proper and most fruitful development of them. To any casual observer it would seem natural that the two fields should be closely related if only because historically women have been active primarily in the family and therefore might be thought to be of central importance in explaining the history of that institution. Yet few readers of women's history or of the history of the family can fail to note the lack of attention one area of study has paid to the other. For example, demographers struggle to explain the decline in fertility in the nineteenth century, yet rarely do they ask how women may have determined that result. Instead, their explanations almost always rely on men's motives. By the same token, much of the writing about women proceeds as though women outside the family were the most common examples of the way women lived in the past. Certainly the lives and activities of many women centered outside the family, and they deserve and need to be described and analyzed. But the inescapable fact of women's history is that until the middle of the twentieth century the characteristic arena of existence and activity of most women has been the family. The family and women, in short, are closely linked, even if the two disciplines are far from congruent. Their academic students should be talking to one another more than they have been. As we shall see, the natural connection between them is now beginning to be recognized and acted upon.

Undoubtedly the most striking difference between the literature on the history of the family and that on the history of women is the driving concern the former has with quantification or numerical generalization. The justification, as in all fields, is that through numbers the historian can escape from particularity, subjectivity, and unrepresentativeness. Perhaps the most striking finding derived from the use of numerical data has been that the so-called nuclear or two-generation family was characteristic of colonial America; the extended family was, as it is today, quite rare. In fact, thanks to the relentless pursuit of the subject, especially by the English scholar Peter Laslett,[3] it is now known that virtually no society of any size in the past exhibited a family structure in which more than two generations lived under the same roof. This finding was central in removing from historical discourse the once widely held view that industrialization (and urbanization) was the principal explanation for the emergence of the modern conjugal family.

Despite this gain, however, studies of household structure have not advanced our knowledge about the family very far. Several historians of the family have complained that neither the rather narrow definition nor the finding itself tells us much beyond the bare fact. Some have pointed out, for example, that a nuclear structure may be only temporary, that at certain stages in the life cycle of the family more than two generations might live under a single roof, or that newly married couples might live with parents before they have children. Moreover, merely counting generations in a household at one time may well obscure the emotional reality of the family: separation may be by dwelling (which the manuscript census would quickly show), but not by substantial distance (which would be difficult, if not impossible, to discover from the manuscript census data). Thus parents might be around the corner, but from the census data alone would appear to be far removed from married children.[4] Since a primary purpose of structural analysis is to ascertain internal familial relations, merely counting bodies under a single roof may obscure the true relations among family members. Consequently, recent studies have begun to examine structural questions that move beyond the issue of the nuclear character of the family, the fact of which, in any case, is no

3. Peter Laslett, "Size and Structure of the Household in England over Three Centuries," *Population Studies,* XXIII (1969), 199–223; Peter Laslett, ed., *Household and Family in Past Time* (Cambridge, Eng., 1972).

4. For telling and informed critiques of the Laslett approach, see Lutz K. Berkner, "The Use and Misuse of Census Data for the Historical Analysis of Family Structure," *Journal of Interdisciplinary History,* V (1975), 721–728, and Maris A. Vinovskis, "From Household Size to the Life Course," *American Behavioral Scientist,* XXI (1977), 263–287. For examples of empirical studies that move beyond household structure, see Howard P. Chudacoff, "New Branches on the Tree: Household Structures in Early Stages of the Family Cycle in Worcester, Massachusetts, 1860–1880," *Proceedings* of the American Antiquarian Society, LXXXVI (1976), 303–320, and his "Newlyweds and Family Extension: The First Stage of the Family Cycle in Providence, Rhode Island, 1864–1865 and 1879–1880," in Tamara K. Hareven, ed., *Transitions: The Family and the Life Course in Historical Perspective* (New York, 1978). For a discussion of the diachronic approach to the family: Tamara K. Hareven, "The Family Process: The Historical Study of the Family Cycle," *Journal of Social History,* VII (1974), 322–330.

longer a debatable question. Some of the most recent demographic work on the southern English colonies, for example, has shown that there were significant differences in sex ratios, mortality, and rates of population growth between the New England and Chesapeake colonies.[5]

Some students of the nineteenth-century family have transcended the old questions about the nuclear family by using the manuscript census data to redefine the family functionally. They contend that no single definition does justice to the flexibility of the institution under changing circumstances and human needs.[6] They have introduced the conception of the "augmented family," that is, the family with outsiders (boarders, who paid for food and lodging, or roomers) rather than relatives. Augmented families never constituted a majority of families at any time, but they were much more common in the nineteenth century than today. Although it seems logical to assume that the presence of boarders and roomers reflected a need for additional family income, in several instances there is no clear correlation between the presence of boarders and family income.[7] As in other such cases, numerical evidence alone cannot answer the question of the meaning to be assigned to the augmented family.

In a further effort to move away from "snapshot" or static conceptions of the family, of which nuclear structure is a prime example, historians of the family have drawn upon modern sociological concepts that stress change over time and thus better serve the needs and concerns of historians. The idea of the family cycle, which was introduced to criticize the conception of nuclear structure, sees families moving through a progression of stages from formation (marriage) to

5. Russell R. Menard, "Immigration to the Chesapeake Colonies in the Seventeenth Century: A Review Essay," *Maryland Historical Magazine*, LXVIII (1973), 323–329; Robert V. Wells, *The Population of the British Colonies in America before 1776: A Survey of Census Data* (Princeton, 1975); Lois Green Carr and Lorena S. Walsh, "Planter's Wife: The Experience of White Women in Seventeenth-Century Maryland," in Michael Gordon, ed., *The American Family in Social-Historical Perspective*, 2d ed. (New York, 1978).

6. John Modell and Tamara Hareven, "Urbanization and the Malleable Household: An Examination of Boarding and Lodging in American Families," *Journal of Marriage and the Family*, XXXV (1973), 467–479.

7. See, for example, Clyde Griffen and Sally Griffen, *Natives and Newcomers: The Ordering of Opportunity in Mid-Nineteenth-Century Poughkeepsie* (Cambridge, Mass., 1978), p. 236, and Susan J. Kleinberg, "Technology's Stepdaughters: The Impact of Industrialization upon Working-Class Women, Pittsburgh, 1865–1890," Ph.D. dissertation, University of Pittsburgh, 1973, 251. The as yet unpublished research of Ralph Mann of the University of Colorado on the two California gold towns of Grass Valley and Nevada City, which he has kindly let me see, also provides examples of middle-class merchants and others housing roomers and boarders under circumstances that seem to rule out economic reasons.

first birth and finally to the death of a partner. Although this conception recognizes the changing and flexible nature of the family, which accumulating historical data document, it still leaves out deviations from those broad stages. As a result, sociologist Glen Elder's conception of the "family life course" has recently been attracting the interest of several family historians. The advantage of the life course idea is that it postulates no general pattern or series of stages for all families, but rather asks how many individuals found themselves in a given situation in the past. By shifting the emphasis from the family to the individual within the family, historians can capture deviations from the family cycle and achieve a closer approximation of social reality. This most recent emphasis upon individuals *within* families has also encouraged some family historians to begin to look at the place of women in and outside families, thus helping to close the once formidable gulf between the two fields.[8]

One consequence of a reliance upon sociological theory and conceptualization has been a tendency toward abstraction as well as quantification. The trend is evident in the contents of the new *Journal of Family History*. Many of the articles suggest that the family is now being studied across the tradtitional boundaries of nations, and in the present as well as the past, that is to say, across the conventional boundaries of historical analysis. The purpose does not seem to be comparative so much as transnational and transtemporal. The family, in short, is taken as a single institution, capable of being examined across time and space, much as sociologists or anthropologists would study an institution. (Paradoxically enough, there is an equally strong though contrary tendency in the literature to emphasize the difference between families *intranationally* in regard to ethnicity, race, and class, about which more will be said a little later.) Insofar as the study of the family is abstracted from the traditional contexts of national cultures and historical periods in which historians have conventionally discussed institutions, to that extent, it would seem, the integration of the history of the family with that of women (which has not exhibited the same drift toward abstraction) or into history in general is likely to be slowed or even rendered impossible.

A related impediment to bringing the history of the family into the mainstream of the past has been identified by a leading student of the family. Historical demography, Maris Vinovskis has warned, must

8. For an excellent introduction to the definition and application of the life course approach, see the essays in Hareven, ed., *Transition,* especially the introduction by Charles Tilly and the essay by Glen Elder, Jr.

move beyond mere statistical analysis and confront "the issue of the interaction of attitudinal and demographic factors and avoid an unnecessary and undesirable split between a social science approach to the study of history and the more traditional, humanistic effort to recapture the essence of the past."[9]

In actual fact, several quantitatively inclined students of the family have already managed to narrow the gap that rightly worries Vinovskis. No one has been more successful in that respect than Daniel Scott Smith, whose several articles drawn from his study of Hingham, Massachusetts, have shown how an imaginative use of statistical evidence can reveal parental attitudes and practices.[10] Maris Vinovskis himself has demonstrated that quantification of the educational experience of women can throw light on which sex makes decisions to control fertility. Peter Uhlenberg's highly skilled demographic work reveals how recent certain patterns of women's lives and family character actually are. Before this century, for example, a majority of women did not experience what is taken for granted today as the life of a typical woman, that is, living until her last child is married and having her husband still alive.[11]

Furthermore, two overlapping aspects of family history have managed to maintain connections with the larger qustions and concerns of traditional history while relating the history of the family to women's history. These are studies of ethnic and of working-class families. Perhaps the most imaginative works of this kind are those by Daniel Walkowitz, which delineate the divergences in family patterns, age of marriage, and other aspects of family life among various ethnic and occupational segments of the working class. Walkowitz's examination of two upstate New York towns certainly call into question generalizations about *the* family.[12] Susan Hirsch's book-length analysis of similar census sources for the industrial city of Newark, New Jersey, during

9. Maris Vinovskis, "Recent Trends in American Historical Demography: Some Methodological and Conceptual Considerations," *Annual Review of Sociology, 1978,* 613.

10. See Daniel Scott Smith, "Parental Control and Marriage Patterns: An Analysis of Historical Trends in Hingham, Massachusetts," *Journal of Marriage and the Family,* xxxv (1973), 419–428, and his article "Family Limitation, Sexual Control, and Domestic Feminism in Victorian America," in Mary S. Hartman and Lois W. Banner, eds., *Clio's Consciousness Raised* (New York, 1974), 119–136.

11. Maris A. Vinovskis, "Socioeconomic Determinants of Fertility," *Journal of Interdisciplinary History,* vi (1976), 375–396; Peter R. Uhlenberg, "A Study of Cohort Life Cycles: Cohorts of Native-Born Massachusetts Women, 1830–1920," *Population Studies,* xxiii (1969), 407–420, and his essay "Changing Configurations of the Life Course" in Hareven, ed., *Transitions.*

12. Daniel J. Walkowitz, "Working-Class Women in the Gilded Age: Factory, Family, and Community Life among Cohoes, New York, Cotton Workers," *Journal of Social History,* v (1972), 464–490, and his "Statistics and the Writing of Working-Class Culture:

the first half of the nineteenth century, however, points toward a different though not necessarily a contradictory conclusion—that in certain important ways working-class families differed only marginally from middle-class families. She found that working-class wives' roles and the extent to which children worked outside the home were very similar to patterns customarily associated with middle-class women and children.[13] These conclusions, however, have not emerged from other studies of working-class or immigrant families, such as those on Italians and Jews.[14]

To complicate the matter still further, not all of these studies of families outside the middle class are congruent in time: some, such as Hirsch's, end with 1860; others, such as Walkowitz's, run to as late as 1880, and still others relate to the opening years of the twentieth century. In short, the extent to which working-class or immigrant families differ among themselves and from middle-class families is still an open question, even in regard to structure and size, and certainly in regard to intrafamilial relations. The as yet unpublished work of Robert Griswold, drawing upon divorce records from two rural California counties, persuasively argues that the familial values of these lower-class families were remarkably like those of the more historically accessible middle-class urban families of the mid-nineteenth century.[15] Perhaps the most significant point to be drawn from these otherwise inconclusive studies is that they have tended to heal the split between what Vinovskis has called the behavioralistic and the humanistic approach to the family. All of them use quantitative evidence, yet always with an eye to linking it to values and attitudes. Such a use of quantification serves also to establish friendly connections to the history of women, which has always been strongly committed to the study of values and attitudes.

No aspect of family history in the United States has received more attention and profited more from recent research than the black family under slavery. Although Herbert Gutman's book embraces in its title the black family after emancipation as well as during slavery, most of the book and most of the insights concern the slave family.

---

A Statistical Portrait of the Iron Workers in Troy, New York, 1860–1880," *Labor History,* xv (1974), 416–460.

13. Susan E. Hirsch, *Roots of the American Working Class: The Industrialization of Crafts in Newark, 1800–1860* (Philadelphia, 1978).

14. Virginia Yans-McLaughlin, *Family and Community: Italian Immigrants in Buffalo, 1880–1930* (Ithaca, N.Y., 1977); Thomas Kessner, *The Golden Door: Italian and Jewish Immigrant Mobility in New City, 1880–1915* (New York, 1977).

15. Robert Griswold, "The Character of the Family in Rural California, 1850–1890," Ph.D. dissertation, Stanford University, 1979.

Gutman's book, in fact, is only the most recent and largest of several important works which have reversed a generation of scholarship that had insisted that slavery prevented the formation of, or at least severely weakened, the family among American blacks.[16] The upshot of the various studies, whether drawn from literary or from quantitative sources, has been the disclosure of strong similarities between blacks and whites in family structure (nuclear) and in intrafamilial relations (male-dominated) both under slavery and after. Age at first marriage and at first birth, it is true, were lower for slave women than for free white women, and though the fertility of both white and black women fell in the nineteenth century, the decline for black women was somewhat slower.[17]

The continuing emphasis upon structure and intrafamilial relations serves to remind us that the history of the family is still so new that its relevance to the study of the past in general has not yet been clearly established. Few family historians, for example, have tried to show what difference it made whether boarders lived with families or not. At least two book-length studies have analyzed what sociologists and psychologists have said about the family in the twentieth century,[18] but they have done little to expand our knowledge of its history since none of the sociological or psychological studies of the family over the past half century have been based on historical investigations. The bare facts of the family's past are still being accumulated.

At least one prominent English historian of the family has suggested that now that it has been recognized that the nuclear family was not a product of industrialization, but arose before it, perhaps the causal direction ought to be reversed. The rise of an industrial society may have been dependent on the prior development of the modern

16. Herbert G. Gutman, *The Black Family in Slavery and Freedom, 1750–1925* (New York, 1976); John W. Blassingame, *The Slave Community: Plantation Life in the Antebellum South* (New York, 1972); George P. Rawick, *From Sundown to Sunup: The Making of the Black Community* (Westport, Conn, 1972); Paul J. Lammermeier, "The Urban Black Family in the Nineteenth Century: A Study of Black Family Structure in the Ohio Valley, 1850–1880," *Journal of Marriage and the Family,* xxxv (1973), 440–456; Elizabeth Pleck, "The Two-Parent Household: Black Family Structure in Late-Nineteenth-Century Boston," *Journal of Social History,* vi (1972), 3–31; Allen Kulikoff, "The Origins of Afro-American Society in Tidewater Maryland and Virginia, 1700 to 1790," *William and Mary Quarterly,* 3d ser., xxxv (1978), 226–259. For an informed critique of some of Gutman's evidence and conclusions, see Stanley L. Engerman, "Studying the Black Family," *Journal of Family History,* iii (1978), 78–101.

17. Stanley L. Engerman, "Black Fertility and Family Structure in the United States, 1880–1940," *Journal of Family History,* ii (1977), 117–138.

18. Christopher Lasch, *Haven in a Heartless World: The Family Besieged* (New York, 1977), and Mark Poster, *A Critical Theory of the Family* (New York, 1978).

companionate family.[19] It would have provided the individualistic mobility and personal autonomy required for the development of urban industrialization as well as giving the nurturance, support, and protection that human beings found necessary for survival in the harsh, competitive environment of early industrialization. But this frankly speculative justification for the study of family history has not been supported by or pursued in empirical studies.

The most promising way in which the study of the family and the history of women are being connected is through scholarly efforts to locate in time the emergence of the modern American family. These studies generally point to several attitudes and institutions that came together at about the same time and that are the hallmarks of the modern family. They are the development of the idea and practice of domesticity, a new concept of the child, the companionate or egalitarian marriage, and the fall in the rate of fertility. All four developments seem to emerge toward the end of the eighteenth and the opening of the nineteenth centuries. Such students of the family as Daniel Scott Smith and Robert Wells and such students of women's history as Nancy Cott and Mary Beth Norton have recently identified these years as the era of transition from the traditional to the modern family.[20] Significantly, too, the documentation is both literary and quantitative. Students of childhood and child rearing have singled out those same years as a turning point in the attitude toward treatment of children.[21] The agreement among the three fields at present is suggestive rather than conclusive, but the evidence is mounting fast.

19. E. Anthony Wrigley, "Reflections on the History of the Family," *Daedalus,* CVI (1977), 83.

20. Smith, "Parental Control and Marriage Patterns"; Robert V. Wells, "Family History and Demographic Transition," *Journal of Social History,* IX (1975), 1–19; Robert V. Wells, "Family Size and Fertility Control in Eighteenth-Century America: A Study of Quaker Families," *Population Studies,* XXV (1971), 73–82; Nancy F. Cott, "Eighteenth-Century Family and Social Life Revealed in Massachusetts Divorce Records," *Journal of Social History,* (1976), 20–43; Nancy F. Cott, "Divorce and the Changing Status of Women in Eighteenth-Century Massachusetts," *William and Mary Quarterly,* 3d ser., XXIII (1976), 586–614, and her book *The Bonds of Womanhood: "Woman's Sphere" in New England, 1780–1835* (New Haven, 1977); Mary Beth Norton, "Eighteenth-Century American Woman in Peace and War: The Case of the Loyalists," *William and Mary Quarterly,* 3d ser., XXXIII (1976), 386–409, and her book *Liberty's Daughters: The Revolutionary Experience of American Women, 1750–1835* (Boston, 1980).

21. John F. Walzer, "A Period of Ambivalence: Eighteenth-Century American Childhood," in Lloyd de Mause, ed., *The History of Childhood* (New York, 1975); Abigail J. Stewart, David G. Winter, and A. David Jones, "Coding Categories for the Study of Child-Rearing from Historical Sources," *Journal of Interdisciplinary History,* V (1975), 687–701; Peter Gregg Slater, *Children in the New England Mind* (Hamden, Conn., 1977).

Particularly significant in bringing together family and women's history is the literature on changes in fertility. Demographers, of course, have long been interested in what they call "the demographic transition"—the shift from large to significantly small families—which occurred in the United States in the middle of the nineteenth century.[22] The fact of the fall in fertility is not in dispute; explaining why that drop occurred is the problem. All students of the subject properly rule out urbanization and industrialization as adequate explanations because the fall took place before industrialization was widespread, and because the decline was almost as sharp in rural areas. Yet the high correlation between the density of population on arable land and the fall in the birth rate does not provide a persuasive explanatory motivation either.[23] As a result, some historical demographers and historians have suggested that women may have played a determining role in bringing down birth rates, a suggestion that is as novel among traditional demographers as it is obvious to historians of women. Peter Uhlenberg's demographic work has also demonstrated that studies of families drawn from the census records can throw a flood of light on women's history, including that of women outside the family.[24]

One aspect of family history has been central to women's history almost from the beginning of the latter's resurgence in the 1960s. It is the interpretation or meaning to be assigned to domesticity or the confinement of married women to household activities in the expanding urban environment of the nineteenth century. At the outset, historians of women placed heavy emphasis on the image—as opposed to the reality, which is harder to capture historically—of domesticity. The unstated implication was that there was a close fit between

22. The best-known estimates of the transition, calculated for each year from 1800 to 1960, are in Ansley Coale, Jr., and Melvin Zelnik, *New Estimates of Fertility and Population in the United States* (Princeton, 1963), 36. The figures are for white women only.

23. Yasukichi Yasuba, *Birth Rates of the White Population in the United States, 1800–1860* (Baltimore, 1961), first demonstrated the correlation between the density of population and the decline in the birth rate which has been corroborated in subsequent studies: Colin Forster and G. S. L. Tucker, *Economic Opportunity and White American Fertility Ratios* (New Haven, 1972), and Richard A. Easterlin, "Factors in the Decline of Farm Family Fertility in the United States: Some Preliminary Research Results," *Journal of American History,* LXIII (1976), 600–612.

24. Smith, "Family Limitation, Sexual Control, and Domestic Feminism in Victorian America"; Wells, "Family History and Demographic Transition"; Carl N. Degler, *At Odds: Women and the Family in America from the Revolution to the Present* (New York, 1980), chap. 8; Peter Uhlenberg, "A Study of Cohort Life Cycles" and "Cohort Variations in Family Life Cycles Experiences of United States Females," *Journal of Marriage and the Family,* XXXVI (1974), 284–292. See also his article "Changing Configurations of the Life Course."

prescription or image and actuality,[25] and that the effect was oppressively restrictive for women. More recently, however, as students have probed the behavior of women and families, the interpretations of domesticity have become more diverse. Some have seen domesticity as a form of limited advancement for women, providing them with opportunities or bases for broadening their sphere of activities.[26] Others have emphasized the deepening of women's self-identity as a result of their social segregation from men.[27] Still others have suggested that many women saw this identity as valuable in itself and thereby laid the groundwork for a later feminism.[28] In short, historians of women have moved from a simple "model of oppression," as Gerda Lerner once called it, to a recognition that women have also been forces in history, as Mary Ritter Beard contended more than thirty years ago.

Uncovering the actual behavior of women within the family has not been easy. Perhaps the most revealing as well as the least representative method has been the use of manuscript or published correspondence, diaries, and journals of women. Significantly enough, when such sources are compared with the prescriptive literature that has been used in the past to ascertain the nature and meaning of domesticity, the congruence between them has often turned out to be marginal, a fact that has evoked warnings against careless or misplaced use of prescriptive literature.[29] On the other hand, as men-

25. Barbara Welter, "The Cult of True Womanhood: 1820–1860," *American Quarterly*, XVIII (1966), 151–174, is by now the classic expression of the idea. It has been built upon and expanded into a theory of change in Gerda Lerner, "The Lady and the Mill Girl: Changes in the Status of Women in the Age of Jackson," *Midcontinent American Studies Journal*, X (1969), 5–15.

26. Keith Melder, "Ladies Bountiful: Organized Women's Benevolence in Nineteenth-Century America," *New York History*, XLVIII (1967), 231–254; Glenda Riley, "The Subtle Subversion: Change in the Traditional Image of the American Woman," *The Historian*, XXXII (1970), 210–227; and Ann Douglas Wood, "Mrs. Sigourney and the Sensibility of the Inner Space," *New England Quarterly*, XLV (1972), 163–181.

27. The idea of sorority was first advanced in Christopher Lasch and William Taylor's early article, "Two 'Kindred Spirits': Sorority and Family in New England, 1839–1845," *New England Quarterly*, XXXVI (1963), 23–41; its classic expression is in Carroll Smith-Rosenberg, "The Female World of Love and Ritual: Relations between Women in Nineteenth-Century America," *Signs*, I (1975), 1–29. Its reflection, in part, in women's novels has been delineated in Helen Papashvily, *All the Happy Endings* (New York, 1956), and Nina Baym, *Woman's Fiction: A Guide to Novels by and about Women in America, 1820–1870* (Ithaca, N.Y., 1978). An indication of its existence below the middle class can be found in Johnny Faragher and Christine Stansell, "Women and Their Families on the Overland Trail, 1842–1867," *Feminist Studies*, II (1975), 150–166.

28. Kathryn Kish Sklar, *Catharine Beecher: A Study in American Domesticity* (New Haven, Conn., 1977).

29. Anne Firor Scott, *The Southern Lady: From Pedestal to Politics, 1830–1930* (Chicago, 1970); Ernest Earnest, *American Eve in Fact and Fiction, 1775–1914* (Urbana, Ill., 1974);

tioned already, there is evidence that the ideals set forth in the middle-class prescriptive literature were accepted by women farther down the social scale. In sum, to ask whether domesticity was principally a matter of social control or one of social identification for women is to miss the complexity of women's place in the family in the past.

The literature in the burgeoning field of sexuality is similarly complicated. One of the by-products of the upsurge in interest in women's history has been a greater willingness on the part of historians to ask questions about sexual behavior in the past. Since sexuality is to women's oppression what color has been to black oppression, sexual attitudes and behavior have been highly visible in the literature of women's history, especially that concerned with the nineteenth century. What meaning should be assigned to the image of the sexless woman which appeared in much popular and even some medical literature of the time? Was there a difference between image and behavior? The meaning as well as the nature of attitudes toward women's sexuality and the actual sexual behavior of women has spawned a controversial literature that has not yet arrived at consensus.[30] Yet it seems fair to say that the most recent writings have tended to be more positive than negative in their assessments of the sexual subordination of women during the nineteenth century. Nancy Cott, for example, has argued that "passionlessness" may well have been a kind of strategy adopted only half-consciously by married women in pursuit of autonomy within the family.[31]

Although it is true that in general most historians of women are

Cott, *Bonds of Womanhood:* Ruth H. Bloch, "Untangling the Roots of Modern Sex Roles: A Survey of Four Centuries of Change," *Signs,* IV (1978), 237–252; and Jay Mechling, "Advice to Historians on Advice to Mothers," *Journal of Social History,* IX (1975), 44–63.

30. Especially critical of nineteenth-century male attitudes and practices are Ben Barker-Benfield, "The Spermatic Economy: A Nineteenth Century View of Sexuality," *Feminist Studies,* I (1972), 45–74, and G. J. Barker-Benfield, *The Horrors of the Half-Known Life: Male Attitudes toward Women and Sexuality in Nineteenth-Century America* (New York, 1976); and Ann Douglas Wood, "'The Fashionable Diseases': Women's Complaints and Their Treatment in Nineteenth-Century America," *Journal of Interdisciplinary History,* IV (1973), 25–52. Critical of that approach are Regina Markell Morantz, "The Perils of Feminist History," *Journal of Interdisciplinary History,* VI (1974), 649–660, and Carl N. Degler, "What Ought to Be and What Was: Women's Sexuality in the Nineteenth Century," *American Historical Review,* LXXIX (1974), 1467–90. In between the extremes would fall Carroll Smith-Rosenberg and Charles Rosenberg, "The Female Animal: Medical and Biological Views of Women and Her Role in Nineteenth-Century America," *Journal of American History,* LX (1973), 332–356.

31. Nancy Cott, "Passionlessness: An Interpretation of Victorian Sexual Ideology, 1790–1850," *Signs,* IV (1978), 219–236. A similar argument is pursued in Degler, *At Odds,* chap. 9.

themselves women, an obvious exception to the rule is in the history of birth control. Three of the four recent books on fertility control have been written by men.[32] Significantly, Linda Gordon, the woman author of one of these four books, was the first to raise the important question of why feminists and women social radicals in the nineteenth century did not publicly support contraception or abortion. To Gordon, as a woman and a feminist, that failure to endorse methods of fertility control presented a problem that required an explanation. Her work shows quite concretely that the study and understanding of the past is advanced by women's participation in the writing of history. They perceive important connections in the past that male historians tend to overlook. The subject of birth control suggests, too, that the role of prescriptive literature in shaping behavior needs to be carefully explored. During the nineteenth century both contraception and abortion were virtually unanimously and vocally condemned by all classes, groups, and institutions, yet both methods of controlling fertility were widely practiced.

Unlike the question of sexuality, women's education has been a historical staple, but it, too, has been affected by new questions put by the revived women's movement. For example, the so-called triumph of women's drive for higher education has been placed in a new perspective—generally a less favorable one—by recent students who have measured it against more feministic standards than the older histories did. Among other things, they suggest that even in regard to higher education there was an enduring tension between women's aspirations as individuals and their traditional subordination in the family.[33] The women's colleges, too, as Debra Herman and Roberta Wein have argued, felt the tension, for in the end they defended their existence by asserting they would turn out better wives and mothers.[34] To date, however, no examination has been made of what was a

32. David M. Kennedy, *Birth Control in America: The Career of Margaret Sanger* (New Haven, 1970); James C. Mohr, *Abortion in America: The Origins and Evolution of National Policy, 1800–1900* (New York, 1978); Linda Gordon, *Woman's Body, Woman's Rights: A Social History of Birth Control in America* (New York, 1976); James Reed, *From Private Vice to Public Virtue: The Birth Control Movement and American Society since 1830* (New York, 1978).

33. Ronald W. Hogeland, "Coeducation of the Sexes at Oberlin College: A Study of Social Ideas in Mid-Nineteenth-Century America," *Journal of Social History*, VI (1972–73), 160–176; Charlotte Williams Conable, *Women at Cornell: The Myth of Equal Education* (Ithaca, N.Y., 1977).

34. Debra Herman, "College and After: The Vassar Experiment in Women's Education, 1861–1924," Ph.D. dissertation, Stanford University, 1979; Roberta Wein, "Women's Colleges and Domesticity, 1875–1918," *History of Education Quarterly*, XIV (1974), 31–47.

significant social decision in the early nineteenth century: the inclusion of girls on an equal basis with boys in public primary and secondary schools. One result of that "decision" was a striking improvement in women's literacy rates, even in rural areas, between the Revolution and 1860; another was that more girls than boys graduated from high school during the last three decades of the nineteenth century and the first seven of the twentieth.

Few aspects of women's history have attracted more attention from historians over the last decade than the work experience of women. The recent scholarly interest concentrates primarily on working-class rather than professional women's work. Thus such questions as the place of women in unions, the relations between class and gender, and the work opportunities of women figure prominently in the literature.[35] Little attention, unfortunately, has been paid to the significant role women workers played in sparking early industrialization. By 1850, for example, women workers made up 22 percent of the labor force in manufacturing, a proportion not equaled again in the nineteenth century. Unlike the situation in family history, statistical analyses have not figured importantly in the literature on the history of women; the contrast between the two fields here is striking even in discussions of women's place in the economy.

From a theoretical point of view, writings on working-class women usually recognize that class cannot be the primary explanation for the oppression of women workers. This insight has been troubling for a number of women historians who take a Marxian approach to history. But the recognition has usually resulted in an effort to combine class and gender as explanatory categories rather than rejection of one or the other.[36] The fact that women's history is at once like and yet unlike the history of other oppressed social groups, that it requires its own explanatory categories, has also given rise to a number of works seeking to come to grips with that challenge to historical explanation.[37]

35. The articles in Milton Cantor and Bruce Laurie, eds., *Class, Sex, and the Woman Worker* (Westport, Conn., 1977), are examples of excellent work along these lines, as are Thomas Dublin's study *Women at Work: The Transformation of Work and Community in Lowell, Massachusetts, 1826–1869* (New York, 1979), and David M. Katzman, *Seven Days a Week: Women and Domestic Service in Industrializing America* (New York, 1978). An exception to the generalization in the text is Barbara J. Harris, *Beyond Her Sphere: Women and the Professions in American History* (Westport, Conn., 1978).

36. See, for example, Eli Zaretsky, *Capitalism, the Family, and Personal Life* (New York, 1976); Heidi Hartmann, "Capitalism, Patriarchy, and Job Segregation by Sex," in Martha Blaxall and Barbara Reagan, eds., *Women and the Workplace: The Implications of Occupational Segregation* (Chicago, 1976).

37. For a convenient collection of important theoretical pieces, see those by Gerda Lerner, Hilda Smith, Juliet Mitchell, and Sheila Ryan Johannson in Berenice A. Car-

Little of the recent literature on working women, however, has directed attention to what is clearly a prime connection between the history of women and the history of the family: the fact that the vast proportion of white working women in the nineteenth and twentieth centuries were not married.[38] Until the 1950s over four-fifths of all married women, regardless of class or race, were outside the paid labor force. It is true that black wives throughout the years before 1950 worked in much greater proportion than white wives. But even among black women the historical tendency was for the proportion to decline.[39]

Before the outburst of new interest in women's history, perhaps the most obvious way in which women came into conventional history was through the fight for the suffrage. Yet this familiarity has not prevented new work from reinterpreting the meaning of the struggle for the vote. William O'Neill was one of the earliest historians to ask why the achievement of the suffrage did not accomplish more for women.[40] In raising that important question he simultaneously laid a foundation for an explanation as to why a new feminist movement erupted in the 1970s. His answer was not simply that women's suffrage was defended more conservatively in the twentieth than in the nineteenth century, as Aileen Kraditor had shown, nor that it was simply a conservative reform, as Alan Grimes had argued.[41] Rather O'Neill contended that women's emancipation was much broader than the suffrage and that to have expected a feminist future to emerge from the achievement of the vote was to misunderstand the nature of true emancipation. (Stanley Lemons did show that the suffrage was not as devoid of positive social and political results as O'Neill had contended, but O'Neill's large point still stood.)[42]

---

roll, ed., *Liberating Women's History: Theoretical and Critical Essays* (Urbana, Ill., 1976). Additional efforts along these lines are William H. Chafe, *Women and Equality: Changing Patterns in American Culture* (New York, 1977), chaps. 3 and 4, and Carl N. Degler, *Is There a History of Women?* (Oxford, 1975).

38. Notable exceptions are Patricia Branca, "A New Perspective on Women's Work: A Comparative Typology," *Journal of Social History*, IX (1975), 129–153, and William H. Chafe, *The American Woman: Her Changing Social, Economic, and Political Roles, 1920–1970* (New York, 1972).

39. Claudia Golden, "Female Labor Force Participation: The Origin of Black and White Differences, 1870 and 1880," *Journal of Economic History*, XXXVIII (1977), 87–108, suggests that the slave experience may account for the differences.

40. William L. O'Neill, *Everyone Was Brave: The Rise and Fall of Feminism in America* (Chicago, 1969).

41. Aileen S. Kraditor, *The Ideas of the Woman Suffrage Movement, 1890–1920* (New York, 1965); Alan P. Grimes, *The Puritan Ethic and Woman Suffrage* (New York, 1967).

42. J. Stanley Lemons, *The Woman Citizen: Social Feminism in the 1920s* (Urbana, Ill. 1973).

If from the standpoint of full emancipation, the suffrage could be shown to be wanting, that point, Ellen DuBois more recently has reminded us, ought not to obscure the deeply radical nature of the suffrage in the context of the late nineteenth century's emphasis on domesticity and the doctrine of the two spheres.[43] No historian, however, has yet published a book-length analysis of the women antisuffragists, even though, as an organized body of opponents to their own enfranchisement, they were not only effective but unique in the history of organized struggles for the vote or for reform in general.[44] We still await, too, an inquiry into women's participation in politics before the vote, for the work of Linda Kerber and Julie Jeffrey have made evident that the material is there, and further that the relation between women and the family may have been a significant part of the story. For more recent periods, studies of modern feminist ideology have emphasized the interaction between women's political goals and social changes in the society at large.[45]

Undoubtedly one of the exciting challenges of women's history is to demonstrate specifically how our conception of the past will change once we recognize that women have been historical forces. As Gerda Lerner has remarked, women in the nineteenth century, before they had the vote, nevertheless still "found a way to make their power felt through organizations, through pressure tactics, through petitioning, and through various other means; these later became models for other mass movements of reform."[46] And some years ago, Ross Paulson tried to draw some important connections between the struggles for women's suffrage and temperance in various countries around the

43. Ellen DuBois, "The Radicalism of the Woman Suffrage Movement: Notes Toward the Reconstruction of Nineteenth-Century Feminism," *Feminist Studies*, III (1975), 63–71.

44. In the meantime, the best work on the antisuffragists is Jane Jerome Camhi, "Women against Women: American Antisuffragism, 1880–1920," Ph.D. dissertation, Tufts University, 1973.

45. Linda Kerber, "The Republican Mother: Women and the Enlightenment—An American Perspective," *American Quarterly*, XXVIII (1976), 187–205, and her article "Daughters of Columbia: Educating Women for the Republic, 1787–1805," in Stanley Elkins and Eric McKitrick, eds., *The Hofstadter Aegis: A Memorial* (New York, 1974); Julie Roy Jeffrey, "Women in the Southern Farmers' Alliance: A Reconstruction of the Role and Status of Women in the Late Nineteenth-Century South," *Feminist Studies*, III (1975), 72–91. See also her *Frontier Women: The Trans-Mississippi West, 1840–1880* (New York, 1979). For more recent periods see Gayle Graham Yates, *What Women Want: The Ideas of the Movement* (Cambridge, Mass., 1975), and Sara Evans, *Personal Politics: The Roots of Women's Liberation in the Civil Rights Movement and the New Left* (New York, 1979).

46. Gerda Lerner, "New Approaches to the Study of Women in American History," *Journal of Social History*, III (1969), 61.

world.[47] Unfortunately, his reach exceeded his grasp of the very broad subject he blocked out for himself. Further study of the role of women in the movement for prohibition is sure to show that not only do the history of women and that of the family intertwine, but if we pay attention to women in the past we will better understand why and how change occurred at all. Recently, Donald Mathews has observed, for example, that the development of southern religion can be understood only by examining the role of women in the churches.[48]

One might have expected that the various studies of social mobility and work in nineteenth-century cities would throw new light on both working women and family life, but none of the dozen or so studies produced in the 1960s and 1970s paid any attention to women except Clyde and Sally Griffen's study of Poughkeepsie. Michael Katz's otherwise thorough analysis of Hamilton, Ontario, treated the family in some detail but inexplicably ignored women workers.[49]

Measured by work produced, the field of women's history is moving ahead most successfully. Already several scholarly journals are publishing work of high quality: *Feminist Studies,* which began in 1974, and *Signs: A Journal of Women in Society and Culture,* which published its first number in 1975. The new interest in women's history has transformed the old but small Berkshire Conference of women historians into a major national convention at which scores of papers on recent research are presented almost annually to audiences of several hundred scholars. In 1979 a comprehensive, two-volume listing of manuscript sources pertaining to the history of women in libraries throughout the United States was published, providing a valuable research tool, as well as yet another measure of the burgeoning interest in the field.[50] More than half a dozen general studies or texts intended for college or high school classes in women's history have already appeared, with more likely to appear in the immediate future. Certainly women's history has attracted more students, teachers, and scholars and produced a larger literature than family history, even though the achievement in the latter field is impressive.

Ironically enough, the same reason that helps to explain why wom-

47. Ross Evans Paulson, *Women's Suffrage and Prohibition: A Comparative Study of Equality and Social Control* (Glenview, Ill., 1973).

48. Donald G. Mathews, *Religion in the Old South* (Chicago, 1977).

49. Griffen and Griffen, *Natives and Newcomers;* Michael B. Katz, *The People of Hamilton, Canada West: Family and Class in a Mid-Nineteenth-Century City* (Cambridge, Mass., 1975).

50. Andrea Hinding, *Women's History Sources: A Guide to Archives and Manuscript Collections in the United States,* 2 vols. (New York, 1979).

en's history has forged ahead more rapidly than family history also helps to account for the slowness with which it has been integrated into history in general. The reason is the strongly ideological or presentist origin of the field. Women's history was obviously developed to meet women's need for a past. Family history, on the other hand, has no social group with a direct interest in its advancement, hence it lacks the energy and personnel that presses women's history forward, unearthing new sources and asking new questions. At the same time, however, that same presentist origin frightens or misleads those historians who do not share or do not recognize women's need to have a history. They forget that all history has developed to serve the need that is felt by all human beings to have an identity rooted in the past. Women, though, have been able to assert their self-consciousness only in recent times. Today, moreover, the same forces of professionalism and scholarly detachment that have operated in more established fields, or in fields without immediate presentist origins such as family history, are also at work in women's history, as the high standard of recent scholarly work makes evident.

Having said this, though, we must still admit that neither women's nor family history has made much headway in being integrated into general history, or, to put the matter more precisely if more mundanely, into college or high school history survey courses or general textbooks. Integration will still require more thought and effort than exhortations, or assertions that women make up half the population, or that everyone comes from a family. For the plain fact is that history, as that word is defined by many citizens and most historians, still does not include those activities women have engaged in; nor is it immediately clear to people outside the field how the history of the family helps us better to understand the past. In sum, what is meant by history or the past will have to be changed before these two subdisciplines become an integral part of it. Neither of them now relates directly to the past as it is understood today. Especially is this true of women's history, since the conventional past was not only conceived (invented?) by men but includes, almost by definition, only those activities in which men have been engaged, while ignoring almost entirely the historical activities of women. That the definition of history ought to include women is no longer debatable; that doubt has been removed by recent scholarship in the field and by the recognition that if we are to understand the past from which all of us have emerged, we must know how women helped to shape it. The challenge is now to rethink our conception of the past we teach and write about so that women and the family are integrally included.

# 14

## Intellectual and Cultural History

### Robert Darnton

A MALAISE is spreading among intellectual historians in the United States. Twenty years ago, they saw their discipline as the queen of the historical sciences. Today she seems humbled. No dramatic dethronement has occurred; but after a realignment of research during the last two decades, she now sits below the salt, surrounded by rude new varieties of sociocultural history and bewildering language—*mentalité, episteme,* paradigm, hermeneutics, semiotics, hegemony, deconstruction, and thick description.

Evidently some historians continue to feel comfortable within the intellectual framework established by Arthur Lovejoy and Perry Miller, for one still finds "unit-ideas" and "mind" amid the overgrowth of trendier terms.[1] But the trend toward self-doubt and beleaguered self-assertion can be found wherever intellectual historians discuss the state of their craft—and the historiographical-methodological discussions have multiplied in the past few years. Murray Murphey began a recent article with a lament: "Thirty years ago intellectual history occupied an envied place in the American university; its courses were full to overflowing and its practitioners—men such as Merle Curti, Ralph Gabriel, and Perry Miller—were famous through-

---

1. The *Dictionary of the History of Ideas* (New York, 1973), 4 vols., ed. Philip P. Wiener and others, can be considered "a monument to Lovejoy," as a reviewer observed in another monumental Lovejoy enterprise, the *Journal of the History of Ideas:* F. E. L. Priestley, "Mapping the World of Ideas," *Journal of the History of Ideas,* xxxv (1974), 527–537. Although the *Dictionary* represents different varieties of intellectual history, it generally treats ideas in the Lovejoy fashion, as concrete entities that can be traced through time and across space. Compare the preface of the *Dictionary* with Lovejoy's prefatory article in the first issue of the *Journal:* "Reflections on the History of Ideas," *Journal of the History of Ideas,* 1 (1940), 3–23. See also George Boas, *The History of Ideas: An Introduction* (New York, 1969), and Rush Welter, "On Studying the National Mind," in John Higham and Paul K. Conkin, eds., *New Directions in American Intellectual History* (Baltimore, 1979), 64–82.

out the profession, and indeed beyond. But thirty years have brought a marked change. Students no longer see intellectual history as the place 'where the action is,' and the profession seems to concur that the 'cutting edge' of historical scholarship lies elsewhere."[2] At the same time, Dominick La Capra sounded the alarm in calling for a conference at Cornell on the future of intellectual history: "In the recent past intellectual history has been shaken by a number of important developments. Social historians have posed questions not answerable through traditional techniques of narrating or analyzing ideas. These questions bear upon the nature of collective 'mentalities' and the genesis or impact of ideas. At times the impetus of social historians seems imperialistic: the reduction of intellectual history to a function of social history and the elevation of social problems to the status of the only truly significant historical problems."[3] The same theme ran through a set of papers presented at a conference on American intellectual history at Racine, Wisconsin, in December 1977.[4] It had emerged seven years earlier in a conference on the state of historical studies held in Rome.[5] It has reappeared regularly at conventions of the American Historical Association.[6] And it can be detected everywhere in the reviews and articles through which intellectual historians try to take one another's pulse. To be sure, many of them claim that they never felt healthier, and they welcome the current crisis as an opportunity to reorient their discipline. But optimists and pessimists agree that a crisis exists and that its outcome hangs on the relations between intellectual and social history.[7]

2. Murray G. Murphey, "The Place of Beliefs in Modern Culture," *New Directions*, 151.

3. Circular (Spring 1979) entitled "The Future of European Intellectual History."

4. John Higham, "Introduction," *New Directions*, xi–xviii.

5. The proceedings of the Rome conference were published in Felix Gilbert and Stephen Graubard, eds., *Historical Studies Today* (New York, 1972), after appearing in issues of *Daedalus*. See especially the papers by Felix Gilbert, "Intellectual History: Its Aims and Methods," and Benjamin I. Schwartz, "A Brief Defense of Political and Intellectual History."

6. The convention at San Francisco in 1973 precipitated a great deal of stocktaking among intellectual historians and contributed to the formation of an Intellectual History Group, which issued its first newsletter in the spring of 1979.

7. As examples of strong views on the crisis, see Paul K. Conkin, "Intellectual History: Past, Present, and Future," in Charles F. Delzell, ed., *The Future of History* (Nashville, 1977), 111, and Gene Wise, "The Contemporary Crisis in Intellectual History Studies," *Clio*, v (1975), 55. For more moderate reactions, see Leonard Krieger, "The Autonomy of Intellectual History," *Journal of the History of Ideas*, xxxiv (1973), 499–516, and David Potter, "History and the Social Sciences," in Don E. Fehrenbacher, ed., *History and American Society: Essays of David M. Potter* (New York, 1973), 40–47. Some French historians have developed similar views of a crisis within their own tradition. See Jean Ehrard and others, "Histoire des idées et histoire sociale en France au

That view derives in part from a sharpened sense of the history of intellectual history in the United States. John Higham and Robert Skotheim have shown that intellectual history and social history came of age together early in the twentieth century, as ingredients in the New History of James Harvey Robinson, Charles A. Beard, Frederick Jackson Turner, and Carl Becker.[8] The two genres seemed new in that they challenged an older view of history as past politics. They worked their way into college curricula as allies, the "intellectual and social history" courses that proliferated in the 1920s and 1930s. The alliance fell apart during the next two decades, however, when Arthur Lovejoy and Perry Miller raised the level of intellectual history by stripping it of any concern for social context. Among Americanists, Miller's success stimulated his successors to chase after abstractions—myths, symbols, and images. They also drew on the attempts of Vernon Parrington, Ralph Gabriel, and Merle Curti to determine the distinctive character of American thought. By the 1960s the American Studies movement had cut American intellectual history free of its moorings in social history and had drifted off in pursuit of a disembodied national mind. At that point, the professors' universities exploded beneath them. Racial conflict, "countercultures," student radicalism, the war in southeast Asia, the collapse of the presidency destroyed the vision of American history as a spiritual consensus. Social historians rushed in, not to fill the vacuum but to pick apart the ruins of the old New History, not to reconstruct a single past but to burrow in different directions. Black history, urban history, labor history, the history of women, of criminality, sexuality, the oppressed, the inarticulate, the marginal—so many lines of inquiry opened up that social history seemed to dominate research on all fronts. The abandoned ally had regained command of the profession.

Some American historians probably would consider this account of their professional past overdramatic or inaccurate. Some have always disparaged intellectual history as unworkable, if not quite unAmerican—"like trying to nail jelly to the wall," in the words of one

XVIIIe siècle: Réflexions de méthode," *Niveaux de culture et groupes sociaux: Actes du colloque réuni du 7 au 9 mai 1966 à l'Ecole normale supérieure* (Paris and The Hague, 1967), 171–188.

8. Much of the following historiographical sketch is based on Robert Skotheim, *American Intellectual Histories and Historians* (Princeton, 1966), and especially the work of John Higham: "The Rise of American Intellectual History," *American Historical Review*, LVI (1951), 453–471; "American Intellectual History: A Critical Appraisal," *American Quarterly*, XIII (1961), 219–233; (with the collaboration of Leonard Krieger and Felix Gilbert) *History* (Englewood Cliffs, N.J., 1965); and *Writing American History: Essays on Modern Scholarship* (Bloomington, Ind., 1970).

old-time, hard-line political historian.[9] And indeed, the home-grown varieties of intellectual history seem stunted in comparison with those of Europe. Europeans do not speak of intellectual history in the American manner but rather to the history of ideas, *histoire des idées, Geistesgeschichte, storia della filosofia*—different names that denote different traditions. Those traditions have rubbed off on American students of European history, especially the students who did their graduate work after 1950, when fellowships, charter flights, and a strong dollar made study abroad more accessible than ever before. Those who remained at home often learned their European history from the European refugees who had flocked to American universities in the 1930s. And those who somehow escaped the immediate influence of Europe still dealt with European subjects, subjects often transmitted in foreign languages and located in a remote past, where there was no difficulty about defining American character or culture. Sources, teachers, and subjects made the intellectual history of Europe inherently cosmopolitan.

Yet the American version of that history has reached a critical point. It has converged with the crisis in American Studies, although it has developed along a different course. The course was set between the world wars by Arthur Lovejoy and Carl Becker. Lovejoy traced the filiation of key ideas over vast stretches of time, while Becker sketched the intellectual climate of entire eras. But each man worked from classic texts, which he could locate easily in his own library. For the next generation of intellectual historians, Crane Brinton demonstrated the importance of following ideas beyond libraries and to "their ultimate refuge in the mind of the common man."[10] By 1950 this approach had crystallized as a course, Harvard's History 134a, "Intellectual History of Europe in the Eighteenth and Nineteenth Centuries," and a textbook, *Ideas and Men.*[11] During the next two

9. William Hesseltine, quoted in Skotheim, *American Intellectual Histories,* 3.
10. Crane Brinton, *English Political Thought in the Nineteenth Century* (New York, 1962; first ed. 1933), 3.
11. See Brinton's definition of the task of intellectual history in *Ideas and Men: The Story of Western Thought* (Englewood Cliffs, N.J., 1963; first ed. 1950), 4, and the course description of History 134a that appeared in the Harvard catalogs of the 1950s and 1960s: "An examination of changes brought about in the sentiments and theories of ordinary Western Europeans in the centuries which witnessed the American, the French, and the Industrial Revolutions. Not primarily a history of formal thought; rather concerned with the penetration downward into the crowd of the theories professed by formal thinkers." The first course on intellectual history in the United States was given by James Harvey Robinson at Columbia in 1904. In the 1930s Brinton hoped that his version of the "method of men" as distinct from the "method of ideas" would bring the history of thought "very close to the now fashionable social history," referring to the New History of Robinson (*English Political Thought,* 4).

decades, H. Stuart Hughes and Peter Gay extended the attempt to trace connections between ideas and men in several studies of the social dimensions of thought. They usually organized their books as Brinton had done, alloting chapters to thinkers and tying them together with dialectical formulas: consciousness and society, antiquity and modernity.[12] Similar concerns inspired a group of gifted biographers, Arthur Wilson, Frank Manuel, and Jacques Barzun.[13] But the emphasis on "the method of men," as Brinton called it, raised the danger that intellectual history would develop into the history of intellectuals and that it would lose touch with the "common man."

Meanwhile, social historians were rediscovering that rare species in Europe, or rather they were reconstructing the common ground of experience for different groups of men and women by using techniques borrowed from demography, economics, and sociology. Some of the impetus for this tendency did not come from social scientists but from a cosmopolitan group of scholars who gathered around Georges Lefebvre in Paris and, like him, reinterpreted the French Revolution from the perspective of peasants and sansculottes.[14] "History from below" became a rallying cry for those who wanted to make contact with the submerged mass of humanity and to rescue the lives of ordinary men and women from oblivion in the past. It spread everywhere in Europe, especially to England, where it reinvigorated a strong tradition of labor history. George Rudé, E. J. Hobsbawm, and E. P. Thompson wrote masterful studies of popular protest and working-class movements, and the journal *Past and Present* championed a view of history as the development of society rather than the unfolding of events. At the same time, a sister journal in France, *Annales: Economies, Sociétés, Civilisations,* was waging a parallel cam-

12. H. Stuart Hughes, *Consciousness and Society: The Reorientation of European Social Thought, 1890–1930* (New York, 1958); *The Obstructed Path: French Social Thought in the Years of Desperation, 1930–1960* (New York, 1968); *The Sea Change: The Migration of Social Thought, 1930–1965* (New York, 1975); and Peter Gay, *The Enlightenment: An Interpretation,* 2 vols. (New York, 1966 and 1969). For comparable discussions of the nature of intellectual history and its methods, see the introductions in Brinton, *Ideas and Men,* and Hughes, *Consciousness and Society;* and Gay, "The Social History of Ideas: Ernst Cassirer and After," in Kurt H. Wolff and Barrington Moore, Jr., eds., *Essays in Honor of Herbert Marcuse* (Boston, 1967), 106–20.

13. Arthur Wilson, *Diderot,* 2 vols. (New York, 1957 and 1972); Frank E. Manuel, *The Prophets of Paris* (Cambridge, Mass., 1962); Jacques Barzun, *Berlioz and the Romantic Century* (Boston, 1950).

14. The group included Albert Soboul, George Rudé, Richard Cobb, and K. D. Tonnesson. The most important book produced by it was Soboul's thesis, *Les sansculottes parisiens en l'an II* (Paris, 1958), although the group became known in the English-speaking world primarily through work published in English by Rudé and Cobb.

paign against *l'histoire événémentielle* and in favor of a related version of social history—history as the long-term interplay of structure and conjuncture, inertia and innovation, *histoire totale.* The catchwords of the so-called *Annales* school sometimes sounded like slogans, but they were given force by a succession of stunning doctoral theses, notably those of C. E. Labrousse, Fernand Braudel, Pierre Goubert, and Emmanuel Le Roy Ladurie. By 1970, social history seemed to turn around the *Past and Present–Annales* axis and to be sweeping everything before it.

It certainly swept a great many American historians off their feet and reinforced the indigenous revival of social history. Radicals called for a fresh look at the American Revolution "from below." Labor historians developed a Thompsonesque view of the history of work. And representatives *en mission* from the *Annales* traveled to campuses throughout the country, after establishing strongholds at Princeton, Ann Arbor, and Binghamton. The vogue seemed to extend everywhere—except to the camp of the intellectual historians. When looked at from the bottom up, the myths and images of the Americanists nearly disappeared from sight, and the ideas and "isms" of the Europeanists could be seen as ideologies or *mentalités*—that is, collective attitudes, which needed to be studied by the methods of the social sciences. Insofar as this approach left any room for the intellectual historian, it threatened to make him over as a sociologist or anthropologist. Robinson, Brinton, and Hughes had hoped to make a juncture with social history. Their successors worried about being cannibalized by it. As Paul K. Conkin put it, they succumbed to the view that "intellectual history has had a brief but glorious past, suffers a beleaguered present, and has no future."[15]

Before attempting to assess the validity of that view, one might try to measure it against some indication of the way American historians have actually behaved, both as teachers and as scholars, since World War II. Of course it would be vain to search for a precise behavior pattern among professors, who reputedly give way to idiosyncrasy and absent-mindedness rather than the herd instinct. But it should be possible to locate areas of emphasis within the profession by taking soundings in three sources: course catalogs, dissertation abstracts, and scholarly journals.

If the catalogs fail to convey the flavor of the lecture hall, they describe the subject matter of courses fully enough to enable one to

15. Conkin, "Intellectual History," 111.

classify courses by genre. To be sure, most courses involve several genres. They cover periods rather than themes—American History, 1865–1945, rather than American Intellectual History since the Civil War—so they cannot be classified under a single rubric. But an important minority of courses, from 17.1 percent of the sample in 1948 to 24.6 percent in 1978, can be classified unambiguously in one of the seven categories in Tables 1 and 2 at the end of this paper. Those courses provide a reasonably accurate indication of shifting emphases in the types of history taught to American undergraduates. Table 1 shows their relative importance in eight major universities at ten-year intervals between 1948 and 1978. Table 2 gives their proportions in the curricula of the eight universities as a whole during the same years.

The picture varied somewhat from campus to campus. Wisconsin developed strength in economic history in the 1940s, while Harvard was becoming a stronghold of intellectual history. But a general tendency prevailed almost everywhere. The eight universities offered eighteen courses (3.4 percent of their total offerings in history) devoted specifically to intellectual history in 1948–49 and seventy-two (6.4 percent) in 1978–79. Thus intellectual history did not arise suddenly, and it did not decline in the face of a surge in social history. True, social history did surge ahead during the 1970s. From a negligible position in the 1940s (seven courses, 1.3 percent of the total), it became the most important specialization in 1978–79 (ninety-five courses, 8.4 percent of the total). But it included so many subspecializations—the history of cities, blacks, workers, women—that it reinforced an earlier tendency for curricula to expand and fragment. The expansion occurred in the 1960s, when such universities as Yale and Indiana doubled their course offerings in history. Many departments broke up their survey courses, relaxed their requirements, and encouraged professors to align teaching more closely with research. The educational diet was enriched, but it was education à la carte; and it must have been difficult to digest for the unsophisticated undergraduate who had to put together a program from a bewildering catalog. (Wisconsin offered 227 history courses in 1968; Princeton had offered 21 in 1948.) In the end he might know something about the rise of the black ghetto in Detroit and nothing about the decline of the Roman Empire.

Intellectual history seems to have resisted the tendency toward fragmentation; and it held its own in the 1970s, when the expansion stopped. Most intellectual historians continued to give survey courses. Whether they made room for some elements of social history by rewriting lectures and reorganizing reading assignments cannot be known without further research, but it seems unlikely that many of them threw away large quantities of lecture notes. Some even repeat their old examination questions. ("If the questions change, the answers remain the same," goes a professorial proverb.) Change in teaching appears to be slow.[16]

Trends move more quickly in research, where social history has indeed gained ground at the expense of intellectual history. Table 3 shows that the percentage of dissertations in social history quadrupled between 1958 and 1978, while the percentage of those in intellectual history dropped slightly. In 1978 there were three times as many doctoral dissertations completed in social history as in intellectual history. Social history even outstripped political history as the most important area of research. In fact, political history declined significantly during the 1960s and 1970s—an indication that "event" history is on the wane in scholarship, even if it continues to be important in teaching. Moreover, the trend will probably accelerate, owing to a time lag. Most of the graduate students who completed their dissertations in 1978 chose their fields of study five to ten years earlier, when the fever for social history was still increasing. Those who chose fields at the end of the 1970s, when the fever was at its height, will extend it as they complete their dissertations throughout the 1980s. Yet their opportunity to affect future generations will be limited, because many of them will not find teaching positions. Tables 2 and 3 confirm the general impression that a critical disparity between supply and demand exists in college teaching. The number of courses in history declined slightly from 1968 to 1978, but the number of dissertations rose, and it has quadrupled since 1958.[17]

16. According to a survey of 200 colleges conducted in 1953, courses on social and intellectual history were quite new in most colleges and were generally taught by younger professors. Unfortunately, the survey did not provide any details about the rate of curricular changes or the relative importance of social and intellectual history, but it did bring together scattered information about the character of the courses: H. L. Swint, "Trends in the Teaching of Social and Intellectual History," *Social Studies*, XLVI (1955), 243–251. A handbook on history offerings in British universities in 1966 shows that nineteen of thirty-five universities provided courses in social history and sixteen provided courses in the "history of ideas" (George Barlow, ed., *History at the Universities* [London, 1966]).

17. According to a survey of history professors organized by David Landes and Charles Tilly in 1968, 14 percent of the respondents specialized in intellectual history and 17 percent in social history, and the social historians were younger (David S. Landes and Charles Tilly, *History as Social Science* [Englewood Cliffs, N.J., 1971]), 28 (the percentages have been calculated from the figures on p. 28). A survey conducted by the American Council of Learned Societies in 1952 gave less clear results, because it confused specialization by genre and by time period and it did not include social history

In order to sound the currents of scholarship among older historians, one can take samples from three of the most general and venerable scholarly journals, the *American Historical Review,* the *Journal of Modern History,* and the *Journal of American History.* Table 4 demonstrates the continued importance of political history, which accounted for a third of the articles from 1946 right through to 1978. Articles on international relations declined, but when taken together with articles on politics, they consistently occupied half the journals. While historians were burying *l'histoire événémentielle* on the Continent, it continued to thrive in the United States. Intellectual history remained healthy—astoundingly stable, in fact, at about a tenth of the scholarly output since the 1940s. And social history shot up, but only during the last ten years.[18]

A comparison of the data from all three sources (Figure 1) suggests the way trends move through the profession as a whole. Their origin remains a mystery. But once they exist, they are picked up first by graduate students, appear next in courses, and then spread through the more established journals, having penetrated the specialized and avant-garde journals earlier. Research sets the pace for teaching, at least among the younger historians. The older ones seem to abide by the kind of history they assimilated as graduate students, perhaps because they are less open to innovation or need it less. In any case, the profession seems remarkably conservative. All three sources show the same pattern of change, but the changes are minimal. The only field that has developed dramatically since World War II is social history. The importance of intellectual history has fluctuated very little—so little, in fact, that its practice seems to belie the jeremiads of its practitioners.

Can one go so far as to conclude that the statistics reveal a colossal case of false consciousness among those who make the study of con-

---

among the genre specializations. Still, it showed the importance of intellectual history at that time. Of 742 historians who identified themselves by genre, 109 (15 percent) called themselves intellectual and cultural historians—more than those in any other category except diplomatic history (136 historians, or 18 percent) (J. F. Wellmeyer, Jr., "Survey of United States Historians, 1952, and a Forecast," *American Historical Review,* LXI [1956], 339–352).

18. Recently the *Journal of American History* has listed all the articles on American history that have appeared in virtually all serious American periodicals, dividing them according to genre. In 1978 it included intellectual history, though not political history, among its generic categories—and it listed 2,131 articles! By compiling and computing them, one gets results that are pretty close to those in Table 4: international relations, 6 percent; intellectual history, 2 percent (but articles on the arts accounted for another 3 percent and articles on religion another 5 percent); social history, 22 percent; and economic history, 4 percent.

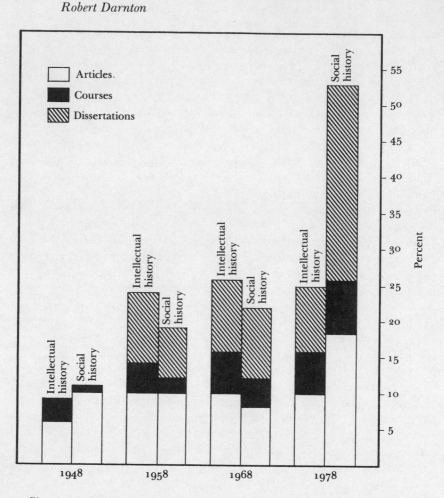

*Figure 1*. Articles, courses, and dissertations in intellectual and social history as percentages of all history articles, courses, and dissertations, 1948–78.

sciousness their speciality? Not really, because the importance of intellectual history has declined relative to that of social history; and although intellectual historians may be just as active as ever, some of them may have an accurate intuitive sense of momentum running down, of innovation passing into other hands. In fact, they might consider this account of their condition as a symptom of its gravity. How outrageous to describe the study of ideas by statistics and graphs! The whole endeavor smacks of the quantification of culture, of the spread of social science to places where it has no business, of the attempt to reduce the life of the mind to the sociology of knowledge. Better to nail jelly to the wall.

Perhaps at this point it would be appropriate to venture a more subjective assessment of tendencies within the field as a whole. Unfortunately, however, intellectual history is not a whole. It has no governing *problématique*. Its practitioners share no sense of common subjects, methods, and conceptual strategies. At one extreme they analyze the systems of philosophers; at the other they examine the rituals of illiterates. But their perspectives can be classified from "high" to "low," and one can imagine a vertical spectrum in which subjects shade off into one another, passing through four main categories: the history of ideas (the study of systematic thought, usually in philosophical treatises), intellectual history proper (the study of informal thought, climates of opinion, and literary movements), the social history of ideas (the study of ideologies and idea diffusion), and cultural history (the study of culture in the anthropological sense, including world views and collective *mentalités*).[19]

No doubt the highest range of ideas will attract scholars as long as anyone feels the challenge of scaling the thought of great men such as Augustine and Einstein. But since World War II, philosophers and literary critics have tended to neglect the historical study of great books, preferring to explore the linguistic dimensions of meaning and the structural significance of texts. Historians have had to supply much of the history of philosophy and the history of literature on their campuses, and the effort has marked their scholarship. Instead of surveying those neighboring fields as outsiders, they have attempted to understand them from within. Carl Schorske, for example, has developed an "internalist" view of philosophy, literature, art, music, and psychology in late-nineteenth-century Vienna.[20] Other

19. Of course it is possible to classify these varieties of history in many ways. The most common distinction separates the history of ideas from intellectual history, but most historians, including Lovejoy, use those terms in an overlapping and inconsistent manner. For attempts to define the field and to sort it into subdivisions, see Maurice Mandelbaum, "The Historiography of the History of Philosophy," *History and Theory*, IV (1965), supplement 5, 33–66; Hajo Holborn, "The History of Ideas," *American Historical Review*, LXXIII (1968), 683–695; and Hayden White, "The Tasks of Intellectual History," *The Monist*, LIII, (1969), 606–630.

20. See the forthcoming collection of Schorske's essays, *Fin-de-Siècle Vienna: Politics and Culture*, and for a comparable view of Viennese culture, Allan Janik and Stephen Toulmin, *Wittgenstein's Vienna* (New York, 1973).

Robert Darnton

historians have limited themselves to one discipline studied over a
longer time period. But like Schorske, they have tried to bring out the
intellectual qualities inherent in their subjects and to avoid the bland-
ness of earlier forms of interdisciplinary study. Morton White, Bruce
Kuklick, and Murray Murphey have studied the history of American
philosophy from the viewpoint of philosophers as well as from that of
historians.[21] Edmund Morgan, Alan Heimert, Sacvan Bercovitch, and
David Hall have carried the study of Puritanism even farther than
where Perry Miller left it.[22] And the internal history of science has
extended farther than ever in many different directions.

With each extension, the historical subfields have become more
rigorous but also more esoteric—a seemingly inevitable tendency,
because historians must specialize in order to follow the specialization
in the growth of knowledge. Yet a countertendency has set in, and it
may indicate that social history has had some impact at the higher
level of the history of ideas. In his highly technical account of the rise
of pragmatism, for example, Kuklick shows how philosophy became
imbedded in the structure of the modern university, and he draws on
Laurence Veysey's sociological study of the university as an institution.[23] In tracing the development of "modernist" ideas in Protestant
theology, William Hutchinson tries to follow their diffusion as well as
their philosophical elaboration.[24] Bruce Frier has demonstrated that
the abstractions of Roman law had important connections with the
real estate market in ancient Rome.[25] And several historians of science, Roger Hahn and Charles Rosenberg in particular, have shown
the significance of interest groups and institutions in the development
of scientific theories.[26] The history of science may prove to be a

21. Morton White, *Science and Sentiment in America: Philosophical Thought from Jonathan Edwards to John Dewey* (New York, 1972) and *The Philosophy of the American Revolution* (New York, 1978); Bruce Kuklick, *The Rise of American Philosophy: Cambridge, Massachusetts, 1860–1930* (New Haven, 1977); and Murray Murphey (with Elizabeth Flower), *A History of Philosophy in America*, 2 vols. (New York, 1977).

22. Edmund S. Morgan, *Visible Saints: The History of a Puritan Idea* (New York, 1963); Alan Heimert, *Religion and the American Mind from the Great Awakening to the Revolution* (Cambridge, Mass., 1966); Sacvan Bercovitch, *The Puritan Origins of the American Self* (New Haven, 1975) and *The American Jeremiad* (Madison, Wis., 1978); and David Hall, *The Faithful Shepherd: A History of the New England Ministry in the Seventeenth Century* (Chapel Hill, N.C., 1972).

23. Laurence Veysey, *The Emergence of the American University* (Chicago, 1965).

24. William R. Hutchison, *The Modernist Impulse in American Protestantism* (Cambridge, Mass., 1976).

25. Bruce Frier, *Landlords and Tenants in Imperial Rome* (Princeton, 1980).

26. Roger Hahn, *The Anatomy of a Scientific Institution: The Paris Academy of Sciences, 1666–1803* (Berkeley, 1971), and Charles Rosenberg, *The Trial of the Assassin Guiteau: Psychiatry and Law in the Gilded Age* (Chicago, 1968).

strategic field for assessing the interplay of social history and the history of ideas, because it has expressed most clearly the tension between internal and external approaches to formal thought. The dichotomy may seem unreal to some specialists, and there seemed to be room for both approaches in Thomas Kuhn's distinction between normal and revolutionary phases in the development of science. But since the initial publication of *The Structure of Scientific Revolutions* (1962), Kuhn has moved toward the "internalist" position and has somewhat altered his notion of paradigm, making it more accommodating to normative and less to sociological notions.[27] Meanwhile, "externalists" have shown how the culture and politics of early-modern England and Weimar Germany influenced the development of Newtonianism and quantum physics.[28] The two tendencies could split the history of science in half, sending it toward sociology on the one hand and toward philosophy and the natural sciences on the other. But it seems more likely that the tension will continue to be creative and that even the most recondite scientific activity will be interpreted within a cultural context.[29]

Contextualization is the strongest feature in the area of the history of ideas that has made the strongest progress during the last decade: the history of political thought. In a series of programmatic articles followed by a set of major books, Quentin Skinner, John Dunn, and John Pocock have argued that one can capture the meaning of a political treatise only by recreating the political idiom of the time in which it was written. They shift the emphasis from text to context, but not in order to smuggle in a reductionist view of ideas, either Marxists or Namierite in inspiration. On the contrary, they assert the autonomy of thought by invoking analytical philosophy and by treating thought as "statements" or "speech-acts" conveying particular meanings. As meaning is bound up in time and language, it cannot inhere in the "unit-ideas" imagined by Lovejoy, which move in and out of

27. Thomas S. Kuhn, "The Relation between History and History of Science," *Daedalus,* Spring 1971, 271–304; "Mathematical vs. Experimental Traditions in the Development of Physical Science," *Journal of Interdisciplinary History,* VII (1976), 1–31; and *Black-Body Theory and the Quantum Discontinuity, 1894–1912* (New York, 1978), a book that must be one of the most severely "internalist" histories of a scientific subject ever written.

28. Margaret C. Jacob, *The Newtonians and the English Revolution: 1689–1720* (Ithaca, N.Y., 1978), and Paul Forman, "Weimar Culture, Causality, and Quantum Theory, 1918–1927: Adaptation by German Physicists and Mathematicians to a Hostile Intellectual Environment," *Historical Studies in the Physical Sciences,* III (1971), 1–115.

29. As an example of a strong "internal" study, see Stillman Drake, *Galileo at Work: His Scientific Biography* (New York, 1978), and, as an "external" view, Daniel Kevles, *The Physicists: The History of a Scientific Community in the United States* (New York, 1978).

minds across the centuries; and it cannot be understood by reading the works of great political theorists as if they could speak directly to us. Modern philosophy has freed the historian to work in a historical mode, to reenact the past by rethinking thought in the manner prescribed by Collingwood. Armed with this procedure, Skinner, Dunn, and Pocock have slashed through the anachronisms in the literature surrounding such major figures as Machiavelli, Hobbes, and Locke. They have cut fresh paths through the history of political thought from the thirteenth to the nineteenth century. And while dealing with thought at the highest level, they have reinforced the social history of ideas at the crucial juncture where ideas merge into ideologies.[30]

The concern for specificity of context has also dominated much of the recent work on the intermediate level of intellectual history. The grand tableau about the spirit of an age and the sweeping treatise on the mind of a nation seem to be dying genres, despite the spirited efforts of Ira Wade, Peter Gay, and Rush Welter to keep them alive.[31] In American studies especially, scholars have turned from the holistic to the institutional view of intellectual life. What passed as national character in the 1950s now looks like the culture of middle-class whites to many younger historians. They tend to see knowledge as power, as the ideological fortification of specific social groups; and so they have concentrated on the intellectual history of professions, professionals, and professionalization—a process that now looks so ubiquitous that it is running a close second to the rise of the middle class as a historical theme.[32] The favorite profession among

30. The literature by and about these historians is now quite extensive. As examples of their programmatic writing, see Quentin Skinner, "Meaning and Understanding in the History of Ideas," *History and Theory*, VIII (1969), 3–53; John Dunn, "The Identity of the History of Ideas," *Philosophy*, XLIII (1968), 85–104; and J. G. A. Pocock, "Languages and Their Implications: The Transformation of the Study of Political Thought," in Pocock, *Politics, Languages, and Time: Essays on Political Thought and History* (New York, 1971), 3–41. Their substantive works are Skinner, *The Foundations of Modern Political Thought*, 2 vols. (Cambridge, Mass., 1978); Dunn, *The Political Thought of John Locke* (Cambridge, Mass., 1969); and Pocock, *The Machiavellian Moment: Florentine Political Thought and the Atlantic Republican Tradition* (Princeton, 1975).

31. Ira O. Wade, *The Structure and Form of the French Enlightenment*, 2 vols. (Princeton, 1977); Gay, *The Enlightenment;* and Rush Welter, *The Mind of America, 1820–1860* (New York, 1975).

32. In addition to the older work by Daniel Calhoun, Roy Lubove, and Corinne Gilb, see George W. Stocking, *Race, Culture, and Evolution: Essays in the History of Anthropology* (New York, 1968); Mary O. Furner, *Advocacy and Objectivity: A Crisis in the Professionalization of American Social Science, 1865–1905* (Lexington, Ky., 1975); Thomas L. Haskell, *The Emergence of Professional Social Science: The American Social Science Association and the Nineteenth-Century Crisis of Authority* (Urbana, Ill., 1977); and, for related views, Thomas Bender, *Toward an Urban Vision: Ideas and Institutions in Nineteenth-Century America* (Lexington, Ky., 1975).

Europeanists seems to be history. Their choice may not be free from bias, but it has resulted in some excellent intellectual biographies, notably John Clive's *Macaulay* and Leonard Krieger's *Ranke*. And in the work of Hayden White, Nancy Struever, Maurice Mandelbaum, Donald Kelley, and Lionel Gossman, the history of history has gone beyond the older historiographical concerns to a fresh consideration of time consciousness and the linguistic nature of thought in the past.[33] The Europeanists seem more sensitive to European currents of philosophy—analytical philosophy in England, poststructuralist thought in France—while the Americanists respond primarily to the American strain in the sociology of knowledge and anthropology.[34]

It may be misleading, however, to distinguish too neatly between the European and American branches of intellectual history. One tendency that brings them together and that also shows the continuity between the older and younger generations of intellectual historians is the emphasis on social thought. The work of Martin Jay and Stuart Hughes, of David Hollinger and Morton White, of Jonathan Beecher and Frank Manuel shows a concern for the social dimensions of thought on both sides of the Atlantic and of the so-called generation gap.[35] The emphasis on social thinkers also stands out in intellectual biography, a genre that has flourished in the United States while faltering on the Continent, especially in France. What makes biography unfashionable in the *Annales* school—its emphasis on individu-

33. Donald R. Kelley, *Foundations of Modern Historical Scholarship: Language, Law, and History in the French Renaissance* (New York, 1972); Nancy Struever, *The Language of History in the Renaissance: Rhetorical and Historical Consciousness in Florentine Humanism* (Princeton, 1970); Hayden White, *Metahistory: The Historical Imagination in Nineteenth-Century Europe* (Baltimore, 1973); Lionel Gossman, "Augustin Thierry and Liberal Historiography," *History and Theory*, xv (1976), supplement 15; and Maurice Mandelbaum, *History, Man, and Reason: A Study in Nineteenth-Century Thought* (Baltimore, 1971). See also George Huppert, *The Idea of Perfect History: Historical Erudition and Historical Philosophy in Renaissance Florence* (Urbana, Ill., 1970); Linda Orr, *Jules Michelet: Nature, History, and Language* (Ithaca, N.Y., 1976); and Charles Rearick, *Beyond the Enlightenment: Historians and Folklore in Nineteenth-Century France* (Bloomington, Ind., 1974).

34. Among the works most often cited by Americanists are Robert K. Merton, *Social Theory and Social Structure* (New York, 1968; first ed. 1949); Peter Berger and Thomas Luckmann, *The Social Construction of Reality* (New York, 1966); more recently Clifford Geertz, *The Interpretation of Cultures* (New York, 1973); and above all Thomas Kuhn, *The Structure of Scientific Revolutions*. At this moment, Foucault stands out among the closely watched avant-garde for Europeanists: see Hayden V. White, "Foucault Decoded: Notes from Underground," *History and Theory*, xii (1973), 23-54.

35. In addition to the works of Hughes, White, and Manuel cited above, see Martin Jay, *The Dialectical Imagination: A History of the Frankfurt School and the Institute of Social Research, 1923-1950* (Boston, 1973); David A. Hollinger, *Morris R. Cohen and the Scientific Ideal* (Cambridge, Mass., 1975); and Jonathan Beecher and Richard Bienvenu, *The Utopian Vision of Charles Fourier* (Boston, 1971).

Robert Darnton

als and events rather than on long-term shifts in structures—makes it appealing to Americans, who thirst for specificity and hunger after connections between social theory and institutional setting. Thus Dorothy Ross has seen the history of psychology through the life of G. Stanley Hall; Barry Karl and John Diggins have seen political science and sociology come of age in the lives of Charles Merriam and Thorstein Veblen; and Peter Paret and Keith Baker have seen a general sociopolitical science take shape through the lives of Clausewitz and Condorcet.[36] Three biographies of Durkheim appeared in 1972; two works on Vico came out in 1975–76; at least a dozen studies of Marx were published in 1977–78; and the bicentennial of the deaths of Voltaire and Rousseau in 1978 brought such an outpouring of books and articles on top of such a vast body of earlier work that the literature on the two great philosophers can hardly be read by a single scholar, especially if he wants to master their own writings, which are now becoming available in the superb editions of Theodore Besterman and R. A. Leigh.[37] The Enlightenment scholar cannot neglect Arthur Wilson's *Diderot* and Robert Shackleton's *Montesquieu*.[38] And if he needs to study the transatlantic dimension of the Republic of Letters, he will have to plow through the vast editions of Jefferson, Adams, and the other Founding Fathers. The great scholarly editions of the 1960s and 1970s are creating new possibilities for the intellectual historian, if they do not overwhelm him.

He will not get relief from the sheer documentary weight of the past if he seeks refuge at the lower level of study that is now becoming known as the social history of ideas; for here he will need to examine not only the works of great writers but also their diffusion, and he will need to study the production and diffusion of lesser literature, too. Social historians of ideas attempt to follow thought through the entire

36. Dorothy Ross, *G. Stanley Hall: The Psychologist as Prophet* (Chicago, 1972); Barry Karl, *Charles E. Merriam and the Study of Politics* (Chicago, 1974); John P. Diggins, *The Bard of Savagery: Thorstein Veblen and Modern Social Theory* (New York, 1978); Peter Paret, *Clausewitz and the State* (New York, 1976); and Keith Baker, *Condorcet: From Natural Philosophy to Social Mathematics* (Chicago, 1975).

37. For representative examples of these works, which are too numerous to be listed, see Dominick La Capra, *Emile Durkheim, Sociologist and Philosopher* (Ithaca, N.Y., 1972); Leon Pompa, *Vico: A Study of the "New Science"* (Cambridge, 1975); Jerrold Seigel, *Marx's Fate: The Shape of a Life* (Princeton, 1978); Ira O. Wade, *The Intellectual Development of Voltaire* (Princeton, 1969); and Judith Shklar, *Men and Citizens: A Study of Rousseau's Social Theory* (Cambridge, Mass., 1969).

38. The late Arthur Wilson was an American who did his graduate work in England. Robert Shackleton is an Englishman who has lectured widely in the United States. Like other historians mentioned in this essay—Pocock, Skinner, and Stone, for example—they represent a strain of scholarship that cannot be identified exclusively with one country and that often goes by the name "Anglo-Saxon" on the Continent.

342

fabric of society. They want to penetrate the mental world of ordinary persons as well as philosophers, but they keep running into the vast silence that has swallowed up most of mankind's thinking. The printed word provides one trail through the emptiness, however, because by following it the historian can get some sense of the lived experience of literature—at least among the literate and after the invention of movable type. Scholars have pursued this path the farthest in England and France, where *histoire du livre* has emerged as a distinct subdiscipline. But Americans also seem to show increasing interest in the history of literacy, popular literature, publishing, and journalism.[39]

It was by studying popular pamphlet literature that Bernard Bailyn renovated the history of the American Revolution.[40] He showed that the view of events among ordinary citizens was as important as the events themselves—that Americans perceived the actions of George III and his ministers through a dense political culture, which they had inherited from their seventeenth-century ancestors and which shaped their behavior throughout the eighteenth century. The work of Popock, Skinner, and Dunn indicated that this culture could be traced back to the Renaissance, provided it were understood as the elaboration of an idiom rather than a great chain of ideas. The beginning of this process became clear from the work of Renaissance scholars—notably Hans Baron, Felix Gilbert, William Bouwsma, Gene Brucker, Marvin Becker, Eric Cochrane, and Donald Weinstein—who showed how civic humanism blossomed, flourished, and withered throughout the tempestuous histories of Florence and Venice. From Italy the ideological current flowed to England, where it was transformed by the Reformation and tinctured by indigenous institutions. Despite the incursions of Namierites and internal quarreling, historians of England, from Christopher Hill to J. H. Hexter, Lawrence Stone, J. H. Plumb, E. P. Thompson, and John Brewer, have agreed on the cen-

39. Aside from the older but still solid work of Richard Altick and Robert Webb, see Elizabeth Eisenstein, *The Printing Press as an Agent of Change: Communications and Cultural Transformations in Early-Modern Europe*, 2 vols. (Cambridge, Eng., 1979), and, for a recent survey of the subject, Raymond Birn, "*Livre et Société* after Ten Years: Formation of a Discipline," *Studies on Voltaire and the Eighteenth Century*, CLV (1976), 287-312. David D. Hall, "The World of Print and Collective Mentality in Seventeenth-Century New England," in Higham and Conkin, eds., *New Directions*, 166-180, suggests ways that French methods could be applied to American history. Several Americanists—notably Stephen Botein, Norman Fiering, and William Gilmore—have already made important contributions to *histoire du livre*, and the discipline is beginning to have an impact on general studies, such as Henry F. May, *The Enlightenment in America* (New York, 1976).

40. Bernard Bailyn, *The Ideological Origins of the American Revolution* (Cambridge, Mass., 1967) and *The Origins of American Politics* (New York, 1968).

tral importance of ideology in English public life during the seventeenth and eighteenth centuries. At that point American historians—Edmund Morgan, Jack Greene, Gordon Wood, and Eric Foner as well as Bernard Bailyn—could grasp the ideological theme, give it some final twists and turns, and show how it determined the character of the new republic. At each stage in the development of this rich strain of historiography, the historians have stressed the way political discourse was imbedded in institutional life. Instead of treating thought as an epiphenomenon of social organization, however, they have tried to show how it organized experience and conveyed meaning among the general citizenry. Instead of contemplating a transcendent spirit, they have tried to re-create a political language. And instead of imposing their own categories on that language, they have let it speak for itself. Thus avoiding reductionism on the one hand and anachronism on the other, they have shown that the study of ideology can serve as a testing ground for problems and methods within the social history of ideas as a whole.[41]

In passing to cultural history, one moves below the level of literacy and onto territory where history and anthropology meet. The meetings usually occur when they converge on subjects classified loosely as popular culture. Historians seem comfortable with the term. With a few exceptions, such as Hayden White, they have not asked whether it stands for a coherent field of study but rather have rushed from subject to subject as occasions arose.[42] The enthusiasm has been

41. The literature on these interlocking subjects is so vast that this account hardly does justice to it. The complex and sometimes contradictory tendencies within it stand out more clearly in debates conducted through journals than in monographs. See Gordon S. Wood, "Rhetoric and Reality in the American Revolution," *William and Mary Quarterly*, XXIII (1964), 3–32; J. G. A. Pocock, "Virtue and Commerce in the Eighteenth Century," *Journal of Interdisciplinary History*, III (1972), 119–134; Aileen Kraditor, "American Radical Historians on Their Heritage," *Past and Present*, no. 56 (August 1972), 136–153; Joyce Appleby, "The Social Origins of American Revolutionary Ideology," *Journal of American History*, LXIV (1978), 935–958; Bernard Bailyn, "The Central Themes of the American Revolution: An Interpretation," in Stephen G. Kurtz and James H. Hutson, eds., *Essays on the American Revolution* (Chapel Hill, N.C., 1973) 3–31; and Robert Kelley, "Ideology and Political Culture from Jefferson to Nixon," *American Historical Review*, LXXXII (1977), 531–562. Recent work on nineteenth-century Britain and America shows a similar tendency to treat culture in a broad, transatlantic perspective: see Daniel Walker Howe, ed., *Victorian America* (Philadelphia, 1976).

42. Hayden V. White, "Structuralism and Popular Culture," *Journal of Popular Culture*, VII (1974), 759–775. White challenges the common distinction between "high" and "low" or elite and popular culture. Given the many directions, upward as well as downward, of cultural currents, his point seems convincing, whether or not one goes on to accept his pointedly "unhistoric" and structuralist view of culture. For a more thorough and more historical survey of the subject, which also does away with the high-low distinction, see Peter Burke, *Popular Culture in Early Modern Europe* (New York, 1978).

greatest in conferences on French history, where Americans and Frenchmen have joined hands in a merry round of reports on carnivals and charivari.[43] At its best—in the work of Natalie Davis, Robert Mandrou, Marc Soriano, and Carlo Ginzburg, for example—this effervescence has stimulated some striking original research.[44] At its worst, it appears trivial and trendy. Whatever its trendiness, the history of popular culture certainly is not new. E. K. Chambers demonstrated its importance at the turn of the century, and long before that Burckhardt had given it a central place in his panorama of Renaissance culture. The complexity and depth of the literature on the subject can be appreciated from Peter Burke's recent survey of it.[45]

Nonetheless, the enthusiasm for popular culture is symptomatic of a shift within social history itself. The pacesetters of the field, such historians as Emmanuel Le Roy Ladurie and Lawrence Stone, who used to fill their books with graphs, demographic statistics, and quantitative models of social structures, have relied entirely on qualitative evidence in their latest work, glossing literary references with references to anthropology.[46] One of the most influential and anthropological books of the decade, Keith Thomas's *Religion and the Decline of Magic,* was criticized for not being anthropological enough—not only by anthropologists but also (at least implicitly) by Thomas's fellow social historian E. P. Thompson.[47] Thompson himself epitomizes the inflection toward cultural history and toward an anthropological mode of understanding among social historians. After attempting to recount the development of working-class con-

43. The most important recent occasions were the conference in Paris in 1977 and in Madison and Stanford in 1975. The proceedings of the latter were published as *The Wolf and the Lamb: Popular Culture in France from the Old Regime to the Twentieth Century,* ed. Jacques Beauroy, Marc Bertrand, and Edward T. Gargan (Saratoga, Calif., 1977).

44. See especially Natalie Zemon Davis, *Society and Culture in Early Modern France* (Stanford, 1975).

45. Burke, *Popular Culture.*

46. Compare Emmanuel Le Roy Ladurie, *Les paysans de Languedoc* (Paris, i966), with Le Roy Ladurie, *Montaillou, village occitan de 1294 à 1324* (Paris, 1975) and *Le carnaval de Romans: De la Chandeleur au mercredi des Cendres, 1579–1580* (Paris, 1979); and compare Lawrence Stone, *The Crisis of the Aristocracy, 1558–1641* (Oxford, 1965) with Stone, *The Family, Sex, and Marriage in England 1500–1800* (New York, 1977). One can detect similar changes in the work of Jean Delumeau, François Furet, Edward Shorter, and many other social historians.

47. Hildred Geertz, "An Anthropology of Religion and Magic," with a reply by Keith Thomas, *Journal of Interdisciplinary History,* VI (1975), 71–109, and E. P. Thompson, "Anthropology and the Discipline of Historical Context," *Midland History,* no. 3 (Spring 1972), 41–55. Thompson later aligned himself with Thomas and against Geertz: "Eighteenth-Century English Society: Class Struggle without Class?" *Social History,* III (1978), 155. But his earlier review contains criticisms that are strikingly similar to Geertz's; see especially his remarks on pp. 51–55.

sciousness within the categories of orthodox Marxism, he has moved back farther into the preindustrial era and deeper into the study of plebeian culture.[48] But where will all the work on maypoles, magic, rough music, wife sales, effigy bonfires, and public executions lead?

The most common way of drawing it all together has been to subsume it under the category of *mentalité*, a convenient Gallicism, which has spread through English and German after making its fortune in France. Despite a spate of prolegomena and discourses on method, however, the French have not developed a coherent conception of *mentalités* as a field of study. They tend to load the term with notions of *représentations collectives* derived from Durkheim and the *outillage mental* that Lucien Febvre picked up from the psychology of his day.[49] Whether *mentalité* will bear the load remains to be seen. But it probably will not survive Americanization any better than *Weltanschauung* did. The first attempts to domesticate it suggest that it will dissolve in discourse about general attitudes.[50]

If so, American historians may not have advanced far beyond a stage of confusing enthusiasm for the study of symbolic behavior among the "inarticulate"—that is, the illiterate, preliterate, and semiliterate, who really manage to express themselves very well through their own cultural forms. But some advance has already occurred, and it has occurred in an empirical way, by digging through difficult sources in order to excavate evidence about those forms. The

48. Compare E. P. Thompson, *The Making of the English Working Class* (New York, 1966; first ed. 1963), with Thompson, "Eighteenth-Century English Society," which provides a retrospective view of his work on time and work discipline, the moral economy of the crowd, rough music, plebeian culture, and criminality. Whether or not Thompson has established his orthodoxy within the camp of the *New Left Review*, he has succeeded in developing a literary and (though he might reject the word) anthropological mode of understanding within social history.

49. The latest French review of the field is Philippe Ariès, "L'histoire des mentalités," in Jacques Le Goff, ed., *La nouvelle histoire* (Paris, 1978), 402–423. The best of the many programmatic articles by the French are George S. Duby, "L'histoire des mentalités," in *L'histoire et ses méthodes (Encyclopédie de la Pléiade*, Paris, 1961), 937–966, and Jacques Le Goff, "Les mentalités, une histoire ambiguë," in Jacques Le Goff and Pierre Nora, eds., *Faire de l'histoire* (Paris, 1974) III, 76–94. For an astute assessment by an outsider, see Rolf Reichardt, "Histoire des mentalités: Eine neue Dimension der Sozialgeschichte am Beispiel des französischen Ancien Régime," *Internationales Archiv für Sozialgeschichte der deutschen Literatur*, III (1978), 130–166. Reichardt also discusses some German literature, where the hesitation between *mentalité* and *Mentalität* parallels the confusion between *mentalité* and *mentality* in English.

50. The term is used loosely throughout several of the essays in Higham and Conkin, eds., *New Directions*. As an example of firmer usage, see James A. Henretta, "Families and Farms: *Mentalité* in Pre-Industrial America," *William and Mary Quarterly*, 3d ser., XXXV (1978), 3–32.

richest material has been unearthed in the field of black history. Peter Wood has used anthropological methods to investigate the nature of language and labor among slaves in South Carolina. Lawrence Levine has drawn on folklore to convey the way blacks coped with adversity through language and laughter. And Eugene Genovese has brought slave religion back to life in a powerful interpretation of slavery as a sociocultural system.[51] Historians of labor, religion, and the family have developed similar strains of research by marrying social and cultural history.[52] The marriage took place long ago in "Third World" studies, where historians have had to learn all they could from anthropologists and anthropologists have often worked in a diachronic dimension.[53] In the study of American Indians, anthropologists have actually been more historical than historians, for the historians' ethnocentric obsession with the white man's burden of guilt has blinded them to the importance of warfare and diplomacy among the Indian tribes themselves throughout the eighteenth and nineteenth centuries.[54]

The tacking between history and anthropology has benefited both disciplines, because they provide complementary ways of reaching the same goal: the interpretation of culture. Moreover, anthropology offers the historian what the study of *mentalité* has failed to provide: a coherent conception of culture, which Clifford Geertz has defined as

51. Peter H. Wood, *Black Majority: Negroes in Colonial South Carolina from 1670 through the Stono Rebellion* (New York, 1974); Lawrence W. Levine, *Black Culture and Black Consciousness: Afro-American Folk Thought from Slavery to Freedom* (New York, 1977); and Eugene D. Genovese, *Roll, Jordan, Roll: The World the Slaves Made* (New York, 1974).

52. For example, Herbert G. Gutman, *The Black Family in Slavery and Freedom* (New York, 1976); Daniel T. Rodgers, *The Work Ethic in Industrial America, 1850-1920* (Chicago, 1978); James Obelkevich, *Religion and Rural Society: South Lindsey, 1825-1875* (Oxford, 1976).

53. Two examples, which draw on traditions of mutual instruction between history and anthropology from various parts of the world, are Karen Spalding, "The Colonial Indian: Past and Future Research Perspectives," *Latin American Research Review*, VII (1972), 47-76, and Irwin Scheiner, "Benevolent Lords and Honorable Peasants: Rebellion and Peasant Consciousness in Tokugawa Japan," in Tetsuo Najita and Irwin Scheiner, eds., *Japanese Thought in the Tokugawa Period, 1600-1868* (Chicago, 1978).

54. Richard White, "The Winning of the West: The Expansion of the Western Sioux in the Eighteenth and Nineteenth Centuries," *Journal of American History*, LXV (1978), 319-343. It would not take a great deal of reading in current anthropology to disabuse historians of the belief that anthropologists sin in three main ways: lack of a time dimension, excessive holism, and concentration on "primitive" societies. See, for example, Clifford Geertz, *Islam Observed: Religious Development in Morocco and Indonesia* (Chicago, 1968), and S. J. Tambiah, *Buddhism and the Spirit Cults in North-East Thailand* (Cambridge, 1970).

*Robert Darnton*

"an historically transmitted pattern of meanings embodied in symbols."[55] Of course it would be easy to fish other definitions out of the anthropological literature. Anthropologists disagree as much as anyone else. But they share a common orientation toward the problems of interpreting culture. They can help the historian reorient his own attempts to solve those problems, and they can set him on course in pursuit of patterns of meaning.

The concern for meaning runs through all the varieties of intellectual history, from the "high" to the "low." It suggests that all are being renovated in ways that cannot be seen in the statistics or heard through the cries of alarm from those who favor older ways. Of course it would be simplistic to divide the profession between innovators and traditionalists or Pollyannas and Jeremiahs. It also would be foolish to deny that some traditional types of intellectual history have suffered during the last ten years. Future historians probably will not produce many treatises on the spirit of an age or the mind of a nation or the linkage in great chains of ideas. There seems to be some drift from the "higher" to the "lower" sectors of the spectrum. But intellectual historians need not worry about disappearing in the rising tide of social history. Although they may feel queasy at times, they are getting their sea legs; they have fresh wind in their sails; and they are moving in new directions.

### NOTE ON TABLES AND FIGURE

Each of the sources used in compiling these tables has advantages and disadvantages. The course catalogs often give quite full descriptions of the courses; and if one assumes a fairly strong correlation between the descriptions and the teaching, they probably provide a valid indication of the relative importance of various history genres. Most courses, however, are not generic. They cover time periods; and it is impossible to know whether emphases have shifted within them unless one undertakes an elaborate survey. Nonetheless, shifts in emphasis should be expressed fairly accurately in the minority of the courses (about 25 percent) that are devoted to specialized genres. The statistical base is broad, and it would have been broader had it been possible to find more complete runs of catalogs. Incomplete statistics were compiled from the catalogs of Columbia University, Chicago University, and the University of California at Los Angeles. They conformed to the pattern of those from the other catalogs, but they contained too many gaps to be used in Tables 1 and 2. The statistics include graduate courses open to undergraduates—the 400-level courses at Harvard, for example—but not graduate seminars intended exclusively for graduate students and listed separately. Mixed generic courses, such as the "social and intellectual history" courses popular in the 1940s, were not entered under either rubric. Those classified as "political" were devoted specifically to politics, according to the catalogs. But the general courses probably emphasized politics heavily, so it may be underrepresented.

55. For the full version of this definition, see Clifford Geertz, "Religion as a Cultural System," in *Interpretation of Cultures,* 89.

348

Thanks to the extensive summaries in *Dissertation Abstracts,* the classification of doctoral dissertations does not pose special problems. But the data could not be traced back to 1948, because too few theses were microfilmed at that time. By 1958 the great majority of history theses appeared in *Dissertation Abstracts.* Foreign dissertations were eliminated from the data. And the monthly reports were compiled for all twelve months of 1958 in order to have statistics large enough to be compared with the six months of reports covered in the statistics for 1968 and 1978. (There were no significant seasonal fluctuations in the reporting.) Thus the number of doctorates in history increased from about 200 in 1958 to about 860 in 1978, and it did not decrease as the job market contracted during the 1970s.

The *Journal of Modern History, Journal of American History,* and *American Historical Review* were chosen for the compilation of the data in Table 4 because of their general character and because they go back to the 1940s. One might expect new trends to appear more quickly in such specialized journals as the *Journal of Social History, Journal of Interdisciplinary History, Journal of the History of Ideas,* and *American Quarterly.* But the siphoning off of avant-garde articles probably occurs at about the same rate in all fields, including the fields represented by the *Negro History Bulletin, Agricultural History,* and *Diplomatic History.* Changes in editors also affect the coverage of journals, and important changes occurred in the editorships of all three of the journals studied. But such changes also take place fairly equally across fields. So it seems valid to use the three older and more established journals in order to measure trends in the scholarship of older and more established historians. The articles were compiled over three-year periods in order to build up an adequate statistical base.

Finally, I should add that I did all the compiling and computing myself, without the help of research assistants, and that I tried to read through all the course descriptions, dissertation abstracts, and journal articles as thoroughly as possible. In the end I developed some intuitive sense of changes within the profession. And if I made errors, they probably are consistent, or at least did not result from hasty work.

350

Table 1. Specialized history courses offered at eight American universities, 1948–78

| University | Political history | Constitutional history | International relations | Intellectual history | Cultural history | Economic history | Social history | Total history courses offered |
|---|---|---|---|---|---|---|---|---|
| Harvard | | | | | | | | |
| 1948-49 | 2 | 2 | 4 | 5 | 0 | 1 | 3 | 82 |
| 1958-59 | 3 | 3 | 2 | 12 | 0 | 1 | 2 | 115 |
| 1968-69 | 4 | 3 | 7 | 14 | 0 | 3 | 4 | 131 |
| 1978-79 | 6 | 1 | 6 | 19 | 3 | 5 | 13 | 177 |
| Yale | | | | | | | | |
| 1948-49 | 2 | 2 | 3 | 3 | 2 | 0 | 1 | 43 |
| 1958-59 | 2 | 0 | 4 | 4 | 2 | 0 | 2 | 67 |
| 1968-69 | 7 | 2 | 10 | 11 | 3 | 5 | 1 | 133 |
| 1978-79 | 4 | 1 | 8 | 12 | 2 | 2 | 13 | 133 |
| Princeton | | | | | | | | |
| 1948-49 | 1 | 1 | 1 | 1 | 0 | 0 | 0 | 21 |
| 1958-59 | 0 | 1 | 3 | 1 | 0 | 2 | 1 | 27 |
| 1968-69 | 1 | 1 | 0 | 3 | 1 | 2 | 1 | 52 |
| 1978-79 | 1 | 1 | 1 | 5 | 2 | 2 | 6 | 62 |
| Indiana | | | | | | | | |
| 1948-49 | 1 | 1 | 2 | 1 | 0 | 0 | 0 | 41 |
| 1958-59 | 0 | 2 | 2 | 0 | 0 | 0 | 0 | 63 |
| 1968-69 | 0 | 4 | 7 | 4 | 0 | 3 | 6 | 135 |
| 1978-79 | 0 | 4 | 6 | 2 | 0 | 4 | 4 | 116 |

| | | | | | | | | |
|---|---|---|---|---|---|---|---|---|
| **Michigan** | | | | | | | | |
| 1948–49 | 0 | 4 | 3 | 3 | 0 | 4 | 0 | 82 |
| 1958–59 | 0 | 4 | 5 | 3 | 3 | 6 | 0 | 132 |
| 1968–69 | 0 | 4 | 5 | 14 | 1 | 7 | 9 | 200 |
| 1978–79 | 0 | 2 | 3 | 14 | 1 | 7 | 16 | 189 |
| **Wisconsin** | | | | | | | | |
| 1948–49 | 0 | 3 | 1 | 1 | 0 | 6 | 0 | 79 |
| 1958–59 | 0 | 2 | 2 | 2 | 0 | 8 | 1 | 107 |
| 1968–69 | 0 | 6 | 10 | 3 | 4 | 13 | 12 | 227 |
| 1978–79 | 0 | 1 | 5 | 4 | 7 | 4 | 13 | 186 |
| **Berkeley** | | | | | | | | |
| 1948–49 | 0 | 5 | 4 | 0 | 3 | 1 | 2 | 97 |
| 1958–59 | 0 | 4 | 6 | 5 | 3 | 0 | 7 | 130 |
| 1968–69 | 0 | 6 | 4 | 7 | 1 | 2 | 8 | 146 |
| 1978–79 | 0 | 0 | 4 | 11 | 0 | 4 | 13 | 148 |
| **Stanford** | | | | | | | | |
| 1948–49 | 0 | 1 | 5 | 4 | 1 | 0 | 1 | 86 |
| 1958–59 | 0 | 2 | 5 | 6 | 1 | 1 | 2 | 104 |
| 1968–69 | 0 | 0 | 7 | 9 | 2 | 1 | 5 | 108 |
| 1978–79 | 3 | 1 | 3 | 5 | 5 | 1 | 17 | 119 |

Table 2. Specialized history courses offered at eight American universities, by subfield, 1948–78

| Courses | 1948–49 | | 1958–59 | | 1968–69 | | 1978–79 | |
|---|---|---|---|---|---|---|---|---|
| | Number | Percent | Number | Percent | Number | Percent | Number | Percent |
| Social history | | | | | | | | |
| Immigration-ethnicity | 3 | — | 0 | — | 2 | — | 8 | — |
| Labor | 1 | — | 1 | — | 0 | — | 6 | — |
| Black | 0 | — | 0 | — | 5 | — | 16 | — |
| Urban | 0 | — | 0 | — | 8 | — | 14 | — |
| Women-family | 0 | — | 0 | — | 1 | — | 13 | — |
| General | 3 | — | 14 | — | 30 | — | 38 | — |
| All social history | 7 | 1.3% | 15 | 2.0% | 46 | 4.1% | 95 | 8.4% |
| Political history | 6 | 1.1 | 5 | 0.7 | 12 | 1.1 | 14 | 1.2 |
| Constitutional history | 19 | 3.6 | 18 | 2.4 | 26 | 2.3 | 11 | 1.0 |
| International relations | 23 | 4.3 | 29 | 3.9 | 50 | 4.4 | 36 | 3.2 |
| Intellectual history | 18 | 3.4 | 33 | 4.4 | 65 | 5.7 | 72 | 6.4 |
| Cultural history | 6 | 1.1 | 9 | 1.2 | 12 | 1.1 | 20 | 1.8 |
| Economic history | 12 | 2.3 | 18 | 2.4 | 36 | 3.2 | 29 | 2.6 |
| All specialized history | 91 | 17.1 | 127 | 17.0 | 247 | 21.9 | 277 | 24.6 |
| Other history | 440 | 82.9 | 618 | 83.0 | 885 | 78.2 | 853 | 75.5 |
| All history | 531 | 100.0% | 745 | 100.0% | 1,132 | 100.1% | 1,130 | 100.1% |

*Table 3.*   Dissertations completed in history, by subfield, 1958–78

| Courses | 1958 (12 months) | | 1968 (6 months) | | 1978 (6 months) | |
|---|---|---|---|---|---|---|
| | Number | Percent | Number | Percent | Number | Percent |
| Social history | | | | | | |
|   Immigration-ethnicity | 3 | 1.5% | 7 | 1.9% | 12 | 2.8% |
|   Labor | 1 | 0.4 | 7 | 1.9 | 13 | 3.0 |
|   Black | 2 | 1.0 | 8 | 2.1 | 21 | 4.9 |
|   Urban | 1 | 0.4 | 2 | 0.5 | 12 | 2.8 |
|   Women-family | 2 | 1.0 | 4 | 1.1 | 14 | 3.2 |
|   General | 5 | 2.5 | 11 | 2.9 | 45 | 10.4 |
|     All social history | 14 | 6.8 | 39 | 10.4 | 117 | 27.1 |
| Political history | 69 | 34.3 | 126 | 33.4 | 102 | 23.7 |
| Constitutional history | 3 | 1.5 | 2 | 0.5 | 1 | — |
| International relations | 21 | 10.5 | 48 | 12.7 | 40 | 9.3 |
| Intellectual history | 21 | 10.5 | 36 | 9.5 | 38 | 8.8 |
| Cultural history | 5 | 2.5 | 12 | 3.2 | 25 | 5.8 |
| Economic history | 15 | 7.5 | 18 | 4.8 | 15 | 3.5 |
|   All specialized history | 148 | 73.6 | 281 | 74.5 | 338 | 78.2 |
| Other history | 53 | 26.4 | 96 | 25.5 | 93 | 21.6 |
|     All history | 201 | 100.0% | 377 | 100.0% | 431 | 99.8% |

*Table 4.* History articles appearing in three scholarly journals, by subfield, 1946–78

| Subfield | 1946–48 | | | | | 1956–58 | | | | | 1966–68 | | | | | 1976–78 | | | | |
|---|---|---|---|---|---|---|---|---|---|---|---|---|---|---|---|---|---|---|---|---|
| | JMH | JAH | AHR | Total | Percent | JMH | JAH | AHR | Total | Percent | JMH | JAH | AHR | Total | Percent | JMH | JAH | AHR | Total | Percent |
| Political history | 12 | 13 | 10 | 35 | 31.8% | 24 | 20 | 8 | 52 | 38.2% | 20 | 26 | 19 | 65 | 35.9% | 36 | 10 | 13 | 59 | 32.6% |
| International relations | 13 | 5 | 6 | 24 | 21.8 | 12 | 11 | 4 | 27 | 19.9 | 14 | 6 | 4 | 24 | 13.3 | 16 | 6 | 3 | 25 | 13.8 |
| Intellectual history | 2 | 1 | 4 | 7 | 6.4 | 1 | 6 | 6 | 13 | 9.6 | 6 | 7 | 6 | 19 | 10.5 | 6 | 3 | 10 | 19 | 10.5 |
| Cultural history | 2 | 2 | 2 | 6 | 5.4 | 0 | 2 | 1 | 3 | 2.2 | 3 | 2 | 3 | 8 | 4.4 | 4 | 3 | 3 | 10 | 5.5 |
| Social history | 0 | 4 | 7 | 11 | 10.0 | 0 | 5 | 8 | 13 | 9.6 | 1 | 10 | 4 | 15 | 8.3 | 14 | 16 | 3 | 33 | 18.3 |
| Economic history | 3 | 4 | 0 | 7 | 6.4 | 1 | 2 | 1 | 4 | 2.9 | 0 | 3 | 5 | 8 | 4.4 | 1 | 3 | 2 | 6 | 3.3 |
| Other | 3 | 10 | 7 | 20 | 18.2 | 5 | 11 | 8 | 24 | 17.6 | 6 | 20 | 16 | 42 | 23.2 | 10 | 9 | 10 | 29 | 16.0 |
| Total | 35 | 39 | 36 | 110 | 100.0% | 43 | 57 | 36 | 136 | 100.0% | 50 | 74 | 57 | 181 | 100.0% | 87 | 50 | 44 | 181 | 100.0% |

354

# 15

# Marking Time: The Historiography
of International Relations

## Charles S. Maier

I

THE history of international relations (including here American diplomatic history as well as that of other countries) cannot, alas, be counted among the pioneering fields of the discipline during the 1970s. At universities and among the educated public that reads and helps to produce serious historical scholarship, diplomatic history has become a stepchild. Promising graduate students are tempted by the methodological excitement attending social history. The output of maturer scholars has been intermittent. Seminal and rich works have indeed appeared. Still, there has been no wave of transforming research during the 1970s comparable to the sustained output on American slavery or labor or the prenational American experience. Nor has there been an acknowledged master. William Langer, the greatest historian of international relations the United States has produced since World War I, turned toward new questions concerning population and society during the two decades before his death in 1977.

This faltering, however, does not exclude many quiet achievements. It can be plausibly argued that the "average" article or monograph was more sophisticated, better researched, less provincial and jejune at the end of the 1970s than was its equivalent twenty years earlier. The discipline has begun to liberate itself from many of the obsessional over-stated dichotomies, especially those that once illuminated but since have hobbled American diplomatic history: idealist or realist; revolutionary or repressive; peaceable or expansionist. Happily, fewer historians feel constrained to explain events within these self-imposed Procrustean alternatives. On the other hand, there is little sense of collective enterprise, of being at the cutting edge of scholarship.

Why this languishing? American diplomatic historians have provided their own self-criticism; narrowly cast inquiries, parochial perspectives, and unfamiliarity with foreign languages and sources have limited not the best, but still too many works.[1] There have also been more general handicaps. The stalemate of diplomatic history reflects in part scholars' recent aversion to writing about elites and the powerful. History from the bottom up takes its toll in a field of human activity that is still largely executed, if not ultimately shaped, from the top down. Intellectual history could innovate by shifting focus from great ideas to *mentalités,* social history by renewing concerns with the bonds of community life. But the history of international relations finds this methodological democratization more difficult. Perhaps the reluctance to deal with decision makers sprang from a bad conscience about the legitimacy of United States power. It may have corresponded to the impulse that took some young doctors into community health care or lawyers away from corporate practice. Throughout the culture one might expose power or resist it, but hardly seek it, or even comfortably describe it without implicit condemnation. Students of history in the 1970s were certainly prepared to probe the pathological, whether in Hitler or in nineteenth-century sexual repression; many seemed less eager, however, to analyze political power except as pathology.

Fields within history, moreover, like those within natural science, go through periods of routine and then bursts of intense creativity. Quantum mechanics or quarks, plate tectonics or quasars, can produce scientific "revolutions" only intermittently. Nevertheless, if history is stimulated by events in the outside world as well as by the internal dynamic of the craft itself, then the 1970s should have been a decade of greater collective creativity. For the deep transformation of the United States' own international position—its self-accepted restraint in the wake of Vietnam, the success of OPEC and the decline of the dollar as an instrument of influence abroad, Washington's groping toward a multipolar balance of power—all might have been expected to provoke deep historical reflection in the field of international relations. To be sure, some of the reaction to events had already helped to prod Cold War "revisionism," whose shattering historiographical effect was loosed during the 1960s. And the lead time for

1. Alexander De Conde, "What's Wrong with American Diplomatic History?" *Newsletter* of the Society for Historians of American Foreign Relations (hereafter cited as SHAFR *Newsletter*); I (May 1970), 1–16; and David S. Patterson, "What's Wrong (and Right) with American Diplomatic History?: A Diagnosis and a Prescription," SHAFR *Newsletter,* IX (September 1978), 1–14.

historical writing and publication is long enough so that the shifts in the American world role of the 1970s may still exert their full influence on the writing of history during the decade to come.

Part of the difficulty may lie in the field's intrinsic resistance to new techniques. In an age when the computer was transforming studies of voting and mobility, international history seemed less able to profit from the new technology. Although some efforts were made to harness the computer for content analysis of speeches and articles and for simulations of crises, such as that of 1914, these displays remained marginal to what most historians deemed important investigations.[2] Similarly, psychoanalytical reconstruction (when not deemed fanciful by skeptics) might illuminate the long-term behavior of a given leader.[3] It seemed less useful, however, for untangling the concatenations of events that the historian of international relations usually addressed.

Rankean exegesis still forms the basis of the craft, and the word "craft" is used deliberately. The fine works in international history were those in which the author demonstrated mastery of broad masses of documentation; the ability to bring in multiple points of view (by applying what has been somewhat grandiloquently termed the multiarchival approach); and, not least, the capacity to re-create the plausible context in which policy debate took place—that is, a feel for the perceived constraints on possible historical choices. These are traditional skills, no easier for being traditional, but not necessarily those that excited new entrants into the profession. Where one finds innovation, it consists more in the systematic inclusion of fields of

2. See J. David Singer, "The Behavioral Approach to Diplomatic History," in Alexander De Conde, ed., *Encyclopedia of American Foreign Policy: Study of the Principal Movements and Ideas*, 3 vols. (New York, 1978),1, 66–77; Charles F. Hermann,*Crises in Foreign Policy: A Simulation Analysis* (Indianapolis, 1969), and Hermann, ed., *International Crises: Insights from Behavioral Research* (New York, 1972); Melvin Small; "The Applicability of Quantitative International Politics to Diplomatic History," *The Historian*, xxxviii (1976), 281–304; and for a recent résumé of such work, *International Studies Quarterly*, xxi, 1 (March 1977), devoted to "International Crisis: Progress and Prospects for Applied Forecasting and Management." For a critique, see Paul W. Schroeder, "Quantitative Studies in the Balance of Power," *Journal of Conflict Resolution*, xxi (1977), 3–22 and 57–74. On possible computer applications, see the responses in the same issue; also Thomas Schoonover, "How Have State Department Officials (or Diplomatic Historians) Behaved?: A View from the Computer," shafr *Newsletter*, vii (September 1976), 12–17.

3. See Rudolph Binion, "From Mayerling to Sarajevo," *Journal of Modern History*, xlvii (1975), 280–316; and Binion, *Hitler among the Germans* (New York, 1977); also Robert G. L. Waite, *The Psychopathic God: Adolf Hitler* (New York, 1977); Otto Pflanze, "Toward a Psychoanalytic Interpretation of Bismarck," *American Historical Review*, lxxvii (1972), 419–444.

activity impinging on foreign-policy decisions than in the application of new techniques. The creative historian of international relations was casting a wide net: he was writing about the structure of bureaucracies, the constraints of domestic and international economic systems, the influences of private interests, of domestic politics, and of larger cultural predispositions—as, in fact, the good historian has always really had to do.

II

Granted that there were no "turnkey" methodologies to be applied, it is still instructive to review what inspiration the traditionally related field of international relations (taught in the United States within departments of political science and not of history) might have provided. Work there centered both on the nature of the international system as a whole and on the processes of decision making within individual states. In the 1960s so-called transnationalism had become one influential model for analysis of international relations. Transnationalism stressed the growing importance of such "functional" linkages as economic intercourse, technology transfers, and the general fabric of "communications." The agents of functionalism were individuals, businesses, or other private groups more than states, and the model in general fitted in with an optimistic and benign pluralism that suffused American social science. It had little influence on historians of international relations, who were generally separated by the compartmentalization of academic life and who remained, in any case, preeminently concerned with the interaction between states. In fact, by the end of the 1970s political scientists were themselves tending to abandon the transnational approach and to stress again relationships of power and hegemony.[4]

Historians found more to borrow in the major analytical approach to decision making, that of "bureaucratic politics." Refining earlier theories of administrative behavior, this interpretive guideline

4. See Joseph S. Nye and Robert O. Keohane, eds., *Transnational Relations and World Politics* (Cambridge, Mass., 1972), among other works. For an emphasis on communications: Karl Deutsch, *The Analysis of International Relations* (Englewood Cliffs, N.J., 1969); and for renewed stress on rivalries between states, see the essays in Peter J. Katzenstein, ed., *Between Power and Plenty: Foreign Economic Policies of Advanced Industrial States* (Madison, Wis., 1978). For an application of the transnationalist emphasis on communications and international linkages to American expansion, see James A. Field, Jr., "American Imperialism: The 'Worst Chapter' in Almost Any Book," *American Historical Review*, LXXXIII (1978), 644–668; also Milton Plesur, *America's Outward Thrust: Approaches to Foreign Affairs, 1865–1890* (DeKalb, Ill., 1971).

suggested that foreign policy emerged less from a purposeful calcula-
tion of national interests than from the pulling and hauling of governmental agencies with their own built-in procedures, or from the
jockeying of individuals, speaking for agencies and seeking to maintain their domestic influence. Adoption of this analytical mode encouraged historians to stress the diverse pressures inside regimes and
at the subcabinet level, to emphasize the unintended consequences of
incremental decisions and the complexity of outcomes.[5] Samuel
Williamson, Jr.'s fine account of Britain's growing military commitment to France before 1914 and Roger Dingman's exploration of
military and civilian contributions to the naval limitations treaty of
1922 both drew on this approach.[6] Still, the major service of bureaucratic politics as an approach consisted more of suggesting new subjects
for historical scrutiny than of supplying a more valid total explanation
of policy. While it helped to reconstruct individual outcomes,
bureaucratic politics was less useful in explaining long-term definitions of interest and national orientation.

Historians, in fact, could just graft the approach onto their own
continuing investigations into the organization of foreign policy. Zara
Steiner, an American transplanted to Cambridge University, had examined the British Foreign Office; Lamar Cecil published a careful
analysis of the imperial German diplomatic corps; Paul Lauren compared French and German organizational responses; Waldo Heinrichs followed Frederick Ilchman in summarizing the professionalization of the State Department.[7] In these and related studies, historians

5. For the early work on organization, see Herbert A. Simon, *Administrative Behavior: A Study of Decision-Making Processes in Administrative Organization* (New York,
1947), and for the application to foreign policy, Richard C. Snyder, H. W. Bruck, and
Burton M. Sapin, eds., *Decision Making as an Approach to the Study of International Politics*
(Princeton, 1954); the now-classic statement of "bureaucratic politics" methodology is
Graham T. Allison, *Essence of Decision: Explaining the Cuban Missile Crisis* (Boston, 1971);
see also Morton H. Halperin, *Bureaucratic Politics and Foreign Policy* (Washington, 1974);
and for another application, Ernest R. May, "The 'Bureaucratic-Politics' Approach:
U.S.-Argentine Relations, 1942-47," coupled with the useful critique of the method by
Guillermo O'Donnell, "Commentary on May," both in Julio Cotler and Richard R.
Fagen, eds., *Latin American and the United States: The Changing Political Realities* (Stan-
ford, Calif., 1974), 129-175. Another critique appears in Stephen D. Krasner, "Are
Bureaucracies Important?" *Foreign Policy*, no. 7 (1972), 159-179.

6. Samuel R. Williamson, Jr., *The Politics of Grand Strategy: Britain and France Prepare
for War, 1904-1914* (Cambridge, Mass., 1969); Roger Dingman, *Power in the Pacific: The
Origins of Naval Arms Limitation, 1914-1922* (Chicago, 1976).

7. Zara S. Steiner, *The Foreign Office and Foreign Policy, 1898-1914* (Cambridge,
England, 1969); Lamar Cecil, *The German Diplomatic Service, 1871-1914* (Princeton,
1976); Paul Gordon Lauren, *Diplomats and Bureaucrats: The First Institutional Responses to
Twentieth-Century Diplomacy in France and Germany* (Stanford, Calif., 1976); Waldo H.
Heinrichs, Jr., "Bureaucracy and Professionalism in the Development of American

emphasized the painful transition from amateurism and the clinging influences of upper-class prejudice. Indeed, for Martin Weil's scathing if somewhat restricted history of the old hands at the State Department, anti-Semitism and clubby parochialism were chief concerns.[8] Richard Challener provided what amounted to a bureaucratic politics approach when he concentrated on the military's pressure for acquisitive and activist American policies before World War I. He found, however, that this pressure remained of limited influence because of the rudimentary channels for civil-military coordination.[9]

Other emerging developments in the study of international relations informed few historical works produced by historians. "Operational codes" stressed the predispositions of statesmen; "cybernetic" models of decision making suggested the limited adaptability of large-scale organizations, the minimal repertory of responses, and the pressures for conformity; theories of "perception" and "misperception" pointed out that one country's actions could be badly misconstrued by another.[10] But these efforts at modeling probably served the historian of international relations less well than, say, anthropological constructs and economic history served social and economic historians. The latter disciplines offered nonhistorical approaches, which for that very reason could encourage the integration of new data and concepts into historical narrative. But too often model building in international politics remained mere generalization from historical episodes. Borrowing back the generalizations to explain further individual events would add little that the historian did not help to generate to begin with. Recycling was not really interdisciplinary systhesis.[11]

Career Diplomacy," in John Braeman et al., eds., *Twentieth-Century American Foreign Policy* (Columbus, O., 1971), to which can be added Richard Hume Werking, *The Master Architects: Building the United States Foreign Service, 1890–1913* (Lexington, Ky., 1977); Frederick Ilchman, *Professional Diplomacy in the United States, 1779–1939* (Chicago, 1961).

8. Martin Weil, *A Pretty Good Club: The Founding Fathers of the U.S. Foreign Service* (New York, 1978).

9. Richard D. Challener, *Admirals, Generals, and American Foreign Policy, 1898–1914* (Princeton, 1973).

10. See Alexander L. George, "The 'Operational Code': A Neglected Approach to the Study of Political Leaders and Decision Making," *International Studies Quarterly*, XIII (1969), 190–222, a concept derived from Nathan Leites, *A Study of Bolshevism* (Glencoe, Ill., 1953); John D. Steinbrunner, *The Cybernetic Theory of Decision* (Princeton, 1976); Robert Jervis, *Perception and Misperception in International Politics* (Princeton, 1976); Klaus Knorr, "Threat Perception," in Knorr, ed., *Historical Dimensions of National Security Problems* (Lawrence, Kan.), 1976, 78–119.

11. See Stanley Hoffmann, "An American Social Science: International Relations," in *Daedalus: Discoveries and Interpretations: Studies in Contemporary Scholarship*, I (Summer 1977), 41–60, for an emphasis on that discipline's use of history. It is revealing that whereas applied economic issues are increasingly central to much new historiography

Political scientists had more success in persuading historians that the "controlled case study" allowed their profession a useful role as a policy science.[12] At the least, Ernest May's *"Lessons" of the Past* pressed home the point that faulty historical analogies (e.g., "Munich") could produce distorted policies.[13] Policy makers had to work with some received version of the past: better that it was not an oversimplified one. Nonetheless, despite the hopeful terrain for collaboration between history and political science, the question remains whether the controlled case study can sufficiently simplify the web of cause and effect for policy guidance and simultaneously remain good history. Is history, in fine, an inductive science? The question is more than a philosophical one at the beginning of the 1980s, as schools and institutes of policy science seek to integrate history into their curricula, their research, and their recommendations.

III

The social sciences were not the only potential stimuli for progress in diplomatic history. In the area of social history, British and French historical research was transforming in its influence. But for American historians of international relations there was no catalytic book comparable, for example, to E. P. Thompson's *Making of the English Working Class*. The continuing debate on the roots of British imperialism associated with Ronald Robinson and John Gallagher, D. C. Platt, and David Fieldhouse did, it is true, involve American participants.[14] Part of the controversy concerned the degree to which economic penetration itself constituted imperialism or led to more for-

---

in international relations, pure economic theory (with the possible slight exception of game theory) has not had an impact on the field. Probably the relevant models are too rigorously deductive; but compare the fecund role played by theories of growth in economic history. It will be interesting to see whether the historiography of the 1980s will be able to draw upon topological "castastrophe theory" in any substantive way.

12. For examples see Alexander L. George and Richard Smoke, *Deterrence in American Foreign Policy: Theory and Practice* (New York, 1974); Richard Smoke, *War: Controlling Escalation* (Cambridge, Mass., 1977); Barry Blechman and Stephen S. Kaplan, *Force without War: United States Armed Forces as a Political Instrument* (Washington, D.C., 1978); Richard K. Betts, *Soldiers, Statesmen, and Cold War Crises* (Cambridge, Mass., 1977). Stanford University, The John F. Kennedy School of Government at Harvard University, and the Brookings Institution were major centers for this effort at applied historical analysis.

13. Ernest R. May, *"Lessons" of the Past: The Use and Misuse of History in American Foreign Policy* (New York, 1973).

14. John Gallagher and Ronald Robinson, "The Imperialism of Free Trade," *Economic History Review*, 2d ser., VI (1953), 1–15; Ronald Robinson and John Gallagher, with Alice Denny, *Africa and the Victorians: The Official Mind of Imperialism* (London,

mal domination. A further question was the degree to which Europeans had been sucked into formal dominion as a response to indigenous power vacuums or tribal rivalries. This latter view influenced the valuable collections on Britain, France, and Germany in Africa edited by Prosser Gifford and William Roger Louis, while Louis's critical book of readings on the Robinson and Gallagher debate traced the continuing arguments.[15] Richard Graham's studies of the British in Brazil and Edmund Burke's monograph on the French in Morocco likewise stressed the interaction between indigenous society and the Europeans.[16] Most recently Louis placed the recurrent issue of the economic component of imperialism in a major book that traced Franklin Roosevelt's constant pressure on his British allies to shed their imperial possessions.[17] The "imperialism of free trade," which had once allegedly motivated British expansion, now became an incentive for America to supplant the British imperial structure. But it was only one such motivation for Louis, whose large-scale study was alert to all the pressures afflicting London's empire: the clashes of great personalities, differing strategic concepts, and, not least, the aspirations of the colonial peoples themselves.

Other British historical work exerted less influence during the 1970s than had A. J. P. Taylor's revisionist account of the origins of World War II, which unleashed transatlantic debate. Christopher Thorne's major work on the Anglo-American alliance against Japan (a good companion piece to Louis), the continuing monographs on the 1930s, and the collective consolidation of research on Sir Edward Grey's diplomacy did not really open new agendas.[18] Namierite

---

1961); D. C. M. Platt, *Finance, Trade, and Politics in British Foreign Policy, 1815–1914* (Oxford, 1968); D. K. Fieldhouse, *Economics and Empire* (London, 1973); and continuing debate over case studies featured by the *Economic History Review*.

15. Prosser Gifford and William Roger Louis, eds., *Britain and Germany in Africa: Imperial Rivalry and Colonial Rule* (New Haven, 1967) and *France and Britain in Africa: Imperial Rivalry and Colonial Rule* (New Haven, 1971); William Roger Louis, ed., *Imperialism: The Robinson and Gallagher Controversy* (New York, 1976), with the editor's own substantial introduction, 2–51. See also Robin W. Winks, "On Decolonization and Informal Empire," *American Historical Review*, LXXXI (1976), 540–556, for some paradoxical transformations of the major themes.

16. Richard Graham, *Britain and the Onset of Modernization in Brazil, 1850–1914* (Cambridge, Eng., 1968); Edmund Burke, *Prelude to Protectorate in Morocco: Precolonial Protest and Resistance, 1860–1912* (Chicago, 1976).

17. William Roger Louis, *Imperialism at Bay: The United States and the Decolonization of the British Empire, 1941–1945* (New York, 1978).

18. Christopher Thorne, *Allies of a Kind: The United States, Britain, and the War against Japan, 1941–1945* (New York, 1978). What allowed and encouraged the publication of such impressive works as Thorne's and Louis's at the end of the 1970s was the opening of massive American and British archival material, including Foreign Office and British Cabinet papers up to thirty years before the present, and State Department files and

analysis applied to foreign policy—exemplified by Maurice Cowling's *Impact of Hitler,* which stressed the narrowness of the political elite, the primacy of domestic partisan interests over any broader concern for the national interest, and the alleged superiority of private diaries, letters, and the like to any public statements—aroused less response in the United States than Namierite analysis of domestic politics once had.[19] British historians led Americans in seriously exploring the role of intelligence, although the popular semischolarly books in this field enjoyed a real vogue among an American public seeking to define the proper role for its own shaken intelligence apparatus.[20]

Military history also remained a British forte; it took a British historian to apply analogies from America's Vietnamese conflict in a plausible way to an earlier era—to Phillip II's effort to crush the revolt of the Netherlands.[21] Nevertheless, Americans did publish some important contributions to the connection between war and foreign policy, or between war and social organization in general, from antiquity to the contemporary epoch. Edward Luttwack strikingly analyzed the political use—and, equally important, the thrifty husbanding—of armed forces in the Roman Empire. His book outlined the cycle of ascendancy and decline in strategic terms: from the flexible allocation of armies permitted by the client states of the first century of the Christian era to the enclosed, unified empire of the Antonines to the third-century ceding of the periphery for the sake of political control at the center. Examining more recent periods, other American scholars continued to focus on the compelling military theory and applications produced by the Germans. Peter Paret's study of Clausewitz appeared together with a splendid new edition of *On War.* Gordon Graig's learned summation of German history from Bis-

---

Chief of Staff papers as well as private and Presidential Library collections. For the varying access see the useful report by Anna K. Nelson, "Foreign Policy Records and Papers: A Case Study of the Preservation and Accessibility of one Group of Documents," SHAFR *Newsletter,* VIII, 2 (June 1977), 14–26; VIII, 3 (September 1977), 13–32; and VIII, 3 (December 1977), 2–16. See also F. H. Hinsley, ed., *British Foreign Policy under Sir Edward Grey* (Cambridge, Eng., 1977).

19. Maurice Cowling, *The Impact of Hitler: British Politics and British Policy, 1933–1940* (London, 1975).

20. F. H. Hinsley's first volume of the official history of British intelligence in World War II was about to appear as this essay was written. See also Michael R. D. Foot, *SOE in France* (London, 1966), and Christopher Andrew, "The British Secret Service and Anglo-Soviet Relations in the 1920's," pt. 1, *Historical Journal,* XX (1977), 673–706; also R. V. Jones, *Most Secret War: British Scientific Intelligence, 1939–1945* (London, 1978); and on the American side, R. Harris Smith, *OSS: The Secret History of America's First Central Intelligence Agency* (Berkeley, 1972).

21. Geoffrey Parker, *The Army of Flanders and the Spanish Road: The Logistics of Spanish Victory and Defeat in the Low Countries' Wars* (New York, 1972).

marck through Hitler had as one central theme the inability of German society to strike the proper balance between organizing a nation to compete in a world of rival states and attaining liberalism at home. Among students of recent war itself, John Lukacs wrote a provocative account of the early years of World War II, Thomas Havens provided an initial exploration of the less familiar home front in Japan, and Gordon Wright's concluding volume for the Langer series drew on almost all major European languages to provide a masterly if too brief systhesis of the military, political, and social history of that transforming conflict.[22]

British works of history continued to provide specimens of self-assured style, even if only very selective stimulus for debate and research. Other national historical traditions supplied no greater ferment. There was no diplomatic history equivalent of the *Annales* influence from France. The well-crafted, exhaustive works of René Girault, Raymond Poidevin, Jacques Bariéty, and others were indispensable for specialists in their respective areas; still, they were organized less around questions to be answered than around categories to be filled in, and the sources examined often remained traditional.[23] The Germans remained preoccupied with their own equivalent of the

22. Edward N. Luttwack, *The Grand Strategy of the Roman Empire* (Baltimore, 1976); Peter Paret, *Clausewitz and the State* (New York, 1976); Carl von Clausewitz, *On War*, ed. Michael Howard and Peter Paret, and trans. with introductory essays by Paret, Howard, and Bernard Brodie (Princeton, 1976); and a fine historical study showing that German military planning could be zany as well as Clausewitzian, Holger H. Herwig, *Politics of Frustration: The United States in German Naval Planning, 1889–1941* (Boston, 1976). On World War II, see John Lukacs, *The Last European War: September 1939/December 1941* (Garden City, N.Y., 1976); Thomas R. H. Havens, *Valley of Darkness: the Japanese People and World War Two* (New York, 1978); and Gordon Wright, *The Ordeal of Total War, 1939–1945* (New York, 1968). See also the synthesis by Russell F. Weigley, *The American Way of War: U.S. Military Strategy and Policy* (New York, 1973). On a contrasting theme, American scholars also studied peace movements and other antiwar efforts, including Peter Brock, *Pacifism in the United States: From the Colonial Era to the First World War* (Princeton, 1972), emphasizing religious strands; Charles Chatfield, *For Peace and Justice: Pacifism in America, 1914–41* (Knoxville, 1971); C. Roland Marchand, *The American Peace Movement and Social Reform, 1898–1918* (Princeton, 1972); Robert L. Beisner, *Twelve against Empire: The Anti-Imperialists, 1898–1900* (New York, 1968); Lawrence S. Wittner, *Rebels against War: The American Peace Movement, 1941–1960* (New York, 1969); Warren F. Kuehl, *Seeking World Order: The United States and International Organization to 1920* (Nashville, 1969); Calvin DeArmond Davis, *The United States and the Second Hague Peace Conference: American Diplomacy and International Organization, 1899–1914* (Durham, N.C., 1976); and Roger Chickering, *Imperial Germany and a World without War: The Peace Movement and German Society, 1892–1914* (Princeton, 1975).

23. René Girault, *Emprunts russes et investissements français en Russie, 1887–1914* (Paris, 1973); Raymond Poidevin, *Les relations économiques et financières entre la France et l'Allemagne de 1898 à 1914* (Paris, 1969); Jacques Bariéty, *Les relations franco-allemandes après la première guerre mondiale* (Paris, 1977). The promising new journal *Rélations Internationales* devoted issues 10 and 11 (1977) to the United States and Europe.

revisionism debate, centered around the work of Fritz Fischer and his students on German expansionism from 1890 to 1918, or, relatedly, on the role of domestic elites in pressing for *Weltpolitik* to resist democratization at home. The theme had been originally treated by Eckart Kehr in 1930, had marked Hans Gatzke's often overlooked American contribution of 1950, and was revived with verve by Hans-Ulrich Wehler in the 1960s. Here there were continuing German-American links: Kehr had had an impact on Charles Beard, Beard on William Appleman Williams, and Wehler in turn acknowledged a large debt to Williams as well as reintroducing Kehr to Germany.[24] Yet despite important German work on the Second Empire and Third Reich, and notable contributions as well to the history of American foreign policy, no major thematic influence emerged from the Federal Republic. Indeed, there, too, the history of international relations had fallen partially under the shadow of social history—not, however, without instructive if excessively polemical debate.[25]

Scholarly communication with other countries remained limited. Richard Webster contributed to the history of Italian imperialism, and Benjamin Brown was a prime mover in having the Italians publish the papers of their conservative statesman Sidney Sonnino, while younger scholars were joining Italians in studying the Mediterranean country's dependency on the British and Americans after 1943.[26] Soviet and East European treatments of diplomatic history remained a matter for specialists, although the continuing publication of diplomatic documents from the interwar period continued to be highly

24. For a summary of the Fischer debate see John A Moses, *The Politics of Illusion: The Fischer Controversy in German Historiography* (London, 1975). See also Hans W. Gatzke, *Germany's Drive to the West* (Drang nach Westen): *A Study of Germany's Western War Aims during the First World War* (Baltimore, 1950); also Hans-Ulrich Wehler's major work, *Bismarck und der Imperialismus* (Cologne, 1969). Eckart Kehr's study of 1930 was translated by Pauline R. and Eugene N. Anderson as *Battleship Building and Party Politics in Germany 1894–1901* (Chicago, 1975), and his essays, edited by Wehler in Germany in 1964, were translated by Greta Heinz and edited by Gordon Craig as *Economic Interest, Militarism, and Foreign Policy: Essays on German History* (Berkeley and Los Angeles, 1977). For the intellectual filiation, see Arthur Lloyd Skop, "The Primacy of Domestic Politics: Eckart Kehr and the Intellectual Development of Charles A. Beard," *History and Theory,* XIII (1974), 119–131.

25. For the recent methodological controversies, which indirectly contest the emphasis on domestic socioeconomic conflicts and ask for a return to classic diplomatic history, see Klaus Hildebrand, "Geschichte oder 'Gesellschaftsgeschichte'? Die Notwendigkeit einer politischen Geschichtsschreibung von internationalen Beziehungen," *Historische Zeitschrift,* no. 223 (1976), 328–357; and Hans-Ulrich Wehler's response, "Kritik und kritische Antikritik," *Historische Zeitschrift,* no. 225 (1977), 347–384.

26. Richard A. Webster, *Industrial Imperialism in Italy, 1908–1915* (Berkeley and Los Angeles, 1975); Sidney Sonnino, *Diario,* ed. Benjamin F. Brown (Bari, 1972) (vol. I of Sonnino, *Opera Omnia*).

welcome. Cooperation with Japanese scholars, especially on the background of the Pacific War and the origins of the Cold War, was advanced at several conferences.[27]

IV

A major source of renewal in any intellectual field is the legacy of earlier work. As Harold Bloom has suggested for poetry, the underlying impulse may be patricidal, and the honing of graduate students on earlier interpretations can yield diminishing returns. Nonetheless, most American historians writing on international relations were studying their own diplomatic history and pursuing earlier debates. The overarching issue remained the causes and the degree of American expansionism—a preoccupation that had become acute during the 1960s. In researching turn-of-the-century imperialism, interwar economic intervention, or the origins of the Cold War, American historians continued to be concerned with the legitimacy of the power that the United States had eagerly or reluctantly brought to bear. In contrast to the debates of the 1960s, however, those of the 1970s no longer counterposed harsh indictments against outraged protestations of idealism. The critics were generally more discriminating; the defenders of American policy conceded that the United States was a nation-state like others, concerned with its own (or its elites') prosperity and security. Post-Vietnam historiography had a more reserved tone.

The debates, however, prolonged the earlier confrontations. In 1959 William Appleman Williams had formulated the suggestive notion of "open-door imperialism," which, like Robinson and Gallagher's "imperialism of free trade," proposed that the most productive economic powers in an international system could enjoy the benefits of imperialism without formal annexation. Such a critique of neocolonialism was hardly new, and it was simultaneously emerging in Latin American *dependencia* theories, which sought to explain the persisting difficulties of regions economically subordinated to the Northern Hemisphere.[28] Walter LaFeber's and Thomas McCormick's studies elaborated the argument, while critics complained that the

27. See Dorothy Borg and Shumpei Okomoto, eds., *Pearl Harbor as History: Japanese-American Relations, 1931–1941* (New York, 1973); and Yonusuke Nagai and Akira Iriye, eds., *The Origins of the Cold War in Asia* (New York, 1977).
28. William Appleman Williams, *The Tragedy of American Diplomacy* (New York, 1959; rev. ed., 1962). Williams's *Roots of the Modern American Empire* (New York, 1969) stressed that commercial-minded farmers powerfully contributed to the expansionist impulse. For dependency theories see Charles Gibson's essay in this volume.

economic thesis downplayed the racialist and social Darwinist milieu of the late nineteenth century, the recrudescence of great-power rivalry, and, in general, the role of chance in the accumulation of an empire.[29] How did one successfully invoke such long-term trends to account for the almost serendipitous annexationism in the wake of 1898? On the other hand, the skeptics often made their case by reducing imperialism to military action and annexation. They declined to interpret formal acquisitions as part of a larger advance of protective tariffs and arms races, and much less as a response to disturbing social conflict at home. Thus while the formal argument continued over the causes of imperialism, the covert issue often remained what exactly should be construed as imperialism.[30]

The nature of the connection between social system and foreign policy also motivated continuing research on the period of World War I and its aftermath. One major starting point was the work of Arno J. Mayer. Following the debates in Washington, London, Paris, Berlin, and later Rome, Mayer traced the international settlement that emerged from a clash among a nationalist Right, a reform-minded but anti-Bolshevik center, and the collectivist Left. Mayer's first book had explained the success that Wilson's "new diplomacy" attained in 1918, but in his large and detailed sequel, Mayer demonstrated how the president's policies lost their reformist impetus as Allied peacemakers reacted to social upheaval in 1919. N. Gordon Levin depicted a Wilson similar to Mayer's: an evangelical spokesman for a liberal capitalist international order. The earlier question of why Wilson had entered the war yielded to the issue of what he sought from the peace to follow.[31]

29. Walter LaFeber, *The New Empire: An Interpretation of American Expansion, 1860–1898* (Ithaca, N.Y., 1963); Thomas J. McCormick, *China Market: America's Quest for Informal Empire, 1893–1901* (Chicago, 1967).

30. See Field, "American Imperialism"; also Robert L. Beisner, *From the Old Diplomacy to the New, 1865–1900* (New York, 1975), for critiques. Marilyn B. Young described how individual initiatives were replaced by a forward government policy in which means and ends often meshed poorly; see her *Rhetoric of Empire: American China Policy, 1895–1901* (Cambridge, Mass., 1968). Ernest R. May, "American Imperialism: A Reinterpretation," *Perspectives in American History*, 1 (1967), 123–283, addressed the issue of how imperialism could find a new, activist constituency by 1898 more than any underlying pressures; May's earlier *Imperial Democracy: The Emergence of America as a Great Power* (New York, 1961) and Bradford Perkins, *The Great Rapprochement: England and the United States, 1895–1914* (New York, 1968); James A. Field, Jr., *America and the Mediterranean World, 1776–1882* (Princeton, 1969); Warren I. Cohen, *America's Response to China: An Interpretative History of Sino–American Relations* (New York, 1971), all in different ways tried to conceptualize the problem of American expansion within the larger framework of international relations.

31. Arno J. Mayer, *Political Origins of the New Diplomacy, 1917–1918* (New Haven,

The objectives suggested by Mayer and Levin struck historians as more fundamental than just the goals of 1918–19. They allegedly revealed the continuing thrust of U.S. policy throughout the twentieth century. Given the interpretive appeal of the primacy of domestic politics, American scholars only slowly began to explore more "old-fashioned" problems of diplomacy.[32] Carl Parrini's concern with the search for capitalist stability marked his investigations of foreign economic policy during and after World War I.[23] Michael Hogan and Burton Kaufman stressed the cooperation of government and business leaders in advancing American interests abroad, much as interpreters of the Hoover era at home were pointing out the interpenetration of private and public sectors.[34] The new monographs on post-war relations with Europe likewise tended to stress the economic dimension; and indeed the financiers' active role that these studies disclosed belied any simple notion of 1920s isolationism. At the same time, however, this research had to take multiple objectives and causal factors into account: the search for political and financial stabilization, ties with the wartime Allies, congressional resistance to active intervention, rivalries in the banking community, and so on. Keith Nelson regretted the limits of American intervention on behalf of financial reconstruction. Although he was preeminently concerned with French policy, Stephen Schuker found the role of American bankers largely sensible and benevolent in trying to settle the agonizing debt and reparations questions of the 1920s. Melvyn Leffler's large-scale investigation of the American interaction with France from the First

---

1959) and *Politics and Diplomacy of Peacemaking: Containment and Counterrevolution at Versailles, 1918–1919* (New York, 1967); N. Gordon Levin, Jr., *Woodrow Wilson and World Politics: America's Response to War and Revolution* (New York, 1968). See also Lloyd E. Ambrosius, "The Orthodoxy of Revisionism: Woodrow Wilson and the New Left," *Diplomatic History*, 1 (1977), 199–214.

32. For a useful "traditional" study of Anglo-American differences, see W. B. Fowler, *British–American Relations, 1917–1918: The Role of Sir William Wiseman* (Princeton, 1969).

33. Carl Parrini, *Heir to Empire: United States Economic Diplomacy, 1916–1923* (Pittsburgh, 1969).

34. Michael J. Hogan. *Informal Entente: The Private Structure of Cooperation in Anglo–American Economic Diplomacy, 1918–1928* (Colombia Mo., 1977); Burton J. Kaufman, *Efficiency and Expansion: Foreign Trade Organization in the Wilson Administration, 1913–1921* (Westport, Conn. 1974). Joan Hoff Wilson, *American Business and Foreign Policy, 1920–1933* (Lexington, Ky., 1971), suggested, however, that the relationship between business and government and within the business community was far less cohesive. And Joseph Tulchin's *Aftermath of War: World War I and United States Policy toward Latin America* (New York, 1971) argued that the State Department backed business interests only to achieve a set of strategic objectives bequeathed by the war, whereas Dana Munro seemed unable to discern any economic structure to American relationships in *The United States and the Caribbean Republics, 1921–1933* (Princeton, 1974).

World War to the depression offered a thorough and well-modulated assessment of intentions and results. Any historian assessing the American role abroad gained useful help in the 1970s by Mira Wilkins's large-scale history of United States multinationals.[35]

Nor did all historians, of course, choose to accent the economic dimension of foreign policy, especially when they turned to the 1930s. While Lloyd Gardner's pioneering work had focused on the economic dimensions of Franklin Roosevelt's foreign policy, the older issues of isolationism and intervention still prompted inquiries.[36] Examining the reaction to Japanese expansion, Dorothy Borg had been struck by the passivity of State Department and presidential responses. Arnold Offner criticized Roosevelt even more harshly, not as a covert economic expansionist but as a hesitant and belated opponent of Nazism. Dismayed historians found that American policy in countering the Holocaust and in admitting Jewish refugees was tragically and needlessly restrictive.[37] The upshot was that while "friendly" historians still credited Roosevelt's achievement in moving a deeply divided and distrustful country to aid Britain and Russia, fight a global war, and remain willing to enter a permanent international organization, they also had to come to terms with his devious political tactics, his sometimes vacuous, sometimes imperial objectives. Robert Dallek's major synthetic narrative of Roosevelt's foreign policy succeeded in holding the achievements and the flaws in balance as he conceded deviousness but emphasized the domestic constraints imposed by the Depression and isolationist sentiment. Dallek also insisted that Roosevelt's postwar objectives, including a U.N. that would encourage

35. See Keith L. Nelson, *Victors Divided: America and the Allies in Germany, 1918–1923* (Berkeley and Los Angeles, 1975); Stephen A. Schuker, *The End of French Predominance in Europe: The Financial Crisis of 1924 and the Adoption of the Dawes Plan* (Chapel Hill, N.C., 1976); Melvyn P. Leffler, *The Elusive Quest: America's Pursuit of European Stability and French Security* (Chapel Hill, N.C., 1979); Mira Wilkins, *The Maturing of Multinational Enterprise: American Business Abroad from 1914 to 1970* (Cambridge, Mass., 1974).

36. Lloyd C. Gardner, *Economic Aspects of New Deal Diplomacy* (Madison, Wis., 1964), could be supplemented by the more specialized recent study of Frederick C. Adams, *Economic Diplomacy: The Export-Import Bank and American Foreign Policy, 1934–1939* (Columbia, Mo., 1976).

37. Dorothy Borg, *The United States and the Far Eastern Crisis of 1933–1938* (Cambridge, Mass., 1964); Arnold A. Offner, *American Appeasement: United States Foreign Policy and Germany, 1933–1938* (Cambridge, Mass., 1969). David Wyman, *Paper Walls: America and the Refugee Crisis, 1938–1941* (Amherst, Mass., 1968); Henry L. Feingold, *Politics of Rescue: The Roosevelt Administration and the Holocaust, 1938–1945* (New Brunswick, N.J., 1970); Arthur D. Morse, *While Six Million Died* (New York, 1968); and Saul S. Friedman, *No Haven for the Oppressed: United States Policy toward Jewish Refugees, 1938–1945* (Detroit, 1973), told a bleak story that raised poignant echoes during the anguish of the boat people in 1978–79.

Americans to continue a world role, and a strong China, were less utopian than critics charged.[38]

The controversy over the Cold War remained probably the major single concern among American historians investigating their country's international role. To some degree the fierceness of the revisionist debate slackened. The harsh judgments of Gar Alperowitz and Gabriel Kolko that the United States bore the burden of responsibility—either because of Truman's peppery aggressiveness or the inherent expansionist requirements of American capitalism—no longer had shock value.[39] Despite its problematic use of documentation, Kolko's first volume, especially, remained the most consistent, critical Left analysis of the United States' search for hegemony. His theses might be elaborated, modified, or passionately rebutted, but they could not be ignored. The 1970s produced some counterstatements to the revisionist interpretations and many efforts at reconciling their critiques with less damaging reconstructions of policy. John Lewis Gaddis's book defended Truman's policy in the context of public opinion, although the often derivative nature of public opinion on issues of foreign policy tended to be slighted. Alonzo Hamby likewise described Truman's foreign policy as a sort of inevitable middle-of-the-road response to polarized American ideological pressures.[40] More suggestively, Thomas Paterson, Lynn Davis, and Daniel Yergin explored the premises of American diplomacy that led policy makers to contest Soviet influence in Eastern Europe and thereby to exacerbate conflict.[41] Yergin sought to temper his basically revisionist

38. Robert Dallek, *Franklin D. Roosevelt and American Foreign Policy, 1932–1945* (New York, 1979). Joseph P. Lash, *Roosevelt and Churchill, 1939–1941: The Partnership That Saved the West* (New York, 1976), continued an older, more heroic conception that seemed increasingly difficult to sustain.

39. Gar Alperovitz, *Atomic Diplomacy: Hiroshima and Potsdam* (New York, 1965); Gabriel Kolko, *The Politics of War: The World and United States Foreign Policy, 1943–1945* (New York, 1968); and Joyce and Gabriel Kolko, *The Limits of Power: The World and United States Foreign Policy, 1945–1954* (New York, 1972).

40. John Lewis Gaddis, *The United States and the Origins of the Cold War* (New York, 1972); Alonzo L. Hamby, *Beyond the New Deal: Harry S. Truman and American Liberalism* (New York, 1973). For Truman there was also Robert J. Donovan, *Conflict and Crisis: The Presidency of Harry S. Truman, 1945–1948* (New York, 1977); and for a useful study of the limited formative role of public opinion and the Cold War the most notable work was Ralph B. Levering, *American Opinion and the Russian Alliance, 1939–1945* (Chapel Hill, N.C., 1976). For critical biographical approaches to other American leaders during the Cold War see Gaddis Smith, *Dean Acheson,* vol. XVI of *The American Secretaries of State and their Diplomacy,* ed. Robert H. Ferrell (New York, 1972)—a series that still remained an important starting point for specialized researches; also Lloyd C. Gardner, *Architects of Illusion* (Chicago, 1972), and Townsend Hoopes, *The Devil and John Foster Dulles* (Boston, 1973).

41. Thomas G. Paterson, *Soviet–American Confrontation: Postwar Reconstruction and the*

critique with evocations of Stalin's domestic repression, but he denied that Stalin's harshness at home made him expansionist abroad. Yergin's identification of the so-called Riga Axioms of State Department officials nurtured in the interwar antibolshevism of that Baltic listening post, and George Kennan's own efforts to explain what he had really meant by "containment," spurred continuing debate over what the postulates of American policy had been.[42]

Yergin still focused on the interactions of individual policy makers, and, except for the role of the aircraft industry, largely omitted the organizational influence of government agencies and private constituencies. Despite the wide-ranging exploitation of manuscript sources, *Shattered Peace* conveyed some of the journalistic feel of 1970s history, with its frequent search for some underlying "story." All of the works cited here lacked the aura of solid, magisterial control that had marked Herbert Feis's work and George Kennan's history.[43] Perhaps the intervening political turmoil, the masses of new papers to assimilate, or the dissertation origins of the newer books precluded the stylistic assurance conveyed by the earlier works. Perhaps, too, it was no accident that the earlier books emanated not from academic historians but from reflective and older public servants. Granted, style could and did serve the cause of apologia; but that very split between high historical style on one side and somewhat brittle, critical narrative on the other testified to the dislocation that the 1960s and early '70s had bequeathed.

Focus on the infrastructure of foreign policy was left to specialized studies.[44] In the case of the second generation of research on use of

*Origins of the Cold War* (Baltimore, 1973); Lynn Etheridge Davis, *The Cold War Begins: Soviet-American Conflict over Eastern Europe* (Princeton, 1974); Daniel Yergin, *Shattered Peace: The Origins of the Cold War and the National Security State* (Boston, 1977).

42. For the containment debate see John Lewis Gaddis, "Containment: A Reassessment," *Foreign Affairs*, LV (July 1977), 873–887; Edward Mark, "The Question of Containment: A Reply to John Lewis Gaddis," *Foreign Affairs*, LVIII (January 1978), 430–440; also Edward Mark, "Charles E. Bohlen and the Acceptable Limits of Soviet Hegemony in Eastern Europe: A Memorandum of 18 October 1945," *Diplomatic History*, III (1979), 201–213; Robert L. Messer, "Paths Not Taken: The United States Department of State and Alternatives to Containment, 1945–1946," *Diplomatic History*, I (1977), 297–320 and documentation, 389–399; Daniel F. Harrington, "Kennan, Bohlen, and the Riga Axioms," *Diplomatic History*, II (1978), 428–437.

43. Herbert Feis, *Roosevelt-Churchill-Stalin: The War They Waged and the Peace They Sought* (Princeton, 1957); George F. Kennan, *Soviet-American Relations, 1917–1920*, 2 vols. (Princeton, 1956–58). For a historical survey of the Cold War suitable for teaching, Walter LaFeber's *America, Russia, and the Cold War*, rev. ed. (New York, 1976), remained balanced and thoughtful. And the reader could still profitably consult William H. McNeill, *America, Britain, and Russia: Their Cooperation and Conflict, 1941–1946* (London, 1953).

44. See, for example, Scott Jackson, "Prologue to the Marshall Plan: The Origins of

the atomic bomb, Barton Bernstein remained sympathetic to Alperovitz's earlier indictment, but reconstructed policy more meticulously. Martin Sherwin's engaging book highlighted the contradictory pressure from the scientific community on the issues of resorting to the weapon and then sharing its secret.[45] In this area, as in others, the thrust of new scholarship was to fill out the historical picture of Cold War origins and to set in chiaroscuro the simpler and starker contrasts left by the historians who wrote in the 1960s.

New published memoirs and papers proved helpful in this steady work, but it was the massive opening of archival sources that was the real prerequisite. Researchers could consult State Department files in theory up through the date of the latest volumes of *Foreign Relations of the United States;* in practice, as of 1978, the "decimal series" comprising the country files ran through 1949 or 1950. The agency-oriented "lot files" were rapidly being opened, while historians were appealing to Executive Order 11652 (updated now with Executive Order 12652) or to "FOI" (the Freedom of Information Act) in order to have reviewed and declassified such sources as otherwise closed Joint Chief of Staff Papers. John Gimbel had drawn upon the massive Allied Military Government (Germany) archives for his studies; exploitation of the counterpart records for occupied Japan (SCAP) was just beginning, and the service secretaries' files were still being declassified.[46]

the American Commitment for a European Recovery Program," *Journal of American History*, LXV (1979), 1043–1068; the articles cited in note 42 above; and relating military planning to Cold War outcomes, Michael S. Sherry, *Preparing for the Next War: America Plans for Postwar Defense, 1941–1945* (New Haven, 1977).

45. Barton J. Bernstein, "The Quest for Security: American Foreign Policy and International Control of Atomic Energy, 1942–1946, " *Journal of American History*, LX (1974), 1003–1044; also Barton J. Bernstein, "Roosevelt, Truman, and the Atomic Bomb, 1941–1945: A Reinterpretation," *Political Science Quarterly*, XC (1975); 23–62; Martin J. Sherwin, *A World Destroyed: The Atomic Bomb and the Grand Alliance* (New York, 1975). More recently, we have an informed and revealing essay on the background of hydrogen-bomb development: David Alan Rosenberg, "American Atomic Strategy and the Hydrogen Bomb Decision," *Journal of American History*, LXVI (1979), 62–87.

46. John Gimbel, *The American Occupation of Germany: Politics and the Military, 1945–1949* (Stanford, Calif., 1968); also Gimbel, *The Origins of the Marshall Plan* (Stanford, Calif., 1976)—but see the alternative view in Jackson, "Prologue to the Marshall Plan." For a sample of work on Japan, see Howard Schonberger, "American Labor's Cold War in Japan," *Diplomatic History*, III (1979), 249–272. Among the published manuscript sources important for the period of the cold war were *The Papers of Dwight David Eisenhower*, vol. VI, *Occupation, 1945*, ed. Alfred D. Chandler and Louis Galambos, and vols. VII–IX, *The Chief of Staff*, ed. Louis Galambos (Baltimore, 1978); and Jean Edward Smith, ed., *The Papers of Lucius D. Clay: Germany, 1945–49*, 2 vols. (Bloomington, Ind., 1974). Forrest C. Pogue's authorized biography of George C. Marshall had not yet reached the period of diplomatic service with the completion of vol. III, *Organizer of Victory, 1943–1945* (New York, 1973). Valuable memoirs included

Marshall Plan (ECA) and subsequent files on European assistance were slowly becoming disengaged from the Agency for International Development (AID), which had inherited them. Even with continuing classification, the mass of documentation was overwhelming. Researchers' carts of archival boxes trundled busily at the National Archives, and the emerging results of doctoral research filled *Diplomatic History*, the new journal of the active Society for Historians of American Foreign Relations. SHAFR, moreover, maintained pressure to open files as rapidly as possible. Specifying papers for mandatory review and declassification was a cumbersome recourse for the historian who needed to survey massive serial holdings. Nevertheless, it still allowed the late 1970s to become a period of fruitful research into contemporary history. The momentum of the arms race was examined in Robert Divine's *Blowing on the Wind;* other authors could explore the role of science and technology in international politics—not with the authority of "official history," as in the fine volumes covering the Atomic Energy Commission, the Army in World War II, or most recently the Joint Chiefs of Staff, but with at least some of the outlines of intragovernmental debate relatively secure.[47]

The contrast emerged when historians sought to deal with the Soviet Union. Adam Ulam's reconstruction was ingenious, if maddeningly undocumented; Vojtech Mastny drew on all of the published East European material as well as Western documentation to write a valiant and plausible account of the internal logic of Soviet policy making from 1941 through 1945. Of course, no equivalent of American documentation was at hand. Mastny's defense that enough data existed to reconstruct Moscow's policy was doubtless partially correct. The notion that Soviet or other archives could ultimately resolve the deepest problems of historical responsibility remains a naive one. On the other hand, archival source material has always remained essential for analyzing the policy process within government agencies, and Mastny found it difficult to pin down the internal steps by which

---

Dean Acheson, *Present at the Creation: My Years in the State Department* (New York, 1970); W. Averell Harriman and Elie Abel, *Special Envoy to Churchill and Stalin, 1941–1946* (New York, 1975); and George F. Kennan, *Memoirs, 1925–1950* (Boston, 1967), and *Memoirs, 1950–1963* (Boston, 1972).

47. *The History of the Joint Chiefs of Staff: The Joint Chiefs of Staff and National Policy:* James F. Schnabel, vol. I, *1945–1947;* Kenneth W. Condit, vol. II, *1947–1949;* James F. Schnabel and Robert J. Watson, vol. III, pts. 1 and 2, *The Korean War* (Wilmington, 1979); Robert A. Divine, *Blowing on the Wind: The Nuclear Test Ban Debate, 1954–1960* (New York, 1978); and for insights into the Eisenhower period, see George B. Kistiakowsky, *A Scientist at the White House: The Private Diary of President Eisenhower's Special Assistant for Science and Technology,* Introduction by Charles S. Maier (Cambridge, Mass., 1976).

Charles S. Maier

Soviet policy evolved. Rather than fall back on a demonic Stalin, however, Mastny emphasized what he felt were the logical needs and historical traditions of a one-party repressive state. And in contrast to the revisionists, he argued, earlier and firmer Anglo-American resistance to Soviet control could have minimized the Cold War.[48] (Ironically, the revisionist-influenced view that Americans deepened the Cold War by unrealistically contesting Soviet objectives in an area they could not control, and the counterrevisionist argument that Washington could have prevented Communist takeovers by firmer resistance, together implied that the in-between course Washington policy makers chose proved the most fruitless of all!)

For the Kennedy, Johnson, and Nixon administrations, historical coverage became primarily a matter of drawing on public sources, interviews, and private collections of papers. Robert Slusser's careful reconstruction of the Berlin crisis of 1961 demonstrated how much could be learned by discriminating collation of the press and official releases.[49] For those wishing to investigate United States policy in East Asia, the Pentagon Papers proved a rich trove. Despite the limits of this compilation, drawn as it was from Defense Department holdings alone, it still represented an immensely revealing accumulation of five administrations' thinking about foreign policy and strategy. While the war had been under way, ravaging Indochina and polarizing universities at home, dissenting historians and other scholars had felt it an urgent task to prepare informed background surveys of U.S. involvement. In the years since the last American troops withdrew, historians have begun the retrospective scholarly effort of probing the origins of the American commitment. For the later initiatives of the 1970s—the abandonment of the dollar's gold backing in 1971, the resumption of relations with China, negotiations over arms control or the status of the Panama Canal, and so on—there was political and economic analysis and informed journalism, sometimes afflicted by the compulsion to make all events breathtaking, but often highly informative.[50]

48. Adam Ulam, *Expansion and Coexistence: The History of Soviet Foreign Policy, 1917–1967* (New York, 1968) and *The Rivals: Russia and America since World War II* (New York, 1971); Vojtech Mastny, *Russia's Road to the Cold War: Diplomacy, Warfare, and the Politics of Communism, 1941–1945* (New York, 1979); and for strategic issues see Thomas W. Wolfe, *Soviet Power and Europe, 1945–1970* (Baltimore, 1970), the product of a RAND researcher.

49. Robert M. Slusser, *The Berlin Crisis of 1961* (Baltimore, 1973).

50. *The Pentagon Papers: The Defense Department History of United States Decision-making on Vietnam*, 4 vols. (Boston, 1971—the "Senator Gravel edition"). For contemporary or near contemporary accounts, see The Committee of Concerned Asian Scholars, *The Indochina Story* (New York, 1970); Chester Cooper, *The Lost Crusade:*

374

V

The overwhelming mass of historical research on American foreign relations concerned the issues of the twentieth century. The debate over the Cold War, the opening of new sources, the fact that the United States emerged as a world power only at the end of the 1800s attracted most scholars to the recent period. Research and writing on the earlier eras thus remained sparse, a rather bleak contrast with the suggestive work on eighteenth- and nineteenth-century political and social history. David Pletcher published a spacious survey of the international setting in which the United States undertook its major continental expansion in the 1840s, drawing on the archives of Madrid, Paris, and London as well as those at home. Pletcher's President Polk emerged as a blustering and truculent leader whose acquisitions would probably have fallen to the United States piecemeal and without the risks of war—a conclusion that suggested, in line with the lessons of the 1970s, that the means and ends of American international objectives could become tragically disproportionate.[51]

The history of expansion raised the question of America's original settlers, whose history claimed special attention in the 1970s—not often from the potentially fruitful viewpoint of international politics! There were some intriguing exceptions. Francis Jennings's *Invasion of America*—a study of cultural, military, and diplomatic interaction—suggestively illustrated the potential for treating the clash of populations from a bicultural perspective. Richard White presented the

*America in Vietnam* (New York, 1970); Frances Fitzgerald, *Fire in the Lake: The Vietnamese and the Americans in Vietnam* (New York, 1972); David Halberstam, *The Best and the Brightest* (New York, 1972). The war prompted sinologist Franz Schurmann to undertake a major interpretative analysis of post-1945 foreign policy: *The Logic of World Power: An Inquiry into the Origins, Currents, and Contradictions of World Politics* (New York, 1974). Other continuing historical work includes Russell H. Fifield, *Americans in Southeast Asia: the Roots of Commitment* (New York, 1973); Donald F. Lach and Edmund S. Wehrle, *International Politics in East Asia since World War II* (New York, 1975); George C. Herring, "The Truman Administration and the Restoration of French Sovereignty in Indochina," *Diplomatic History*, 1 (1977), 97–117. Gary R. Hess, "Franklin Roosevelt and Indochina," *Journal of American History*, LIX (1972), 353–368; and Walter LaFeber, "Roosevelt, Churchill, and Indochina, 1942–1945," *American Historical Review*, LXXX (1975), 1277–1295; Leslie H. Gelb with Richard K. Betts, *The Irony of Vietnam: The System Worked* (Washington, D.C., 1979); William Shawcross, *Sideshow: Kissinger, Nixon, and the Destruction of Cambodia* (New York, 1979). Some of the more notable books addressing current foreign-policy questions as historical issues included John Newhouse, *Cold Dawn: The Story of SALT* (New York, 1973); Walter LaFeber, *The Panama Canal: The Crisis in Historical Perspective* (New York, 1978); William B. Quandt, *Decade of Decision: American Policy toward the Arab-Israeli Conflict, 1967–1976* (Berkeley and Los Angeles, 1977).

51. David M. Pletcher, *The Diplomacy of Annexation: Texas, Oregon, and the Mexican War* (Columbia, Mo., 1973).

Western Sioux not merely as victims but as a virtual khanate of the prairie, pursuing their own expansionist nomadism at the expense of weaker tribes. The picture that Richard Metcalf provided of Rhode Island settlers being pulled into Indian political rivalries really was a counterpart to the dynamics of expansion that Robinson and Gallagher suggested for the British in Africa. And in general the most exciting work on Indian–white interaction deserved to be read in conjunction with the history of other cultural borderlands, such as Father Robert Burns's work on medieval Spain.[52]

It remains disappointing, however, that American historians did not turn back with more vigor to the foreign policy of the early Republic. For Americans of the 1970s, who were themselves emerging from years of intense divisiveness, the half century after 1775 should have proved compelling as an era of ideological self-definition and bitter disagreement over foreign policy. Outside the framework of biography, however, relatively little was published. Perhaps the most interesting work was that of Ernest May, whose *Making of the Monroe Doctrine* introduced to the early period the analytical methods May had earlier applied to more recent diplomatic history. For May, careful testing of hypotheses made the 1823 Monroe Doctrine explicable primarily in terms of electoral politics. Since Secretary of State John Quincy Adams feared being tarred with the brush of appeasement of England in the upcoming presidential campaign, he persuaded Monroe to act independently in announcing that the Latin American republics were not to be subjugated. Investigation of domestic pressures has consistently marked May's work, from his study of German, British, and American policies during World War I to his analysis of the constituency behind imperialism to the most recent work.[53] But these pressures, for May, have not been those of the social or economic system as a whole; thus he diverges from Left historians who likewise stress the primacy of domestic politics. Rather, the formative influences remain the contingent and more fragmented exertions of

52. Francis Jennings, *The Invasion of America: Indians, Colonialism, and the Cant of Conquest* (Chapel Hill, N.C., 1975); also Alden T. Vaughan, *New England Frontier: Puritans and Indians, 1620–1675* (Boston, 1965); Richard White, "The Winning of the West: The Expansion of the Western Sioux in the Eighteenth and Nineteenth Centuries," *Journal of American History*, LXV (1978), 319–348; P. Richard Metcalf, "Who Should Rule at Home?: Native American Politics and Indian–White Relations," *Journal of American History*, LXI (1974), 651–665; Robert I. Burns, S. J., "Christian–Islamic Confrontation in the West: The Thirteenth-Century Dream of Conversion," *American Historical Review*, LXXVI (1971), 1386–1434; and see note 69 below.

53. Ernest R. May, *The Making of the Monroe Doctrine* (Cambridge, Mass., 1975) and *The World War and American Isolation* (Cambridge, Mass., 1959); and the works cited on imperialism and bureaucratic politics above.

specific professional groups or bureaucracies; and the explanation they help to provide does not respond to the general question "Why imperialism?' or "Why war?" but rather "Why this war or this initiative at this time?" The result is to answer testable questions, but at the cost of skirting some of the larger and imponderable ones.

Even the Bicentennial failed to inspire serious foreign-policy studies, perhaps because the leading historians of early America remained preoccupied with the political and ideological dimensions of the revolutionary transformation. Only scattered effort was devoted to analysis of the Atlantic system, in which the ragged American war became geopolitically and economically too costly for London. William Stinchcombe had followed the implementation of the French alliance, and Jonathan Dull also derived a rewarding study by rigorously placing America on the periphery of the Anglo–Franco–Spanish conflicts after 1763.[54] Dull's book presented the Revolution in the context of Vergennes's effort to prevent further erosion of France's position; and he provocatively argued that France finally aided the colonies not because Saratoga made their victory seem likely but because continuing weakness made assistance a necessity if the Americans were merely to survive. Beyond these studies, several historians reexamined the early national dilemmas in navigating between world rivals: Lawrence Kaplan surveyed the foreign policy of the period from 1763 to 1801; Richard B. Morris narrated the making of the Peace of Paris against an exciting canvas; and James Hutson contested Felix Gilbert's influential view of the diverse sources of the Founding Fathers' diplomacy in order to insist on their hard-bitten realism about the international order.[55]

54. William C. Stinchcombe, *The American Revolution and the French Alliance* (Syracuse, N.Y., 1969), stresses the dependency of the Americans and the transitory nature of the pact; Jonathan Dull, *The French Navy and American Independence: A Study of Arms and Diplomacy* (Princeton, 1975).

55. For the United States in the Ango–French conflict, see Frederick W. Marks, *Independence on Trial: Foreign Affairs and the Making of the Constitution* (Baton Rouge, 1973); Charles R. Ritcheson, *Aftermath of Revolution: British Policy toward the United States, 1783–1795* (Dallas, 1969), evaluating positively Jay's diplomacy; Albert H. Bowman, *The Struggle for Neutrality: Franco-American Diplomacy during the Federalist Era* (Knoxville, Tenn., 1974); and Alexander De Conde, *The Quasi-War: The Politics and Diplomacy of the Undeclared War with France* (New York, 1966). On other issues: Richard B. Morris, *The Peacemakers: The Great Powers and American Independence* (New York, 1965); Paul A. Varg. *Foreign Policies of the Founding Fathers* (East Lansing, Mich., 1963); Lawrence Kaplan, *Colonies into Nation: American Diplomacy, 1763–1801* (New York, 1972); James H. Hutson, "Intellectual Foundations of Early American Diplomacy," *Diplomatic History*, 1 (1977), 1–19; and Felix Gilbert, *To the Farewell Address: Ideas of Early American Foreign Policy* (Princeton, 1961).

VI

The assignment for this essay includes assessment not only of American diplomatic history but the history by Americans of other societies' foreign relations. In theory a common concern with the international system should have linked the two enteprises, but revealingly this was often not the case. American diplomatic history often remained conceptually a subfield of United States history. While in the 1970s scholars from abroad researched at the National Archives or the presidential libraries and contributed significant monographs, by and large the product remained home-grown. In contrast, Americans concerned with international relations abroad often remained in closer touch with scholars from the countries they studied than they did with their colleagues in U.S. diplomatic history.

Both groups benefited significantly from the opening of new documentation. For the United States the newly accessible archives allowed breakthroughs in the history of the 1940s; in the case of Europe, it was interwar history that benefited. Whereas the generation of William Langer, Raymond Sontag, and, somewhat earlier, Sidney Fay had worked largely from edited national documentary collections, such as *Die grosse Politik*, American researchers now could consult the archives directly. Indeed, the massive German Foreign Ministry and cabinet documents of 1918–45 were largely available on microfilm and superbly catalogued by George O. Kent. The equivalently rich Public Record Office holdings were open to within thirty years of the current date and allowed for the rush of new works that reevaluated appeasement and British relations with Germany, France, and the United States. The opening of French Foreign Ministry holdings at the Qai d'Orsay allowed primary research on the 1920s and occasionally later periods. The records of other important civilian and military agencies were also becoming accessible, as were new personal manuscript collections. Where the bulk of raw documentation became overwhelming, objective and inclusive edited collections—Weimar cabinet protocals, the *Documents Diplomatiques Français*, the post-1945 Japanese Finance Ministry official history (for those with the language), and, of course, *Foreign Relations of the United States*—were increasingly indispensable for at least initial research.

The result of the new collections was that American scholars joined in effect an international team to explore recent diplomatic history. Norman Rich and Gerhard Weinberg published major studies of Nazi foreign policy. Rich tended to stress objectives, Weinberg events, but both tellingly documented the traditional view of Hitlerian expansion.[56] Other scholars looked at the budgetary, economic, and

378

strategic pressures that lay behind appeasement, including the threats to Britain in the Far East. Younger American scholars contributed to a far more subtle picture of Anglo-French policy making during the 1930s than the earlier dichotomy of appeasers and anti-Nazis had allowed.[57] At the end of the 1970s, Edward W. Bennett, a historian outside the university, published his fine detailed study of early German rearmament and the disarray it met in the West. Bennett's book, which followed an earlier trenchant monograph on Depression diplomacy, was far broader in theme and chronological span than his modest title indicated.[58] George Baer and John Coverdale augmented the research on Germany with monographs on Italian policy.[59]

American contributions to the history of the 1920s were equally fruitful, and they treated the problems of that decade on their own terms and not merely as an overture to the accelerated crises that followed. Arno Mayer's reexamination of Versailles from the viewpoint of domestic politics (discussed above) established the originality and the comprehensiveness of what American scholarship might offer. Jon Jacobson delved into the Briand-Austin-Chamberlain-Stresemann negotiations after Locarno primarily from the perspective afforded by the German documents, but clearly depicted how wearying were the issues, how limited the settlements. Stephen Schuker's study, cited above, concentrated on the financial vulnerability that compelled the French to renounce the Ruhr occupation and accept a settlement that undermined their aspirations to prevent German revival. The book was an important synthesis of international political and economic material with impressive exploitation of public and private archives. My own work concentrated on the parallel conservative recoveries in France, Germany, and Italy during the 1920s, but had to treat overarching international issues such as reparations and inflation as a formative influence on parallel

56. Norman Rich, *Hitler's War Aims*, 2 vols. (New York, 1973–74); Gerhard L. Weinberg, *The Foreign Policy of Hitler's Germany: Diplomatic Revolution in Europe, 1933–36* (Chicago, 1970).

57. Robert Paul Shay, *British Rearmament in the Thirties: Politics and Profits* (Princeton, 1977); Bradford Lee, *Britain and the Sino-Japanese War, 1937–1939* (Stanford, Calif., 1973). Robert Young's *In Command of France* (Cambridge, 1978) was an important Canadian reassessment.

58. Edward W. Bennett, *German Rearmament and the West, 1932–1933* (Princeton, 1979); also Bennett, *Germany and the Diplomacy of the Financial Crisis, 1931* (Cambridge, Mass., 1962). Useful in the related field of military influence was Gaines L. Post, Jr., *The Civil-Military Fabric of Weimar Foreign Policy* (Princeton, 1973).

59. George W. Baer, *The Coming of the Italian-Ethiopian War* (Cambridge, Mass., 1967) and *Test Case: Italy, Ethiopia, and the League of Nations* (Stanford, Calif., 1976); John F. Coverdale, *Italian Intervention in the Spanish Civil War* (Princeton, 1975).

domestic developments. International politics fed back to influence the domestic divisions that had themselves helped to structure alignments across frontiers.[60] In general, American researchers demonstrated as much and sometimes more and earlier initiative than their European colleagues in exploiting the nongovernmental archives of interest groups, bankers, political parties, and the like. Out of the cumulative research on both sides of the Atlantic, however, was emerging a new consensus on European international relations that was more sensitive to American intervention, more alert to constraints of public finance, less critical of the Versailles settlement and reparations (though this new view hardly penetrated outside the academy), and, in general, more sympathetic to French dilemas and more critical of post-1919 British policy (in contrast, say, to Richard Ullman, whose fine multivolume work had focused not on the German problem but on the Soviets after the Revolution).[61]

Because of the new archival sources and the continuing interest in the related issue of National Socialism, research on European international history centered on the interwar period. Study of wartime diplomacy and the Cold War in Europe was also beginning, although the Europeans themselves were proportionally more active in the latter area—probably because they sensed that their own societies had assumed their contemporary institutional structure largely in the flux of the early postwar years. On the other hand, scholarship in nineteenth-century European diplomacy largely languished. International relations entered, of course, into such works as Fritz Stern's *Gold and Iron,* but not as the central theme.[62] The major American work on the nineteenth-century international system was probably Paul Schroeder's brilliant and paradoxical analysis of British and Austrian policies during the Crimean War. Read in conjunction with earlier work on Metternich and the origins of World War I, Schroeder's book formed part of a sustained argument that England

60. Jon Jacobson, *Locarno Diplomacy: Germany and the West, 1925-1929* (Princeton, 1972); Schuker, *End of French Predominance in Europe:* Charles S. Maier, *Recasting Bourgeois Europe: Stabilization in France, Germany, and Italy in the Decade after World War I* (Princeton, 1975). See also Sally Marks, *The Illusion of Peace: International Relations in Europe, 1918-1933* (New York, 1976); Walter A. McDougall, *France's Rhineland Diplomacy, 1914-1924* (Princeton, 1978); and Kenneth Paul Jones, "Discord and Collaboration: Choosing an Agent General for Reparations," *Diplomatic History,* I (1977), 118-137. On German policy see also F. Gregory Campbell, *Confrontation in Central Europe: Weimar Germany and Czechoslovakia* (Chicago, 1975).

61. Richard H. Ullman, *Anglo-Soviet Relations, 1917-1921,* 3 vols. (Princeton, 1961-72).

62. Fritz Stern, *Gold and Iron: Bismarck, Bleichröder, and the Building of the German Empire* (New York, 1977).

under liberal leadership, more than Austria under conservative, had proved the principal long-term force undermining nineteenth-century stability. Schroeder, however, did not glorify Austrian conservatism ideologically, as Henry Kissinger's earlier treatment of Metternich had tended to do; for instead of finding a coherent Viennese concept of European equilibrium, Schroeder discerned only improvised but adaptive responses.[63]

American scholars remained active in investigating the international history of Latin America. The Mexican revolution served several historians as a focal point for the diplomacy of the great powers. While the outstanding contributions were by British historian Peter Calvert and the former German scholar Friedrich Katz (now, however, resident in the United States),[64] American researchers also reexamined Wilsonian diplomacy in Mexico. They stressed not the president's search for self-determination but ignorance of local conditions and his rigid moralism. In addition, Hans Schmidt published a sobering account of the American occupation of Haiti that highlighted the social and racial tension between white American marines and Black Haitians, while Dick Steward contributed an updated analysis of the Good Neighbor policy. Two able investigations of Brazil's international role under Vargas emphasized somewhat different findings, in part because the cut-off dates chosen were different. Following Brazil's economic diplomacy through the 1930s, Stanley Hilton suggested that the Brazilians managed to keep the German economic option open despite Washington's pressure. Focusing more on the war years, Frank McCann analyzed how Vargas used the alliance with Washington against Germany to counter British economic influence and Argentine rivalry. Both books implied that the potentially dependent power had exploited its diplomatic resources with skill and foresight.[65]

63. Paul W. Schroeder, *Austria, Great Britain, and the Crimean War: The Destruction of the European Concert* (Ithaca, N.Y., 1972). Cf. Schroeder, "World War I as Galloping Gertie: A Reply to Joachim Remak" *Journal of Modern History*, XLIV (1972), 319–345; and Schroeder, *Metternich's Diplomacy at Its Zenith, 1820–1823* (Austin, Tex., 1962). Cf. Henry A. Kissinger, *A World Restored* (Boston, 1957). For another recent example of scholarship in this area see Alan J. Reinerman, "Metternich, Alexander I, and the Russian Challenge in Italy, 1815–1820," *Journal of Modern History*, XLVI (1974), 262–276.

64. See Peter Calvert, *The Mexican Revolution, 1910–1914: The Diplomacy of Anglo-American Conflict* (Cambridge, Eng., 1968), sophisticated and critical of the United States and Friedrich Katz's massively documented account of German failure, *Deutschland, Diaz, and die mexicanische Revolution: Die deutsche Politik in Mexico, 1870–1920* (Berlin, 1964).

65. See Kenneth J. Grieb, *The United States and Huerta* (Lincoln, Neb., 1969), critical of Wilson's moralist intervention; also P. Edward Haley, *Revolution and Intervention: The*

The 1970s also brought the application of the multiarchival approach to the history of international relations in Asia, where linguistic obstacles had long been a deterrent. Akira Iriye's work on Pacific rivalry after the Washington Conference was pioneering in this demanding work of international historical reconstruction; and Stephen Pelz's monograph on the breakdown of naval limitation (along with Dingman's study of the Washington Conference cited earlier) also worked from the archives in Tokyo as well as those of Washington and London.[66] Michael Hunt likewise pursued a genuine bilateral approach in investigating how China and the United States, despite their common interest in keeping Russian and Japanese influence out of Manchuria, failed to cooperate, in large part because of the perpetuation of American stereotypes about the Chinese.[67] On the other hand, John Dower's forthcoming biography of the postwar Japanese prime minister, Yoshida Shigeru, emphasizes the common quest of Japanese and American elites for capitalist stability after 1945: an interpretive framework that illuminates much of the postwar recovery but should not be allowed to obscure the detailed texture of how different groups in a reemerging Japan (or similarly in postwas Europe) could play off the divergent approaches for stabilization advocated by U.S. authorities.

The prejudices of American diplomats so tellingly documented by Michael Hunt press home the importance of the theme that Iriye has recently stressed: the role of cultural systems in shaping international relations.[68] But further differentiation is still required; for the research area of cultural systems currently distinguishes two historical

---

*Diplomacy of Taft and Wilson with Mexico, 1910–1917* (Cambridge, Mass., 1970); Hans Schmidt, *The United States Occupation of Haiti, 1915–1934* (New Brunswick, N.J., 1971); Dick Steward, *Trade and Hemisphere: The Good Neighbor Policy and Reciprocal Trade* (Columbia, Mo., 1975); Stanley Hilton, *Brazil and the Great Powers, 1930–1939: The Politics of Trade Rivalry* (Austin, Tex., 1975); Frank D. McCann, Jr., *The Brazilian-American Alliance, 1937–1945* (Princeton, 1973). I am indebted to David M. Pletcher's review essay, "United States Relations with Latin America: Neighborliness and Exploitation," *American Historical Review*, LXXXII (1977), 39–59, for initial orientation in this literature.

66. Akira Iriye, *After Imperialism: The Search for a New Order in the Far East, 1921–1931* (Cambridge, Mass., 1965); Stephen E. Pelz, *Race to Pearl Harbor* (Cambridge, Mass., 1974).

67. Michael H. Hunt, *Frontier Defense and the Open Door: Manchuria in Chinese-American Relations, 1895–1911* (New Haven, 1973). See also, for related themes, John E. Schrecker, *Imperialism and Chinese Nationalism: Germany in Shantung* (Cambridge, Mass., 1971); Akira Iriye, *Pacific Estrangement: Japanese and American Expansion, 1897–1911* (Cambridge, Mass., 1972), Charles E. Neu, *An Uncertain Friendship: Theodore Roosevelt and Japan, 1906–1909* (Cambridge, Mass., 1967); and for a later period, Barbara W. Tuchman, *Stilwell and the American Experience in China, 1911–45* (New York, 1971).

68. See Akira Iriye, "Culture and Power: International Relations as Intercultural Relations," *Diplomatic History*, III (1979), 115–128; and for applied examples, Iriye, ed., *Mutual Images: Essays in American-Japanese Relations* (Cambridge, Mass., 1975); also the

themes. It encompasses the broad collisions of peoples that occur when the state framework is vague or fragmented or overarchingly imperial (e.g., the American frontier, Christian–Moorish border-lands, the Balkans, West Africa).[69] But as Iriye applied the idea, it suggests research on the national value systems of highly organized states. Moreover, he has used the term to include the economic framework of international relations as well as the structure of values; and it may prove more analytically fruitful to distinguish economic motivation from cultural predispositions in future historical analysis. The research objective is important but still in need of clarification.

Meanwhile, the centrality of cultural presuppositions has never really been absent from the work of John K. Fairbank and other historians of the Chinese "world order." Indeed, the recent initially released volume (Number x) of *The Cambridge History of China* stresses the world view of a Peking under assault from barbarian Westerners and domestic rebels. Joseph Fletcher's contributions, especially, reconstruct the priorities of Ch'ing foreign policy, oriented primarily not toward the Pacific but toward the maintenance of suzerainty in Central Asia. Fletcher's scholarship, which spans the empires and languages from the Pacific to the Indian Ocean and the Mediterranean, is perhaps the most "international" of all American contributions, although it still seems more concerned with charting the conquests, regimes, and migrations of people than with conceptual explanation of the historical transformations in Asia.[70]

VII

This survey began by claiming that despite notable individual contributions, the field of diplomatic history has flagged in recent years. There are some reasons to believe, however, that a renewed sense of collective purpose may be at hand. Increasingly scholars in many fields are rediscovering the autonomy of the international system and

earlier similar plea by John K. Fairbank, "Assignment for the '70's," *American Historical Review*, LXXXIV (1969), 861–879.

69. See note 52 above and, for examples, David Jacoby, "The Encounter of Two Societies: Western Conquerers and Byzantines in the Peloponnesus after the Fourth Crusade," *American Historical Review*, LXXVIII (1973), 873–906; Robert S. Smith, *Warfare and Diplomacy in Pre-Colonial West Africa* (London and New York, 1976), a British contributor; and Andrew C. Hess, *The Forgotten Frontier: A History of the Sixteenth-Century Ibero-African Frontier* (Chicago, 1978).

70. Joseph Fletcher, "Ch'ing Inner Asia c. 1800," "Sino-Russian Relations, 1800–1862," and "The Heyday of the Ch'ing Order in Mongolia, Sinkiang, and Tibet," all in John K. Fairbank, ed., *The Cambridge History of China*, vol. x, pt. 1 (Cambridge, Eng., 1978), 35–106, 318–350, 351–408. See also John K. Fairbank, ed., *The Chinese World Order: Traditional China's Foreign Relations* (Cambridge, Mass., 1968).

the persistence of conflict among states. Perhaps this perception results from the readjustment of American power and the slow dissolution of a frozen bipolar international system. It may also accompany the awareness that within national societies old social divisions and new constraints on economic growth resist institutional solutions. The decline of buoyant confidence may be hard on bold policies but may be good for the historiography of international relations. The chastened public mood has undercut the persuasiveness of theories that postulated conflict-free industrial societies. These predictions of the 1950s and 1960s had, in effect, resumed the optimistic sociologies of modernization outlined by Comte, Saint-Simon, and others, who believed that industrial society would eliminate the causes of international conflict. Today there seems greater receptivity to "Mediterranean" notions of cycles and conflicts, to a Thucydidean or Machiavellian feel for the balance of power.

One interesting harbinger of this renewed emphasis is the fact that theorists on the Left are themselves stressing international social and economic systems, such as the relationship between core and periphery. The idea is hardly new, but its revival and application to Europe has proven suggestive. Marxian synthesizers have stressed the historical roots of the international division of labor in the early modern era. Theorists of revolution and political development have increasingly emphasized the bureaucratic state as an autonomous force and not a passive "executive committee" for the ruling class.[71] Hence while Marxian inspiration in the 1950s and 1960s usually led the historian in the West to stress the primacy of internal politics and the role of domestic elites in manipulating foreign policy for their internal advantage, contemporary Marxism has stimulated renewed concern with the state and with international conflict. The more Marxian, in some respects, the more Rankean!

What is more, contemporary fiscal difficulties throughout the West—default or near bankruptcies on the part of municipalities, tax revolts, persistent inflation—press home the lesson that any state's international influence depends on the resources it can extract or the renunciation of private consumption it can enforce on its own citizens or on those of its allies. (Obviously this burden diminishes to the

---

71. See Immanuel Wallerstein, *The Modern World-System: Capitalist Agriculture and the Origins of the European World-Economy in the Sixteenth Century* (New York, 1976); Perry Anderson, *Lineages of the Absolutist State* (London, 1975); Theda Skocpol, *States and Social Revolutions* (New York, 1978). For non-Marxist work on the emergence of the state and state system, see the essays in Charles Tilly, ed., *The Formation of National States in Western Europe* (Princeton, 1975).

degree that continued growth allows for both public and private surpluses, but constant growth has been an exception throughout most of history.) Hence today's economic circumstances encourage interest in the contribution of the international rivalry of the early modern era to the rise of the bureaucratic state, or in the repercussions of international crisis and national consolidation in the 1850s and 1860s, or in the interlocking economic difficulties and nationalist rivalries of the 1920s and 1930s. Research on these periods of systemic crisis opens up fruitful cooperative possibilities between historians and practitioners of political economy (by which is meant the conflicts over scarce resources and the role of political power in structuring market relationships). Suggestive studies of the international economic system under London's leadership at the turn of the century, of interwar monetary arrangements, and of the Bretton Woods architecture of American economic hegemony illustrate these possibilities.[72]

As historians of international relations assimilate this approach into their own discipline, there is promise that they will overcome the once liberating but now constraining dichotomy between *Primat der Aussenpolitik* and *Primat der Innenpolitik*. The latter, often revisionist emphasis served well those historians who wished to stress the domestic roots of expansion and to overcome historical apologetics. It allowed wide categories of explanation to be brought to bear on policy formation. International history gained immeasurably by its thoughtful application. Nevertheless, its practitioners often slighted the fact that national leaders, after all, must seek to resolve what loom as real international dilemmas. They cannot separate domestic and foreign challenges since the approval earned by responding to one set of problems conditions the freedom of action to deal with the other. Doubtless the international system is influenced recursively by the domestic forces within its constituent societies: Metternich and Castlereagh constructed a tissue of relationship among rulers different from those improvised by statesmen after the full impact of urbanization and universal suffrage had been felt. Nonetheless, the realm of international relations assumes at least relative autonomy.

72. See Marcello De Cecco, *Money and Empire* (Oxford, 1976), the work of an Italian economist; Stephen V. O. Clarke, *Central Bank Cooperation, 1924-1931* (New York, 1967); Charles P. Kindleberger, *The World in Depression, 1929-1939* (Berkeley and Los Angeles, 1973); Benjamin M. Rowland, ed., *Balance of Power or Hegemony: The Interwar Monetary System* (New York, 1976); Alfred E. Eckes, *A Search for Solvency: Bretton Woods and the International Monetary System, 1941-1971* (Austin, Tex., 1975); Fred L. Block, *The Origins of International Economic Disorder: A Study of United States International Monetary Policy from World War II to the Present* (Berkeley and Los Angeles, 1977).

International hisory must, and currently does, give indications of probing the simultaneity of relationships.

There is a related gain to be made from reshifting focus somewhat away from decision making and policy formation pure and simple. Certainly the concentration on decision making was useful: it encouraged testable questions, and it encouraged the systematic canvassing of wider and wider influences on what ultimately happened. Ernest May, for example, summarized his effort as one "of placing oneself at a point in the past and asking: what kind of analysis would have produced the most accurate prediction of what was to occur?"[73] He cross-tested comparative scenarios to explain particular outcomes. Nonetheless, the historian must also keep in mind the system as system: that is, not as a metaphysical entity but as a series of interacting outcomes not readily deducible from a summing up of individual policies. This task involves continuing alertness to the repercussions of decision, to the unforeseen linkages among events, the structure as a whole. As Paul Schroeder has written:

> To put it simply, I do not believe that analyzing foreign policy in terms of the determinants of decisions is the most important or satisfactory way of understanding what happens in international relations and why. It is less important to know why statesmen took certain actions than to know what reactions and results those actions produced in the international arena, and why under the prevailing system they led to these results and not others, and how these actions affected the system itself.[74]

Schroeder has drawn the conclusion, which seems to me more confining than it should be, that diplomatic history should not be integrated into other broader history before it has been explored under its own logic. In part this is true: as Hobbes pointed out three centuries ago, the international system *is* unique, precisely in the absence of any common sovereign. It is that field of human activity where law is at best normative and participants ultimately have to invoke the threat of force or force itself. Historians as well as theorists have to confront this continued irreducible challenge of national rivalries. Indeed, the challenge is more than one of methodology alone: it involves the continued functioning of the discipline as such. An era of arms races, of rivalries over scarce natural resources, of the reemergence of a new multipolar balance of power, reveals anew that the Hobbesian postu-

73. May, *Making of the Monroe Doctrine*, 254.
74. Schroeder, *Austria, Great Britain, and the Crimean War*, xiv.

late persists. It is shortsighted for history faculties at such a juncture to downgrade the field or discourage its perpetuation.

On the other hand, to insist on the relevance of the history of international relations does not mean just to call for a return to following cables and negotiations. Rather, it seems to this reviewer of the discipline, at least, that research on the international system *as system* must mandate investigation of domestic and international pressures as part of one structure. An international system, as noted, is distinguished by the absence (or sometimes the contested legitimacy) of a common sovereign. It may comprise a set of statesmen or bureaucratic spokesmen who identify their objectives with the interests of the molecular states traditionally posited as the formal actors. But it also includes the classes, interests, and cultural and ethnic groups seeking an architecture across the frontiers of national authority to preserve their influence within them. Given these multiple attributes, the appropriate goal cannot simply be reduction to an earlier "classic" diplomatic history. Nor, on the other hand, can it be to subsume the history of international relations under some broader rubric; for the minimal Hobbesian criterion of the international system does justify a unique discipline. Rather that discipline itself must be responsive to useful explanatory approaches from other historical or social science fields—not in a faddish or spurious syncretic way, but with discrimination. In this respect, the history of international relations might profitably develop, as many have recognized, into "international history" that would analyze political structures, cultural systems, and economic arrangements within the persisting framework of a world of competing territories. Historians and analysts of international relations, no matter what their political preferences, now seem ready to accept the systemic intertwining of domestic and international influences and not to insist that one set of causes or another be given primacy. If this realization, which has been slowly nurtured throughout the 1970s, is indeed acted upon by scholars, then the decade to come should witness an exciting resumption of international history.

# PART THREE

## MODES OF GATHERING
## AND ASSESSING
## HISTORICAL MATERIALS

# 16

## Oral History in the United States

### Herbert T. Hoover

I N recent years it has become fashionable for directors of oral history centers to claim credit for the "growth industry" of academia. Their boast has been misleading in some ways. Financial support for the gathering and processing of interviews has been sparse; and without funds in sufficient quantity to sustain a variety of full-fledged, ongoing projects across the country, oral historians have improved scholarship in only select areas of historical interest. The movement has operated on the periphery of academia; and because it has not been close to the center of the community of publishing scholars, it has functioned without consistent standards and has had no major impact upon the general tenor of historiography. Nevertheless, the claim to remarkable growth has been justified in other ways. Total interview production has increased steadily since the introduction of electronic recorders at mid-century. Practitioners have refined the mechanics of gathering, processing, and preserving interviews. If they have not created a bona fide growth industry over the past thirty years, they have at least transformed a hit-and-miss technique into a semiprofessional practice and have offered the fruits of their labors for general use by historians.

The gathering of knowledge transmitted by word of mouth is of course among the oldest means of collecting historical information. It has been used by Europeans since Herodotus made his queries about the heroic deeds of participants in the Persian Wars during the fifth century B.C. It has been employed by Latin Americans since Bartolomé de Las Casas gathered hearsay evidence for his polemics against Spanish brutality to the Indians during the sixteenth century, and has been practiced by writers in the United States since English colonials began to chronicle the growth of settlement along the Atlantic seaboard in the seventeenth century.

American authors have been erratic in their use of oral research. Until the post–Civil War years they relied heavily on interviews without much concern about the reliability of their respondents. Then most of them became reluctant to use oral sources at all, because a new school of professional historians excluded interviewing from its "scientific" research scheme for fear that human memory would distort the record of the past preserved in documents. As long as advocates of Rankean objectivity dominated the profession, knowledge garnered among eyewitnesses was used as a prime source mainly by scholars in other disciplines researching historical subjects about which printed sources were scarce, such as American Indian ethnohistory and westering movements on the trans-Mississippi frontier.

Professional historians continued to look askance at oral research until the 1930s, when attacks upon scientific history eroded their biases somewhat, and accomplished authors in sister disciplines presented reasons for the increased use of interviews. After blending documentary and oral source materials into the life story of Sitting Bull, Stanley Vestal noted the most obvious advantage of interviews over other types of sources: "We are altogether too apt to allow more authority to the printed page than it deserves. In an interview one has many opportunities to test the honesty, capacity and knowledge of an informant. But when we read, we listen in the dark."[1] Following a frustrating search for personal information to include in his biography of Grover Cleveland, Allan Nevins called for efforts to fill gaps in historical knowledge through a "systematic attempt to obtain, from the lips and papers of living Americans who have led significant lives, a fuller record of their participation in political, economic and cultural life."[2]

Interest in the use of interviews continued to grow during the 1940s, for two reasons. One was the loss of written information due to the growth of transportation and communication systems. Instead of exchanging letters, public officials and corporation leaders could travel by automobile or airplane to meet face to face, or use the telephone to achieve speed and secrecy in communication. The other reason was reluctance among national leaders to keep complete records because of the increasing accessibility of public documents. "Fearing next decades's graduate students," high-ranking officials "became reluctant to put in writing the real reasons for some of their

1. *Sitting Bull: Champion of the Sioux* (Boston, 1932), 4.
2. *The Gateway to History* (Garden City, N.Y., 1956), 8.

actions," and those reasons could be recorded only by personal interviews.[3]

Two oral research centers began work almost simultaneously to prevent the permanent loss of vital historical information. The Forest History Society has claimed that "since its inception in 1947" its researchers have "been actively engaged in oral history interviewing." For several years the interviewers confined their efforts to investigations on the history of lumbering in the north-central states, and recorded the reminiscences of their respondents with pen and paper. By 1953, however, they had enlarged the design of their research to investigate the history of forest products industries across the United States and Canada, had acquired tape recorders to preserve the words of their respondents verbatim, and had established the first tape library created expressly to preserve the findings of oral research about the history of a major industrial undertaking.[4]

Allan Nevins founded the other center, at Columbia University, in 1948. Like the historians of forestry, he began cautiously; at first he restricted his efforts to biographical interviews with knowledgeable public leaders from his own area. A secretary, who accompanied him, scribbled notes and hurried home to type them up for revision by the respondents. But after a year or so Nevins broadened the scope of his work, too, and began to gather recollections and personal papers from people influential in various spheres as well as to launch special projects on the histories of institutions that had helped to shape the course of American history. He purchased electronic recorders to preserve reminiscences with greater accuracy. He installed transcribers to transform recorded interviews into typescripts for future use by scholars, raised funds to extend the life of his work among prominent leaders and institutions, and opened a library that has become the largest repository for transcribed interviews in the United States.[5]

Through the 1950s the movement grew slowly but significantly. In 1951 Owen Bombard initiated work on the life and industrial achievements of Henry Ford that would produce a collection of more than 400 interviews. During the years 1953–58 William Owens supervised the taping of reminiscences on the growth of the Texas oil industry from the time the Lucas Gusher blew at Spindletop in 1901

3. Arthur Schlesinger, Jr., "On the Writing of Contemporary History," *Atlantic Monthly*, CCXIX (March 1967), 71.

4. Barbara D. Holman, *Oral History Collection of the Forest History Society: An Annotated Guide* (Santa Cruz, Calif., 1976), iv.

5. Allan Nevins, "Oral History: How and Why It Was Born," *Wilson Library Bulletin*, XL (1966), 600–601.

through the tidelands crisis following World War II. Forrest Pogue initiated a tape series at the George C. Marshall Research Library to supplement documentary sources on the general's career. Nevins gathered interviews about the administration of Franklin D. Roosevelt. The University of California at Berkeley founded an office for oral research that since has become a model for others to emulate in the collection of interviews about regional history.[6]

As these several new archival projects took shape, academicians looked for ways to use oral research. Professors encouraged graduate students to experiment with interviews while preparing theses and dissertations. The program committee of the Southern History Association arranged the session "Living Subjects as Historical Sources" at the annual conference of the association in 1958 for the purpose of precipitating discussion about techniques of oral research. Venturesome scholars began to draw more heavily on oral sources for the preparation of their manuscripts. The most successful was T. Harry Williams, who later described his attitude as he did his work on Huey Long in the early 1960s: "I became increasingly convinced of the validity of oral history. Not only was it a necessary tool in compiling the history of the recent past, but it also provided an unusually intimate look into the past."[7]

The movement gained momentum during the early 1960s with the enlargement of research budgets on major university campuses. Archivists at Tulane University gathered tapes to supplement a collection of manuscripts on the history of jazz. Professors at Texas Tech University conducted interviews about the life of artist Peter Hurd, the history of the XIT Ranch, and other southwestern leaders and institutions. Historians at Cornell University investigated the history of agriculture and food processing in the state of New York, and later did oral research on labor history, industrial leaders, and institutions of national prominence. The director of the Wisconsin State Historical Society opened a center on the campus at Madison to gather and to preserve reminiscences about the history of the western Great Lakes region.[8]

6. Louis Starr, "Oral History," *Encyclopedia of Library and Information Science*, xx, 445-446; Chester V. Kielman, "The Texas Oil Oral History Project," *Wilson Library Bulletin*, xl (1966), 616-618; Forrest C. Pogue, "The George C. Marshall Oral History Project," *Wilson Library Bulletin*, xl (1966), 607-615.

7. *Huey Long* (New York, 1969), ix.

8. Gary L. Shumway, comp., *Oral History in the United States: A Directory* (New York, 1971), 49, 57, 69-87, 98; Richard B. Allen, "The New Orleans Jazz Archive in Tulane," *Wilson Library Bulletin*, xl (1966), 619-623; Gould P. Colman, "Oral History at Cornell," *Wilson Library Bulletin*, xl (1966), 624-628.

Meanwhile, work on modern presidencies became a project of special interest that continued through the 1970s. After Nevins completed his interviews on Franklin Roosevelt, others questioned respondents about Eleanor Roosevelt and several high-ranking officials on the New Deal staff, and these interviews were placed in the library at Hyde Park. Louis Starr, who succeeded Nevins as director of the Columbia center, gathered one collection on the administration of Dwight Eisenhower, and John Wickman, of the Eisenhower Memorial Library at Abilene, started another. John Fuchs began oral research on Harry Truman for the library at Independence. Arthur Schlesinger, Jr., initiated an interview series on John F. Kennedy's administration, at the request of the president's family following his assassination, and this work was carried on under the auspices of the Office of Presidential Libraries at the National Archives.

Late in the 1960s, Joe B. Frantz supervised a staff that initiated work for the University of Texas on the life and times of Lyndon B. Johnson, which has since been enlarged and refined by interviewers from the Johnson Memorial Library. An independent Hoover Presidential Library Association began to gather a tape collection for deposit at West Branch, Iowa. Before the Watergate scandal, interviewers from Whittier College and California State College at Fullerton did independent oral research on the early career of Richard M. Nixon. Daniel Reed, assistant archivist for the Office of Presidential Libraries, has recently made plans for the collection of interviews about the administrations of Gerald Ford and Jimmy Carter. Oral research on modern presidencies, begun by Nevins in the late 1950s and expanded by others in the early 1960s, has mushroomed into an extensive enterprise that to date has been the only major oral history program sponsored largely by federal agencies.[9]

9. Shumway, *Oral History,* 4, 60, 68; personal interview with Daniel J. Reed, Office of Presidential Libraries, National Archives, May 1, 1979. Considering the amount of information that is lost in phone conversations and personal conferences by public officials every day, oral history work by federal agencies has been disappointing. But there have been other scattered efforts. The Social Security Administration has collected interviews about pioneers in the social security movement. The Air Force Academy, the Naval Academy, and the Army Military Research Center at Carlisle Barracks have assembled for their respective branches small tape collections on modern military operations. The National Park Service has taped interviews to supplement documentary records of its various programs. In cooperation with government agencies, the Firestone Library at Princeton University has sponsored the Dulles Oral History Collection to supplement its holdings on John Foster Dulles, and the George C. Marshall Library has gathered more than 300 interviews on its subject (Shumway, *Oral History,* 22, 49, 50, 63, 82, 96). In recent years, too, Charles Morrissey has directed a special project entitled "Former Members of Congress," with funding from the National Endowment for the Humanities, which will produce interviews with approxi-

*Herbert T. Hoover*

Approximately ninety oral history offices were in operation across the country by 1966.[10] Recognizing the need for a clearinghouse and agency to guide the oral history movement in the future, veteran practitioners gathered that year at Arrowhead, California, and discussed the founding of a national organization. Out of their meeting came the Oral History Association, which has grown into a society of some 1,400 members whose activities have more than satisfied the expectations of the founders of the organization. The OHA has published a quarterly newsletter, a bibliography, and a journal entitled *The Oral History Review.* It has sponsored annual conferences where practitioners and administrators have assembled to exchange information. It has served as a forum through which scholars who have used interviews in their research have been able to share their accomplishments. The association has arranged displays of the best equipment and has offered workshops for newcomers on the techniques and uses of oral research.

A new dimension was added to the movement in the late 1960s. While "elitists" enlarged their work among persons who had "led significant lives" and institutions that had caused major changes in American society, a group of practitioners emerged to experiment with oral research at the grass-roots level. In an atmosphere of social rebellion, class conflict, and racial tension, they worked the ghettos and hinterlands of America to "recreate the history of those who have been ignored in the past." Their intention was that "through the medium of the voices of the people themselves history would recognize the lives and contributions to the culture of blacks, Chicanos, women, workers," American Indians, and others who were "once considered outcast groups."[11]

The most productive among the fledgling "bottom-uppers" were

mately 100 leading legislators, and the Capitol Historical Society contemplates work on congressional staff members. But there is need for more consistent efforts to record the motives and activities of leading officials and agencies in the federal government (telephone interview with Richard Baker, Senate Historian of the United States Congress, May 1, 1979).

10. Manfred Waserman, comp., *Bibliography on Oral History 1975* (New York, 1975). iii.

11. Ron Grele, "Can Anyone Over Thirty Be Trusted?: A Friendly Critique of Oral History," *Oral History Review,* VI (1978), 39. The only substantial work accomplished at the grass roots before the 1960s was that done by untrained researchers employed by Federal Writers Projects. In the years 1936–38, work relief interviewers gathered some 2,000 interviews on slavery, which were typical of the products of WPA research efforts. Although several scholars have found them useful, others have noted their obvious deficiencies. The words of the respondents were not recorded verbatim, and the respondents were reminiscing about events that had occurred more than half a centruy earlier at a time when they were inclined to hide or repress their feelings.

those who entered the field in 1966, when Doris Duke, the American Tobacco Company heiress, offered financial support for oral research among Native Americans. In response to proposals that were far more idealistic than realistic, her executive secretary, May MacFarland, contracted to send substantial sums of money over a period of five years to regional centers at the universities of Utah, Arizona, New Mexico, Oklahoma, South Dakota, Illinois, and Florida. Because the seven Duke projects were set up by men and women who knew little about the intricacies of oral research, some of them never accomplished the purpose intended by their benefactor. But three were notably successful. Under the capable supervision by C. Gregory Crampton, the Utah center has collected and processed more than 1,000 taped interviews on the histories of mountain and interior basin tribes. Through the persistent efforts of Samuel Proctor, the Florida project has made belated progress in reconstructing the history of the Catawba federation. With guidance from Joseph Cash, the Duke project at the Univeristy of South Dakota has gathered and processed more than 1,000 interviews among tribes scattered between the upper Mississippi Valley and the Pacific Northwest. And the South Dakota project has survived, under the direction of the writer and Judy Zabdyr, as a reorganized center with legislative support to carry on work among Indians and non-Indians alike across the northern prairies and Great Plains.

The beginning of work on tribal histories was paralleled by the opening of many new projects on regional history. Among those that have continued to operate to the present, the one at the Wisconsin–River Falls Research Center has been fairly typical. Since its establishment in 1967, it has survived on meager funds with volunteer staff to assemble and transcribe interviews that "produce a vivid and multifaceted profile of life in the valley of the St. Croix River from the time of its settlement [by non-Indians] up to the recent past."[12]

The introduction of grass-roots interviewing and the enlargement of regional research completed a pattern in the oral history movement which has not changed appreciably except for the quantity of production. It comprises projects of four general types: biographical studies, institutional investigations, special group surveys, and regional histories. A catalog published in 1971 listed 230 collections with all of these components represented.[13] Another in 1975 identified

12. *Voices from the St. Croix Valley: A Guide to the Oral History Collection* (River Falls, Wis., 1978), Introduction.
13. Shumway, *Oral History*, 3.

316 collections, and suggested similar diversity by listing sources of funding for their development. Universities and colleges had sponsored 155 collections, public libraries had maintained 48, ethnic and professional groups had supported 29, and various societies and special groups had sustained 84.[14] A later survey, in 1978, gave an estimate of some "500 projects in operation," plus "probably the same number contemplated, already finished or in the process of formation."[15]

While the oral history movement more than doubled in size as an archival enterprise during the 1970s, it also branched out to affect formal education. The most far-reaching development in the use of interviews as a classroom assignment has occurred at the precollege level, drawing its inspiration from the pioneering efforts of an imaginative social studies teacher at Rabun Gap–Nacoochee School in rural Appalachia. At the outset of the 1970s, Eliot Wigginton became frustrated by the lethargy of his students and sent them into the surrounding community to interview old-timers about the past. After considerable experimentation and personal effort to improve interviewing techniques, Wigginton began to release segments of his students' interviews in publications on Appalachian folk history under the title *Foxfire,* and began to promote oral research as a panacea for sagging interest among secondary school students of history.[16] The Foxfire technique soon became a nationwide practice, not only because other social studies instructors were quick to imitate Wigginton, but also because the model proved as useful to students in schools with limited resources as to those enrolled in systems with ample funding.

An exemplary project has been completed in a small hamlet on the edge of the remote Pine Ridge Reservation in western South Dakota. It has both enriched the experiences of the novice interviewers and preserved details of an important episode that might otherwise have been lost. A small group of Indian students published a booklet called *Wanbli* (Eagle), based on interviews with their elders, which describes how, after the war between the Sioux and the United States Army in the 1870s, federal officials tried to persuade Chief Lip and his band of 635 Upper Brules to settle on the Rosebud Reservation, where they seemed to belong. Lip's followers preferred to camp with Oglalas, however, and after years of delay and negotiation they finally per-

14. Starr, "Oral History," 451–452.
15. Grele, "Can Anyone Over Thirty Be Trusted?," 36.
16. Thad Sitton, "The Descendants of Foxfire," *Oral History Review,* VI (1978), 20–35.

suaded Indian Office personnel to enroll them on the Pine Ridge Reservation. Because of their determination, the community of Wanbli was founded, and it has survived as a vital component in the society of one of the largest Indian tribes on the North American continent.[17]

A development similar to that initiated by Wigginton for secondary schools has taken shape on college and university campuses since the mid-1970s. Hoping to remedy declining enrollments, many historians have sought to revive interest in the study of the nation's past with out-of-class assignments on family history through the use of personal interviews. This technique has been promoted by special sessions in the annual workshops offered for teachers at small colleges by the Newberry Library in Chicago, and it has been improved by special training in oral research techniques on many campuses. Most of the history departments have arranged interim seminars or one-semester courses; but a few have developed full-blown curricula. Beloit College has offered a baccalaureate degree in oral history, for instance, and California State College at Fullerton has begun to provide a combination of formal instruction and practical experience that leads to the award of a master's degree in oral research techniques.[18]

Important as oral history has become as a teaching tool, it remains primarily in the domain of scholarship; hence its state of development must be judged according to its merits as an archival enterprise. That basic skills required for carrying on all types of projects have been developed satisfactorily is evident in the contents of the handbooks that have appeared during the past ten years. Willa Baum, of the Berkeley center, has prepared two fine publications—*Oral History for the Local History Society* and *Transcribing and Editing Oral History*—for those who interview eminent Americans or conduct regional research.[19] Cullom Davis and his colleagues have written *Oral History: From Tapes to Type* for similar groups of researchers.[20] The late Ramon Harris and several associates in South Dakota published *The Practice of Oral History*, which addresses the particular problems of oral historians who work with ethnic groups and local historical societies.[21]

The basic skills have been worked out, but the broader considerations that ultimately determine the quality of the products of oral history have yet to receive sufficient attention to elevate oral research above its semiprofessional condition. The immaturity of the move-

17. *Wanbli* (n.p., n.d.)
18. Grele, "Can Anyone Over Thirty Be Trusted?," 36.
19. Nashville, 1969, 1974; Nashville, 1977.
20. Chicago, 1977.
21. Glen Rock, N.J., 1975.

ment has been evident in the articles that have appeared in the journal of the OHA; except for those in the 1977 and 1978 issues of the *Review,* they have read like show-and-tell reports on individual projects. The unrefined condition of oral research has also been reflected in some of the suggestions that have been advanced as means for its improvement. A group of scholars wrote recently from the campus of a major university that the key to better performance might be the revision of interviewing strategy through psychological analysis of the adversary relationship between interviewer and interviewee. Most veteran interviewers agree, however, that an adversary relationship should never exist. Others have suggested that the best method of improvement might be the subjection of collections to some kind of general evaluation, like the book review—one supposes for the purpose of coercing interviewers and transcribers into doing better work. A past president of the OHA has even contended that the way to improve oral history is to elevate its status to one of a "discipline," with its own special goals and definition of history.

The problem of quality control in an oral history collection must be addressed in the context of half a dozen other criteria, which can serve both as standards for the improvement of ongoing projects and as bases for judgments about the reliability of collections that have been completed in the past. The first is the general design of the project that produced a collection. Just as an author should know what a book is going to be about before he or she begins to write it, so should a project director establish topical boundaries for an oral research effort before it begins. This was one concern that provoked Barbara Tuchman to complain about the "artificial survival of trivia of appalling proportions," with "people being invited merely to open their mouths, and ramble effortlessly and endlessly into a tape recorder," leaving behind them only "a few veins of gold and a vast mass of trash."[22] Project directors who send interviewers out to conduct "open-ended" interviews about myriad subjects with ill-defined boundaries, such as "black history" and "man's reaction to world affairs," almost inevitably assemble collections that will be of little use to anyone, because few scholars will have the patience required to search for the small "veins of gold" in the great heaps of "trash."

A second consideration involves funding. Directors have enthusiastically launched countless projects with great potential only to fall short of producing useful documentary material because they failed

22. "Distinguishing the Significant from the Insignificant," *Radcliffe Quarterly,* LVI (March 1972), 9-10.

to arrange for enough money to pay the bills. Oral research is very expensive. Nevins wrote that while he directed the Columbia center in the 1950s he could not "operate even a sternly economical but efficient office for less than $40,000 a year, and costs rose."[23] Indeed they did, and they continue to rise in times when academic institutions grow increasingly parsimonious in the allocation of funds for research, and when foundations and public endowments become more and more hesitant to put money into projects that have little visibility or potential for effecting immediate social change. Some project directors have tried to compensate for the scarcity of funds by drafting students to conduct interviews, and by either stockpiling unprocessed tapes or enlisting volunteers to type them into transcripts. Tactics such as these are ill-advised attempts to circumvent the fact that a project cannot operate professionally, and produce sources worthy of use for serious scholarship, at much less than about $250 an interview. The budget is therefore a reasonable measure of the quality of the materials one might expect to find in a project's library.

A third factor, which is related to budgetary considerations, comprises the criteria used during the selection of interviewers. "Scratch an oral historian," wrote OHA president Waddy Moore recently, "and you are just as likely to find a folklorist, sociologist, economist, someone from the field of communications, medicine, government, business, literature, entertainment, and so the list goes on."[24] These are not oral historians! Nor are undergraduate students in need of tuition money, laymen who happen to belong to the groups from which respondents are to be selected, or historical society members who have a "great interest in history." The person who conducts interviews should possess credentials that reflect advanced training in the particular field of history under study, personality traits that are conducive to relaxed conversation with various kinds of respondents, and some prior success in establishing rapport among groups of people with backgrounds unlike his or her own.

Next comes the matter of how oral researchers go about their work. Every experienced interviewer is familiar with the requirements. Like Allan Nevins, the interviewer must first "prepare himself by reading files of newspapers, going through official reports, begging wives for old letters and diary notes, and talking with associates."[25] From these sources he must extract a list of central questions to explore, much as

23. Nevins, "Oral History," 601.
24. "Critical Perspectives," *Oral History Review*, VI (1978), 2.
25. Nevins, "Oral History," 601.

the writer drafts a tentative table of contents for a book he or she is about to write. With the list of questions in hand, the interviewer must select respondents who are reputed to have answers, as well as special knowledge about a variety of related questions that the interviewer can add to his list as he goes along. The interviewer must observe proper protocol: dealing with an ethnic group, for example, by working through its established leaders, or being careful to contact individuals in the pecking order that exists in any group of respondents. He must investigate the background of each interviewee before the occasion of an interview, in order to tailor his approach to his respondent's personal proclivities. Finally, he must prepare himself mentally for each interview, so that he can react with enthusiasm to the information his respondent provides, and at the same time present a relaxed bearing that invites the respondent to lead the conversation. Herin lies the "art" of oral research. Only those who have mastered it can bring back reliable material.

Fifth among major considerations is processing. Those project directors who have stored taped interviews with ample precautions to prevent their destruction by electronic print-through or magnetic fields have accomplished only half the task. Every interview should be transcribed by a patient typist whose ear is specially trained for this work, edited by a person who understands the elements of style as well as the general subjects covered by the respondents, and indexed by someone who is competent to categorize information into useful subjects. A small percentage of the scholars who use oral sources prefer to listen to original tapes, but most of them will take time to use only those materials that have been thoroughly processed, and scholars should always examine the quality of staff and the procedures used for the preparation of transcripts in a collection before putting them to use in the development of a manuscript.

Finally there is the issue of use rights. Most scholars simply assumed the right to information gathered in personal interviews until 1967, when Arthur Schlesinger, Jr., addressed this question amid controversy over the ownership of the Kennedy tapes. "The basic premise of the oral history idea," he said, "is that the person interviewed retains absolute and total control over the interview."[26] Shortly thereafter most project directors devised simple release forms, which respondents were asked to sign as agreements to present their interviews as gifts to some project or institution; and this procedure was considered adequate until a new federal copyright law went into

26. "On the Writing of Contemporary History," 71.

effect on January 1, 1978. Since then, wise project directors have employed attorneys to draft more elaborate release forms for the signatures of both respondents and interviewers. Until all of the implications of the new copyright code are clarified through litigation, both project directors and scholars must exercise care about gaining assurance that the contents of interviews are properly released for general use—by both the respondents and the interviewers, who share ownership as co-authors.

Oral research cannot rise above its semiprofessional status until those engaged in the collecting and processing of interviews work consistently according to all of these criteria, and the prospect that very many will do so in the near future is bleak. If rated honestly by these standards, all but a small percentage of the projects and centers now in operation across the United States would receive low grades, and doubtless none would deserve perfect scores. Oral history remains an unrefined technique, but the condition of the movement should not deter scholars from using oral sources, if they are careful to evaluate the quality of collections before drawing information from them. Indeed, doubts about the value of interviews used judiciously as prime sources for scholarship should by now have been put to rest by the high quality of notable books that have been prepared through oral research.

The best works have been biographical studies. Stanley Vestal's *Sitting Bull* remains an exemplary work in this genre, even though it was researched before the term "oral history" was in common use and before tape recorders came onto the market. Its quality can only inspire admiration in readers who are familiar with sources on the subjects it explores. Supplementing scattered documentary materials and questionable secondary works with interviews he conducted among Indian people on the northern Great Plains, Vestal re-created the life and times of one of the most influential and famous Indian leaders in American history in a volume that remains by far the best to appear on the Hunkpapa warrior and medicine man.

T. Harry Williams has created an even better model in *Huey Long*. It received mixed reviews at the time of its publication. One critic likened Williams to an archaeologist who returned from an excavation to heap useless debris upon his unsuspecting audience. Others, however, recognized the extraordinary contribution he had made by using interviews to fill gaps in the documentary materials about the public career of a man who understandably failed to keep written records. For this work Williams was justly awarded the Pulitzer Prize. Theodore Rosengarten took a different approach to biography in *All*

*God's Dangers.*[27] While a graduate student at Harvard, he traveled to Alabama with hopes of researching the history of a defunct Alabama sharecroppers' union, and, after many recording sessions, pieced together instead the life story of Nate Shaw in a volume that presents oral history at its best. Through his reminiscences, the black farmer has offered a perspective on the past century of southern history that could have been preserved in no other way.

Merle Miller presented biography in another fashion with his *Plain Speaking: An Oral Biography of Harry S. Truman.*[28] This book was panned by reviewers when it appeared. One complained that it was not biography at all, but a recitation of earthy "Trumanisms" interspersed with unwelcome intrusions by the interviewer. Another believed that Miller had failed to put the "hard questions" to his respondent. But many oral historians appreciated how capably Miller had dealt with his testy, aging respondent, and how much effort he put into gleaning from Truman and others who were close to him dimensions of the late president's public life that would otherwise have been lost. The text of *Plain Speaking* is a fair representation of the kind of dialogue that takes place in many interviews. Alex Haley has presented still another example of the value of interviews to biographical inquiry with his well-known *Roots.*[29] Following leads and clues to his "furtherest-back person" and applying research skills he had developed from experience as a journalist, Haley tracked his ancestry back to Gambia, West Africa, with tape recorder in hand.[30]

*The Emergence of UAW Local, 1936–1939: A Study in Class and Culture* illustrates the value of oral research to the writing of institutional history.[31] Following Nevins's advice to first immerse himself in documents that pertained to the history of United Auto Workers Local 229, Peter Friedlander conducted intensive interviews with a past president and several other members of the union that sprang up in the Polish district of suburban Detroit during the 1930s. With his findings, he wrote a sophisticated study that presented the history of the local as an example of the class conflict and social change that have accompanied the movement for collective bargaining in the twentieth century.

27. New York, 1974. See also Rosengarten's interesting essay, "Stepping Over Cockleburs: Conversations with Ned Cobb," in Marc Pachter, ed., *Telling Lives: The Biographer's Art* (Washington, D.C., 1979), 104–31.

28. New York, 1973.

29. Garden City, N.Y., 1976.

30. "My Furtherest-Back Person—The African," *New York Times Magazine,* July 16, 1972, 12–16.

31. Pittsburgh, 1975.

Oral investigations into the histories of special groups have generated a variety of publications. The only one of substance on American Indians has been *To Be an Indian: An Oral History,* by Joseph Cash and Herbert T. Hoover, which, like Rosengarten's biography of Nate Shaw, offers up oral history without comments by the editors.[32] It presents the viewpoints of Indian people about major developments in the history of Indian–white relations in the northern Great Plains region during the past century. *Hillbilly Women,* by Kathy Kahn, "tells what it means to be a woman when you are poor, when you are proud, and when you are a hillbilly" in "southern Appalachia," in a presentation of segments from about twenty interviews interspersed with photographs and comments by the editor.[33] *Hannah's Daughters: Six Generations of an American Family, 1876–1976,* by Dorothy Gallagher, gives an intimate picture of the experiences of frontier women in the state of Washington with a sequence of reminiscences by women of several generations in a single family.[34] *Hard Times: An Oral History of the Great Depression* and "Hard Times, 1970: An Oral History of the Recession," by Studs (Louis) Terkel, include interview segments gathered by a Chicago radio broadcaster with exceptional ability to get respondents to bare their emotions concerning the hardships they have endured under economic stress.[35] Terkel edited his interviews far too extensively, as his critics have charged, and concentrated more on the flow of his narrative than upon the accuracy of his interpretations. Nevertheless, he has published a valuable body of material that suggests that people have turned inward during hard times, and have tended to fix more blame upon themselves than upon the faulty economic systems that have affected them.

An excellent regional study appeared in 1976 under the title *Our Appalachia.* Laurel Shackelford and William Weinberg selected interviews for publication from a collection gathered by a four-college consortium, based at Alice Lloyd College, in Pippa Passes, Kentucky, in the early 1970s, and with them presented a social history of central Appalachia through the second and third quarters of the twentieth century.[36] Photographs accompany a text comprising the words of the respondents along with interpretive comments by the editors.

These books, which demonstrate the best features of the growing body of literature in biography, institutional investigations, group

32. New York, 1971.
33. Garden City, N.Y., 1973.
34. New York, 1976.
35. New York, 1970; *New York Times Magazine,* December 20, 1970, 10–11, 46–51, 54.
36. New York, 1977.

surveys, and regional studies that have evolved from oral research in recent years, also reflect continuing trends in the oral history movement. In the late 1970s, projects were established that have indicated a somewhat greater diversity of institutional interests. One group of researchers has started to work on an "Oral History of the AFL-CIO Labor Movement" for the Meany Center for Labor Studies in Silver Spring, Maryland, while another has opened a project on the "Social History of Neenah, Wisconsin's Prominent Paper Manufacturing Families." Special group studies launched in recent years have been more ambitious than those established in the 1960s. The Armenian Assembly Charitable Trust recently received funding for "Oral Histories of Armenians in America." The Association for the Study of Afro-American Life has begun work with principal leaders for an "Oral History of Black Americans." A group in St. Paul, Minnesota, has initiated an interview series on second-generation Finnish people scattered in mining communities across northern Michigan, Wisconsin, and Minnesota. Historian Edward Sundberg and his wife, Gerda, are broadening the scope of an old project that they operate from their home in Watersonville, California, which seeks to explore the "American-Scandinavian Ethnic Heritage" thoroughly. Not only have they traversed the North American continent to interview immigrants, but they have also made several trips to Europe to gather supplementary information. "We have just returned from our research trip to Denmark, Finland and Sweden," they wrote to their colleagues in oral history during the fall of 1978, "to visit remigrants" and to "talk with emigration experts" abroad. While in Scandinavia, they interviewed twenty-nine remigrants and collected information to explain past trends in the migration of Scandinavians to the United States.

As oral historians have expanded their interests in institutional and cultural studies during recent years, they have also extended provincial research into urban communities. In 1978 historians Robert Trennert and Wesley Johnson opened a project on the history of Phoenix, Arizona, for example. The director of the Bronx Historical Society has begun work with respondents on the history of the Bronx, and two scholars have started to explore the oral history of a small urban community in Oviedo, Florida. In other words, historians in cities and towns of varying sizes have begun to recognize the importance of personal reminiscences to the understanding of the history and condition of urban culture.

The diversity and breadth of projects established during recent years suggest increasing interest in oral research among professional historians as well as technicians and archivists. The publications that have been prepared through the use of interviews demonstrate the potential that oral research has to improve scholarship. Despite the deficiencies that have prevented the oral history movement from rising above its semiprofessional status through the 1970s it has become an important fixture in the profession, one whose influence on historiography in the United States is likely to increase as rapidly as funds become available to support its progress.

# 17

## *Psychohistory*

### Peter Loewenberg

L OVE has to be reinvented," said Rimbaud. History too needs to be reinvented by every historian and each generation. The task of this generation has been to dilate the traditional meanings and definitions of historical research to include the behavioral and human sciences. Psychohistory, one of the newest methods of historical research, combines historical analysis with social science models, humanistic sensibility, and psychodynamic theory and clinical insights to create a fuller, more rounded view of the past. The psychohistorian is aware of the dynamic interaction of character, society, human thought and action. This awareness is consonant with the historian's traditional commitment to the unity of man and culture, of life and ideas, in past and present. Although historians have always recognized the existence of the nonrational and the irrational in history, their categories of explanation have too often been limited to the utilitarian, materialistic, or intellectual rationality of motives. Now we have enlarged and refined concepts of explanation of human conduct to include the emotional and unconscious basis of historical thought and action.

Historians now recognize more clearly than ever the integral, subjective, relationship between researchers and their work. We also acknowledge that there is no external, objective, criterion of what is admissible, relevant, or excludable and unimportant in history. Historians of each age redefine categories of evidence in the light of the needs, sensibilities, and perceptions of their age. Among the new realizations is that not only social and political contexts but also personal life and family settings predispose historians to given kinds of materials, values, research problems, and interpretations.[1]

I wish to thank Frank Otto Gatell, Edward Goldman, Daniel W. Howe, John Modell, and Eric Monkkonen for aiding me in the preparation of this essay.
1. George Devereux, *From Anxiety to Method in the Behavioral Sciences* (The Hague

The forces of passion and irrationality that are all about us, as well as in us, are so overwhelming in history that only by the utmost stretching of all plausibility can they be denied. Many historical phenomena elude the analyses of utilitarian and material categories of explanation. Historians scrupulously and painstakingly ascertain whether an event has taken place and when it occurred. Yet in explaining the event they have too often been content with the amateur maxims of common sense and the nonexplanation of historical "accident" to cover blunders by historical actors, the coincidence of events, or subjective feelings in the historian that are too uncomfortable to face. The attribution of historical events to "accidents" is usually the historian's way of saying: "I do not know and cannot look any further."

Historians see in their material only what they are prepared to perceive. Thus the value of any conceptual framework lies in the new combinations of data or inferences from the data it allows the historian to derive as he confronts and interprets documents and the other raw material of history. A knowledge of psychodynamics sensitizes historical researchers to nuances of shifting relationships in the documentary material that they might not otherwise notice and respond to. Psychohistorians use the same sources as other historians: government documents, diaries, journals and memoirs, cultural and literary artifacts, account books and fiscal data. They observe them, however, with different lenses.

A psychological contribution to history consists of three essentials. It seeks evidence of the unconscious in human behavior as demonstrated by life styles, adaptations, creativity and sublimations, character, slips of speech, hearing and writing, errors, accidents, dreams, neuroses and psychoses, and human action or inhibition. Second, psychohistory is a genetic approach; it is not only psychological but also truly *historical*. It emphasizes the importance of origins, antecedents, and patterns of repetition. Thus it is developmental—stressing the longitudinal growth and adaptation of the person all his life, including events and behaviors learned from infancy, childhood, adolescence, and adulthood. Third, psychohistory is oriented to dynamic psychology in which the present reality interacts at all times with and is related to the individual's personal and social past in the unconscious. Psychohistory also gives due place to the aggression, sexuality, passions, fantasy, and emotional states of the inner world of its subjects. It rejects the myth of the asexuality and innocence of child or adult, man or woman. Psychohistory recognizes that the emotional

and Paris, 1967); Peter Loewenberg, "Why Psychoanalysis Needs the Social Scientist and the Historian," *International Review of Psychoanalysis*, IV (1977), 305-315.

Peter Loewenberg

meaning of an event, symbol, or image is determined by the fantasies of the subject rather than being externally ascribed.

Psychohistorians seek patterns, repetitions, deviant cases, and their meanings in the private and often unconscious world of their subjects and of themselves.[2] They pursue visible traces of the unconscious and its defenses. Psychohistory is, to paraphrase what Freud said of psychoanalysis, a general history. Freud's own view of his work was that "the main value of my synthesis lies in its linking together the neurotic and normal processes."[3] The human personality is indivisible. The processes we know clinically are just as relevant to this morning's newspaper or yesteryear's diary or legislative conflict as to a patient's neurotic sympton. It was Marc Bloch who said: "Historical facts are, in essence, psychological facts. Normally, therefore, they find their antecedents in other psychological facts."[4] Although historians have always recognized the role of emotions and irrationality in human action, they now have begun to account for a proportion of previously inexplicable behavior by seeking patterns of explanation using the insights that the sciences of psychodynamics have developed in this century.[5]

Historians study past human actions, thoughts, and motives. This is

2. See the excellent introduction by Peter N. Carroll, "Some Theoretical Assumptions and Implications of Psychohistory," in *The Other Samuel Johnson: A Psychohistory of Early New England* (Rutherford, N.J., 1978).

3. Freud to Wilhelm Fliess, November 14, 1897, in *The Origins of Psycho-Analysis: Letters to Wilhelm Fliess, Drafts and Notes, 1887–1902*, ed. Marie Bonaparte, Anna Freud, Ernst Kris, trans. Eric Mosbacher and James Strachey (New York, 1954), letter no. 75, 234. Peter Gay makes a persuasive case for psychoanalysis as the "general psychology," meaning "a branch of science capable of supplying laws for normal as well as neurotic behavior, of accounting for successful as well as stunted human development." Therefore it is the psychology particularly suited to historical explanation: "All history must be in significant measure psychohistory" (Introduction to *Art and Act: On Causes in History: Manet, Gropius, Mondrian* [New York, 1976], 21–22, 19). For an opposing view, see Hayden White, who thinks that genius and neurosis are mutually exclusive: "When it is a matter of dealing with a thinker or writer of manifest genius, the application of a theory such as psychoanalysis, which was devised for the study of neurotics and psychotics, appears to be a mistake"(*Metahistory: The Historical Imagination in Nineteenth-Century Europe* [Baltimore, 1973], 431). However, see White on the origins of creativity: "Knowledge is a product of a wrestling not only with the 'facts' but with one's self" (ibid., 192).

4. *The Historian's Craft*, trans. Peter Putnam (New York, 1953), 194.

5. The most complete bibiographical survey of psychohistory is Faye Sinofsky et al., "A Bibliography of Psychohistory," *History of Childhood Quarterly*, 11 (1975), 517–562. An impressive survey of the literature from ancient to modern is Thomas W. Africa, "Psychohistory, Ancient History, and Freud: The Descent into Avernus," *Arethusa*, XII (1979), 5–33. See also George M. Kren and Leon Rappoport, "Clio and Psyche," *History of Childhood Quarterly*, I (1973), 151–163; Peter Loewenberg, "History and Psychoanalysis," in *The International Encyclopaedia of Psychiatry, Psychology, Psychoanalysis, and Neurology* (New York, 1977), V 363–374.

also what the psychoanalyst studies in his patients.[6] When dealing with issues of motivation, both disciplines are committed to the theory of overdetermination. Only a poor historian would maintain that a major historical event had but one cause. We must necessarily look to many levels of causation and appraise the significance of each. Freud too insisted upon the overdetermined nature of the affects, dreams, and symptoms of psychic life. Thus both disciplines seek multiple explanations for single phenomena; both disciplines follow the law of the conservation of evidence. No detail is so minor that it can be ignored, no deviant case is so trivial that it may be overlooked. This distinguishes history and psychoanalysis from the social and the natural sciences that seek to fit or subsume individual events under general covering laws of behavior. The epistemological problem is identical for the historian and the psychoanalyst. They must both reconstruct, or recreate in their minds, the life of their subjects.[7]

The formal summons to the historical profession to engage seriously with psychoanalysis and apply it in research and conceptualization came from William L. Langer in a presidential address to the American Historical Association in December 1957.[8] Langer's personal experience in psychoanalysis favorably disposed him to its application in historical research. He also came to appreciate its value for research through his role as chief of the Research and Analysis branch of the Office of Strategic Services (OSS) and organizer of the Board of National Estimates for the Central Intelligence Agency. Psychodynamic studies of foreign leaders, texts, and propaganda by American intelligence services contributed to intelligence gathering and evaluation and strengthened his conviction of the value of psychodynamics for the historian's armamentarium.[9]

6. For a discussion of the similarities of clinical and historical method, see Hans Meyerhoff, "On Psychoanalysis and History," *Psychoanalysis and the Psychoanalytical Review*, XLIX (1962), 3-20.

7. Michael T. McGuire, *Reconstructions in Psychoanalysis* (New York, 1971); Samuel Novey, *The Second Look: The Reconstruction of Personal History in Psychiatry and Psychoanalysis* (Baltimore, 1968).

8. "The Next Assignment," *American Historical Review*, LXVIII (1958), 283-304. For the earliest uses of psychoanalysis by historians, see Preserved Smith, "Luther's Early Development in the Light of Psychoanalysis," *American Journal of Psychology*, XXIV (1913), 360-377, and Harry Elmer Barnes, *Psychology and History* (New York, 1925). Langer's famous chapter 3, "The Triumph of Imperialism," in *The Diplomacy of Imperialism* (New York, 1935), is a sensitive psychological treatment of popular fantasies.

9. The background to his call for historians to use psychoanalysis was revealed in Langer's posthumous memoir. He was introduced to the personal value of psychoanalysis in 1938 when he was seized with great anxiety while lecturing, sometimes feeling that he "was facing a hostile group, ready to attack me at any moment." Public speaking then became a "chronic ordeal" for him, "to be avoided whenever

The necessity of professional training in two disciplines has been reflected in mental health specialists' criticism of the crude methods of historians who write psychological history.[10] Conversely, historians criticize clinicians who are not historians, yet offer interpretations of history.[11] The model of interdisciplinary teams and collaboration by specialists at the interface of the disciplines has not been a generally successful solution. The ultimate synthesis must take place in the mind of a psychohistorian professionally trained in both disciplines if the research and conceptualizations are to have integrity as both historical and psychological accounts.

A development in America since 1956 has been the return to the traditional model, as it evolved on the European continent and in Great Britain, of the professional training of nonmedical researchers in psychoanalysis. Systematic postdoctoral training of social scientists, historians, and humanists, including didactic analysis, seminars, and the supervision of clinical control cases, now takes place in psychoanalytic institutes. In 1977, California officially recognized the importance of psychoanalytic clinical training and practice "as an adjunct to teaching, training or research."[12] A new professional identity and a new historical discipline are emerging. Instead of historians and critics who do armchair psychoanalysis, or clinicians who dabble in history and the humanities, academically trained professional historians now conduct programs of research, teaching, and administration in their respective fields in universities, and also practice as clinicians, keeping in daily contact with unconscious processes and defenses of both themselves and their patients. The new academic historian-psychoanalysts are products of a merger in methods and

possible." He entered psychoanalysis, which he found "a most effective method for learning about oneself," with Jenny Waelder. This is the same Jenny Waelder Hall who was consulted by his brother, Walter Langer, in 1943 while he was writing a psychoanalytic study of Hitler for the OSS. William L. Langer, *In and Out of the Ivory Tower: The Autobiography* (New York, 1977), 168–172, 180–193, 218–223, 247–250; Walter C. Langer, *The Mind of Adolf Hitler: The Secret Wartime Report* (New York, 1972), 19. For examples of psychoanalytical studies of Axis propaganda and leaders in World War II, see Peter Loewenberg, "Psychohistorical Perspectives on Modern German History," *Journal of Modern History*, XLVII (1975), 229–279, especially 253–274.

10. *The Psychiatrist as Psychohistorian,* Report on the Task Force on Psychohistory of the American Psychiatric Association (Washington, D. C., 1976).

11. Hans W. Gatzke, "Hitler and Psychohistory: A Review Article," *American Historical Review*, LXXVIII (1973), 394–401; and the controversy it generated in *American Historical Review*, LXXVIII (1973), 1155–63; and the review by Dietrich Orlow, "The Significance of Time and Place in Psychohistory," *Journal of Interdisciplinary History*, v (1974), 131–138.

12. California Business and Professions Code, Division 2, chap. 5.1, sec. 2529-30, "Research Psychoanalysts."

perspectives at an early stage of career development, usually shortly after the completion of graduate training. Instead of the previous collaboration between specialists at the interface of two fields, these few hybrid scholars have created a personal fusion of style, discipline, and method within their own minds. Dual training is especially important in psychohistory precisely because, unlike other methods of history, psychodynamic study has as its substance repressed emotional material. Painful, frightening, anxiety-inducing, disgusting, or shameful feelings are too easy for the historian to obviate and avoid in his or her research and writing. Historians will be less likely to run away from these feelings, or not to see them at all, if they have faced them personally.[13] The interchange must be constant, unconscious, instantaneous, spontaneous, and intrapsychic rather than interpersonal. "In this conncection," said Freud, "the psychoanalytic mode of thought acts like a new instrument of research."[14] Thus Freud's famous vision of 1926 has been realized:

If—which may sound fantastic today—one had to establish a university of psychoanalysis,... analytic instruction would include disciplines which are remote from the physician and which he does not come across in his work: cultural history, mythology, the psychology of religion, and literary criticism. Without a good orientation in these fields, the analyst stands helpless before a great part of his material.[15]

A new historical subdiscipline now exists whose practitioners are not psychoanalysts doing history or historians using psychoanalysis, but psychohistorians.

Several of America's scholarly journals, such as *The American Historical Review,* the *Journal of Modern History, The Journal of Interdisciplinary History,* and *The Historian,* have devoted special issues to psychohistory. *The Journal of Psychohistory* (formerly known as *The History of Childhood Quarterly*), which is dedicated to the history of childhood and the family, the psychohistory of individuals and groups, and the

13. For a dissenting view on the need for professional training in psychodynamics for psychohistorians, see Fred Weinstein and Gerald M. Platt, *Psychoanalytic Sociology: An Essay on the Interpretation of Historical Data and the Phenomena of Collective Behavior* (Baltimore, 1973), 1, n. 1.
    14. "The Claims of Psycho-Analysis to Scientific Interest" (1913), *Standard Edition of the Complete Psychological Works of Sigmund Freud,* trans. and ed. James Strachey in collaboration with Anna Freud, 24 vols. (London, 1953-1974), XIII, 185 [henceforth *S.E.*]
    15. "Die Frage der Laienanalyse," *Studienausqabe,* ed. Alexander Mitscherlich et al., 11 vols. (Frankfurt am Main, 1975) [henceforth *Studien*]. "Ergänzungsband," 336-337. The translation is mine.

proposition that the long-neglected history of childhood is the basis for psychohistory, was founded in 1973. The Group for the Use of Psychology in History, an affiliate of the American Historical Association, publishes *The Psychohistory Review,* which contains articles, reviews, bibliography, and discussion of teaching methods. According to a recent survey, courses in psychohistory are currently offered at approximately thirty major American colleges and universities.[16] Psychohistory has been offered as a field of doctoral study in history at UCLA, Yale, Kansas State University, SUNY–Stony Brook, Princeton, MIT, and Boston University. It has also been offered as an "outside" field at such other graduate schools as Wisconsin and Berkeley.

The historical profession has, on the whole, been wary of, if not antagonistic to, the use of psychoanalytic perceptions in historical research and interpretation.[17] Critics object that psychobiographers too often make inferential leaps from adult behavior to infantile experiences, ignoring intervening developments and variables. This charge, frequently well founded, raises an issue about the quality of psychohistory being written rather than the purpose or potential value of the enterprise itself. Some writers have used psychological categories as weapons with which to attack and discredit political figures,[18] in expositions that make leaps directly from infantile traumata to public political conduct. But much of the hostility has been defensive because psychoanalysis, unlike other historical methods, deeply involves the subjectivity of the researcher. Often one of the unconscious motives for studying history is to displace conflict to the past. Therefore attempts to confront and deal with conflict in the immediacy of current research are met with hostility. Some recent commen-

16. Survey by John Fitzpatrick as cited in George M. Kren and Leon H. Rappoport, eds., *Varieties of Psychohistory* (New York, 1976), 2, 14, n. 3. A most sophisticated engagement with the problems of psychohistory is Saul Friedländer, *History and Psychoanalysis: An Inquiry into the Possibilities and Limits of Psychohistory* (New York, 1978).

17. E. J. Hundert, "History, Psychology, and the Study of Deviant Behavior," *Journal of Interdisciplinary History,* II (1972), 453–472; Philip Pomper, "Problems of a Naturalistic Psychohistory," *History and Theory,* XII (1973), 367–388; Jacques Barzun, *Clio and the Doctors: Psycho-History, Quanto-History, and History* (Chicago, 1974), and reviews by Fred Weinstein in *Journal of Modern History,* XLVIII (1976), 117–118, and Peter Loewenberg in *Clio: An Interdisciplinary Journal of Literature, History, and the Philosophy of History,* v (1975), 123–127. See also Robert Coles, "Shrinking History," *New York Review of Books,* February 23 and March 8, 1973; Geoffrey Barraclough, "Psycho-history Is Bunk," *Guardian* (Manchester and London), March 3, 1973); Gerald Izenberg, "Psychohistory and Intellectual History," *History and Theory,* XIV (1975), 139–155. Izenberg writes as though ideas could not have more than a single (rational) determinant or referent.

18. See the notorious example by Sigmund Freud and William C. Bullitt, *Thomas Woodrow Wilson: A Psychological Study* (Boston, 1967).

tators have issued calls for historians to utilize nonpsychoanalytic psychological models in their research.[19] Many of the conceptual differences between schools of psychodynamics turn out to be fictive when they are applied in empirical cases. The problem of theory choice is in many ways simpler for historians than for clinicians. Historians may be eclectic and choose explanatory models to elucidate their material from whatever theories appear to be most useful. Historians require of a theory of behavior only that it be historical, that it be sufficiently rich and complex to explain the manifold problems of human behavior encountered by the historian, and that the theory be consistent and structurally coherent. Most psychohistorians reject nonpsychoanalytic psychologies for use in historical research because of their ahistorical, nondevelopmental character and because they are either so simplistic that they explain only elementary traits or so lacking in structural coherence as to be unusable by historians. "In the last analysis," argues Saul Friedländer, "only the psychoanalytic (or psychoanalytically influenced) theories can furnish psychohistory with an adequate general framework, for these theories are the only ones that satisfy the criteria which *for the historian* are fundamental."[20]

The reciprocal relationship between history and psychoanalysis dates from Freud's work on culture and history in the early years of this century. He wrote widely on aesthetics and freely used literary, artistic, and anthropological examples to demonstrate his ideas, including discourses on the beginnings of social contract and the psychodynamics of religion, group leadership, poetic creativity, and biography.

Further developments have taken place in modern psychoanalytic theory and clinical practice, and in historical investigation as psychoanalysis has become assimilated as a research tool and interpre-

19. Terry H. Anderson, "Becoming Sane with Psychohistory," *The Historian*, XLI (1978), 1–20; Peter C. Hoffer, "Is Psychohistory Really History?," *Psychohistory Review*, VII (1979), 6–12. See also other explicitly nonpsychoanalytic studies in psychohistory in the same issue: Harvey Asher, "Non-Psychoanalytic Approaches to National Socialism," 12–31; and Uri Wernick, "Cognitive Dissonance Theory, Religious Reality, and Extreme Interactionism," 22–28. George D. Jackson calls on psychohistorians to follow the theories of Carl Rogers and Abraham Maslow: "Lenin and Psychohistory," *Canadian Slavonic Papers*, XIX (1977), 207–222. For consciously nonpsychoanalytic psychohistory, see Richard C. Raack, "When Plans Fail: Small Group Behavior and Decision-Making in the Conspiracy of 1808 in Germany," *Journal of Conflict Resolution*, XIV (1970), 3–19. Raack utilizes cognitive dissonance theory; see Leon Festinger, *A Theory of Cognitive Dissonance* (Stanford, 1957); Charles M. Radding, "The Evolution of Medieval Mentalities: A Cognitive-Structural Approach," *American Historical Review*, LXXXIII (1978), 577–597.
20. Friedländer, *History and Psychoanalysis*, 11.

tive modality among historians and social scientists. Ego psychology
and character analysis are particularly important and welcome to historians because they are based on the evidence of adult behavior.
They do not require reconstruction of infantile experience or reduc-
tions to originology, the behavior and patterns of accommodating to
the world exist in adulthood, and the evidence is historical. Clinically
all aspects of personality are related—style of work and social intercourse, creativity, sexuality, attitudes toward money, intellectual style,
fantasies, modes of conflict, and transferences. It is on these levels of
ego functioning that interpretations are made to the patient. The
historian has many of these kinds of data of personality and ego
functioning at his disposal. If he looks at them with an eye for the
psychological relationships of various kinds of historical evidence,
many connections that were not previously apparent will appear, for
human beings are integral in many more ways than they consciously
realize. The historian may now seek psychologically informed structures of behavior that make relationships and connections out of
hitherto discrete or incomprehensible pieces of behavior.

Psychoanalysis, which has developed certain formulations derived
from extensive clinical experience, may supply the latent content behind manifest fantasies and meanings that the historian notes. Thus
repetition of a maladaptive pattern in varied life situations is one of
the indicators that unconscious processes are at work. Such repeated
patterns of provocation and deadlocked conflict in adult life provided
a key to the interpretation of Woodrow Wilson by Alexander and
Juliette George.[21]

One of the most useful of all psychodynamic clinical categories for
the historian is the idea of character. Wilhelm Reich delineated the
exterior characterological attributes in terms of character "armor"—
that is a focus on actual behavior and ideas, such as living one's life by
a program, thoroughness, pedantry, and evenness of attention and
feeling which in some cases amounts to an affect block.[22] A feature of
Reich's conceptualization and clinical technique that has not yet been
exploited by historians is its significance for intellectual artifacts such
as literature, philosophy, and history itself. Reich demonstrated that
*modes of thought* such as circumstantial, ruminative thinking, or emphasis on restraint and control, or indecision, doubt, and distrust are

21. George and George, *Woodrow Wilson and Colonel House: A Personality Study* (New
York, 1956, 1964). See Bernard Brodie, "A Psychoanalytic Interpretation of Woodrow
Wilson," *World Politics*, IX (1957), 413–422.
22. Reich, *Character Analysis* (New York, 1949), 193–200.

all indicative of character structure. The reliance on what is observable and easily identifiable, in contrast to what is inner, makes Reich's approach appealing and especially useful to the historian. The external features that would denote a compulsive character structure include a character armor of flat, affectless tone, and an attempt to avoid emotional engagement by intellectualization or by denying the existence of emotions.

Some current psychohistorians write with pre-1930s models of psychodynamics,[23] as though ego psychology had never been developed, as though Freud as early as World War I had not already conceptualized and dealt with problems of the individual's adaptation to reality, work that was extended by Anna Freud, Heinz Hartmann, Ernst Kris, and Rudolph Loewenstein.

Freud built one half of the bridge that the psychohistorian must complete, for the dimension of time is also basic to the historian's discipline. In both historical studies and psychoanalysis there is no more productive or crucial question than "Why now?" The elaboration of plans coupled with an inability to bring them to consummation in the life of the British general Sir Henry Clinton led Wyatt and Willcox to seek a psychoanalytic interpretation on the model of Freud's "Those Wrecked by Success."[24] The critical question was, why could Clinton not act in his own interest at the appropriate time?

The leading American ego psychologist is Erik H. Erikson, who has integrated personal, psychosocial, and historical experience in his concept of identity.[25] Erikson conceptualized eight epigenetic stages,

23. For an example of how psychohistory should *not* be written, both because it lacks all sensitivity to ego psychology and adaptation and because here psychodiagnostics are used as a weapon for political purposes, see Dana Ward, "Kissinger: A Psychohistory," *History of Childhood Quarterly*, II (1975), 287–349. Whatever one may think of Henry Kissinger's diplomacy, he certainly has shown a great capacity to adapt creatively to new personal, social, and political situations.

24. *S.E.*, XIV, 316–331; Frederick Wyatt and William B. Willcox, "Sir Henry Clinton: A Psychological Exploration in History," *William and Mary Quarterly, 3d ser.*, XVI (1959), 3–26; Willcox, *Portrait of a General: Sir Henry Clinton in the War of Independence* (New York, 1964).

25. Erik H. Erikson, *Childhood and Society* (New York, 1950, 1963: citations are to the revised second edition); *Identity and the Life Cycle: Selected Papers* (New York, 1959); *Identity: Youth and Crisis* (New York, 1968); *Dimensions of a New Identity* (New York, 1974); *Life History and the Historical Moment* (New York, 1957). For an appreciation, see Robert Coles, *Erik H. Erikson: The Growth of His Work* (Boston, 1970); for a sometimes savage critique see Paul Roazen, *Erik H. Erikson: The Power and Limits of a Vision* (New York, 1976). For a balanced discussion by a psychoanalytically trained historian, see John J. Fitzpatrick, "Erik H. Erikson and Psychohistory," *Bulletin of the Menninger Clinic*, XL (1976), 295–314; see also the "Special Issue on Erik H. Erikson," *Psychohistory Review*, V (1976).

or "ages of man" in which phase-specific biological developments meet psychosocial crises of growth. Thus the progressive development of the individual from birth through infancy, childhood, youth, adolescence, adulthood, and maturity to death is of importance to historians because in addition to infancy it emphasizes later periods of life, especially adolescence, as critical times for reworking earlier problems and integrating new solutions. Erikson defines personal identity as "the accrued confidence that the inner sameness and continuity prepared in the past are matched by the sameness and continuity of one's meaning for others."[26] A psychosocial identity is the sense of continuity between one's personal, family, ethnic, and national past and one's current role and interaction with the present. It means that one may say: "The way you see me now is the way I really am, and it is the way of my forefathers."[27]

Erikson's contribution to history is to use the lives of such creative individuals as Martin Luther[28] and Mohandas Gandhi[29] to elaborate on the psychosocial identity crises of a specific historical movement. Thus Erikson treats Luther not in psychogenetic terms alone but also as the expression of a social and economic class in movement, a northern European consciousness, and a crisis of faith in the early sixteenth century. While he gives due credit to the theme of Luther's anality, he finds this characterological trait in the adult modes of a stubborn sticking to principle and an uncompromising certainty in his own rectitude. The excremental experiences, language, and imagery of Luther are invoked by Erikson, but not with a pejorative intent. The admiration and respect of the biographer for his subject as a *persona* and for Luther's historical role is evident throughout.

The concepts of psychosocial and historical identity present an opening for the discussion of national groups in terms of the kinds of identities they cultivate in their young. Erikson did this in three brilliant concluding sections of *Childhood and Society*. There he portrays German, American, and Russian identity formation as adolescents experience it. The descriptions are clinical and literary, after the manner of a psychologically sophisticated anthropologist. Instead of employing survey techniques and statistical modes, Erikson uses cul-

26. *Childhood and Society,* 261.
27. Ibid., 129.
28. *Young Man Luther: A Study in Psychoanalysis and History* (New York, 1958, 1962). This work, as befits great and provocative studies, already has a historiography of its own. See Donald B. Meyer, "A Review of *Young Man Luther: A Study in Psychoanalysis and History*," in *History and Theory,* 1 (1961), 291–297; Roger A. Johnson, ed., *Psychohistory and Religion: The Case of Young Man Luther* (Philadelphia, 1977).
29. *Gandhi's Truth: On the Origins of Militant Nonviolence* (New York, 1969).

tural artifacts including folk songs, myth, films, and pseudo-autobiography such as *Mein Kampf.* His clinically and personally (Erikson grew up in Baden) informed account of how a young German of the first third of this century experienced his home, his mother and father, school, youth groups, *Wanderjahre,* the military, and national belonging is highly convincing.[30] In each case Erikson uses personalities, either such mythical ones as "Joe Hill," the idealized subject of an American folk song, or a cultural creation such as Maxim Gorky's "The Mother," or a historical figure such as Adolf Hitler as he portrayed himself. The essay on Germany, which is a classic of its kind, views Hitler's *Mein Kampf* as a skillful projection of the image of an adolescent who never gave in, who refused to surrender to the domineering father, and who insisted on protecting the loving mother—an image designed to appeal to the unconscious fantasies engendered by German family patterns.

Until recently Erikson's work was criticized only on historical grounds. Recently a social and theoretical critique of his model has developed.[31] Nevertheless, his ego psychological model has understandably had great influence on and appeal to historians. The special power of the psychobiographer's use of ego psychology is the attention to the historical actor's adaptation of the forces of his upbringing to the needs of the reality situation, rather than a focus on clinical pathology. Thus Richard Bushman, for example, explores the way Benjamin Franklin became a superb diplomat and conciliator from learning to cope with his demanding father and brothers.[32] Cushing Strout likewise deals with William James's work inhibitions in the ego psychological terms of his mechanisms of defense,[33] and David Musto relates John Quincy Adams's identity formation to strong family pressures internalized since childhood.[34] Robert Tucker's biography of Josef Stalin is Eriksonian in its smooth integration of emotional life

30. "Autobiographic Notes on the Identity Crisis," *Daedalus,* "The Making of Modern Science: Biographical Studies," IC (1970), 730–759.

31. See, for example, Howard I. Kushner, "Pathology and Adjustment in Psychohistory: A Critique of the Erikson Model," *Psychocultural Review,* I (1977), 493–506, and "Americanization of the Ego," *Canadian Review of American Studies,* X (1979), 95–101.

32. Bushman, "On the Use of Psychology: Conflict and Conciliation in Benjamin Franklin," *History and Theory,* V (1968), 225–240. See also Bushman, "Jonathan Edwards as Great Man: Identity, Conversion, and Leadership in the Great Awakening," *Soundings,* LII (1969), 15–46, and "Jonathan Edwards and Puritan Consciousness," *Journal of Scientific Study of Religion,* V (1966), 383–396.

33. Strout, "Ego Psychology and the Historian," *History and Theory,* VII (1968), 281–297.

34. Musto, "The Youth of John Quincy Adams," *Proceedings of the American Philosophical Society,* CXIII (1969), 269–282.

themes and politics. For example, he relates the violent beatings Stalin's father administered to his mother and the boy's futile efforts to protect her to Stalin's imagery of "lashing across their mugs, good and hard, and without letup" in political discourse, and his instructions to judges to administer such lashings literally.[35]

The psychological aspect of ideologies, including racism, is so important that it cannot be overlooked in any study of the subject. Studies of the psychodynamics of anti-Semitism have provided models for the integration of historical, social, and psychological variables in research. Racial prejudice may be seen as a cultural Rorschach test because it serves as a projection of all of those forces and fantasies with which a culture is ill at ease and which it needs to repress. By these defense mechanisms all of the attributes that are most repressed or conflictual in a culture are ascribed to the ethnic outgroups. They may be viewed as dominated by libidinal or aggressive drives—being dirty, sexual, lazy, or irresponsible—and may also be seen as stereotypes of ambition, intelligence, and shrewdness. In the case of Nazi propaganda images of Jews, for example, the contradictions were blatant. The Jews were portrayed as being both lazy and striving, inept and brilliant, Bolsheviks and capitalists.[36]

The historiography of the relations between the white, black, red, and yellow ethnic groups in American history has necessarily utilized the theories and clinical findings of psychoanalysis as well as ethnography and cultural anthropology.[37] A nation with a moving frontier, and which in three centuries displaced the native population, necessarily had complex and ambivalent feelings toward the American Indians. From their arrival, European settlers in North America had to deal with natives who already occupied the continent. The often violent displacement of the American Indians had its psychological concomitants in rationalizations of civilizing missions, religious justifications, projections of sexual and aggressive impulses onto the Indi-

35. Tucker, *Stalin as Revolutionary, 1879–1929: A Study in History and Personality* (New York, 1973), 74. See also Tucker, "The Rise of Stalin's Personality Cult," *American Historical Review*, LXXXIV (1979), 347–366.
36. Peter Loewenberg, "Psychodynamik des Antijudentums," in Walter Grab, ed., *Jahrbuch des Instituts für Deutsche Geschichte* (Tel Aviv), I (1972), 145–158.
37. Winthrop Jordan, *White over Black: American Attitudes toward the Negro, 1550–1812* (Chapel Hill, N.C., 1968); Joel Kovel, *White Racism: A Psychohistory* (New York, 1970); Peter Loewenberg, "The Psychology of Racism," in Gary B. Nash and Richard Weiss, eds., *The Great Fear: Race in the Mind of America* (New York, 1970), 186–201; and Loewenberg, "Racism and Tolerance in Historical Perspective," in Peter Orleans and William Ellis, jr., eds., *Race, Change, and Urban Society* (Beverly Hills, Calif., 1971), 561–576.

ans, and paternalism.[38] The recent biography of Jackson by Michael Rogin views his life in the context of early-nineteenth-century America's struggle with the problem of Indian "removal," paternalism, violence, and war.[39]

No problem in American social and political life has been greater or has received more psychohistorical attention than the human saga of domination, adaptation, and resistance which began in Negro slavery and is yet to be resolved. Stanley Elkins's famous psychological conceptualization of the middle-passage and slave experience using the analogy of the Nazi concentration camp has stimulated a considerable historiography of its own.[40] White majority relations with minority populations in various regions of the United States followed the national patterns of discrimination with a psychology of phobia, paranoid projections, and displacement in the case of Oriental minorities in the far West[41] and of Mexican-Americans in the Southwest.[42]

38. Gary B. Nash, *Red, White, and Black: The Peoples of Early America* (Englewood Cliffs, N.J., 1974), and "The Image of the Indian in the Southern Colonial Mind," *William and Mary Quarterly*, 3d ser., XXIX (1972), 197-230; Wilbur R. Jacobs, "The Fatal Confrontation: Early Native-White Relations on the Frontiers of Australia, New Guinea, and America—A Comparative Study," *Pacific Historical Review*, LX (1971), 293-309, and *Dispossessing the American Indian: Indians and Whites on the Colonial Frontier* (New York, 1972).

39. Rogin, *Fathers and Children: Andrew Jackson and the Subjugation of the American Indian* (New York, 1975). See the thoughtful review essay by Lewis Perry in *History and Theory*, XVI (1977), 174-195, and the caustic one by Elizabeth Fox-Genovese, "Psychohistory versus Psychodeterminism: The Case of Rogin's Jackson," *Reviews in American History*, III (1975), 407-418.

40. Elkins, *Slavery: A Problem in American Institutional and Intellectual Life* (Chicago, 1959); Ann J. Lane, ed., *The Debate over "Slavery": Stanley Elkins and His Critics* (Urbana, Ill., 1971); Kenneth Stampp, "Rebels and Sambos: The Search for the Negro's Personality in Slavery," *Journal of Southern History*, XXXVII (1971), 367-392; David Brion Davis, *The Slave Power Conspiracy and the Paranoid Style* (Baton Rouge, 1970). Eugene Genovese attacked a psychological approach to slaveholding in *The World the Slaveholders Made* (New York, 1969), 143-144, but five years later he found that guilt played an important role among slave owners; see *Roll, Jordan, Roll* (New York, 1974), 120-123, 453.

41. Gunther Barth, *Bitter Strength: A History of the Chinese in the United States, 1850-1870* (Cambridge, Mass., 1964); Stuart C. Miller, *The Unwelcome Immigrant: The American Image of the Chinese, 1785-1882* (Berkeley and Los Angeles, 1969); Roger Daniels, *The Politics of Prejudice: The Anti-Japanese Movement in California and the Struggle for Japanese Exclusion* (Berkeley and Los Angeles, 1962); Alexander Saxton, *The Indispensable Enemy: Labor and the Anti-Chinese Movement in California* (Berkeley and Los Angeles, 1971).

42. Robert Coles, *Eskimos, Chicanos, Indians*, vol. IV of *Children of Crisis* (Boston, 1977). Mauricio Mazon, "Illegal Alien Surrogates: A Psychohistorical Interpretation of Group Stereotyping in Time of Economic Stress," *Aztlan*, VI (1975), 305-324; Rodolfo Alvarez, "The Psycho-historical and Socioeconomic Development of the Chicano

The psychohistorian must strive to comprehend not only primitive aggressive and libidinal drive behavior and universal infantile fantasies, but also their varied expression at given times and places in history by men and institutions. The methodological link between universal modes of the unconscious and the particular social setting must be made. Historians need studies of how the life experiences, political constellations, critical personal traumas (expulsion from home, death of a parent, early illness) of leaders and activists and such social traumas as war, famine, and depression have conditioned styles of leadership and the nature of group functioning. A group that has experienced a common historical event or situation constitutes a cohort and may possess common features or patterns of response that can be identified decades later.[43] Some traumas, such as the atomic bombing of Hiroshima, which Robert Jay Lifton studied, are so overwhelming that all age groups are hit with the blow at once.[44] Other prolonged traumas, such as the blockade and starvation of Germany in World War I, affected some groups (such as young children) more intensely than others. Psychoanalytic concepts of phase specificity must therefore be used by the historian to examine the impact of a particular kind of deprivation on a given age group at a certain historical time.[45]

The antebellum generation, typified by Abraham Lincoln, is treated in psychoanalytic terms by George Forgie as a cohort that forged its identity against the legacy of a powerful generation of Founding Fathers—heroes all, men who could never be equaled without a crisis and a struggle that was even greater than theirs. Thus Forgie casts the political and ideological issues of slavery and union in a new perspective of emotions and fantasies based on the psychodynamics of generational oedipal conflict.[46]

---

Community in the United States," *Social Science Quarterly,* LIV (1973), 920–942, and "The Unique Psycho-Historical Experience of the Mexican-American People," *Social Science Quarterly,* LII (1971), 15–29.

43. Norman B. Ryder, "The Cohort as a Concept in the Study of Social Change," *American Sociological Review,* XXX (1965), 843–861, and "Cohort Analysis," in *International Encyclopedia of the Social Sciences,* 2d ed. (New York, 1968), II, 546–550.

44. Lifton, *Death in Life: Survivors of Hiroshima* (New York, 1967), and *History and Human Survival: Essays on the Young and Old, Survivors and the Dead, Peace and War, and on Contemporary Psychohistory* (New York, 1971).

45. Peter Loewenberg, "The Psychohistorical Origins of the Nazi Youth Cohort," *American Historical Review,* LXXVI (1971), 1457–1502.

46. Forgie, *Patricide in the House Divided: A Psychological Interpretation of Lincoln and His Age* (New York, 1979). Forgie interestingly applies the common childhood experience of the family romance in which children fantasy that they are in fact the children, not of ordinary mundane parents, but of heroes.

When dealing with small groups—for example, the leadership of a political party or a financial power elite—historians have relied on quantitative economic and social data that produce external evidence such as income, education, membership in associations and clubs, and comparative intellectual development. This kind of evidence, while it may be statistically broad, is necessarily collected without emotional depth. It is thin in the perception of common dynamic development and phase-specific emotional experiences that the members of a group have had. One of the major problems historians confront is that of bridging the gap between personalities and institutions— finding the juncture between individuals and the organization or power structure they shaped or to which they belonged.

The problem now in the forefront of conceptual synthesis is integrating the singular personal experience that lends itself to psychoanalytic explanation and the larger social matrix of historical developments. Wilfred Bion has applied Kleinian theory to the functioning of groups in what has come to be known as the "Tavistock" model of group dynamics.[47] The aim of a Tavistock "work group" is to study the emotional "work" of a group independently of any reality task that groups conventionally have to perform. This strategy enables the members to observe in their behavior and emotions how the psychological processes of group functions occur.

The relevance to history and politics of group fantasies is readily apparent. Such groups as cabinets and parliaments, general staffs and governing committees also have emotional agendas. Steven Brown and John Ellithorp applied Bion's categories in their study of Senator Eugene McCarthy's 1968 campaign for the United States presidency.[48] An exciting innovation in the training of historians occurred at Yale University in 1967 when David Musto and Boris Astrachan gave a group of history graduate students a Bion Tavistock group experience with the intention that they should apply what they learned through the emotional experience to the study of groups functioning in history.[49]

Historians of the future will explore and capture the common emotional dimensions of the lives of a generation which may cut across

---

47. Bion, *Experiences in Groups and Other Papers* (New York, 1959).
48. Brown and Ellithorp, "Emotional Experiences in Political Groups: The Case of the McCarthy Phenomenon," *American Political Science Review*, LXIV (1970), 349-366. For an application of psychodynamics to leadership groups, see Irving L. Janis, *Victims of Group Think: A Psychological Study of Foreign-Policy Decisions and Fiascoes* (Boston, 1972).
49. Musto and Astrachan, "Strange Encounter: The Use of Study Groups with Graduate Students in History," *Psychiatry*, XXXI (1968), 264-276.

traditional lines of status or class. What psychohistory offers historians is a new and subtler category of inner emotional evidence with which to complement their "surface" or external statistical data, which usually define a temporal era or a social or leadership subgroup. Historians might examine and compare the emotional experiences and maturational development of an entire leadership caste, such as the top echelon of National Socialism. In-depth longitudinal studies of the ego development, object relations, gender identity, and character structure of such elite groups as various "kitchen cabinets," parliamentary factions, the Committee of Public Safety in the French Revolution, and the early Bolsheviks or of such small groups as the Anabaptists during the Reformation may bring forth emotional common denominators that are all the more decisive for being only partly conscious. It is only in the realm of feelings that the individual can be fully understood. Unique persons can best be comprehended in their full cultural contexts, which means in relation to the lives of others with whom they have deeply rooted emotional affinities. In both cases, the group and the individual, the explanation of motive, of deep-seated fears and aspirations, runs from the single person to his peers and then back to the unique psyche as the dialectic of feeling and thought, leader and group, stasis and action, is played out in history.[50]

Biography, which studies the individual in depth and intensity, has been the classic forum for the blending of history and psychoanalysis, which is also an individual clinical method *par excellence.* As Donald Meyer stated, "psychoanalytic biography constitutes a perspective, or a focus, from which history can organize all its narratives, no matter how vast a range of social data these may comprehend."[51] Biographies of political leaders from classic to modern times,[52] artists and

50. H. Stuart Hughes, "History and Psychoanalysis: The Explanation of Motive," in *History as Art and as Science: Twin Vistas on the Past* (New York, 1964), 42–67.

51. In Mazlish, *Psychoanalysis and History,* 179.

52. Thomas W. Africa, "The Mask of an Assassin: A Psychohistorical Study of M. Junius Brutus," *Journal of Interdisciplinary History,* VIII (1978), 599–626; Fawn M. Brodie, *Thaddeus Stevens: Scourge of the South* (New York, 1959), and *Thomas Jefferson: An Intimate History* (New York, 1973); Elizabeth W. Marvick, "Childhood History and Decisions of State: The Case of Louis XIII," *History of Childhood Quarterly,* II (1974), 135–200; E. Victor Wolfenstein, *The Revolutionary Personality: Lenin, Trotsky, Gandhi* (Princeton 1967) and *Personality and Politics* (Belmont, Calif., 1969); Bruce Mazlish, *The Revolutionary Ascetic: Evolution of a Political Type* (New York, 1976); Peter Loewenberg, "Theodor Herzl: A Psychoanalytic Study in Charismatic Political Leadership," in Benjamin B. Wolman, ed., *The Psychoanalytic Interpretation of History* (New York, 1971), 150–191; David H. Donald, *Charles Sumner and the Coming of the Civil War* (New York, 1960).

writers,[53] explorers and adventurers,[54] and philosophers and scientists[55] have been enriched by psychoanalytic understanding. We also have contemporary leadership studies of such political figures as John F. Kennedy, Lyndon Johnson, Henry Kissinger, Richard Nixon, Jimmy Carter, and Jerry Brown, with varying results.[56] Many of these studies have crossed the line between biography and journalism.

A development of considerable significance is the growing application of psychoanalytic object relations theory to historical problems. Object relations theory is derived from the first year of life, when the child is learning to distinguish self from nonself, subject from object. To the infant all sources of pleasure, such as the mother's breast, are viewed as a part of the self and as "good." Sources of discomfort, such as pressure in the colon or a pain in the stomach, are believed to be outside of the self and "bad." This primitive "splitting" serves as a model for the defense mechanism of projection in later life. Projection is the tendency to take feelings or qualities that belong to the subject and to attribute them to persons or objects in the external world. The assumption of object relations theory is that adult functioning and relations with the persons and problems of the outer world are patterned on the first relations of the infant to its primary

53. Maynard Solomon, *Beethoven* (New York, 1977). Editha and Richard Sterba, *Beethoven and His Nephew: A Psychoanalytic Study of Their Relationship* (New York, 1954, 1971), is particularly interesting in making use, more than a century after Beethoven's death, of oral tradition in Heiligenstadt, the suburb of Vienna where he lived. This is an application of Marc Bloch's research technique of "understanding the past by the present," *Historian's Craft*, 43, 47. David J. Fisher, "Sigmund Freud and Romain Rolland: The Terrestrial Animal and His Great Oceanic Friend," *American Imago*, XXXIII (1976), 1–59. The most creative psychoanalytic approach to literary texts, and of great value for historical texts as well, is Norman N. Holland's "reader's response" method, which utilizes "countertransference" or the subjective feelings of the researcher as a tool of cognition; see Holland, *The Dynamics of Literary Response* (New York, 1968).

54. Fawn M. Brodie, *The Devil Drives: A Life of Sir Richard Burton* (New York, 1967); John E. Mack, *A Prince of Our Disorder: The Life of T. E. Lawrence* (Boston, 1976); William G. Neiderland, "An Analytic Inquiry into the Life and Work of Heinrich Schliemann," in Max Schur, ed., *Drives, Affects, Behavior* (New York, 1965), II, 369–396.

55. Jerrold Seigel, *Marx's Fate: The Shape of a Life* (Princeton, 1978); Arthur Mitzman, *The Iron Cage: An Historical Interpretation of Max Weber* (New York, 1969); Bruce Mazlish, *James and John Stuart Mill: Father and Son in the Nineteenth Century* (New York, 1975); Frank E. Manuel, *A Portrait of Isaac Newton* (Cambridge, Mass., 1968); Bennett Simon and Nancy Simon, "The Pacifist Turn: An Episode of Mystic Illumination in the Autobiography of Bertrand Russell," *Journal of the American Psychoanalytic Association*, XX (1972), 109–121; Nelson H. Minnich and W. W. Meissner, "The Character of Erasmus," *American Historical Review*, LXXXIII (1978), 598–624.

56. Nancy Clinch, *The Kennedy Neurosis* (New York, 1973); Doris Kearns, *Lyndon Johnson and the American Dream* (New York, 1976); Bruce Mazlish, *Kissinger: The European Mind in American Policy* (New York, 1976), and *In Search of Nixon: A Psychohistorical Inquiry* (New York, 1972); Mauricio Mazon, "Young Richard Nixon: A Study in Political Precocity," *The Historian*, XLI (1978), 21–40.

mothering figure. Object relations theory is attractive to social scientists because it does not require an instinctual theory of love and aggression, as libido theory does. It merely postulates that individuals relate as they have learned to, or were programmed to, according to the unconscious fantasies of infancy.[57] Kleinian psychoanalytic theories were used by John Demos in a study of New England witchcraft,[58] and Kohutian theories of narcissism have influenced Christopher Lasch and Ann Douglas.[59]

Three psychohistorical studies of Bismarck provide examples of how varied psychodynamic models may illuminate even a carefully studied historical subject and complement one another conceptually. Charlotte Sempell describes Bismarck's maternal deprivation.[60] Otto Pflanze, using a Reichian psychodynamic model, treats Bismarck's arrogant character as an external defense against underlying passive-dependent needs.[61] Judith Hughes relies on a Fairbairnian object-relational model of Bismarck's relations with his mother to explain his adult mode of exploiting and misusing other people, including his son Herbert and his political counterplayers.[62]

Among psychohistorical techniques used by the U.S. Office of Strategic Services in World War II was a personality study of Adolf Hitler.[63] The particular value of this study for historians is that it used Hitler's own text as the primary source for interpretation; this is the kind of evidence that historians have in abundance and interpret in

57. Object-relational analysis is applied as a conceptual framework in my "Unsuccessful Adolescence of Heinrich Himmler," *American Historical Review,* LXXVI (1971), 612–641. This schema may be particularly useful for secondary, noncharismatic leaders.

58. Demos, "Underlying Themes in the Witchcraft of Seventeenth-Century New England, *American Historical Review,* LXXV (1970), 1311–26.

59. Lasch, *The Culture of Narcissism: American Life in an Age of Diminishing Expectations* (New York, 1978); Douglas, *The Feminization of American Culture* (New York, 1977, 1978), especially 419–420. For the work of Heinz Kohut, see his "Thoughts on Narcissism and Narcissistic Rage," *Psychoanalytic Study of the Child,* XXVII (1972), 360–400; "Forms and Transformations of Narcissism," *Journal of the American Psychoanalytic Association,* XIV (1966), 243–262; *The Analysis of the Self: A Systematic Approach to the Psychoanalytic Treatment of Narcissistic Personality Disorders* (New York, 1971); and *The Restoration of the Self* (New York, 1977).

60. Sempell, "Bismarck's Childhood: A Psychohistorical Study," *History of Childhood Quarterly,* II (1974), 107–124.

61. Pflanze, "Toward a Psychoanalytic Interpretation of Bismarck," *American Historical Review,* LXXVII (1972). 419–444.

62. Hughes, "Toward the Psychological Drama of High Politics: The Case of Bismarck," *Central European History,* X (1978), 271–285.

63. Walter C. Langer, Ernst Kris, and Bertram D. Lewin, "A Psychological Analysis of Adolph Hitler" (Washington, D. C., 1944); and Walter C. Langer, *The Mind of Adolf Hitler.*

the regular course of their work.[64] This wartime intelligence psychobiography of Hitler was of value to R. G. L. Waite in his psychohistory of Hitler and the Third Reich, which also uses more recently discovered documents and data, such as the Soviet autopsy report indicating that Hitler had only one testicle.[65] The significance of such data is not trivial or incidental. The integral nature of human psychodynamics—the fact that all elements of the person, even the most apparently disparate aspects of fantasy or behavior, are related to each other—means that politics cannot be separated from the person. If Hitler had a genital malformation and consequently the fantasies to which it gave rise, it undoubtedly affected his ideas, images, and actions concerning masculinity and femininity, brutality and compassion, hardness and softness, strength and weakness, perfection and mutilation. The personal data, as Waite demonstrates, illuminate and explicate the public record.

Rudolph Binion pursues actual traumas that he demonstrates or infers in Hitler's life, from his experiences in infancy, when he was presumably overindulged by a mother made anxious by the loss of earlier children, to his mother's death from breast cancer when he was eighteen, to his being gassed in World War I, to the Final Solution.[66]

A definitive biography of Hitler must give close attention to his successes and adaptations, and they were numerous, as in the party crisis of 1925–26 and his diplomacy of the 1930s. A balanced psychohistorical view must also look with care at those points in Hitler's life and politics at which he failed to see reality and adjust to it, for example at the Dunkirk evacuation and the Russian campaign. This is an ego-psychological approach in that it focuses on and evaluates historically the points at which the ego functions of reality testing, perception, and tolerance of stress, frustration, ambiguity, and ambivalence were intact in Hitler's decision making and those at which they were vitiated or overwhelmed by forces of the unconscious.

On the other side of the Atlantic, a major area in which psychoanalytic insight has been applied to historical processes is colo-

64. Peter Loewenberg, review in *Central European History*, VII (1974), 262–275; for a recent interpretation of the latent emotional content of Hitler's writings and speeches, see Richard A. Koenigsberg, *Hitler's Ideology: A Study in Psychoanalytic Sociology* (New York, 1975).

65. Waite, *The Psychopathic God* (New York, 1977); Lev Bezymenski, *The Death of Adolf Hitler: Unknown Documents from Societ Archives* (New York, 1968).

66. Binion, *Hitler among the Germans* (New York, 1976). See my critique in "Psychohistorical Perspectives," 241–244, and George M. Kren, "Psychohistorical Interpretations of National Socialism," *German Studies Review*, I (1978), 150–172.

nial and revolutionary America. Among group phenomena on which psychoanalytic perceptions have been brought to bear are Puritan childhood,[67] the Salem witch trials,[68] and the American Revolution.[69] David Horowitz has reinterpreted the colonial resentment of England and the politics of the American revolution by synthesizing these economic and political events with the psychology resulting from the virtually perpetual Indian wars of early American history. Peter N. Carroll places the biography of Samuel Johnson of New England in the context of generational and religious developments. Philip Greven offers a model that relates political attitudes toward England and revolution to child raising and the moral severity of particular styles or "temperaments" of Protestantism practiced in colonial and revolutionary America. He distinguishes three varieties of Protestant belief and behavioral systems: the evangelical, the moderate, and the genteel—each with its own child-rearing standards, morality, and attitude toward authority, expressed in politics as well as personal conduct and theology.[70] The psychohistorical interpretation of emotional themes in American culture has been highly developed, including interpretations of frontier violence,[71] love,[72] and politics.[73]

67. Philip J. Greven, Jr., *The Protestant Temperament: Patterns of Child-Rearing, Religious Experience, and the Self in Early America* (New York, 1977), and *Four Generations: Population, Land, and Family in Colonial Andover, Massachusetts* (Ithaca, N.Y., 1970); John Demos, *A Little Commonwealth: Family Life in Plymouth Colony* (New York, 1970).

68. Demos, "Underlying Themes in the Witchcraft of Seventeenth-Century New England"; Emery J. Battis, *Saints and Sectaries: Anne Hutchinson and the Antinomian Controversy in Massachusetts Bay Colony* (Chapel Hill, N.C., 1962).

69. Edwin G. Burrows and Michael Wallace, "The American Revolution: The Ideology and Psychology of National Liberation," in *Perspectives in American History*, vi (1972), 167-306; Winthrop Jordan, "Familial Politics: Thomas Paine and the Killing of the King, 1776," *Journal of American History*, lx (1973), 294-308.

70. Horowitz, *The First Frontier: The Indian Wars and America's Origins, 1607-1776* (New York, 1978); Carroll, *The Other Samuel Johnson;* Greven, *The Protestant Temperament.*

71. Richard Slotkin, *Regeneration through Violence: The Mythology of the American Frontier, 1600-1860* (Middletown, Conn., 1973); John G. Cawelti, *The Six-Gun Mystique* (Bowling Green, O., 1976); Richard Hofstadter and Michael Wallace, eds., *American Violence: A Documentary History* (New York, 1970).

72. Leslie Fiedler, *Love and Death in the American Novel* (New York, 1960), is a classic; see also his *Return of the Vanishing American* (New York, 1968).

73. Richard Hofstadter, *The Paranoid Style in American Politics* (New York, 1965), and *The American Political Tradition* (New York, 1955), especially 134, 210-211, 231. See the psychological interpretation of Hofstadter's work by Daniel W. Howe and Peter E. Finn, "Richard Hofstadter: The Ironies of An American Historian," *Pacific Historical Review*, xliii (1974), 1-23. See also the works of David Brion Davis, *The Slave Power Conspiracy*, and Davis, ed., *The Fear of Conspiracy: Images of Un-American Subversion from the Revolution to the Present* (Ithaca, N.Y., 1971). For conspiracy fantasies in the American Revolution, see Bernard Bailyn, *The Ideological Origins of the American Revolution* (Cambridge, Mass., 1967), 144-159.

Among the most creative applications of psychoanalytic insight to cultural and intellectual history is research on the fecund culture of *fin-de-siècle* Vienna, a milieu that spawned much that is the essence of modern art, literature, theater, music, philosophy, statecraft, and psychology. Carl E. Schorske has integrated politics, art, and literature with psychological dimensions of Viennese culture in a series of sweeping and superbly sensitive studies.[74] William McGrath has developed the political and psychological implications of the aesthetic commitments of a generation of middle-class Viennese intellectuals who shaped the rich political, literary, musical, and psychological milieus of Vienna in the 1890s.[75] Peter Gay has stressed the German cultural origins of Freud's thought and sensitively explored the psychological dilemmas of Jewish assimilation and self-hatred in Central Europe.[76]

Because psychological history is based on a developmental model, researchers have explored the history of childhood and the family and historians of the family have naturally looked at intergenerational relationships.[77] The classic study that has influenced the development of the field is Philippe Aries's *L'enfant et la vie familiale sous l'ancien régime* (Paris, 1960).[78] Aries proposes that "childhood" as a category of life developed among the aristocracy and bourgeoisie of Western Europe in the sixteenth and seventeenth centuries. Previously "the idea of childhood," by which Aries means "an awareness of the par-

74. "Generational Tension and Cultural Change: Reflections on the Case of Vienna," *Daedalus*, CVII (1978), 111–122; "Politics and Patricide in Freud's *Interpretation of Dreams*," *American Historical Review*, LXXVIII (1973), 328–347; "Politics and the Psyche in *Fin de Siècle* Vienna, Schnitzler, and Hofmannsthal," *American Historical Review*, LXVI (1961), 930–947.

75. *Dionysian Art and Populist Politics in Austria* (New Haven, 1974); "Freud as Hannibal: The Politics of the Brother Band," *Central European History*, VII (1974), 31–57. See also the critique by Stanley Rothman and Phillip Isenberg, ibid., 58–78, and the reply by McGrath, ibid., 79–83.

76. Gay, *Freud, Jews, and Other Germans: Masters and Victims in Modernist Culture* (New York, 1978). See also my "Insiders and Outsiders," *Partisan Review*, XLVI (1979), 461–470. For a problematic treatment of German and Jewish historical interaction in terms of the psychology of "myths," see Sidney M. Bolkosky, *The Distorted Image: German Jewish Perceptions of Germans and Germany, 1918–1935* (New York, 1975), and my critique in *History and Theory*, XVI (1977), 361–367. For an analysis of these same psychological "myths" and mechanisms as currently reenacted in Near Eastern politics, see Jay Y. Gonen, *A Psychohistory of Zionism* (New York, 1975) and my review essay in *History of Childhood quarterly*, III (1975, 300–305).

77. Tamara K. Hareven, "The History of the Family as an Interdisciplinary Field," *Journal of Interdisciplinary History*, II (1971), 399–414.

78. Trans by Robert Baldick as *Centuries of Childhood: A Social History of Family Life* (New York, 1962). See the persuasive critique by Demos that Aries fails to be developmental in viewing childhood: *Little Commonwealth*, 130.

ticular nature of childhood, that particular nature which distinguishes
the child from the adult, even the young adult, . . . did not exist."[79]
Most of the subsequent American work on Europe has also focused
on early modern France,[80] and on the upper and middle classes.[81] A
notable exception because of its emphasis on ordinary people is Edward Shorter's *Making of the Modern Family.*[82]

Changes in the concept of childhood in America have been related
to the development of adolescence as a phase of life between childhood and adulthood.[83] Historians of childhood in America have also
studied the history of changes in public policies between state and
nonstate roles in strengthening the family.[84] David Potter developed
an interpretation of American national character and history based
on a neo-Freudian model of viewing culture and personality "in an
integral sense, as a totality." Potter pointed out the meaning for the
American character of the emotional implications of bottle feeding
for mother-child intimacy, the importance of disposable diapers for
indulgent toilet training, and the new emotional factors in marriage
when its economic functions are diminished.[85]

It is difficult to apply a clinical schema to a national polity without
an intervening level of sociocultural concepts and empirical studies of
processes to make the linkage between a mode of parenting and a
pattern of national or group behavior. Until this intermediate link is
available, historians will have microcosmic studies of mother-child
interaction on the one hand and action in history on the other, but
they will be unable to relate the two spheres to each other in a given

79. *Centuries of Childhood,* 29.
80. For example, David Hunt, *Parents and Children in History: The Psychology of Family Life in Early Modern France* (New York, 1970).
81. For an interesting comparative treatment of the interaction of upper-class and working-class youth in English and German university towns, see John R. Gillis, *Youth and History: Tradition and Change in European Age Relations, 1770–Present* (New York, 1974).
82. New York, 1975. Shorter criticizes Aries precisely on this point of ignoring the lower classes, thus presenting skewed results (170, 192). See, however, the critique of Shorter by Christopher Lasch, *Haven in a Heartless World* (New York, 1977), 168, 219, n. 4.
83. Joseph F. Kett, *Rites of Passage: Adolescence in America, 1970 to the Present* (New York, 1977); John Demos and Virginia Demos, "Adolescence in Historical Perspective," *Journal of Marriage and the Family,* XXXI (1969). See also Gillis, *Youth and History.*
84. Robert Bremner et al., eds., *Children and Youth in America: A Documentary History* (Cambridge, Mass., 1970–1974), 3 vols. See also Bernard Wishy, *The Child and the Republic: The Dawn of Modern American Child Nurture* (Philadelphia, 1968).
85. Potter, *People of Plenty: Economic Abundance and the American Character* (Chicago, 1954), 194, 198, 203–204. For the most useful synthesis of the field of culture and personality with psychodynamics, see Robert A. LeVine, *Culture, Behavior, and Personality* (Chicago, 1973).

case. What is needed is a solid series of studies of mothering, family patterns, childhood and adolescent socialization, and adaptive processes for each historical period and geographical and cultural area. Historians of the family have begun to fill in some of the gaping areas of ignorance.[86] The history of childhood and of the family and collective biography are now moving to the forefront of historical interest. The family and the collectivity of a small group are seen as mediating agencies between social class and the individual. The economic and national consciousness of individuals are established at the crucial periods of life when psychic patterns are imparted unconsciously—in the family. Thus a psychological history of the family, childhood, and generations may provide the crucial psychohistorical link between Freud and Marx, between the micro-individual level and the macro-social economic scene, in each epoch of history.[87]

As a research and explanatory model, psychohistory is value-neutral. It has been used in the service of both radical and conservative cultural positions. Freud, who was a skeptic, saw an immortal combat between man's biological drives and the demands of historical culture. He believed that human culture is in unalterable conflict with the demands of man's instinctual life, and that "the price of progress in civilization is paid in forfeiting happiness through the heightening of a sense of guilt."[88] This heritage, which recognizes the fundamentally ambiguous nature of history, is very much alive among humanists.[89]

Psychohistory is also a powerful mode for criticizing the cultural and behavioral norms of the Western world, its family and work

86. "The Family in History," special issue of *Journal of Interdisciplinary History*, II (1971); John Demos and Sarane S. Boocock, eds., *Turning Points: Historical and Sociological Essays on the Family*, supplement to *American Journal of Sociology*, LXXXIV (1978); Tamara K. Hareven, ed., *Family and Kin in Urban Communities, 1700–1930* (New York, 1977), and *Transitions: The Family and the Life Course in Historical Perspective* (New York, 1978); John Modell, Frank F. Furstenberg, Jr., and Theodore Herschberg, "Social Change and Transitions to Adulthood in Historical Perspective," *Journal of Family History*, I (1976), 7–32; Lloyd de Mause, ed., *The History of Childhood* (New York, 1974).

87. See the judicious evaluation by Frank E. Manuel, "The Use and Abuse of Psychology in History," *Daedalus*, C (1977), 187–213; Robert A. Pois, "Historicism, Marxism, and Psychohistory: Three Approaches to the Problem of Historical Individuality," *Social Science Journal*, XIII (1976), 77–91.

88. "Das Unbehagen in der Kultur," *Studien*, IX, 260; "Civilization and Its Discontents" (1930), *S.E.*, XXI, 134.

89. Hans Meyerhoff, "Freud and the Ambiguity of Culture," *Partisan Review*, XXIV (1957), 117–130; Philip Rieff, *Freud: The Mind of the Moralist* (New York, 1959), and *The Triumph of the Therapeutic: Uses of Faith after Freud* (New York, 1966); Lionel Trilling, *Freud and the Crisis of Our Culture* (Boston, 1955), and *Sincerity and Authenticity* (Cambridge, Mass., 1972); Robert Waelder, *Progress and Revolution: A Study of the Issues of Our Age* (New York, 1967).

ethos, patterns of aggression, and interpersonal relations.[90] In some cases the critics, writing what may be termed "meta-psychohistory," include a postulated utopian future.[91] Other interpretations have stressed adaptation to change, internalization of social norms, and integration of personality in historical setting. The chief synthesizer of social analysis with psychoanalytic ego psychology and object relations theory was Talcott Parsons.[92] Fred Weinstein and Gerald Platt have successfully applied Parsons's psychoanalytic object relations model of social internalization to psychohistory.[93]

Psychohistory provides a new tool for historians to analyze their data and interpret the complex configurations of human behavior in the past. American historians have applied it both crudely and well, both daringly and conservatively. To historians of the next decades falls the task of moving beyond beginnings to explain mankind's past and current predicaments with greater sophistication than we have yet been able to do.

90. Russell Jacoby, *Social Amnesia: A Critique of Conformist Psychology from Adler to Laing* (Boston, 1975); Eli Zaretsky, *Capitalism, the Family, and Personal Life* (New York, 1976); Mark Poster, *Critical Theory of the Family* (Somers, Conn., 1978); Lasch, *Haven in a Heartless World* (New York, 1977) and *The Culture of Narcissism*; Paul Roazen, *Freud: Political and Social Thought* (New York, 1970). A variant of this culture critical approach is the psychohistorical interpretation of the Nazi death camps; see Richard L. Rubenstein, *The Cunning of History: The Holocaust and the American Future* (New York, 1975) and "Religion and the Origins of the Death Camps: A Psychoanalytic Interpretation," in Rubenstein, *After Auschwitz: Radical Theology and Contemporary Judaism* (Indianapolis, 1966), 1–44.

91. Herbert Marcuse, *Eros and Civilization: A Philosophical Inquiry into Freud* (Boston, 1955); Norman O. Brown, *Life against Death: The Psychoanalytical Meaning of History* (Middletown, Conn., 1959). Frank E. Manuel has exposed utopias to psychohistorical analysis: "Toward a Psychological History of Utopias," in *Utopias and Utopian Thought* (Boston, 1967), 69–98.

92. Talcott Parsons, *Social Structure and Personality* (Glencoe, Ill., 1964), and, with Robert F. Bales, *Family, Socialization, and Interaction Process* (Glencoe, Ill., 1955).

93. Weinstein and Platt, *The Wish to Be Free: Society, Psyche, and Value Change* (Berkeley and Los Angeles, 1969), and *Psychoanalytic Sociology;* see also Weinstein and Platt, "The Coming Crisis of Psychohistory," *Journal of Modern History*, XLVII (1975), 202–228.

# 18

## Quantitative Social-Scientific History

### J. Morgan Kousser

QUANTITATIVE social science launched its invasion of American history during the years 1957 to 1961.[1] In 1957, Lee Benson, a historian schooled in sociology, published a sweeping critique of "impressionistic" treatments of nineteenth-century American elections and called on historians to expand their definition of primary sources beyond newspapers and manuscripts to include quantifiable data. Four years later Benson added practice to preachment, relying heavily on a quantitative analysis of election returns to produce a brilliant and original interpretation of American politics in the 1830s and '40s. In a paper delivered in 1957, two Harvard economists, Alfred H. Conrad and John R. Meyer, reinvigorated the discussion of an old historical problem and initiated the new "econometric history" by demonstrating the profitability both of slavery and of applying modern economic theory and techniques to history. By 1960, the "cliometricians," as they were jibingly labeled, were holding annual conferences at Purdue to coordinate research efforts and criticize each other's papers. A year before, the historian Merle Curti, assisted by several other historians and his psychologist wife, Margaret, published a quantitative historical study of community social structure and mobility, which, along with the work of Stephan Thernstrom, inspired legions of students to take up the "new social history."[2]

1. Of course, historians, especially economic historians, have always counted or used such implicitly quantitative phrases as "more," "less," "most." But the rapid development in social science theory and statistical methods in the postwar era and the continuing revolution in data-processing technology have given a qualitatively different cast to quantitative history in the last two decades.

2. Benson, "Research Problems in American Political Historiography," reprinted in his *Toward the Scientific Study of History* (Philadelphia, 1972), 3–80, and *The Concept of Jacksonian Democracy: New York as a Test Case* (Princeton, 1961); Conrad and Meyer,

_J. Morgan Kousser_

The response of the historical profession's elite was rapid, but by no means single-minded. To the sometimes strident demands of the devotees of the new history that traditionally trained historians "retool, rethink, reform, or be plowed under," as one older economic historian caricatured the new program, some historians at first reacted with fright, irrationality, and something close to panic. Arthur Schlesinger, Jr., whose description of Whig and Jacksonian electoral coalitions had failed Benson's systematic numerical tests, retreated behind a hastily erected wall of dogma. "Almost all important questions," Schlesinger proclaimed, "are important precisely because they are _not_ susceptible to quantitative answers." In a presidential address to the American Historical Association, Carl Bridenbaugh issued a jeremiad against the infiltrating priests of the new religion, warning his fellow historians never to "worship at the shrine of that Bitch-goddess, QUANTIFICATION."[3]

Others kept their wits a bit better, declaring the historical faith broad enough to encompass another sect. Reminding his readers that enthusiasm for social science had repeatedly waxed and waned within the American historical profession in the twentieth century, C. Vann Woodward suggested that "rhetorical indignation and the neo-Luddite posture of our conservatives are not effective responses. Smashing computers is not quite the answer." If Woodward seemed to yearn for a revolution that would overthrow the contemporary regime of historical craftsmen who were "even more addicted than those of earlier generations to over-specialization and narrowness of subject matter," whose "monumental patience" produced such "unimpressive conclusions," he was doubtful about the revolutionaries' prospects for victory and skeptical of their utopian visions.[4]

A third response to the social-scientific proselytizers, especially popular among graduate students and younger historians, was fraternization and—usually timid—collaboration. Thus, a traditionally trained historian who found Guttman scaling helpful in his study of the mid-

---

"The Economics of Slavery in the Antebellum South," in Robert William Fogel and Stanley L. Engerman, eds., _The Reinterpretation of American Economic History_ (New York, 1971), 342–361; Curti, _The Making of an American Community: A Case Study of Democracy in a Frontier County_ (Stanford, 1959).

3. All of the quotations are from C. Vann Woodward, "History and the Third Culture," _Journal of Contemporary History_, III (April 1968), 29–30.

4. Woodward, "Third Culture," 30, 24. For a similar response, see Harold D. Woodman, "Economic History and Economic Theory," _Journal of Interdisciplinary History_, III (1972), 323–350. The "sectarian" epithet is in widespread use. See, for example, J. H. Hexter, "Fernand Braudel and the _Monde Braudelien_," _Journal of Modern History_, XLIV (1972), 386.

nineteenth-century British Parliament, William O. Aydelotte, nevertheless carefully qualified his endorsement of the use of quantitative methods. "Quantification," he remarked in a set of essays advocating its employment in historical study "is merely an ancillary tool, one of several, that can, for certain classes of questions, be of some help." From 1965 to 1970, 120 historians, many of them no less hesitant than Aydelotte, attended summer seminars in historical data analysis at the University of Michigan.[5]

Nonetheless, by 1970 the noisy initial skirmishes were over. Formidable beachheads of research had been established in social and political history, while in economic history the cliometric generals had won decisive victories. The econometric historians were powerful enough to take over the strongest disciplinary journal, the *Journal of Economic History*, while their social and political counterparts started new ones—the *Journal of Social History* (1967), *Historical Methods* (1967), and the *Journal of Interdisciplinary History* (1970). The body of work based on the analysis of quantitative data was impressive. In political history, the "ethnocultural thesis" rested on examinations of patterns of voting returns in ethnically and religiously homogeneous geographic areas; the theory of "critical elections," on correlations of election returns by area across time; and various hypotheses about the behavior of particular legislative bodies, on Guttman scaling and factor analyses of roll calls.[6] In social history, scholars tabulated the extent to which individual family heads remained in the same area or the same occupational rank over time; demographers charted changes in marriage, birth, and death rates, as well as in family size and type, while other social historians graphed patterns of wealth and landholding and alterations in those patterns. Economic historians

5. Aydelotte, *Quantification in History* (Reading, Mass. 1971), 34; Robert P. Swierenga, "Clio and Computers: A Survey of Computerized Research in History," *Computers and the Humanities*, v (1970), 5.

6. Benson, *Concept of Jacksonian Democracy;* Paul Kleppner, *The Cross of Culture: A Social Analysis of Midwestern Politics, 1850–1900* (New York, 1970); Michael F. Holt, *Forging a Majority: The Formation of the Republican Party in Pittsburgh, 1848–1860* (New Haven, 1969); Ronald P. Formisano, *The Birth of Mass Political Parties: Michigan, 1827–1861* (Princeton, 1971); Walter Dean Burnham, *Critical Elections and the Mainsprings of American Politics* (New York, 1970); William O. Aydelotte, "Voting Patterns in the British House of Commons in the 1840s," *Comparative Studies in Society and History,* v (1963), 134–163; Joel H. Silbey, *The Shrine of Party: Congressional Voting Behavior, 1841–1852* (Pittsburgh, 1967); Thomas B. Alexander, *Sectional Stress and Party Strength: A Study of Roll-Call Voting Patterns in the United States House of Representatives, 1836–1860* (Nashville, 1967).

7. Stephan Thernstrom, *Poverty and Progress in a Nineteenth Century City* (Cambridge, Mass., 1964); John Demos, *A Little Commonwealth: Family Life in Colonial Plymouth* (New York, 1970); Philip Greven, *Four Generations: Population, Land, and Family in*

used statistical techniques and neoclassical theory in their often strikingly novel treatments of economic growth, slavery, human and non-human capital formation, demographic and technological change, and fiscal and monetary policy.[8] More self-consciously theoretical than the others, the cliometricians developed the explicit counterfactual model. Usually trained as economists, they sprinkled their work liberally with regression equations and complex supply and demand curves.[9] By contrast, scholars in the other two fields typically identified themselves with the concerns and more literary style of history, in which most of them had received their degrees. By the end of the 1960s, then, a growing band of quantifiers had moved beyond propagandizing and built a scholarly edifice that was grand enough to inspire a new review article industry.[10]

In the 1970s, quantifiers gained legitimacy in the historical profession, greatly extended their range of topics and geographical areas, and, for the first time, became visible to the lay public.[11] In 1974 and 1975 heavily quantitative works by Stephan Thernstrom and Robert W. Fogel and Stanley L. Engerman won Bancroft prizes, and other books that relied largely on numerical evidence captured honors disbursed by the American and Southern Historical Associations.[12] Fogel

---

*Colonial Andover* (Ithaca, N.Y., 1970); Kenneth A. Lockridge, *A New England Town: The First Hundred Years* (New York, 1970); Jackson Turner Main, *The Social Structure of Revolutionary America* (Princeton, 1965).

8. Fogel and Engerman, *Reinterpretation: Purdue Faculty Papers in Economic History, 1956-1966* (Homewood, Ill., 1967).

9. Robert W. Fogel, "The Specification Problem in Economic History," *Journal of Economic History,* XXVII (1967), 283-308; Lance E. Davis, "Specification, Quantification, and Analysis in Economic History," in G. R. Taylor and L. F. Ellsworth, eds., *Approaches to the Study of American Economic History* (Charlottesville, Va., 1971), 106-120.

10. For a sampling, see Allan G. Bogue, "United States: The 'New' Political History," *Journal of Contemporary History,* III (1968), 5-28; Jerome M. Clubb and Howard W. Allen, "Computers and Historical Studies," *Journal of American History,* LIV (1967), 599-607; Morton Rothstein et al., "Quantification and American History: An Assessment," in Herbert J. Bass, ed., *The State of American History* (Chicago, 1970), 298-329; Fogel, "The New Economic History: Its Findings and Methods," in Fogel and Engerman, *Reinterpretation,* 1-12.

11. Harry S. Stout, "Quantitative Studies and the American Revolution," *Computers and the Humanities,* X (1976), 257-264.

12. Thernstrom, *The Other Bostonians: Poverty and Progress in the American Metropolis, 1880-1970* (Cambridge, Mass. 1973); Fogel and Engerman, *Time on The Cross,* 2 vols. (Boston, 1974); Joan W. Scott, *The Glassworkers of Carmaux: French Craftsmen and Political Action in a Nineteenth-Century City* (Cambridge, Mass., 1974); Thomas B. Alexander and Richard E. Beringer, *Anatomy of the Confederate Congress: A Study of the Influences of Member Characteristics on Legislative Voting Behavior* (Nashville, 1972); F. Sheldon Hackney, *Populism to Progressivism in Alabama* (Princeton, 1969); James T. Lemon, *The Best Poor Man's Country: A Geographical Study of Early Southeastern Pennsylvania* (Baltimore, 1972).

and Engerman's belligerently cliometric *Time on the Cross,* which has reportedly sold more than 20,000 copies, was the subject not only of many popular reviews but of news stories in *Time* and *Newsweek.*[13] American scholars pushed the quantitative frontiers back into the Middle Ages and out to China, Japan, Africa, Latin America, and Eastern Europe.[14] When an article on the styles of Vivaldi, Zeno, and Ricci containing not only five reproductions of paintings but also two tables and four graphs appeared in a journal founded to disseminate the new history, it was a pretty good sign that quantification had arrived.[15]

A less impressionistic indication of its growing acceptance was the increase in the extent to which articles published in mainstream professional journals were based on quantitative data. Table 1 is a table of tables.[16] Since not every "quantitative" article is equally quantitative, and since the number of pages in each journal differs somewhat from issue to issue and from year to year, even excluding book reviews, bibliographies, social notes, and advertisements, I formed an index of the amount of quantitative material published by simply counting the number of tables and dividing that figure by the number of pages devoted to original articles, research notes, and review articles. Table 1 contains the results in tables per page, multiplied by 100 for ease of reading, for eighteen years' worth of issues of five leading journals, which together roughly represent the scholarly interests of most pro-

13. For a sampling, see *Atlantic,* August 1974, 78–82; *Commentary,* August 1974, 68; *New Yorker,* September 30, 1974, 128–130; *Newsweek,* May 6, 1974, 77; *Time,* June 17, 1974, 98–100.

14. Val R. Lorwin and Jacob M. Price, eds., *The Dimensions of the Past: Materials, Problems, and Opportunities for Quantitative Work in History* (New Haven, 1972); Gilbert Rozman, "County-level and Prefectural-level Population Data in Eighteenth and Nineteenth Century China," and David M. Deal, "County Level Economic Data in Twentieth-Century China," both delivered at the December 1978 meeting of the American Historical Association.

15. David Burrows, "Style in Culture: Vivaldi, Zeno, and Ricci," *Journal of Interdisciplinary History,* IV (1973), 1–23.

16. There is no accurate way to estimate the number of quantitative or social-scientific historians, for three reasons. First, publications that might be characterized as quantitative history appear in too wide a range of historical and social-scientific journals to keep track of—in the *American Economic Review* and the *American Political Science Review,* in *Social Science Quarterly* and *Political Science Quarterly,* in *Population Studies* and *Computers and the Humanities,* as well as in many of the hundred or so strictly historical journals. Second, many of the historians who employ quantifiable data or notions drawn from social science do so only occasionally and do not consider themselves "quantitative" historians, or shift their identities depending on the nature of their current research. Third, many social scientists who deal from time to time or even most of the time with data drawn from the past do not consider themselves primarily historians. It therefore makes more sense to speak of changes in the use of numerical methods rather than in the size of a nonexistent "community" of quantitative historians.

Table 1. Tables per page (× 100) in five leading historical journals, 1961–78

| Year | AHR | JAH | JMH | JSH | W&M | All five journals |
|---|---|---|---|---|---|---|
| 1961 | 1 | 00 | 0 | 3 | 2 | 1 |
| 1962 | 0 | 0 | 1 | 1 | 4 | 1 |
| 1963 | 0 | 1 | 1 | 1 | 1 | 1 |
| 1964 | 0 | 1 | 9 | 9 | 2 | 1 |
| 1965 | 0 | 0 | 1 | 0 | 4 | 1 |
| 1966 | 3 | 0 | 0 | 1 | 3 | 2 |
| 1967 | 00 | 2 | 0 | 4 | 4 | 2 |
| 1968 | 5 | 2 | 00 | 3 | 5 | 3 |
| 1969 | 5 | 5 | 2 | 4 | 4 | |
| 1970 | 1 | 10 | 1 | 7 | 2 | 4 |
| 1971 | 2 | 4 | 3 | 1 | 10 | 4 |
| 1972 | 3 | 3 | 5 | 4 | 5 | 4 |
| 1973 | 3 | 7 | 1 | 5 | 9 | 5 |
| 1974 | 4 | 6 | 5 | 7 | 5 | 5 |
| 1975 | 1 | 5 | 3 | 3 | 4 | 3 |
| 1976 | 3 | 10 | 1 | 7 | 7 | 6 |
| 1977 | 1 | 11 | 2 | 5 | 2 | 4 |
| 1978 | 2 | 6 | 5 | 8 | 8 | 6 |
| 1961–64 | 00 | 00 | 00 | 2 | 2 | 1 |
| 1965–69 | 3 | 2 | 1 | 2 | 4 | 2 |
| 1961–69 | 2 | 1 | 1 | 2 | 3 | 2 |
| 1970–73 | 2 | 6 | 2 | 4 | 6 | 4 |
| 1974–78 | 2 | 8 | 3 | 6 | 5 | 5 |
| 1970–78 | 2 | 7 | 3 | 5 | 6 | 5 |
| 1961–78 | | | | | | |
| Number of tables | 151 | 291 | 119 | 203 | 398 | 1,162 |
| Number of pages | 7,636 | 7,012 | 6,215 | 5,523 | 8,830 | 35,216 |

Note: One zero indicates that no tables appeared at all. Two zeroes mean that fewer than 0.5 table was printed for every 100 pages of text.

fessional historians in America: the American Historical Review, the Journal of American History, the Journal of Modern History, the Journal of Southern History, and the William and Mary Quarterly. Their combined circulation in 1978 was approximately 48,500.[17]

17. The eighteen-year period was chosen to balance the numbers of volumes before and after 1970. Any graph or matrix containing at least six cell entries of actual numbers was counted as a table, whether it appeared in footnotes, appendices, or text, and whether it was labeled as a figure or table or not. Matrices or figures not based on real numbers were ignored, as were all equations unless the latter were grouped together to form a table. It was not feasible to weight tables by the number of entries, but, in general, the size of tables grew over time. Since all entries in Table 1 are based on raw data rounded off to two decimal places, the multiyear figures at the foot of the table may differ slightly from averages of the yearly figures.

The most striking feature of Table 1 is the growth in tables per page from the beginning to the end of the period. From 1961 to 1964, three of the five journals averaged less than one table for every 100 pages of text, and the overall average was slightly over one. In thirteen of the forty-five journal-years during the 1960s, no tables were published in any issue. By contrast, each of the journals averaged more than one table for every 200 pages for every year during the 1970s, and the overall average nearly quintupled from the 1961-64 period to that of 1974-78. A chi-square test on that part of the table containing yearly data for each of the five journals reveals that the chance was less than one in a thousand that such a pattern would have been produced if the average number of tables per page had been the same in every year—that is, had they not grown with the passage of time. To obtain a better indication of the trend, we can relax a few statistical assumptions and run a linear least-squares regression of the ninety tabular entries for individual journals for individual years on time ($t = 1, 2, \ldots, 18$). The resulting parameter estimates are

$$\text{tables/pages} (\times \ 100) = 0.280 + 0.302 \ (\text{time}).$$

Thus, in each year during the 1960s and 1970s, the average journal which printed 500 pages of text published one and a half more tables ($5 \times 0.302$) than it had the previous year.[18] The time trend by itself explains 32.7 percent of the variance in the number of tables per page. More complex equations and procedures could be tried, but the assumptions have already been strained a good deal, and the result is clear enough—the amount of published material that displayed a quantitative bent expanded markedly after 1965.

A few differences between journals may also be noted. The *AHR*, which serves the widest audience and covers the broadest range of geographic areas and longest time span of the five, published the fewest tables, and the *JMH*, which concentrates on European history, the next fewest. United States historians of Europe and non-Western countries are apparently less prone to quantify than are Americanists. The fact that the *William and Mary Quarterly*, a journal of colonial America, printed more tables than any of the other four demonstrates the plentitude of pre-1800 quantitative data for this hemisphere, while the fact that the *JAH* and *JSH* showed the most marked growth in the number of tables belies the rather conservative reputations of those journals.

18. The intercept term or the number of tables printed per 100 pages in 1961 predicted by the equation is 0.280. If the trend continues, in 1985 the average journal will print 7.5 tables per 100 pages ($0.280 + 24 \times 0.302 = 7.528$).

**439**

Table 2. Tables per page (× 100) in three specialized American journals and two European journals, 1961–78

| Year | JEH | JIH | JSocH | ANN | VSWG |
|---|---|---|---|---|---|
| 1961 | 9 | | | 9 | |
| 1962 | 17 | | | 6 | |
| 1963 | 12 | | | 5 | |
| 1964 | | | | | |
| 1965 | | | | | 4 |
| 1966 | | | | | 6 |
| 1967 | | | 11 | | 9 |
| 1968 | | | 9 | | |
| 1969 | | | 8 | | |
| 1970 | | 6 | 8 | | |
| 1971 | | 10 | 11 | | |
| 1972 | | 12 | 12 | | |
| 1973 | | 13 | 10 | | |
| 1974 | | 15 | 18 | | |
| 1975 | 18 | 20 | 13 | | |
| 1976 | 19 | 17 | 8 | 24 | 14 |
| 1977 | 20 | 20 | 18 | 12 | 16 |
| 1978 | | 17 | 10 | 9 | 13 |
| | | | | | |
| 1961–69 | 13 | | 9 | 7 | 6 |
| 1970–78 | 19 | 15 | 12 | 15 | 15 |
| Number of tables | 580 | 762 | 579 | 596 | 160 |
| Number of pages | 3,520 | 5,224 | 4,901 | 4,845 | 1,611 |

Note: The *Journal of Social History* and *Journal of Interdisciplinary History* were founded in 1967 and 1970, respectively. The other three journals were sampled for three years each from each decade.

Table 2 charts the number of tables per page for selected years of five organs of social scientific history. The *Journal of Economic History*, the *Journal of Interdisciplinary History*, and the *Journal of Social History* are based in the United States, although they publish articles on the history of a great many countries and often contain papers by foreign scholars. *Annales: Economies, Sociétés, Civilisations* is the leading French journal of historical social science, and *Vierteljahrschrift für Sozial- und Wirtschaftsgeschichte* is West German. All of these journals published more tables per page than the five mainstream American journals, and all showed an increase in the number of tables from the 1960s to the 1970s. The gap between the mainstream and specialized journals, however, closed a bit over the period, as a comparison of Tables 1 and 2 shows. As expected of the leading journal in the area most identified with quantification, the *JEH* published more (and longer) tables than any of the others. The sample of the *JEH*, *ANN*, and *VSWG* is too small to determine whether there were any significant differences in

440

the journals of various countries, but the numbers appear to be fairly close. The quantitative revolution is not confined to America.

But quantification may involve more than simply counting and calculating elementary descriptive statistics. If the number of tables seemed to reach a plateau during the 1970s, they were increasingly sophisticated, as regression and correlation coefficients, Lorenz curves, and discriminant, probit, and logit analyses began to supplement raw counts of data. Tables 3 and 4 chart the growth in the number of "sophisticated" tables, that is, those that presented more than counts, percentages, and simple measures of central tendency and dispersion.

As a comparison of Tables 1 and 3 shows, historians in America have increasingly realized the usefulness of counting, but relatively few seem to have reached the level of an introductory one-semester statistics course, or at least few authors and editors believe that their readers have. The contrasts among journals and between the beginning and end of the period parallel those in Table 1. The number of "sophisticated" tables rose from none in 1961–64 to 84 in 1974–78, and nearly five-sixths of that increase came in two journals, the *JAH* and *W&M.* Even so, the five journals averaged only one sophisticated table per 100 pages in the last period.

Table 4, which displays the number of sophisticated tables per page in the more specialized American and foreign journals, demonstrates both the general growth in expertise and an important distinction between social historians on the one hand and economic and political historians on the other. The *JEH,* which averaged only three sophisticated tables per year in the early 1960s, progressed to twenty-six per year in the late 1970s. The *JIH,* which publishes in all three subfields of social scientific history, averaged only slightly fewer methodologically advanced tables per page in the 1970s than the *JEH.* The nature of the data typically available made it apparent much earlier in economic and political than in social history that one had to go beyond mere counting to get interesting results.[19] For much economic and

19. Thus, social historians do not appear to have noticed the extensive effort by sociologists, political scientists, and economists to overcome the so-called ecological fallacy. Through the use of regression and other techniques, it is possible to tease a great deal more reliable information about individuals from aggregate data than had been thought possible. For examples of the most recent work on the topic, see John L. Hammond, "New Approaches to Aggregate Electoral Data," *Journal of Interdisciplinary History,* IX (1979), 473–492; Laura Irwin Langbein and Allan J. Lichtman, *Ecological Inference* (Beverly Hills, Calif., 1978), and Langbein and Lichtman's paper, "Comparing Tests for Aggregation Bias: Party Realignment in the 1930s," Presented at the 1979 meeting of the Midwest Political Science Association.

Table 3. Number of "sophisticated" tables per page (× 100) in five leading historical journals, 1971–78

| Year | AHR | JAH | JMH | JSH | W&M | All five journals |
|---|---|---|---|---|---|---|
| 1961 | 0 | 0 | 0 | 0 | 0 | 0 |
| 1962 | 0 | 0 | 0 | 0 | 0 | 0 |
| 1963 | 0 | 0 | 0 | 0 | 0 | 0 |
| 1964 | 0 | 0 | 0 | 0 | 0 | 0 |
| 1965 | 0 | 0 | 0 | 0 | 00 | 00 |
| 1966 | 0 | 0 | 0 | 0 | 0 | 0 |
| 1967 | 0 | 0 | 0 | 0 | 0 | 0 |
| 1968 | 00 | 00 | 0 | 0 | 0 | 00 |
| 1969 | 0 | 0 | 0 | 0 | 1 | 00 |
| 1970 | 0 | 5 | 0 | 0 | 0 | 1 |
| 1971 | 0 | 0 | 0 | 00 | 1 | 00 |
| 1972 | 0 | 0 | 0 | 1 | 1 | 00 |
| 1973 | 0 | 1 | 0 | 0 | 00 | 00 |
| 1974 | 0 | 2 | 00 | 00 | 2 | 1 |
| 1975 | 00 | 2 | 0 | 0 | 00 | 1 |
| 1976 | 2 | 1 | 0 | 3 | 0 | 1 |
| 1977 | 0 | 7 | 0 | 0 | 0 | 1 |
| 1978 | 0 | 2 | 0 | 0 | 0 | 00 |
| | | | | | | |
| 1961–64 | 0 | 0 | 0 | 0 | 0 | 0 |
| 1965–69 | 00 | 00 | 0 | 0 | 00 | 00 |
| 1961–69 | 00 | 00 | 0 | 0 | 00 | 00 |
| | | | | | | |
| 1970–73 | 0 | 1 | 0 | 00 | 1 | 00 |
| 1974–78 | 00 | 3 | 00 | 1 | 00 | 1 |
| 1970–78 | 00 | 2 | 00 | 00 | 1 | 1 |
| | | | | | | |
| 1961–78 | 00 | 1 | 00 | 00 | 00 | 00 |
| Percent of all tables, 1961–78 | 6 | 27 | 1 | 6 | 8 | 11 |
| N | 9 | 78 | 1 | 13 | 31 | 132 |

Note: Zero means no tables at all. Two zeroes mean less than 0.5 tables per 100 pages.

political data are available only for aggregates, such as counties, states, or industries, while information that is recorded for individuals is often either too bulky and intricate to yield its pattern to simple procedures, as in the case of legislative roll calls, or indecipherable without more complex treatment, as in the use of price-quantity pairs to estimate supply and demand curves. While the degree of statistical expertise requisite for the practice of economic and political history may have somewhat slowed progress and raised barriers to entry into these branches of the discipline, there have been benefits as well. Because political and especially economic historians are used to em-

*Table 4.* Number of "sophisticated" tables per page (× 100) in five specialized journals

| Year | JEH | JIH | JSocH | ANN | VSWG |
|---|---|---|---|---|---|
| 1961 | 0 | | | 1 | |
| 1962 | 2 | | | 0 | |
| 1963 | 00 | | | 0 | |
| 1964 | | | | | |
| 1965 | | | | | 0 |
| 1966 | | | | | 0 |
| 1967 | | | 0 | | 0 |
| 1968 | | | 1 | | |
| 1969 | | | 0 | | |
| 1970 | | 0 | 0 | | |
| 1971 | | 2 | 0 | | |
| 1972 | | 4 | 1 | | |
| 1973 | | 7 | 00 | | |
| 1974 | | 00 | 00 | | |
| 1975 | 4 | 1 | 0 | | |
| 1976 | 4 | 4 | 0 | 1 | 0 |
| 1977 | 3 | 2 | 3 | 1 | 00 |
| 1978 | | 3 | 2 | 00 | 0 |
| | | | | | |
| 1961–69 | 1 | | 00 | 00 | 00 |
| 1970–73 | | 3 | 00 | | |
| 1974–78 | | 2 | 1 | | |
| 1970–78 | 4 | 3 | 1 | 1 | 00 |
| 1961–78 | 3 | | 1 | 1 | 00 |
| Percent of all tables, 1961–78 | 15 | 18 | 5 | 5 | 1 |
| N | 88 | 137 | 33 | 31 | 1 |

ploying more advanced techniques, they find it much more natural than social historians do to posit multivariate explanations and attempt to sort out the separate influences of many independent variables on some dependent variable. Since their data sets often contain information not only on individual actions but on the social settings of behavior as well, those who study politics or the economy are, ironically, rather more prone to emphasize the importance of variations in the social context of human acts than are social historians.

That social history would benefit from the application of more complex statistical techniques to data collected at both the individual and aggregate levels appears plain.[20] That social historians are mov-

20. For an example, see Michael P. Weber and Anthony E. Boardman, "Economic Growth and Occupational Mobility in Nineteenth Century Urban America: A Reappraisal," *Journal of Social History*, 11 (1977), 52–74. The situation in social history has not changed much since 1970. See Rothstein, "Quantification and American History," 312.

ing in this direction is not so clear. Although Table 4 evidences a slight trend toward a higher level of methodological expertise in the social history journals, throughout the period the *JSocH, ANN,* and *VSWG* published far fewer sophisticated tables than the *JEH* and *JIH,* and in all three social history journals, the percentage of tables that went beyond counting and other simple measures fell below that in four of the five mainstream journals (compare the penultimate rows in Tables 3 and 4).[21]

What has quantitative social-scientific history achieved in the two decades since its emergence? First, its practitioners have shown that old topics may be viewed in novel ways or that old evidence may be supplemented by material unusable before the advent of modern data-processing equipment. Now, for the first time, the attitudes of the pre-survey electorate, (i.e., pre-1935) rather than just those of politicians and newspaper editors, have become prime objects of attention.[22] Instead of looking at cities or rural communities only from the limited points of view of those who left written records, we can follow the life courses of groups of ordinary people, seeking to explain their differing experiences by variations in the areas where they lived, the economic conditions they faced, their ethnic and class positions, and so on.[23] Fundamental facts about the lives of slaves, peasants, and proletarians, as well as of slaveholders, gentry, and bourgeoisie, can, through the use of social-scientific theory and statistics, be analyzed rigorously.[24]

Second, infected by the social scientists' penchant for overt generalization, historians are beginning to talk more readily about new topics, of systems and structures, rather than merely events: of the traits of broad political eras, rather than single elections; of the

21. For good discussions of the primarily descriptive use of quantification in France, see Price and Lorwin, *Dimensions of the Past,* 97–139, and Robert Forster, "The Achievements of the Annales School," *Journal of Economic History,* XXXVIII (1978), 58–76.

22. Lee Benson, "An Approach to the Scientific Study of Past Public Opinion," in his *Scientific Study of History,* 105–59.

23. See, for example, many of the essays in two volumes edited by Tamara K. Hareven, *Anonymous Americans: Explorations in Nineteenth-Century Social History* (Englewood Cliffs, N.J., 1971), and *Family and Kin in Urban Communities, 1700–1930* (New York, 1977), and the citations in Hareven's introductory essay to the latter volume, 1–15.

24. Fogel and Engerman, *Time on the Cross;* Tamara K. Hareven and Maris A. Vinovskis, eds., *Family and Population in Nineteenth-Century America* (Princeton, 1978), William O. Aydelotte et al., eds., *The Dimensions of Quantitative Research in History* (Princeton, 1972), 56–225; Roger L. Ransom and Richard Sutch, *One Kind of Freedom: The Economic Consequences of Emancipation* (Cambridge, Eng. 1977).

structure of wealth holding, rather than individual stories of mobility or riches; of the determinants of economic growth, rather than the experiences of single firms; of changes in the forms of collective violence, rather than unique strikes.[25] Family reconstitution and statistical studies of other available demographic records allow historians to recover an implicit history of patterns of births, marriages, and deaths which was unknown to those actually living at the time.[26] What could be further from the traditional narrative of events, or more basic to the existences of the masses of people?

This is not to claim that historians who draw on the techniques of the social sciences always seek to make large generalizations, or that they usually try to perform rigorous tests of alternative explicit mathematical models.[27] Indeed, my impression is that most recent books and essays by historians who count are overloaded with mere description, insufficiently theoretical, or shackled to questions posed by traditional historiography; and several essayists have warned that quantitative history may devolve into "mindless empiricism" or "quantitative antiquarianism."[28] To borrow terms from Thomas Kuhn,

25. Good recent reviews of the political history literature include Philip Vander-Meer, "The New Political History: Progress and Prospects," *Computers and the Humanities*, XI (1977), 265-278; Allan G. Bogue, "Recent Developments in Political History: The Case of the United States," in *The Frontiers of Human Knowledge* (Uppsala, Sweden, 1978), 79-109. See also Paul Kleppner, *The Third Electoral System, 1853-1892: Parties, Voters, and Political Cultures* (Chapel Hill, N.C. 1979); J. Morgan Kousser, *The Shaping of Southern Politics: Suffrage Restriction and the Establishment of the One-Party South, 1880-1910* (New Haven, 1974); Lee Soltow, *Men and Wealth in the United States, 1850-1870* (New Haven, 1975); Jeffrey G. Williamson, *Late Nineteenth-Century American Development: A General Equilibrium History* (Cambridge, Eng. 1974); Charles Tilly, ed., *Historical Studies of Changing Fertility* (Princeton, 1978); Charles Tilly et al., *The Rebellious Century, 1830-1930* (Cambridge, Mass., 1975).

26. Charles Tilly, "The Historical Study of Vital Processes," in Tilly, ed., *Changing Fertility*, 3-55; and Maris A. Vinovskis, "Recent Trends in American Historical Demography: Some Methodological and Conceptual Considerations," *Annual Review of Sociology*, IV (1978), 603-627, are the best introductions to the literature.

27. Some early enthusiasts seemed to believe, either naively or optimistically, that working with quantitative data and computers would necessarily compel historians to "follow the scientific method." See Robert P. Swierenga, "Computers and American History," *Journal of American History*, LX (1974), 1061, and Richard Jensen, "Quantitative American Studies: The State of the Art," *American Quarterly*, XXVI (1974), 227.

28. Quotations from Charles Tilly, "Computers in Historical Analysis," *Computers and the Humanities*, VII (1973), 334; and John B. Sharpless and Sam Bass Warner, Jr., "Urban History," *American Behavioral Scientist*, XXI (1977), 224. See also Joel H. Silbey, "Clio and Computers: Moving into Phase II: 1970-1972," *Computers and the Humanities*, VII (1972), 79; Jerome M. Clubb, "The 'New' History as Applied Social Science: A Review Essay," ibid., IX (1975), 250-251; and my review of Kleppner, *Third Electoral Era*, forthcoming in *Journal of American History*. A systematic content analysis of 349 articles published from 1967 to 1976 in ten history journals found that only 37 percent of the articles contained explicit hypothesis tests and that even in the three most social-

without a "Copernican Revolution" in a discipline, how can one expect the products of one period of "normal science" to differ very much from those of the next? It may be, however, that some of Kuhn's critics are correct, that we should not expect changes to be so radical and swift, but rather to arrive gradually and piecemeal, that the very criticisms aimed at conservative quantifiers will eventually produce a consensus about a new paradigm for historical study, and that we can best project the eventual trend in social-scientific history by concentrating on the most advanced segments of the profession.[29]

A focus on that group, the economic historians, reveals a third achievement of social-scientific historians. Despite the sometimes fratricidal battles among quantifiers, many of their arguments can, at least in principle, be fairly satisfactorily resolved. That some of their disputes do not involve nonterminating matters of opinion raises the possibility—which has been discussed for decades, if not centuries— that history may become, at least in part, a science.[30] To take the most notorious example, in the wake of the cliometricians' cockfight over *Time on the Cross,* too many onlookers failed to notice that most of the arguments were about methodological specifics: Was the sample representative? Were the assumptions for the estimates reasonable? Were the basic data biased? Were the best statistical procedures employed? Were the inferences logical? Despite the fact that many details were obscurely presented in their hastily prepared second vol-

---

scientific of the journals (*JEH, JIH,* and *JSocH*), only 44 percent of the articles were analytical in this sense (D. N. Sprague, "A Quantitative Assessment of the Quantification Revolution," *Canadian Journal of History,* xiii [1978], 177-192).

29. Critiques of Kuhn's *Structure of Scientific Revolutions* (Chicago, 1962) include Stephen Toulmin, "Does the Distinction between Normal and Revolutionary Science Hold Water?" in Imre Lakatos and Alan Musgrave, eds., *Criticism and the Growth of Knowledge* (Cambridge, Eng., 1970), 39-48; and John Urry, "Thomas S. Kuhn as Sociologist of Knowledge," *British Journal of Sociology,* xxiv (1973), 469. It may be, of course, that the historical discipline is in a prescientific stage, and that it is the initial acceptance of a paradigm, rather than replacement of one by another, that is at issue. Or perhaps history is not sufficiently like physics, on which Kuhn's notions were primarily based, for the concept of paradigm shifts to be strictly applicable to the discipline.

30. By "scientific" here, I mean not that historians will discover universal laws but merely that they will establish a widespread consensus among scholars on a set of important if narrow facts (for example, that slavery was profitable for the average slave owner), that their findings will be replicable, and that systematic research that builds on earlier firmly grounded results is possible. In this sense, history has always been scientific to a degree. The difference is that much social-scientific theory, especially in economics, is based on explicit assumptions and statistical methodology on explicit rules of inference, and that the range of facts that can be established by such means is comparatively wide. A similar distinction is drawn in Stanley L. Engerman, "Recent Developments in American Economic History," *Social Science History,* ii (1977), 78.

ume, Fogel and Engerman willingly provided their data, clarified their equations, and retraced their processes of reasoning for the benefit of even their most antagonistic critics. Since both sides shared a commitment to the same basic theory and rules of statistical inference, the debate produced some light as well as much heat, Although important differences of interpretation may well remain if the controversy is ever concluded, it seems likely that nearly all economic historians will eventually agree on the basic facts about slave living conditions, as they do now on the question of whether or not slavery was profitable (it was).[31] In contrast, it is much more difficult to resolve disagreements based on impressionistic evidence, since it is much harder to exchange *Verständnisse* than computer tapes. Most of the major points in *Time on the Cross* are verifiable or falsifiable; most of those in Eugene Genovese's *Roll, Jordan, Roll,* with which it shared the Bancroft Prize, are not.[32]

The fourth achievement of quantitative history has been the accumulation of intellectual capital, the amassing in machine-readable form of several enormous and numerous smaller data sets that will pay intellectual dividends for years to come. In economic history, the regional, sectoral, and national accounts estimates of the National Bureau of Economic Research studies and the Parker-Gallman, Bateman-Foust, and Ransom-Sutch census samples have laid the foundations for impressive scholarly edifices, and the groundbreaking studies of American wealth by Lee Soltow and Alice Hanson Jones should soon foster similarly rapid development.[33] In political history, the massive file of electoral and congressional data at the

31. Some historians have read Robert W. Fogel's coy essay "The Limits of Quantitative Methods in History," *American Historical Review*, LXXX (1975), 329-350, as implying fairly severe restrictions on the ability of such methods to transform the discipline. Read carefully and in conjunction with *Time on the Cross* and his later essay, "Cliometrics and Culture: Some Recent Developments in the Historiography of Slavery," *Journal of Social History*, XI (1977), 34-51, the "limits" seem to be set at a very large, if finite, number.

32. Paul A. David et al. *Reckoning with Slavery: A Critical Study in the Quantitative History of American Negro Slavery* (New York, 1976); Donald N. McCloskey, "The Achievements of the Cliometric School," *Journal of Economic History*, XXXVIII (1978), 23; Eugene D. Genovese, *Roll, Jordan, Roll: The World the Slaves Made* (New York, 1974). For a lovely, if less explosive, example of the productivity of cliometric controversy, see Robert E. Gallman, "The Statistical Approach: Fundamental Concepts as Applied to History," in Taylor and Ellsworth, eds., *Approaches*, 63-86.

33. NBER. *Trends in the American Economy in the Nineteenth Century* (Princeton, 1960) and *Output, Employment, and Productivity in the United States after 1800* (Princeton, 1966); William N. Parker, ed., *The Structure of the Cotton Economy of the Antebellum South* (Berkeley, 1970); Alice Hanson Jones, *American Colonial Wealth: Documents and Methods*, 3 vols. (New York, 1977); Soltow, *Men and Wealth;* Ransom and Sutch, *One Kind of Freedom.*

University of Michigan's Inter-University Consortium for Political and Social Research, initally set up by Lee Benson, Warren E. Miller, and others, has buttressed a great deal of scholarship.[34] In social history, Theodore Hershberg's 2.5 million computerized records at the Philadelphia Social History Project, the large number of social and geographic mobility studies inspired by Thernstrom's work, and the considerable body of European and American demographic data, especially Ansley Coale's European Fertility Project and the large data file now being developed by Robert Fogel and his collaborators, appear to foreshadow increasing returns.[35] It must be noted, however, that a great many computer-ready data remain in the hands of individual researchers, despite repeated arguments that their centralization would be of major benefit to the scholarly community.[36] Such centralization would facilitate the replication, with somewhat different methods or objectives, of individual studies, as well as the linkage of diverse data sets in order to provide better tests of hypotheses. Surely a comprehensive program to secure these widespread holdings and make them accessible to all scholars should become a crucial priority of professional committees on quantification and funding agencies.

The limited exposure of a great many historians to social-scientific theory and statistics, and the thorough training of a much smaller number, constitute the fifth accomplishment of quantitative historians. In 1971, David S. Landes and Charles Tilly concluded in *History as Social Science* that "the history student of today must learn social science statistics, computer techniques, model-building, and ancillary skills."[37] To gauge the profession's progress toward that goal, I sent questionnaires to the approximately 125 history departments that

34. The ICPSR's historical and contemporary archive holdings are detailed in its *Guide to Resources and Services, 1978–1979* (Ann Arbor, Mich. 1979).

35. Theodore Hershberg et al., "Occupation and Ethnicity in Five Nineteenth-Century Cities: A Collaborative Inquiry," *Historical Methods Newsletter,* VII (1974), 174–216; ibid., IX (1976), 43–181; Thernstrom, *Other Bostonians,* 223; Larry T. Wimmer, "The Economics of Mortality in North America, 1650–1910," *The Center for Historical Population Studies Newsletter,* Spring, 1979, 12–13. For citations of the numerous studies of Coale and other demographers and historians, see Michael R. Haines, "Age-Specific and Differential Fertility in Durham and Easington Registration Districts, England, 1851 and 1861," *Social Science History,* II (1977), 23–52.

36. Price and Lorwin, *Dimensions of the Past,* 24–25; Preston Cutler, et al., "Report on the Status of Mathematical Social Science and the Roles of the National Science Foundation and the Mathematical Social Science Board" (n.p., 1976), 33; J. Morgan Kousser, "The Agenda for 'Social Sicence History,'" *Social Science History,* I (1977), 390.

37. Landes and Tilly, eds., *History as Social Science* (Englewood Cliffs, N.J., 1971), 75. For similar positions, see Swierenga, "Computers and American History," 1067–68; Rothstein, "Quantification and American History," 315.

have graduate programs, and received at least partially completed replies from eighty-three of them. Fifty-three of these departments, which accounted for 64 percent of the returned questionnaires and 42 percent of those sent out, offered a course in methodology or statistics. Nearly all such courses, which enrolled an average of eight students each, lasted for a single quarter or semester and were taught by historians. The statistics component of these courses was elementary, compared to analogous ones in the social sciences: none required calculus, only forty-two took the student through bivariate regression, thirty-three introduced multivariate regression, and only eight went on to more advanced levels. Introductory graduate-level methods courses in economics and increasingly in psychology, sociology, and political science presume a knowledge of elementary calculus, linear algebra, and some probability theory, and proceed well beyond ordinary least-squares regression analysis. On the theoretical side, only eight history departments had offerings in social-scientific theory, but thirty-one encouraged their students to take theory courses in other departments.

While nineteen schools offered graduate subfields in quantitative history or permitted the substitution of quantitative training for a language requirement, and perhaps 500 students have taken methodology courses in departments outside history over the last few years, only five departments that responded to the questionnaire required all students to take at least one methodology course. Clearly, there was something of a generational split over quantification, for while the respondents, who were usually the "house quantifiers" in each department, reported that students in 71 percent of the schools were more interested in taking methods courses or reading historical works based on statistics than their predecessors a few years ago, only 22 percent thought that their faculty colleagues enthusiastically supported attempts to provide students with statistical training. Of the students who had taken methodology courses, about 64 percent were in United States history, 22 percent in modern European, 5 percent in pre-modern European, and 4 percent in Latin American; the rest were scattered or in unspecified fields.

In addition to departmental offerings, approximately 750 graduate students and younger professors have attended the summer training programs that began at the University of Michigan in 1968, the Newberry Library in Chicago in 1972, and The Johns Hopkins University in 1976. All offer short (four to eight weeks), intensive introductory statistics courses for historians at approximately the same level as most regular term courses. In addition, the Newberry gives courses contemporaneously in numerous areas of social history and provides encouragement and continuing advice to its 400 alumni, a small number of whom go on to take more sophisticated methods courses in social science departments. Michigan's summer program, which caters to political scientists, concentrates much less of its attention on historians than does the Newberry's, but provides many more advanced statistics courses, of which a small but growing number of historians take advantage. Tiny compared to the other two, the Hopkins program, while open to all, essentially serves Hopkins graduate students.[38]

While the training currently available may be sufficient to overcome the "math anxiety" that haunts many historians and to enable them to read and evaluate many books and articles now being produced in social and political history, a four-week or one-term course that avoids calculus and linear algebra can hardly prepare anyone to comprehend fully most present scholarship in economic history or the more advanced pieces in other fields, to conduct serious and technically advanced statistical research, or even to proceed to more complex topics through self-education, since a grounding in mathematics is necessary to grasp such methods firmly. Those who brave disciplinary boundaries and adjust to another field's jargon and set of concerns will probably emerge more thoroughly trained than students who do not venture outside history departments; but the often stiff prerequisites for social science statistics courses and the lack of encouragement for such training from senior professors revealed in my survey will inhibit all too many history students and younger faculty from taking full advantage of programs offered in other departments.

Moreover, the present structure of rewards offers students little incentive to become really well trained. Since history departmental search and promotion committees, as well as referees and editors for journals and presses, usually have too little methodological or theoretical expertise to distinguish between accomplished and journeyman quantifiers, rational students and younger faculty members will invest just enough of their energy in acquiring such skills to be sure of satisfying the committees and publishers. Those untenured historians spurred to improve their skills by a simple desire to learn and understand will rarely be able to divert enough time from their teaching duties and publishing imperatives to become expert at theory or

38. Information on the summer programs was graciously provided by Jerome M. Clubb (Michigan), Louis Galambos (Johns Hopkins), and Richard Jensen (Newberry). In addition, summer intitutes at Cornell in 1967 and Harvard in 1973 taught approximately fifty more students.

statistics. Tenured historians will usually be too absorbed in substantive projects to upgrade their skills or will rationalize their unwillingness to retool by muttering the dogma about old canines and new tricks. In the short term, the profession might overcome these structural problems by adding competent methodologists from history or social science departments to search and promotion committees (just as a small but increasing number of journals and presses are employing the services of methodologically expert referees) and by prevailing upon funding agencies to set up a program of two-year postdoctoral training fellowships for historians.[39]

In the longer term, history departments are condemning many of their graduates to technological obsolescence by not requiring that they take even token methodology courses. By offering only elementary statistics and very few theory courses, departments are fostering dilettantism—as such historians as Lawrence Stone acknowledge and approve. Asserting that historians can and "should" dip into social scientific fields merely to seek "a specific idea or piece of information," that "there is nothing wrong with poking about in a social science," and that the most historians "can usually hope to achieve is the somewhat superficial overview of the enthusiastic undergraduate interested in the field," Stone opposes more thorough statistical and theoretical training for graduate students in the discipline and in this connection openly disdains "that most idiotic of proverbs that a little knowledge is a dangerous thing."[40] Sad to say, Stone's advocacy of amateurism is echoed in practice by too many social scientists, whose dabbling in history is no more productive of creditable historical social science than historians' dabbling is of excellent social-scientific history.[41]

39. To attract the very best students away from the security of immediate tenure-track positions, the postdoctoral program would at first have to offer stipends at higher amounts than entry-level jobs pay. To train people well, the program would have to require that students master at least some calculus and linear algebra before beginning it; otherwise, the first year would be devoted to completing what should be prerequisites, the second to polishing the thesis and job seeking, and little would be accomplished except a reduction in unemployment. Each postdoctoral student should be attached to both history and social science departments so that he or she can obtain both guidance (from historians) and the most advanced course training (from social scientists).

40. Stone, "History and the Social Sciences in the Twentieth Century," in Charles F. Delzell, ed., *The Future of History* (Nashville, 1977), 18–19, 36–37.

41. A theoretical social scientist once constructed an elaborate mathematical model to determine which house of Congress would act first when trying to overturn a veto by the president of the United States. He abandoned the paper when informed, while delivering it at a conference, of the constitutional provision (Art. I, Sec. 7) dictating that the first attempt to override had to occur in the house in which the bill originated.

## J. Morgan Kousser

By shuttling students off to other departments to take theory and methods courses, then, history departments are missing an opportunity to integrate social-scientific and traditional historical training, a combination that would benefit both sides. Yet only two of the history departments rated in the top ten in the recent Ladd-Lipset survey (Michigan and Wisconsin) offer graduate students the option of taking rigorous programs in theory or methods as a normal part of the history regimen, while two of the remaining eight (Princeton and Stanford) do not even give introductory methodology courses in their departments.[42] No doubt sweeping changes in historical graduate training will come first in less established schools, where those opposed to or skeptical of quantification are less firmly entrenched—at such places as Carnegie-Mellon, with its new "applied history" program, or the California Institute of Technology, where social-scientific history is beginning to be offered as a field of concentration in an interdisciplinary Ph.D. degree program.[43]

Since it is impossible in a short essay even to list all of the uses historians in America have made of quantitative methods in the 1970s, I shall try to make a limited assessment and to project future trends by focusing briefly on the eight volumes published at the time of this writing under the auspices of the History Advisory Committee of the Mathematical Social Science Board.[44] The products of conferences in which most of the leading quantifiers took part, these volumes contain samples of some of the profession's most quantitatively advanced work. The varied topics addressed in these collections of essays—fertility, the family, race relations, slavery, mobility, the cities, the British economy, electoral and legislative behavior, and public policy—indicate the wide scope of current research. Because there has been no coordinated direction of research (as there has in France), because the subjects themselves are so diverse, and because social-scientific research in all

42. The Ladd-Lipset ratings are in *The Chronicle of Higher Education,* January 15, 1979, 6. The facts about departmental offerings come from the questionnaires and university catalogs.

43. Landes and Tilly, *History as Social Science,* 33–34, made a similar point with different examples.

44. Donald N. McCloskey, ed., *Essays on a Mature Economy: Britain after 1840* (Princeton, 1971); Aydelotte et al., eds., *Dimensions of Quantitative Research;* Stanley L. Engerman and Eugene D. Genovese, eds., *Race and Slavery in the Western Hemisphere* (Princeton. 1975); Leo F. Schnore, ed., *The New Urban History: Quantitative Explorations by American Historians* (Princeton, 1975); William O. Aydelotte, ed., *The History of Parliamentary Behavior* (Princeton, 1977); Joel H. Silbey et al., eds., *The History of American Electoral Behavior* (Princeton, 1978); Tilly, *Changing Fertility;* Hareven and Vinovskis, *Family and Population.*

of these areas began relatively recently, these volumes do not consist of summaries or even preliminary syntheses. Indeed, with one partial exception, there are no real textbooks yet in social-scientific history, even though several books of readings and two very elementary statistics texts for historians appeared in the early 1970s.[45]

The essays in the MSSB volumes reflect the three major uses that historians have made of mathematics and statistics: exploring the basic patterns in previously unexamined data, challenging or confirming older descriptions or explanations, and offering tentative interpretations or new frameworks to guide future research. In uncharted areas, nearly any explorer who counts counts; that is to say, even simple methods can yield significant findings. For example, the compilation of data on the country-by-country destinations of African slaves by Philip D. Curtin and others and the computation of rates of return on the British slave trade by Roger Anstey carry profound implications for questions of comparative slave treatment and the value of slave lives in the Americas, as well as the origins of British capitalism. By charting the lines of House and Senate careers, H. Douglas Price throws new light on the growth of political professionalism in the United States, with all the implications of that development for problems of power and policy. Other papers use more complex statistical techniques in an essentially inductive, exploratory manner.[46] Thus, Kathleen Neils Conzen employs factor analysis to sort out the socioeconomic traits of residential areas of antebellum Milwaukee; William O. Aydelotte, Guttman scaling to determine the extent and timing of the split in the British Conservative party in the

45. The partial exception—because it focuses entirely on economic growth—is Lance E. Davis et al., *American Economic Growth: An Economist's History of the United States* (New York, 1972). Several fine books of readings include Robert P. Swierenga, ed., *Quantification in American History: Theory and Research* (New York, 1970); Don Karl Rowney and James Q. Graham, Jr., eds., *Quantitative History: Selected Readings in the Quantitative Analysis of Historical Data* (Homewood, Ill., 1969); Fogel and Engerman, *Reinterpretation;* Joel H. Silbey and Samuel T. McSeveney, eds., *Voters, Parties, and Elections: Quantitative Essays in the History of American Popular Voting Behavior* (Lexington, Mass., 1972); and Lee Benson et al., eds., *American Political Behavior: Historical Essays and Readings* (New York, 1974). The two statistics texts are Charles M. Dollar and Richard J. Jensen, *Historian's Guide to Statistics: Quantitative Analysis and Historical Research* (New York, 1971), and Roderick Floud, *An Introduction to Quantitative Methods for Historians* (Princeton, 1973).
46. Given the inductive uses to which historians often put complex statistical techniques, it is virtually astounding that they have paid so little attention to the Tukey techniques of exploratory data analysis. For examples of what such techniques can do, see Burton Singer, "Exploratory Strategies and Graphical Displays," *Journal of Interdisciplinary History,* VII (1976), 57-70; and John L. McCarthy and John W. Tukey, "Exploratory Analysis of Aggregate Voting Behavior: Presidential Elections in New Hampshire, 1896-1972," *Social Science History,* II (1978), 292-331.

1841-46 Parliament; and Nancy H. Zingale, a combination of analysis of variance and correlational analysis to unravel the skeins of voting behavior in Minnesota.[47]

Other contributors operationalize and test the notions of impressionistic historians and popular thinkers. Peter H. Smith finds the 1916-17 Mexican Constitutional Convention delegates neither young nor underprivileged, and his skillful delineation and explanation of convention cleavages, based on the techniques of factor analysis and automatic interaction detection, disclose that no consistent social patterns lay behind splits among the delegates. Gerald H. Kramer and Susan J. Lepper attempt to disentangle the effects of incumbency, seniority, and presidential coattails from those of economic conditions in determining votes for American congressmen through a complicated set of regression analyses. Gilbert Shapiro and Philip Dawson systematically analyze the content of French revolutionary *cahiers* and correlate the results with an index of ease of entry into the nobility in an effort to determine whether bourgeois and aristocrats who lived in areas of relatively free social mobility were more or less likely to be revolutionary than denizens of less fluid jurisdictions.[48]

Finally, some of the papers, especially those by economists, import mathematicizable theories from other disciplines and specify their implications for historical problems. Two examples will suffice. In a brilliant synthetic essay, Richard A. Easterlin blends sociological theories with those of the so-called new home economics to concoct a model of family fertility decisions, thus providing a rational structure of individual choice for demographic history, which is perhaps the least theoretical field of social-scientific history. In another paper that is likely to reshape much empirical work, Joseph A. Swanson and Jeffrey G. Williamson develop an abstract mathematical discussion of the locational decisions of firms which draws attention to quite different determinants of comparative urban growth than previous theories had.[49]

The MSSB volumes typify the vanguard of the field in other ways as

47. See the essays by Curtin and others in Engerman and Genovese, eds., *Race and Slavery,* 3-130, 495-506; Price, in Aydelotte, ed., *Parliamentary Behavior,* 28-62; Conzen, in Schnore, ed., *Urban History,* 145-183; Aydelotte, in Aydelotte et al., eds., *Dimensions of Quantitative Research,* 319-346; and Zingale, in Silbey et al., eds., *History of American Electoral Behavior,* 106-136.

48. Smith, in Aydelotte, ed., *History of Parliamentary Behavior,* 186-224; Kramer and Lepper, in Aydelotte et al., eds., *Dimensions of Quantitative Research,* 256-284; and Shapiro and Dawson, in ibid., 159-191.

49. Easterlin, in Tilly, ed., *Historical Studies of Changing Fertility,* 57-133; Swanson and Williamson, in Schnore, ed., *New Urban History,* 260-273.

*Table 5.* Some characteristics of the eight Mathematical Social Science Board volumes*

| Discipline of authors | Percent pages by | Tables/page × 100 | "Sophisticated" tables/page × 100 | Number of theoretical tables, graphs |
|---|---|---|---|---|
| History | 37% | 31 | 6 | 5 |
| Economics | 24 | 18 | 3 | 33 |
| Interdisciplinary | 15 | 22 | 8 | 0 |
| Political science | 10 | 21 | 10 | 1 |
| Sociology, anthropology | 8 | 22 | 2 | 0 |
| Demography, geography | 3 | 20 | 6 | 4 |
| Unidentified | 2 | 32† | 0 | 0 |
| Total | 99 | 25 | 6 | 43 |
| N | 2,775 (pages) | 681 (tables) | 161 (tables) | 43 |

*Volumes listed in footnote 44.
†Not included in other columns.

well. As a comparison of Table 5 with the earlier data on scholarly journals will show, these books contain a higher proportion of numerical tables per page than either the mainstream or the specialized magazines, and a much higher proportion of the MSSB tables go beyond counts, percentages, and measures of dispersion and central tendency. Moreover, the eight works contain a good many of what might be termed "theoretical tables": supply and demand curves, simulations, hypothetical demographic patterns, and the like. Finally, historians did not dominate the conferences on which these tomes are based. Only a minority of the pages were filled with articles written solely by people with Ph.Ds in history. Approximately the same amount of space represented contributions by economists and collaborators from two or more fields. The volumes thus reflect an observation perhaps more strikingly symbolized by the fact that the president of the Social Science History Association in the third year of its existence (1979–80) was a political scientist, Warren E. Miller: quantitative social-scientific history is genuinely interdisciplinary.

Indeed, its interdisciplinary character has always been its strength and is now the guarantee of its continued vigor. The importation of new and fruitful theories, methods, and modes of thought always stimulates a field's development, and social-scientific history is the entrepôt for the products of many disciplines: economics, political science, sociology, demography, geography, and even some segments of anthropology. The frequent collisions between, for instance, economists armored with theory and historians who habitually, and all too often (from the economists' point of view) correctly, question whether the assumptions of some theory are met in the particular context usually result in improvements in both models and history. Furthermore, although declining job opportunities and the consequent cuts in the quantity and probably the quality of history graduate students have decreased the role of graduate training in fostering the transition to a quantitatively literate profession, the employment situation is better in social science departments.[50] As a result, the number of professionals interested in historical social science should continue to grow, regardless of trends in the number of historians. And since the average social scientist will be better trained in theory and statistics than the average historian, the intellectual quality of social-scientific history may well rise whether or not history graduate training becomes more quantitatively rigorous. Finally, if these prognostications are even approximately correct, they raise a serious dilemma for the historical profession in America. The social-scientific merchants have developed not only an extensive trade, but a large demand within the historical community for their valuable products and a comprador class to look after their interests in the new territory. Isolationism would be ill advised even if it were possible.[51] Can the average citizens of the increasingly colonized country afford to remain semiliterate in the traders' language?

50. So far as I know, there have been no systematic surveys of graduate-student quality over time, and even firmly based impressions must await the publication of first books by the generation of the late 1970s; but rational risk-averse American students who desired either to maximize their future income streams, guarantee some minimum level of economic security, or have sufficient leisure to pursue intellectual activities with a minimum of impediments would have been ill advised to choose a career in history rather than economics, sociology, law, or business after about 1970.

51. For such advice on history's alleged ills, see Jacques Barzun, *Clio and the Doctors: Psycho-History, Quanto-History, and History* (Chicago, 1974).

I want to thank my colleagues John F. Benton, Lance E. Davis, Nicholas Dirks, Daniel J. Kevles, and Terrence McDonald for comments on this essay, although they would not want to be held responsible for the resulting document.

My general viewpoint and many specific points so closely parallel those in the excellent set of review essays edited by Allan G. Bogue and Jerome M. Clubb for *American Behavioral Scientist*, XXI (1977), 163–310, especially Bogue and Clubb's "History, Quantification, and the Social Sciences," ibid., 167–186, that I can no longer sort out those ideas that I had independently from those I stole from that set of essays. To avoid repetition I shall display the booty without further acknowledgment.

# 19

## Comparative History

### George M. Fredrickson

S URVEYING recent comparative work by American historians is not an easy task; for there is no firm agreement on what comparative history is or how it should be done.[1] All history that aims at explanation or interpretation involves some type of explicit or implicit comparison, but to isolate "comparative history" as a special trend within the profession requires a reasonably precise and restrictive definition. One can, first of all, distinguish comparative history from history that uses the "comparative method" in a relatively brief or casual fashion, more as a heuristic device than as a sustained method or approach. The limited use of a generalized "comparative perspective" or exotic analogy as a way of shedding additional light on some phenomenon in a single nation or society is not comparative history in the full sense.[2] Neither is the type of study—so important in the "new social history"—that closely examines a particular community or social action in terms of conceptual schemes or categories that are applicable to the study of similar entities in other contexts.[3] If

1. Some recent discussions of the nature of comparative history which present varying definitions and approaches are Fritz Redlich, "Toward a Comparative Historiography: Background and Problems," *Kyklos*, XI (1958); 362–389; William H. Sewell, "Marc Bloch and the Logic of Comparative History," *History and Theory*, VI (1967), 208–218; Robert F. Berkhofer, Jr., *A Behavioral Approach to Historical Analysis* (New York, 1969), 250–269; C. Vann Woodward, "The Comparability of American History," in Woodward, ed., *The Comparative Approach to American History* (New York, 1968), 3–17; Carl Degler, "Comparative History: An Essay Review," *Journal of Southern History*, XXXIV (1968), 425–430; and Maurice Mandelbaum, "Some Forms and Uses of Comparative History," unpublished paper delivered at the Convention of the American Historical Association, San Francisco, 1978.

2. This approach is employed in many of the essays in Woodward, ed., *Comparative Approach*.

3. A large proportion of the articles in the excellent journal *Comparative Studies in Society and History* (1958—) are actually of this nature.

"microcosmic" studies with comparative implications are ruled out, so are "macrocosmic" works that attempt to describe international developments of some kind without a prime concern for analyzing and comparing the variable responses of particular societies.[4]

What remains is a relatively small but significant body of scholarship that has *as its main objective* the systematic comparison of some process or institution in two or more societies that are not usually conjoined within one of the traditional geographical areas of historical specialization.[5] It is only in work of this sort that comparison per se is consistently at the core of the enterprise. In other types of history sometimes described as comparative, the main concern is placing some local phenomenon in a broader geographical context, revealing the general trends prevailing in a given region or throughout the world, tracing some idea or influence across national or cultural boundaries, or describing a particular case in terms that may lend themselves to comparison.

The object of comparative history in the strict sense is clearly a dual one: it can be valuable as a way of illuminating the special features or particularities of the individual societies being examined—each may look different in the light of the other or others—and also useful in enlarging our theoretical understanding of the kinds of institutions or processes being compared, thereby making a contribution to the development of social-scientific theories and generalizations. But the practitioners of comparative history may differ on the priority that they assign to these two aims. Those in the humanistic "historicist" tradition will normally give preference to the former, while those who consider history as nothing more than contemporary social science applied to the past will tend to favor the latter.[6] To some extent, although not consistently, this difference of priorities follows disciplinary lines. It is impossible to discuss comparative history without recognizing the contribution of historically oriented sociologists, political

4. Much work in comparative sociology can thus be excluded. A search for uniformities that can be described only on a very abstract plane clearly inhibits a detailed comparison involving the kinds of variables that historians normally stress.

5. Charles Tilly, Louise Tilly, and Richard Tilly, *The Rebellious Century, 1830–1930* (Cambridge, Mass., 1975), constitutes a major methodological contribution to comparative historical analysis. But the fact that its comparisons are limited to closely related Western European societies places it outside the scope of this essay.

6. For a defense of the "historicist" approach to comparative history, see Redlich, "Toward a Comparative Historiography." A historian who defends the social-scientific mode is Lee Benson. See especially Benson's proposal for a comparative approach to the causes of the American Civil War based on "typologies, analytic models, theories of internal war" in *Toward the Scientific Study of History: Selected Essays* (Philadelphia, 1972), 309–326.

scientists, anthropologists, and economists. But their work tends to differ from that of those who are squarely in the historical profession by its greater concern for generating and testing theories or models that are either of potentially universal application or at least readily transferable to a number of social situations other than those being directly examined.

Unfortunately, the body of work that qualifies as comparative history in the strict sense is characterized both by its relative sparseness and by its fragmentation. Comparative history does not really exist yet as an established field within history or even as a well-defined method of studying history. Unlike "the new social history" or even psychohistory, it does not possess a self-conscious community of inquirers who are aware of each other's work and build on it or react critically to it. Most of those who do comparative history do not define themselves as comparative historians in any general or inclusive sense. Those interested in the comparison of one kind of institution or process often seem unaware of the cross-cultural work being done on other kinds of phenomena. Scholars working on particular topics in the comparative history of certain traditionally juxtaposed areas, such as the United States and Latin America, often make no reference to relevant work being done on other parts of the world.

Because of the sparseness and fragmentation of comparative studies, it is difficult to describe general trends over such a relatively short period as a decade. To gain a coherent view, it is necessary to consider works published in the 1960s as well as the 1970s and view them in relation to special lines or traditions of comparative inquiry. To grasp one important tendency, it is useful to go back to 1966, a year that saw the publication of two unusually ambitious studies in comparative history—C. E. Black's *Dynamics of Modernization*[7] and Barrington Moore's *Social Origins of Dictatorship and Democracy*.[8] These two books provided competing paradigms for doing comparative history in the grand manner, which is nothing less than an attempt to compare the essential dynamics of entire societies. Black's work was rooted in modernization theory, which, according to him, described "the process by which historically evolved institutions are adapted to the rapidly changing functions that reflect the unprecedented increase in man's knowledge, permitting control over his environment, that accompanied the industrial revolution."[9] In this initial study, he

7. *The Dynamics of Modernization: A Study in Comparative History* (New York, 1966).
8. *Social Origins of Dictatorship and Democracy: Lord and Peasant in the Making of the Modern World* (Boston, 1966).
9. Black, *Dynamics of Modernization*, 7.

looked at the process worldwide, and, concentrating on the political dimension, identified seven distinct patterns of "political moderniza-tion." Black has remained a dedicated promoter and practitioner of "comparative modernization" studies.[10] In 1975 he collaborated with seven other authors, three of whom were fellow historians, to produce *The Modernization of Japan and Russia,* a magisterial product of inte-grated team scholarship which combined richness of historical detail with a consistent theoretical framework.[11] The work was genuinely interdisciplinary—the other contributors were two economists and two sociologists—and relentlessly comparative; at no time is the reader so absorbed in one society that he is unaware of the other. It is the most successful example to date of the social-scientific approach to comparative history and suggests that the wave of the future for this kind of work may well be joint efforts by historians and comparative sociologists or economists.

Moore's *Social Origins* provided a quite different model. It was also concerned with "modernization" as a comparable process occurring throughout the world, but the important variable for Moore was the role of social classes, especially the peasantry, and not the interrela-tion of state formation, cultural traditions, and technological de-velopment that is central for Black and his collaborators. In compar-ing the agrarian sources of modernity in England, France, the United States, China, Japan, and India, Moore distinguished three different paths to the modern world: one leads to capitalist democracy by way of bourgeois revolution, a second to fascism ("revolution from above"), and a third to communism through the revolutionary mobilization of the peasantry. Moore's neo-Marxian class analysis of-fered a clear alternative to the conventional modernization paradigm as a theoretical scheme for comparing the transition from preindus-trial to industrial society in various parts of the world. No other work comparable to his in scope and incisiveness has appeared, but in the same neo-Marxian vein were Eric R. Wolf's *Peasant Wars of the Twen-tieth Century*[12] and Immanuel Wallerstein's *Modern World-System.* Strictly speaking, however, Wallerstein's influential study was not

10. See Cyril E. Black, ed., *Comparative Modernization: A Reader* (New York, 1976). This collection contains some essays on the comparative history of modernization. Particularly notable is "Education and Modernization in Japan and England," by Marius B. Jansen and Laurence Stone (214–237), originally published in *Comparative Studies in Society and History,* ix (1967), 208–232.

11. Cyril E. Black et al., *The Modernization of Japan and Russia: A Comparative Study* (New York, 1975).

12. New York, 1969. Wolf describes and compares agrarian uprisings in Mexico, Russia, China, Vietnam, Algeria, and Cuba.

comparative at all, because its frame of reference was a single "European world-economy" that had its origins in the sixteenth century. But its distinction between "core," "semi-peripheral," "peripheral," and "external" areas and its discussion of the kinds of processes that occur in each offered a provocative set of hypotheses to guide the work of comparative historians with a Marxian orientation.[13]

Most of the comparative history that has been done by Americans since the 1960s has not had the grand scope and commitment to a single overarching theory that characterizes the work of Black, Moore, and Wallerstein. It has been concerned less with the dynamics of entire societies than with the role and character of particular ideas, institutions, modes of social and political action, or environmental challenges in a small number of national settings, most often only two. It has tended to be eclectic, adhoc, or casual in its use of social theory and usually retains as its main purpose the better comprehension of particular societies or groups of related societies rather than the discovery of universal laws of social development or the driving forces of world history. Hence it is closer than the work of the "grand manner" comparativists to the conventional tendency of historians to look for particularity, complexity, and ambiguity. Yet the very act of comparison requires categories that are comparable and some presuppositions about what is constant and predictable in human motivation or behavior. Without such assumptions, one could write parallel histories but not comparative ones. Hence comparative historians with more modest ambitions than Black, Moore, and Wallerstein are inevitably driven to a kind of "middle range" social theorizing that is generally more defensible when it is made explicit. Some of the questions that comparativists have difficulty evading are the extent to which people in comparable circumstances are impelled by "idealist" or "materialist" motives; the appropriateness of such concepts as class, caste, race, ethnic group, and status group to describe particular forms of social stratification; and the cross-cultural meaning of such terms as equality, democracy, fascism, racism, and capitalism. One of the great values of comparative history is that it forces such issues to the forefront of consciousness and demands that they be resolved in some fashion that is neither parochial nor culture-bound.

It must be conceded, however, that the usual impulse that has led

13. *The Modern World-System: Capitalist Agriculture and the Origins of the European World-Economy in the Sixteenth Century* (New York, 1974). An essay that applies some of the insights of Moore and Wallerstein to the comparative study of revolutions is Theda Skocpol, "France, Russia, and China: A Structural Analysis of Social Revolutions," *Comparative Studies in Society and History,* XVIII (1976), 175–210.

Americans to do comparative history has not been so much a desire for cosmopolitan detachment or conceptual clarity as the hope that they can learn something new about American history by comparing some aspect of it with an analogous phenomenon in another society. The subjects of comparative historical study which have aroused the greatest interest and stimulated the most work in the United States are clearly those that arise from a sense that some central feature of the American experience has an obvious parallel elsewhere. The fact that other societies have arisen out of a process of settlement and geographic expansion has spawned comparative colonization and frontier studies; the existence elsewhere in the Americas of black servitude has led to a substantial outpouring of comparative work on slavery and race relations; and, most recently, the awareness that the struggle for women's rights and equality with men has not been unique to the United States has resulted in the first signs of a comparative historiography of women and sex roles. An efficient way to sum up the most characteristic manifestations of comparative history in the United States is to deal with each of these subareas individually before taking note of a small amount of work that deals with other subjects and suggests additional comparative possibilities.

The comparative study of colonization and frontier expansion derives from a post–World War II reaction against dominant traditions in American historiography which viewed the United States in isolation from the rest of the world and asserted a uniqueness that was never verified—as any claim to uniqueness must be—by a sustained use of the comparative method. Frederick Jackson Turner's celebrated hypothesis that "the American way of life," and more specifically its legacy of democracy and individualism, resulted from the frontier experience and not from the transplantation of European culture and ideologies was reexamined in a cross-cultural perspective. Frontier historians and historical geographers have produced a literature, mostly in the form of articles or essays, juxtaposing the westward movement in the United States with frontier expansion in Canada, Australia, South Africa, Argentina, and Brazil; some have looked even farther afield and examined Roman, medieval European, Russian, and Chinese frontiers in the light of the Turner thesis.[14] What

14. See especially Walker D. Wyman and Clifton B. Kroeber, eds., *The Frontier in Perspective* (Madison, Wis., 1957); Richard Hofstadter and Seymour Martin Lipset, eds., *Turner and the Sociology of the Frontier* (New York, 1968); and David Harry Miller and Jerome O. Steffen, eds., *The Frontier: Comparative Studies* (Norman, Okla., 1977). Actually most of the essays published or reprinted in these collections are not directly comparative but deal exclusively with individual frontiers. Important exceptions are A.

has emerged is a distinct impression that frontier expansions have varied so greatly in their causes and consequences that it is questionable whether one can speak of "the frontier" as a distinctive historical process with predictable results. In 1968, however, Ray Allen Billington attempted to resurrect a neo-Turnerian claim for American uniqueness by arguing that many of the differences between frontiers can be accounted for by varying physical conditions. The American frontier differed from all others in its consequences, he asserted, because nowhere else was "the physical environment conducive to exploitation by propertyless individuals *and* the invading pioneers equipped by tradition to capitalize fully on that environment."[15]

This cross-cultural testing of the Turner thesis has led to some suggestive comparative insights about the effect of physical environments and preexisting institutions or values on the establishment of new settler communities, but it has not resulted in book-length studies of historiographic significance. A major reason for this lack of development beyond the essay has been a widespread tendency among American historians in general to repudiate Turner's thesis that the frontier had a decisive effect on American society, politics, or "national character." In 1968, Seymour Martin Lipset concluded after a brief review of comparative frontier studies that doubt had been cast on Turner's contention that "the frontier experience was the main determinant of American egalitarianism." What happened on other frontiers pointed to the importance in the American case of "values derived from the revolutionary political origins and the Calvinist work ethos."[16] As frontier history moved to the periphery of American historiography, the impulse to do comparative frontier studies waned. But the recent vogue of American Indian history and a tendency to redefine the frontier as "an intergroup situation"[17] (Turner and his followers had conceived of the frontier as "open land" and had grossly neglected the native American side of the process) has inspired renewed interest in comparative frontier history as a way of making sense of the interactions of the white settlers and indigenous

L. Burt, "If Turner Had Looked at Canada, Australia, and New Zealand when He Wrote about the West" (Wyman and Kroeber, 59–77); Marvin W. Mikesell, "Comparative Studies in Frontier History" (Hofstadter and Lipset, 152–171); and David Henry Miller and William W. Savage, Jr., "Ethnic Stereotypes and the Frontier: A Comparative Study of Roman and American Experiences" (Miller and Steffen, 109–137).

15. Billington, "The Frontier," in Woodward, ed., *Comparative Approach*, 77.

16. Lipset, "The Turner Thesis in Comparative Perspective: An Introduction," in Hofstadter and Lipset, eds., *Turner*, 12.

17. Jack D. Forbes, "Frontiers in American History and the Role of the Frontier Historian," *Ethnohistory*, XVI (1968), 207.

peoples in a variety of contexts, especially the North American, South African, and Latin American.[18]

A serious attempt has also been made to develop a comparative perspective on European settlement in North America and elsewhere based on premises radically different from those of the frontier school. In *The Founding of New Societies* (1964) Louis Hartz sought to substitute a kind of cultural and ideological determinism for Turner's environmentalism to explain why the United States had become a unique kind of "liberal" society.[19] Collaborating with specialists on the history of settlement in Latin America, South Africa, Canada, and Australia, Hartz further developed the thesis, anticipated in his *Liberal Tradition in America*,[20] that European colonists and the societies they founded were shaped less by frontier processes and experiences than by their European antecedents. He argued that each settler society represented a particular "fragment" of an evolving European civilization, the nature of which was predetermined by the mind-set and social background of the original colonists. Since each "new society" contained at the outset only one element of a European dialectic that included "feudalism," "liberalism," and "radicalism," it lost "the impetus for change that the whole provides."[21] Latin American civilization, therefore, represented an immobilized feudalism, the United States an ossified liberalism, and Australia an atrophied form of the proletarian radicalism of the early industrial revolution. The grand schema that Hartz set out in his introduction and in his essay on the United States was only partly sustained by the other contributors. Although they made an effort to remain within the framework that he had laid down, they were not entirely successful, suggesting that the scheme may have been too rigid and deterministic to do justice to complex historical situations. Although the "fragment" theory provoked considerable discussion for a time, it did not in fact become a guiding paradigm for subsequent comparative history.

The ideas and actions of colonizers nevertheless remains a viable

18. A symposium volume comparing the American and South African frontiers is in preparation, under the editorship of Howard Lamar and Leonard Thompson of Yale University.

19. Hartz, *The Founding of New Societies: Studies in the History of the United States, Latin America, South Africa, Canada, and Australia* (New York, 1964), with contributions by Kenneth D. McRae, Richard M. Morse, Richard N. Rosencrance, and Leonard M. Thompson.

20. Hartz, *The Liberal Tradition in America: An Interpretation of American Political Thought since the Revolution* (New York, 1955).

21. Hartz, *Founding of New Societies*, 3.

subject for comparative study. James Lang's *Conquest and Commerce* juxtaposed and contrasted the political structures and economies of the colonial systems or empires established by Spain and England in the New World from the beginnings of settlement until the end of the eighteenth century.[22] After giving a detailed portrait of each pattern, Lang concluded with a comparison that threw into sharp relief the major differences accounting for the divergent outcomes of simultaneous efforts at imperial reorganization in the late eighteenth century. By focusing on the view from the metropole rather than on the internal development of colonial societies, he provided a useful perspective for understanding the degree to which politically dependent "frontier" societies were in fact influenced or manipulated by outside or metropolitan forces.

The most highly developed subject of comparative historical study in the United States is the character and consequences of a single institution that developed initially within the colonial systems treated by Lang—Afro-American slavery. More than the study of frontiers or "the founding of new societies," comparative work on slavery and race relations has resulted in a substantial body of literature that has developed its own set of issues and stimulated an ongoing debate. Among the reasons that comparative history "took off" in this field rather than others are (1) the assumption that slavery as a concept is realtively easy to define, at least when compared with "frontier"; (2) the great public preoccupation in the 1960s and early 1970s with the race issue in the United States; and (3) the stimulus of a well-formulated thesis about the differences between slave societies and their legacies in Anglo and Iberian America around which the discussion could revolve. The Tannenbaum-Elkins thesis, developed in the 1940s and 1950s, postulated a Latin American pattern of mild slavery and "open" race relations that was ascribed mainly to the persistence and enforcement of Catholic-hierarchical traditions. This pattern was contrasted with that in British America, where, it was argued, Protestantism, capitalistic individualism, and a high degree of local autonomy for slaveholders resulted in a peculiarly harsh and closed system of servitude that left behind it a heritage of blatant discrimination against all those of African ancestry.[23] Herbert S. Klein's *Slavery*

22.  Lang, *Conquest and Commerce: Spain and England in the Americas* (New York, 1975).
23.  See Frank Tannenbaum, *Slave and Citizen: The Negro in the Americas* (New York, 1946); and Stanley Elkins, *Slavery: A Problem in American Institutional and Intellectual Life* (Chicago, 1959).

*in the Americas* attempted to confirm this basic view of differences between the two patterns through a detailed comparison of slavery in Cuba and Virginia.[24]

David Brion Davis presented the first really substantial challenge to the Tannenbaum-Elkins thesis in *The Problem of Slavery in Western Culture*.[25] Although this work was mainly a history of ideas about slavery within an international context rather than a comparative history in the strict sense, it contained a long section showing the basic similarities of slave institutions in British and Latin America. Arguing that slavery necessarily involved some kind of tension or compromise between the conception of the bondsman as property or thing and the recognition of his essential humanity, Davis suggested that Tannenbaum and Elkins had exaggerated the extent to which the legal systems of British and Iberian America stressed different sides of this inescapable duality. He also cast doubt on the assumption that Latin American slaves were treated less harshly by their masters. In a later essay summarizing his argument, Davis conceded that "American slavery took a great variety of forms," but attributed the differences less to the cultural-legal traditions stressed by Tannenbaum and Elkins than to "economic pressures and such derivative factors as the nature of employment, the number of slaves owned by a typical master, and the proportion of slaves in a given society."[26] The stage of economic development in particular regions, he concluded, was probably more important for distinguishing slave regimes than was the national or cultural background of the slave owners. Subsequent comparative studies of slave conditions have tended to sustain Davis's position. The work of Franklin Knight, Carl Degler, and others has deepened our sense of how economic and demographic conditions shaped the treatment and governance of slaves in fairly predictable ways that were to a great extent independent of cultural and legal traditions.[27]

But Davis had left open an avenue for cross-cultural contrast by

24. Klein, *Slavery in the Americas: A Comparative Study of Cuba and Virginia* (Chicago, 1967).

25. Davis, *The Problem of Slavery in Western Culture* (Ithaca, N.Y., 1966), 223–288. A provocative earlier attack on the Tannenbaum-Elkins thesis appeared in Marvin Harris, *Patterns of Race in the Americas* (New York, 1964), 65–94. But its thin documentation and polemical tone limited its influence among historians.

26. Davis, "Slavery," in Woodward, ed., *Comparative Approach*, 130.

27. See Franklin W. Knight, *Slave Society in Cuba during the Nineteenth Century* (Madison, Wis., 1970) and *The African Dimension in Latin American Societies* (New York, 1974), 5–49; Carl N. Degler, *Neither Black nor White: Slavery and Race Relatioins in Brazil and the United States* (New York, 1971), 25–92; and H. Hoetink, *Slavery and Race Relations in the Americas: An Inquiry into Their Nature and Nexus* (New York, 1973), 3–86.

acknowledging the validity of Tannenbaum's contention that manumission was easier to obtain and much more extensive in Iberian America than in British settlements and that subsequent distinctions between freedmen and whites were less rigid. What he was questioning was the extent to which this difference resulted from "the character of slavery."[28] In an essay entitled "The Treatment of Slaves in Different Countries" Eugene Genovese helped to clarify the issue and pointed toward a possible synthesis by distinguishing among various kinds of "treatment." Where Tannenbaum's followers went wrong, he suggested, was in contending that slaves were better treated on a day-to-day basis in Latin America than in the United States and then using this alleged contrast to explain the readier access of "the black slave as a black man" to "freedom and citizenship."[29] There was in fact no necessary causal relationship and hence no contradiction between studies showing that physical treatment was dependent on material conditions and those claiming a significant cross-cultural difference between patterns of racial mobility and differentiation.

In the early 1970s, therefore, day-to-day conditions of slave life were less and less taken as a basis for contrasting British American and Latin American slave societies. The generalization that slavery in this sense was milder in Latin America than in the United States appeared to be almost totally discredited. But the difference that Tannenbaum had also found in the racial attitudes and policies arising first during the slave era in relation to manumission and free people of color and then persisting after emancipation now came to the forefront as something that needed to be explained independently of the harshness or mildness of plantation regimes. The most important and successful study that clearly distinguished the determinants of slave conditions from those of race relations was Carl Degler's *Neither Black nor White: Slavery and Race Relations in Brazil and the United States* (1971). Degler argued that demographic factors, particularly the persistence of an international slave trade that provided relatively inexpensive bondsmen, actually made slavery a harsher institution in Brazil than in the United States. In the latter case, the earlier closing of the trade and the need for domestic reproduction of the slave force resulted in better material conditions and less flagrant cruelty. At the same time, however, the American system produced a

28. Davis, *Problem of Slavery in Western Culture*, 262.

29. Genovese, "The Treatment of Slaves in Different Countries: Problems in the Application of the Comparative Method," in Laura Foner and Eugene D. Genovese, eds., *Slavery in the New World: A Reader in Comparative History* (Englewood Cliffs, N.J., 1969), 203.

more restrictive attitude toward manumission and imposed a racial caste system on freedmen and their descendents that had no real analogue in Brazil. Although he documented a tradition of color prejudice and discrimination in Brazil, Degler found that a "mulatto escape hatch" provided a chance for upward mobility for many Brazilians of African descent. He explained this difference from the more rigid American form of racial stratification in terms of larger differences between Brazilian and American social and cultural development. The contrast between a rapidly modernizing, politically democratic, and formally egalitarian society and one that has been characterized by underdevelopment and the persistence of a hierarchical social order provided a contextual basis for understanding why race relations have differed in the two countries.

Despite its extremely favorable reception, *Neither Black nor White* has not been followed by similarly ambitious and detailed comparisons of the historical origin or background of race patterns in two or more New World societies. An important article by Donald L. Horowitz, published in 1973, drew attention to the circumstances surrounding early miscegenation and to the security needs of various slave societies as key variables in determining whether or not an intermediate mulatto or "colored" group emerged.[30] For the most part, however, the trend in the 1970s has been away from the direct comparison of slave societies and the racial systems associated with them. As evidenced by volumes emanating from "comparative" conferences, the scholars of various disciplines who are interested in New World slavery and race relations have been devoting themselves mainly to applying new and more sophisticated approaches and techniques, particularly those involving quantification, to the study of individual cases.[31] Explicit comparison has been left largely in the hands of editors and reviewers, who have been understandably reluctant to draw sweeping comparative generalizations from such a complex mass of new data. In the long run, this particularism may lead to better and more subtle comparisons; but for the moment its stress on the shaping effect of local economic, demographic, and ecological

30. Donald L. Horowitz, "Color Differentiation in the American Systems of Slavery," *Journal of Interdisciplinary History*, III (1973), 509–541.

31. See David W. Cohen and Jack P. Greene, eds., *Neither Slave nor Free: The Freedmen of African Descent in the Slave Societies of the New World* (Baltimore, 1972); Stanley L. Engerman and Eugene D. Genovese, eds., *Race and Slavery in the Western Hemisphere: Quantitative Studies* (Princeton, 1975); and Vera Rubin and Arthur Tuden, eds., *Comparative Perspectives on Slavery in New World Plantation Societies,* Annals of the New York Academy of Science, vol. 292 (New York, 1977).

contexts makes cross-cultural contrast more difficult and problematic than it has been in the past.

Somewhat distinct from the mainstream of interdisciplinary comparative slavery and race-relations studies are efforts to deal cross-culturally with slaveholding classes, antislavery movements, and the causes and consequences of emancipation. Instead of focusing on the enduring structural features of multiracial slave societies, this body of work has concentrated on historical processes and transformations with a crucial political dimension. The landmark study of this kind was the first long essay in Eugene Genovese's *World the Slaveholders Made* which differentiated between slaveholding classes in various parts of the Americas and tried to account for their divergent responses to the threat of abolition.[32] The important variable for Genovese was the nature of class consciousness among planter groups as determined by their relations both with dominant classes in a metropole and with their own slaves. Although not systematically comparative, Robert Brent Toplin's *Abolition of Slavery in Brazil* frequently referred to analogous developments in the United States and lent support to some of Genovese's arguments.[33] In a 1972 article, Toplin made direct comparisons between slaveholder reactions to abolitionism in the two contexts.[34] David Brion Davis's *Problem of Slavery in the Age of Revolution* dealt with antislavery movements on both sides of the Atlantic in the late eighteenth and early nineteenth centuries.[35] Like his earlier work, this study was more in the genre of "international history" than an example of sustained comparative analysis, but it did provide considerable insight into how the hegemonies of social class could influence antislavery attitudes and actions in various settings. In 1978, C. Vann Woodward and I both published essays pointing beyond slavery itself and comparing emancipations and the subsequent establishment of new racial orders in a variety of situations.[36]

My use of the Cape Colony of South Africa as one of three cases

32. Genovese, *The World the Slaveholders Made: Two Essays in Interpretation* (New York, 1969), 3–113.

33. Toplin, *The Abolition of Slavery in Brazil* (New York, 1971).

34. Toplin, "The Specter of Crisis: Slaveholder Reactions to Abolitionism in the United States and Brazil," *Civil War History*, XVIII (1972), 129–138.

35. Davis, *The Problem of Slavery in the Age of Revolution, 1770–1823* (Ithaca, N.Y., 1975).

36. George M. Fredrickson, "After Emancipation: A Comparative Study of White Responses to the New Order of Race Relations in the American South, Jamaica, and the Cape Colony of South Africa," and Woodward "The Price of Freedom," in David G. Sansing, ed., *What Was Freedom's Price?* (Jackson, Miss., 1978), 71–92 and 93–113.

may be part of a new trend to look beyond the Americas for forced-labor or racial situations suitable for comparison with those in the United States. William Wilson's sociohistorical analysis of race relations in the United States and South Africa in *Power, Racism, and Privilege*[37] and Kenneth P. Vickery's 1974 article "Herrenvolk Democracy and Egalitarianism in South Africa and the U.S. South"[38] suggested the potentialities of a comparative approach to the development of patterns of racial inequality in North America and South Africa.[39] The introduction to the volume edited by Suzanne Miers and Igor Kopytoff, *Slavery in Africa,*[40] and the comparative essay that provides the conceptual framework for Frederick Cooper's *Plantation Slavery on the East Coast of Africa*[41] have begun the process of integrating indigenous African slave systems into the universe of cross-cultural slavery studies. Work is also in progress comparing American slavery and Russian serfdom.[42] A pioneer effort to extend the comparative study of race relations into modern ubran situations on both sides of the Atlantic is Ira Katznelson's *Black Men, White Cities: Race, Politics, and Migration in the United States, 1900–1930, and Britain, 1948–1968.*[43]

If the civil rights movement of the 1960s gave an impetus to slavery and race relations as a field of study with a comparative dimension, something similar is now beginning to occur in the new field of women's history that is associated with the recent revival of feminism in the United States. The role and status of women are obviously subjects readily accessible to cross-cultural analysis. As yet, however, comparative women's history has not produced any major hypotheses that lend themselves to testing in a variety of situations. All we have, in fact, are a small number of isolated studies that do not bear any clear and direct relationship to each other. The most important of these are Ross Evans Paulson's *Women's Suffrage and Prohibition,*[44] an analysis of

37. Wilson, *Power, Racism, and Privilege: Race Relations in Theoretical and Sociohistorical Perspectives* (New York, 1973).
38. *Comparative Studies in History and Society,* XVI (1974), 309–328.
39. A forthcoming study of my own, *The Arrogance of Race: Patterns of Inequality in American and South African History,* will attempt a detailed and systematic comparison of white-supremacist attitudes, ideologies, and policies.
40. Miers and Kopytoff, eds., *Slavery in Africa: Historical and Anthropological Perspectives* (Madison, Wis., 1977).
41. Cooper, *Plantation Slavery on the East Coast of Africa* (New Haven, 1977), 1–20.
42. By Peter Kolchin, who has presented papers on this topic at historical meetings.
43. London, 1973.
44. Paulson, *Women's Suffrage and Prohibition: A Comparative Study of Equality and Social Control* (Glenview, Ill., 1973).

the interaction between feminist and temperance movements in the United States, England, and the Scandinavian countries (with asides on France, Australia, and New Zealand); Roger Thompson's *Women in Stuart England and America,*[45] an attempt to explain why women were apparently better off in the colonies than in the mother country; and, most recently, Leila Rupp's *Mobilizing Women for War,*[46] an ingenious comparison of the nature and success of propaganda directed at increasing female participation in World War II in the United States and Germany. Because this body of work lacks a common focus, theme, or set of theoretical assumptions, it is clearly premature to speak of a comparative historiography of women and sex roles in the same sense that one can point to a tradition of comparative slavery or frontier studies.

During the past decade or so, there have also been a small number of "one-shot" comparative works that have not as yet been followed up. Perhaps the most significant of these was Robert Kelley's *Transatlantic Persuasion,* a study of liberal-democratic ideologies and spokesmen in the United States, England, and Canada in the mid to late-Victorian period.[47] But Kelley's pursuit of uniformities and his conviction that he was really dealing with a single transatlantic phenomenon inhibited his use of comparative analysis. Another kind of comparativist would have been more alert to differences that would require explanation. Some of the essays in C. Vann Woodward's *Comparative Approach to American History* suggested some excellent possibilities for comparative history that have still not been pursued systematically. John Higham's short but provocative discussion of how American immigration looks in relation to the experience of "other immigrant receiving countries," such as Canada, Argentina, Brazil, and Australia, provided an open invitation for detailed comparisons of immigration and ethnicity.[48] David Shannon's fine essay "Socialism and Labor" revived the old question of why socialism failed to develop in the United States in the way it did in other industrial nations.[49] The current vogue of labor history should eventually inspire some brave scholars to attempt sustained comparisons of the political role of labor in the history of the United States and other modern societies. The

45. Thompson, *Women in Stuart England and America: A Comparative Study* (Boston, 1974).

46. Rupp, *Mobilizing Women for War: German and American Propaganda, 1939–1945* (Princeton, 1978).

47. Kelley: *The Transatlantic Persuasion: The Liberal Democratic Mind in the Age of Gladstone* (New York, 1969).

48. Higham, "Immigration," in Woodward, ed., *Comparative Approach,* 96–98.

49. Shannon, "Socialism and Labor," in ibid, 238–252.

possible rise of a new focus of comparative historical interest—the maintenance of public order—may be heralded by two books published in 1977, one comparing police activity in New York and London in the mid-nineteenth century[50] and the other analyzing problems of public security in Ireland during the era of World War I and in Palestine in the late 1930s.[51]

When all is said and done, however, the dominant impression that is bound to arise from any survey of recent comparative work by American historians is not how much has been done but rather how little.[52] What we have been considering is in fact a very small fraction of the total output of American historians. The percentage would shrink even further were we to limit our attention to the work of those who are historians in the strict disciplinary sense. Such notable comparativists as Moore, Wolf, Wallerstein, Hartz, Lang, Wilson, and Katznelson have in fact been trained in other disciplines. A main reason for what was earlier referred to as the "sparseness" of comparative work is the way the historical profession is organized in the United States. Historians receive most of their predoctoral training in the history of a single nation or culture area. Teaching and publication are similarly specialized. There are, to my knowledge, no professorships of comparative history at major institutions.[53] There is no journal devoted exclusively to comparative history, although *Comparative Studies in Society and History* provides a forum for historians along with comparativists from other disciplines. The absence of doctoral programs, professorships, and journals devoted to comparative history per se has clearly had an inhibiting effect on the development of this mode of historical analysis. Since reputations and successful careers are the products of intense geographical specialization, young

50. Wilbur R. Miller, *Cops and Bobbies: Police and Authority in New York and London, 1830-1870* (Chicago, 1977).

51. Tom Bowden, *The Breakdown of Public Security: The Case of Ireland, 1916-1921, and Palestine, 1936-1939* (Beverly Hills, Calif., 1977).

52. In addition to the works already cited, however, a small number of comparative essays or articles deserve to be mentioned. Daniel Walker Howe, "The Decline of Calvinism: An Approach to Its Study," *Comparative Studies in Society and History,* XIV (1972), 302-327, is a good example of how to compare the fate of a common set of ideas in different societies. C. K. Yardley's "The 'Provincial' Party and the Megalopolises: London, Paris, and New York, 1850-1910," ibid., xv (1973), 51-88, is an important attempt at comparative urban history, a field that remains surprisingly underdeveloped. John A. Garraty, "The New Deal, National Socialism, and the Great Depression," *American Historical Review,* LXXVIII (1973), 907-944, represents the first results of an inquiry into the effects of the Depression on major industrial nations. It demonstrates the usefulness of examining the impact of an international cataclysm, such as a depression or a world war, on two or more comparable societies.

53. Tufts University, however, is in the process of establishing one.

historians launch into comparative work at some risk to their future prospects. Established scholars can afford the luxury of a foray into cross-cultural analysis, but are reluctant to go too far lest they lose touch with the main lines of development in their own field of specialization. This is especially true because historians are more uncomfortable than sociologists, for example, with generalizations that are not based on detailed knowledge and some immersion in primary sources. It thus becomes necessary for would-be comparativists to develop what amounts to a second or even a third field of specialization, almost equivalent to their original area of expertise, if they wish to go beyond "comparative perspective" and do sustained comparative history that will be respected by experts on each of the societies that they are examining. Understandably, therefore, few historians are willing to devote the time and energy that such an enterprise involves. Unless comparative history becomes a distinct field or recognized subdiscipline within history, in the manner of comparative sociology, politics, or literature, it is unlikely that it will become a major trend within the profession. Perhaps the decision to make comparative history the theme of the 1978 convention of the American Historical Association reflected some tentative movement in this direction. But for the moment, most comparative history is done by scholars who are either based in another discipline or taking an extended holiday from their normal role as historians of a single nation or cultural area.

# 2 0

## The Teaching of History

### Hazel Whitman Hertzberg

I N the 1960s and 1970s American historians knew a great deal
more about the history of what they were teaching than about
the history of what they were doing in the classroom. Interest in
the history of history teaching was virtually nonexistent among historians in general and historians of education in particular. The earlier
development of a modest historiographical tradition came to a virtual
halt after World War II. Thus the crisis that enveloped history teaching in the 1970s was without a literature that might have helped to
explain it. Initially the crisis seemed to be about jobs and enrollments:
deeper dimensions emerged subsequently.

In examining the teaching of history in the 1960s and 1970s, I shall
focus primarily on the curriculum and methods of instruction in the
secondary school, college, and university, bypassing history in the
elementary school not because it is unimportant but because the evidence is scanty and inconclusive.

History as a separate, widespread, and major subject of instruction
in the schools, colleges, and universities of the United States is only
about a century old. In the last decades of the nineteenth century, the
high school developed from the academy, and the university was
born. The first generation of professional historians who helped to
found the university and to shape the new curricula of the college and
high school returned from Germany with a vision of history that
encompassed a commitment to both specialized research and civic
responsibility, a vision they translated into American terms. They
displaced the patrician amateurs of the nineteenth century and
moved history into the educational system, transforming it into a
teaching profession.[1]

1. John Higham, *History* (Englewood Cliffs, N.J., 1965), 11.

474

The professionalization of history, symbolized by the founding of the American Historical Association in 1884, was part of a larger movement to establish history as a major subject at every level, from little red schoolhouses through the new universities. Because the American educational system was decentralized—no Ministry of Education existed in Washington to dictate curricula, materials, or methods of teaching—the establishment of history was accomplished through a complex of voluntary organizations, institutional mandates, and state and local regulations. In this process the new professionals played a decisive role.

At the beginning of the 1880s history hovered at the outskirts of American education, but by World War I it was comfortably settled at the center. In the 1880s history was taught only sporadically in the common schools, and somewhat more frequently in the academies and high schools.[2] College history developed rapidly in the '80s; the history seminar became a major mode of instruction in graduate schools during the same decade.[3] Beginning with the 1892 National Education Association Committee of Ten, the various national committees that created history curricula for the secondary and elementary schools were dominated by historians.[4] The 1899 AHA Committee of Seven recommended a secondary school curriculum much like that of the college: ancient, medieval and modern European, English, and American history and civil government.[5] By 1916 this pattern had been widely adopted.[6] The Ph.D. became virtually mandatory for college teaching at the major universities, while history was required for teacher certification in most states.[7] Influential regional associations of college and school history teachers, formed around the turn of the century, published proceedings, syllabi, sourcebooks, and other curricular material. The *History Teacher's Magazine,* founded in 1909 and shortly thereafter supervised by an AHA advisory committee, covered history teaching at all levels of instruction except graduate education. History textbooks for schools and colleges were

2. Rolla M. Tryon, *The Social Sciences as School Subjects* (New York, 1935), 132–151.

3. Herbert B. Adams, *The Study of History in American Colleges and Universities* (Washington, D.C., 1887).

4. See for example, [NEA] *Report of Committee of Ten on Secondary School Studies* (New York, 1894).

5. [AHA] Committee of Seven, *The Study of History in Schools: Report to The American Historical Association* (New York, 1899).

6. Tryon, *Social Sciences,* 179–183.

7. Lawrence R. Veysey, *The Emergence of the American University* (Chicago, 1965), 176; Bessie L. Pierce, *Public Opinion and the Teaching of History in the United States* (New York, 1926), 56.

written by distinguished historians who were leaders in the movement to establish history. The burgeoning history classes in schools and colleges were thus supported by professional activities and furnished with curricular materials. In the school, history was typically taught through the recitation; in the graduate school, through the seminar. The typical mode of instruction in the college is not so certain. By the end of the period history had become not only a major subject in the schools but also increasingly a required one.[8]

But even as the Committee of Seven pattern triumphed in the schools, its critics, on the increase both inside and outside the profession, were calling for a curriculum more suited to the present age. The reform impulses of the Progressive period, the growth of cities, immigration, mushrooming school populations, the rising "science of pedagogy," and the growth of the teachers' colleges—all contributed to discontent with the curricular status quo. In the historical profession, scientific history was challenged by the "New History," which called for a history that would draw on the social sciences and speak to the present, a history that would be more than "past politics."

The 1916 report by the NEA Committee on the Social Studies provided a rallying point and a platform. The desire to include the social sciences and social issues was reflected in the term "social studies," although its meaning has been endlessly debated ever since. The 1916 report defined "the cultivation of good citizenship" as the "conscious and constant" purpose of social studies, a citizenship based on national ideals while encompassing the "world community." To this end, the committee proposed a junior cycle (grades 7–9) of geography, European history, American history, and civics, and a senior cycle (grades 10–12) of European history, American history, and problems of democracy ("POD")—social, economic, and political. History was to pay due attention to Latin America and the Orient. The selection of historical topics should depend, the committee urged, not on their "relative proximity in time" or on their importance from an adult or sociological point of view but on the degree to which they could be related to "the present life interests of the pupil, or can be used by him in his present processes of growth."[9]

James Harvey Robinson, a prominent advocate of the New History and one of the committee's few historians, was also its most influential member. The report quoted him liberally. The recommended cur-

8. Pierce, *Public Opinion,* 52.
9. [NEA] *The Social Studies in Secondary Education* (Washington, D.C., 1916), 9, 12, 39, 44.

riculum kept history and civics as the curricular core while accommodating the social sciences, social problems, and other topical approaches. It proved to be both functional and durable, becoming in the next half century the typical pattern of social studies instruction.

What were some of the factors that may have accounted for history's dynamic thrust between the 1880s and World War I ? First and most fundamental was the phenomenal growth in educational enrollments at all levels, even though most Americans still did not go beyond elementary school. It was on this expanding base, which provided increasing numbers of jobs for persons trained in history, that Clio's American house was built.

Second, the formation of the AHA before the professional organization of other social sciences gave historians several advantages. Not only were they present at the creation of major sectors of the educational system, but history was one of the "new" subjects in the battle against the old classical curriculum in the high schools and colleges. That the history advocated by the new professionals was "scientific" helped to gain its acceptance and gave it a central role in establishing the research function of graduate education.

Third, historians early formed an alliance with the National Education Association, identifying history with the historic role of the schools in the education of citizens in a democratic society. Civic education was broadly conceived as including not only the national past but the history of the Western and ancient worlds. It encompassed the study of civics or government, with which history was closely associated.[10]

Fourth, with the emergence of the New History in the Progressive period came a new group of historians—such men as James Harvey Robinson, Charles A. Beard, and Carl L. Becker—whose historical interests coincided with the rising educational demands for history teaching more closely allied to contemporary problems and to the social sciences. Like the "scientific historians" with whom they did battle, they believed in the civic mission of education. In each phase of the rise of history teaching there were, it seems, major historians whose history matched the needs of the day.

Fifth, the caliber of historians who helped to establish history in the schools, colleges, and universities was stunning. The seven men whom John Higham identified as the scholars of enduring distinction who received their undergraduate training between 1880 and 1905—

10. N. Ray Hiner, "Professions in Process: Changing Relations between Historians and Educators, 1896–1911," *History of Education Quarterly*, XII (1972), 34–56.

Charles McLean Andrews, Charles A. Beard, Carl L. Becker, James Henry Breasted, Edward A. Channing, Charles Homer Haskins, and Frederick Jackson Turner—were all involved in school history, as well as history in the colleges and universities.[11] Their vision and that of such other historians as Andrew C. McLaughlin and Herbert Baxter Adams, who helped to establish history as a teaching as well as a research profession, was a spacious one. It arose from a view of progress that saw the historical sweep of the West in general and of American civilization in particular as an upward struggle of profound significance to humanity. It encompassed the whole of the American educational system, the education of citizens as well as specialists, and viewed the study and teaching of history as essential to the progress of a democratic society. It was also informed by experience. Most of these leaders had contact with all levels of education, and produced instructional materials for the schools and colleges, source materials for the researcher, and major works of history.

After World War I, history education in the colleges and schools followed roughly parallel paths with a stronger emphasis on Western civilization in the colleges and on American history in the schools. A reformation of the college curriculum began after World War I to counter the waning popularity of electives and the incoherence of curricula. Introductory history in higher education was revitalized largely through the growth of courses in Western civilization which were often part of "general" or "liberal" education reforms.[12] The grandparent of them all was the famous "contemporary civilization" course instituted at Columbia College in 1919. "Western civ" (and varieties thereof) became the typical introductory history course. The American history survey was offered in almost all colleges and universities by the 1940s. These introductory history courses were also beneficiaries of the general education movement after World War II.

In the secondary schools, world history/European history and American history, as recommended by the 1916 NEA Committee on the Social Studies, gradually displaced the older Committee of Seven pattern, downplaying ancient history, consolidating English with European history, broadening history beyond Europe and the United States, and establishing "problems of democracy" as the capstone in the senior year. Partially in response to the 1916 report, the National Council for the Social Studies was formed in 1921, led by historians,

11. Higham, *History*, 57.
12. Higham also attributes to "Western civ" the renewal of the function of the historian as a generalist in a present-minded culture, a process that "surely encouraged the newer areas of research into which historians were moving" (*History*, 42).

political scientists, and educators, most of whom were engaged in teacher education. It also reflected a desire for the professionalization of social studies teachers as well as dissatisfaction with the existing historical and social science professional bodies. Among the disciplinary associations, only the AHA maintained a close and continuing relationship with NCSS, although there were difficult moments. The last major effort by the historical profession, as represented by the AHA, to work closely with the schools occurred in the 1930s with the AHA's Commission on the Social Studies, whose chairman was August C. Krey and whose guiding spirit was Charles A. Beard. Unlike earlier national commissions, however, this one did not recommend a curriculum.[13] The commission's report consisted of a series of individual volumes on various aspects of social studies education, most of which rest in undeserved out-of-print oblivion. The AHA gave the royalties from the commission's publications to help subsidize the NCSS journal, *Social Education*. The subsidy ended in 1954, but the journal was published "in collaboration with the American Historical Association," as its cover proclaimed, until 1968.[14]

But long before the late 1960s, when this relationship officially ended, the distance between the AHA and the schools had been widening. The separation seems to have been due in large part to the growing emphasis on research training for the Ph.D. and a concomitant lessening of interest in teaching. By the mid-1950s a new and numerous postwar generation of Ph.D.s was entering teaching. Increasing specialization supported by increasing affluence resulted in a tremendous proliferation of specialized courses while the general introductory courses fell into disfavor. The days when senior professors took pride in teaching the undergraduate survey seemed to be over, and many of their doctoral students adopted a similar attitude. Dexter Perkins's 1956 presidential address to the AHA, "And We Shall Gladly Teach," argued that the greatest challenge to the historian was

13. See Charles A. Beard and George S. Counts, *Conclusions and Recommendations of the Commission* (New York, 1934). Among the other volumes were Charles A. Beard, *The Nature of the Social Sciences in Relation to Objectives of Instruction* (New York, 1934) and *A Charter for the Social Sciences in the Schools* (New York, 1932); Henry Johnson, *An Introduction to the History of the Social Sciences* (New York, 1932); Tryon, *Social Sciences;* Merle E. Curti, *The Social Ideas of American Educators* (New York, 1935); William C. Bagley, *The Teacher of the Social Studies* (New York, 1937); Ernest Horn, *Methods of Instruction in the Social Studies* (New York, 1937); Charles E. Merriam, *Civic Education in the United States* (New York, 1934).

14. Louis M. Vaneria, "The National Council for the Social Studies: A Voluntary Organization for Professional Service," unpublished Ph.D. dissertation, Teachers College, Columbia University, 1958, 167–172, 213–217. The NCSS periodical, *Social Education,* was a continuation of the *History Teacher's Magazine.*

the challenge of the classroom.[15] But the growing number of students in history classes provided the illusion that history's place was secure and that problems of classroom teaching were not significant.

While Cleo magistra dozed, a new movement to reform the schools by reforming the curriculum was stirring. During the 1950s the schools were widely attacked for offering an education inadequate to the citizens of a great power with world responsibilities. Especially in mathematics, sciences, and languages, American education was deemed inferior to European schools in general and the USSR's in particular. The curriculum was soft, it was alleged, the teachers were ill prepared, many students couldn't read, and able students were neglected. The launching of Sputnik uncorked unprecedented amounts of government and foundation funds for curriculum development. In the early 1960s the movement spread to the social studies, now relabeled "the social sciences," and focused largely on the "new" subjects: anthropology, enconomics, and sociology. The latter had strong backing from their respective learned societies, although by no means as complete as that for history in the earlier period.

The social studies wing of the new movement became known as "the new social studies." Based in the universities, the movement largely bypassed the teachers' colleges and schools of education (the pejorative term was "educationists"), the NCSS, and even teachers in the schools. The curriculum developers proposed instead to go directly to the students. The role of the teacher was essentially to deliver specially designed curricular materials to them, through carefully designated procedures.

The new social studies showed clearly the influence of reform's chief theoretician, Jerome Bruner. Students were to learn the "structure" of the disciplines, to employ their methodologies, and to engage in "inquiry" and "discovery" by using a wide array of materials, including films, filmstrips, records, and other audiovisual devices. Most of the new social studies projects were directed to able students. With "excellence" as their watchword, the reformers advocated "conceptual teaching" as being an efficient and powerful aid to learning. The meaning of "concepts," as of "structure," was often unclear, especially when applied to history. In-depth studies and "postholing," in which limited data made it easier for students to learn by discovery, were aspects of the new social studies more adaptable to history teaching. The movement emphasized Benjamin S. Bloom's taxonomy of the

15. Perkins, *American Historical Review,* LXII (1957), 291–309.

levels of intellectual operations, the careful creation of objectives, and learning processes rather than content.[16]

The new social studies were thought of as an "interdisciplinary" or "multidisciplinary" affair, but the problem of how the overall curriculum was to be rebuilt or modified to relate the several disciplines to each other or to provide coherent "scope and sequence" was not addressed. Area studies, which had been growing in the 1950s, were recognized as an important curricular ingredient, but they did not fit easily into a separate disciplinary approach. Citizenship education—as represented by the traditional civics, government, and "problems of democracy" courses—was ignored, or assumed to take care of itself when intellectually able and inquiring citizens were produced. The new social studies were unified by a shared approach and shared methodologies, not by a conception of shared content or shared civic purposes. Clearly something had to give. History, it was agreed, had to move over.

Educational reform is typically ahistorical, and the new social studies were no exception.[17] The reformers were uninformed about previous curricular reforms, even those in their own discipline. Most of the project developers had little previous contact with schoolrooms. The movement was to a large extent antihistorical as well, partly because history's commanding position in the schools was an inconvenience, partly because of the ahistorical stance of many of the social sciences.

The new social studies movement was financed far more generously than any previous social studies reform. In the early 1960s funds for project development flowed liberally from the National Science Foundation, the U.S. Office of Education, and private foundations. The project developers, needing an organization of their own, created in 1963 the Social Science Education Consortium, an invited group of social scientists and project developers eventually broadened to include "methods" educators and curriculum supervisors. For some years the ssec maintained a correct but distant relationship to the National Council for the Social Studies.

16. See Jerome Bruner, *The Process of Education* (New York, 1960); John Haas, *The Era of the New Social Studies* (Boulder, Colo., 1978), for a history of the movement written by a participant. For a comparison of the new social studies with the source study movement (1880s–1916) see Hazel W. Hertzberg, *Historical Parallels for the Sixties and Seventies: Primary Sources and Core Curriculum Revisited* (Boulder, Colo., 1971).

17. See Arno A. Bellack, "History of Curriculum Thought and Practice," *Review of Educational Research*, XXXI (1969), 283–291.

History was included in the new social studies on the understanding that it was a social science. Some projects, such as the Anthropology Curriculum Study Project and the High School Geography Project, both sponsored by their respective learned societies, developed units suitable for use in history courses. A few, such as the Educational Development Center, developed a whole new social studies curriculum. EDC's "Man: A Course of Study" (MACOS) included some history for the elementary grades, and made history the focus of its secondary school materials.

The two specifically historical projects, which emphasized the use of primary sources and "the historian's mode of inquiry," were Edwin Fenton's Carnegie-Mellon Curriculum Development Center and the Amherst Project, headed by Richard H. Brown and Van R. Halsey. The Amherst Project created units that could be incorporated into American history courses. The Fenton project was more ambitious: some texts and materials handled European and American history with a strong social science emphasis, and others dealt with economics, political science, behavioral science, and humanities. The project most closely allied to citizenship education was the Harvard Social Studies Project, headed by Donald W. Oliver and James P. Shaver, organized around persisting and controversial public issues and often using historical materials.[18]

Throughout most of the 1960s, social studies curricular reform and the new social studies were synonymous. History was discussed within this context. A few critics attacked the "new history" (the new social studies history, not the James Harvey Robinson "New History") for focusing too narrowly on history, as well as for sundry other sins, such as neglecting content, failing to meet the needs and interests of the child, and detaching the past from current problems.[19] All but the first criticism were also made by many of history's supporters. Some educators in both camps questioned the validity of "structure" and the overuse and/or originality of the "inquiry method," as well as its value as a basis for organizing the curriculum. Most writers on school history in the 1960s simply assumed history's central place in the curriculum while accepting the incorporation of social science into his-

18. For descriptions and evaluations of the new social studies projects, see Norris M. Sanders and Marlin L. Tanck, "A Critical Appraisal of Twenty-six National Social Studies Projects," *Social Education,* XXXIV (1970), 383–446, and the entire November issue of *Social Education,* XXXVI (1972). For Fenton's views, see his *New Social Studies* (New York, 1967).

19. See Albert S. Anthony, "The Role of Objectives in the 'New History,'" *Social Education,* XXXI (1967), 574–580. See also in the same issue "Edwin Fenton Replies," 580–583, and "Richard H. Brown Replies," 584–587.

tory neutrally or enthusiastically.[20] With a few exceptions, however, these writers were outside the new social studies movement. They could not match the élan or the creative energy of the reformers: willy-nilly they tended to be cast as defenders of a status quo of which they were also seasoned critics. The new social studies appeared to be making significant inroads into the leadership of social studies education, if not the classroom.

But the societal concerns of the 1960s were precisely those that the new social studies neglected: civil rights, the antiwar movement, the cities, the poor, blacks and other "minorities," "slower students," and what educators called the "affective domain" (emotions and feelings) as distinct from the "cognitive domain." Nor were the new social studies part of the '60s attack launched by the "new romantics" which pictured the schools as heartless, joyless, stiffly academic, and unresponsive to the individual and "cultural" needs of students, a critique almost the reverse of the '50s attacks out of which the new social studies had grown. In the late 1960s, just as the new social studies were ready to disseminate their wares, the full force of the student revolt disrupted the colleges and quickly spread to the schools.

The social studies response to the turmoil in the schools and in society did not take the form of a movement with a well-developed ideology, or even a name. As we moved into the 1970s the watchword was "relevance" to social problems and self-realization. The student, who in the new social studies had been modeled after the academic scholar, was now cast as the social activist in search of a personal or group identity. The pages of *Social Education* quickly filled with articles on social problems and how to teach them, often using new social studies methodologies, such as "inquirey" and "discovery." "Valuing," a minor theme in the 1960s, became a major one in the late 1960s and '70s. The new emphasis was both ahistorical and antihistorical. The past was relevant only when it dealt with matters of burning social or personal concern. The idea of a common American past, including the melting pot as a creator of American nationality, was junked by both the new social studies and the social problems/personal realization approach, to be replaced by a fragmented past and cultural pluralism as a theory of nationality and an article of faith. Minicourses mushroomed and computers made feasible their scheduling. Many history courses were broken into discrete bits even while retaining

20. For a summary of these views, see J. Wade Carruthers, "*Social Education* Looks at the History Curriculum: An Eleven-Year View," *Social Education*, XXXI (1967), 93–98, 107.

their old titles. Requirements were relaxed or jettisoned. The newest wave had a much more direct and immediate impact on the schools than had the new social studies. The latter, however, began to incorporate some of the new topics and emphases into their materials.

By the early 1970s, these two competing trends had reached an uneasy accommodation, finding common ground in objectives, concepts, inquiry, a concern with processes, and a tacit agreement to overlook scope and sequence. The NCSS Curriculum Guidelines, published in 1971, illustrate this liaison.[21] Based on "knowledge," "abilities," "valuing," and "social participation" as the four curriculum components, and with a strong emphasis on diversity, flexibility, and student involvement, the guidelines provided a checklist of sixty-five items for evaluation of social studies programs. Although history remained the most common social studies subject in the schools, in the guidelines it was relegated to a mere listing as one of the social sciences on which the curriculum should draw and a few other brief mentions. School history was singled out as "often bland, merely narrative, repetitious, inattentive to the non-Western world; it is distorted by ignoring the experiences of Blacks, Chicanos, native American Indians, Puerto Ricans, and Oriental Americans." Government or civics didn't fare much better. Except for a few strictures about out-of-date geography and political science, the other social sciences emerged unscathed. "Enduring or pervasive social issues," such as "economic injustice, conflict, racism, social disorder, and environmental imbalance," were recommended as appropriate content from kindergarten through high school. The United States as a "nation" was treated with embarrassment, the preferred terms being "society," "culture," or "the real social world." The knotty problem of curricular organization was to be handled by "structural elements" drawn from the social sciences, social issues, or student and community concerns, or from social participation. A slightly revised version of the guidelines, published in 1979, showed that the accommodation had held. The chief differences were an expanded list of issues, such as sexism, which had meanwhile emerged, a strong infusion of a "global issues" approach, and a few references to "citizenship education."[22]

New textbooks in the 1970s fell smartly into line with the social studies detente. In a provocative 1979 *New Yorker* series on the history of American history texts, Frances FitzGerald describes the '70s

21. "Social Studies Curriculum Guidelines," *Social Education*, XXXV (1971), 853–869.
22. "A Revision of the NCSS Curriculum Guidelines," *Social Education*, XLIII (1979), 261–278.

textbooks as invaded by the new social studies version of the social sciences, marked by uncertainty and confusion about the American past and present, and peopled with historical or contemporary examples of '60s and '70s protest movements, notably blacks and other "minorities" and women, without much regard for their integration into the narrative or into a coherent view of the nature of American nationality. Her account of how '70s texts were manufactured, standardized, and adopted should give pause to those concerned about how and what people learn in school history, and about the integrity of historical scholarship. One may quarrel with FitzGerald's treatment of individual texts and historical topics as well as with her interpretation of the history of history teaching, but the series raised significant questions about the quality of textbooks which needed to be addressed.[23]

The traditional curricular pattern established by the 1916 NEA Committee had "finally been shattered," Richard E. Gross reported in a 1977 survey of the status of the social studies. Between 1961 and 1973 total secondary school enrollments had risen by 59 percent, but social studies enrollments (at least since 1972) were mixed, ranging from significant increases to moderate or drastic decreases, with a "debacle" in the primary grades. In both 1961 and 1973, U.S. history, U.S. government, and world history enrolled the largest number of social studies students. The first two held their own in terms of percentage of rising enrollments, the third did not. Absolute enrollments in civics and "problems of democracy" fell drastically. The number of high schools offering U.S. history dropped from 73 percent in 1961 to 53 percent in 1973, and in world history from 68 percent to 49 percent.[24] Significant increases occurred in state and local history and in area studies. The spectacular growth areas were in the social sciences: sociology, economics, and psychology, the latter being the fastest growing course.

The Gross survey reported that the actual impact of the new social studies in the classroom remained somewhat mysterious. Many teachers claimed that they were using methodologies associated with the new social studies. They also reported, however, that actual use of the new social studies project materials was minimal, and many had not even heard of the projects. Textbooks, curriculum guides, and

23. Frances FitzGerald, "Rewriting American History," *New Yorker,* LV (February 26, 1979), 41–77; (March 5, 1979), 40–91; (March 12, 1979), 48–106.
24. These 1961 figures, not included in the Gross report, are from National Center for Education Statistics, *Course Offerings, Enrollments, and Curriculum Practices in Public Secondary Schools, 1972–73* (Washington, D.C., 1976), 12.

485

in-service programs seemed to be the channels through which versions of the new social studies seeped into the classroom; they did not do so through teachers' membership in professional organizations or teachers' reading of professional literature.

Other trends reported were sometimes contradictory or fragmenting: the growth of minicourses, values education, electives, back-to-basics, local options, specialized ethnic offerings, law and citizenship education, performance objectives/competencies, and a decrease in social studies requirements.

The social studies curriculum was a "patchwork" that lacked any clear scope and sequence, Gross declared. Although he found some reaction against "the mini-course bandwagon, specialized offerings in ethnic studies, and the anarchical curriculum itself," he did not see a countervailing trend toward greater curricular coherence. Gross urged the development of a national curricular framework with a "core of socio-civic learnings" to aid local districts in curricular revision, one that would make the social studies "more basic to the maintenance and extension of democratic values and to the future of this nation than is any other disciplinary area." The alternative, he concluded, was a balkanized and steadily declining curricular field. He did not suggest that history had or did not have a role to play in the curricular reconstruction he proposed.[25] Nor did the survey report on the serious situation in the job market for social studies teachers in many schools.

Perhaps the celebration of the Bicentennial, along with a rising popular interest in the past during the last half of the 1970s, gave the strongest boost to school history. These factors were reflected in curricular attention to "roots," families, communities, and oral history. Museums developed lively school programs and instructional materials.[26] A reaction against minicourses, a concern with the way the jumble of topics and courses was to be integrated in student minds, and tightened school budgets, which discouraged expensive "innovations," were factors of mixed impact not necessarily favoring history or the social studies as a whole. In the back-to-basics movement, the social studies were not defined as "basic." Teachers had difficulty in defending the value of social studies, including history, to school boards, administrators, and students. Students earlier attracted by

25. Richard E. Gross, "The Status of the Social Studies in the Public Schools of the United States: Facts and Impressions of a National Survey," *Social Education*, XLI (1977), 194–200, 205.

26. See, for example, *Family Work Community: Museum Catalog of Teaching Materials* (Old Sturbridge, Mass., n.d. [but 1979]).

social activism were concentrating on getting good grades and getting ahead, and often preferred subjects with more immediate payoff.[27]

This is a mixed picture. I do, however, see a nascent revival of interest in school history at the end of the decade. This estimate is based more on personal contact than on indications in the literature. There was the recent success of "History Day" in several states, in which secondary school students created projects, wrote papers, or gave performances on some aspect of a national topic. Participation by secondary school teachers in the AHA regional conferences for all history teachers was also encouraging. At the end of the 1970s historians formed an interest group (SIGHT) within NCSS.

I have thus far concentrated on the schools in discussing the changing position of history in the 1960s and '70s. The colleges and universities, however, were also part of the overall crisis. In the late 1960s the dimensions of the crisis were unclear and the responses uncertain.

One response was to seek hard facts. Exactly what had happened to history degrees, enrollments, and curricula? By the mid-1970s surveys began to appear. Most reviewed the current situation with little attention to long-term trends. (For the latter, see Tables 1 and 2.)[28] By 1976, history's share of bachelor's degrees had fallen to 3.06 percent, below the 1955 figure. While degree figures after 1976 were not available, several studies of students' prospective majors were ominous: in 1975, 1.3 percent planned to major in "history and culture"; in 1978, only 0.7 percent.[29]

The survey that attracted the most attention in the profession was issued in 1975 by a committee of the Organization of American Historians headed by Richard S. Kirkendall. It reviewed the status of history in the schools and colleges and concluded that "history is in a state of crisis." While noting many state and regional variations, the committee found declining enrollments in the colleges and a trend away from history courses in the schools. In both, the dropping of various types of requirements was a contributing and probably a major factor. Teacher certification requirements, which affect enrollments in college courses as well as the teaching of history in the

27. Celestino Fernandez et al., "High School Students' Perceptions of Social Studies," *Social Studies*, LXVII (1976), 51–57. See also James P. Shaver et al., "The Status of Social Studies Education: Impressions from Three NSF Studies," *Social Education*, XLIII (1979), 150–153.

28. I am indebted to C. Dale Whittington, a doctoral student at Teachers College, Columbia University, for making these tables.

29. "Fields of Study Chosen by Students," *Chronicle of Higher Education*, XI (September 15, 1975), 18–19, and "Characteristics of 1978–79 College Freshmen," *Chronicle*, XVII (January 22, 1979), 14–15.

*Table 1*.  Bachelor's and first professional degrees conferred in history and the social sciences, 1949–76

| Year | Total bachelor's degrees | Social science as percent of total | History as percent of social science | History as percent of total |
|------|------|------|------|------|
| 1949 | 366,634 | 9.78% | 29.25% | 2.86% |
| 1955 | 287,401 | 13.13 | 26.70 | 3.32 |
| 1961 | 401,113 | 13.53 | 29.05 | 3.93 |
| 1968 | 671,591 | 18.11 | 29.11 | 5.27 |
| 1976 | 934,400 | 13.69 | 22.36 | 3.06 |

Sources: U.S. Department of Commerce, Bureau of the Census, *Statistical Abstract of the United States*, 1950, 1954, 1957, 1960, 1963, 1965, 1966, 1968, 1977; U.S. Department of Health, Education, and Welfare, National Center for Education Statistics, *Earned Degrees Conferred*, 1972–73 and 1973–74, and *Digest of Education Statistics*, 1977–78.

*Table 2*.  Bachelor's degrees in history and the social sciences, 1968–76

| Year | Social science as percent of total | History as percent of social science | History as percent of total |
|------|------|------|------|
| 1968 | 18.11% | 29.11% | 5.27% |
| 1970 | 18.63 | 28.08 | 5.23 |
| 1972 | 17.85 | 27.55 | 4.92 |
| 1974 | 15.95 | 24.56 | 3.92 |
| 1976 | 13.69 | 22.36 | 3.06 |

Sources: See note to Table 1.

schools, were reported to be quite fluid: requirements were strongest in the South, weakest in the East. State and local laws mandating the teaching of history in the schools showed signs of erosion.[30]

Long-term trends in the Ph.D. were described by Frank Freidel in his 1976 presidential address to the Organization of American Historians. Freidel noted that the output of trained historians rose geometrically from the 1920s level of 50 a year to almost 1,200 in 1972, nearly 500 of whom were in American history. The overwhelming majority of all professional historians (i.e., Ph.D. holders) ever trained in the United States were alive and active in 1976, most of them teaching in colleges and universities.[31]

Surveys of four-year liberal arts colleges and two-year community

30. Richard S. Kirkendall, "The Status of History in the Schools," *Journal of American History*, LXII (1975), 557–570.
31. Frank Freidel, "American Historians: A Bicentennial Appraisal," *Journal of American History*, LXIII (1976), 5–20.

colleges showed that institutions where history enrollments and student interest in history were decreasing far outnumbered those with rising or stable enrollments and interest. The demise of general education requirements in the four-year colleges, especially Western or world civilization, had had a devastating impact on enrollments, many respondents reported. History was required for graduation in virtually all of the community colleges outside of New England and the Mid-Atlantic region, where the figure was only 30 percent. In the four-year colleges American history and Third World history were better off than European history; the latter also declined in community colleges. While Third World interest increased, American and Western/world civilization courses declined in the two-year colleges. In both types of institutions, historians were teaching classes composed primarily of nonmajors (90 percent in the four-year colleges, 52 percent in the community colleges).[32]

The '70s efforts to get at the facts confirmed that there was indeed a crisis in the teaching of history. To what did historians attribute this state of affairs? The student revolt against the "irrelevant" past was widely accepted as a major reason. Other factors were the financial problems of academia, the shrinking job market, student interest in practical vocational education, and the back-to-basics movement. The popularity of social sciences other than history, especially in the high school, was another theme. But extended analysis of these factors was rare. Discussion tended to be confined to assertion rather than searching explanation.

Some historians accepted the view that history was irrelevant. David H. Donald wrote in 1977 that because the abundance that sustained the United States throughout its history had ended, "the 'lessons' taught by the American past are today not merely irrelevant but dangerous." "Our problems grow constantly larger," Donald wrote, while "the chances of solving them drastically diminish." Some teachers of history seemed to share Donald's forthright views.[33]

Herbert London's analysis of history's troubles attributed them to the effects on historical scholarship of three major movements: exis-

32. See Hugh B. Hammett, Charles F. Sidman, Thomas Longin, and Henry P. French, Jr., "Can the Teaching of History Survive 1984?," *History Teacher*, x (1977), 229–248. See also Warren L. Hickman, "The Erosion of History," *Social Education*, XLIII (1979), 18–22; Jack Friedlander, "The Status of History in the Two-Year College," *AHA Newsletter*, XVI (April 1978), 6–7.

33. David H. Donald, "Our Irrelevant History," *AHA Newsletter*, xv (December 1977), 3–4. In the same issue see challenges to Donald's view by Edward L. Keenan, 4–5, and Blanche Wiesen Cook, 5–6. See also Christopher Lasch, *The Culture of Narcissism: American Life in an Age of Diminishing Expectations*, (New York, 1978), xiii–xviii.

tentialism, revisionism, and romanticism. Existentialism, he wrote in 1971, made "the accumulated experience of the past an absurd curiosity." He characterized revisionism as a reaction against the '50s consensus historians who renounced Beardian progressivism and tended to dwell on the virtues of America's past. The revisionists were a "disparate group of thinkers" united by "an opposition to the status quo." While the radical historians contributed significantly to a discipline that "for a time sadly neglected the deep-seated conflicts in American life," in so doing they were guilty of "failing to understand their adversaries and of judging them by standards that in themselves may be ephemeral." Romanticism, London asserted, "disregards reason and the past." History could be fairly described as "tradition that has lost a considerable part of its legitimacy."[34]

A number of historians attributed decline to the profession's neglect of the broad humanizing function of history in favor of increasingly narrow specialization. Immersed in specialized historical research, Charles G. Sellers asserted in the late 1960s, historians had "remained complacently indifferent to the freshman and sophomore courses that offered the only opportunities for historical learning to the vast majority of students, and to the history courses in the schools that afford the only opportunity for historical learning to the vast majority of the population." Sellers suggested that the college could learn from the "learning by discovery" in the new school history, which eschewed coverage in favor of asking "what the student can be expected to do with the subject in terms of his own development.[35]

A similar charge, but with a different remedy, was advanced by William H. McNeill. Since the 1950s, McNeill wrote, historians had focused on specialized research and failed to recognize any obligation to find something of general import to teach all students.

> The study of history cannot be expected to recover centrality in college curricula unless and until we have something to teach that speaks to general concerns of ordinary citizens. Specialized "post-hole" courses in subjects of arcane professional debate will not do. Their meaning depends on the pre-existence of opinions about the past to be tested and modified by precise investigation. But without a generalized picture of the past to alter, such courses float in a vacuum that makes them all but meaningless for ordinary students. . . . Better than any other discipline,

34. Herbert London, "The Relevance of 'Irrelevance': History as a Functional Discipline," *NYU Education Quarterly*, II (1971), 9–15.
35. Charles G. Sellers, "Is History on the Way out of the Schools and Do Historians Care?," *Social Education*, XXXIII (1969), 509–516.

history can define shared, public identities—national, civilizational, human, as well as local, ethnic, sectarian. For obvious practical reasons, college courses must concentrate at the introductory level on shared identities.[36]

Some critics located the problem in a more general repudiation by both students and faculty of a "common core" of knowledge: "whether certain values can be transmitted, whether the transmission of such values is a desirable educational objective, and whether anything like a common culture can be communicated to student bodies of widely disparate tastes and ambitions" are questions that need to be confronted, Stephen R. Graubard wrote in 1975. "Anything resembling the earlier consensus about subjects that ought to be universally taught, so that students may experience and share a common sense of the past, is rapidly disappearing. . . . An intellectual change has occurred, comparable in some ways to what happened in the nineteenth century when those who taught the classics were compelled to abandon their 'monopolies.' "[37]

Then there were the historians who attributed history's problems to poor teaching. Teaching was rarely studied at the postsecondary level; the leaders of the profession ignored it; history professors were lulled by captive audiences into assuming that they were teaching well when in fact they often were not. School history teachers imitated university instructors whose methods were quite unsuitable for teaching high school students. Poor history teaching in the schools was blamed on the teachers' failure to understand the nature of history, which in turn resulted in college students who lacked an understanding of chronological development or a sense of history.[38]

Probably the most frequent explanation of history's problems was that the wrong history was taught. Historians asserted that much of the history taught was no better than myth, that history was irrelevant to the needs of blacks and women and other "minorities," that history was too impersonal and did not involve students, that it was too political and not sufficiently cultural or social. A few warned that if the

36. William H. McNeill, "History for Citizens," *AHA Newsletter*, XIV (March 1976), 4-6.

37. Comments by Stephen R. Graubard in "Teaching History Today," *AHA Newsletter*, XIII (Novemeber 1975), 5-6.

38. See, for example, Gilbert C. Fite, "The Historian as Teacher: Professional Challenge and Opportunity," *Journal of Southern History*, XLI (1975), 3-18; Mark M. Krug, "On the Crisis in the Teaching of History," *Illinois Schools Journal*, LVIII (1978), 20-26; Ira Marienhoff, "A High School Teacher Looks at College Teaching," *AHA Newsletter*, V (April 1967), 13-16.

American history taught focused too exclusively on past American transgressions, the result might be a repudiation of the past as too heavy a burden to bear, and consequently even less interest in history.[39]

Since change through time is fundamental to historical thought, it is somewhat surprising that so few historians seem to have asked whether this aspect of history may present unique problems to students, and if so, why. In Great Britain a number of investigators made empirical studies of how students learn history, largely within a Piagetian framework, and have applied their findings to teaching.[40] A few such studies were conducted here before World War II. Some American social scientists, such as Erik Erikson and Kenneth Keniston, noted the conflicts about the past which arise in adolescence and youth.

One analysis attributed part of history's problems to the widespread emergence of new conceptions of time and change which particularly affected students. I have posited three basic conceptions of time and change in three types of societies. In the traditional model characteristic of tribal and peasant societies, change is incorporated into a seamless past-present-future. In the progressive model, characteristic of urbanizing, industrializing societies, the present is thought of as somewhat detached from the past and as moving toward a better future, while change is regarded as being both inevitable and good. In the "now" model, a subordinate but influential conception characteristic of postindustrial societies, the past and future become detached from the intense and endless present in which change erupts. Each transition is accompanied by a profound societal crisis. In the traditional model, history is an aspect of religion and myth; in the progressive, it is secularized; in the now, it is irrelevant. In the nineteenth and twentieth centuries in the United States, the progress-

39. See Edgar Bruce Wesley, "Let's Abolish History Courses," *Phi Delta Kappan*, XLIX (1967), 3–8; Linda Greene, "Justice in America: Persistent Myth," *Social Education*, XXXVII (1973), 637–639; James A. Banks, "Teaching for Ethnic Literacy: A Comparative Approach," *Social Education*, XXXVII (1973), 738–750; Peter J. Frederick, "Is Someone in the Classroom with Clio?," *History Teacher*, V (1971), 7–19; Alice P. Kenney, "Fact and Feeling for the 'Now' Generation," *History Teacher*, IV (1970), 21–26; Russell H. Bostert, "Teaching History," in Steven M. Cahn, ed., *Scholars Who Teach: The Art of College Teaching* (Chicago, 1978).

40. See, for example, E. A. Peel, "Some Problems in the Psychology of History Teaching," in W. H. Burston and D. H. Thompson, eds., *Studies in the Nature and Teaching of History* (New York, 1967); R. N. Hallam, "Piaget and Thinking in History," in Martin Ballard, ed., *New Movements in the Study and Teaching of History* (Bloomington, Ind., 1970); G. Jahoda, "Children's Concepts of Time and History," *Educational Review*, XV (1963), 87–104.

ive model of time and change predominated, and it was in this period that history was professionalized and that adolescence as a distinct and prolonged life stage came into being. Following World War II, the "now" model emerged. Its growth was due partially to affluence because only an affluent society could afford to delay the entrance of large numbers of persons into the labor market or to underemploy them, and to support the widespread experimentation and the variety of institutions, many of them temporary, in which nowness found its home; partially to the rapid pace of change, so rapid that traditional social institutions had great difficulty in adjusting to it; and partially to television, with its intense focus on the new and its sudden temporal reversibilities. Adolescents and youth, whose numbers increased as a result of the post–World War II baby boom, were the groups most affected. In adolescence, in Eriksonian terms, one struggles with and finds a new identity. As both Erikson and Piaget point out, this struggle involves a confrontation with one's past and with history. It is characterized by some alienation from the past, by ambivalence toward or rejection of history, and by the acquisition of new temporal conceptions as an essential part of an evolving cognitive structure. This analysis seeks to explain both the lack of enthusiasm for history long noted in the schools and the more recent open revolt against history by students with such different immediate concerns as reforming society and getting jobs. The teaching of history, I contend, rather than ignoring the special problems history presents, can help students come to grips with the past, a process that is essential to their own cognitive growth.[41]

Several other historians also dealt with the linkage between adolescence and history. Martin E. Sleeper's investigations, based on Erikson and Piaget, revealed that history readily coexists in two disparate categories in the minds of adolescents: a sense of the past as it bears on one's own personal development, in which the adolescent imagination is most lively and powerful, and formal history, worth studying but without personal relevance and meaning, in which thinking is far less speculative and hypothetical. These categories are united only through the perception of a particular event that seems salient to both the individual and the societal past. Sleeper's view is based largely on students who are competent in history.[42]

41. Hazel W. Hertzberg, "Alienation from the Past: Time, Adolescence, and History" (paper, Teachers College Conference on History in the Schools, 1977).
42. Martin E. Sleeper, "The Uses of History in Adolescence," *Youth and Society,* IV (1973), 259–274, and "A Developmental Framework for History Education in Adolescence," *School Review,* LXXXIV (1975), 91–107. See also John B. Poster, "The Birth of the

The explanatory literature of the 1970s was thus fairly sparse, although suggestive. No historian seems to have investigated in any depth college students' views of history or how they learn it. It seems clear, on the basis of the literature in England and the United States, that at different stages of life students have quite different conceptions of history and learn differently. But we know very little about adult conceptions of history and how they may have changed through time. I suspect that looking at history from these varied perspectives not only would be of immediate practical utility but would enrich our understanding of what constitutes historical thinking and a sense of the past.

Not until the mid-1970s did most historians in higher education connect the troubles they faced with history's troubles in the schools, and take measures encompassing both. While the AHA's History Education Project (HEP) in the late 1960s encouraged experimentation in history teaching, the immediate concern of the professional associations was the rapidly growing unemployment among new Ph.Ds. This was a matter of special concern to women, blacks, and other "minorities," who evolved programs to increase their numbers in a profession that in higher education was still largely male and white. *History Teacher,* a quarterly journal begun in 1968, was taken over in 1972 by the Society for History Education, thus giving the profession for the first time in decades a periodical devoted to all aspects of history teaching at all levels of education. Neither the *American Historical Review* nor the *Journal of American History* carried articles on teaching, a policy that continued in the 1970s. The *Network News Exchange,* a newsletter also published by SHE, was started in 1975. The AHA's Teaching Division, headed by a vice-president, was set up in 1974; and the *AHA Newsletter* initiated a regular column on the teaching of history. The OAH's Committee on the Status of History in the schools and colleges was formed in 1974; the *OAH Newsletter* from its inception carried material on history teaching. The AHA Teaching Division cosponsored a series of regional teaching conferences for teachers at all levels of education. Teaching sessions multiplied at the AHA and OAH annual meetings. Here the division between doing history and teaching it was perpetuated, "almost as if two different and often nonintersecting conventions were being held at

---

Past: Children's Perceptions of Historical Time," *History Teacher,* VI (1973), 587–598; Hazel W. Hertzberg, "The Now Culture: Implications for Teacher Training Programs," *Social Education,* XXXIV (1970), 271–279; Michael A. Zaccaria, "The Development of Historical Thinking: Implications for the Teaching of History," *History Teacher,* XI (1978), 323–340.

the same time and in the same place," as Warren I. Susman pointed out.[43] Other programs related to teaching were the NEH summer seminars for college teachers, which included a substantial number devoted to history, as did NEH programs for teachers' institutes and curriculum development in the elementary and secondary schools. A further development was the establishment in 1976 of the National Coordinating Committee for the Promotion of History, which included the AHA, the OAH, and other professional associations and interested groups beyond academia. The NCC thus represented a broadening trend in the definition of who would be included in "the profession."

That colleges and universities had begun to offer training programs for other than academic historical careers was evident in the findings of a 1978 NCC survey. The forty-eight programs reported were described as new, small, often interdisciplinary, and including professionals from the fields for which candidates were preparing. Most had internships, a clear break with traditional training. The programs fell under three broad categories: archives and information management, cultural resources management (historic preservation and museums), and applied research (corporations, consulting firms, government). Three-quarters of the new programs offered a two-year master's degree, the remainder the baccalaureate, the doctorate, or the M.A. and the doctorate.[44]

By the mid-1970s also, formal training in college teaching was offered in the graduate history departments of thirty-two public and private universities, although the traditional one-to-one apprenticeship relationship between professors and their teaching assistants was still the predominant pattern. The new programs varied from casual to highly structured, and included attention to the philosophy and/or methods of college teaching as well as the philosophy of history and historiography. A few institutions offered the Doctor of Arts degree, instituted at Carnegie-Mellon in 1967, which replaced the exclusively research-oriented dissertation with a teaching-oriented product. It closely resembled the much older Doctor of Education, which arose for similar reasons.[45]

43. Warren I. Susman, "Annual Report, Vice-President, Teaching Division," [AHA] *Reports of the Vice-Presidents, 1978* (Washington, D. C., 1978), 13.
44. Arnita A. Jones, "Clio Confronts Adam Smith: A Survey of National Trends in the Adjustment of Training Programs for Historians," *OAH Newsletter*, vi (January 1979), insert, n.p. See also Robert Kelley, "A Note on Teaching: The Graduate Program in Public Historical Studies," *History Teacher*, xi (1978), 227–228.
45. Maxine Seller, "The Training of the College History Teacher: A Teaching Division Survey," *AHA Newsletter*, xv (January 1977), 6–8.

Some historians addressed themselves to general problems in undergraduate history education. Samuel P. Hays advocated "a curriculum based on different contexts of human life in terms of social structure and social change," organized "so as to facilitate the student's understanding of systematic varieties of human experience in the past, and thereby facilitate entry into varieties of human experience in the present." Such a curriculum would be organized "not around countries or time periods, as is the custom, but around thematic problems concerning the types of human contexts of life," treated comparatively. Hays suggested such topics as the community, the family, ethnocultural groups and their relationships, socioeconomic inequality, and types of processes of social change. As ways for students to become directly involved in investigations that tied their experience to broader historical phenomena, he suggested family genealogies and community studies. Such an approach, Hays argued, could provide an effective two-way communication between student and teacher, facilitate a more common perspective between history and some of the social sciences, and help us to "realize how our study is neither, strictly speaking, a social science nor a humanities subject."[46]

The use of comparative history from a somewhat different perspective was advocated by Russell H. Bostert. History teachers should share certain assumptions, Bostert wrote: first "that all generations tend to be present-minded" and that few history courses will be meaningful to any generation of students unless they help them to understand the present, and second that it is possible by an act of self-transcendence to put oneself in the past and "deal with it in a way that seeks neither heroes nor villains, but an understanding of both." The first assumption can sometimes result in "isolating and concentrating upon history's transgressions and derogations as seen from the present." A likely result, Bostert warned, "will be to spawn historical judgments that add up to a severe condemnation of the American experience." Such judgments may elicit counterjudgments designed to "save" the American past, while students, "attracted to the voices of dissent in their own history, will pay less attention to continuity than discontinuity, finding in the latter a key to hoped-for changes in the future." A normative approach, Bostert believed, is likely to confront the teacher with a growing polarization of views about the past, especially the American past. Comparative history could help teachers to cope with polarization without taking an innocuous middle course,

46. Samuel P. Hays, "History and the Changing University Curriculum," *History Teacher*, VIII (1975), 64-72.

Bostert argued. Slavery, imperialism, racism, violence, and the treatment of ethnic minorities were topics recommended for this treatment.[47]

Experimentation in undergraduate teaching was the typical subject of 1970s literature. At the University of Kansas, a new program based on a self-assessment offered new courses of direct advantage to other departments and professional schools, a series of general-interest topical courses for casual students, and a new structure combining non-prerequisite core lectures with a variety of satellite specialized discussion/research courses, careful student advising, and research or support for faculty and a visiting-scholar program. In a two-year period, course enrollments and the number of departmental majors rose substantially.[48]

The introductory undergraduate course, the traditional staple of the undergraduate history curriculum, did not escape reexamination. Some historians abandoned the survey altogether. Others experimented with Western or world civilization, American history, and courses that included all. "Western civ," some critics pointed out, had developed in a specific historical context, largely in response to the changing position of the United States in the world and as an aspect of a liberal education. Its basic assumption of the unilinear progress of the West toward human freedom had given it an organizing principle that many historians no longer found valid. Some of those who shared this view advocated global history for citizens of a global age. But they disagreed on the form this history should take. William H. McNeill, for example, argued that a course of general significance for undergraduates as citizens was needed, and that failure to agree on one was an admission that historians have nothing to teach young people that they ought to know. Such a course was not only necessary but possible. "Each scale of history has an appropriate conceptualization and amount of detail," he wrote. "An adequate principle can make a world history or a national history just as accurate and far more exciting than any Ph.D. thesis is likely to be." Giles Constable substituted for the single introductory survey a series of one-term correlated courses, covering broad geographical areas of the world and planned along common lines and around common problems, as a conceptual framework in which to bring out both the particular and the general characteristics of specific historical material. This approach, Consta-

47. Bostert, "Teaching History," 5-13.
48. Charles Sidman, "Teaching History Today," *AHA Newsletter,* XIII (October 1975), 5-7. See also Paul Cappuzello, Mark Schlesinger, et al., *Recent Trends in History Curriculum and Pedagogy* (Bowling Green, Ky., 1976).

ble argued, was feasible in any department with at least one teacher each in American, European, and Third World history.[49]

But many historians, unwilling to give up "Western civ," suggested ways of reorganizing it. Lewis W. Spitz proposed revealing "the continuity of certain problems in Western culture and the recurrence of some difficulties and solutions to these problems" by teaching "how different historical situations shape what it is possible for people to do and to be." Spitz described a new required course with several alternative tracks, taught not only by historians but by faculty from other departments, such as classics, philosophy and religion, art, music, and drama. Certain historical and cultural readings constituted a common core for all of the tracks.[50]

The '70s literature on college American history survey courses showed more concern for methodologies and materials than for broader conceptual problems. Richard A. Waller's 1975 review of changes in the U.S. survey course revealed widespread citicism of the traditional lecture method, repetition of content and coverage, "irrelevance," and inept use of audiovisual techniques. Laboratory courses that "deemphasize content coverage and emphasize the historian's method" constituted the most common way of circumventing or supplementing the lecture method. To formal literary sources were added artifacts, ephemera, recorded speeches, political cartoons, and pop-culture items. Students investigated the history of their own families or communities, often using oral history. Some institutions called attention to changing historical interpretations. The American-studies approach continued. Black history, women in history, ethnic, Indian, peace, state and local history, and pop culture, especially films, were favored topics. A comparative focus was one of the most striking developments: themes or institutions in American history were compared with similar ones elsewhere, often in an attempt to overcome parochialism. A concern with processes characterized much of the literature; in some instances the emphasis was shifted deliberately and decisively from learning content to learning processes.[51]

Examples of the types of changes advocated for high school U.S. history may be seen in the 1974 NCSS Yearbook, *Teaching American History: A Quest for Relevancy*, which combined '60s and '70s issues with

49. "Beyond Western Civilization: Rebuilding the Survey," *Network News Exchange*, II (Spring 1977), 4–16; papers by William H. McNeill, 4–6; Giles Constable, 9–12.

50. Paper by Lewis W. Spitz in ibid., 6–9.

51. Robert A. Waller, "The United States History Survey Course: Challenges and Responses," *History Teacher*, VIII (1975), 199–207.

new social studies methodologies. "A study of history can readily serve as a vehicle by which students can learn an applicable mode of inquiry, develop useful concepts, successfully empathize with the past, continue to clarify values, learn to recognize and to cope with suspected myths and stereotypes, and to ask critical questions about the past, present, and future," the editor wrote. The historical topics selected for "sample lessons" were a pre-1800 Indian group, a Confederate soldier's life during the Civil War, the women's equal rights movement, Appalachian coal miners, the melting-pot "myth" in relation to "black culture," the American city, "Who is qualified for the presidency?" and the environment.[52]

What was lacking in the discussions of the American history course was attention to the kinds of problems that engaged historians in the brisk debate on Western civilization/world cultures. In reading the literature, I have the impression of either studied avoidance or extreme delicacy in attaching any overall meaning or direction or coherence to American history. Yet the teaching of the history of a country to its citizens, especially in the troubled 1970s, surely deserved consideration of such questions.

If, as many historians contended, the conception of American history as a history of progress (whether through consensus or conflict) had been shattered, how was this shattering development to be dealt with? What alternative conceptions should be offered? If the liberal tradition was vigorously challenged, how should the challenge be treated in the classroom? How were differing conceptions of the nature of American nationality to be handled and what were their implications for "history for citizens"? If for many historians detachment had gone aglimmering, how did the substitution of personal engagement and moral judgment affect what and how the historian taught? If history teachers should quickly incorporate new interpretations or emphases into their teaching, how were they to do so? Or, to ask a prior question that remained unexamined, was it necessarily desirable for them to do so? What themes or emphases were appropriate to the American history survey and why? What consequences might be expected from specific answers to these questions, not only for students' understanding of history, but for their views of their own country and their relationship to it? Similar questions, of course, could be asked of the teaching of all history. They were more urgent for the teacher of American history whose students would not be specialists than for the

52. Allan O. Kownslar, ed., *Teaching American History: A Quest for Relevancy* (Washington, D.C., 1974), 12.

teacher of undergraduate majors or graduate students. Most of the literature in the 1970s ignored such questions, assumed a position that at best answered them implicitly, or referred to them only briefly.[53]

The range of literature of the 1970s on teaching history in schools and colleges was probably unparalleled in undergraduate—and perhaps even secondary school—history instruction. It was eclectic, interesting, and often exuberant. The proliferating topics included the history of blacks, ethnic groups, women, families, communities, states and localities, ecology and the environment, law, architecture, the city, novels, films, music, movies, and drama; the list is not exhaustive. Some topics were proposed as separate courses, others as approaches in broader courses. Methodologies and materials included films, filmstrips, television, audio and video tapes, role playing, simulation, games, computer-assisted instruction, and team teaching. The use of oral history was widely reported. What struck the seasoned reader of this literature was how closely the reforms proposed for school classrooms and for higher education resembled each other. They shared strengths of able description, earnestness of purpose, and concern for students.

Certainly the literature had its serious weaknesses. For example, the particular teaching problems inherent in proposed new topics were largely overlooked. An interesting exception—and there were others—was Gerda Lerner's analysis of the teaching of women's history. Another problem was fragmentation and its consequences. As Henry Bausum wrote, "Valuable as such topics may be in shedding light on specific problems, they threaten to leave today's student with an even narrower historical consciousness than that provided by the widely criticized political history of yesteryear."[54] Yet another weakness was the absence of provisions for evaluation. In the early stages of an innovation, innovators understandably resist evaluation because the results are likely to be inconclusive. By the time a project is well along, unfortunately, the innovators are likely to lose interest in

53. Aspects of some of these problems are addressed in Myron A. Marty, "Nationality and History Education: National History in International Times," *History Teacher*, XII (1978), 45–55, and in the same issue by Eugene L. Asher, "Nationality and History Education: The Social Uses of History in the School Curriculum," 57–64; John Jarolimek, "Born-Again Ethnics: Pluralism in Modern America," *Social Education*, XLIII (1979), 204–209. See also, R. Freeman Butts, "The Revival of Civic Learning," *Social Education*, XLIII (1979), 359–364.

54. Gerda Lerner, "Teaching Women's History," *AHA Newsletter*, XIV (May/June 1976), 3–6; Henry Bausum, "The Social Function of History," *AHA Newsletter*, XV (May/June 1977), 7.

evaluation. Thus the literature of innovation was full of successes but notably lacking in failures, a circumstance that weakens its usefulness to potential imitators.[55]

Did the new approaches make any difference in student attitudes toward history or in student learning? One of the rare attempts to find out employed two versions of the same new course, one using the traditional lecture and the other using lectures plus experimental "focus" groups on particular topics. The most striking result was the lack of difference. Students in both classes claimed new knowledge and positive attitudes toward history. They did equally well on objective and essay examinations and expressed about the same interest in taking more history courses. From these results both traditionalists and innovators could cautiously take heart.[56]

These weaknesses were compounded by another: the persistent ahistorical quality of the literature on teaching. Reformers tend to dismiss "traditional" teaching as inadequate without further ado, definition, or differentiation, often basing their views on their limited personal experience or that of their offspring. The accounts of the 1970s contained few references to relevant earlier experiments and almost none earlier than the 1960s. Yet most innovations had counterparts in the past that could be highly instructive. There are "new" ideas waiting in the records which do not have to be reinvented, only resuscitated and adapted. Without a cumulative body of research and development, it is difficult to see how long-term improvement of teaching can take place. In the 1970s the presentism that so many historians deplored as characteristic of our society and of our students was well settled in one wing of Clio's house.

The dark continent of the 1970s was the history of history teaching itself. The few forays into this cloudy territory were in school history, where a discontinuous historiographical tradition languished. Several studies focused on the period of history's rise in the schools, one on the use of primary sources and the core curriculum since the 1880s, a scattering on the work of Harold Rugg, Harry Elmer Barnes, and the new social studies.[57] Toward the close of the decade an increase in

55. See Myron A. Marty, "Trends and Trendiness in Teaching Undergraduate History," *Teaching History*, 1 (Fall 1976), 41–47.

56. James J. Lorence and Bryan Hendricks, "Is Innovative Teaching More Effective?: Teaching the Focus-Group Strategy in the Freshman American Survey," *History Teacher*, xii (1979), 187–198.

57. In addition to Hiner, "Professions in Process... 1896–1911"; Haas, *Era of the New Social Studies;* and Hertzberg, *Historical Parallels,* already cited, see N. Ray Hiner, "Professions in Process: Changing Relations among Social Scientists, Historians, and Educators, 1880–1920," *History Teacher*, vi (1973), 201–218; David Muschinske,

historical allusions in articles about teaching perhaps foreshadowed an interest in creating or reviving a significant and needed field of historical investigation.

The teaching of history in our time could hardly escape the turmoil of our time. The characteristics of history teaching in the last two decades—specialization, fragmentation, experimentation, "excellence," "relevance," confidence in the new, narrowness or uncertainty of purpose, segmentation, presentism—all were part of currents running deep in American life.

By the end of the 1970s, history's status throughout the educational system had been deeply shaken, yet it remained an important subject enrolling large numbers of students. How the teaching of history would fare in the 1980s would depend both on developments far beyond the profession and on the choices historians themselves made.

It seems to me that at the decade's end at least two societal trends, one well under way, the other just emerging, could affect history's future favorably if historians were able to work with them. In the 1970s Americans took the past into their own hands in a popular revival of historical interest in TV, trade books, films, historical societies, historic preservation and restoration, houses and neighborhood reconstruction, museum attendance, even antiques and clothing. The revival was personal, visual, concrete, dramatic, and participatory. Some historians tapped into this revival; many feared it as misleading, inaccurate, and romanticized. Few examined the question of why, at a time when an "appetite for history" was growing in the country, it was declining in the schools and colleges.[58] Popular movements in the past have affected the teaching of history, but only when a genuine mutuality of interest developed did the teaching of history benefit. I believe that popular interest in history bespoke a deep longing for historical roots in uncertain times, a search for individual and collective meaning from which people could draw sustenance, a reaction against a disposable society—and a disposable past.

The second factor is more speculative. I can state it only briefly. At

"American Life, the Social Studies, and Harold Rugg," *Social Studies,* LXV (1974), 246-249; Raymond J. Cunningham, "Is History Past Politics?: Herbert Baxter Adams as Precursor of the 'New History,'" *History Teacher,* IX (1976), 244-257; Justus D. Doenecke, "Harry Elmer Barnes: Prophet of a Usable Past," *History Teacher,* VIII (1975), 265-276; Peter F. Carbone, Jr., *The Social and Educational Thought of Harold Rugg* (Durham, N.C., 1977). History in higher education is dealt with tangentially in Frederick Rudolph, *Curriculum: A History of the American Undergraduate Course of Study since 1636* (San Francisco, 1977).

58. John Lukacs, "What Is Happening to History?", unpublished paper, 1979, 6.

the end of the 1970s the United States was entering a period of transformation as a result of the inevitable change in the nature, supply, and distribution of energy, one that will result in major changes in the way we think, feel, and pursue our ways of life. The imperative of conservation, with its husbanding of limited resources, requires a temporal perspective radically different from the imperative of unlimited consumption, with its assumption of unlimited resources. Perhaps this transformation will engender a need for a past both sustaining and explanatory. It was in a period of transformation in American life that history arose and became established in the American educational system. A century later, the conditions of the new period and the status of history were very different, but history was equally needed.

For the future of history teaching two developments within the profession in the 1970s seem to be most significant. The first was the emergence of a new generation of historians committed to the importance and improvement of teaching. They had considerable experience with classroom experiment and had produced a body of literature on teaching. They had not yet, however, been able to move teaching in its manifold aspects to within hailing distance of the sanctum occupied by research unrelated to teaching. The second factor was the breaching of boundaries dividing historians in the schools and colleges from historians in the world outside, teachers of history at various educational levels from each other, and history in the minds of teachers from history in the minds of students. These boundaries had at least been crossed, though tentatively and never in force.

While these developments were encouraging, they did not match the gravity of the crisis, which was a crisis not only for historians but also for the American people. For a century historians had the formal teaching of the past in their keeping. It was in the classroom that most Americans confronted the glories and follies of their own past and the past of humankind. I shall not argue how fundamental historical consciousness is to the future of our society, how destructive the consequences if only stray bits and pieces of history fall haphazardly into people's minds, how harmful the results of a national historical lobotomy.

At the close of the 1970s history's position in the classrooms and curricula of American schools and colleges was based essentially on the dwindling capital created by earlier generations of historians. Institutional inertia had been history's curricular protector—as well as its insidious enemy. Even history's research function could not indefinitely flourish if the educational base on which it rested continued to crumble. The renewal of the teaching of history, so vital to the society, so essential to the profession, had only begun.

What history teaching needed was theories, historical analyses, and unifying ideas sufficiently powerful to re-create a sense of purpose, sufficiently broad to encompass all who teach and learn history, sufficiently applicable to reshape the curriculum and inform teaching, and sufficiently persuasive to convince students and the public that history in the schools and colleges was worth studying. Such developments would require profound changes in the structure and direction of the profession. Whether American historians would so commit themselves to the study and practice of teaching was, at the beginning of the 1980s, a question that could not yet be answered.

# THE CONTRIBUTORS

ALLAN G. BOGUE (b. 1921) is the Frederick Jackson Turner Professor of American History at the University of Wisconsin. He received his Ph.D. from Cornell University in 1951. He is the author of *Money at Interest: The Farm Mortgage on the Middle Border* (1955) and *From Prairie to Corn Belt: Farming on the Illinois and Iowa Prairies in the Nineteenth Century* (1963), and co-editor of *American Political Behavior: Historical Essays and Readings* (1973) and *The History of American Electoral Behavior* (1978). His study *Radicalism in the Civil War Senate of the United States* is forthcoming. He has served as president of the Agricultural History Society and of the Social Science History Association.

WILLIAM J. BOUWSMA (b. 1923) is Sather Professor of History at the University of California, Berkeley. He received his Ph.D. from Harvard University in 1950. His publications include *Concordia Mundi: The Career and Thought of Guillaume Postel* (1958); *Venice and the Defense of Republican Liberty* (1968); and *The Culture of Renaissance Humanism* (1973). He has served as president of the American Historical Association (1978), the Society for Italian Historical Studies (1973–75), and the Society for Reformation Research (1963).

DAVID BRODY (b. 1930) is Professor of History at the University of California, Davis. He received his Ph.D. from Harvard University in 1958. His publications include *Steelworkers in America: The Nonunion Era* (1960); *The Butcher Workmen: A Study of Unionization* (1964); *Labor in Crisis: The Steel Strike of 1919* (1965); and *Industrial America in the Twentieth Century* (1967). His *Workers in Industrial America: Essays on the Twentieth Century Struggle* is forthcoming. He has served as Visiting Professor of American Labour History at Warwick University in England (1972–73), as Senior Fulbright Lecturer at Moscow State University (1975), and as seminar director (for labor leaders) in the Program for the Professions of the National Endowment for the Humanities (1977, 1978).

KATHLEEN NEILS CONZEN (b. 1942) is Associate Professor of American Urban History at the University of Chicago. She received her Ph.D. from the

University of Wisconsin in 1972. Her publications include *Immigrant Milwaukee, 1836-1860: Accomodation and Community in a Frontier City* (1976); "Local History as Case Study" (1978); and a forthcoming essay, "Cultural Maintenance, Assimilation, and the Rural Ethnic Community." Professor Conzen is a member of the executive boards of The Social Science History Association and the Immigration History Society, and has taught in the Urban History Workshop of the Newberry Library's Summer Institute for Family and Community History.

PHILIP D. CURTIN (b. 1922) is Professor of History at The Johns Hopkins University. He received his Ph.D. from Harvard University in 1953. His publications include *Two Jamaicas* (1955); *The Image of Africa* (1964), which was awarded the Robert Livingston Schuyler Prize of the American Historical Association; *The Atlantic Slave Trade: A Census* (1969); and *Economic Change in Pre-Colonial Africa: Senegambia in the Era of the Slave Trade* (1975). In 1961 he was founding chairman of the African Studies Program at the University of Wisconsin. He served as president of the African Studies Association, 1970-71; chairman of the SSRC-ACLS Joint Committee on African Studies, 1971-73; and as vice-president representing the United States in the International Congress of Africanists, 1969-73.

ROBERT DARNTON (b. 1939) is Professor of History at Princeton University. He was a Rhodes Scholar at Oxford University and received his D.Phil. there in 1964. His publications include *Mesmerism and the End of the Enlightenment in France* (1968) and *The Business of Enlightenment: A Publishing History of the Encyclopédie, 1775-1800* (1979). His essay "The High Enlightenment and Low-Life of Literature in Prerevolutionary France" received the 1971 prize of the American Society for Eighteenth-Century Studies. His essay "The Encyclopédie Wars of Prerevolutionary France" received the same prize in 1973, as well as the Koren Prize from the Society for French Historical Studies.

CARL N. DEGLER (b. 1921) is the Margaret Byrne Professor of American History at Stanford University. During 1973-74 he served as Harmsworth Professor of American History at Oxford University. He received his Ph.D. from Columbia University in 1952. His publications include *Out of Our Past: The Forces That Shaped Modern America* (1959); *Neither Black nor White: Slavery and Race Relations in Brazil and the United States* (1971), which was awarded the Pulitzer Prize and the Bancroft Prize; *The Other South: Southern Dissenters in the Nineteenth Century* (1974); and *At Odds: Women and the Family in America from the Revolution to the Present* (1980). He is a member of the editorial boards of *Signs: Women in Culture and Society* (since 1974) and the *Journal of Family History* (since 1977). In 1974-75 he served as president of the Pacific Coast Branch of the American Historical Association, and in 1979-80 as president of the Organization of American Historians.

JOHN HOPE FRANKLIN (b. 1915) is the John Matthews Manly Distinguished Service Professor at the University of Chicago. In 1962–63 he served as Pitt Professor of American History and Institutions at Cambridge University. He received his Ph.D. from Harvard University in 1941. His publications include *From Slavery to Freedom: A History of Negro Americans* (1947 *et seq.*); *The Militant South, 1800–1860* (1956); *Reconstruction: After the Civil War* (1961); and *A Southern Odyssey: Travelers in the Antebellum North* (1976). He is general editor of the University of Chicago Press Series of Negro American Biographies and Autobiographies (1969–). He has served as president of the American Historical Association (1979), the Organization of American Historians (1974–75), the Southern Historical Association (1970–71), the American Studies Association (1966–67), and the United Chapters of Phi Beta Kappa (1973–76). In 1976 he was selected to be the Jefferson Lecturer in the Humanities by the National Endowment for the Humanities.

GEORGE M. FREDRICKSON (b. 1934) is Professor of History at Northwestern University. He received his Ph.D. from Harvard University in 1964. His publications include *The Inner Civil War: Northern Intellectuals and the Crisis of the Union* (1965); *The Black Image in the White Mind: The Debate on Afro-American Character and Destiny* (1971), which received the Annisfield-Wolf Award in Race Relations; and a forthcoming volume entitled *The Arrogance of Race: Patterns of Inequality in American and South African History*. In 1973 and 1975 he directed National Endowment for the Humanities Seminars for College Teachers on the topic "Comparative Perspectives on the History of Slavery and Race Relations."

CHARLES GIBSON (b. 1920) is the Irving A. Leonard Distinguished University Professor of History at the University of Michigan. He received his Ph.D. from Yale University in 1950. His publications include *The Inca Concept of Sovereignty and the Spanish Administration in Peru* (1948); *Tlaxcala in the Sixteenth Century* (1952); *The Aztecs under Spanish Rule* (1964); and *Spain in America* (1966). He has served on the Board of Advisory Editors to the *Handbook of Latin American Studies* since 1968, as well as two terms on the editorial board of the *Hispanic American Historical Review*. He served as president of the American Historical Association in 1977.

JOHN WHITNEY HALL (b. 1916) is the A. Whitney Griswold Professor of History at Yale University. He received his Ph.D. from Harvard in 1950. His publications include *Tanuma Okitsugu: Forerunner of Modern Japan* (1955); *Village Japan* (1959); *Twelve Doors to Japan* (1965); *Government and Local Power in Japan, 500 to 1700* (1966); *Japan from Prehistory to Modern Times* (1970): and *Japan in the Muromachi Age* (1977). From 1958 until 1968 he served as chairman of the Association for Asian Studies Conference on Modern Japan, and from 1968 to 1971 as chairman of the ACLS-SSRC Joint Committee on Japanese Studies. He has served as director and president of the Association of Asian

Studies (1958–61, 1967–68), since 1968 as chairman of the American Delegation to the Conference on U.S.-Japan Educational and Cultural Interchange. Since 1974 he has been chairman of the Japan-U.S. Friendship Commission.

HAZEL W. HERTZBERG (b. 1918) is Professor of History and Education at the Teachers College of Columbia University. She received her Ph.D. from Columbia University in 1968. Her publications include *Teaching a Pre-Columbian Culture: The Iroquois* (1966); *The Search for an American Indian Identity: Modern Pan-Indian Movements* (1971); *Historical Parallels for the Sixties and Seventies: Primary Sources and the Core Curriculum Revisited* (1971); "The Now Culture: Some Implications for Teacher Training Programs" (1973); and "Alienation from the Past: Time, Adolescence, and History" (1977). She is a member of the Social Science Education Consortium and the National Council for the Social Studies, and has served as a consultant to school districts and local teachers' groups on the new social studies.

HERBERT T. HOOVER (b. 1930) is Professor of History and Director of the Oral History Center at the University of South Dakota. He received his Ph.D. from the University of Oklahoma in 1966. His publications include *To Be an Indian: An Oral History* (1971); *The Practice of Oral History* (1975); *The Chitimacha People* (1975); and *The Sioux* (1979). He has conducted more than 500 interviews during the past decade, including oral history projects on fourteen Sioux and Winnebago reservations. He has also completed oral history projects at various religious institutions and conducted interviews with public figures.

MICHAEL KAMMEN (b. 1936) is the Newton C. Farr Professor of American History and Culture at Cornell University. He received his Ph.D. from Harvard University in 1964. His publications include *A Rope of Sand: The Colonial Agents, British Politics, and the American Revolution* (1968); *People of Paradox: An Inquiry Concerning the Origins of American Civilization* (1972), which was awarded the Pulitzer Prize; *Colonial New York: A History* (1975); *A Season of Youth: The American Revolution and the Historical Imagination* (1978); and *"What Is the Good of History?": Selected Letters of Carl L. Becker, 1900–1945* (1973).

NIKKI R. KEDDIE (b. 1930) is Professor of History at the University of California, Los Angeles. She received her Ph.D. in 1955 from the University of California, Berkeley. Her publications include *Religion and Rebellion in Iran: The Tobacco Protest of 1891–92* (1966); *An Islamic Response to Imperialism* (1968); *Scholars, Saints, and Sufis: Muslim Religious Institutions since 1500* (1972); *Women in the Muslim World* (1978); and *The Middle East and Beyond* (1979). She spent the academic years 1959–60 and 1973–74 in Iran.

J. MORGAN KOUSSER (b. 1943) is Professor of History at the California Institute of Technology. He received his Ph.D. from Yale University in 1971.

His publications include *The Shaping of Southern Politics: Suffrage Restriction and the Establishment of the One-Party South, 1880–1910* (1974); "Ecological Regression and the Analysis of Past Politics" (1973); "The 'New Political History': A Methodological Critique" (1976); and "The Agenda for 'Social Science History'" (1977). He is chairman of the Social Science History Association's Methodology Network and a member of the editorial board of the *Journal of American History.*

PETER J. LOEWENBERG (b. 1933) is Professor of History at the University of California, Los Angeles. He received his Ph.D. in history in 1966 from the University of California, Berkeley, and in psychoanalysis in 1976 from the Southern California Psychoanalytic Institute, where he is now a faculty member and a practicing research psychoanalyst. His publications include "The Psychohistorical Origins of the Nazi Youth Cohort" (1971); "The Unsuccessful Adolescence of Heinrich Himmler" (1971), which was awarded the Franz Alexander Essay Prize of the Southern California Psychoanalytic Institute; "Psychohistorical Perspectives on Modern German History" (1975); "Why Psychoanalysis Needs the Social Scientist and the Historian" (1977); and "History and Psychoanalysis" (1977). He has been a member of the editorial board of the *Journal of the American Psychoanalytic Association*, a contributing editor to the *Journal of Psychohistory*, and currently serves on the board of editors of the *Psychohistory Review.*

WILLIAM H. McNEILL (b. 1917) is the Robert A. Millikan Distinguished Service Professor of History at the University of Chicago. He received his Ph.D. from Cornell University in 1947. His publications include *The Rise of the West* (1963), which received the National Book Award; *Europe's Steppe Frontier, 1500–1800* (1964); *Venice: The Hinge of Europe, 1081–1797* (1974); *Plagues and People* (1976); and *Metamorphoses of Greece since World War II* (1978). He has been editor of the *Journal of Modern History* since 1971, and served in 1974–75 as chairman of the American Historical Association's Committee on Teaching.

CHARLES S. MAIER (b. 1939) is Professor of History at Duke University. He received his Ph.D. from Harvard University in 1967. His publications include *Recasting Bourgeois Europe: Stabilization in France, Germany, and Italy in the Decade after World War I* (1975), which was awarded the Herbert Baxter Adams Prize and the George Louis Beer Prize of the American Historical Association; *The Origins of the Cold War and Contemporary Europe* (editor) (1979); and "Between Taylorism and Technocracy: European Ideologies and the Vision of Industrial Productivity in the 1920s," *Journal of Contemporary History*, v (1970), which received the Klaus Epstein Memorial Prize. He has been a Visiting Professor at the University of Bielefeld (West Germany), and is currently a staff associate of the Brookings Institution and chairman of the Joint Committee on Western Europe of the Social Science Research Council and the ACLS.

*The Contributors*

KARL F. MORRISON (b. 1936) is Professor of Medieval History at the University of Chicago. He received his Ph.D. from Cornell University in 1961. His publications include *The Two Kingdoms: Ecclesiology in Carolingian Political Thought* (1964); *Rome and the City of God: An Essay on the Constitutional Relationship of Empire and Church in the Fourth Century* (1964); *Carolingian Coinage* (1967); and *Tradition and Authority in the Western Church, ca. 300–1140* (1969). He has served as councillor in the Medieval Academy of America (1972–75) and as president of the Midwest Medieval Conference and of the Medieval Association of the Midwest (1976–77).

JAY SAUNDERS REDDING (b. 1906) is the Ernest I. White Professor Emeritus of American Studies and Humane Letters at Cornell University. He received an M.A. from Brown University in 1932 and the D.Litt. in 1963. His publications include *To Make a Poet Black* (1939); *No Day of Triumph* (1942), which won the Mayflower Award for Distinguished Writing; *They Came in Chains* (1950); *On Being Negro in America* (1952); *The Lonesome Road* (1958); and *Cavalcade* (1971), an anthology of Afro-American writing. From 1965 until 1970 he served as director of the Division of Research and Publication of the National Endowment for the Humanities. He is a member of the Board of Directors of the American Council of Learned Societies.

PETER N. STEARNS (b. 1936) is the Heinz Professor of History at Carnegie-Mellon University. He received his Ph.D. from Harvard University in 1963. His publications include *European Society in Upheaval: Social History since 1800* (1967); *1848: The Revolutionary Tide in Europe* (1974); *Lives of Labor: Work in Maturing Industrial Society* (1975); *Old Age in European Society* (1977); *Paths to Authority: The Middle Class and the Industrial Labor Force in France, 1820–1848* (1978); and *Be a Man!: Males in Modern Society* (1979). He has been the editor of the *Journal of Social History* since 1967. He received the Koren Prize of the Society for French Historical Studies in 1964 and the Newcomen Award of the *Business History Review* in 1965.

# INDEX

In this index primary emphasis is placed on developments and problems within the historical profession in the United States during the 1970s. Many substantive historical phenomena (e.g., the crusades, the Renaissance, the American Revolution) are not indexed because they can be readily located by chapter topic within the pertinent essays. Bibliographical material found in the footnotes is not indexed. With the exception of well-known journals (e.g., *American Historical Review, Journal of American History, Journal of Modern History*), almost all journals and historical newsletters are indexed by subject matter (e.g., the *Journal of World History* is listed under *World History*).

Abrahamian, Ervand, 145
Abu-Lughod, Janet, 152
Abzug, Robert H., 306
Adams, Herbert Baxter, 478
Adams, Jeremy, 67, 72
Adams, Robert McC., 137
Adams, William Y., 125–26
*Adams Chronicles*, 14
Affirmative action and minority history, 118
Africa, U.S. attitudes toward, 113–15
*African Economic History*, 128
*African Heritage Studies Foundation*, 118
*African Historical Studies*, 115. See also *History in Africa*.
African history, 27, 113–30
*African History, Journal of*, 117
African Studies Association, 118
African studies programs, 115, 123, 128
Afro-American Life, Association for the Study of, 406
Agricultural history, 124, 128–29, 143. See also Rural history.
Ahmad, Feroz, 150
Akita, George, 167
Alba, Victor, 200
Alexander, Thomas B., 236

Algar, Hamid, 144–45
Alitto, Guy, 177
Alperowitz, Gar, 370, 372
Alpers, Edward A., 127
American Association for State and Local History, 12, 273–74
American Council of Learned Societies, 173
*American Heritage*, 12
American Historical Association, 12, 19, 27, 45, 114, 184, 328, 411, 434, 437, 475, 477, 479, 487, 495; Committee of Seven, 475–76; History Education Project, 494
*American Historical Review*, 161, 335, 413, 438–39, 442, 494
*American Oriental Society, Journal of*, 161
American Revolutionary Bicentennial celebration, 14, 273, 486
Amherst Project (history education), 482
Andrews, Charles McL., 478
*Annales: Economies, Sociétés, Civilisations*, 331–32, 440, 443–44
*Annales* mode of historical scholarship, 26, 30, 35–36, 89–92, 105, 210, 275, 341–42
Annan, Noel, 44

Anstey, Roger, 453
Anthropology, 41-42, 163, 166-67, 189-92, 199, 223, 228, 296-97. *See also* Social science and social theory.
Anthropology Curriculum Study Project, 482
Appleby, Joyce Oldham, 89
Aptheker, Herbert, 294, 305
Arab Asia, history of, 150-53
Arab-Israeli issues, 152-53
Archaeology, 21, 189
Area studies, 21, 113-15, 122-23, 132-34, 157-59, 184
Ariès, Philippe, 429
Armenian Assembly Charitable Trust, 406
Art: as historical evidence, 69; history of, 52, 64, 67, 69, 73, 189
Asante Collective Biography Project, 126
*Asantesem*, 126
Asia, U.S. attitudes toward, 157, 161, 171, 179-80, 183
Asian Studies, Association for, 158, 162, 164, 170, 173, 185
*Asian Studies, Bibliography of,* 158, 162, 184
*Asian Studies, Journal of,* 162-63, 180
*Asiatic Society of Japan, Transactions of,* 162
Austen, Ralph, 121
Astrachan, Boris, 423
Aydelotte, William O., 247, 435, 453

Baer, George, 379
Bailyn, Bernard, 10, 38, 45, 276, 343-44
Baker, Keith, 111, 342
Banani, Amin, 140, 143
Bancroft, George, 293
Bancroft, Hubert H., 187
Banker, James R., 86
Bannon, John Francis, 201
Bariéty, Jacques, 364
Barlow, Robert, 189
Barnes, Harry Elmer, 501
Baron, Hans, 83, 86, 343
Barzun, Jacques, 32, 331
Bassett, John Spencer, 19
Bastin, John, 181
Bates, Ulku, 137
Baum, Willa, 399
Bausum, Henry, 500
Baxter, James Phinney, 20
Bay, Edna C., 122
Bayat, Mangol, 145
Beale, Howard K., 43-44
Beard, Charles A., 43, 237, 329, 365, 477-79

Beard, Mary Ritter, 319
Beardians, 490
Beck, Lois, 153
Becker, Carl L., 5, 22, 43, 329-30, 477-78
Becker, Marvin B., 83-84, 343
Beecher, Jonathan, 341
Behavioralism, 232-33, 240, 244-45. *See also* Social science and social theory.
Bellah, Robert, 171
Bemis, Samuel Flagg, 20
Benda, Harry, 179-82
Bender, Thomas, 289
Bendix, Reinhard, 82
Bennett, Edward W., 379
Bennett, Norman, 115
Benson, Lee, 32, 231-32, 234-35, 240-42, 249, 433, 448
Bercovitch, Sacvan, 338
Berger, D. H., 181
Berger, Gordon, 168
Berkes, Niyazi, 149
Berkshire Conference, 325
Berlanstein, Leonard R., 91
Berlin, Ira, 300-301
Bernard, Leon, 84
Bernstein, Barton, 372
Bernstein, Gail, 169
Bernstein, Irving, 255
Berry, Sara S., 128
Besterman, Theodore, 342
Biggerstaff, Knight, 162
Billington, Ray Allen, 463
Bingham, Woodbridge, 162, 173
Binion, Rudolph, 427
Biography, use of, 100, 188, 424-25
Bion, Wilfred, 423
Bireley, Robert, 81
Black, C. E., 459-61
Black history, 21, 213-14, 221, 292-307. *See also* Slavery.
Blassingame, John W., 295-97
Bloch, Marc, 23, 53, 410
Bloom, Benjamin S., 480
Blum, Jerome, 110
Bodde, Derk, 173, 175
Bodnar, John, 257
Bogue, Allan G., 32, 231-51, 280, 505
Bohmer, David A., 249
Bolitho, Harold, 171
Bolton, Herbert E., 187, 201
Bombard, Owen, 393
Borah, Woodrow, 190, 197
Borg, Dorothy, 369
Borton, Hugh, 162
Bostert, Russell H., 496-97

Bourne, E. G., 187
Bouwsma, William J., 78–94, 343, 505
Bowser, Frederick, 191
Bowsky, William M., 83
Boxer, Charles, 171
Bradford, William, 19
Brady, Thomas A., Jr., 84
Braibanti, Ralph, 183
Brandes, Stuart, 264
Braudel, Fernand, 30, 79, 332; followers of, 220–21. *See also Annales* mode of scholarship.
Braverman, Harry, 263–64
Breasted, James Henry, 478
Brenner, Robert, 80
Breslow, Marvin Arthur, 89
Brewer, John, 343
Bridenbaugh, Carl, 88, 434
Brinton, Crane, 45, 330–32
Broderick, Francis L., 306
Brody, David, 252–69, 505
Bronx Historical Society, 406
Brown, Benjamin, 365
Brown, George W., 117
Brown, Kenneth L., 122
Brown, L. Carl, 153
Brown, Richard H., 482
Brown, Steven, 423
Brown, W. Norman, 184, 186
Browne, E. G., 145
Brucker, Gene A., 83, 85, 343
Bruner, Jerome, 480
Buck, Lawrence P., 87
Bullard, Melissa Meriam, 93
Bulliet, Richard, 136–37
Burckhardt, Jakob, 345
Burgin, Miron, 195
Burke, Edmund, 154, 362
Burke, Peter, 345
Burnham, Walter Dean, 238–39
Burns, Robert Ignatius, 66–67, 376
Bushman, Richard, 419
Buttinger, Joseph, 181
Byzantine history, 63

Cady, John, 181–82
Cahen, Claude, 132, 136
Calvert, Peter, 381
Cambridge Population Studies Group, 226, 275
Campbell, Angus, 238
Carnegie-Mellon Curriculum Development Center, 482
Carper, Laura, 297
Carroll, Peter N., 428

Carter, Charles H., 80–81
Cash, Joseph, 397, 405
Castles, Lance, 182
Cecil, Lamar, 359
Challener, Richard, 360
Chambers, E. K., 345
Chambers, Richard, 153
Chandler, Alfred D., 264
Chaney, William A., 64–65, 72
Chang, Richard, 167
Chang Chung-li, 176–77
Chang Hsin-pao, 177
Channing, Edward A., 478
Charanis, Peter, 63
Childhood, history of, 430–31
*Childhood, History of, Quarterly,* 413
China, history of, 159–60, 172–79
Chinese Thought, Committee on, 173–74
Chojnacki, Stanley, 83, 93
Chow Tse-tsung, 178
Chrisman, Miriam U., 84, 87
Church, William F., 81
Church history, 66–68, 87–89, 100
Civil War centennial celebration, 13–14
Clark, Kenneth, 295
Clark, Norman, 291
Clasen, Claus-Peter, 87
Cline, Howard F., 188, 190, 199
Cliometrics. *See* Economic history; Quantitative methods.
Clive, John, 341
Coale, Ansley, 448
Cochran, Bert, 255
Cochran, Thomas C., 234, 236
Cochrane, Eric, 83, 343
Cohen, David William, 123
Cohen, Paul, 177
Cohen, William B., 120
Collaborative projects, growth of, 45, 79–80, 92, 172–73, 412–13; in Latin American history, 192
Collingwood, R. G., 340
Collins, Robert O., 120
Commager, Henry Steele, 23, 294
Commons, John R., 253, 256
Communism and writing of history, 106–7. *See also* Marxist historical thought.
Community history, 289. *See also* Local history.
Comparative history, 78–80, 84, 120–21, 133, 457–73
*Comparative Studies in Society and History,* 472
Conant, Kenneth John, 55

Conference on Taisho (1970), 168
Conkin, Paul, 332
Conrad, Alfred H., 433
Constable, Giles, 497-98
Conzen, Kathleen Neils, 261, 270-91, 453, 505
Cook, Sherburne F., 189-90, 197
Cooper, Frederick, 128, 470
Cott, Nancy, 317, 320
Cottam, Richard W., 143
Coverdale, John, 379
Cowling, Maurice, 363
Cragg, Gerald R., 89
Craig, Albert M., 166-67
Craig, Gordon A., 110, 363
Crampton, C. Gregory, 397
Crane, Robert, 184
Creel, Herrlee G., 162, 173-75
Crew, Phyllis Mack, 88
Crime, history of, 209, 219, 222
Crowley, James B., 169
Cultural history, 100-101, 117, 123, 327-54
Cumbler, John T., 258
Curti, Margaret, 433
Curti, Merle, 279, 282, 327, 329, 433
Curtin, Philip D., 113-30, 453, 506

Dallek, Robert, 369
Darnton, Robert, 327-54, 506
Davidson, Basel, 306
Davis, Bitton, 91
Davis, Cullom, 399
Davis, David Brion, 466-67, 469
Davis, James C., 83-84, 93
Davis, Lynn, 370
Davis, Natalie Zemon, 90, 228, 345
Davison, Roderic, 148
Dawley, Alan, 257, 261, 268
Dawn, C. E., 154
Dawson, Philip, 454
Death, history of, 221, 223
Degler, Carl N., 308-26, 466-68, 506
Demography, 53-54, 70-71, 92, 138, 193, 224-25, 227, 310, 318. *See also* Quantitative methods.
Demos, John, 276-77, 426
Dependency theory, 202
Detachment and historical inquiry, 23, 51, 54-55
Devereux, Robert, 149
De Voto, Bernard, 22
De Vries, Jan, 80, 91
Diggins, John, 342
Dike, Kenneth O., 117, 127

Dingmam, Roger, 359, 382
Diplomatic history, 80-81, 119, 355-87
*Diplomatic History*, 373
Divine, Robert, 373
Dols, Michael, 138
Donald, David H., 489
Dore, R. P., 170
Douglas, Ann, 426
Douglas, Mary, 41
Dower, John, 382
Doyle, Don Harrison, 280
Dublin, Thomas, 261, 268
Dubofsky, Melvin, 255
DuBois, Ellen, 324
DuBois, W. E. B., 293, 304-6
Dubs, Homer, 173
Duignan, Peter, 120, 122
Duke, Doris, 397
Dull, Jonathan, 377
Dunbar, Tony, 297
Dunn, John, 339-40, 343
Dunning, William, 293
Durkheim, Emile, 342, 346
Duus, Peter, 166, 168
Dykstra, Robert R., 280

East Asian history, 27, 159-64
Easterlin, Richard A., 227, 454
Eastern European history, 106, 108, 111
Eastman, Lloyd, 178
Economic history, 27, 36, 80, 92-93, 101-2, 127-29, 137, 192, 253
*Economic History, Journal of*, 435, 440-43
Education, history of, 215-17, 223, 321-22
Educational Development Center, 482
Edwards, Richard, 263
Egypt, history of, 150-53
Ehrenkreutz, Andrew, 138
Ehret, Christopher, 124
Eisenstein, Elizabeth, 81-82
Elder, Glen, 311
Elison, George, 171-72
Elisseeff, Serge, 165
Elkins, Stanley, 280, 306, 421, 465-66
Ellithorp, John, 423
Elphick, Richard, 121
Emerson, Rupert, 182-83
Employment problems, 28, 44, 75, 103, 118-19, 129-30, 206, 334-35
English, Paul, 136, 143
Engerman, Stanley, 226, 294-95, 436-47, 446-47
Entner, M. D., 146
Eppse, Merl R., 294

Erikson, Erik, 186, 417-19, 492-93
Ershkowitz, Herbert, 245
Essex Institute (Salem, Mass.), 12
Ethnic history, 21, 101, 205-6, 218, 257-58, 262
Ethnohistory, 65, 189, 193. *See also* anthropology.
European Fertility Project, 448
European influences on U.S. historians, 89-90, 95, 104-5, 108-9, 202, 210, 256, 266-67, 275, 309, 331-32, 361, 364-65

Fairbank, John K., 162, 166, 173-74, 177, 383
Faler, Paul, 257
Family history, 34, 92-93, 101, 122, 191, 205-6, 208, 218, 219, 221-22, 224, 228, 259, 308-26, 431
*Family History, Journal of,* 313
Far Eastern Association, 162-63, 185
Far Eastern Studies Committee, American Council of Learned Societies, 162
Fay, Sidney B., 378
Fèbvre, Lucien, 53, 346
Fei Hsiao-t'ung, 173
Feierman, Steven, 124
Feis, Herbert, 20, 371
Feith, Herbert, 182
Feldberg, Michael, 258
Feldman, Gerald, 112
*Feminist Studies,* 325
Fenton, Edwin, 482
Fetter, Bruce, 122
Feuerwerker, Albert, 177
Fieldhouse, David K., 361
Finberg, H. P. R., 290
Findley, Carter, 150
Fine, Sidney, 255
Fischer, Fritz, 365
Fitzgerald, C. P., 160
FitzGerald, Frances, 484-85
Fletcher, Joseph, 383
Fogel, Robert W., 32, 226, 294-95, 436-37, 446-48
Foner, Eric, 344
Foner, Philip, 256
Ford, Henry, 24
Ford Foundation, 132, 161, 235
Foreign-language competence, 119, 133, 158, 160-61, 163, 184, 356
Foreign Relations, Society for Historians of American, 373
*Foreign Relations of the United States,* 372
Forest Historical Society, 393
Forgie, George, 422

Formisano, Ronald P., 241-42
Forster, Robert, 10, 79, 92, 111
Foundations, role of, 132, 157, 161, 165, 173, 234-35, 273, 302, 397, 401, 481
Fox, Daniel, 306
*Foxfire* books, 398
Franklin, John Hope, 9, 11-15, 292, 294, 302, 507
Frantz, Joe B., 395
Fredrickson, George M., 469-70, 507
Freedom of Information Act, 372
Freeman, E. A., 45
Freeze, Gregory L., 112
Freud, Anna, 417
Freud, Sigmund, 410-11, 413, 417, 431
Friedlander, Peter, 262-63, 404
Friedländer, Saul, 415
Frier, Bruce, 338
Frisch, Michael, 290
Frye, Richard N., 135

Gabriel, Ralph, 327, 329
Gaddis, John Lewis, 370
Galenson, Walter, 253
Gallagher, Dorothy, 405
Gallagher, John, 361, 366, 376
Gann, Lewis H., 120, 122
Gardner, Lloyd, 369
Garlock, Jonathan, 261-62
Garthwalte, Gene, 140
Gatzke, Hans, 365
Gay, Peter, 110, 331, 340, 429
Geanakoplos, Deno John, 79
Geertz, Clifford, 41, 181-82, 185, 228, 347
Gemery, Henry, 128
Gendzier, Irene, 151-52
Genealogy, 14. *See also* Family history.
Generational differences, 20, 29, 98-99, 116, 142, 145, 155, 237-38, 449; in Islamic history, 132-34, 142; in labor history, 255-56; in Latin American history, 188-89, 198-99; in political history, 237-38
Genovese, Eugene, 216, 228, 297-98, 347, 447, 467, 469
Geography and history, 21, 42, 105, 126, 143, 291
George, Alexander, 416
George, Juliette, 416
George C. Marshall Research Library, 394
Gibb, H. A. R., 134
Gibson, Charles, 187-202, 507
Gifford, Prosser, 120, 362

Gilbert, Felix, 19, 82–83, 343, 377
Gillin, Donald, 178
Gimbel, John, 372
Ginzburg, Carlo, 345
Girault, René, 364
Glacken, Clarence J., 82
Goitein, S. D., 134–35
Goldthwaite, Richard, 92
Golembek, Lisa, 137
Goodfield, June, 38
Goodrich, L. Carrington, 172–74
Gordon, Linda, 321
Gossman, Lionel, 341
Gottschalk, Louis, 20
Goubert, Pierre, 332
Grabar, Oleg, 137
Graduate training, 27–28, 75–76, 115–16, 160–61, 449–51, 488–89; Ph.D. dissertations, 28, 56–63, 103, 334, 353
Graham, Richard, 362
Gramsci, Antonio, 35, 216, 225
Gran, Peter, 141, 151
Graubard, Stephen R., 491
Gray, Sir Edward, 362
Green, Constance McL., 20, 275
Greene, Jack P., 79, 344
Greenfield Village (Dearborn, Mich.), 24
Greven, Philip, 212–13, 276–77, 428
Grieder, Jerome, 177
Griffin, Clyde, 325
Griffin, Sally, 325
Grimes, Alan, 323
Griswold, Robert, 315
Gross, Richard E., 485–86
Grossman, Maria, 87
Group for the Use of Psychology in History, 414
Grundler, Otto, 87
Grunebaum, G. E. von, 134, 154–55
Gundersheimer, Werner L., 83
Gutman, Herbert, 252, 258, 266–68, 283, 296, 315–16
Guttman scaling, 248, 434–45, 453

Hackett, Roger, 168
Haeger, John W., 175
Hafkin, Nancy J., 122
Hahn, Roger, 112, 338
Hakone Conference (1960), 169–70
Haley, Alex, 14, 43, 306–7, 404
Hall, D. G. E., 180
Hall, David, 338
Hall, Ivan, 168
Hall, John Whitney, 9, 157–86, 170, 172, 507–8

Hall, Van Beck, 246
Halsey, Van R., 482
Hamby, Alonzo, 370
Hammarberg, Melvyn, 242
Handlin, Oscar, 254
Hanke, Lewis, 188, 201
Hanley, Susan, 170
Harding, Robert R., 91
Hareven, Tamara, 259
Haring, Clarence H., 187
Harlan, Louis, R., 304
Harms, Robert, 127
Harootunian, Harry D., 167–68, 171
Harris, Ramon, 399
Harrison, Brian, 256
Hart, David Montgomery, 125
Hartmann, Heinz, 417
Hartwig, Gerald, 127, 129
Hartz, Louis, 464, 472
Harvard Social Studies Project, 482
Harvard-Yenching Institute, 162
Haskins, Charles Homer, 50–53, 55–56, 63, 74, 478
Hauser, William, 171
Havens, Thomas, 168, 364
Hays, Samuel P., 35, 241, 286, 496
Heimert, Alan, 338
Heinrichs, Waldo, 359
Henige, David P., 124–25
Henry Francis du Pont Winterthur Museum, 12–13
Henry E. Huntington Library and Art Gallery, 13
Herbert Hoover Institute, 120
Herbert Hoover Presidential Library Association, 395
Herlihy, David, 57, 83, 92
Herman, Debra, 321
Hershberg, Theodore, 448
Hertzberg, Hazel W., 474–504, 508
Hess, Andrew C., 79
Hexter, J. H., 88, 251, 343
High School Geography Project, 482
Higham, John, 19, 23, 34, 329, 471, 477
Hill, Christopher, 343
Hilton, Stanley, 381
Hirsch, Susan, 314–15
Hirschberg, Julia, 198
Historical Association (U.K.), 27
*Historical Methods Newsletter*, 235, 435
*Historical Scholarship in America* (1932), 19
*Historical Studies Today* (1971), 19
History, interest in, 14–15, 43–44, 104; among students, 102, 206
*History* (1965), 19

History Advisory Committee, MSSB, 251
*History and Theory,* 82
History Day, 15
*History in Africa: A Journal of Methodology,* 125
*History Teacher,* 494
*History Teacher's Magazine,* 475
Hitti, Philip, 132
Ho Ping-ti, 176
Hobsbawm, E. J., 24, 205, 210, 255–56, 264, 283, 331
Hodgson, Marshall, 138, 154
Hofstadter, Richard, 20, 231–32, 254
Hogan, Michael, 368
Hogendorn, Jan, 128–29
Hollinger, David, 341
*Holocaust,* 14
Holod, Renata, 137, 140
Holt, Michael F., 236
Holt, Thomas, 302
Hoover, Herbert T., 391–407, 508
Horowitz, David, 428
Horowitz, Donald L., 468
Hourani, Albert, 140
Hsiao Kung-chuan, 176
Huang, Ray, 176
Hucker, Charles O., 174–76
Hudson, Michael, 152
Huggins, Nathan I., 295, 299–300, 306
Hughes, H. Stuart, 331–32, 341
Hughes, Judith, 426
Hume, David, 68
Hummel, Arthur, 173
Humphreys, Stephen, 138
Hunt, Michael, 382
Huppert, George, 83, 91
Hurewitz, Jacob C., 152
Hurst, G. Cameron, 172
Hutchinson, William R., 338
Hutson, James, 377

Ilchman, Frederick, 359
Inalcik, Halil, 134
India, history of, 183–86
Industrialization, 24, 193. *See also* Labor history.
Institutions, social, 34, 215–17
Intellectual history, 36, 67–69, 100, 228–29, 327–54
Interdisciplinary developments: in African history, 122–29; in Asian history, 161–63, 166–67, 175–76, 181; in black history, 293–95, 297–98; in community history, 275, 279, 282, 291; in comparative history, 459–61; in diplomatic history, 358–62; in early modern European history, 82–83, 96; in family history, 312–13, 316; in intellectual history, 331, 337, 341, 344–45, 347–48; in Islamic history, 133–34, 136–38, 141–43, 151; in Latin American history, 188–90, 199; in medieval history, 50, 53, 64–65, 76; in modern European history, 106, 108; in political history, 232–36, 240–51; in psychohistory, 408–13, 415, 417, 424–25; in social history, 218–25; in teaching of history, 482. *See also* Methodology, developments in; Social science and social theory.
Iran, history of, 142–46
Iriye, Akira, 382–83
Irwin, Graham, 117
Irwin, Paul, 125
Isaacman, Allen, 122
Islam: history of, 134–38, 151–53; U.S. attitudes toward, 142, 146, 150, 155
Issawi, Charles, 141–43

Jacobson, Jon, 379
Jameson, J. Franklin, 22
Jansen, Marius, 167–68, 170
Japan, history of, 159–60, 164–72
Japan Foundation, 165
Japanese Studies, center for, 166
Jay, Martin, 341
Jeffrey, Julie, 324
Jennings, Francis, 375
Jensen, Richard J., 32, 241–42
Jewish history, 101
Johnson, Chalmers, 179
Johnson, Wesley, 406
Jones, Alice Hanson, 447
Jones, Gareth Stedman, 266
Jones, Howard Mumford, 110
Jones, William I., 129
*Journal of American History,* 335, 438–39, 442, 494
*Journal of Interdisciplinary History,* 236, 413, 435, 440–41, 443
*Journal of Modern History,* 335, 413, 438–39, 442
Kahin, George, 182–83
Kahn, Kathy, 405
Kammen, Michael, 19–46
Kaplan, Lawrence, 377
Kaplan, Steven L., 91
Karl, Barry, 342
Karpat, Kemal, 150

Katz, Friedrich, 381
Katz, Michael, 282–83, 325
Katzman, David M., 259
Katznelson, Ira, 470, 472
Kaufman, Burton, 368
Kazemzadeh, Firuz, 145
Keddie, Nikki R., 131–56, 508
Kehr, Eckart, 365
Kelley, Donald R., 80, 82, 341, 471
Keniston, Kenneth, 492
Kennan, George, 371
Kent, George O., 378
Kerber, Linda, 324
Kerr, Malcolm, 152
Kettering, Sharon, 81
Key, V. O., Jr., 238–40
Khadduri, Majid, 152
Kilby, Peter, 129
Kiley, Cornelius, 172
Kilson, Martin, 306
Kingdon, Robert M., 84
Kirkendall, Richard S., 487
Kirkland, Edward C., 20
Kissinger, Henry, 381
Kitzinger, Ernst, 64–65, 72
Klaits, Joseph, 88
Klapisch, Christiane, 92
Klein, Herbert S., 128, 465
Kleinberg, Susan, 259
Kleppner, Paul, 241–43, 262
Knight, Franklin, 466
Knight, Peter, 259
Kolko, Gabriel, 370
Konvitz, Josef W., 84
Kopytoff, Igor, 470
Korman, Gerd, 261
Kousser, J. Morgan, 32, 240, 243, 433–56, 508–9
Kracke, E. A., Jr., 176
Kraditor, Aileen, 323
Kramer, Gerald H., 454
Krey, August C., 479
Krieger, Leonard, 19, 341
Kris, Ernst, 417
Kristeller, Paul Oskar, 86
Kubler, George, 189
Kublin, Hyman, 169
Kuhn, Philip A., 176
Kuhn, Thomas, 339, 445–46
Kuklick, Bruce, 338

Labor history, 21, 101, 214, 252–69
*Labor History*, 254
Labrousse, C. E., 332
LaCapra, Dominick, 328

Ladurie, Emmanuel LeRoy, 332, 345
LaFeber, Walter, 366
Lampard, Eric, 285
Land, James, 465, 472
Landes, David S., 32, 37, 40, 102, 151, 448
Lane, Frederic C., 83
Langbein, John H., 92
Langer, William L., 20, 355, 378, 411
Language skills. *See* Foreign-language competence.
Lanning, John Tate, 188
Lapidus, Ira M., 135–36
Lasch, Christopher, 221, 229, 426
Laslett, Peter, 311
Latin America, U.S. attitudes toward, 200–201
Latin American history, 27, 187–202
*Latin American History, Research Review of*, 199
Latin American Studies Association, 199
Latourette, Kenneth S., 174
Lauren, Paul, 359
Laurie, Bruce, 258
Lazarsfeld, Paul, 240
Lebra, Joyce, 168
Lefebvre, Georges, 331
Leffler, Melvyn, 368
Legal history, 187, 246–47
Leigh, R. A., 342
Leiscester School (U.K.), 274
Leisure, history of, 205, 215, 221–23
Lemons, Stanley, 323
Leonard, Irving A., 188
Lepper, Susan J., 454
Lerner, Daniel, 182
Lerner, Gerda, 319, 324, 500
Levenson, Joseph R., 175, 177
Levin, N. Gordon, 367–68
Levine, Lawrence, 300, 306, 347
Lewis, Bernard, 134, 147, 149, 155
Lewis, Hylan, 297
Lewis, John, 179
Life cycle, history of, 221, 417–18. *See also* Childhood, history of; Old age, history of; youth, history of.
Lifton, Robert Jay, 422
Lipset, Seymour Martin, 463
Little, David, 89
Litwack, Leon, 299
Liu, James T. C., 175
Liu, Kwang-ching, 175, 177
Local history, 21, 42–43, 270–80, 290–91
Lockhart, James, 191, 198
Lockridge, Kenneth A., 276–77

Lockwood, William W., 167, 170
Loemker, Leroy E., 88
Loewenberg, Peter J., 408–32, 509
Loewenstein, Rudolph, 417
Logan, Rayford, 292
London, Herbert, 489–90
Lougee, Carolyn C., 91
Louis, Wm. Roger, 120, 362
Lovejoy, Arthur, 327, 329, 330, 339
Lovejoy, Paul, 128
Lowe, E. A., 55
Lukacs, John, 364
Luttwack, Edward, 363
Lybyer, A. H., 146

McAlister, John T., 182
McCall, Daniel, 123
McCann, Frank, 381
McCormack, Garran, 178
McCormick, Thomas, 366
McDaniel, Robert, 145
McGee, J. Sears, 88
McGrath, William, 429
McKeown, Thomas, 225
McKitrick, Eric, 280
McKnight, Brian E., 176
McLaughlin, Andrew C., 478
McNeill, William H., 79, 95–112; 490, 497, 509
McSeveney, Samuel, 242
McVey, Ruth, 182
Maier, Charles S., 110, 355–87, 509
Main, Gloria, 37
Main, Jackson Turner, 246
Maitland, Frederick William, 74
Major, J. Russell, 81
Makdisi, George, 138
Mandelbaum, Maurice, 110, 341
Mandrou, Robert, 345
Manuel, Frank, 331, 341
Marder, Arthur, 111
Mardin, Serif, 149
Marsot, Afaf, 151
Martines, Lauro, 83–85
Marx, Karl, 25
Marxist historical thought, 25–26, 36, 80, 100, 105–7, 202, 322, 384, 431, 460–61. *See also* Radical historians.
Masao, Maruyama, 168–69, 171
Mass, Jeffrey, 172
Massignon, Louis, 136
Mastny, Vojtech, 373–74
Material culture, history of, 136
Mathematical Social Science Board, History Advisory Committee, 235, 452–55

Mathews, Donald, 325
May, Ernest R., 40, 361, 386, 476
May, Henry F., 23
Mayer, Arno J., 367–68, 379
Mazzaoui, Michel, 140
Meacham, Standish, 111
Meany Center for Labor Studies, 406
Medicine, history of, 129, 138, 214–15, 223
Medieval Academy, 50, 52, 55
Medieval history, 49–77
Medieval Japanese studies, Institute for, 172
Meier, August, 300
Meisner, Maurice, 179
Meiss, Millard, 55, 69, 72
Merriman, Roger B., 187
Metcalf, Richard, 376
Methodology, developments in, 31–32, 36, 125, 209–11, 281, 357–58, 386–87, 400–402, 409–10, 449–52, 481. *See also* Interdisciplinary developments.
Metro History Fair (Chicago), 15
Metzger, Thomas, 177
Meyer, Donald, 424
Meyer, John R., 433
Michael, Franz, 173, 177
Middle Eastern history, 27, 131–56
Miers, Suzanne, 470
Military history, 35, 99–100, 363–64
Miller, Frank, 169
Miller, Joseph C., 124
Miller, Merle, 404
Miller, Perry, 276, 327, 329, 338
Miller, Warren E., 445, 448
Minear, Richard, 169
Ming Biographical History Project, 173
Mintz, Sidney, 41
Miskimin, Harry A., 80
Mississippi Valley Historical Association, 12. *See also* Organization of American Historians.
Mitchell, Richard P., 151
Mobility, 34, 223, 225, 227, 282
Modernization theory, 149–50, 155, 169–70, 459–60; in family history, 316–17; in Latin American history, 193, 196–97; in social history, 218–21, 225, 228; in political history, 245–46. *See also* Social science and social theory.
Molho, Anthony, 83
Mommsen, Theodor, 76
Monter, William, 84
Montgomery, David, 255, 264, 268
Moore, Barrington, 459–61, 472

Moore, Waddy, 401
Moote, A. Lloyd, 81
Moral judgments, 23–24
Morey, Charles Rufus, 55
Morgan, Edmund, 276, 338, 344
Morison, Samuel E., 20, 23
Morley, James, 170
Morris, Richard B., 377
Morrison, Karl F., 49–77, 510
Morse, Richard B., 200
Motley, John Lothrop. 43
Moynihan, Daniel P., 296
Murdock, George P., 123
Murphey, Murray, 327, 338
Murra, John, 191
Musallam, Basim, 138
Musto, David, 419, 423
Myrdal, Gunnar, 294

Nader, Helen, 93
Naff, Thomas, 141
Najita, Tetsuo, 166, 168, 171
Nakamura, James, 167
Narrative history, 29, 65–66
National Archives (U.S.), 13–14
National Bureau of Economic Research, 447
National Coordinating Committee for the Promotion of History, 28, 495
National Council for the Social Studies (1921), 478, 481, 487–88, 498
National Defense Education Act, 161, 185
National Education Association, 477
National Education Association, Committee of Ten (1892), 475–76
National Endowment for the Humanities, 10, 14, 27, 235, 302, 495
National Historic Preservation Act of 1966, 273
National Historical Publications and Records Commission, 13
National Park Service, 13
National Science Foundation, 235, 481
Nationalism (ethnocentrism), 22, 100, 113–14
Near East Program, Princeton University, 132–33
Negro history. *See* Black history; Slavery.
Nelson, Donald, 263–64
Nelson, Keith, 368
*Network News Exchange,* 494
Nevins, Allan, 20, 392–95, 401, 404
Newberry Library Family and Community History Center, 226, 236, 399, 449–50

Nichols, Roy F., 20, 237
Nivison, David S., 175
Noble, David F., 264
Norman, E. H., 166–68, 170
North, Robert, 179
Northrup, David, 127
Norton, Mary Beth, 317
Notehelfer, F. B., 169

Oberling, Pierre, 145
Oberman, Heiko A., 87
Obichere, Boniface, 117
Offner, Arnold, 369
Old age, history of, 220. *See also* Life cycle, history of.
Oliver, Donald W., 482
O'Neill, William, 323
Oral history, 391–407
Oral History Association, 396, 400
Oral history centers, 393–95
*Oral History Review,* 396, 400
Oral tradition, 123–25, 300
Organization of American Historians, 12, 487, 495; Committee on the Status of History, 494
Orientalism, 131–35, 139, 153, 155, 159–61; decline of, 173
Osborne, Milton, 182
Owen, Roger, 141
Owens, William, 393
Ozment, Steven E., 84, 87

Paetow, Louis, 55
Painter, Nell Irvin, 302
Palmer, Robert R., 79, 82
Pan American Institute of Geography and History, 201
Paret, Peter, 342, 363
Parrington, Vernon L., 329
Parrini, Carl, 368
Parry, John H., 110
Parsons, Stanley B., 242
Parsons, Talcott, 432
*Past and Present,* 331
Paterson, Thomas, 370
Patterson, K. David, 129
Paulson, Ross Evans, 324, 470
Paxton, Robert O., 105
Peace Corps, 115–16, 124
Pelz, Stephen, 382
Pelzer, Karl, 180
Pepper, Suzanne, 178
Perkins, Dexter, 479
Perlman, Selig, 253–54, 265, 268–69
Peru, history of, 191

Petrovich, Michael B., 111
Pflanze, Otto, 426
Philadelphia Social History Project, 260, 448
Phillips, Mark, 82
Phillips, Ulrich B., 293
Philosophy of history, 32, 328–30
Pierson, Peter, 80
Pike, Ruth, 84
Pittau, Joseph, 167
Platt, D. C., 361
Platt, Gerald, 432
Pleck, Elizabeth, 34, 259
Pletcher, David, 375
Plumb, J. H., 343
Pocock, J. G. A., 82, 85–86, 339–40, 343
Pogue, Forrest, 394
Poidevin, Raymond, 364
Political history, 25–26, 35, 194–95, 231–51, 447–48
Political Research History Data Archive, 235, 238, 448
Polk, William R., 152–53
Polsby, Nelson W., 246
Pomper, Gerald, 238
Posnansky, Merrick, 117
Potter, David M., 20, 296, 430
Prescott, William H., 187–88
Presidential libraries (U.S.), 13, 395
Price, H. Douglas, 453
Pritchard, Earl H., 162
Proctor, Samuel, 397
Professionalization of history, 19, 22, 340–41, 359–60, 475
Prosopography, 196, 198, 243–44, 286
Psychohistory, 21, 36, 39–40, 408–32
*Psychohistory, Journal of,* 413
*Psychohistory Review,* 414
Public history, 44–45. *See also* Employment problems.
Pye, Lucian, 183
Pyle, Kenneth, 166, 169

Quantitative methods, 21, 32–33, 36–37, 53–54, 70–71, 81, 93, 102, 190–91, 196–97, 200, 211, 221, 225–30, 232–33, 235–36, 243, 261–62, 275, 281, 285, 294, 310, 314–15, 449
Quarles, Benjamin, 292
Quataert, Donald, 150

Rabb, Theodore K., 88
Radical historians, 24–25, 153, 212, 216–17, 220–21, 235. *See also* Marxist historical thought.

Ramsauer, Ernest E., 150
Ranger, Terence, 117
Ranum, Orest, 80, 84
Rapp, Richard Tilden, 84
Rawlinson, John, 177
Read, Conyers, 40
Redding, Jay Saunders, 292–307, 510
Reed, Daniel, 395
Reformation history, 84, 87
Reich, Wilhelm, 416–17, 426
Reid, James, 140
Reill, Peter H., 83
*Reinterpretation of American History and Culture,* 231
Reischauer, Edwin O., 162, 165–66
Riasanovsky, Nicholas V., 111
Ricard, Robert, 188
Rich, Norman, 378
Ricoeur, Paul, 68
Robinson, James Harvey, 77, 329, 332, 476–77, 482
Robinson, Richard D., 150
Robinson, Ronald, 361, 366, 376
Rockefeller, John D., Jr., 13
Rockefeller Foundation, 161
Rodgers, Daniel T., 260
Roelker, Nancy Lyman, 80
Roff, William R., 182
Rogin, Michael P., 421
Roosen, William, 81
Roosevelt, Franklin D., 13, 395
Roosevelt, Theodore, 45
*Roots* (Haley), 14, 273
Rosenberg, Charles, 338
Rosengarten, Theodore, 303, 403–4
Ross, Dorothy, 342
Rotberg, Robert I., 122
Rothkrug, Lionel, 88
Rowen, Herbert H., 80
Roys, Ralph, 189
Ruch, Barbara, 172
Rudé, George, 256, 331
Rudin, Harry R., 119
Rudwick, Elliott M., 300
Rugg, Harold, 501
Ruigh, Robert E., 81
Rupp, Leila, 471
Rural history, 21, 274, 280. *See also* Agricultural history.
Rusk, Jerrold G., 239–40
Rustow, Dankwart, 150
Rutman, Darrett, 289

Safran, Nadav, 151–52
Said, Edward W., 131, 154–55

Samaha, Joel B., 92
Sansom, George B., 160, 165
Saxton, Alexander, 258
Scalapino, Robert, 168
Scalogram. *See* Guttman scaling.
Scheiner, Irwin, 167, 171
Schiffron, Harold, 178
Schirokauer, Conrad, 175
Schlesinger, Arthur M., Jr., 32, 231–32, 395, 402, 434
Schlesinger, Arthur M., Sr., 271, 281
Schmidt, Hans, 381
Schorske, Carl, 337–38, 429
Schram, Stuart, 179
Schroeder, Paul, 380–81, 386
Schuker, Stephen, 368, 379
Schurmann, Franz, 179
Schwartz, Benjamin, 175, 179
Schwartz, Susan, 198
Science, history of, 63, 100, 103, 215, 338–39
Scott, Joan Wallach, 112
Scruggs, Otey M., 306
Seigel, Jerrold E., 86
Sellers, Charles G., 490
Semantics, 67–68
Sempell, Charlotte, 426
Sennett, Richard, 282
Sexuality, history of, 34, 219, 227, 320–21
Shackelford, Laurel, 405
Shackleton, Robert, 342
Shade, William G., 245
Shannon, David, 471
Shapiro, Gilbert, 454
Sharman, Lyon, 178
Sharp, Lauriston, 181
Sharpless, John, 285
Shaver, James P., 482
Shaw, E. K., 149
Shaw, Stanford J., 140, 148–49
Sheehan, James J., 110–11
Sheldon, Charles, 171
Sheridan, James, 178
Sherwin, Martin, 372
Shively, Donald, 170
Shorter, Edward, 430
Siffin, William J., 183
*Signs: A Journal of Women in Society and Culture*, 325
Silberman, Bernard, 168
Silbey, Joel H., 234
Simpson, Lesley B., 189–90, 197
Skinner, G. William, 176
Skinner, Quentin, 339–40, 343
Skotheim, Robert, 329

Slavery, 101, 193, 214, 217–18, 421, 462, 465–70. *See also* Black history.
Slavic history, 103, 106, 108, 111
Sleeper, Martin E., 493
Slusser, Robert, 374
Smail, John R. W., 183
Smaldone, Joseph P., 122
Smith, Daniel Scott, 314, 317
Smith, John, 19, 42
Smith, M. G., 125
Smith, Peter H., 198, 454
Smith, Thomas C., 167, 170
Smith, Wilfred C., 153
Smith-Rosenberg, Carroll, 34
*Social Education*, 479, 483
Social history, 27, 34–35, 92–93, 101, 188, 192, 205–30, 261, 328–36
*Social History, Journal of*, 435, 440, 443–44
Social science and social theory, 21, 26, 173, 175, 182–83, 185–86, 189–92, 223, 232–36, 238. *See also* Behavioralism; Dependency theory; Interdisciplinary developments; Modernization theory.
Social Science Education Consortium, 481
*Social Science History*, 236
Social Science History Association, 236, 455
*Social Science in Historical Study* (1954), 19
Social Science Research Council, 19, 235, 272
Society for History Education, 494
Soltow, Lee, 447
Sontag, Raymond, 378
Soriano, Marc, 345
Soucek, Priscilla, 137
South Asia, history of, 183–86
Southeast Asia, history of, 27, 179–83
*Southern History, Journal of*, 438–49, 442
Southern History Association, 12, 394
Spanish history, 93
Specialization, 11, 50–51, 56, 63–64, 76–78, 80–81, 103, 118, 122, 158, 163–64, 180–81, 200–202, 232–33; in comparative history, 458–59; in diplomatic history, 378; in intellectual history, 329–39, 341; in medieval history, 56–57, 63; in modern European history, 98–101, 109–10; in women's and family history, 308–10, 315, 325–26
Spector, Stanley, 177
Spence, Jonathan, 176–77
Spencer, Herbert, 175
Spitz, Lewis W., 87, 498
Spodek, Howard, 185
Sports history. *See* Leisure, history of.

Stampp, Kenneth, 295, 306
Starn, Randolph, 93
Starr, Louis, 395
State historical agencies, 12
Stearns, Peter N., 205-30, 259, 510
Steinberg, David J., 180-82
Steiner, Zara, 359
Stern, Fritz, 380
Stern, Samuel, 136
Steward, Dick, 381
Stinchcombe, William, 377
Stites, Richard, 112
Stone, Lawrence, 91-92, 111, 226, 343, 345, 451
Strauss, Gerald, 84
Strayer, Joseph R., 54-55
Strout, Cushing, 419
Struever, Nancy S., 86, 341
Stucker, John J., 240
Sullivan, Richard, 57
Sundberg, Edward, 406
Sundberg, Gerda, 406
Susman, Warren I., 495
Swanson, Joseph A., 454
Swierenga, Robert P. 32
Swisher, Earl, 177

Tackett, Timothy, 91
Taft, Philip, 253-54, 256
Tannenbaum, Frank, 465-67
Taylor, A. J. P., 362
Taylor, Frederick W., 263
Taylor, George, 173
Teachers for East Africa, 116, 124
Teng Ssǔ-yü, 177
Tentler, Leslie, 259
TePaske, John, 197
Terkel, Louis (Studs), 405
Textbooks, 102, 484-85; publication patterns in, 103-4
Thernstrom, Stephan, 214, 227, 282, 285, 433, 436, 448
Thomas, Keith, 345
Thompson, E. P., 24, 210, 256-57, 264, 266-68, 283, 343, 331-32, 345-46, 361
Thompson, Leonard, 117, 121
Thompson, Roger, 471
Thompson, Virginia, 182
Thorne, Christopher, 362
Thrupp, Sylvia, 74
Tierney, Brian, 57, 68, 72
Tignor, Robert, 121, 151
Tilly, Charles, 30, 110, 225, 247, 448
Tilly, Louise, 110
Tilly, Richard, 110

Tilman, Robert O., 183
Toplin, Robert Brent, 469
Totman, Conrad, 171
Trager, Frank N., 182-83
Treadgold, Donald W., 110
Trennert, Robert, 406
Trevor-Roper, Hugh, 113
Trexler, Richard C., 90
Trinkaus, Charles, 85-86
Tsunoda, Ryusaku, 165
Tuchman, Barbara, 43, 400
Tucker, Robert C., 111, 419
Turkey, history of, 146-50
Turner, Frederick Jackson, 21, 43, 237, 256, 279-80, 329, 462-64, 478
Turner, Victor, 41
Typologies, 41, 223-24, 277

Udovitch, Abraham L., 137, 142
Uhlenberg, Peter, 314, 318
Ulam, Adam, 373
Ullman, Richard, 380
Ulman, Lloyd, 253
U.S. Office of Education, 481
Urban history, 21, 122, 214, 274, 280-89
Urbanization, 35

Van Niel, Robert, 182
Vansina, Jan, 117, 123-25
Van Slyke, Lyman, 179
Van Tine, Warren, 255, 262
Varley, Paul, 172
Vasilier, A. A., 63
Vestal, Stanley, 392, 403
Veysey, Laurence, 39, 43, 338
Vickery, Kenneth P., 470
Vidal, Gore, 43
*Vierteljahrschrift für Sozial- und Wirtschaftsgeschichte*, 440, 443-44
Vinovskis, Maris, 227, 313-15
Vryonis, Speros, Jr., 64-65, 72, 137

Wade, Ira, 340
Waite, R. G. L., 427
Wakeman, Frederic, Jr., 176
Walker, Mack, 111
Walkowitz, Daniel, 258, 268, 314-15
Wallace, Anthony F. C., 41, 291
Waller, Richard A., 498
Wallerstein, Immanuel, 79-80, 147, 460-61, 472
Walton, Robert C., 84
Walzer, Michael, 88-89
Ward, Robert, 170

Ware, Norman, 254
Warner, Sam Bass, Jr., 283, 285-86
Washington, Booker T., 304-5
Watt, John R., 176
Wauchope, Robert, 190
Weber, Eugen, 111
Weber, Max, 89, 126, 171
Webster, Richard, 365
Wehler, Hans-Ulrich, 365
Weil, Martin, 360
Wein, Roberta, 321
Weinberg, Gerhard L., 111, 378
Weinberg, William, 405
Weiner, Myron, 185
Weinstein, Donald, 83, 343
Weinstein, Fred, 432
Weinstein, James, 256
Wells, John E., 176
Wells, Robert, 317
Welter, Rush, 340
Wendell, Charles, 151
Wertheimer, Barbara Mayer, 255
Whig interpretation of history, 85, 88, 92-93
White, Hayden V., 32-33, 341, 344
White, Morton, 338, 341
White, Richard, 375
Whitehead, Alfred North, 77
Whitmore, John, 182
Wickman, John, 395
Wigginton, Eliot, 398-99
Wilbur, C. Martin, 173, 178
Wilcox, Donald J., 82
Wilkie, James, 197-98
Wilkins, Mira, 369
Wilks, Ivor, 117, 126
Willcox, William B., 417
*William and Mary Quarterly,* 438-42
Williams, T. Harry, 394, 403
Williams, William Appleman, 365-66
Williamson, Jeffrey G., 454
Williamson, Joel R., 306
Williamson, Samuel, Jr., 359
Wilson, Arthur, 331, 342
Wilson, George, 169
Wilson, John G., 89
Wilson, Monica, 121
Wilson, R. Jackson, 22
Wilson, William, 470, 472

Wisconsin-River Falls Research Center, 397
Wisconsin School of Labor History, 256
Wisconsin State Historical Society, 394
Witke, Charles, 64-65, 72
Witt, Ronald G., 86
Wolf, Eric R., 460, 472
Wolper, Stanley, 184, 186
Women, history of, 21, 35, 73, 91, 101, 122, 191, 205-6, 208, 213-14, 220-21, 308-26, 462, 470-71
Wood, Gordon S., 344
Wood, Peter, 347
Woods, John, 139-40
Woodside, Alexander, 181
Woodson, Carter G., 117
Woodward, C. Vann, 21, 231-32, 254, 294-95, 297, 434, 469, 471
Work, history of, 223, 228. *See also* Labor history.
Works, John A., Jr., 124
*World History, Journal of,* 35
World War I, 150, 260, 263, 293, 355
World War II and historical thought, 131-34, 138, 143, 157, 160-61, 167-68, 170-72, 179, 188, 231-32, 253-54, 263, 265, 332, 335, 462, 474, 492
Wou, Odoric, 178
Wright, Arthur, 173-75
Wright, Gordon, 24, 364
Wright, James E., 242
Wright, Marcia, 120
Wright, Mary C., 20, 175, 178
Wyatt, David K., 182
Wyatt, Frederick, 417

Yale Center for Parliamentary History, 88
Yamamura, Kozo, 170-71
Yans-McLaughlin, Virginia, 257
Yergin, Daniel, 370-71
Youth, history of, 208-9, 221. *See also* Life cycle, history of.

Zabdyr, Judy, 397
Zabih, Sepehr, 146
Zagorin, Perez, 89
Zavala, Silvio, 188
Zingale, Nancy H., 454
Zophy, Jonathan W., 87

**Library of Congress Cataloging in Publication Data**

Main entry under title:
The Past before us.

"Prepared for presentation on the occasion of the Fifteenth International Congress
of Historical Sciences, held in Bucharest, Romania, August 1980."
    Includes index.
    1. Historiography—United States—Congresses.   I. Kammen,
Michael G.   II. American Historical Association.
D13.P36      901      79-25785
ISBN 0-8014-1224-2